Major Problems in the History
of the American South

MAJOR PROBLEMS IN AMERICAN HISTORY SERIES

GENERAL EDITOR
THOMAS G. PATERSON

Major Problems in the History of the American South
Volume I: The Old South

DOCUMENTS AND ESSAYS

EDITED BY
PAUL D. ESCOTT
WAKE FOREST UNIVERSITY

DAVID R. GOLDFIELD
UNIVERSITY OF NORTH CAROLINA, CHARLOTTE

D. C. HEATH AND COMPANY
Lexington, Massachusetts   Toronto

Acquisitions Editor: James Miller
Developmental Editor: Sylvia Mallory
Production Editor: Cathy Labresh Brooks
Designer: Sally Thompson Steele
Production Coordinator: Lisa Arcese
Permissions Editor: Margaret Roll

Cover: Mississippi River Plantation by John Barnard
Minnesota Historical Society/Aldus Archive, London

Published simultaneously in Canada.

Printed in the United States of America.

International Standard Book Number: 0-669-13157-1

Library of Congress Catalog Card Number: 89-85075

10 9 8 7 6 5 4 3

For Lauren and David
and
Eleanor and Erik

Preface

Historian David M. Potter has written that the South has been "a kind of Sphinx on the American land." Nothing in the two volumes of *Major Problems in the History of the American South* will challenge that description of a great American enigma. We hope, though, that readers will become more enlightened by these volumes' documents and essays as they search to know what the South was and is. If nothing else, southern history and southern historiography teach humility. The South, less a geographical region than a state of mind, is a fickle place, and writers have grasped it about as well as they might a greased pig. But for all who have endeavored to unlock its essence, the fun has been in the hunt and in the insights that come from what English professor Fred Hobson has called "the southern rage to explain." The selections in this book, like those in the other volumes of D. C. Heath's Major Problems in American History Series, are intended to interest readers in that quest to explain.

In this first volume, we begin the hunt by offering a small sampling of what others—with no agreement, of course—have described as distinctive about the South. In subsequent chapters, we take the reader on a basically chronological tour through southern history from the pre-Columbian Indian settlements to the dislocations of Reconstruction. We have selected documents that evoke the atmosphere of the times as well as inform readers of the major issues that southerners have confronted. In choosing the essays, we have attempted to strike a balance between the classic literature and the exciting scholarship on the South published during the past decade. We have avoided any particular ideological bent and have tried to present both sides of a story—a difficult task, because most southern stories have too many sides to count. Most of all, we want readers to reach their own conclusions about the major interpretive problems in southern history. Chapter introductions, as well as headnotes to the documents and essays, help set the questions in historical and interpretive perspective. Since so much fine work has focused on the South (as the lists of books and articles for further reading at the end of each chapter attest), it is inevitable that we have omitted someone's favorite essay or document. We will be happy to redress grievances in future editions. Please let us know your preferences.

Numerous friends and colleagues contributed to the two volumes. Early on, we polled some southern historians on the essays and documents that they believed ought to appear here. Their replies were helpful and heartening. We particularly want to note the insights of Edward L. Ayers, Paul H. Bergeron, David L. Carlton, Michael B. Chesson, Janet L. Coryell, Mary A. DeCredico, John Duffy, Raymond Gavins, Jack Temple Kirby, William Link, Melton McLaurin, James Tice Moore, Theda Perdue, Lawrence N. Powell, James M. Russell, Edward M. Steel, Jr., Thad Tate, William Bruce Wheeler, and Jon Wiener. Detailed and extremely helpful written reviews of draft tables of contents were provided by Edward L. Ayers, F. N. Boney, Robert F. Martin, Mary Beth Norton, Lawrence N. Powell, Howard N. Rabinowitz, and Terry L. Seip. Becky Bell of the Country Music Foundation, David E. Alsobrook of the Jimmy Carter Library, Cheryl Roberts of the Urban Institute at the University of North Carolina, Charlotte, and the staffs at Atlanta mayor Andrew Young's office and the Lyndon B. Johnson Library in Austin, Texas, were especially helpful in gathering documents for us. Barbara Lisenby and her interlibrary loan staff at the University of North Carolina, Charlotte, and Carrie Thomas of the Z. Smith Reynolds Library at Wake Forest University relentlessly tracked down both primary-source documents and essays. Finally, we were fortunate to work with a professional and congenial group at D. C. Heath, particularly Sylvia Mallory, James Miller, Cathy Labresh Brooks, and Margaret Roll. Thomas G. Paterson, the editor of the Major Problems in American History Series, provided timely assistance and encouragement.

As in all of our work, the patience and support of our families have been most important. We dedicate this book to our children, who are enjoying the benefits of growing up in the South.

P.E.

D.G.

Contents

C H A P T E R 4
The American Revolution
Page 148

C H A P T E R 5
The South in the New Nation
Page 208

C H A P T E R 6
The Old South
Page 244

C H A P T E R 7
Slavery and Southern Blacks
Page 292

C H A P T E R   8
The Nonslaveholding Whites
Page 338

C H A P T E R   9
Women's Culture in the Old South
Page 378

C H A P T E R 10
Sectionalism and Slavery
Page 421

C H A P T E R 11
The Sectional Crisis and Secession
Page 453

What Is the South?

✕

Historian Michael O'Brien noted that "no man's South is the same as another's." Although there is general agreement that the South is (or at least was,
at some time) distinctive from other parts of the United States, there is no consensus on either the nature or the duration of that difference. Definitions of the
South have stressed everything from the obvious (for example, climate and white
supremacy) to the obscure (the line below which grits replace hash browns).

Part of the problem is that there are many Souths. The folks who lived in
the South Carolina lowcountry were very different in terms of ethnicity, accent,
ideology, occupation, religion, music, and language from the people of the southern Appalachians. There are distinctions within states—lowcountry versus upcountry, piedmont versus coastal plain, and delta versus piney woods. These disparities have led some to contend that the South is more a state of mind than a
geography.

Yet some thing or things draw these disparate areas together, and observers
since the first settlements have tried to identify what, in fact, constitutes "the
South." The task is more than a mere intellectual exercise. As with the study of
any ethnic group, distinction helps to define identity. And the study of the South
has helped to define our national identity as well. The South has often served as
a counterpoint, both good and bad, to the rest of the country. In learning what
is special about the South and how it became that way, we are learning about
our national culture as well.

✕ E S S A Y S

W. J. Cash's *The Mind of the South* is among the most eloquent and forceful
statements of a southern identity, though the Charlotte journalist's emphasis on
the continuity of southern history has provoked sharp responses from some historians, among them Yale University's C. Vann Woodward. The first two essays
present Cash's and Woodward's differing views. Defining southern distinctiveness is a major academic industry and in fact, as Wake Forest historian David
L. Smiley notes in the next essay, has become a distinctive element in itself.
Assuming the South's difference, the obvious question is, "Different from
what?" Sheldon Hackney, historian and president of the University of Pennsyl-

vania, demonstrates in the last essay that the North had a significant hand in creating a distinctive South, and the South often functioned as a mirror image of the rest of the nation.

The Continuity of Southern History

W. J. CASH

There exists among us by ordinary—both North and South—a profound conviction that the South is another land, sharply differentiated from the rest of the American nation, and exhibiting within itself a remarkable homogeneity.

As to what its singularity may consist in, there is, of course, much conflict of opinion, and especially between Northerner and Southerner. But that it is different and that it is solid—on these things nearly everybody is agreed. Now and then, to be sure, there have arisen people, usually journalists or professors, to tell us that it is all a figment of the imagination, that the South really exists only as a geographical division of the United States and is distinguishable from New England or the Middle West only by such matters as the greater heat and the presence of a larger body of Negroes. Nobody, however, has ever taken them seriously. And rightly.

For the popular conviction is indubitably accurate: the South is, in Allen Tate's phrase, "Uncle Sam's other province." And when Carl Carmer said of Alabama that "The Congo is not more different from Massachusetts or Kansas or California," he fashioned a hyperbole which is applicable in one measure or another to the entire section.

This is not to suggest that the land does not display an enormous diversity within its borders. Anyone may see that it does simply by riding along any of the great new motor roads which spread across it—through brisk towns with tall white buildings in Nebraska Gothic; through smart suburbs, with their faces newly washed; through industrial and Negro slums, medieval in dirt and squalor and wretchedness, in all but redeeming beauty; past sleepy old hamlets and wide fields and black men singing their sad songs in the cotton, past log cabin and high grave houses, past hill and swamp and plain. . . . The distance from Charleston to Birmingham is in some respects measurable only in sidereal terms, as is the distance from the Great Smokies to Lake Pontchartrain. And Howard Odum has demonstrated that the economic and social difference between the Southeastern and Southwestern states is so great and growing that they have begun to deserve to be treated, for many purposes, as separate regions.

Nevertheless, if it can be said there are many Souths, the fact remains that there is also one South. That is to say, it is easy to trace throughout the region (roughly delimited by the boundaries of the former Confederate States of America, but shading over into some of the border states, notably Kentucky, also) a fairly definite mental pattern, associated with a fairly definite social pattern—a complex of established relationships and habits of thought, sentiments, prejudices, standards and values, and associations of ideas, which, if it is not common strictly to every group of white people in the South, is still common in one appreciable measure or another, and in some part or another, to all but relatively negligible ones.

It is no product of Cloud-Cuckoo-Town, of course, but proceeds from the common American heritage, and many of its elements are readily recognizable as being simply variations on the primary American theme. To imagine it existing outside this continent would be quite impossible. But for all that, the peculiar history of the South has so greatly modified it from the general American norm that, when viewed as a whole, it decisively justifies the notion that the country is—not quite a nation within a nation, but the next thing to it.

To understand it, it is necessary to know the story of its development. And the best way to begin that story, I think, is by disabusing our minds of two correlated legends—those of the Old and the New Souths.

What the Old South of the legend in its classical form was like is more or less familiar to everyone. It was a sort of stage piece out of the eighteenth century, wherein gesturing gentlemen moved soft-spokenly against a background of rose gardens and dueling grounds, through always gallant deeds, and lovely ladies, in farthingales, never for a moment lost that exquisite remoteness which has been the dream of all men and the possession of none. Its social pattern was manorial, its civilization that of the Cavalier, its ruling class an aristocracy coextensive with the planter group—men often entitled to quarter the royal arms of St. George and St. Andrew on their shields, and in every case descended from the old gentlefolk who for many centuries had made up the ruling classes of Europe.

They dwelt in large and stately mansions, preferably white and with columns and Grecian entablature. Their estates were feudal baronies, their slaves quite too numerous ever to be counted, and their social life a thing of Old World splendor and delicacy. What had really happened here, indeed, was that the gentlemanly idea, driven from England by Cromwell, had taken refuge in the South and fashioned for itself a world to its heart's desire: a world singularly polished and mellow and poised, wholly dominated by ideals of honor and chivalry and *noblesse*—all those sentiments and values and habits of action which used to be, especially in Walter Scott, invariably assigned to the gentleman born and the Cavalier.

Beneath these was a vague race lumped together indiscriminately as the poor whites—very often, in fact, as the ''white-trash.'' These people belonged in the main to a physically inferior type, having sprung for the most part from the convict servants, redemptioners, and debtors of old Virginia and Georgia, with a sprinkling of the most unsuccessful sort of European peasants and farm laborers and the dregs of the European town slums. And so, of course, the gulf between them and the master classes was impassable, and their ideas and feelings did not enter into the make-up of the prevailing Southern civilization.

But in the legend of the New South the Old South is supposed to have been destroyed by the Civil War and the thirty years that followed it, to have been swept both socially and mentally into the limbo of things that were and are not, to give place to a society which has been rapidly and increasingly industrialized and modernized both in body and in mind—which now, indeed, save for a few quaint survivals and gentle sentimentalities and a few shocking and inexplicable brutalities such as lynching, is almost as industrialized and modernized in its outlook as the North. Such an idea is obviously inconsistent with the general assumption of the South's great difference, but paradox is the essence of popular thinking, and millions—even in the South itself—placidly believe in both notions.

These legends, however, bear little relation to reality. There was an Old South, to be sure, but it was another thing than this. And there is a New South. Industrialization and commercialization have greatly modified the land, including its ideology. . . . Nevertheless, the extent of the change and of the break between the Old South that was and the South of our time has been vastly exaggerated. The South, one might say, is a tree with many age rings, with its limbs and trunk bent and twisted by all the winds of the years, but with its tap root in the Old South. Or, better still, it is like one of those churches one sees in England. The facade and towers, the windows and clerestory, all the exterior and superstructure are late Gothic of one sort or another, but look into its nave, its aisles, and its choir and you find the old mighty Norman arches of the twelfth century. And if you look into its crypt, you may even find stones cut by Saxon, brick made by Roman hands.

The mind of the section, that is, is continuous with the past. And its primary form is determined not nearly so much by industry as by the purely agricultural conditions of that past. So far from being modernized, in many ways it has actually always marched away, as to this day it continues to do, from the present toward the past.

The Discontinuity of Southern History

C. VANN WOODWARD

Among the major monuments of broken continuity in the South are slavery and secession, independence and defeat, emancipation and military occupation, reconstruction and redemption. Southerners, unlike other Americans, repeatedly felt the solid ground of continuity give way under their feet. An old order of slave society solidly supported by constitution, state, church and the authority of law and learning and cherished by a majority of the people collapsed, perished and disappeared. So did the short-lived experiment in national independence. So also the short-lived experiment in Radical Reconstruction. The succeeding order of Redeemers, the New South, lasted longer, but it too seems destined for the dump heap of history.

Perhaps it was because Cash wrote toward the end of the longest and most stable of these successive orders, the one that lasted from 1877 to the 1950's, that he acquired his conviction of stability and unchanging continuity. At any rate, he was fully persuaded that "the mind of the section . . . is continuous with the past," and that the South has "always marched away, as to this day it continues to do, from the present toward the past." Just as he guardedly conceded diversity in advancing the thesis of unity, so he admits the existence of change in maintaining the thesis of continuity, change from which even the elusive Southern "mind" did not "come off scot-free." But it was the sort of change the French have in mind in saying, *"Plus ça change, plus c'est la même chose."* Tidewater tobacco, up-country cotton, rampaging frontier, flush times in Alabama and Mississippi, slavery, secession, defeat, abolition, Reconstruction, New South, industrial revolution—*toujours la même chose!* Even the Yankee victory that "had smashed the Southern world" was "almost entirely illusory," since "it had left the essential Southern mind and will . . . entirely unshaken. Rather . . . it had operated enormously to fortify and confirm that mind and will." As for Reconstruction, again, "so far from having reconstructed the Southern mind in the large and in its essential character, it was still this Yankee's fate to have strengthened it almost beyond reckoning, and to have made it one of the most solidly established, one of the least reconstructible ever developed."

The continuity upon which Cash is most insistent is the one he sees between the Old South and the New South. He early announces his intention of "disabusing our minds of two correlated legends—those of the Old and New South." He promises in Rankean terms to tell us "exactly what the Old South was really like." He concedes that there was a New South as well. "Nevertheless, the extent of the change and of the break between the Old South that was and the New South of our time has been vastly exaggerated." The common denominator, the homogenizing touchstone is his "basic Southerner" or "the man at the center." He is described as "an exceedingly simple fellow," most likely a hillbilly from the backcountry, but fundamentally he is a petit bourgeois always on the make, yet ever bemused by his vision of becoming, imitating, or at least serving the planter aristocrat. Cash's crude Irish parvenu is pictured as the prototype of the planter aristocrat. Cash is confused about these aristocrats, mainly I think because he is confused about the nature and history of aristocracy. He admires their "beautiful courtesy and dignity and gesturing grace," but deplores their "grotesque exaggeration" and their "pomposity" and suspects that the genuine article should have been genteel. He grudgingly acknowledges their existence, but denies the legitimacy of their pretenses—all save those of a few negligible Virginians. He seems to be saying that they were all bourgeois, that therefore the Old South was bourgeois too, and therefore essentially indistinguishable from the New South. New and Old alike were spellbound by the spurious myth of aristocracy. This and the paradoxical fact that those parvenu aristocrats actually took charge, were a real ruling class, and the continuity of their rule spelled the continuity of the New South with the Old.

The masses came out of the ordeal of Civil War with "a deep affection for these captains, a profound trust in them," a belief in the right "of the master class to ordain and command." And according to Cash, the old rulers continued to ordain and command right on through the collapse of the old order and the building of the new. He detects no change of guard at Redemption. So long as the industrialists and financiers who stepped into the shoes of the old rulers gave the Proto-Dorian password and adopted the old uniforms and gestures, he salutes them as the genuine article. In fact they were rather an improvement, for they represent "a striking extension of the so-called paternalism of the Old South: its passage in some fashion toward becoming a genuine paternalism." Cash enthusiastically embraces the thesis of Broadus Mitchell's "celebrated monograph" that the cotton-mill campaign was "a mighty folk movement," a philanthropic crusade of inspired paternalists. The textile-mill captains were "such men as belonged more or less distinctively within the limits of the old ruling class, the progeny of the plantation." Indeed they were responsible for "the bringing over of the plantation into industry," the company town. Even "the worst labor sweaters" were "full of the ancient Southern love for the splendid gesture," fulfilling "an essential part of the Southern paternalistic tradition that it was an essential duty of the upper classes to look after the moral welfare of these people."

To the cotton mills the neopaternalists add the public schools for the common whites and thus "mightily reaffirm the Proto-Dorian bond." The common poverty acted as a leveler (back to the Unity thesis) and brought "a very great increase in the social solidarity of the South," a "marked mitigation of the haughtiness" of the old captains, now "less boldly patronizing," and "a suppression of class feeling that went beyond anything that even the Old South had known." The common white felt "the hand on the shoulder . . . the jests, the rallying, the stories . . . the confiding reminders of the Proto-Dorian bond of white men." That, according to Cash, was what did in the Populist revolt and the strikes of the lint-head mill hands as well. For from the heart of the masses came "a wide, diffuse gratefulness pouring out upon the cotton-mill baron; upon the old captains, upon all the captains and preachers of Progress; upon the ruling class as a whole for having embraced the doctrine and brought these things about."

Of course Cash professes not to be taken in by Progress like the rednecks and the lint-heads. He realizes that Progress and Success had their prices and he sets them down scrupulously in the debit column of his ledger. "Few people can ever have been confronted with a crueler dilemma" than the old planter turned supply merchant to his former huntin' and fishin' companion as sharecropper: "The old monotonous pellagra-and-rickets-breeding diet had at least been abundant? Strip it rigidly to fatback, molasses, and cornbread, dole it out with an ever stingier hand . . . blind your eyes to peaked faces, seal up your ears to hungry whines. . . ." And that sunbonnet, straw-hat proletariat of the paternalistic mill villages? By the turn of the century they had become "a pretty distinct physical type . . . a dead white skin, a sunken chest, and stooping shoulders. . . . Chinless faces, microcephalic foreheads, rabbit teeth, goggling dead-fish eyes, rickety limbs, and stunted bodies. . . . The women were characteristically stringy-haired and limp of breast at twenty, and shrunken hags at thirty or forty." Something admittedly was happening to the captains, too, what with "men of generally coarser kind coming steadily to the front." And in "all the elaborate built-up pattern of leisure and hedonistic drift; all the slow, cool, gracious and graceful gesturing of movement," there was a sad falling off, a decay of the ideal. "And along with it, the vague largeness of outlook which was so essentially a part of the same aristocratic complex; the magnanimity . . ."

Admitting all that, "But when the whole of this debit score of Progress is taken into account, we still inevitably come back to the fact that its total effect was as I have said." *Plus ça change!* "Here in a word, was triumph for the Southern will . . . an enormous renewal of confidence in the general Southern way." In [Henry W.] Grady's rhetoric, "Progress stood quite accurately for a sort of new charge at Gettysburg." To be sure, Southern Babbitts eventually appeared, but even they were "Tartarin, not Tartuffe . . . simpler, more naïve, less analytical than their compatriots in Babbittry at the North. . . . They go about making money . . . as boys go about stealing apples . . . in the high-hearted sense of being embarked upon capital sport." Yet, like the planter turned supply merchant or captain of industry, "they looked at you with level and proud gaze. The hallmark of their breed was identical with that of the masters of the Old South—a tremendous complacency." And Rotary, "sign-manual of the Yankee spirit"? Granting "an unfortunate decline in the dignity of the Southern manner," it was but "the grafting of Yankee backslapping upon the normal Southern geniality. . . . I am myself," Cash wrote, "indeed perpetually astonished to recall that Rotary was not invented in the South." And does one detect "strange notes—Yankee notes—in all this talk about the biggest factory, about bank clearings and car loadings and millions"? Strange? Not for Jack Cash. "But does anybody," he actually asked, "fail to hear once more the native accent of William L. Yancey and Barnwell Rhett, to glimpse again the waving plume of, say, Wade Hampton?"

How could he? How could any historian? He sometimes reminds one of those who scribble facetious graffiti on Roman ruins. He betrays a want of feeling for the seriousness of human strivings, for the tragic theme in history. Looking back from mid-twentieth century over the absurd sky-scrapers and wrecked-car bone piles set in the red-clay hills, how could he seriously say that the South believed it "was succeeding in creating a world which, if it was not made altogether in the image of that old world, half-remembered and half-dreamed, shimmering there forever behind the fateful smoke of Sumter's guns, was yet sufficiently of a piece with it in essentials to be acceptable." A great slave society, by far the largest and richest of those that had existed in the New World since the sixteenth century, had grown up and miraculously flourished in the heart of a thoroughly bourgeois and partly puritanical republic. It had renounced its bourgeois origins and elaborated and painfully rationalized its institutional, legal, metaphysical, and religious defenses. It had produced leaders of skill, ingenuity, and strength who, unlike those of other slave societies, invested their honor and their lives, and not merely part of their capital, in that society. When the crisis came, they, unlike the others, chose to fight. It proved to be the death struggle of a society, which went down in ruins. And yet here is a historian who tells us that nothing essential changed. The ancient "mind," temperament, the aristocratic spirit, parvenu though he called it—call it what you will, *panache* perhaps—was perfectly preserved in a mythic amber. And so the present is continuous with the past, the ancient manifest in the new order, in Grady, Babbitt, Rotary, whatever, *c'est la même chose.*

I am afraid that Cash was taken in by the very myth he sought to explode—by the fancy-dress charade the New South put on in the cast-off finery of the old order, the cult of the Lost Cause, the Plantation Legend and the rest. The new actors threw themselves into the old roles with spirit and conviction and put on what was for some a convincing performance. But Cash himself, even though he sometimes took the Snopeses for the Sartorises, plainly saw how they betrayed to the core and essence every tenet of the old code. "And yet," he can write,

> And yet—as regards the Southern mind, which is our theme, how essentially superficial and unrevolutionary remain the obvious changes; how certainly do these obvious changes take place within the ancient framework, and even sometimes contribute to the positive strengthening of the ancient pattern.
>
> Look close at this scene as it stands in 1914. There is an atmosphere here, an air, shining from every word and deed. And the key to this atmosphere . . . is that familiar word without which it would be impossible to tell the story of the Old South, that familiar word "extravagant."
>
> [Then, after a reference to the new skyscrapers in the clay hills:]
>
> Softly; do you not hear behind that the gallop of Jeb Stuart's cavalrymen?

The answer is "No"! Not one ghostly echo of a gallop. And neither did Jack Cash. He only thought he did when he was bemused.

After some years in the profession, one has seen reputations of historians rise and fall. The books of Ulrich Phillips and later Frank Owsley began to collect dust on the shelves, and one thinks of Beard and Parrington. In America, historians, like politicians, are out as soon as they are down. There is no comfortable back bench, no House of Lords for them. It is a wasteful and rather brutal practice, unworthy of what Cash would agree are our best Southern traditions. I hope this will not happen to Cash. The man really had something to say, which is more than most, and he said it with passion and conviction and with style. Essentially what he had to say is something every historian eventually finds himself trying to say (always risking exaggeration) at some stage about every great historical subject. And that is that in spite of the revolution—any revolution—the English remain English, the French remain French, the Russians remain Russian, the Chinese remain Chinese—call them Elizabethans or Cromwellians, Royalists or Jacobeans, Czarists or Communists, Mandarins or Maoists.

That was really what Cash, at his best, was saying about Southerners, and he said it better than anybody ever has—only he rather overdid the thing. But in that he was merely illustrating once more that ancient Southern trait that he summed up in the word "extravagant." And, for that matter, his critic, poured in the same mold, may have unintentionally added another illustration of the same trait. If so, Jack Cash would have been the first to understand and not the last to forgive. Peace to his troubled spirit.

Quest for a Central Theme

DAVID L. SMILEY

In the history of Southern history in America the central theme has been the quest for the central theme. Local and state historians, students of regionalism and sectionalism, along with authors of American history surveys, have agreed in accepting the hypothesis that there is an American South and that it has had, historically, a unifying focus at its center. Furthermore, it has become customary among many historians to emphasize sectionalism as a key factor in American political history and to seek the causes for the apparent division of national patriotism. The man in the street, though his views may be hazy or overemotional, is confident that there are distinctive social and political patterns, perhaps traceable to a unique agricultural base, which combine to make the regions below the Potomac a recognizable entity, and most Americans at one time or another have engaged in the pursuit of a central theme in Southern history.

In its broadest sense the attempt to generalize regional folkways into an American South is part of the search for a national identity. Since the days of Noah Webster's early crusade for American English orthography and usage and Ralph Waldo Emerson's 1837 appeal for an American culture—Oliver Wendell Holmes called it "our intellectual Declaration of Independence"—Americans have earnestly sought to define the elusive qualities of their civilization and have squirmed uncomfortably when critics such as Harriet Martineau or Charles Dickens ridiculed their efforts. There are interesting parallels between the national response to Dickens' *American Notes* and the Southern umbrage at the publication of Fanny Kemble's *Georgia Journal*. Still, the search for a national identity went on, and alongside it, as if in overt denial of a homogeneous national character, the search for Southern distinctiveness continued.

The reasons for the dichotomy in the national personality are complex and often obscure. At the same time that it served the purposes of American patriotism to sound a bold trumpet for a native civilization, it was politically advantageous to assent to the proposition that that civilization contained two "nations," opposites in fundamental aspects. The subsequent defeat

David L. Smiley, "The Quest for the Central Theme in Southern History." Reprinted with permission from *The South Atlantic Quarterly*, Vol. 71:3 (Summer 1972), pp. 307–325. Copyright 1972 by Duke University Press.

of one "nation" by the other had the effect, on both sides, of inspiring each to glamorize its superior civilization and to denigrate that of the other as alien, un-American, and lacking in enduring and essential values. Especially was this activity prevalent among Southerners, where it took the form of reverence for the Lost Cause and allegiance to the cult of the Old South. In paying homage to a mythical past they were but acting out a characteristic common to peoples defeated by material or military force, i.e., the tendency to emphasize the superiority of less tangible qualities which their civilization allegedly produced in great quantity. This happened in the post–Civil War South at a thousand veterans' campfires, in political orations on days set aside to the memory of the dead, and in graduation addresses replete with scholarly appurtenances, and soon the emphasis began to appear in presumably objective histories and biographies of the Confederacy and its leaders.

In these expressions, down to the latest Rebel yell or defiant wave of the Confederate battle flag, there was the axiomatic acceptance of the belief that there was in fact an American South and that it possessed clearly defined traits which set it apart from the rest of the nation. In some instances, notably in the rhetoric of ambitious politicians and regional promoters, these assumptions conveyed overtones of immediate advantage to the author. A widely accepted central theme or distinguishing characteristic of the American South, for example, might affect a person's vote for or against a party, a personality, or a platform. On other occasions it might encourage or discourage decisions concerning the migration of industries and the choice of sites for capital investments, or the transfer of individual talents to sunnier climes or a more favorable labor situation.

At the same time, other statements of the central theme emerged from the labors of those committed to the highest obligations of scholarship: to sift the evidence and to generalize its meaning into an idea whose purpose is to enlarge understanding and to stimulate additional study and thought. In each case the motivation, though vastly different in purpose and effect, remains confused and unclear, and a study of the themes and forces which have attracted scholarly attention is significant in illuminating the problems and clarifying the objectives of the broader quest for national identity.

Basically and historically the effort to express the essence of the American South in a central theme has turned upon two related streams of thought. One has been to emphasize the causal effects of environment, while the other has put uppermost the development of certain acquired characteristics of the people called Southern. The work of the scholar Ulrich B. Phillips well illustrates the dual thrust of the endeavor. The South, he declared in a famous article, was a section dominated by racial conflict. It was "a land with a unity despite its diversity, with a people having common joys and common sorrows, and, above all, as to the white folk a people with a common resolve indomitably maintained—that it shall be and remain a white man's country." The "cardinal test of a Southerner and the central theme of Southern history," he said, was the desire to preserve the supremacy of the white race.

A few months after the article appeared, however, Phillips published

Life and Labor in the Old South, in which he defined the South in terms of environmental causation. "Let us begin by discussing the weather," he wrote, "for that has been the chief agency in making the South distinctive." Behind the central theme of white supremacy Phillips could now discern a determinative meteorological pattern. Climate encouraged the production of staple crops, he declared, and staple crops promoted the plantation as the most efficient institution for their cultivation; the plantation's demand for large quantities of cheap labor led to slave importations; the presence of large numbers of Africans resulted in turn in a continuing race problem and the effort to maintain white supremacy. The acquired characteristic of racism now became a "house that Jack built" upon the foundation of a causative weather pattern.

Although critics have eroded much of Phillips' work, searchers for the central theme continued to follow the twin trails that he blazed. Generally they have undertaken to document either the theme of a dominant pattern of life or they have looked beyond the characteristic itself to seek geographical, meteorological, or psychological determinants of the significant traits. Sometimes a student has combined all of these in a single sentence. "The South," wrote Wendell H. Stephenson, "is a geographical location, a group of factors that differentiated the region and its inhabitants from other sections of the United States, and a state of mind to which these factors gave rise."

Thus, in one way or another, seekers for the central theme in Southern history have illustrated Phillips' observations that the South was either the home of a peculiar behavior pattern—all but universally present among people who considered themselves Southern and all but universally absent elsewhere in the land (the inheritance theory)—or a place where men's lives were molded by impersonal forces of climate or geography (the environmental view).

Perhaps the earliest assumption among those in quest of the central theme has been that the South is the product of a dictatorial environment. Phillips himself spoke of climate, in the form of heavy rainfall and an overheated sun, as causative factors in Southern life. Deluges eroded the topsoil, packed plowed lands, and ran off in floods, he said, and these rains conditioned the soils of the South. The sun was "bakingly hot"; it parched vegetation and enervated Europeans. Clarence Cason agreed that the South was a hot land. It was that part of the United States where the mercury reached 90 degrees in the shade at least one hundred afternoons a year. According to the climate theory, the tyrant sun slowed life to a languid crawl, impelled men to choose the shaded sides of streets, and induced cooks to concoct gastronomical delights to tempt heat-jaded appetites. It also dictated an emphasis upon staple crops, and as a consequence influenced the labor system of the South. Cason related with approval the Mississippi proverb that "only mules and black men can face the sun in July" in support of the comforting philosophy that only dark-skinned menials, presumably equipped by an all-wise Creator to endure the heat, should perform physical labor.

The idea that the central theme of Southern history may be found in the environment, in a causal relationship between a tropical climate and a peculiar way of life, has been a persistent one. In 1778 Judge William Henry Drayton told the South Carolina Assembly that "from the nature of the climate, soil and produce of the several states, a northern and southern interest naturally and unavoidably arise," and this view found ready acceptance. In his *Notes on Virginia* Thomas Jefferson remarked that "in a warm climate, no man will labor for himself who can make another labor for him." For this reason, he said, "of the proprietors of slaves a very small proportion indeed are ever seen to labor." Not only did the sun dictate a Southern interest and an aversion to toil; it also purified the Anglo-Saxon blood lines. In 1852 a newspaper editor pointed out that South Carolina lay in the same latitude as Greece and Rome, which was a "pretty good latitude for a 'breed of noble men.'" Six years later an observer commented that the "gentleman and lady of England and France, born to command, were especially fitted for their God given mission of uplifting and Christianizing the Negroes because they were softened and refined under our Southern sky." These views continued into the present century. Hamilton J. Eckenrode declared that in the warm climate of the American South a superior Nordic race became "tropicized" and thus improved in quality, and Francis B. Simkins also defined the South as the result of an adjustment of Anglo-Saxon peoples to a subtropical climate. He went on to deplore the modern preference for sun-tanned women and architectural styles that broke with the ante-bellum tradition, and—perhaps with tongue in cheek—he regarded all admiration for Southern temperatures as a form of Yankee carpetbaggery. "Because of the tyranny of books and magazines imported from strange climates," he said, Southerners had lost their fear of the sun, and in so doing had denied their birthright. They were "prompted to construct artificial lakes, treeless lawns, and low-roofed houses without porches or blinds."

Such is the environmental view—the causal effects of climate upon Southern folkways—and its inaccuracies are manifest. There is no unity in Southern climate, for the section includes startling variations in pattern and is wholly temperate rather than tropical in nature. William A. Foran pointed out that it was climate of opinion rather than climate in fact that influenced the configurations of life and thought among Europeans inhabiting the Southern regions of North America. "The Great South of 1860," Foran said, "began at Mason's and Dixon's line, just twenty-five miles south of the Liberty Bell on Independence Square, and ranged on through fifteen degrees of latitude." It encompassed almost every type of North American climate, "from pleasantly-tempered Virginia and magnolia-scented Charleston to the arctic blizzards of Texas. . . . Can historians speak glibly of a southern climate, much less of a tropical one," he asked, "of a land whose rainfall varies from zero to seventy inches a year?"

But the important question concerns the causal relationship between high temperatures and a distinctive life style. Even if there were a demonstrable meteorological unity to Southern weather, that would not of itself determine a particular social order, an agricultural pattern, or a way of life. That it did so in fact is the basic assumption of the advocates of the environmental theory. Yet climate neither forecast nor foreordained a staple crop-slave labor-race segregation cycle such as Phillips and others have described. Edgar T. Thompson explicitly rejected the Phillips thesis. "The plantation was not to be accounted for by climate," he said; the climate-plantation-slavery syndrome was instead a defense mechanism. "A theory which makes the plantation depend upon something outside the processes of human interaction, that is, a theory which makes the plantation depend upon a fixed and static something like climate," he declared, "is a theory which operates to justify an existing social order and the vested interests connected with that order."

Whatever forces produced the plantation—perhaps a complex combination of the English manorial tradition and the immediate need for a social unit that could provide a measure of economic independence and military defense—it has existed in low-country regions of the South as an important institution. Many seekers for the central theme have considered it, therefore, as the distinctive characteristic of Southern life. First used to describe a group of "planted" colonists, the word came to mean a system of farming with tenants, indentured servants, peons, or slaves working under the direction of proprietors who owned great estates and who used their wealth and social position to play active roles in their communities' affairs. As a close-knit social and political group, the planters exerted an influence that was indeed often predominant. In some regions they were able to define their interests as those of the entire population, and their way of life as typical of the whole. With the enthusiastic co-operation of nostalgic novelists, poets, song composers, and advertising agents, the plantation and its gentlemen of distinction became the epitome of the Southern ideal. For a generation prior to the Civil War its proponents were able to impose the "plantation platform" of opposition to national banks, internal improvements at federal government expense, and tariffs of protection upon the policies of the general government. At the same time, opponents of the Jeffersonian agricultural Arcadia and the Calhounian logic of dominant particularism came to view the plantation as the symbol of all that was evil or amiss about America. It represented wealth amassed by exploiting an immoral labor system, disunionist and antinationalistic sentiments, support for policies that tied the whole country to a humiliating economic colonialism, and political power resting upon a snobbish and superficial aristocracy. For these reasons, enemies of the plantation regarded it as "un-American." Still, it served as a definition of the South. The plantation system was an ancient one; in varying forms it antedated the rise of chattel slavery, and after emancipation it persisted in fact and fancy as a distinctive entity. It was also fairly well distributed over the coastal plains and river valleys, regions earliest settled and seat of preponderant voting strength, and it extended into a roughly similar topography as settlement advanced into the Southwest. The plantation pattern of production was therefore general enough to serve as an archetype, however superficial, of a recognizable Southern society.

The great estate, with its paternalistic Massa and Missus, and the values it allegedly conserved, has provided much of the romantic Southern tradition. "The plantation," said Sheldon Van Auken, "is central to any understanding of the South." Since before there were white men in New England, he declared, it has been the most significant aspect of a South differentiated by it from the rest of the nation. More than other forms of economic and social organization the plantation provided security to laborers and a satisfying way of life to its operators. It set the standards for the entire South, Van Auken concluded, and it has remained the ideal image of the South. Earlier, Francis P. Gaines studied the plantation as a Southern tradition and declared that "the supremacy of the great estate in the thinking of the South cannot be successfully challenged."

But despite the plantation's exalted place in tradition, at no time was it the typical pattern of life in the Southern regions. It was a hothouse flower that could not hold its own in the low country and could not survive the cooler breezes of the uplands. Many students, including both Gaines and Van Auken, pointed out that the plantation did not penetrate into the hilly regions where yeoman farmers predominated and where a different way of life prevailed; except for isolated regions in the Virginia tidewater and the South Carolina low country, it did not monopolize life anywhere. The Owsleys have demonstrated that the plantation was not typical even of the Alabama black belt and was becoming less important in the decade of the 1850's. And according to Avery Craven, by 1860 Virginia and Maryland had "come largely to the small farm and the small farmer." The governor of Virginia reported that the state was no longer characterized by the "large plantation system," but had developed into an agriculture of "smaller horticultural and arboricultural farming." . . .

The plantation was, presumably, the home of other significant factors in the Southern image—the planter and his code of honor, and the institution of slavery—and students turned to these as central characteristics. As Avery Craven put it, "Only two factors seem to have contributed to the making of anything Southern—an old-world country-gentleman ideal and the presence of negroes in large numbers." The small minority of well-to-do planters lived in conscious imitation of the old English squires, stocking their homes with books and musical instruments, importing furnishings and clothing, and providing tutors for their children. In their personal relationships the more refined among them practiced a gallant chivalry. "When you institute a comparison between the men of the North and the South, does it not result in favor of those of the South?" a speaker in the Kentucky constitutional convention of 1849 asked. "Has not the South acquired for itself a character for frankness, generosity, high-toned honor, and chivalry which is unknown in the North?"

This was the country-gentleman ideal as a characteristic of the South. Though many planters ignored the demands of the code, in theory it set Cavalier Southerner apart from Roundhead Yankee. It provided a theme for the Southern Agrarians, who saw in it a conservative civilization which had, in the words of John Crowe Ransom, come "to terms with nature." Living "materially along the inherited line of least resistance," the planters sought "to put the surplus of energy into the free life of the mind." But to emphasize the country-gentleman as the typical inhabitant of the Southern regions, and to pretend that he alone possessed a code of disinterested obligation to public service or polite manners, ignored a host of other types equally Southern and overlooked commendable contributions to statecraft made by men who lived in other quadrants of the country.

Much more common as a unifying factor was another by-product of the plantation system of production, slavery and the Negro. Thomas P. Govan declared that the South was that part of the United States in which slavery continued for sixty years after it was abandoned elsewhere, but was in all other respects similar to the rest of the country. The only important sectional conflict in America, he said, arose from the fact that Negroes were held as slaves; emancipation eliminated the single Southern distinctive and removed the cause of its desire to be independent. The subsequent insistence upon white supremacy, Govan contended, merely meant that Southerners acted like other men of European origins when they confronted large numbers of people of differing ethnic types. To define the South as the land of white supremacy, he concluded, overlooked the very real racism among non-Southern Americans and incorrectly suggested that only Southerners were capable of bigotry and intolerance. Yet Charles S. Sydnor cited the presence of the Negro as the most popular of the monocausationist theories explaining the differences between Southerners and other Americans.

The plantation also fostered a rural environment with its strange mixture of the polished and the primitive, and some students have defined the South in terms of its folkways. Andrew N. Lytle stated the central theme as a "backwoods progression" of an agrarian Arcadia, and others of the Agrarian School have emphasized the essential "South-ness" of a slowed pace of life, enjoyment of living, and leisure for contemplation and meditation. John Hope Franklin saw a different product of a rural South. It was a land of violence whose peoples possessed a "penchant for militancy which at times assumed excessive proportions." The Southern reputation for pugnacity, he added, "did not always command respect, nor even serious consideration; but it came to be identified as an important ingredient of Southern civilization."

Another critique of the Agrarian School came from David Potter. Declaring that the agrarian formula fitted the South remarkably badly, he defined the section as a place where older folkways persisted. "The culture of the folk survived in the South long after it succumbed to the onslaught of urban-industrial culture elsewhere," he said. "It was an aspect of this culture that the relations between the land and the people remained more direct and more primal in the South than in other parts of the country." In addition, relationships of people to one another "imparted a distinctive texture as well as a distinctive tempo to their lives." Americans regarded the South with a kind of nostalgia, he noted; its basis was not an ideal utopian society that never existed, but a "yearning of men in a mass culture for the life of a folk culture which really did exist."

Thus the climate and its alleged offspring, the plantation, the planter, the staple crop, and the Negro, all set in a rural scene surrounded by primitive folkways, have provided students with the ingredients for a central theme. Another avenue into the character of the Southern regions has been to pursue the second of Phillips' hypotheses and to describe the South on the basis of social patterns. Charles S. Sydnor suggested both the problem and the possibilities. Southern historians, he pointed out, studied a region which had no definite boundaries and therefore faced the prior necessity of delimiting their subject. In doing so, they pioneered in the study of social history. They considered the distinctive traits of the people called Southern and then sought "to discover the geographical incidence of these characteristics." Thus the student of the South "was driven from the problem of area back to the prior problem of essence," Sydnor declared; "his initial task was to discover what the Old South was. From the nature of the case he was compelled to be a social historian."

Elaborating upon his own analysis, in another article Sydnor listed some distinctively Southern culture patterns. Among them he described an inherited way of life modeled after that of the English gentry, slavery, malaria, hookworm, lynching, farm tenancy, the advocacy of states' rights, mockingbirds, and a unique attitude toward law and order. Following Sydnor's suggestions, other South-seekers offered additional criteria: the South is the place where people celebrate Christmas but not the Fourth of July with fireworks; it is where cooks add salt pork to the extended boiling of green vegetables; it is the domain of hominy grits; it is the land of one-party politics, one-horse plowing, and one-crop agriculture. Charles F. Lane declared that "the preference for the mule as a draft animal is one of the least-considered traits characterizing Southern culture" and proposed a map showing the mule population of the country as a way of marking boundaries around the South.

Other observers defined the South as the center of Protestant evangelical fundamentalism. Edwin McNeill Poteat declared that "the South is religiously solid" in much the same way that it was, to him, politically solid. To most Southerners heresy remained heresy, he said, and "they still in the main submit readily to demagogy in the pulpit, and enjoy the thrill of denominational competition." The religious South exhibited a "more homogeneous quality than any other section," Poteat concluded. There was some agreement with this idea. "The distinctiveness of the Old South," said Francis B. Simkins, "is perhaps best illustrated by its religion. Historic Protestantism was reduced to the consistencies of the Southern environment without sacrificing inherent fundamentals." Charles W. Ramsdell noted that religious fundamentalism was a Southern characteristic, and pointed out its effects in the reaction to the biological discoveries of the evolution of species, the effort to prohibit the manufacture and sale of beverage alcohol by constitutional amendment, and the resurgence of the Ku Klux Klan.

Another proposal in the quest for cultural distinctives held that the South was a collection of "settlement characteristics." The geographer Wilbur Zelinsky catalogued these traits as the pattern in which men house themselves. "In the course of field observations of house types, urban morphology, farmsteads, and other settlement characteristics," he said, "I have discovered a constellation of traits that are apparently co-terminous with the South and function collectively as a regional label." Some of the traits he emphasized were houses placed well back from the street and from each other, low or nonexistent curbings, sidewalk arcades in front of town shops, a central location for courthouses in county seats, a large number of rural nonfarm homes, a lack of "spatial pattern" to farm buildings, and a high rate of building abandonment. "The observer can be reasonably certain that he is within the Southern culture area when the bulk of these traits recur with great frequency," Zelinsky concluded, "and particularly when they are assembled into one or another of the regional house types."

Related to the description of the South as a land of rather slovenly dwelling patterns is David Bertelson's idea that the distinguishing characteristic of Southerners is laziness. By his definition, however, they were afflicted not with a lack of energy but with a dearth of social unity. Southerners sought individual rather than social goals and were motivated by a desire for private gain, he said. They were prototypes of the "robber barons" who sought wealth without social responsibility, and were so thoroughly committed to economic motivation that the relatively un-self-seeking abolitionists baffled them. To Bertelson the South was an individualistic, chaotic economy in an America whose other inhabitants held some idea of community purpose, and this gave Southerners a sense of apartness and led both to the formation and to the failure of the Confederacy. Before and during the war, he said, the idea that labor meant liberty for private gain destroyed all efforts to create community and strengthened the view of outsiders that Southerners were lazy.

A similar view was that of Earl E. Thorpe, who also argued that freedom was a chief characteristic of Southerners. To Thorpe, however, its emphasis was upon sexual license. Easy access to black females who "desperately wanted displays of recognition and affection" meant that there was less repression in the South than elsewhere, and freedom led to romanticism, hedonism, and pugnacity. The Southern white male, confronting the criticism of a more inhibited outside world, became militant in the defense of his society and his frequently deceived womenfolk. Thorpe thus described a Freudian South lying just below the land of Id, a harem of sexual freedom rather than a place of economic individualism.

Another recent proposal, offered by C. Vann Woodward, held that the only distinguishing feature that may survive the social revolution of the post-1945 era is the memory of the Southern past. "The collective experience of the Southern people," he said, has made the South "the most distinctive region of the country." It was an experience that repudiated the most cherished aspects of the American self-image, for it was a record of poverty in a land of plenty, pessimism and frustration among a people wedded to optimism and unending success, and guilt complexes in a naively innocent America. Indeed, Woodward comes close to saying that the central theme of Southern history is Southern history. However helpful the idea may be in interpreting the dreary years after Appomattox, it ignores the peculiarities and events that caused such an aberrant history in the first place.

Another currently popular thesis, also based upon the harsh unpleasantness that surrounds much of Southern existence, contends that the Southerner is more inclined to romanticism than are other Americans. The Southerner is distinguished by his preference for fantasy and myth. "The quality that makes him unique among Americans," said T. Harry Williams, is his ability to conjure up "mind-pictures of his world or of the larger world around him—images that he wants to believe, that are real to him, and that he will insist others accept." George B. Tindall suggested the possibility that "we shall encounter the central theme of Southern history at last on the new frontier of mythology," and he listed some of the myths about the South that have at one time or another gained support: the Pro-Slavery South, the Confederate South, the Demagogic South, the States' Rights South, the Lazy South, and the Booster South. "There are few areas of the modern world," he declared, "that have bred a regional mythology so potent, so profuse and diverse, even so paradoxical, as the American South." Here again the searcher finds the results of an allegedly distinctive South, one of the inheritance family of character traits, but provides little illumination as to its cause.

The effort to locate the South by defining it as a single characteristic produced still another statement of the central theme. Outlined by Avery Craven and Frank L. Owsley and amplified by others, it argued that the South was the product of attacks from without. In this view the South was a state of mind, a conscious minority reacting to criticism by forging a unity as a defense mechanism. Opposition drew people together in defense of their peculiarities when their natural course would have been to fight among themselves. It began, according to Craven, with the tariff controversy in the 1820's and it became full grown in the abolition crusade.

Frank L. Owsley further developed the theme that the South came into being only when it became the victim of outside attack. "There was very little defense or justification of slavery until the commencement of a vigorous abolitionist assault from the North," he said. But "the attack upon slavery and the South resulted in the development of a philosophical defense of slavery. . . . So violent and dangerous did this new crusade appear to Southerners that a revolution in Southern thought immediately took place." Owsley declared that attacks upon the South had continued since the Civil War, but these merely succeeded in making the section more united than before. Charles W. Ramsdell, B. B. Kendrick, and A. B. Moore, along with others, defended the "outside attack" thesis, while Frank E. Vandiver emphasized an "offensive-defensive" pattern of Southern response to external criticism. Implicit in this argument is the assumption that a united South began as a Yankee invention.

The contention that the idea of a South grew out of external attacks produced its corollary—that the South was the result of a conscious effort to create a sense of unity among a diverse population with conflicting interests. In the effort, Southern leaders used all available arguments—climate, race, soil, staple-crop similarities, the agrarian philosophy with its country-gentleman ideal and the plantation as a romantic tradition, and slavery as a positive good. Some of them dramatized, if they did not actually invent, attacks from without as aids to their campaign for sectional unity. "If there is a central theme," said Robert S. Cotterill, "it is the rise of Southern nationalism." The study of the emergence of a divergent nationalism attracted many scholars. The South "was an emotion," Avery Craven wrote, "produced by an assumption on the part of outsiders of a unity there which did not exist, by propaganda within which emphasized likenesses rather than differences and created a unity of fear where none other existed."

In the conscious effort to create a South, every hint of attack from outside the section came as a godsend. William Lloyd Garrison and his abolition newspaper might well have passed unnoticed had not Southern publicists called attention to him by putting a price upon his head. Critics of the Southern system such as Elijah P. Lovejoy in Illinois and Cassius M. Clay in Kentucky found themselves the objects of violent mob resistance. In 1859 Edmund Ruffin, an energetic Southern unifier, expressed gratitude for the John Brown raid upon Harpers Ferry because of its beneficial effects upon "the sluggish blood of the South," and he took it upon himself to send samples of Brown's pikes to the governors of the slave states lest they forgot. After the war, Reconstruction again called forth a movement for white unity in the face of political and economic coercion—new attacks from without—and into the twentieth century there appeared leaders willing to evoke memories of the past as weapons against proposed changes in existing social or educational arrangements.

The flaw in the hypothesis of a movement to unify a people in the face of real or imaginary attacks from without has two aspects. First, as with all devil theories of historical motivation, it assumes almost magical powers of clairvoyance among promoters of the movement; and second, what it describes are but activities common to politicians practicing their profession wherever found, not uniquely Southern behavior at all. It was not surprising that Southern leaders should appeal for unanimity in support of their programs and candidacies; indeed, it would require explanation had any not done so. And that they could have foreseen the consequences of their conduct places a severe strain upon credulity.

From this confusing and sometimes contradictory survey of central themes in Southern history and life the suspicion emerges that the American South defies either location or analysis. It appears to be in fact an enigma challenging comprehension, "a kind of Sphinx on the American land." Its geographical boundaries are imprecise at best, and the characteristics of its population resist valid generalization. To say this is not to say that the South does not exist; it is to suggest that it exists only as a controlling idea or belief upon which men acted, risked, and died. The idea of the South is real; it is one of the most important ideas in American history, and that gives it significance.

The South idea has played a fundamental role in national development. In the early days of the Republic, as part of the debate between Thomas Jefferson and Alexander Hamilton which formed the basis of the first party divisions under the Constitution, the idea of a South contributed to the definition of public policy. As the internal dispute became more heated, it entered into the compromises that Americans made over the admission of Missouri, in the tariff settlement in 1833, and in the agreements of 1850. The idea appeared in party platforms and in the selection of candidates, and in 1860 it was an essential element in the division within the Democratic party.

The idea of a South produced an internal civil war whose outcome established the American nation. That result might have occurred in the absence of civil war, and also without the South idea, temporarily expressed as a Confederacy of states hostile to national union. But as it happened, the emergence of American nationality depended upon the idea of a South that posed a challenge to national citizenship and solidarity. In the postwar settlement—the constitutional amendments comprised in the peace treaty between the sections—the idea of the South profoundly affected the nature of the re-established Union upon national and pluralistic foundations. Later, when war emotions had cooled and industrial production expanded, it was the idea of the South that influenced the form and the content of the reactionary compromises of 1877. In the twentieth century the idea of a South re-emerged as men debated the meaning of national citizenship and the civil liberties the nation owed its citizens.

The American South is therefore not a place or a thing; it is not a collection of folkways or cultural distinctives. It is an idea. Those of whatever persuasion or tradition who believe themselves to be Southern are indeed Southern, and the South exists wherever Southerners form the predominant portion of the population. The study of the idea of Southness is thus a part of intellectual history, or, because it is an exercise in faith, it belongs among the academic offerings in the department of religion.

Perhaps a more fruitful question for students of the American South would be, not *what* the South is or has been, but *why* the idea of the South began, and *how* it came to be accepted as axiomatic among Americans. Whose interests were served when people spoke and thought of the South as an entity? How did the agents of the opinion-forming and opinion-disseminating institutions transmit the idea that allegiance to a section should transcend loyalty to the nation? What have been the effects upon American history of the belief in the idea of a South? Answers to these questions will go far to remove the study of the South from the realm of classifying and cataloguing to the tasks of probing causes and effects and the weighing of motivations. These are the true functions of the historian.

The South as a Counterculture

SHELDON HACKNEY

All around us extraordinary crises threaten to intrude into the serenity of our daily lives, and we are aware as seldom before of the striking disjunction between the personal and the public realms. At this time, when the habits of mind formed by our national historical experiences with individualism, affluence, progressive growth and military victory seem to be interfering with our ability to face up to the problems of racial justice, poverty, environmental despoliation and war, we should ask how our regional heritage speaks to our present needs. As the nation's largest and oldest counterculture, the South has much to teach us.

This, no doubt, seems a bizarre assertion to those familiar with the making of the contemporary counterculture. Much of the impetus for the cultural rebellion of youth lately has come from the assault of the civil rights movement on the South in the 1960s, so it would be a supreme irony if there were strong resemblances between the culture of the South and the culture created by young Americans seeking alternative values.

As analyzed sympathetically by Theodore Roszak in *The Making of a Counter Culture*, today's counterculture is at bottom a revolt against the dehumanizing effect of scientific and technological values, and against the bureaucratic society whose very efficiency depends upon desensitizing people to individual needs and differences. Artificial barriers that separate people, be they psychological, institutional, or social, say the current rebels, have to be torn down. In contrast to the ideal of material progress through rational analysis, the counterculture focuses on the quality of life and the need for individuals to have more power over the decisions that affect their lives.

The revolt against authoritarianism in favor of the New Left's ideal of participatory democracy has become more generally a revolt against authority of any kind. Only personal experience can serve as the basis of belief, a precept that should be appreciated by Southern Protestants who trace their form of worship back to the frontier. . . .

. . . In simplistic terms, it is a matter of the heart versus the head. There is a widespread feeling that the life of reason has failed us because so many barbarities are perpetrated in its name and so many evils exist within its sight. The technocratic rationalism of the war in Vietnam is the thing that lends it a special horror.

Furthermore, so the argument goes, technocracy and bureaucracy stultify spontaneity and thus make individual authenticity impossible. In con-

"The South as a Counterculture" by Sheldon Hackney. Reprinted from *The American Scholar*, Volume 42, Number 2, Spring 1973. Copyright © 1973 by the author. By permission of the publisher.

trast to the innovative thinkers of the late nineteenth and early twentieth centuries, such as Sigmund Freud, who were interested in the nonrational in order to control it better, we are confronted with Normal O. Brown, who argues that civilization's discontents will remain unless currently repressed instinctual drives are released from control by the superego. At the risk of putting the matter even more simplistically, the counterculture is a protest against the commercialization of life.

What are we to make of all this from our special vantage point in the South? I begin with history, because I accept as truth what Jack Burden says in Robert Penn Warren's novel, *All the King's Men*: "If you could not accept the past and its burden there was no future, for without one there cannot be the other, and . . . if you could accept the past you might hope for the future, for only out of the past can you make the future."

The key to the Southern past is that Southerners are Americans who have taken on an additional identity through conflict with the North. The process differentiating the South from the American non-South in the early nineteenth century was based on divergent economic interests growing from differing labor systems, and depending in part upon the Southern context of a sparse, occupationally homogeneous population and the lack of an urban middle class. With that beginning, the Southern sense of separateness has been constructed of many layers of defensiveness, particularism, isolation, guilt, defeat and the reactions to changes initiated from without: abolitionism, the Civil War, Reconstruction, poverty, depressions, industrialization and lately the civil rights movement. Through all this, white Southerners learned to see themselves as an oppressed minority with a giant sense of grievance, an identity they share with blacks, although for different reasons.

The counterattack of the Southern press against the hypocrisy and self-righteousness of the North during the Second Reconstruction is but another activation of this traditional defensive mentality. The same siege mentality can be seen subtly at work among historians and others who attribute the slow pace of modernization in the South to the region's colonial status and the imperial domination of Northern economic interests. Furthermore, the sense of persecution can be seen influencing the literature of the region. When Quentin Compson in *Absalom! Absalom!* comes to call on Rosa Coldfield before going off to Harvard, he is reminded, as he must have been a thousand times before, of the Yankee's persecution of the South. "So," says Rosa Coldfield, "I don't imagine you will ever come back here and settle down as a country lawyer in a little town like Jefferson since Northern people have already seen to it that there is little left in the South for a young man."

Nevertheless, Southerners are Americans, and in a real sense the need to be different was forced upon them by circumstances and by outsiders. The resulting approach-avoidance relationship of South to North explains why one finds in the South the coexistence of hyper-Americanism and cultural peculiarity.

The "approach" side of this curious psychological transaction can be seen best since the Civil War in the New South movement, beautifully dissected by Paul Gaston in *The New South Creed*, one of whose messages is that a conquered people frequently will imitate its conquerors. The chief tenet of the New South crusade is that industrialization is the way to secular salvation, and its optimistic dogma has from the first been that the South is destined to be the most prosperous place on earth, a new Eden. The bearers of these glad tidings were not only wise men out of the North, but local prophets as well, of whom Henry Grady was the most renowned in the nineteenth century. Today's champions of the New South tend to be the more institutional, hungry utilities and state industrial development offices, but the message is the same: The South is the land of milk and honey, or at least of water and electricity, and one can move into this land of low taxes and docile labor with little of the difficulty experienced by the children of Israel.

Southerners, when operating on the "avoidance" side of the American mirror, traditionally have had to define themselves in opposition to a presumed American norm, and in that sense at least, the South is a real counterculture. When the South was first created, the North was becoming the special carrier of Yankee commercial culture with its stress upon hard work, thrift and the cash basis of value. The mythical Southern planter, created in novels as an alternative to the emerging Yankee, was therefore a noneconomic man, the result of the South's need for a myth that would distinguish it from, and make it morally superior to, the North. . . .

The planters of the legend, explains William R. Taylor in *Cavalier and Yankee*, were exemplars of noncompetitiveness. They were generous, loving, gentle, noble and true to their word. Rather than the instinctive nobility of the unspoiled savage, however, the planter had the benefits of a benign and salubrious country life and rigorous training in a civilized code. But it was not the code of the Yankee. The legendary planter was free of personal ambition, particularly of the material sort, and his natural impulses were disciplined, not by calculation of gain, but by his concern for family and racial traditions, by rigid standards of decorum and a complicated code of personal honor. That our fictive hero was also weak, improvident, indolent and ineffectual betrays a flaw of disbelief on the part of his creators and explains why (Oh, confounder of women's liberation) Scarlet O'Hara always ended up running Tara. Southern writers shared more than they realized of the mainstream cultural values of the nation.

Northern writers, conversely, played an important part in the creation of the plantation legend, but for reasons differing from those of their Southern brothers. Faced with severe social dislocations growing out of geographic mobility, industrialization, immigration and urbanization, some Northerners began to fear the erosion of the old republican style of life characterized by simplicity and prudence. In growing numbers during the decades before the Civil War, such men began to focus their discontent on the planter and the slave system upon which he depended, as the primary threat to the Puritan virtues upon which the republic was founded. At the same time, many other Northerners were becoming painfully aware that

the helter-skelter process of social mobility in America could not monitor the conditions under which men competed, and thus could not guarantee
the moral worth of the men who succeeded. The image of the Yankee as
an acquisitive, grasping, uncultivated and amoral man was not acceptable
to many sensitive Northerners. Some reacted by imputing to the Yankee
a transcending social virtue. They argued in effect that the ascetic, single-
minded, materialistic and opportunistic Yankee benefited society by making
a profit. Others, however, helped to create the planter or the Southern
gentleman as the counterpoint to the Yankee. The Southern gentleman was
made to possess all of the virtues that the Yankee lacked. He had honor
and integrity, indifference to money questions and business, a decorous
concern for the amenities of life and a high sense of social responsibility.
In the age of democratic expansion, anxious men sought an antidemocratic
Good Society and they found it in the mythical, static, Southern plantation.

Southern intellectuals responded obligingly by spending an enormous
amount of energy romantically constructing Biblical or feudal or classical
Greek alternatives to the liberal capitalism of the nation at large. John C.
Calhoun, to an extent, and George Fitzhugh, more fundamentally, attacked
the dehumanization inherent in the wage slavery of free enterprise. According to Fitzhugh in his books, *Sociology for the South or The Failure
of Free Society* and *Cannibals All: or, Slaves Without Masters*, free competition was only legalized exploitation. It was merely freedom for the
strong to oppress the weak. Anticipating Herbert Marcuse, one of the
political philosophers of the New Left, Fitzhugh pointed out that not only
was physical wretchedness the result of this war of all against all, but
psychological wretchedness as well. For under capitalism one man's success
was marked by another man's failure; fortunes shifted rapidly, and the
result was that the human personality was marked by insecurity, anxiety
and unhappiness. To complete his rejection of Jefferson, Fitzhugh advocated strong and positive action by the government to build up industries
and cities in the South. Rejecting the doctrine of progress and the principle
of equality, Fitzhugh held that only within the framework of absolute dependence and superiority could genuine reciprocal affection exist between
human beings. A society seeking solutions in fantasy could scarcely get
further away from the American consensus.

After the Civil War, the mutual symbolic interaction of North and South
continued under the new conditions. While the myth of the New South
was being created in a great rush of popular fervor, the myth of the Old
South was simultaneously being created, packaged and marketed in the
North and the South. Reflecting this divided mind of the South, Joel Chan-
dler Harris recorded his Uncle Remus stories at the same desk where he
wrote for the *Atlanta Constitution* editorials infused with New South boosterism. Harris, George Washington Cable, Thomas Nelson Page, Mary
Noailles Murfree and their fellow writers in the 1880s established the pri-
macy of Southern themes in American letters. Archaic romance and local
color stories appealed to Northern audiences facing the reality of rapid
social change in their daily lives. Southern sensibilities called for pathos

balanced with the theme of sectional reconciliation. Through it all ran an intense sense of place and awareness of the past-in-the-present that are trademarks of Southern literature. The stock Southern character, for Northern as well as Southern writers, was still the embodiment of noncommercial nobility, the counterpoint to the shrewd but crude robber baron who ruled the Gilded Age.

The Agrarians, a group of Southern intellectuals centered at Vanderbilt University in the 1920s and 1930s, did not perpetuate this cavalier myth, but they were nonetheless engaged in the old Southern sport of defining an alternative to the national consensus. As their manifesto, *I'll Take My Stand*, put it in 1930, "All the articles bear in the same sense upon the book's title-subject: all tend to support a southern way of life against what may be called the American way; and all as much as agree that the best terms in which to represent the distinction are contained in the phrase, Agrarian versus Industrial." It was a frontal assault on the principles of Northern and modern civilization, a continuing comparison between the disordered present and the heroic past, which has always been the currency of groups disturbed by change.

The Agrarians, echoing George Fitzhugh, denied the virtue of machine-produced wealth and decried the brutalization of man and the philistinization of society that inevitably resulted from an industrial order. As humanists, they insisted that labor, the largest item in human life, should be enjoyed. This was impossible under industrialism. The art and culture they held most valuable was that which grew out of natural folk ways of doing, living and thinking. All else was superficial. Present day devotees of the *Whole Earth Catalog*, organic gardening and the handicraft industry would find this pretty heavy stuff.

More abstractly, the Agrarians placed the relationship of man to nature close to the center of their philosophy. They believed that "there is possible no deep sense of beauty, human heroism of conduct, and no sublimity of religion, which is not informed by the humble sense of man's precarious position in the universe." In other words, "there is more in the land than there is in the man," or, as John Crowe Ransom put it, "Nature wears out man before man can wear out nature. . . . It seems wiser to be moderate in our expectations of nature, and respectful; and out of so simple a thing as respect for the physical earth and its teeming life, comes a primary joy, which is an inexhaustible source of arts and religions and philosophies." The thing that differentiates these romantic conservatives most clearly from their descendants among today's youthful counterculturists is that the Agrarians linked community with continuity. They thought that "tradition is not simply a fact, but a fact that must be constantly defended." Nevertheless, paradoxical as it might seem, there is a large area of agreement between the culture of the South as understood by the Agrarians and the contemporary counterculture.

Like all paradoxes, the similarity between the culture of the South and the counterculture has its limitations. The world view of Southern Protestantism, which dominates the mind of the region, makes a virtue out of suffering in a way members of the counterculture would not understand or accept, even though the emphasis upon redemption through a personal conversion experience might find some resonance among young Americans seeking instant salvation along various secular and spiritual paths. Just as the counterculture is unthinkable in a country lacking the affluence provided by the work ethic in league with technocracy, Southern culture would not long survive apart from the rationalism whose hegemony it was created to challenge. The problems of human survival are not going to be solved by consulting the *I Ching* or Tarot cards.

Even so, at the present, when ten times more college students take courses in astrology than in astrophysics, when middle Americans, numbered by their lives as members of endless audiences, are in search of affective relationships, the South has much to offer. To an increasingly fragmented world the South offers an integrated view of life. There is no such thing as being "in fashion" now; styles in clothes and in most areas of life are too various and are multiplying too rapidly for a single standard to exist even for a short time. Contemporary art runs a gamut from the Wyeths to Helen Frankenthaler, and style has become a collective noun. Such currently popular writers as Donald Barthelme and Jerzy Kosinski render life into brilliant snippets of experience that coagulate without melding. Compare this to the vision of William Faulkner in which past, present and future are linked together; in which individuals don't merely rub up against each other in fleeting encounters but are enmeshed in each other's lives; in which individual lives over long periods of time are bound together by their connection to place. There is a wholeness to life in the South, even in its harsh and ugly aspects, and this is a useful antidote to a world in which increasing individuality means increasing isolation.

The price of wholeness is finitude. Freedom and the power to act are circumscribed when one is tied to a community. Rather than something that a counterculture must construct in the future after all the restraints of organized society have been cast off, community for Southerners is a set of conditions and obligations to be fulfilled through courage and honor. Strangely enough, Southerners, both white and black, do not feel alienated from themselves even though they feel alienated from the national sources of economic and political power.

It may also seen strange to find illegal defiance of national authority coexisting so comfortably in the South with superpatriotism, but that is a consequence of the dual identity of Southerners, and grows out of their double history. As C. Vann Woodward points out in *The Burden of Southern History*, the South's experiences with defeat, poverty and guilt have set it apart from the nation. In contrast to the national belief that problems have solutions, Southerners harbor the countervailing suspicion that there are limits to human power.

There is a salutary humanistic lesson in discovering the vine of fate entangling Southern history. Whether that vine is wisteria or kudzu may vary according to ideological taste, but the message that there are areas of life not susceptible to rational control or bureaucratic manipulation strikes a resonant note. As a perceptive journalist observed of a group of irate town fathers in Mississippi who had just been struck by another federal court edict, "Of course, they are not really surprised because, being Southerners and therefore fatalistic, they live always half expecting disaster." . . .

Southern history forces us to be aware not only of complexity, but also of defeat and failure. It would be wrong to reject or oppose the improvement in social welfare that will come from the intrusion of the machine into the garden, but we should oppose the Icarian notion that change comes without costs, and that the South will be immune from history. Only through such a constant realization do we have a chance to industrialize and humanize at the same time, to walk the thin line between defeatism and morally obtuse boosterism.

In striving to live with our past without being oppressed by it, the proper stance is one of ambivalent judgment, an ironic distance between oneself and his history that energizes rather than immobilizes. The modern man facing his existential predicament might well be guided by the lesson contained in the following Hasidic legend recorded by Elie Wiesel in his book, *Souls on Fire:*

> One of the Just Men came to Sodom, determined to save its inhabitants from sin and punishment. Night and day he walked the streets and markets preaching against greed and theft, falsehood and indifference. In the beginning, people listened and smiled ironically. Then they stopped listening: he no longer even amused them. The killers went on killing, the wise kept silent, as if there were no Just Man in their midst.
>
> One day a child, moved by compassion for the unfortunate preacher, approached him with these words. "Poor stranger. You shout, you expend yourself body and soul; don't you see that it is hopeless?"
>
> "Yes, I see," answered the Just Man.
>
> "Then why do you go on?"
>
> "I'll tell you why. In the beginning I thought I could change man. Today, I know I cannot. If I still shout today, if I still scream, it is to prevent man from ultimately changing me."

FURTHER READING

David Bertelson, *The Lazy South* (1967)
James Branch Cabell, *Let Me Lie* (1947)
F. Garvin Davenport, *Myth and Southern History* (1970)
Carl N. Degler, *Place over Time: The Continuity of Southern Distinctiveness* (1977)
———, "Thesis, Antithesis, Synthesis: The South, the North, and the Nation," *Journal of Southern History* 53 (1987), 3–18
John Hope Franklin, *The Militant South* (1956)
———, "The Great Confrontation and the Problem of Change," *Journal of Southern History* 38 (1972), 3–20
Wilson Gee, "The Distinctiveness of Southern Culture," *South Atlantic Quarterly* 37 (1939), 119–29
Patrick Gerster and Nicholas Cords, eds., *Myths and Southern History* (1974)
C. Hugh Holman, *The Immoderate Past: The Southern Writer and History* (1977)

Lewis M. Killian, *White Southerners* (1970)
Florence King, *Southern Ladies and Gentlemen* (1975)
Jack Temple Kirby, *Media-Made Dixie* (1978)
A. Cash Koeniger, "Climate and Southern Distinctiveness," *Journal of Southern History* 54 (1988), 21–44
Sharon McKern, *Redneck Mothers, Good Ol' Girls, and Other Southern Belles* (1979)
Grady McWhiney, *Southerners and Other Americans* (1973)
Bill C. Malone, *Southern Music/American Music* (1979)
U. B. Phillips, "The Central Theme of Southern History," *American Historical Review* 34 (1928), 30–43
David M. Potter, "The Enigma of the South," *Yale Review* 51 (1961), 142–51
Francis Butler Simkins, *The Everlasting South* (1963)
William R. Taylor, *Cavalier and Yankee* (1961)
Frank E. Vandiver, ed., *The Idea of the South: Pursuit of a Central Theme* (1964)
Alice Walker, "The Black Writer and the Southern Experience," *New South* 25 (1970), 23–26
C. Vann Woodward, *The Burden of Southern History* (1961)
Howard Zinn, *The Southern Mystique* (1964)

CHAPTER
2

Red, White, and Black

Historians of the colonial South have discovered that whites—Spaniards, French, and English—did not happen on an empty wilderness in the New World. Along the South Atlantic and Gulf coasts and as far into the interior as the Appalachian Mountains, Indian tribes and confederations had built towns, and they farmed and hunted vast territories. Unfortunately, almost all of what we know of the first southern civilization consists of indirect evidence gleaned from the accounts of whites, from archaeological sites, and from transcribed comments of descendants. The Indians who inhabited the South in the sixteenth century were nonliterate people, and their numbers dwindled rapidly once whites introduced unaccustomed diseases into the New World environment. We are still sorting out such basic questions as who these people were, the various alliances they formed, and their cultures. Once we have a better understanding, we can assess the nature and impact of the Indians' contact with both white and black southerners.

The introduction of blacks from Africa and the West Indies added to the diversity of the southern colonial population. The interaction between whites and native Americans after 1619 expanded to include blacks, though there is evidence that Indians were at least aware of Africans through earlier Spanish and French contacts. The growth of the black population, especially after 1680, has enabled historians to develop a deeper cultural portrait of the uprooted Africans than has been possible for the Indians. Therefore, the questions we ask have advanced beyond the basic issues of identification. What, for example, was the extent of cultural interaction between black and white southerners in the colonial era, and how did it vary from colony to colony? What preconceptions did blacks and whites bring to their encounters with each other? When and how did slavery emerge as an important labor system? And what were the roles of economic expediency and racial attitudes in the formalization of slavery?

人 *D O C U M E N T S*

Much of what little we know about the southeastern Indians comes from contemporary whites' perceptions. Usually these observations are layered with the prejudices of sixteenth- and seventeenth-century Europeans encountering a culture quite different from their own. Despite this drawback, several accounts demonstrate sensitivity and provide valuable insights. Such is the case with the paintings of John White, who accompanied Sir Walter Raleigh's first expedition to Roanoke Island, near present-day North Carolina, in 1585. Four of the paintings are reproduced in the first document. That colony, and a subsequent settlement on Roanoke Island—the famous Lost Colony—did not survive. Two decades later, a more successful venture at Jamestown, Virginia, provides us with another detailed account of Indian civilization, this time through the descriptions of Captain John Smith. Though somewhat of an autocrat to his fellow colonists, Captain Smith held a keen appreciation for native American culture and for the meaning of the Indian-white encounter, as the next excerpt indicates. The third document, written by Gabriel Díaz Vara Calderón, bishop of Cuba, later in the seventeenth century, reflects a different relationship between white European and native American. The Spanish were intent on converting the Indians to the Catholic faith and established their settlements—missions—to carry out that goal, as well as to pacify the Indians.

The institution of slavery evolved slowly until the late seventeenth century. Georgia was a holdout in the trend toward slavery. But as the series of documents in the fourth selection encompassing the period 1735 to 1750 reveals, sentiment for slave labor quickly mounted in the colony, culminating in the repeal of the act prohibiting slavery there. In the half-century from 1700 to 1750, the southern colonies increasingly formalized master-slave relationships and restricted the liberties of slaves, as the fifth document, from South Carolina, reflects. These regulations emerged alongside the sharp upsurge in slave importations, as well as rising fears over slaves' growing numbers. The South Carolina statute was a direct response to a brief, but bloody, slave revolt in 1739 in the Stono River district, 20 miles outside of Charleston. Slaves worked out their own accommodation to the restrictions, including leaving their masters for extended periods of time. The last excerpt, from Colonel Landon Carter's diary, demonstrates both the exasperation of a leading Virginia planter and the support runaways received from the larger slave community.

John White Depicts Indian Life, 1585

Indian Village of Pomeiooc

Indian Woman and Young Girl

Indian Village of Secoton

Cooking Fish

John Smith on the Natives of Virginia, 1612

The land is not populous, for the men be fewe; their far greater number is of women and children. Within 60 miles of James Towne there are about some 5000 people, but of able men fit for their warres scarse 1500. [The Indian population figures for Smith's day are under review, but no consensus seems to have been reached as yet.] To nourish so many together they have yet no means because they make so smal a benefit of their land, be it never so fertill. 6 or 700 have beene the most hath beene seene together, when they gathered themselves to have surprised Captaine Smyth at Pamaunke, having but 15 to withstand the worst of their furie. [This maximum show of fighting men (probably exaggerated by Smith) only confirms Smith's conviction that the land of Virginia was not populous. England's second city, Norwich, then had twice as many inhabitants as Powhatan's entire "empire."] As small as the proportion of ground that hath yet beene discovered, is in comparison of that yet unknowne, the people differ very much in stature, especially in language, as before is expressed. Some being very great as the Sesquesahamocks; others very little, as the Wighcocomocoes: but generally tall and straight, of a comely proportion, and of a colour browne when they are of any age, but they are borne white. Their haire is generally black, but few have any beards. The men weare halfe their heads shaven, the other halfe long; for Barbers they use their women, who with 2 shels will grate away the haire, of any fashion they please. The women are cut in many fashions agreeable to their yeares, but ever some part remaineth long. They are very strong, of an able body and full of agilitie, able to endure to lie in the woods under a tree by the fire, in the worst of winter, or in the weedes and grasse, in Ambuscado in the Sommer. They are inconstant in everie thing, but what feare constraineth them to keepe. Craftie, timerous, quicke of apprehension and very ingenuous. Some are of disposition fearefull, some bold, most cautelous [wary and wily], all Savage. Generally covetous of copper, beads, and such like trash. They are soone moved to anger, and so malitious, that they seldome forget an injury: they seldome steale one from another, least their conjurers should reveale it, and so they be pursued and punished. That they are thus feared is certaine, but that any can reveale their offences by conjuration I am doubtfull. Their women are carefull not to bee suspected of dishonesty without the leave of their husbands. Each household knoweth their owne lands and gardens, and most live of their owne labours. For their apparell, they are some time covered with skinnes of wilde beasts, which in winter are dressed with the haire, but in sommer without. The better sort use large mantels of deare skins not much differing in fashion from the Irish mantels. Some imbrodered with white beads, some with copper, other painted after their manner. But the common sort have scarce to cover their nakednesse but with grasse, the leaves of trees, or such like. We have seen some use mantels made of Turky feathers, so prettily wrought and woven with threeds that nothing could bee discerned but the feathers. That was exceeding warme and very handsome. But the women are alwaies covered about their midles with a skin and very shamefast [modest] to be seene bare. They adorne themselves most with copper beads and paintings. Their women some have their legs, hands, brests and face cunningly imbrodered [tattooed] with diverse workes, as beasts, serpentes, artificially wrought into their flesh with blacke spots. In each eare commonly they have 3 great holes, whereat they hange chaines bracelets or copper. Some of their men weare in those holes, a smal greene and yellow coloured snake, neare halfe a yard in length, which crawling and lapping her selfe about his necke often times familiarly would kisse his lips. Others wear a dead Rat tied by the tail. Some on their heads weare the wing of a bird, or some large feather with a Rattell. Those Rattels are somewhat like the chape of a Rapier but lesse, which they take from the taile of a snake. [The ''chape'' is the metal cap covering the tip of the scabbard of a rapier, dagger, etc. This is most likely the earliest specific mention of the American rattlesnake.] Many have the whole skinne of a hawke or some strange fowle, stuffed with the wings abroad. Others a broad peece of copper, and some the hand of their enemy dryed. Their heads and shoulders are painted red with the roote *Pocone* braied to powder mixed with oyle, this they hold in somer to preserve them from the heate, and in winter from the cold. Many other formes of paintings they use, but he is the most gallant that is the most monstrous to behould.

Their buildings and habitations are for the most part by the rivers or not farre distant from some fresh spring. Their houses are built like our Arbors of small young springs [saplings] bowed and tyed, and so close covered with mats, or the barkes of trees very handsomely, that notwithstanding either winde, raine or weather, they are as warme as stooves, but very smoaky, yet at the toppe of the house there is a hole made for the smoake to goe into right over the fire.

Against the fire they lie on little hurdles of Reedes covered with a mat borne from the ground a foote and more by a hurdle of wood. [Smith refers to the rectangular frames lifting the Indian beds slightly from the ground.] On these round about the house they lie heads and points one by th'other against the fire, some covered with mats, some with skins, and some starke naked lie on the ground, from 6 to 20 in a house. Their houses are in the midst of their fields or gardens which are smal plots of ground. Some 20, some 40. some 100. some 200. some more, some lesse, some times from 2 to 100 of those houses togither, or but a little separated by groves of trees. Neare their habitations is little small wood or old trees on the ground by reason of their burning of them for fire. So that a man may gallop a horse amongst these woods any waie, but where the creekes or Rivers shall hinder.

Men women and children have their severall names according to the severall humor of their Parents. Their women (they say) are easilie delivered of childe, yet doe they love children verie dearly. To make them hardy, in the coldest mornings they wash them in the rivers and by painting and ointments so tanne their skins, that after a year or two, no weather will hurt them.

The men bestowe their times in fishing, hunting, wars and such manlike exercises, scorning to be seene in any woman-like exercise, which is the cause that the women be verie painefull and the men often idle. The women and children do the rest of the worke. They make mats, baskets, pots, morters, pound their corne, make their bread, prepare their victuals, plant their corne, gather their corne, beare al kind of burdens and such like.

Their fire they kindle presently [quickly] by chafing a dry pointed sticke in a hole of a little square peece of wood, that firing it selfe, will so fire mosse, leaves, or anie such like drie thing, that will quickly burne. In March and Aprill they live much upon their fishing weares, and feed on fish, Turkies and squirrels. In May and June they plant their fieldes and live most of Acornes, walnuts, and fish. But to mend their diet, some disperse themselves in small companies and live upon fish, beasts, crabs, oysters, land Torteyses, strawberries, mulberries, and such like. In June, Julie, and August they feed upon the rootes of *Tocknough* berries, fish and greene wheat. It is strange to see how their bodies alter with their diet, even as the deare and wilde beastes they seeme fat and leane, strong and weak. Powhatan their great king and some others that are provident, rost their fish and flesh upon hurdles as before is expressed, and keepe it till scarce times. . . .

For fishing and hunting and warres they use much their bow and arrowes. They bring their bowes to the forme of ours by the scraping of a shell. Their arrowes are made some of straight young sprigs which they head with bone, some 2 or 3 inches long. . . .

In their hunting and fishing they take extreame paines; yet it being their ordinary exercise from their infancy, they esteeme it a pleasure and are very proud to be expert therein. And by their continuall ranging, and travel, they know all the advantages and places most frequented with Deare, Beasts, Fish, Foule, Rootes, and Berries. At their huntings they leave their habitations, and reduce themselves into companies, as the Tartars doe, and goe to the most desert places with their families, where they spend their time in hunting and fowling up towards the mountaines, by the heads of their rivers, where there is plentie of game. For betwixt the rivers the grounds are so narrowe, that little commeth there which they devoure not. It is a marvel they can so directly passe these deserts, some 3 or 4 daies journey without habitation. Their hunting houses are like unto Arbours covered with mats. These their women beare after them, with Corne, Acornes, Morters, and all bag and baggage they use. When they come to the place of exercise, every man doth his best to shew his dexteritie, for by their excelling in those quallities, they get their wives. Forty yards will they shoot levell, or very neare the mark, and 120 is their best at Random. [Shooting "at random" meant with speed, but without careful aim; shooting "level" meant carefully, with direct aim.] At their huntings in the deserts they are commonly 2 or 300 together. Having found the Deare, they environ them with many fires, and betwixt the fires they place themselves. And some take their stands in the midst. The Deare being thus feared by the fires and their voices, they chace them so long within that circle that many times they kill 6, 8, 10, or 15 at a hunting. They use also to drive them into some narrowe point of land; when they find that advantage and so force them into the river, where with their boats they have Ambuscadoes to kill them. When they have shot a Deare by land, they follow him like blood hounds by the blood and straine and oftentimes so take them. Hares, Partridges, Turkies, or Egges ["egges" seems out of place; perhaps a garbled spelling of "geese"], fat or leane, young or old, they devoure all they can catch in their power. In one of these huntings they found Captaine Smith in the discoverie of the head of the river of Chickahamania, where they slew his men, and tooke him prisoner in a Bogmire, where he saw those exercises, and gathered these observations. . . .

One Savage hunting alone, useth the skinne of a Deare slit on the one side, and so put on his arme, through the neck, so that his hand comes to the head which is stuffed, and the hornes, head, eies, eares, and every part as arteficially counterfeited as they can devise. Thus shrowding his body in the skinne by stalking he approacheth the Deare, creeping on the ground from one tree to another. . . .

When they intend any warres, the Werowances usually have the advice of their Priests and Conjurers, and their Allies and ancient friends, but chiefly the Priestes determine their resolution. Every Werowance, or some lustie fellow, they appoint Captaine over every nation. They seldome make warre for lands or goods, but for women and children, and principally for revenge. They have many enimies, namely all their westernely Countries beyond the mountaines, and the heads of the rivers. Upon the head of the Powhatans are the Monacans, whose chiefe habitation is at Russawmeake, unto whome the Mouhemenchughes, the Massinnacacks, the Monahassa-nuggs, and other nations pay tributs. Upon the head of the river of Top-pahanock is a people called Mannahoacks. To these are contributers the Tauxsnitanias, the Shackaconias, the Outponcas, the Tegoneaes, the Whon-kentyaes, the Stegarakes, the Hassinnungas, and diverse others, all con-federats with the Monacans though many different in language, and be very barbarous living for most part of wild beasts and fruits: Beyond the moun-taines from whence is the head of the river Patawomeke, the Savages report inhabit their most mortall enimies, the Massawomekes upon a great salt water, which by all likelyhood is either some part of Cannada some great lake, or some inlet of some sea that falleth into the South sea. . . .

Their manner of trading is for copper, beades, and such like, for which they give such commodities as they have, as skins, fowle, fish, flesh, and their country corne. But their victuall is their chiefest riches.

There is yet in Virginia no place discovered to bee so Savage in which the Savages have not a religion, Deare, and Bow, and Arrowes. All things that were able to do them hurt beyond their prevention, they adore with their kinde of divine worship; as the fire, water, lightning, thunder, our ordinance, peeces, horses, etc. But their chiefe God they worship is the Divell. Him they call *Oke* and serve him more of feare then love. [Oke was the malevolent, vengeful god of the Powhatan tribe.] . . . They say they have conference with him, and fashion themselves as neare to his shape as they can imagine. In their Temples they have his image evill favouredly carved, and then painted and adorned with chaines copper, and beades, and covered with a skin, in such manner as the deformity may well suit with such a God. By him is commonly the sepulcher of their kings. Their bodies are first bowelled, then dryed upon hurdles till they bee verie dry, and so about the most of their jointes and necke they hang bracelets or chaines of copper, pearle, and such like, as they use to weare, their inwards they stuffe with copper beads and covered with a skin, hatch-ets and such trash. Then lappe they them very carefully in white skins and so rowle them in mats for their winding sheetes. And in the Tombe which is an arch made of mats, they lay them orderly. What remaineth of this kinde of wealth their kings have, they set at their feet in baskets. These Temples and bodies are kept by their Priests.

For their ordinary burials they digge a deep hole in the earth with sharpe stakes and the corpes being lapped in skins and mats with their jewels, they lay them upon sticks in the ground, and so cover them with earth. The buriall ended, the women being painted all their faces with black cole [charcoal, soot, burned wood] and oile, doe sit 24 howers in the houses mourning and lamenting by turnes, with such yelling and howling as may expresse their great passions.

In every Territory of a werowance is a Temple and a Priest 2 or 3 or more. Their principall Temple or place of superstition is at Uttamussack [site of the principal Pamunkey temple] at Pamaunke, neare unto which is a house Temple or place of Powhatans.

Upon the top of certaine redde sandy hils in the woods, there are 3 great houses filled with images of their kings and Divels and Tombes of their Predecessors. Those houses are neare 60 foot in length built arbor wise after their building. This place they count so holy as that but the Priestes and kings dare come into them; nor the Savages dare not go up the river in boats by it, but that they solemnly cast some peece of copper, white beads or *Pocones* into the river, for feare their *Oke* should be offended and revenged of them. . . .

In this place commonly is resident 7 Priests. . . . Their devotion was most in songs which the Chiefe Priest beginneth and the rest followed him. . . .

Although the countrie people be very barbarous, yet have they amongst them such governement, as that their Magistrats for good commanding, and their people for du subjection, and obeying, excell many places that would be counted very civill. The forme of their Common wealth is a monarchicall governement, one as Emperour ruleth over many kings or governours. Their chiefe ruler is called Powhatan, and taketh his name of the principall place of dwelling called Powhatan. But his proper name is Wahunsonacock. Some countries he hath which have been his ancestors, and came unto him by inheritance, as the countrie called Powhatan, Arrohateck, Appamatuke, Pamaunke, Youghtanund, and Mattapanient. All the rest of his Territories expressed in the Map, they report have beene his severall conquests. In all his ancient inheritances, hee hath houses built after their manner like arbours, some 30 some 40 yardes long, and at every house provision for his entertainement according to the time. At Werowocomoco, he was seated upon the Northside of the river Pamaunke, some 14 miles from James Towne, where for the most part, hee was resident, but he tooke so little pleasure in our neare neighbourhood, that were able to visit him against his will in 6 or 7 houres, that he retired himself to a place in the deserts at the top of the river Chickahamania betweene Youghtanund and Powhatan. His habitation there is called Orapacks where he ordinarily now resideth. He is of parsonage ["personage"; personal appearance] a tall well proportioned man, with a sower looke, his head somwhat gray, his beard so thinne that it seemeth none at al, his age neare 60; of a very able and hardy body to ensure any labour. About his person ordinarily attendeth a guard of 40 to 50 of the tallest men his Country doth afford. Every night upon the 4 quarters of his house are 4 Sentinels each standing from other a flight shoot, and at every halfe houre one from the Corps du guard doth hollowe, unto whome every Sentinell doth answer round from his stand; if any faile, they presently send forth an officer that beateth him extremely.

A mile from Orapakes in a thicket of wood hee hath a house in which he keepeth his kind of Treasure, as skinnes, copper, pearle, and beades, which he storeth up against the time of his death and buriall. Here also is his store of red paint for ointment, and bowes and arrowes. This house is 50 or 60 yards in length, frequented only by Priestes. At the 4 corners of this house stand 4 Images as Sentinels, one of a Dragon, another a Beare, the 3 like a Leopard [the "Dragon" was surely a wolf, and the "Leopard" a lynx] and the fourth like a giantlike man, all made evillfavordly ["made to look ugly"], according to their best workmanship.

He hath as many women as he will, whereof when hee lieth on his bed, one sitteth at his head, and another at his feet, but when he sitteth, one sitteth on his right hand and another on his left. As he is wearie of his women, hee bestoweth them on those that best deserve them at his hands. When he dineth or suppeth, one of his women before and after meat, bringeth him water in a woden platter to wash his hands. Another waiteth with a bunch of feathers to wipe them insteed of a Towell, and the feathers when he hath wiped are dryed againe. His kingdome descendeth not to his sonnes nor children, but first to his brethren, whereof he hath 3. namely Opitchapan, Opechancanough, and Catataugh, and after their decease to his sisters. First to the eldest sister then to the rest and after them to the heires male and female of the eldest sister, but never to the heires of the males. . . .

. . . Powhatan began to expostulate the difference betwixt peace and war, after this manner.

Captaine Smith you may understand, that I, having seene the death of all my people thrice [Powhatan is apparently referring to drastic reverses or epidemics in his lifetime of which we have now little or no record], and not one living of those 3 generations, but my selfe, I knowe the difference of peace and warre, better then any in my Countrie. But now I am old, and ere long must die, my brethren, namely Opichapam, Opechankanough, and Kekataugh, my two sisters, and their two daughters, are distinctly each others successours, I wish their experiences no lesse then mine, and your love to them, no lesse then mine to you; but this brute from Nansamund that you are come to destroy my Countrie, so much affrighteth all my people, as they dare not visit you; what will it availe you, to take that perforce, you may quietly have with love, or to destroy them that provide you food? [The bruit, or rumor, from Nansemond "that from the *Chesapeack* Bay a Nation should arise, which should dissolve and give end to his Empier" was confirmed by William Strachey.] what can you get by war, when we can hide our provision and flie to the woodes, whereby you must famish by wronging us your friends; and whie are you thus jealous of our loves, seeing us unarmed, and both doe, and are willing still to feed you with that you cannot get but by our labours? think you I am so simple not to knowe, it is better to eate good meate, lie well, and sleepe quietly with my women and children, laugh and be merrie with you, have copper, hatchets, or what I want, being your friend; then bee forced to flie from al, to lie cold in the woods, feed upon acorns, roots, and such trash, and be so hunted by you, that I can neither rest, eat, nor sleepe; but my tired men must watch, and if a twig but breake, everie one crie there comes Captaine Smith, then must I flie I knowe not whether, and thus with miserable feare end my miserable life; leaving my pleasures to such youths as you, which through your rash unadvisednesse, may quickly as miserably ende, for want of that you never knowe how to find? Let this therefore assure you of our loves and everie yeare our friendly trade shall furnish you with corne, and now also if you would come in friendly

manner to see us, and not thus with your gunnes and swords, as to invade
your foes.

Bishop Calderón on the Mission Indians of Florida, 1675

On the coast of the northern border, 30 leagues from Cape Canaveral,
[where] the canal of Bahama disembogues, is located, on the 30th parallel
of latitude, the city of Saint Augustine. . . . It is the capital of the provinces
of Florida and has more than 300 Spanish inhabitants, soldiers and married
people. . . .

. . . It has a parish church . . . for the teaching of Christian doctrine
and the administering of the sacraments to the Indians who usually attend
to the cultivating of the lands of the residents of the Post [Saint
Augustine]. . . .

Going out of the city, at half a league to the north there is a small
village of scarcely more than 30 Indian inhabitants, called Nombre de Dios,
the mission of which is served from the convent. Following the road from
east to west, within an extent of 98 leagues there are 24 settlements and
missions of Christian Indians, 11 belonging to the province of Timuqua and
13 to that of Apalache. . . .

In the four provinces of Guale, Timuqua, Apalache and Apalachocoli
there are 13,152 Christianized Indians to whom I administered the holy
sacrament of confirmation. They are fleshy, and rarely is there a small one,
but they are weak and phlegmatic as regards work, though clever and quick
to learn any art they see done, and great carpenters as is evidenced in the
construction of their wooden churches which are large and painstakingly
wrought. The arms they employ are bow and arrows and a hatchet they
call *macâna*. They go naked, with only the skin [of some animal] from the
waist down, and, if anything more, a coat of serge without a lining, or a
blanket. The women wear only a sort of tunic that wraps them from the
neck to the feet, and which they make of the pearl-colored foliage of trees,
which they call *guano* and which costs them nothing except to gather it.
[*Guano* is a general term for any sort of palm tree or leaf. He evidently
refers to clothing of Spanish moss.] Four thousand and eighty-one women,
whom I found in the villages naked from the waist up and from the knees
down, I caused to be clothed in this grass [*yerba*: the use of this word
indicates that the writer did not recognize the material] like the others.

Their ordinary diet consists of porridge which they make of corn with
ashes [lye hominy], pumpkins, beans which they call *frijoles*, with game
and fish from the rivers and lakes which the well-to-do ones can afford.
Their only drink is water, and they do not touch wine or rum. Their greatest
luxury is [a drink] which they make from a weed that grows on the seacoast,
which they cook and drink hot and which they call *cazina*. It becomes very
bitter and is worse than beer, although it does not intoxicate them and is
beneficial. They sleep on the ground, and in their houses only on a frame
made of reed bars, which they call *barbacoa*, with a bear skin laid upon
it and without any cover, the fire they build in the center of the house

serving in place of a blanket. They call the house *bujío*. It is a hut made in round form, of straw, without a window and with a door a *vara* [2.8 feet] high and half a *vara* wide. On one side is a granary supported by 12 beams, which they call a *garita,* where they store the wheat, corn and other things they harvest.

During January they burn the grass and weeds from the fields preparatory to cultivation, surrounding them all at one time with fire so that the deer, wild ducks and rabbits, fleeing from it fall into their hands. This sort of hunting they call *hurimelas.* Then they enter the forests in pursuit of bears, bison and lions which they kill with bows and arrows, and this they call *ojêo.* Whatever they secure in either way they bring to the principal cacique, in order that he shall divide it, he keeping the skins which fall to his share. Offering is made to the church of the best parts, and this serves for the support of the missionary priest, to whom they are in such subjection that they obey his orders without question.

In April they commence to sow, and as the man goes along opening the trench, the woman follows sowing. All in common cultivate and sow the lands of the caciques. As alms for the missionaries and the needy widows, they sow wheat in October and harvest it in June. This is a crop of excellent quality in the province of Apalache, and so abundant that it produces seventy *fanegas* [a *fanega* is about a bushel and a half] from one *fanega* sown.

Each village has a council house called the great *bujío,* constructed of wood and covered with straw, round, and with a very large opening in the top. Most of them can accommodate from 2,000 to 3,000 persons. They are furnished all around the interior with niches called *barbacôas,* which serve as beds and as seats for the caciques and chiefs, and as lodgings for soldiers and transients. Dances and festivals are held in them around a great fire in the center. The missionary priest attends these festivities in order to prevent indecent and lewd conduct, and they last until the bell strikes the hour of las *ánimas.*

These Indians do not covet riches, nor do they esteem silver or gold, coins of which do not circulate among them, and their only barter is the exchange of one commodity for another, which exchange they call *rescate.* [*Rescate* is a good Spanish word of Latin origin, meaning "ransom" but with "barter" as a secondary meaning.] The most common articles of trade are knives, scissors, axes, hoes, hatchets, large bronze rattles [*cascabeles grandes de bronce. Cascabeles* are properly small bells of the type used on harness], glass beads, blankets which they call *congas,* pieces of rough cloth [*jerguetas*], garments and other trifles.

As to their religion, they are not idolaters, and they embrace with devotion the mysteries of our holy faith. They attend mass with regularity at 11 o'clock on the holy days they observe, namely, Sunday, and the festivals of Christmas, the Circumcision, Epiphany, the Purification of Our Lady, and the days of Saint Peter, Saint Paul and All Saints Day, and before entering the church each one brings to the house of the priest as a contribution a log of wood. They do not talk in the church, and the women are separated from the men; the former on the side of the Epistle, the latter on the side of the Evangel. They are very devoted to the Virgin, and on Saturdays they attend when her mass is sung. On Sundays they attend the *Rosario* and the *Salve* in the afternoon. They celebrate with rejoicing and devotion the Birth of Our Lord, all attending the midnight mass with offerings of loaves, eggs and other food. They subject themselves to extraordinary penances during Holy Week, and during the 24 hours of Holy Thursday and Friday, while our Lord is in the Urn of the Monument, they attend standing, praying the rosary in complete silence, 24 men and 24 women and the same number of children of both sexes, with hourly changes. The children, both male and female, go to the church on work days, to a religious school where they are taught by a teacher whom they call the *Athequi* [Indian word meaning "interpreter"] of the church; [a person] whom the priests have for this service; as they have also a person deputized to report to them concerning all parishioners who live in evil.

The Debate over Slavery in Georgia, 1735–1750

Minutes of the Georgia Privy Council, 1735

April 3, 1735.

An Act for rendering the Colony of Georgia more Defencible by Prohibiting the Importation and use of Black Slaves or Negroes into the same.

Whereas Experience hath Shewn that the manner of Settling Colonys and Plantations with Black Slaves or Negroes hath obstructed the Increase of English and Christian Inhabitants therein who alone can in case of a War be relyed on for the Defence and Security of the same, and hath Exposed the Colonys so settled to the Insurrections Tumults and Rebellions of such Slaves and Negroes and in Case of a Rupture with any Foreign State who should Encourage and Support such Rebellions might Occasion the utter Ruin and loss of such Colonys, For the preventing therefore of so great inconveniences in the said Colony of Georgia. We the Trustees for Establishing the Colony of Georgia in America humbly beseech Your Majesty That it may be Enacted And be it Enacted that from and after the four and twentieth day of June which shall be in the Year of Our Lord One Thousand Seven hundred and thirty five if any Person or Persons whatsoever shall import or bring or shall cause to be imported or brought or shall sell or Barter or use in any manner or way whatsoever in the said Province or in any Part or Place therein any Black or Blacks Negroe or Negroes such Person or Persons for every such Black or Blacks Negroe or Negroes so imported or brought or caused to be imported or brought or sold Bartered or used within the said Province Contrary to the intent and meaning of this Act shall forfeit and lose the Sum of fifty pounds Sterling Money of Great Britain. . . .

Diary of the Earl of Egmont, 1735–1738

Wednesday, 3 [September 1735]. The Scots settled at Joseph's Town having applied for the liberty of making use of negro slaves, we acquainted one of their number, who came over to solicit this and other requests made by them to us, that it could not be allowed, the King having passed an Act against it, of which we read part to him. . . .

Monday, 17 [November 1735]. A letter was read from Mr. Samuel Eveleigh that he had quitted his purpose of settling in Georgia, and was returned to Carolina, because we allow not the use of negro slaves, without which he pretends our Colony will never prove considerable by reason the heat of the climate will not permit white men to labour as the negroes do, especially in raising rice, nor can they endure the wet season when rice is to be gathered in. . . .

Thursday, 24 [November 1737]. . . . That Mr. —— Mackay had without leave on his own head settled on —— Wilmington Island and employed negroes. N. B. Smart care must be taken of this, for many are disposed to follow his example.

Remonstrance of the Inhabitants of Savannah, 1738

SAVANNAH, 9th December, 1738.
To the Honorable the Trustees for Establishing the Colony of Georgia in America.

May it please your Honors: We whose names are underwritten, being all settlers, freeholders and inhabitants in the province of Georgia, and being sensible of the great pains and care exerted by you in endeavoring to settle this colony, since it has been under your protection and management, do unanimously join to lay before you, with the utmost regret, the following particulars. . . . Timber is the only thing we have here which we might export, and notwithstanding we are obliged to fall it in planting our land, yet we cannot manufacture it for a foreign market but at double the expense of other colonies; as for instance, the river of May, which is but twenty miles from us, with the allowance of negroes, load vessels with that commodity at one half of the price that we can do; and what should induce persons to bring ships here, when they can be loaded with one half of the expense so near us; therefore the timber on the land is only a continual charge to the possessors of it, though of very great advantage in all the northern colonies, where negroes are allowed, and consequently, labor cheap. We do not in the least doubt but that in time, silk and wine may be produced here, especially the former; but since the cultivation of the land with white servants only, cannot raise provisions for our families as before mentioned, therefore it is likewise impossible to carry on these manufactures according to the present constitution. It is very well known, that Carolina can raise every thing that this colony can, and they having their labor so much cheaper will always ruin our market, unless we are in some measure on a footing with them. . . . Your honors, we imagine, are not insensible of the numbers that have left this province, not being able to support themselves and families any longer. . . .

The want of the use of negroes, with proper limitation; which, if granted, would both occasion great numbers of white people to come here, and also render us capable to subsist ourselves, by raising provisions upon our lands, until we could make some produce fit for export, in some measure to balance our importation. We are very sensible of the inconveniences and mischiefs that have already, and do daily arise from an unlimited use of negroes; but we are as sensible that these may be prevented by a due limitation, such as so many to each white man, or so many to such a quantity of land, or in any other manner which your Honors shall think most proper.

Diary of the Earl of Egmont, 1739

Wednesday, 17 Jany. 1738/9. I. Col. Oglethorpe wrote again to the Trustees, to shew further inconveniences arrising from the allowing the use of Negroes, *viz.* 1. That it is against the principles by which the Trustees associated together, which was to releive the distressed, whereas we should occasion the misery of thousands in Africa, by setting Men upon using arts to buy and bring into perpetual slavery the poor people, who now live free there. 2. Instead of strengthning, we should weaken the Frontiers of America. 3. Give away to the Owners of slaves that land which was design'd as a Refuge to persecuted Protestants. 4. Prevent all improvements of silk and wine. 5. And glut the Markets with more of the American Comodities, which do already but too much interfere with the English produce.

James Oglethorpe to the Trustees of Georgia, 1739

SAVANNAH 12th March 1738/9.

Gentlemen, . . . Mr. Williams is very angry, and hath got the poor People of Savannah, many of whom are deeply in Debt to him, to sign the Petition for Negroes, which affirms that white men cannot work in this Province. This Assertion I can disprove by hundreds of Witnesses, all the Saltzburghers, the people at Darien, many at Frederica, and Savannah, and all the Industrious in the Province. The idle ones are indeed for Negroes. If the Petition is countenanced the Province is ruined. Mr. Williams and Doctor Talfeur will buy most of the Lands at Savannah with Debts due to them, and the Inhabitants must go off and be succeeded by Negroes. Yet the very debtors have been weak enough to sign their Desire of Leave to sell.

Diary of the Earl of Egmont, 1739–1740

[Tuesday], 13 March 1738/9. The Saltsburgers at Ebenezer wrote and sign'd a Counter-representation to that sent by the Inhabitants of Savannah, earnestly desiring of Genl. Oglethorpe that Negroes and change of Tenure may not be allow'd of in the Province. In it they express their happy

condition, and desire the encouragement they had might be given to others to joyn them.

The Reverend John Martin Bolzius to the Reverend George Whitefield, 1745

EBENEZER Dec. 24th 1745.

Revd. and Dear Sir, Besides the Blessings, the Lord was pleased to impart to my Soul in your and Mrs. Whitefield's Conversation, I felt many Griefs and troubles in my heart Since my Return from Bethesda and Savannah, arising from the unhappy News, I heard at Savannah and from your Self, that you are induced to petition the Honble. Trustees for giving their Consent to the Introduction of Negroes into this our Colony, for which you think to be Under Necessity with Respect to the Maintainance of the Orphan House. Dont be amazed, Sir at my Boldness to write to you in this Secular Affair, in which I would not meddle at all, if not the Love to your Worthy person, to my Congregation and to this Colony Oblidged me to it. For the Introduction of Negroes inconsistent with the prayseworthy Scheme of the Honble. Trustees our Lawful and Bountiful Superiours, will be very Mischievous to the happy Settling of this Colony, and Especially to the poor white Labouring people in many Respects, and the Sighs of them would be unprofitable for you or any other, who joins with the principles and aims of the Wishers for Negroe Overseer. A Common white Labourer white Man of the meaner Sort can get his and his Family's Livelyhood honestly in Carolina, except he embraces the Sorry Imploy of a Negroe Overseers. A Common white Labourer in Charles-Town (I am told) has no more Wages, than a Negroe for his work *Viz*. 7 *s*. Cur. or 12 *d*. Sterl. a Day, for which it is in my Opinion impossible to find Victuals, Lodging and washing, much less Cloaths. In case he would Settle and Cultivate a plantation, is not all good and Convenient Ground at the Sea Coasts and Banks of the Rivers taken up in Large Quantities by the Merchants and Other Gentlemen? Consequently the poor white Inhabitants are forced to possess Lands, remote from the Conveniencys of Rivers and from Town to their great Disappointment to Sell their produce. Being not inclined to give their Produce of their Plantations or Other Sort of Work for Such a Low price, as Negroes can afford, they find no market, then they are discouraged and Obliged to Seek their Livelihood in the Garrisons, Forts, Scout-Boats, Trading Boats or to be imploy'd amongst the Negroes upon a Gentleman's Plantation, or they are forced to take Negroes upon Credit, of which they will find in Process of time the Sad Consequences on Account of their Debts. I hear the Negroes in Carolina learn all Sorts of trade, which takes away the bread of a poor white trades' man Like wise.

I have Considered the Strength of your Arguments by which you seem to be induced to promote the Introduction of Negroes, as far as it lyes in your power.

First you think the Providence of God has Appointed this Colony rather for the work of black Slaves than for Europians, because of the hot Climate, to which the Negroes are better used than white people.

But, Dear Sir, give me Leave to say, that every honest Labourer amongst us will testify the Contrary and that in some parts of Germany in the Middle of the Summer being the Only Season there to make Hay, and to bring in their Crop, is as hot as here. And if it be so, that in the 3 Months of the Summer it is too hot for white people to work with the hoe in the field, is it so with the plow Can they not Chuse the Morning and Afternoon Hours for Labouring in the Field? Have they not 9 Months in the Year time Enough to prepare the Ground for Europian and Countrey Grain? Which preference they enjoy not in the Northern Parts, by Reason of the Deep Snow and the Exceeding Cold Weather. . . .

II. Your Second Argument for the Introduction of Negroes was, that the Trustees have laid out about 250,000 Pounds Sterl. for Establishing this Colony, and almost to no purpose. . . . There are so many Thousands of Protestants in Germany, who would embrace eagerly an Invitation to this Colony, if they could meet with Encouragement, as they will in time, and it is a Thousand pity, that you will help to make this Retirement and Refuge for poor persecuted or Necessitous Protestants, a Harbour of Black Slaves, and deprive them of the benefit to be Settled here. . . .

III. Your third Argument was, that you have laid out great Sums of Money for Building and Maintaining the Orphan House, which you could not continue without Negroes, and this be the Case of Other Gentlemen in the Colony.

But let me intreat you, Sir, not to have regard for a Single Orphan House, and to Contribute Some thing Mischievous to the Overthrow of the prayseworthy Scheme of the Trustees with Respect to the whole Colony.

IV. Your Last Argument for Negroes was, as I remember, that you intended to bring them to the Knowledge of Christ.

But, Sir, my Heart wishes, that first the White people in the Colony and Neighbourhood may be brought to the Saving and Experimental Knowledge of Christ. As long as they are for this World, and take Advantage of the poor black Slaves, they will increase the Sins of the Land to a great Heighth. If a Minister had a Call to imploy his Strength and time to Convert Negroes, he has in Carolina a Large Field. Dont believe, Sir, the Language of those persons, who wish the Introduction of Negroes under pretence of promoting their Spiritual Happiness, as well as in a Limited Number and under some Restrictions. I am sure, that if the Trustees allow'd to one thousand White Settlers so many Negroes, in a few Years you would meet in the Streets, So as in Carolina, with many Malattoes, and many Negroe Children, which in process of time will fill the Colony. The Assembly in Carolina have made good Laws and Restrictions in favour of the White people, but how many are, who pay regard and Obedience to them? not better would fare the Restrictions and Good Laws of the Trustees. I will not mention the great Danger, to which we are exposed by the Introduction of Negroes with Respect to the Spaniards, and it is a Groundless thing, to say, that one of the Articles of Peace with Spain must be not to give Shelter to the Negroes at Augustine, who would run away.

Repeal of the Act Excluding Negroes, 1750

May it please Your Majesty,

The Trustees for establishing the Colony of Georgia in America in pursuance of the Powers and in Obedience to the Directions to them given by Your Majesty's most Gracious Charter humbly lay before Your Majesty the following Law Statute and Ordinance which they being for that purpose assembled have prepared as fit and necessary for the Government of the said Colony and which They most humbly present under their Common Seal to Your most Sacred Majesty in Council for your Majesty's most Gracious Approbation and Allowance.

> An Act for repealing an Act Intituled (An Act for rendering the Colony of Georgia more defensible by prohibiting the Importation and Use of Black Slaves or Negroes into the same) and for permitting the Importation and Use of them in the Colony under proper Restrictions and Regulations, and for other Purposes therein mentioned.

Whereas an Act was passed by his Majesty in Council in the Eighth Year of his Reign Intituled (an Act for rendering the Colony of Georgia more defensible by prohibiting the Importation and Use of Black Slaves or Negroes into the same) by which Act the Importation and Use of Black Slaves or Negroes in the said Colony was absolutely prohibited and forbid under the Penalty therein mentioned and whereas at the time of passing the said Act the said Colony of Georgia being in its Infancy the Introduction of Black Slaves or Negroes would have been of dangerous Consequence but at present it may be a Benefit to the said Colony and a Convenience and Encouragement to the Inhabitants thereof to permit the Importation and Use of them into the said Colony under proper Restrictions and Regulations without Danger to the said Colony as the late War hath been happily concluded and a General Peace established. Therefore we the Trustees for establishing the Colony of Georgia in America humbly beseech Your Majesty that it may be Enacted And be it enacted That the said Act and every Clause and Article therein contained be from henceforth repealed and made void and of none Effect and be it Further Enacted that from and after the first day of January in the Year of Our Lord One thousand seven hundred and fifty it shall and may be lawful to import or bring Black Slaves or Negroes into the Province of Georgia in America and to keep and use the same therein under the Restrictions and Regulations hereinafter mentioned and directed to be observed concerning the same And for that purpose be it Further Enacted that from and after the said first day of January in the Year of Our Lord One thousand seven hundred and fifty it shall and may be lawful for every Person inhabiting and holding and cultivating Lands within the said Province of Georgia and having and constantly keeping one white Man Servant on his own Lands capable of bearing Arms and aged between sixteen and sixty five Years to have and keep four Male Negroes or Blacks upon his Plantation there and so in Proportion to the Number of such white Men Servants capable of bearing Arms and of such Age as aforesaid as shall be kept by every Person within the said Province.

South Carolina Restricts the Liberties of Slaves, 1740

I. *And be it enacted,* . . . That all negroes and Indians, (free Indians in amity with this government, and negroes, mulattoes and mustizoes, who are now free, excepted,) mulattoes or mustizoes who now are, or shall hereafter be, in this Province, and all their issue and offspring, born or to be born, shall be, and they are hereby declared to be, and remain forever hereafter, absolute slaves. . . .

XXIII. *And be it further enacted* by the authority aforesaid, That it shall not be lawful for any slave, unless in the presence of some white person, to carry or make use of fire arms, or any offensive weapons whatsoever, unless such negro or slave shall have a ticket or license, in writing, from his master, mistress or overseer, to hunt and kill game, cattle, or mischievous birds, or beasts of prey, and that such license be renewed once every month, or unless there be some white person of the age of sixteen years or upwards, in the company of such slave, when he is hunting or shooting, or that such slave be actually carrying his master's arms to or from his master's plantation, by a special ticket for that purpose, or unless such slave be found in the day time actually keeping off rice birds, or other birds, within the plantation to which such slave belongs, lodging the same gun at night within the dwelling house of his master, mistress or white overseer. . . .

XXXII. *And be it further enacted* by the authority aforesaid, That if any keeper of a tavern or punch house, or retailer of strong liquors, shall give, sell, utter or deliver to any slave, any beer, ale, cider, wine, rum, brandy, or other spirituous liquors, or strong liquor whatsoever, without the license or consent of the owner, or such other person who shall have the care or government of such slave, every person so offending shall forfeit the sum of five pounds, current money, for the first offence. . . .

XXXIV. And *whereas,* several owners of slaves have permitted them to keep canoes, and to breed and raise horses, neat cattle and hogs, and to traffic and barter in several parts of this Province, for the particular and peculiar benefit of such slaves, by which means they have not only an opportunity of receiving and concealing stolen goods, but to plot and confederate together, and form conspiracies dangerous to the peace and safety of the whole Province; *Be it therefore enacted* by the authority aforesaid, That it shall not be lawful for any slave so to buy, sell, trade, traffic, deal or barter for any goods or commodities, (except as before excepted,) nor shall any slave be permitted to keep any boat, perriauger or canoe, or to raise and breed, for the use and benefit of such slave, any horses, mares, neat cattle, sheep or hogs, under pain of forfeiting all the goods and commodities which shall be so bought, sold, traded, trafficked, dealt or bartered for, by any slave, and of all the boats, perriaugers or canoes, cattle, sheep or hogs, which any slave shall keep, raise or breed for the peculiar use, benefit and profit of such slave. . . .

XXXVII. And *whereas,* cruelty is not only highly unbecoming those who profess themselves christians, but is odious in the eyes of all men who have any sense of virtue or humanity; therefore, to refrain and prevent barbarity being exercised towards slaves, *Be it enacted* by the authority aforesaid, That if any person or persons whosoever, shall wilfully murder his own slave, or the slave of any other person, every such person shall, upon conviction thereof, forfeit and pay the sum of seven hundred pounds, current money, and shall be rendered, and is hereby declared altogether and forever incapable of holding, exercising, enjoying or receiving the profits of any office, place or employment, civil or military, within this Province. . . .

XXXVIII. *And be it further enacted* by the authority aforesaid, That in case any person in this Province, who shall be owner, or shall have the care, government or charge of any slave or slaves, shall deny, neglect or refuse to allow such slave or slaves, under his or her charge, sufficient cloathing, covering or food, it shall and may be lawful for any person or persons, on behalf of such slave or slaves, to make complaint to the next neighboring justice, in the parish where such slave or slaves live or are usually employed. . . .

XLIII. And *whereas,* it may be attended with ill consequences to permit a great number of slaves to travel together in the high roads without some white person in company with them; *Be it therefore enacted* by the authority aforesaid, That no men slaves exceeding seven in number, shall hereafter be permitted to travel together in any high road in this Province, without some white person with them. . . .

XLV. And *whereas,* the having of slaves taught to write, or suffering them to be employed in writing, may be attended with great inconveniences; *Be it therefore enacted* by the authority aforesaid, That all and every person and persons whatsoever, who shall hereafter teach, or cause any slave or slaves to be taught, to write, or shall use or employ any slave as a scribe in any manner of writing whatsoever, hereafter taught to write, every such person and persons, shall, for every such offence, forfeit the sum of one hundred pounds current money.

XLVI. And *whereas,* plantations settled with slaves without any white person thereon, may be harbours for runaways and fugitive slaves; *Be it therefore enacted* by the authority aforesaid, That no person or persons hereafter shall keep any slaves on any plantation or settlement, without having a white person on such plantation or settlement.

Landon Carter on the Problem of Runaway Slaves, 1766

12. [March] *Wednesday.*

At night found that my ox carter, Simon, was run away and examined Billy the foreman who said he complained of the belly ake and went away, The Overseer being an [illegible] ordnance at Court.

24. *Thursday.*

Simon, one of the Outlaws, came home. He run away the 12th of March and by being out and doing mischief was outlawed in all the Churches 2 several Sundays and on the 10th of this month having a great suspicion that he was entertained at my home quarter where his Aunt and Sisterinlaw lives, Mr. Carter's favourite maid; I had him R[illegible] watched by Talbot and Tom with Guns loaded with small shot and Toney withdrew. Just at dark according to my suspicion they came along my lane; over the Lucern field talking loudly as if secure they should be concealed When Talbot commanding them to stand, upon their running, shot Simon in the right leg foot and ham. He got away and Simon has stayed out ever since then so that he has been now shot to this day 14 days. . . .

 . . . It seems that Simon the runaway was shot at only about 11 days agoe. And he did not come in himself; for Mangorike Will seeing a smoke yesterday amongst Some Cedars by the side of the corn field when he was working; at night went to see what it was, and was long hunting for it as smoke is but rarely seen in the night. At last he got to some burnt Coals and saw no one there, but creeping through the Cedars he came to a fire burning and Simon lying by it; Who instantly started up to run away, but Billy was too swift and after a small struggle made him surrender and brought him in to Tom and Nassau who concealed this from me, in order to make as if the fellow came in himself. Willy says he was not lame last night, although he has now strummed it on account of his leg being shot. I shall punish him accordingly. . . .

25. *Friday.*

 . . . My man Bart came in this day, he has been gone ever since New year's day. His reason is only that I had ordered him a whipping for saying he then brought in two load of wood when he was coming with his first load only. This he still insists on was truth. Although the whole plantation asserts the contrary, and the boy with him. He is the most incorrigeable villain I beleive alive, and has deserved hanging; which I will get done if his mate in roguery can be tempted to turn evidence against him.

Bart broke open the house in which he was tyed and locked up; he got out before 2 o'clock but not discovered till night. Talbot is a rogue. He was put in charge of him. I do imagine the gardiner's boy Sam, a rogue I have suspected to have maintained Bart and Simon all the while they have been out. And I sent this boy with a letter to the Island ferry at breakfast, but he never returned although he was seen coming back about 12 and was seen at night by Hart George at night pretending to be looking for his Cattle. I kept this fellow up two nights about these fellows before And have given Rit the Miller a light whipping as having fed them by the hands of Gardiner Sam. . . .

27. *Sunday.*

Yesterday my son brought a story from Lansdown old Tom, that Johnny my gardiner had harboured Bart and Simon all the while they were out,

Sometimes in his inner room and sometimes in my Kitchen Vault. Tom had this from Adam his wife's grandson That they were placed in the Vault in particular the day my Militia were hunting for them.

This Simon owned, and the boy Adam repeated it to me; but Tom of Landsdown said that George belonging to Capn. Beale saw them in my quarter when he came from setting my Weir. It seemed to me so plausible that I sent Johnny [to] Goal and locked his son in Law Postilion Tom up. Note: every body denied they had ever seen them and in Particular Mrs. Carter's wench Betty, wife to Sawney, brother of Simon, denied that she had ever seen them; as she did to me with great impudence some days agoe. However Capn. Beale's George this day came to me and before Mrs. Carter told the story and in Simon's hearing That coming from the Weir he went into Frank's room and then into Sawney's room, when Simon came in to them. So that favourites and all are liars and villains.

These rogues could not have been so entertained without some advantage to those who harboured them; from whence I may conclude the making away of my wool, wheat etc., and the death of my horses.

⅄ *E S S A Y S*

In his book *The Only Land They Knew* (1981), the late anthropologist J. Leitch Wright, Jr., of Florida State University creatively synthesized the meager source material available to provide a comprehensive view of the southeastern Indians before and during their early contact with Europeans and Africans. The excerpt reprinted in the first essay indicates the diversity of Indian civilizations in the Southeast and the tragic consequences of European settlement. Edmund S. Morgan, who taught history at Yale University, answers the important question of why Virginians established slavery as their primary labor system during the late seventeenth century. In the second essay, he carefully recounts the conditions in Virginia and abroad that accounted for the shift away from white indentured servants to black slaves. The final selection, by St. Olaf College historian Joan R. Gundersen, explores a relationship that scholars have just begun to analyze: that between white and black women. In this study of a parish in colonial Virginia, Gundersen relates the complex gender connections across racial and status lines that affected the lives of black and white women alike.

The Original Southerners

J. LEITCH WRIGHT, JR.

During the first part of the sixteenth century English, French, Spanish, and Portuguese mariners sailed along the North American Atlantic Coast and sometimes were shipwrecked or went ashore for refreshment. Ponce de

---

León, Verrazzano, and the Cabots skirted the shoreline, and occasionally a De Soto penetrated deep into the interior. From their accounts it is possible to catch a glimpse of the Indians they found and of their life-style and culture. But these natives had not suddenly appeared on the scene. Where had they come from, and what cultural changes had they undergone over the centuries? For this there is not a single eyewitness account, and it is necessary to rely on the archaeologist, linguist, folklorist, and ethnologist. Although a few little-understood petroglyphs and pictographs are scattered throughout parts of the South, these Indians were clearly a nonliterate people. . . .

It has not been ascertained with certainty when or from where man first arrived in the South. Archaeologists have uncovered as much of the story as is known. While not ruling out intrusions from Europe, Africa, or the Orient, there is a consensus, or nearly so, that man crossed the ice bridge over the Bering Strait and spread over much of North and South America. Recent archaeological evidence suggests the traditional date of twenty thousand years ago is possibly too late and that man first crossed the Bering Strait perhaps forty thousand or more years ago. The latest archaeological excavations in the Eastern woodlands have supported this theory.

By radiocarbon measurement and other scientific means of dating it has been shown that man has been around not just for a few thousand years but for sixteen thousand or more. Discoveries at Russell Cave in northeastern Alabama disclose an aboriginal occupation extending back about eight thousand years, and excavations at Flint Run, Virginia (near Front Royal), push the date back to 11,500 years. A similar site at Meadowcroft in southwestern Pennsylvania dates back to fourteen thousand B.C. One of the most significant discoveries in the South has been made 47 feet below the surface at Warm Mineral Springs near the Gulf in southwestern Florida. Here divers have retrieved a ten-thousand-year-old human skull from a submerged cave. Subsequent discoveries at an even lower depth suggest the presence of man for up to thirteen thousand years. The latter date, if verified, represents the earliest proven existence of man in the South and there are indications that even this date will have to be pushed back further.

Little is known about earliest man in the South. His religion, language, and social and political relationships are almost a complete mystery. To help describe how Indians advanced from one level of social complexity to another, anthropologists have identified four major cultural periods or traditions: Paleo, Archaic, Woodland, and Mississippian. A minority of contemporary archaeologists contend that a fifth period, Early Man, is emerging, which includes the most ancient Indians such as those at Warm Mineral Springs and Meadowcroft. At this point little is known about Early Man, and it may well be that in fact he did not exist. Paleo man was a nomadic hunter, best known for killing large, now extinct animals with stone-tipped spears or by stampeding them into various kinds of traps to their deaths. Life for Indians in the Archaic tradition was more sophisticated. Depending far less on large game animals, instead they exploited their environment more intensively. They hunted smaller animals with darts thrown from an *atlatl* or spear thrower; gathered nuts, berries, and shellfish; and became more sedentary. In some places they made a crude pottery tempered with vegetable fibers. In the Woodland Period, ca. 1000 B.C. to A.D. 700, the aborigines continued to rely primarily on hunting and gathering. But the use of pottery became widespread, and rudimentary agriculture supplemented their diet. Artifacts recovered from Woodland Period burial mounds, including pipes, stone and copper gorgets, wooden carvings, pottery effigies, and earrings, indicate the cultural advance. Such exotic materials as obsidian, shells from the Gulf of Mexico, and mica reveal that the Woodland Indians were more "cosmopolitan" or had more wide-flung relationships than did Archaic people. Burial mounds up to 40 or more feet in height scattered throughout the South perhaps best separate the Woodland Indians from their predecessors.

The Mississippian tradition, one of the most notable Indian cultures, beginning sometime after A.D. 700 and lasting up to or after white contact, is important for our purposes. This was the era of the mound builders, who constructed truncated platform temple mounds up to 100 feet tall, with religious and political structures on their flat tops. Frequently there was not just a single isolated temple mound but several spread over acres in planned clusters. From the top of the principal mound the priest could see villagers working in outlying fields. Indians brought in countless basketloads of dirt on their backs to construct the mounds, and villages provided the agricultural surplus to support a priestly and political elite.

The organized labor necessary to construct these mounds implies a structured political organization. At the time of white contact an indeterminate number of powerful tribes, chiefdoms, or confederations existed. Some of the better known are the Powhatan Confederation (Tsenacommacah) in Tidewater Virginia, the Natchez on the lower Mississippi River, the Calusa Kingdom in southern Florida, the Apalachee in northern Florida, and the Cofitachiqui in South Carolina. The Natchez, the Apalachee, and the Cofitachiqui were in the mainstream of the Mississippian tradition, while the Algonquians in Virginia, who had no temple mounds, and the Calusa in southern Florida, a maritime people, were on the fringe of Mississippian culture.

The Cofitachiqui chiefdom, occupying a central position in present-day South Carolina, was one of the most powerful societies in the South. De Soto visited the celebrated Queen of Cofitachiqui, the seat of whose domain was perhaps at Silver Bluff on the Savannah River below Augusta or more likely on the Wateree River near Camden. De Soto's chroniclers were clearly impressed by the numerous houses, large mounds, and the grand wooden, mat-covered temple containing bones of deceased natives, whose entrance was defended by intricately carved armed wooden giants. The Queen and her attendants wore long pearl necklaces; the Spaniards and their horses together could not possibly carry all of the pearls, reputedly weighing thousands of pounds. The Queen's armory held an enormous

FORTS

INDIAN TOWNS AND
PLACE NAMES

SOUTHERN   INDIANS

R S. DAWDY

quantity of copper-tipped pikes, maces, battle axes, and, according to some accounts, fifty thousand bows and quivers. For all the known opulence and size of Cofitachiqui, it is not at all clear today whether the Indians there spoke a Siouan, Muskhogean, or some other language, what the bounds of the Queen's realm were, and where her capital was located.

In addition to the Indians of Cofitachiqui, from the earliest times whites also came into direct or indirect contact with the Yuchi at one or another place in the South. In the folk history of these people, who comprised a separate linguistic family, there is the tradition that they had descended from a powerful empire. Yet almost nothing is known about this elusive Indian society. Even more mystery surrounds the Westos and Ricahecrians, who appeared so menacingly on the South Carolina and Virginia frontiers in the seventeenth century. Were they Iroquoian, Muskhogean, or Siouan speakers? Were they different or perhaps the same people? What was the extent and nature of their chiefdom? Spaniards and Frenchmen encountered, painted, and described Timucuans on the Atlantic Coast of present-day northern Florida and southern Georgia. Whether these Indians belonged in the Muskhogean family, as seems likely, or whether it is more proper to link them with Arawakan speakers of the Caribbean and northern South America is still not clear. An appalling number of Southern Indian languages became extinct without having been recorded; it is probable, in fact, that whole families of languages have disappeared without a trace.

Such linguistic diversity, which was greater than that of modern Western Europe, should not obscure the fact that remarkable cultural similarities existed throughout the South. Sixteenth-century Indians were essentially farmers and as such lived far more complicated lives than the hunter-gatherers associated with Russell Cave and Warm Mineral Springs. Maize—Indian corn—was the staff of life. Developed in South America and Mexico, it had made its way north during the Woodland Period. Northern flint corn spread into New England and the Mid-Atlantic states, and varieties of flint corn or popcorn early appeared in the South. Adapted to a warm, moist climate and proceeding along the Gulf of Mexico, southern dent (gourd seed) corn at a much later date, perhaps even after contact, also began to be grown in the South. It had a larger ear and produced a higher yield than flint. Dent and other varieties of corn assumed greater importance in native life and culture. During the Mississippian Period it was difficult to imagine either a large palisaded town containing houses and temple mounds or an isolated residence without an adjoining maize field. Maize itself, along with the Corn Mother goddess and the annual Green Corn festival, played a vital role in the lives of Mississippian people. They did not rely solely on maize. Beans, varieties of peas indigenous to America, squash, and sunflowers were grown. Tobacco culture was widespread not only in the South but throughout North and South America. It was not normally smoked for pleasure but was used in religious and political ceremonies and for medicinal purposes. Countless stone and clay pipes, some finely wrought, attest to tobacco's importance. Aware of the narcotic qualities of this plant, medicine men carried its leaves in their bundles and administered it internally or externally to their patients.

Since the beginnings of agriculture in the South around 1000 B.C. in the early Woodland Period, Indians had perfected farming techniques. By the sixteenth century they had progressed far beyond any primitive slash-and-burn type of agriculture. After Europeans arrived, whether Spaniards in Florida or Englishmen at Jamestown, when they attempted to grow crops, they often turned to the natives for advice. Excavations of middens (trash heaps), fire pits, and an occasional cornfield itself have disclosed much about aboriginal agriculture. An equally important source, perhaps the best one for the sixteenth century, consists of written and pictorial accounts made by the whites. These include narratives of the De Soto expedition and drawings made by the French Huguenot Jacques Le Moyne of the Florida Indians and by the English artist John White at Roanoke Island. An impression frequently derived from such sources is that women performed most of the labor, that agriculture was "squaw" work, while the men lounged about except when off to war or away hunting. This point of view is pervasive and has been perpetuated in numerous works, including Edmund S. Morgan's recent study of seventeenth-century Virginia. The author characterizes the natives of Raleigh's Roanoke Island and of John Smith's Jamestown as "idle" and compares them with the English settlers, whom he regards as equally indolent.

This perception distorts the fact that the sixteenth-century natives were agriculturists and had been for centuries. They usually lived in towns and had their fields in the countryside. What European observers frequently saw and commented on and what White and Le Moyne painted were the small town garden plots, perhaps 100 by 200 feet, which, tended by women, were relied upon until crops in the main fields ripened. Men did much of the work in the principal fields. They cleared them, no easy task, as any white farmer carving out a homestead on the frontier could testify. They girdled large trees with stone axes and knives and used fire and stone implements to help fell the trunks. Time and fire disposed of stumps. In one sense it was easier for Indians than whites to clear an area, because before contact large trees were likely to be farther apart. The natives deliberately burned the forests when lightning did not do the work for them. The effect was to keep down the underbrush, make the woods more open, and facilitate the hunting of larger animals. Even so, the effort required to clear forests for cultivation was enormous, and countless Indian "old fields" scattered throughout the South attest to the Indians' toil. Whites eagerly sought out these clearings to escape such backbreaking work. Natives did not have plows or beasts of burden and broke the ground with hoes consisting of wooden handles with stones, conch shells, or large animal bones at the ends. Available evidence indicates that men with such implements did the heavy work and prepared the ground while women with baskets of corn and beans made holes with pointed sticks and dropped in the seeds.

Maize was the staple, and over centuries the aborigines had learned how to cultivate it more efficiently. Whereas not until the eighteenth-century agricultural revolution did Europeans normally stop sowing broadcast and begin planting in rows, Indians at a much earlier date grew crops in a regular fashion. That is what the women with pointed sticks were doing. Natives planted maize at stated intervals and hilled it; as the stalk grew they piled up more dirt. This helped establish a better root system, strengthened the stalk, trapped moisture in the soil, kept down weeds, and ensured a higher yield. Native practices of not disturbing the soil between hills, planting different crops in the same field, and relying heavily on bottom lands, which presumably were flooded and naturally fertilized, allowed them to use the same field for a long period before exhausting the soil. Beans often were grown in the same field as maize. The corn stalk became a natural support for these "pole" beans, and together maize and beans provided most of the vegetable protein necessary for a balanced diet. Beans also restored nitrogen to the soil, which corn had depleted. King Carter in Virginia and Abraham Lincoln's ancestors in the Mississippi Valley were relentlessly driven westward in search of virgin lands. Indians did not confront those pressures to such a degree, though in time they abandoned some fields and opened up new ones.

The first European observers sometimes remarked that the aborigines harvested two or even three crops of maize a year, but unfortunately they did not usually explain how. A Timucuan practice in Florida was to plant one crop in the early spring and another in the summer on the same ground. It was also possible to grow dent, sweet, pop, and other varieties of corn, which matured at different intervals. In some fashion natives harvested maize throughout much of the summer and fall.

Large fields were owned communally, and vital decisions on what and when to plant were made by the village chief and elders. Agricultural labor was organized and disciplined as it had been for the erection of temple mounds. Any surplus was stored for use until the next harvest or to feed visitors. Granaries took several forms. Some were wattle-and-daub buildings with tightly thatched roofs and sunken clay-lined floors; others were log "corn cribs" raised off the ground on poles; and shallow clay-lined storage pits filled with food and covered with earth and stones at times were used. Indians did not build fences and hedgerows to ward off predators; with no roaming horses, cattle, or swine until after white arrival, they were not as necessary. But birds, deer, and raccoons provided indigenous enemies enough. During the growing season Indian women and children guarded the fields. Le Moyne's and White's pictures portray granaries, fields, planting techniques, and the simple wooden structures used to house sentinels protecting crops.

If sixteenth-century Southern Indians were agriculturalists, they nevertheless had not completely abandoned hunting. For centuries their ancestors had hunted and gathered, and Indians of the late Mississippian tradition still hunted for food, clothed themselves with furs and skins, and collected acorns, walnuts, tuckahoe, chinquapins, and strawberries. It would be impossible to explain or to comprehend native religious beliefs and clan structure without taking into account this hunting tradition. Even so, hunting and gathering clearly were secondary to agriculture and game merely supplemented maize and beans. Much of the earliest information on aboriginal hunting practices concerns tribes living on the Atlantic Coast, such as the Timucuans in Florida or the Powhatans in Virginia. To a degree they were on the periphery of the great maize-growing centers in the interior, and there is some question as to how typical their experience was. But if these sixteenth- and early-seventeenth-century Timucuans and Algonquians provide any example at all, the continuing importance of hunting is obvious. White described how, after crops were harvested in the fall, able-bodied men and at least some of the women moved to temporary quarters in the interior and hunted for one to three months. During these winter months meat may have become more of a staple than maize.

Natives pursued all types of game but especially deer, which abounded. Venison more than any other meat was cooked over Indian fires, and it was doe or buckskin that was likely to clothe a Southern Indian of either sex. In addition to their symbolic importance, bears were valued partly for their fur and meat and especially for their oil. It was used as a condiment with food or rubbed over the body as protection against insects, as a cosmetic, sometimes scented, and as a ritual unguent. Europeans noted that the coarse black hair of many a young female glistened as a result of being greased with bear oil. Meat not consumed immediately was smoked, though rarely salted, and taken to the village for future use. Indians stalked game with bows and arrows, sometimes concealing themselves under a deer's skin in order to get within range. Continuing an ancient practice, natives sometimes made a ring of fire, driving all game, large and small, to the center or to the end of a peninsula, where they could easily be dispatched. The aborigines also fashioned ingenious traps to snare their quarry. Whatever their method, the natives did not slaughter game indiscriminately but killed only that necessary for food and clothing. They lived close to—and regarded themselves as inseparable from—nature, considering the deer, bear, eagle, fox, buffalo, and other animals to be their brothers.

Maize culture and the higher civilization and greater population density associated with it had flowed into the South from an even more southerly region, namely, Meso-America. Perhaps this culture had advanced overland from Mexico via Texas, perhaps by water through the West Indies, or probably by both routes. It may well be that important aspects of Southern culture had evolved locally. In any case, many features of a higher civilization had progressed from somewhere to the south toward the north. At the time of white contact hunting remained far more important for those Indians who lived in the northern part of what was to become the United States. The Algonquians are a case in point. Having first spread over Canada, they thrust themselves southward into New England, the mid-Atlantic states, and finally into the Virginia and North Carolina Tidewater. In general they depended as much on hunting as on agriculture, if not more, for subsistence. The Algonquians of Powhatan's Confederacy in Virginia and the Pamlico and Machapunga of eastern North Carolina had not been on the scene too many centuries before the Europeans arrived.

It is in the Virginia and Carolina Tidewater where the mixing of the Northern hunting-oriented culture with the Southern maize-agrarian civilization can best be documented. Powhatan's subjects had much in common with the Algonquian Delaware, Mohegan, and Pequot to the north. But they had just as much and probably more in common with the Mississippian temple mound civilization to the south. This included the busk or Green Corn ceremony, fire hunting, "bone houses" for the remains of important chiefs, bamboo knives, woven feather mantles, basket traps for fish, cranial deformation, and fish poisoning. A feature conspicuously missing in the Tidewater was the temple platform mound. There is one essential point to keep in mind, however. James Fenimore Cooper's characterization of the Mohegans in New York, the Puritans' description of the New England Indians, and the French portrayal of Algonquian life in the St. Lawrence Valley, all emphasizing the Indians as hunters, becomes more distorted the farther south one looks along the Atlantic Coast.

So far only incidental mention has been made of fishing. A reliance on shellfish dates back to the earliest period, as excavations at Muscle Shoals on the Tennessee River attest. Shell middens many feet tall along the Atlantic and Gulf coasts demonstrate the importance of clams and oysters. One need only glance at Le Moyne's and White's drawings to realize that the Indians did more than gather these mollusks. They fished with spears, bows and arrows, and bone hooks; built rock weirs and channeled fish into basket traps; and threw pounded walnut bark or roots of the devil's shoe-string (*Tephrosia*) into a stream to stupefy fish so they could be easily caught. Part of the catch was smoked and preserved. Until Franciscans established missions and promoted agriculture, Guale Indians in coastal Georgia still depended primarily on marine life from tidal waters.

In most respects European fishing techniques were superior to those of the aborigines, though in regard to the Calusa one wonders. They were a maritime folk whose large canoes ranged the open sea. The Calusa were not typical Southern Indians, and in any case much of their remarkable history remains to be told. As has been seen, the Powhatans were closer to the Mississippian culture. During the winter of 1609–10 Jamestown settlers living right on the river experienced the rigorous "starving time," when their numbers shrank from some five hundred to sixty. The Jamestown experience made it obvious that whites had much to learn from the natives.

The spread of agriculture and adoption of a sedentary life-style allowed time for artisans to perfect their crafts. Indians became proficient in basket-making, carpentry, woodworking, pipemaking, weaving, pottery, certain kinds of metal work, and tanning. Both sexes were artisans, though some crafts seemed to be identified with one or the other. Over the centuries Indians had perfected the art of basketry, making a wide range of colorful and utilitarian split-cane baskets. Some were flat, shallow ones employed in preparing and serving food; a considerable number were large and tightly woven with lids for storage; others were used for gathering nuts and berries; special types of baskets were containers or hampers for bones of deceased ancestors; and porters utilized large ones with arm straps or more likely with tumplines for their chests or foreheads to carry heavy loads of clay and foodstuffs. Basket-makers also made large utilitarian mats and tightly woven shields for warriors. . . .

Pottery had appeared in the South around 2000 B.C. in the Georgia-Florida region during the late Archaic era. Indians never discovered the pottery wheel, but over the centuries they perfected techniques of tempering and firing. Most ceramics were utilitarian pots and bowls, though by the Mississippian era many were artistically formed, decorated, and painted.

Other types of pottery included water bottles, beads, human and animal effigies, pipes, ear spools, ear bobs, burial urns, and storage vessels.

The few surviving textiles from burials and textile impressions deliberately made on pottery give some indication of the ability of aboriginal weavers. They wove animal hair and vegetable and bark fibers into clothes, sandals, and nets.

Just before white contact Southern Indians still relied heavily on stone implements such as projectile points, scrapers, knives, mortars, and pestles. Stoneworkers who chiseled, flaked, ground, and polished stone were highly skilled, as were artisans who engraved elaborate designs on shells or manufactured various types of wampum. It would be erroneous to assume, however, that Indians knew nothing of metal. They made a number of decorative and utilitarian objects out of lead, and for centuries they had acquired and used copper from local sources, the Great Lakes region, or west of the Mississippi River. Hammering and incising with stone or bone tools and annealing the copper with skill, they fashioned beads, bracelets, earrings, ceremonial knives and axes, gorgets, and breast plates. Surviving examples of the latter, almost a foot by two feet in size, with component parts riveted together, are elaborately decorated with an eagle, hawk, or similar motif. These artifacts, some of which were up to five hundred years old at the time of contact and were associated with the Southeastern Ceremonial Complex, reflected a far greater knowledge of metallurgy than is commonly ascribed to the Southern Indians.

The typical Indian at the time of contact was sedentary, living in a town. Scattered throughout the South, villages frequently were palisaded, containing from only a handful up to hundreds of houses. Population ranged from under a hundred to thousands, and over the long span of history the Mississippian was the typical Southern townsman. At the time of the American Revolution Charleston, the largest city south of Philadelphia, contained but twelve thousand inhabitants; Williamsburg, even when the legislature was in session, numbered less than two thousand; and Spanish St. Augustine, whose population numbered almost three thousand in 1763, for most of the eighteenth century was the second largest city south of Philadelphia. Even in 1861 Wilmington, North Carolina, with not quite ten thousand people, was the largest city in the entire state. By almost any standard the white South was rural. But it had not always been that way. For centuries before contact and for some time afterward towns dotted this region, and it is improper to refer to a rural South until after Europeans arrived. One reason for confusion is that we know a good deal about the development of Williamsburg, Norfolk, Charleston, Savannah, and St. Augustine, whereas, in contrast, we are not even sure of the locations of such Indian centers as Cofitachiqui, Mabila, and the capital of the province of Apalachee, each of whose populations numbered in the thousands.

Towns varied in size and appearance. Those that were palisaded and fortified were likely to be on a tribe's or chiefdom's exposed frontier. Larger urban centers in the maize-growing Mississippian area probably contained one or a series of platform temple mounds with houses on top. The typical rectangular or round dwelling was of wattle-and-daub construction and had a thatch roof. Sometimes bark or mats covered the sides and roof, and the floor might be made of puddled clay. Towns generally shared certain key features. One was the square ground. Located in a level, well-defined area, it was enclosed by four wooden shedlike structures. Here elders and clan leaders sat in assigned spots as they conducted business, participated in rituals, or listened to a visiting dignitary. Important towns were likely to have a large circular town house. Perhaps located on a platform mound close by the square ground, it had clay walls and an enormous roof, more often than not with a hole in the center for smoke, and contained scores or even hundreds of seats. Used more extensively in winter than in summer, this "rotunda" was the scene of important business and rituals. A visitor on approaching a town saw first not a cathedral spire but a pole 50 or more feet in height erected on a small mound in the ceremonial ground for use in ball games, which . . . were so important in the Indians' culture. Eagle effigies, animal skulls, and sometimes enemy scalps graced the top of this ball pole. When Spanish missionaries arrived on the scene, they did not approve of the ball game or perhaps even understand its vital role in village life. All they saw was monstrous phallic symbols dotting the landscape. An ossuary or bone house might be found in or close to the towns. Certain mortuary practices were similar throughout the south. Bones of the deceased, particularly those of leaders, were cleaned and at the appropriate time removed to a sacred charnel house and stored in boxes or baskets. As has been mentioned, granaries were commonplace. Any town of consequence had a hot house, like a sauna. To an extent the large rotunda might serve this purpose. More properly the hot house or sweat house was a small, separate, tightly sealed structure where stones were heated and thrown into water. Indians regularly purged and cleansed themselves by first sweating and then plunging into a nearby cold stream.

Early white explorers and modern ethnologists and archaeologists have disclosed numerous characteristics of aboriginal towns. But they have had less to say about, or have almost completely ignored, those natives who lived in the countryside. Early narratives fleetingly mention habitations sprinkled about. Numerous houses outside Mabila reportedly were scattered through the fields a crossbow shot or two from each other. As De Soto traveled up the center of the Florida peninsula, from time to time he encountered houses strung out over four leagues. When in the mid-seventeenth century the English began to settle Carolina and in the early eighteenth century the French arrived in Louisiana, natives were reported to be living in straggling, dispersed houses. The problem with these latter sources is that they refer to a century and a half to two centuries after white contact, and there is no assurance that they accurately depict earlier patterns of settlement. Before Europeans arrived towns were obviously numerous and important, but the extent of the nonurban settlements at that time is not at all clear. Knowledge about rural dwellers is important for a number of reasons, certainly if one is trying to count the total population.

Much is known about the social and political relationships of the surviving historical Southern Indians. As one moves back to the period of contact, however, the story becomes more obscure. The first Europeans were closer to the mark than is generally realized in referring to Indian "kings" and "emperors." These designations in time became so overworked and outdated as to be almost meaningless. But at the time of contact powerful chiefdoms existed, including the Cofitachiqui, Powhatan, Natchez, and Calusa. Powhatan had but to snap his fingers and an unfortunate Indian or the captive John Smith would be brought before him for execution. When the Natchez Sun died, his subjects staged an elaborate funeral which included immolation of his wives. De Soto's chroniclers recount how the Queen of Cofitachiqui was carried about in state in her litter and how her word was law over a large area. The sway of the Calusa chief Carlos was felt over much of southern Florida from the Gulf to the Atlantic Coast. In the eighteenth and nineteenth centuries much was made of the Creek Confederacy centered in the states of Alabama and Georgia. Although many chiefs claimed to be absolute king or ruler, in fact there never was any counterpart to a Carlos, Natchez Sun, or Queen of Cofitachiqui. In the sixteenth century, however, powerful, cohesive regional chiefdoms seemed to have been the norm. But if any ruler of the Aztec or Inca type had ever combined them into a larger state, we do not know about it.

Politically no far-flung polity existed in the South, yet culturally one did. Before white contact a new phenomenon known variously as the eagle, hawk, buzzard, or Southern cult, or the Southeastern Ceremonial Complex, spread over much of the region. Its origins and progress are debatable. It may have been transmitted from Meso-America or evolved locally. Some specialists argue that it suddenly swept over the South just before contact in the same fashion the Ghost Dance religion later galloped over the plains in the nineteenth century. It seems probable, especially in light of recent archaeological evidence, that the Southeastern Ceremonial Complex had evolved and flourished over a long time and had been around three, four, or even more centuries before Columbus's voyage. Associated with this complex were fire and sun worship and such motifs as the eagle, hawk, or buzzard; sun circles, bi-lobed arrow, forked eye, hand and eye, and cross, which can be found engraved on copper and shell. The great platform temple mounds of the Mississippian tradition are also identified with the Southeastern Ceremonial Complex. The highest point of this culture apparently was just before or at the time of white contact.

More important than religion or anything else in regulating an Indian's conduct was clan membership. In no way can aboriginal culture be understood without taking this into account. Sharp differences existed between whites and Indians, and the fact that Southern Indians typically traced their lineage through females was as responsible as anything for the confusion. Both whites and Indians used such familiar terms as father, mother, sister, and brother, but with entirely different meanings. Europeans, raised in the tradition of primogeniture and entail, had difficulty comprehending that when an Indian spoke of his father in fact he might be referring to one of his uncles, and when speaking of his sister he might really mean his first or second cousin. It was difficult, if not impossible, for a father to hand down his possessions and office to his natural son, but he could to his nephew, that is, his sister's son.

All of this makes sense only when one comprehends the fact that clan membership was matrilineal. The mother's brother was more important to a child than his biological father, who was of a different clan. The child's eldest uncle of the same "blood" assumed responsibility for educating and disciplining the child. An Indian youth had brothers and sisters in the same sense as Europeans did, but this same Indian youth also called the children of his mother's sisters his own brothers and sisters. Clans were a related group tracing their lineage in an intricate fashion through the female line, and they were symbolically associated with such totems as turtle, snake, bear, wind, deer, and raccoon. Various clans were represented in any given town. Clan membership determined one's conduct in rituals and political gatherings, prescribed where one sat at the square ground, and decreed whom one should treat with respect or familiarity and whom one could court. Indians visiting a remote town for the first time could expect to be housed and entertained by fellow clansmen, even if they were perfect strangers.

Aboriginal economic concepts and methods of property holding differed markedly from those of Europeans. Knowledge of precontact native thought and practices is naturally incomplete, but certain characteristics seem obvious. At the lowest level individual Indians or families "owned" or enjoyed the use of small tracts, while at the village or tribal level land was normally owned communally; and capitalism, the profit motive, and the Protestant work ethic were largely foreign to the aborigines. Hunting grounds seem to have had definite bounds and were regulated by towns or possibly chiefdoms. Clothing, arms, ornaments, and similar personal effects were owned individually, but no strong tradition of storing up treasures on this earth was apparent. Those who had surplus wealth were expected to distribute it generously, and much of what remained—fortunately for archaeologists—was buried with the deceased.

Southern Indians looked and dressed quite differently from the whites, and much is known about this thanks to Le Moyne's and White's drawings and contemporary written accounts. Although posterity has referred to the natives as red men, in fact, as the earliest Europeans noted, pigmentation might be brown, tawny, olive, yellow, or copper.

Indians—at least the men—were comparatively tall, usually around 5 feet, 6 inches, and sometimes 6 feet or more, and thus taller than their European counterparts. Women were likely to be shorter, averaging not much more than 5 feet. Both sexes were well proportioned, with athletic builds and few deformities. Early English Puritan types in Virginia, either with Freudian perversity or in an attempt to attract more immigrants, enthusiastically described young Indian women with white teeth and twinkling eyes, smooth skins, and loose deerskin mantles exposing well-formed breasts. A deerskin breechcloth for the men and a skirt for the women was the universal attire. At times, especially for use in the summer or in the semitropical lower South, women's skirts and men's breechcloths were delicately woven or plaited out of fiber. For the colder months mantles of deer, bear, or buffalo skins, woven feathers, and Spanish moss provided warmth. Leggings, leather moccasins, and woven sandals protected legs and feet. Coarse black hair grew long, and women and occasionally men let it hang down in the back or to one side. Males sometimes tucked all of their hair on top and at other times shaved part of their heads, leaving a crown or some hair as a potential scalp to tempt any enterprising enemy warrior. Elaborate tattooing was widespread, and the amount of one's body covered seemed to have varied with one's status. Ornaments, worn by men and women alike, included earbobs, necklaces, bracelets, and gorgets fashioned out of clay, copper, bone, and shell.

Contemporary written sources and modern ethnographic studies give some idea about native religious beliefs. The Cherokees can be used as an example, not because they necessarily represented typical Southern Indians, but because more information about them is available. They divided the cosmos into three parts: the Upper World, the Earth, and the Under World. The Sun, Moon, Thunder, and other spirits of the Upper World represented the most important and powerful gods. Below them were men, plants, and animals of this world, while snakes, frogs, underground springs, and so forth were identified with the frightful monster Uktena of the nether regions. A complex system of symbols, rites, and taboos was associated with native religions. For example the eagle, who was of this world, soared and came into contact with the Upper World. Indians venerated this bird, and the eagle, his feathers, and the eagle tail dance figured prominently in religious and political ceremonies. Only after elaborate purification could a picked warrior be sent to hunt and kill an eagle. Anything else would bring down the wrath of the gods.

The Sun and the closely related Corn God lived in the Upper World. The annual Green Corn festival or busk lasted for several days after the new corn ripened. Homage was paid to the Sun, Corn, and similar deities as Indians began their new year. Led by a singer intoning sacred chants, Indians purged themselves with emetics, fortified themselves with herbal medicines, extinguished old fires, laid logs at the cardinal points, and, in homage to the Sun God, kindled a fire by friction. This new fire was taken to each house in town. At the busk ceremonies young boys received war names; unpunished crimes, with a few exceptions, were pardoned; and spouses of either sex could with little difficulty discard their partners. Dancing, celebrating, and feasting on roasted ears of new corn and other food followed the lighting of the new fire.

Indians lived essentially in a law-abiding society. Not that there was an absence of crime and punishment, but they were innocent of a number of the moral lapses of which they were accused. Whites charged young Indians girls with being lascivious and promiscuous, as most certainly they were by European standards. If they could afford it, men might have as many wives as they chose. Despite these differences, Indians had clear notions about marriage and adultery. Young girls normally had sexual relations before marriage, and divorce was easy, yet once a marriage had been agreed upon by the partners and clans involved, it was binding. Husbands and wives who committed adultery could show bruises, broken bones, missing noses, ears, and hair, or worse. These punishments, and those for murder and the like, were meted out by the clan. If the culprit could not be caught, another member of the offending clan had to pay. Clan or blood vengeance was the mainstay of criminal justice and, though harsh, worked reasonably well.

Warfare played an important role in Indian life. Based on the skimpy evidence available it appears to have been of less significance before whites arrived. Indians fought each other in ways familiar to Europeans. A chief commanded his massed army of warriors equipped with spears, war clubs, and bows and protected by leather or woven shields. Forces met in the open field; ambushes, raids by small parties, a single warrior slipping into the heart of an enemy town, and fighting from cover played a role, but a subordinate one, in native warfare.

There seems little question that Indians scalped their victims before Europeans arrived and that they burned at least some of their captives. It has been argued that Europeans, who had been burning witches and heretics for centuries, introduced this practice into America. That is unlikely. Guiding colonists into the Carolina back country early in the eighteenth century, Saponi Indians pointed out large mounds of rocks alongside the trail as they added still another stone to each pile. It marked the place where valiant warriors had been burned or otherwise killed in the past. The spot was well known, and Indians passing by still heard voices, taunts, and cries. How many were burned and how many enslaved or adopted is unclear.

Medicine was inseparable from native religion. The priest was religious leader and doctor at the same time. Over the centuries Indians had determined the curative and painkilling properties of assorted plants, including the narcotics tobacco and Jimson weed; yaupon holly leaves as a stimulant; willow bark, similar to aspirin, as a painkiller; dogwood bark, chinquapins, and persimmons as astringents; magnolia bark and ginseng as general cure-alls; wild cherry for coughs; sassafras as a tonic, salve, and "blood purifier," and so on. The list is long. Medicine men were skilled in treating wounds and snakebites, sucking out impurities with a hollow reed or bone and subsequently treating the victim with drugs. Patients were often diagnosed as being out of harmony with the gods and forces of the universe. Medicine men, who were also conjurers, sang and chanted at the patient's bedside, attempting to appease or drive out the appropriate spirit. By today's standards Indian medical practices were primitive, but so too was European medicine. It was not always clear how a decoction of feces, urine, or stag's penis promoted a white patient's recovery. The Virginian William Byrd had good reason to want to escape from eighteenth-century doctors, to treat himself, and not to pay a fee to prolong his agony, and some of the better practitioners of the age hurried George Washington into the grave.

Europeans portrayed the Indians as taciturn and not given to emotional outbursts, which was partly true. In public meetings they were respectful and attentive, not given to interrupting or quarreling directly with a speaker. This is not to imply that the aborigines never laughed or enjoyed themselves. Based on evidence of a later period it seems obvious they had a keen sense of humor, sometimes wry and subtle, sometimes bawdy. Indians of both sexes and all ages played games; gambled with wooden dice, straws, and seeds; or wagered on the outcome of a footrace or ball game. It was unlikely that a town would go for long without a dance. Led by the singer who had a drum or gourd rattle, men and women, the latter with tortoise-shell rattles attached to their legs, followed the leader in single or double file in various dances, perhaps one honoring the exploits of a war or hunting party, perhaps a formal eagletail dance, or perhaps a frolic having little symbolism.

Numerous excavated chunky stones testify how popular the game of chunky was. Indians threw spears at rolling stones to see who could come closest to where the stone stopped. The ball games, one a forerunner of modern day lacrosse and the other pelota, rivaled chunky in popularity. Using the ball pole as a goal, neighboring towns played one another, and for days beforehand men trained, took medicine, and participated in traditional rites. Rules were simple, and serious injuries common. These games were usually but not always less bloody than open warfare and at times were a substitute for hostilities. In pelota an aggressive player might swallow the buckskin ball, only slightly larger than a musket ball, before dashing off to the goal. If he were discovered, opponents stomped on the victims's stomach until he coughed it up.

Music played a role in precontact culture, and natives used several instruments, including drums, flutes, and rattles. Flutes were recorder-like instruments made of thick, hard cane; deep wooden platters and hollow logs covered with skins served as drums; while gourd or turtle shells filled with pebbles were made into rattles. Natchez musicians in the eighteenth century reportedly used a banjo-like instrument, but whether this was indigenous or imported from Africa is unclear. The singer, an important official in most ceremonies, sometimes accompanied by drums, rattles, and flutes, sang while villagers danced. But the lyrics and melodies of these early chants and songs for the most part have been lost.

One of the most controversial questions is how numerous the Southern Indians were when whites arrived. A dense population suggests intensive agriculture, a high culture, and also a frightful population decline after contact. If the population was relatively sparse, it indicates that the mortality rate, though high because of exposure to new diseases, was not out of line with that of Europeans, who also were regularly swept away by pestilences. A small population made the question of appropriating native lands less bothersome, because if there were few Indians around, obviously there was room enough for everyone. . . .

. . . The key to the catastrophic sixteenth-century depopulation was pandemics set off by white and African newcomers. . . .

. . . There is some question as to whether the Indians were friendly or hostile to Columbus and his contemporaries, but there is little debate that native bodies were gracious hosts to strange viruses and bacteria. For centuries, and for all practical purposes apparently forever, the American Indians had been isolated. Suddenly they were exposed to such scourges as smallpox, measles, chicken pox, scarlet fever, typhus, influenza, and whooping cough from Europe and malaria, yellow fever, and dengue fever from Africa. Over the years Old World inhabitants had built up immunity to many of these maladies, and in time they became less virulent "childhood diseases." But in America, where there was no immunity, the diseases raged with all their pristine fury. Their effect can be compared to the Black Death (bubonic and pneumonic plague), which in the fourteenth century reduced Europe's populace by almost one-third. The difference in America was that the Indians suddenly had to confront not just one alien disease but a variety of microparasites often coming almost simultaneously from both Europe and Africa. . . .

. . . The very fact that the Southern Indians were agriculturalists and lived in towns and villages made them all the more vulnerable to new diseases. Epidemics rapidly spread from one urban center to another, sweeping away a high percentage of the population. Smallpox, although in the 1970s finally eradicated throughout the world, at an earlier period was the greatest killer and one of the more loathsome diseases for the Indians. It was caused by a virus that spread from person to person in minute droplets expelled from mouth and nose. In the sixteenth century hardly ever was a European on hand to record the victims' high fevers, pains, and pus-filled blisters and the ensuing unprecedented mortality. But for the aborigines this and similar diseases were terrifying. . . .

. . . The Southern Indians, along with those in the Greater Antilles, the Isthmus of Panama, and northern South America had achieved remarkable cultural advances and in time presumably would have moved on to the levels achieved by the Aztecs and Incas. But Ponce de León, De Soto, and John Smith could not wait.

The Origins of Slavery in Virginia

EDMUND S. MORGAN

Slavery is a mode of compulsion that has often prevailed where land is abundant, and Virginians had been drifting toward it from the time when they first found something profitable to work at. Servitude in Virginia's tobacco fields approached closer to slavery than anything known at the

Reprinted from *American Slavery, American Freedom: The Ordeal of Colonial Virginia* by Edmund S. Morgan, by permission of W. W. Norton & Company, Inc. Copyright © 1975 by W. W. Norton & Company, Inc.

time in England. Men served longer, were subjected to more rigorous punishments, were traded about as commodities already in the 1620s.

That Virginia's labor barons of the 1620s or her land and labor barons of the 1660s and 1670s did not transform their servants into slaves was probably not owing to any moral squeamishness or to any failure to perceive the advantages of doing so. Although slavery did not exist in England, Englishmen were not so unfamiliar with it that they had to be told what it was. They knew that the Spaniards' gold and silver were dug by slave labor, and they themselves had even toyed with temporary "slavery" as a punishment for crime in the sixteenth century. But for Virginians to have pressed their servants or their indigent neighbors into slavery might have been, initially at least, more perilous than exploiting them in the ways that eventuated in the plundering parties of Bacon's Rebellion. [Bacon's Rebellion was an armed conflict in 1676 pitting land-hungry poor whites and politically ambitious gentlemen against Virginia Governor Berkeley, his corrupt partisans, and the frontier Indians, whose land titles Berkeley protected. The rebellion failed.] Slavery, once established, offered incomparable advantages in keeping labor docile, but the transformation of free men into slaves would have been a tricky business. It would have had to proceed by stages, each carefully calculated to stop short of provoking rebellion. And if successful it would have reduced, if it did not end, the flow of potential slaves from England and Europe. Moreover, it would have required a conscious, deliberate, public decision. It would have had to be done, even if in stages, by action of the assembly, and the English government would have had to approve it. If it had been possible for the men at the top in Virginia to arrive at such a decision or series of decisions, the home government would almost certainly have vetoed the move, for fear of a rebellion or of an exodus from the colony that would prove costly to the crown's tobacco revenue.

But to establish slavery in Virginia it was not necessary to enslave anyone. Virginians had only to buy men who were already enslaved, after the initial risks of the transformation had been sustained by others elsewhere. They converted to slavery simply by buying slaves instead of servants. The process seems so simple, the advantages of slave labor so obvious, and their system of production and attitude toward workers so receptive that it seems surprising they did not convert sooner. African slaves were present in Virginia, . . . almost from the beginning (probably the first known Negroes to arrive, in 1619, were slaves). The courts clearly recognized property in men and women and their unborn progeny at least as early as the 1640s, and there was no law to prevent any planter from bringing in as many as he wished. Why, then, did Virginians not furnish themselves with slaves as soon as they began to grow tobacco? Why did they wait so long?

The answer lies in the fact that slave labor, in spite of its seeming superiority, was actually not as advantageous as indentured labor during the first half of the century. Because of the high mortality among immigrants to Virginia, there could be no great advantage in owning a man for a lifetime rather than a period of years, especially since a slave cost roughly twice as much as an indentured servant. If the chances of a man's dying during his first five years in Virginia were better than fifty-fifty—and it seems apparent that they were—and if English servants could be made to work as hard as slaves, English servants for a five-year term were the better buy.

If Virginians had been willing to pay the price, it seems likely that they could have obtained Negro slaves in larger numbers than they did. During the first half of the century the Dutch were busy dismantling the Portuguese empire and, in the process, taking over the African slave trade. They promoted the development of English sugar plantations in the West Indies and supplied those plantations with enough slaves to give Barbados (founded twenty years after Virginia) a black population of 5,000 by 1645 and 20,000 by 1660. Virginia could scarcely have had a tenth the number at either date. Yet the Dutch were heavily engaged in the purchase of Virginia tobacco. They would surely, in the course of that trade, have supplied Virginians with slaves if the Virginians had been ready to pay.

That Virginia's tobacco planters would not pay, while Barbados' sugar planters would, requires explanation, for mortality was evidently as heavy in Barbados as in Virginia. If servants for a term were a better buy for Virginians, why not for Barbadians?

Up until the 1640s, when the principal crop in Barbados was, as in Virginia, tobacco, the labor force was mainly composed, as in Virginia, of white servants. But a shift from tobacco to cotton and then to sugar in the early 1640s made the islands less attractive than the mainland for servants who crossed the ocean voluntarily. Sugar production required such strenuous labor that men would not willingly undertake it. Sugar planters, in order to get their crops grown, harvested, and processed had to drive their workers much harder than tobacco planters did. Richard Ligon in the late 1640s was scandalized to see how the Barbados planters beat their servants in order to get the work out of them. Moreover, when a servant turned free, he found land much scarcer than in Virginia or Maryland. And even if he could hire a plot, at high rents, sugar production (unlike tobacco) required a larger outlay of capital for equipment than he could likely lay hands on. For these reasons, when Barbados servants became free, they frequently headed for Virginia or other mainland colonies. The sugar planters may thus have bought slaves partly because they could not buy servants unless the servants were shanghaied, or "barbadosed" as the word was at the time, or unless they were sent as prisoners, like the captured Scottish and Irish soldiers whom Cromwell shipped over. A dwindling supply of willing servants may have forced a switch to slaves.

It is possible that the conversion to slavery in Virginia was helped, as it was in Barbados, by a decline in the number of servants coming to the colony. The conditions that produced Bacon's Rebellion and the continuing discontent thereafter did not enhance the colony's reputation. Moreover, by the third quarter of the century there was less pressure on Englishmen to leave home. Complaints of overpopulation in England had ceased, as statesmen and political thinkers sought ways of putting the poor to work. Certainly the number of white immigrants to Virginia does seem to have declined. But if this was a factor in the conversion process, another, probably of greater consequence, was the decline of heavy mortality toward midcentury, for as life expectancy rose, the slave became a better buy than the servant.

The point at which it became more advantageous for Virginians to buy slaves was probably reached by 1660. In that year the assembly offered exemption from local duties to Dutch ships bringing Negroes. But in the same year Parliament passed the Navigation Acts, interdicting both the export of tobacco from the colonies to the Netherlands and any trade by Dutch ships in the colonies. The result was to delay Virginia's conversion to slavery. The mother country attempted to compensate for the severing of the Dutch slave trade through a royally sponsored English trading company, the Royal Adventurers, which was reorganized and rechartered in 1672 as the Royal African Company. These companies enjoyed a monopoly of supplying all the colonies with African slaves until 1698; but the men who ran them never gained sufficient familiarity with Africa or the slave trade to conduct the business successfully. And even though their monopoly could not be effectively enforced, especially against knowledgeable private traders, both tobacco and sugar planters complained that it prevented them from getting the number of workers they needed. Virginia thus began to change to slave labor at a time when she had to compete with the sugar planters for a smaller supply of slaves than would have been available had the freer conditions of trade still existed under which Barbados had made the conversion.

In the competition for slaves after 1660 the sugar planters still enjoyed some advantages. Although sugar and tobacco were both "enumerated" commodities that must be shipped only to England or to another English colony, England did not collect nearly so heavy an import tax on sugar as on tobacco. Consequently, a larger percentage of the price paid by the consumer went to the grower. Moreover, the price of slaves in the West Indies was less than in Virginia, because the islands were closer to Africa, so that costs of transportation and risk of loss on the "Middle Passage" were therefore less. The figures for slave imports into Barbados, Jamaica, and the Leeward Islands in the last quarter of the century are all far above those for Virginia. That Virginia was able to get any at all was owing to the fact that while slaves had become a profitable investment for tobacco growers, the profitability of growing sugar had declined.

It is impossible to reconstruct from surviving data the returns that could be expected on capital invested in growing tobacco in Virginia in comparison with the same amount invested in growing sugar in the West Indies at different periods in the seventeenth century. It is clear, however, that by the end of the seventeenth century and probably by the third quarter of it the tobacco growers had one strong advantage in the longevity of their laborers. A smaller proportion of their profits had to go into labor replacement and was available to meet the higher initial cost of a slave. Life expectancy in Barbados, especially for the black population, continued to be low throughout the seventeenth and most of the eighteenth century. The slaves on Barbados plantations had to be replaced at the rate of about 6 percent a year. It is estimated that between 1640 and 1700 264,000 slaves were imported into the British West Indies. The total black population in 1700 was about 100,000. In the next century, between 1712 and 1762 the importation of 150,000 slaves increased the Barbados black population by only 28,000. By contrast, while Virginia imported roughly 45,000 slaves between 1700 and 1750 (figures from the seventeenth century are sporadic), the black population increased from perhaps 8,000 or 10,000 to over 100,000. In Virginia not only had the rate of mortality from disease gone down, but the less strenuous work of cultivating tobacco, as opposed to sugar, enabled slaves to retain their health and multiply. To make a profit, sugar planters worked their slaves to death; tobacco planters did not have to. A slave consequently had a longer period of usefulness in Virginia than in the West Indies. The return on the investment might be less in the short run, but more in the long run.

The gap between the ability of Virginia and West Indies planters to pay for slaves was also narrowed in the course of the century by changes in the market price of their respective crops. The selling price of muscovado sugar in the islands during the 1640s, when the planters were converting to slavery, was perhaps 60 shillings the hundredweight (it brought 80 shillings at wholesale in London). In the 1650s and 1660s it dropped to about 30 shillings, in the 1670s to about 15, and in the 1680s to as low as 10, with some recovery in the 1690s. Tobacco reached 10 shillings the hundredweight in the 1660s and 1670s and stayed there with occasional ups and downs for half a century.

What these prices meant in profits for the planters depended in large measure on the comparative productivity of sugar and tobacco workers; and, in the absence of actual records of production, that is less easy to determine. No significant innovations in technology occurred in the growth or processing of either crop before the nineteenth century, and by 1660 both sugar and tobacco planters were thoroughly familiar with their respective crops and with ways of maximizing production. Contemporary estimates of productivity per hand on sugar plantations vary widely, but a fair medium might be 1,500 pounds a year. Because of Virginia's fickle weather the tobacco harvest probably varied more from year to year than the sugar harvest, and a man might grow a smaller but better and higher-priced crop by reducing the number of leaves left on each plant. Any estimates of productivity are therefore even more tenuous than those for sugar. It is likely, however, that by the 1660s a man would make less than 1,000 pounds of tobacco in a lean year, but more than 2,000, perhaps much more, in a good year. In the long run a man's labor for a year would probably make about the same weight of tobacco in Virginia as of sugar in the islands. But the tobacco worker could at the same time grow enough corn to sustain himself. And in the most favorable locations, especially on the York and, to a lesser degree, the Rappahannock, he could grow a variety of tobacco (known as sweet-scented) which brought a higher price and weighed more in relation to bulk (reducing freight costs) than the ordinary Orinoco.

In addition, tobacco continued to enjoy the advantage, which it had always had, of requiring a smaller outlay of capital for production equipment. And land, if scarcer than it had been, was still much cheaper in Virginia than in the islands. The far greater number of slaves delivered to the sugar islanders indicates that sugar remained the more attractive risk to English capital investment. Nevertheless, tobacco was so close a competitor that before the 1680s slaves were being shipped from Barbados for sale in Virginia.

In financing the extra cost of slaves, Virginians were not wholly dependent on upswings in the tobacco market. They could draw on capital accumulated during the first half century. Their earnings from tobacco (apart from any they returned to England) had been invested . . . in cattle and hogs and servants. When they wanted to buy slaves in Barbados, they could send cattle and hogs in exchange. Land in the West Indies was too valuable to be devoted to food products, and sugar planters were eager to buy live cattle as well as barreled beef and pork. They needed live cattle not only to turn their mills but also to dung their land as the canes exhausted it. Virginia joined with New England in supplying the need; and though no figures exist to show the volume of the trade, there is a good deal of evidence in county court records of contact between Virginia and Barbados in the seventeenth century. But the extra capital to buy slaves came not only from livestock. In spite of the low profits of tobacco growing after 1660, there were the entrepreneurial profits of the merchant planters and the substantial amounts accumulated by the judicious use of government office.

More important perhaps than the capital generated locally was that attracted from England by the new competitive position of tobacco. Substantial men who might earlier have headed for Barbados now came to Virginia, supplied with funds to purchase or rent land and labor. And men with small amounts of capital, insufficient for the initial outlay of a sugar plantation, could make a good start in Virginia. . . .

Englishmen with spare cash came to Virginia also because the prestige and power that a man with any capital could expect in Virginia was comparatively much greater than he was likely to attain in England, where men of landed wealth and gentle birth abounded. Well-to-do immigrants and their sons, who came to Virginia after midcentury, dominated the colony's politics, probably in default of male survivors of earlier successful immigrants. But the fortunes gathered by those early immigrants during the deadly first half century were not necessarily lost or dispersed. Capital still accumulated in the hands of widows and joined in profitable wedlock the sums that well-heeled immigrants brought with them. The Ludwells, Byrds, Carters, Spencers, Wormeleys, Corbins, and a host of others not only shared the spoils of office among themselves, but also by well-planned marriages shared the savings gathered by their predecessors. In Lancaster County, of the twelve persons who were listed for more than twenty tithables between 1653 and 1679, one was a widow and nine of the remaining eleven married widows.

These were the men who brought slavery to Virginia, simply by buying slaves instead of servants. Since a slave cost more than a servant, the man with only a small sum to invest was likely to buy a servant. In 1699 the House of Burgesses noted that the servants who worked for "the poorer sort" of planters were still "for the most part Christian." But the man who could afford to operate on a larger scale, looking to the long run, bought slaves as they became more profitable and as they became available.

How rapidly they became available and how rapidly, therefore, Virginia made the switch to slave labor is difficult to determine, partly because the Royal African Company monopoly made it necessary to conceal purchases from illicit traders. . . .

But the planters in Virginia, as in the West Indies, were more eager to buy slaves than to pay for them. During the first five years of the new century, they overextended their credit, and the company was faced with a multitude of protested bills of exchange. By 1705 the Virginia assembly was so disturbed by the rising indebtedness that it tried to slow down the traffic, dropping an import duty on servants while retaining one on slaves. But by then the conversion to slave labor had already been made. According to Edmund Jennings, writing in 1708, virtually no white servants had been imported in the preceding six years. This was not the end of white servitude in Virginia, but henceforth white servants were as much the exception in the tobacco fields as slaves had been earlier. Between 1708 and 1750 Virginia recorded the entry of 38,418 slaves into the colony.

Virginia had developed her plantation system without slaves, and slavery introduced no novelties to methods of production. Though no seventeenth-century plantation had a work force as large as that owned by some eighteenth-century planters, the mode of operation was the same. The seventeenth-century plantation already had its separate quartering house or houses for the servants. Their labor was already supervised in groups of eight or ten by an overseer. They were already subject to "correction" by the whip. They were already often underfed and underclothed. Their masters already lived in fear of their rebelling. But no servant rebellion in Virginia ever got off the ground.

The plantation system operated by servants worked. It made many Virginians rich and England's merchants and kings richer. But it had one insuperable disadvantage. Every year it poured a host of new freemen into a society where the opportunities for advancement were limited. The freedmen were Virginia's dangerous men. They erupted in 1676 in the largest rebellion known in any American colony before the Revolution [Bacon's Rebellion], and in 1682 they carried even the plant-cutting rebellion further than any servant rebellion had ever gone. The substitution of slaves for servants gradually eased and eventually ended the threat that the freedmen posed: as the annual number of imported servants dropped, so did the number of men turning free.

The planters who bought slaves instead of servants did not do so with any apparent consciousness of the social stability to be gained thereby. Indeed, insofar as Virginians expressed themselves on the subject of slavery, they feared that it would magnify the danger of insurrection in the colony. They often blamed and pitied themselves for taking into their families men and women who had every reason to hate them. William Byrd told the Earl of Egmont in July, 1736, that "in case there shoud arise a Man of desperate courage amongst us, exasperated by a desperate fortune, he might with more advantage than Cataline kindle a Servile War," and make Virginia's broad rivers run with blood. But the danger never materialized. From time to time the planters were alarmed by the discovery of a conspiracy among the slaves; but, as had happened earlier when servants plotted rebellion, some conspirator always leaked the plan in time to spoil it. No white person was killed in a slave rebellion in colonial Virginia. Slaves proved, in fact, less dangerous than free or semi-free laborers. They had none of the rising expectations that have so often prompted rebellion in human history. They were not armed and did not have to be armed. They were without hope and did not have to be given hope. William Byrd himself probably did not take the danger from them seriously. Only seven months before his letter to Egmont, he assured Peter Beckford of Jamaica that "our negroes are not so numerous or so enterprizeing as to give us any apprehention or uneasiness."

With slavery Virginians could exceed all their previous efforts to maximize productivity. In the first half of the century, as they sought to bring stability to their volatile society, they had identified work as wealth, time as money, but there were limits to the amount of both work and time that could be extracted from a servant. There was no limit to the work or time that a master could command from his slaves, beyond his need to allow them enough for eating and sleeping to enable them to keep working. Even on that he might skimp. Robert Carter of Nomini Hall, accounted a humane man, made it a policy to give his slaves less food than they needed and required them to fill out their diet by keeping chickens and by working Sundays in small gardens attached to their cabins. Their cabins, too, he made them build and repair on Sundays. Carter's uncle, Landon Carter of Sabine Hall, made his slaves buy part of their own clothes out of the proceeds of what they grew in their gardens.

Demographically, too, the conversion to slavery enhanced Virginia's capacity for maximum productivity. Earlier the heavy concentration in the population of men of working age had been achieved by the small number of women and children among the immigrants and by the heavy mortality. But with women outliving men, the segment of women and their children grew; and as mortality declined the segment of men beyond working age grew. There was, in other words, an increase in the non-productive proportion of the population. Slavery made possible the restoration and maintenance of a highly productive population. Masters had no hesitation about putting slave women to work in the tobacco fields, although servant women were not normally so employed. And they probably made slave children start work earlier than free children did. There was no need to keep them from work for purposes of education. Nor was it necessary to divert productive energy to the support of ministers for spiritual guidance to them and their parents. The slave population could thus be more productive than a free population with the same age and sex structure would have been. It could also be more reproductive than a free population that grew mainly from the importation of servants, because slave traders generally carried about two women for every three men, a larger proportion of women by far than had been the case with servants. Slave women while employed in tobacco could still raise children and thus contribute to the growth of the productive proportion of the population. Moreover, the children became the property of the master. Thus slaves offered the planter a way of disposing his profits that combined the advantages of cattle and of servants, and these had always been the most attractive investments in Virginia.

The only obvious disadvantage that slavery presented to Virginia masters was a simple one: slaves had no incentive to work. The difference, however, between the incentive of a slave and that of a servant bound for a term of years was not great. The servant had already received his reward in the form of the ocean passage which he, unlike the slave, had been so eager to make that he was willing to bind his labor for a term of years for it. Having received his payment in advance, he could not be compelled by threats of withholding it. Virginia masters had accordingly been obliged to make freer use of the lash than had been common in England. Before they obtained slaves, they had already had practice in extracting work from the unwilling. Yet there was a difference. If a servant failed to perform consistently or ran away, if he damaged his master's property either by omission or commission, the master could get the courts to extend the term of his servitude. That recourse was not open to the slaveowner. If the servant had received his reward in advance, the slave had received the ultimate punishment in advance: his term had already been extended.

Masters therefore needed some substitute for the extended term, some sanction to protect themselves against the stubbornness of those whom conventional "correction" did not reach. Their first attempt in this direction was an act, passed in 1661, that is sometimes cited as the first official recognition of slavery in Virginia. In it the assembly tried to handle the most common form of servile intractability, by making a servant who ran away with a slave responsible for the loss incurred to the master by the absence of the slave. The law read, "That in case any English servant shall run away in company with any negroes who are incapable of makeing satisfaction by addition of time, *Bee it enacted* that the English so running away in company with them shall serve for the time of the said negroes absence as they are to do for their owne by a former act [the act requiring extra service for double the length of the absence]."

Though this measure tells us something about the relationship between servants and slaves in these early years, it was a deterrent more to servants than to slaves. And it did nothing for the master who could not get what he considered an adequate amount of work out of his slave by the methods that had sufficed for servants. One way might have been to offer rewards, to hold out the carrot rather than the stick. A few masters tried this in the early years, . . . offering slaves freedom in return for working hard for a few years, or assigning them plots of land and allowing them time to grow tobacco or corn crops for themselves. But to offer rewards of this kind was to lose the whole advantage of slavery. In the end, Virginians had to face the fact that masters of slaves must inflict pain at a higher level than masters of servants. Slaves could not be made to work for fear of losing liberty, so they had to be made to fear for their lives. Not that any master wanted to lose his slave by killing him, but in order to get an equal or greater amount of work, it was necessary to beat slaves harder than servants, so hard, in fact, that there was a much larger chance of killing them than had been the case with servants. Unless a master could correct his slaves in this way without running afoul of the law if he misjudged the weight of his blows, slaveowning would be legally hazardous. So in 1669 the assembly faced the facts and passed an act that dealt with them forthrightly:

> *An act about the casuall killing of slaves.*
> Whereas the only law in force for the punishment of refractory servants resisting their master, mistris or overseer cannot be inflicted upon negroes [because the punishment was extension of time], nor the obstinacy of many of them by other than violent meanes supprest, *Be it enacted and declared by this grand assembly,* if any slave resist his master (or other by his masters order correcting him) and by the extremity of the correction should chance to die, that his death shall not be accompted Felony, but the master (or that other person appointed by the master to punish him) be acquit from molestation, since it cannot be presumed that prepensed malice (which alone makes murther Felony) should induce any man to destroy his own estate.

With this act already on the books in 1669, Virginia was prepared to make the most of slavery when slaves began to arrive in quantity. Later legislation only extended the principles here recognized, that correction of slaves might legally be carried to the point of killing them. The most important extensions had to do with runaways. As the numbers of slaves increased and the plantation quarters were placed farther from the house of the master, runaway slaves would frequently hide out in the woods, visiting the quarters by night, where their friends or families would shelter and share food with them. To eliminate this problem, the assembly provided that the names of such outlying slaves should be proclaimed at the door of every church in the country, after divine worship, and then if the runaways did not turn themselves in, it would "be lawful for any person or persons whatsoever, to kill and destroy such slaves by such ways and means as he, she, or they shall think fit, without accusation or impeachment of any crime for the same." The public would compensate the master for the loss of slaves thus killed. If one was captured alive, the owner might apply to the county court "to order such punishment to the said slave, either by dismembring, or any other way, not touching his life, as they in their discretion shall think fit, for the reclaiming any such incorrigible slave, and terrifying others from the like practices."

This was no idle threat. Though the words of the law—"reclaiming," "dismembering," "discretion"—seem to soften the shock, the law authorizes not merely an open season on outlying slaves, but also the deliberate maiming of captured slaves, by judicial order. One gets a glimpse of the law in action in the records of the Lancaster County court for March 10, 1707/8:

> Robert Carter Esq. Complaining to this Court against two Incorrigible negroes of his named Bambarra Harry and Dinah and praying the order of this Court for punishing the said Negroes by dismembring them It is therefore ordered That for the better reclaiming the said negroes and deterring others from ill practices That the said Robert Carter Esq. have full power according to Law to dismember the said negroes or Either of them by cutting of[f] their toes.

Such was the price of slavery, and Virginia masters were prepared to pay it. In order to get work out of men and women who had nothing to gain but absence of pain, you had to be willing to beat, maim, and kill. And society had to be ready to back you even to the point of footing the bill for the property you killed.

It has been possible thus far to describe Virginia's conversion to slavery without mentioning race. It has required a little restraint to do so, but only a little, because the actions that produced slavery in Virginia, the individual purchase of slaves instead of servants, and the public protection of masters in their coercion of unwilling labor, had no necessary connection with race. Virginians did not enslave the persons brought there by the Royal African Company or by the private traders. The only decision that Virginians had to make was to keep them as slaves. Keeping them as slaves did require some decisions about what masters could legally do to make them work. But such decisions did not necessarily relate to race.

Or did they? As one reads the record of the Lancaster court authorizing Robert Carter to chop off the toes of his slaves, one begins to wonder. Would the court, could the court, could the general assembly have authorized such a punishment for an incorrigible English servant? It seems unlikely that the English government would have allowed it. But Virginians could be confident that England would condone their slave laws, even though those laws were contrary to the laws of England.

The English government had considered the problem in 1679, when presented with the laws of Barbados, in which masters were similarly authorized to inflict punishment that would not have been allowed by English law. A legal adviser, upon reviewing the laws for the Lords of Trade, found that he could approve them, because, he said "although Negros in that Island are punishable in a different and more severe manner than other Subjects are for Offences of the like nature; yet I humbly conceive that the Laws there concerning Negros are reasonable Laws, for by reason of their numbers they become dangerous, and being a brutish sort of People and reckoned as goods and chattels in that Island, it is of necessity or at least convenient to have Laws for the Government of them different from the Laws of England, to prevent the great mischief that otherwise may happen to the Planters and Inhabitants in that Island."

It was not necessary to extend the rights of Englishmen to Africans, because Africans were "a brutish sort of people." And because they were "brutish" it was necessary "or at least convenient" to kill or maim them in order to make them work.

The killing and maiming of slaves was not common in Virginia. Incidents like Robert Carter's application to dismember his two slaves are rare in the records. But it is hard to read in diaries and letters of the everyday beating of slaves without feeling that the casual, matter-of-fact acceptance of it is related to a feeling on the part of masters that they were dealing with "a brutish sort of people." Thomas Jones, of Williamsburg, was almost affectionate about it in writing his wife, away on a visit, about her household slaves. Daphne and Nancy were doing well, "But Juliet is the same still, tho I do assure you she has not wanted correction very often. I chear'd her with thirty lashes a Saturday last and as many more a Tuesday again and today I hear she's sick."

Possibly a master could have written thus about a white maidservant. Certainly there are many instances of servants being severely beaten, even to death. But whether or not race was a necessary ingredient of slavery, it *was* an ingredient. If slavery might have come to Virginia without racism, it did not. The only slaves in Virginia belonged to alien races from the English. And the new social order that Virginians created after they changed to slave labor was determined as much by race as by slavery.

Race and Gender in Eighteenth-Century Virginia

JOAN R. GUNDERSEN

Phillis, a black slave, and Elizabeth Chastain LeSueur, her mistress, worked and raised families together for over thirty-two years in King William Parish, Virginia. In their small world, about thirty miles west of Richmond, shared ties of gender created a community of women but not a community of equals. The bonds of race and slavery provided constraints that divided the experience of Phillis from that of Elizabeth. Like most women of their day, they left but a faint trail through the records. Elizabeth Chastain LeSueur was probably the older, born about 1707, while all that is certain about Phillis is that she was born before 1728. Both women died sometime after David LeSueur's estate went through probate in early 1773. Both bore and raised children, worked at the many domstic tasks assigned to women in the colonies, and experienced the growth of slavery in their region. The

Joan Rezner Gundersen, "The Double Bonds of Race and Sex: Black and White Women in a Colonial Virginia Parish," *Journal of Southern History* LII (1986). Copyright 1986 by the Southern Historical Association. Reprinted by permission of the Managing Editor.

similarities and differences between their lives (and the lives of the other women of the parish) reveal much about the ways gender and race interacted in the lives of colonial women.

The lives of black women such as Phillis have yet to be explored in depth by the new social historians. We have, however, learned something about the lives of women like her mistress. Elizabeth Chastain LeSueur. . . . But just as the experience of white women such as Elizabeth Chastain LeSueur differed from that of white males in the colonies, the black female's experience in slavery differed from the male's, and to ignore that difference would be to misunderstand the nature of slavery. Gender not only separated female slaves from males, it also forged bonds with white women. After all, black women lived among whites, and in order fully to understand their lives, it is necessary to compare their experiences with those of white women. Only then can we begin to understand what it meant to be black and female in colonial Virginia.

This essay looks at slavery from a comparative female perspective in King William Parish during the eighteenth century. The findings suggest that the bonds of a female slave were twofold, linking her both to an interracial community of women and setting her apart as a slave in ways that make evident the special burden of being black and female in a white, patriarchal society. The local parish records, including tithe records for nearly every year between 1710 and 1744, provide a unique opportunity to illuminate the role of the black woman in a small plantation setting and to document the development of slavery within a new community just as it became the major labor source for the colony.

The slave women who arrived at King William Parish in the early eighteenth century did not make a simple transfer from an African past to an English colonial present (even with intermediary stops). Rather, they came to a community itself in transformation from a French Protestant refugee culture to an English colonial one. The Virginia House of Burgesses created King William Parish for Huguenot refugees who settled at Manakin Town in 1700. Changing county boundaries placed the settlement at various times in Henrico, Goochland, Cumberland, and Chesterfield counties before 1777. The tiny handful of slaves present before 1720 belonged to a community in which French was the dominant language. The decade of the 1720s, during which the first expansion of the slave population occurred, is also the period in which the Huguenot community leadership and property passed into the hands of those who, like Elizabeth Chastain LeSueur, either had arrived in Virginia as infants or had been born there. An epidemic in 1717–1718 greatly disrupted the community and its institutions, speeding the transfer of leadership to a new generation.

The economy of King William Parish, based on wheat and other grains, was also in transition, and the adoption of slavery was a reflection of this change. The first black women thus had to adapt to both a culture and an economy in transition. In the 1720s some land passed into English hands, and tobacco became a secondary crop. Slavery and tobacco together grew in importance in the parish over time. English interlopers did not introduce either slavery or tobacco, but they did provide a bridge to the agricultural patterns of the rest of the colony. The first slaveholding families in the community, including Elizabeth LeSueur's family, were French, and the purchase of slaves signified their claim to be members of the gentry.

When Abraham and Magdalene Salle purchased Agar, an adult black female, in 1714, she joined a handful of other blacks at Manakin. The only other black woman, Bety, had arrived in the parish the year before. Agar began and ended her three decades of service in Manakin as part of a black female population outnumbered by black men, but for a decade in the middle (1720–1730), she was among the majority or was part of an evenly divided black population. Since black and white women in the Chesapeake were also outnumbered by men, Agar was part of a double minority. In King William Parish the circumstances of immigration had created nearly even sex ratios for both races. By 1714, for example, the white community had only slightly more adult men than women. Recent studies throughout the Chesapeake have documented the shortage of black women in slave communities, and while the sex ratio at King William Parish favored men, it was seldom as severe as that reported for other areas. Thus the sense of being part of a female minority was less obvious than elsewhere in the colony. . . .

Throughout Agar's life at Manakin (1714–c. 1748) she was constantly part of a racial minority, for whites outnumbered blacks until after 1750. By the late 1730s black men and women comprised half of the tithables of King William Parish. Since white women were excluded from the count of tithables, and since there were many more white children than black, Agar and other blacks were still part of a minority in the community, but among a majority of those who worked the fields. Agar probably died in the late 1740s, a few years after the LeSueurs purchased Phillis. Phillis lived in a community almost evenly divided between whites and blacks and between men and women, but belonging to a numerical majority did not loosen either the bonds of slavery or gender.

Ironically, black women had an opportunity for a more normal family life than did black men because they were less desirable purchases. Because black women were outnumbered by men in King William Parish, it was easier for women to form families. Even so, the evidence suggests that black women took their time. Several factors complicated a black woman's search for a partner. The dispersed patterns of ownership meant few black women lived in a slave quarter or with other blacks. Initially blacks, and especially black women, were scattered singly or in small groups among those families who owned slaves. Over one-third of the families owned some slaves or rented them. No family before 1744 paid taxes on more than six blacks over age sixteen. Before 1744 only two or three families owned enough slaves to have both adult males and females. Thus black women had to search for mates on nearby farms. Furthermore, many black women lived relatively short times in Manakin, disappearing from the tithe records after only a few years. Bety, the first female slave in the parish, for example, appears on only four tithe returns. Such transience delayed the process of forming a family. In the early years this experience did not necessarily set black women apart from whites; immigrants of whatever race tended to marry later. As the community aged, however, the black woman's delay in starting a family did set her apart, for native-born white women began families earlier than their immigrant sisters, black or white.

There is only fragmentary evidence to suggest whether the slaves of Manakin were imported directly from Africa, or the West Indies, or if they were purchased from other colonial owners. Almost all slaves bore Anglicized names. The names of the slaves do suggest that the same kinds of compromises between African and English cultures that Peter H. Wood found in South Carolina also existed in colonial Virginia. The process of having the county courts decide the age of young immigrant slaves has identified a small percentage of the black population in King William Parish as imports. Importers usually registered newly arrived Africans at a county in the Tidewater and then brought them upriver for sale. Thus the records in the King William Parish area do not normally distinguish between slaves imported from abroad and those born elsewhere in Virginia.

Whatever these names may reveal about the origins of Manakin's black residents, black and white women were subjected to the same gender-imposed cultural restraints in naming. Of course, only white males had the security of a stable surname, but putting that issue aside, naming patterns reveal a subtle power structure in which gender played as important a role as did race. It is fitting that the first black woman resident in King William Parish was called Bety, because Bett (Beti, Bety, Betty) would prove to be one of the most common names for slave women in the parish. Of the 737 blacks studied, the 336 women bore only 71 names. Nine of these names were used seventeen times or more and account for over half of all the women. Conversely, the 401 men bore 117 names, only 5 of which were used seventeen times or more, representing only one-quarter of all male names. Thus the men bore more individualistic names. The men's names included those with more recognizable African roots such as Ebo, Manoc, and Morocco. The women's names were more Anglicized. The most common female names among slaves were western names that closely resembled African ones, such as Betty and Jude. Hence the names represent a compromise of cultures. It is possible that the lack of recognizable African roots reflected the insistence by owners that black women fit the cultural norms for women while accepting the idea that black men might be "outlandish."

Slave naming patterns may have been affected by the French community. Manakin whites bear frustratingly few names, especially among women. Nine women's names account for over 90 percent of the more than 600 white women associated with the Manakin community before 1776. While both black and white women drew their names from a much smaller pool than did men, the pool of black names had a diversity to begin with only eventually matched by white families who added new names through intermarriage. That black women shared the same names more frequently than black men parallels the pattern of the white community. But there was a further commonality among women's names that cut across racial lines. Slave names were often the diminutives of white names, for example, Betty for Elizabeth and Will for William. White women also were known by diminutives such as Sally, Patsy, and Nancy. They appear this way even in formal documents such as wills. Nicknames and diminutives are not used for adult white males. Hence diminutives were shared by women, both black and white, but not by all groups of men. White women shared in unaltered form several common names with black women, including Sarah, Hannah, and Janne. Male slaves did not bear the same names as white males, although a white youth might be called by a nickname such as Tom, which was also a common slave name. On legal documents and at adulthood, however, white men claimed the distinction granted by the formal versions of their names. Slaveowners apparently found it more necessary to distinguish between white and black males than to distinguish between white and black females by changing the form of their names or choosing names for slaves not used by whites. Such distinctions in naming patterns helped to reinforce the status and power of white men.

The records unfortunately do not reveal who did the naming of black women, whether immigrant blacks influenced the choice of names assigned them or whether owners or mothers chose the names of black children. Control over the power of naming was an important indicator of the power relationship that existed between owner and slave, but general cultural constraints also shaped the choices made by whoever exercised that power. Tradition greatly limited the naming patterns of whites. The oldest children bore grandparents' names, the next oldest were their parents' namesakes, and younger children were named for siblings of their parents. Occasionally a family would use the mother's family name as a first name for a younger child. However, the important point is that general cultural constraints determined naming patterns, not individuals, and the gender constraints of Virginia meant that women of both races shared a naming experience that offered them fewer choices, accorded them less individuality, and reinforced a dependent status.

Childbirth is an experience shared by women of all races, but in King William Parish the patterns of childbearing reveal another way in which black women lived within a community of women and yet encountered a separate experience. Next to the ordinary rhythms of work, childbirth may have been the most common experience for women. Pregnancy, childbirth, and nursing provided a steady background beat to the lives of women in the colonies. Recent research has shown that colonial white women made childbirth a community event, infused with rituals of support by other women, and that these rituals of lying-in were shared with black women. The evidence from Manakin, however, suggests that the risks of childbirth were greater for black women than for white. Although they may have participated in the rituals surrounding childbirth, black women were the center of attention less frequently because they had fewer children; moreover, participation in this women's culture required them to abandon some of their African traditions. Truly, childbirth was a bittersweet experience for black women.

The fragmentary King William Parish Register includes the records of births of slaves among forty-eight owners for the years from 1724 to 1744. The parish register reveals only the owner's name, not the mother's, but since most white families claimed only one or two black women it is possible to trace the childbearing history of individual women. The average birth interval was about 28 months, but was often less than two years. The experience of Marie, a slave of Jean Levillain, illustrates the point. Marie's first two children were born 19 months apart, followed by intervals of 24, 25, 11, 14, and 30 months. In general, for the black women of Manakin, the most frequent interval was 20 months. Fifty-six percent of the birth intervals were between 15 and 34 months. However, another quarter of the intervals fell into a block running 36 to 47 months. The interval between births, however, was much more ragged than these figures suggest. Many women had long gaps in their childbearing histories. Other women had few or no children. For example, Pegg, the slave of Barbara Dutoy, had only one child in twelve years.

While the average and median for childbirth intervals were similar for black and white women in the parish, there were also major differences. The black woman was much more likely to have an intermittent history of childbirth with long gaps, ending much sooner than it did for the whites of Manakin. Birth intervals for whites were more tightly clustered around 24 months than black births. Seventy-four percent of the white births fell in the interval between 15 and 34 months. Elizabeth Chastain LeSueur, for example, bore children every two to three years with almost clockwork regularity from 1728 to 1753, while her slave Phillis had two children 30 months apart and then had no more children for at least seven years.

The child-spacing patterns for black and white women of King William Parish provide important clues to the adaptation of black women to American slavery and their participation in a community culture surrounding childbirth. African customs of nursing were different from those of Europeans. In Africa women often nursed children for more than three years, abstaining from sexual relations during that period. Black women continued these patterns in the Caribbean slave communities, as did seventeenth-century blacks in the Chesapeake. The secondary cluster of birth intervals of three to four years suggests that a number of immigrant black women, including Phillis, continued that tradition in the Manakin area. European women, however, nursed for a shorter time and had resultingly closer birth intervals of about two years. Marie and a number of other black women in the parish adopted the shorter European traditions of nursing. Whether this adoption of European custom came at the urging of owners or as part of a cultural accommodation by black women, the result was that Marie and others like her had one more bond with white women.

In another way, however, the birth intervals explain how childbirth set black and white women apart, for black women had many fewer children per mother than the white women did. . . .

That most black women were immigrants and most whites were native-born accounts for some of the difference in numbers of children, for immigrant women often delayed starting families while searching for mates or found their marriages disrupted. Others reached menopause before they had been in the Manakin area twenty years. The gaps in the middle of black women's childbearing years, however, are at least as significant as any shortening of the years at risk by late starts. Those mid-life gaps in childbearing were due in part to black life expectancy. Africans and other immigrants to the South had high death rates, even in the more healthful eighteenth century. Disruptions caused by the death of a partner could inhibit the total number of children a woman bore, especially while the black community was small, for finding a new partner might take years. Although white women also lost partners, by 1730 the population of King William Parish was colonial-born and more resistant to the endemic fevers. Thus their marriages were more stable. The slave population, however, continued to be heavily immigrant and thus continued to have a higher rate of marriage disruption. Transfers of ownership and removal to other areas increased the possibility of separation from partners and hence lowered the number of children born.

Childbearing was a part of the rhythm of a woman's life, but that rhythm had a different beat for black women. All twelve of Elizabeth LeSueur's children were born in October, November, or December. Phillis's known childbirths, however, were in April and October. Two-thirds of King William Parish's black births, however, occurred between February and July. The months of August through January saw relatively few black births. Black women, then, usually conceived during the months of May through October. The white women of Manakin show a much different pattern of births. Births were heavy in the fall and early spring and lowest in June, July, and August. White conceptions were lowest in the fall; blacks were lowest in the deep winter. Black women thus were in the later stages of pregnancy during the heavy labor season of spring planting. Surely this affected their health.

The puzzling question of why black women had their children on a different cycle from white women has no ready solution. Black women were certainly not planning their pregnancies in order to receive reduced work loads during the spring, because there is evidence that the loads were not reduced. It is possible that black men and women had more contact with each other during the summer and fall while they were tending and harvesting crops. In the cold months black women may have been kept close to the plantation house working on domestic projects such as spinning, and thus were not free to meet with their partners. White women had no such constraints. Opportunity for conception increased when the cold months brought white men closer to the hearth fires.

The white women of Manakin expected their children to survive to adulthood. A black woman could not. King William Parish death records are fragmentary, so slave deaths appear only in a few cases where the record of birth includes a note of the infant's death. Circumstantial evidence, however, suggests high infant and child mortality. Only 44 out of 151 of the slave children whose births were recorded in the parish register appear in any other legal and church record, and for some that second appearance was as a child. Death explains many of the disappearances. For example, Beti, slave of Gideon Chambon, bore children Jean (John) in 1727 and Marye in 1733. When Chambon's estate inventory was filed in 1739 neither child appeared on the list. Given Chambon's age and economic condition, the most likely explanation is that the children died, not that he sold or gave them away. Similarly, Magdalene, born in 1744, does not appear in any records after the filing of John Harris's will when she was seven. Owners registered two and three children by the same name over the years. John Chastain, for example, registered the births of black new-borns named Fillis on March 24, 1745/6 and June 12, 1753. Only one slave of that name appears on his estate inventory. Likewise, Bartholomew Du-puy's slave Sara bore sons named Jack in both 1727 and 1730. Apparently they were doing what many families also did following the death of a white child, that is, replacing it by another of the same name.

The work patterns of black women fostered the high death rate among their children by exhausting mothers and making infant care difficult. The experiences of Aggy, a slave of the Levillain family, provide some clues to the relationship between work, childbearing, and infant mortality. Aggy (Agar) had been born in Manakin on August 7, 1733, as the slave of Jean Levillain; she passed by will to Jean's son Anthony Lavillain in 1746. Four years later, when Aggy was seventeen, Anthony died intestate, leaving Aggy the property of Anthony's newborn daughter Mary and the subject of an administered estate for the next fifteen years. Aggy's first child was born when she was eighteen. Two years later she had another. Throughout those years she worked in the fields, while the administratrix of the estate, Elizabeth Lavillain Young Starkey, recorded expenses for "nursing" both small children. The youngest, a girl, died by age three. In 1763 Aggy, by then thirty, again became pregnant. The pregnancy was not easy, however, for the records show payments to Mrs. Chastain for treating Aggy "when sick" and attending Aggy's lying-in.

Aggy's life illustrates the black pattern of work and childbearing in King William Parish. Beginning in her teens Aggy had two children spaced two years apart, but then there was a ten-year gap before she had another child. From 1754 to 1756 Aggy was hired out. Then she returned to work with the other slaves growing tobacco, wheat, and corn for the estate. John Levillain, Anthony's brother and, after 1754, Mary's guardian, did see that Aggy got medical treatment during her difficult later pregnancy, but the records Levillain filed with the court for income to the estate credit her with the same share of work on the crops as other slaves, so he had not reduced her work. Such practices would increase the risk of infant mortality.

The records for the Manakin area do not reveal much about the birth customs for black women, but Charlotte Chastain's appearance during Ag-gy's lying-in was not the only time a white midwife was paid for the delivery of a black woman's baby in the Manakin area. Thus while the Manakin families might not have been rich enough to provide the elaborate lying-ins for black women that Mary Beth Norton has described, the birth experience was not left entirely to the black community. Since we also know that black women helped at the births of white children, the physical act of giving birth may have been one of the most significant ways in which black and white women served each other in a single community.

As with the other aspects of their lives, work both separated and brought black women together with whites. Virginia's tithe laws made clear the distinctions. White women such as Elizabeth Chastain LeSueur were not counted in figuring the tithe. In fact, they only appeared on the tithe lists when widowed with slaves or male children sixteen years or over. On the other hand, black women like Phillis were counted. Ironically, it is easier to trace black women from year to year in the community since they are listed on the tithes than it is to trace white women. Eventually, in 1769, free black women received the same exemption as white women, but slave women remained a part of the tithe. In other words, black women were considered a basic part of the agricultural labor force in a way that white women were not. Undoubtedly, Phillis had spent part of her time working in the LeSueur fields. When the LeSueurs purchased her they had no children old enough to help with farm work, and David and Elizabeth LeSueur were planting without any regular help. Phillis's arrival assured Elizabeth that she could withdraw from occasional help in the fields to her many household duties and garden.

While white women seldom worked away from home, black women sometimes did. Slave rentals kept the labor supply flexible, cut costs for care by owners, and provided an income for widows and orphans. Two major sources for rental slaves were estates managed to provide an income for widows and orphans, and wealthy farmers who hired out their surplus women and children slaves. Women slaves were hired out more frequently than men. Thus black women might be separated from family and friends in order to secure the income that allowed a white woman to remain on the family farm. Agar, who had arrived at Manakin in 1714, spent the 1730s hired out by the widow Magdalene Salle, while the family's other adult slave, Bob, stayed on the plantation. Only when Magdalene's son came of age and assumed management of the plantation did Agar return to the plantation. Widow Barbara Dutoy also rented her slaves to other residents of Manakin from 1726 to 1733. In both cases rental gave the widow an income without the worry of planting. It allowed minimum disruption to the widow's life, but at the expense of disrupting the slave woman's life. . . .

. . . The rental of female slaves thus seems to have been an integral part of the Manakin labor system, allowing aspiring farmers to add to their small labor forces while providing income for widows and orphans. Once again the community's perception of black women primarily as field hands set black and white women apart.

Phillis might have spent much of her time in the fields, but she also worked with Elizabeth LeSueur on the many tasks associated with women's work. Domestic work was not a single occupation but a variety of highly skilled tasks shared by women on the plantation. For example, clothmaking occupied both white and black women in the Manakin area. When David

LeSueur died in 1772, the family owned working farms in both Buckingham and Cumberland counties. Only the home plantation in Cumberland, however, had cotton, wool and cotton cards, a wool wheel, two spindles, four flax wheels, and parts for two looms. Elizabeth obviously oversaw and worked with Phillis and Phillis's two grown daughters in the making of a variety of cloth. The LeSueurs were not unusual, for inventories throughout the Manakin region mention several crops including flax, the tools necessary to produce linen thread, and, somewhat less frequently, looms for weaving. The Lavillain estate, for example, purchased two spinning wheels. These wheels were for the use of Aggy and Nan, slaves of the estate who continued to be credited with a share of the crops of tobacco and grains. John Levillain simply added cloth production to the women's field duties. The usefulness of women in the tasks of cloth production may have encouraged owners to purchase women slaves. From its beginning the colony at Manakin provided Virginia cloth, used to clothe slaves and the poor. Black women worked with white women in this production on the small farm, thus providing another way in which a community of women cut across racial lines.

The smallness of slaveholdings and the relatively short life expectancies of owners created major instabilities in the lives of black women that exceeded the uncertainties of life for their white mistresses. Although owners recognized that black families existed, and while there is convincing evidence that kinship ties were strong among blacks, the value of slaves as property meant that black family stability was tied to the life cycle of their owners. Short life expectancies and parental willingness to establish adult children on farms of their own as soon as possible accelerated the cycle in the Manakin area. Life patterns in the late seventeenth and early eighteenth centuries were such that most Chesapeake parents expected to die before all their children came of age. One result of this expectation was the willingness of parents to give adult children their shares of the estate when they came of age or married. For example, Elizabeth Chastain's brother John and sister Judith were already living on their shares of land when their father Peter wrote his will. Thus even a long-lived owner was no guarantee of stability in a slave family.

Most blacks in the Manakin area changed hands upon the death of an owner or the coming of age of a child of the owner. Because slaves were valuable legacies to children, they were often divided among several heirs. Daughters, especially, received slaves as their share of the estate, either as dowries or legacies. With slaveholdings small, black families were divided at each period of change within the white family. Most bequests in the Manakin area (except for life interests to widows) were of one or two slaves. David LeSueur, for example, granted each of his eight surviving children one slave. Phillis, her two oldest children, and another male (probably husband to her daughter) stayed with their mistress, Elizabeth Chastain LeSueur, but all of Phillis's younger children and grandchildren were scattered. Owners when possible left very small children with slave mothers or bequeathed the slave mother to a married son or daughter and the slave's children to the children of the son or daughter. Thus black women received some recognition of bonds with children not accorded to men. In fact, the estate appraisers often perceived infants and mothers as one, giving a single value to a mother and her small child. Frequently they did not even bother to list the infant's name.

Black women might wait for years before the pain of such divisions became real. While the marriage of older children of the owners caused some separation among black families, the major estate divisions came when the owner died. Many estates remained intact for years awaiting the coming of age of minor children or the remarriage or death of a widow. Thus the fate of black women (and men) depended on the fate of their white mistresses. For example, Kate was a slave of Anthony Rapine when he died in 1737. Rapine gave his wife, Margaret, a life interest in half the estate with all eventually to go to his daughter, Maryanne Martin. Since Maryanne and her husband lived with the Rapines, Kate's life went on unchanged. In 1740 she bore a daughter, Hannah. Three years later Maryanne Martin was widowed and soon after she remarried. She deeded Kate and Hannah to her year-old son, Peter Martin, shortly before remarrying. In 1747, ten years after Anthony Rapine died, the estate was finally divided between Margaret Rapine and Thomas Smith, who had married the now-deceased Maryanne. Kate and Hannah (by then age seven) were listed together on the inventory and passed into Smith's possession. He then turned Kate and Hannah over to Peter's new guardian in 1749. At last, after twelve years, Kate and Hannah were forced to move. The black woman on a larger estate had a better chance of remaining with kin following the death of an owner. The few large estates included in the study divided slaves on the basis of where they lived, often giving a particular farm and its slaves to an heir.

The slave woman lived and worked in a very small community at Manakin. Since each family owned only a few slaves, a black community could not exist on a single plantation. The farms at Manakin were small enough (the original allotments were 133 acres each) that visiting between farms would be possible, and thus a wider community might have existed. The birth patterns, however, suggest that such visiting was limited. Although the dispersed black population might have hindered the formation of a black community, the tasks of the black woman put her in constant contact with whites. Family members on a small farm labored in the fields alongside the slaves, and women's chores such as spinning might be done with the wife and daughters of the owner. Historians have speculated that slaves who lived on small plantations or in areas isolated from a black community probably adopted white values and customs more readily than those who could fashion a creole life-style with other blacks. For the black woman this meant partial acceptance into the special world of women's society. Such acceptance made more poignant the contrast in birth rates, child mortality, and family stability between blacks and whites.

Life for black women in the Manakin area was filled with insecurity. Some risks, such as childbirth, were shared with white women, but others were not. As part of a double minority black women enjoyed a favorable marriage market, but dispersion of holdings threatened the families formed by black women with separation. Some slaves on large plantations could begin to develop distinct creole societies near Manakin, but that was possible only after 1750 and only for a small proportion of slaves. Slave rentals, which affected women more than men, added another dimension of instability to that ensured by the short life spans of spouses and owners. The decisions made by widows to remarry, farm, or hire out slaves for income not only determined whether white families would remain intact, but whether black ones would too. Most black women in the Manakin area lived on small farms or quarters where their field work was supplemented by sharing in the household tasks of the white women on the farm. The "bonds of womanhood" surrounded her life as much as the bonds of slavery, beginning with the very choice of a name. Childbearing was especially frustrating for the black woman, filled with the pain of frequent infant death, heavy workloads when pregnant, and separation from children. But childbirth also meant sharing in a woman's network that stretched across racial lines. The life of a black woman was thus constantly subjected to the cross-pressures of belonging to a woman's subculture without full membership.

人 *F U R T H E R   R E A D I N G*

James Axtell, *The Invasion Within: The Contest of Cultures in Colonial North America* (1985)

T. H. Breen and Stephen Innes, *"Myne Owne Ground": Race and Freedom on Virginia's Eastern Shore, 1640–1676* (1980)

Wesley Frank Craven, *The Southern Colonies in the Seventeenth Century* (1949)

Philip D. Curtin, *The Atlantic Slave Trade: A Census* (1969)

Basil Davidson, *The Growth of African Civilization: West Africa 1000–1800* (1965)

David Brion Davis, *The Problem of Slavery in Western Culture* (1966)

Gary C. Goodwin, *Cherokees in Transition: A Study of Changing Culture and Environment Prior to 1775* (1977)

Melville J. Herskovits, *The Myth of the Negro Past* (1941)

Charles M. Hudson, *The Southeastern Indians* (1976)

Francis Jennings, *The Invasion of America: Indians, Colonialism, and the Cant of Conquest* (1975)

Winthrop D. Jordan, *White over Black: American Attitudes Toward the Negro, 1550–1812* (1969)

Winthrop D. Jordon and Sheila L. Skemp, eds., *Race and Family in the Colonial South* (1987)

Daniel C. Littlefield, *Rice and Slaves: Ethnicity and the Slave Trade in Colonial South Carolina* (1981)

Daniel R. Mannix, *Black Cargoes: A History of the Atlantic Slave Trade, 1518–1865* (1962)

Russell R. Menard, "From Servants to Slaves: The Transformation of the Chesapeake Labor System," *Southern Studies* 16 (1977), 355–90

Gerald W. Mullin, *Flight and Rebellion: Slave Resistance in Eighteenth-Century Virginia* (1972)

Abraham P. Nasatir, *Borderland in Retreat: From Spanish Louisiana to the Far Southwest* (1976)

Gary B. Nash, *Red, White, and Black: The Peoples of Early America* (1982)

Theda Perdue, *Slavery and the Evolution of Cherokee Society, 1548–1866* (1979)

David B. Quinn, *Set Fair for Roanoke: Voyages and Colonies, 1584–1606* (1985)

Bernard W. Sheehan, *Savagism and Civility: Indians and Englishmen in Colonial Virginia* (1980)

Mechal Sobel, *The World They Made Together: Black and White Values in Eighteenth-Century Virginia* (1987)

Thad W. Tate and David L. Ammerman, eds., *The Chesapeake in the Seventeenth Century: Essays on Anglo-American Society* (1979)

Clarence L. Ver Steeg, *Origins of a Southern Mosaic: Studies of Early Carolina and Georgia* (1975)

Betty Wood, *Slavery in Colonial Georgia, 1730–1775* (1984)

Peter Wood, *Black Majority: Negroes in Colonial South Carolina from 1670 through the Stono Rebellion* (1974)

J. Leitch Wright, Jr., *Anglo-Spanish Rivalry in North America* (1971)

———, *Creeks and Seminoles: The Destruction and Regeneration of the Muscogulge People* (1986)

Colonial Society Matures

木

More than two decades ago, colonial historians began a systematic study of New England towns. Borrowing the methods of European social scientists, they explored such concepts as community and culture and such institutions as the family, church, and politics. Within the past decade, studies of southern communities have paralleled and expanded upon the pathbreaking scholarship of New England historians. The lag owed less to the availability of appropriate sources than to the fact that the colonial South rarely offered the discrete community structure exemplified by New England settlement. Fortunately, scholars have discovered that the absence of specific geographic boundaries is not an obstacle to creative community studies.

This work has led historians to focus on the eighteenth century as a crucial period in the colonial South's maturation—a time when the social structure, political ideology, and economic institutions of the Old South first emerged in recognizable form. Scholars have identified at least five elements in this maturation process: the increasing separation of black and white worlds, the growing economic distance among whites, the development of a cash-crop agriculture based on slave labor, changes in family structure and relationships, and the emergence of a coherent set of political beliefs. These elements did not evolve without challenge—from slaves, landless whites, dissenting political and religious movements, and ultimately the British. In turn, the challenges resulted in a constant shaping and reshaping of these basic features of eighteenth-century southern life and eventually influenced the American Revolution and the society that emerged from that conflict.

Although historians have identified the elements of a mature society, questions remain. How did each element vary from colony to colony? What were the relationships among them? Did some general factor account for all of them? Historians have argued for the causal importance of tobacco, demography, or slavery, but the answer remains unclear. Finally, as the colonists moved away from the coast, how did they transfer the Tidewater culture to the interior? What modifications occurred, if any?

✗ *D O C U M E N T S*

The first document offers glimpses of the lives of Virginia's elites from two different perspectives. Devereux Jarratt was the son of a humble farmer-artisan in Virginia. He rose from his simple boyhood in the 1730s to a respected position as an Anglican (and, after the Revolution, Episcopal) minister. His autobiography, written in 1806, provides one of the few detailed accounts of the life and attitudes of common folk in Virginia. The excerpts from that work reveal the social inadequacy that Jarratt felt while growing up, as well as the high living and completely secular life of the elite. In 1773, Philip Fithian arrived at Robert Carter's Virginia estate, Nomini Hall, from New Jersey to serve as tutor to the Carter children. Fithian's journal is a valuable source on elite life in colonial Virginia. Although his Presbyterian upbringing prevented him from endorsing the life-style he encountered, it is clear that he enjoyed his stay—at least a bit. In many respects, staple-crop agriculture defined the economic and social lives of the planters. It is not too farfetched to talk about a tobacco "culture" in Virginia and a rice "culture" in South Carolina. The second document, from Landon Carter's diary, reveals how much of the planter's ego and reputation were wrapped up in tobacco leaves. In addition, Carter's comments shed light on the strained relationship with his son Robert. Family relations are important in the third selection as well, and again they are connected to staple agriculture. The difference is that the plantation master is not a venerable patriarch but a teenaged girl, Eliza Lucas, who not only adeptly managed her father's properties but successfully introduced indigo cultivation into South Carolina. The excerpts from her letterbook show that she was also proficient at couching her language in the feminine conventions of the time in order to ward off her absent father's desire for her marriage (though a few years later she married widower Charles Pinckney). The excerpt from the Anglican minister Charles Woodmason in the fourth document serves as a lively vignette of the Carolina backcountry on the eve of the Revolution. Woodmason performed missionary work in the interior and offered an unflattering portrait of the inhabitants. But he appreciated their grievances as enumerated in the petitions he helped to formulate. The Regulators, as the backcountry dissenters were called, directed their charges, reprinted here in the last document, at low-country legislators.

Two Observations on the Life-styles of Virginia's Rich and Famous

Reverend Devereux Jarratt: The View of a Commoner, 1740s–1750s

Our food was altogether the produce of the farm, or plantation, except a little sugar, which was rarely used; and our raiment was altogether my mother's manufacture, except our hats and *shoes,* the *latter* of which we never put on, but in the winter season. We made no use of *tea* or *coffee* for breakfast, or at any other time; nor did I know a single family that made any use of them. Meat, bread and milk was the ordinary food of all my acquaintance. I suppose the *richer sort* might make use of *those* and other luxuries, but to such people I had no access. We were accustomed to look upon, what were called *gentle folks*, as beings of a superior order. For my part, I was quite shy of *them*, and kept off at a humble distance. A *periwig*, in those days, was a distinguishing badge of *gentle folk*—and when I saw a man riding the road, near our house, with a wig on, it would so alarm my fears, and give me such a disagreeable feeling, that, I dare say, I would run off, as for my life. Such ideas of the difference between *gentle* and *simple*, were, I believe, universal among all of my rank and age. . . .

. . . During the 5 or 6 years I continued with my brothers, I do not remember ever to have seen or heard any thing of a religious nature; or that tended to turn my attention to the great concerns of eternity. I know not, that I ever heard any serious conversation respecting God and Christ, Heaven and Hell. There was a church, in the parish, within three miles of me, and a great many people attended it, every Sunday. But I went not once in a year. And if I had gone ever so often, I should not have been much the wiser: for the parish minister was but a poor preacher—very unapt to teach or even to gain the attention of an audience. . . .

. . . *Cards, racing, dancing*, &c. which are still the favourite sport and diversion of the wicked and ungodly, were then much in vogue. In these I partook, as far as my time and circumstances would permit, as well on Sundays as any other day. . . .

It was on a Sunday, P.M. when I first came to the house—an entire stranger, both to the gentleman and his lady. Though they had sent their niece and daughter to me, for about three months, yet I had no personal acquaintance with them, as the school had been made up, without my presence. The interview, on my part, was the more awkward, as I knew not how to introduce myself to strangers, and what style was proper for accosting persons of their dignity. However I made bold to enter the door, and was viewed, in some measure, as a phenomenon. The gentleman took me, (if I rightly remember) for the son of a very poor man, in the neighbourhood, but the lady, having some hint, I suppose, from the children, rectified the mistake, and cried out, *it is the school-master*.

Philip Fithian: The View of a Northerner, 1773, 1774

Thursday, December 30, 1773

Dr Franks is moving. he has lived in the House adjoining our School. The morning is fine, I rose by eight, breakfasted at ten, Miss Prissy & Nancy are to-Day Practising Music one on the Forte Piano, the other on the Guitar. their Papa allows them for that purpose every Teusday, & Thursday. Ben is gone to the Quarter to see to the measuring the crop of Corn. On his return in the Evening, when we were sitting & chatting, among other things he told me that we must have a House-warming, seeing we have now got possession of the whole House—It is a custom here whenever any *person* or *Family* move into a *House*, or repair a house they have been living in before, they make a *Ball* & give a Supper. . . .

. . . After considering a while I consented to go, & was dressed—we set away from Mr Carters at two; Mrs *Carter* & the young Ladies in the Chariot, Mrs Lane in a Chair, & myself on Horseback—As soon as I had handed the Ladies out, I was saluted by Parson *Smith;* I was introduced into a small Room where a number of Gentlemen were playing Cards, (the first game I have seen since I left Home) to lay off my Boots Riding-Coat &c—Next I was directed into the Dining-Room to see Young Mr *Lee;* He introduced me to his Father—With them I conversed til Dinner, which came in at half after four. The Ladies dined first, when some Good order was preserved; when they rose, each nimblest Fellow dined first—The Dinner was as elegant as could be well expected when so great an Assembly were to be kept for so long a time.—For Drink, there was several sorts of Wine, good Lemon Punch, Toddy, Cyder, Porter &c.—About Seven the Ladies & Gentlemen begun to dance in the Ball-Room—first Minuets one Round; Second Giggs; third Reels; And last of All Country-Dances; tho' they struck several Marches occasionally—The Music was a French-Horn and two Violins—The Ladies were Dressed Gay, and splendid, & when dancing, their Silks & Brocades rustled and trailed behind them!— But all did not join in the Dance for there were parties in Rooms made up, some at Cards; some drinking for Pleasure; some toasting the Sons of america; some singing "Liberty Songs" as they call'd them, in which six, eight, ten or more would put their Heads near together and roar, & for the most part as unharmonious as an affronted—Among the first of these Vociferators was a young Scotch-Man, Mr *Jack Cunningham;* he was nimis bibendo appotus; noisy, droll, waggish, yet civil in his way & wholly in-offensive—I was solicited to dance by several.

Sunday, March 6, 1774

I rose at eight— . . .

Breakfasted at half after nine. Mr Lane the other Day informed me that the *Anabaptists* in *Louden County* are growing very numerous; & seem to be increasing in afluence; and as he thinks quite destroying pleasure in the Country; for they encourage ardent Pray'r; strong & constant faith, & an intire Banishment of *Gaming, Dancing,* & Sabbath-Day Diversions. I have also before understood that they are numerous in many County's in this Province & are Generally accounted troublesome—Parson *Gibbern* has preached several Sermons in opposition to them, in which he has labour'd to convince his People that what they say are only whimsical Fancies or at most Religion grown to Wildness & Enthusiasm!—There is also in these counties one Mr *Woddel,* a presbiterian Clergyman, of an irreproachable Character, who preaches to the people under Trees in summer, & in private Houses in Winter, Him, however, the people in general dont more esteem than the Anabaptists Preachers; but the People of Fashion in general coun-tenance, & commend him. I have never had an opportunity of seeing Mr *Woddel,* as he is this Winter up in the Country, but Mr & Mrs *Carter* speak well of him, Mr & Mrs *Fantleroy* also, & all who I have ever heard mention his Name. . . .

Thursday, August 25

. . . *Ben* is in a wonderful *Fluster* lest he shall have no company to-morrow at the Dance—But blow high, blow low, he need not be afraid; *Virginians* are of genuine Blood—They will dance or die!

Landon Carter Displays an Ego Wrapped in Tobacco Leaves, 1770

July 6. Friday This morning just as I expected having said I should make very little in either Corn or tobacco I was told by the most insolent as well as most impudent person amongst men (my son) That was because I would follow my own way. Pray Sir, what are my ways? Planting your tobacco drye. That Sir is evidently all the tobacco I have that looks tollerable and in the same field though on the other side of the run it was planted in a season where it is not near so well standing and does not look half so well. Then, Your ground was lighter by G———. By the same oath it is if possible a million of times harder and stiffer.

I was then asked as I planted the same time as they did at Marsk why was not my tobacco as forward. Sir you don't know what you say. In the first place, that tobacco is forwarder than Marsk. In the next Marsk tobacco is sweet scented and of a quicker growth; and that earth I'll be sworn not half so stiff as mine. To which the dutifull child replyed I would swear anything. An impudent rascal. But so it is, a scoundrel determined to abuse his father will be contradictory and as Confident about what he does not know.

He then told me I always broke my ground up wet. I answered this year it really was so; and I was obliged to do it or not break it up at all, for it had not been drye since the September gust, and indeed before, from the 23rd of August. I was answered that was Strange when his wheat at Hickory Thicket had wanted rain All the Spring. To be sure Sir, that might be, and mine be too wet; besides the dryness and the Coldness of the Spring, though it baked, it had not dryed it; for it was evident on the turning those hills they turned up in moist Clods which the hoes were obliged to pound fine.

In short, this man is a brute to his father. . . . If I ask him why richer lands in my neighbourhood don't exceed me in cropping, Then I am answered they make better tobacco. Ask why they don't Sell better, then I am boldly told they do which is too gross a falsehood for a man to utter. . . .

August 23. Thursday But I know in this neighbourhood people are very fond of speaking meanly of their neighbour's Crops and I am certain mine has been so characterised. However, when I ride out, I declare I do not see any so good and although I have so much missing yet by the quantity I tend without any accident things going on just as they do I will venture a wager with the best of them both as to quantity and quality. . . .

August 31. Friday It seems my Son Robert is now once more determined to tend only Orleans Tobacco and never to prime it, laying aside his own reason and possibly adopted the following of others. For as to not priming Tobacco, although they would carry more leaves to the house, I will venture a wager that a plant primed and topped to 10 leaves should be thicker and weigh more than one of these unprimed plants. I have tried it before, have won a wager upon it, and this is the reason why my Tobacco every year is thicker in the leaf and carries a better grain to the felling of every one of these unpriming Gentlemen than any they make.

September 6. Thursday It has been moist and rainy from the beginning of this month till now and we have cut some Tobacco so thick to the admiration of some Gentlemen here on Tuesday last, the 2nd day of the Court, that one of them ignorantly was going to separate the leaf, immagining it had been double. . . .

September 8. Saturday . . . I was pleased to hear Mr Carter, forgetfull of his constant endeavours to expose any management of my crop, now obliged to own the real goodness of it. But still, as if unwilling to app[rove] the management, it is all impute[d to] the accident of the rains; but to ask why the same accident has not be[en so to] others as much is to make a [two lines torn and faded].

I say whoever attempts to make crop[s] or anything without the assistance of heaven? Why then should it be called an accident when my crop turns out well, because the rains have helped me, anymore than the same may be said as to the management of others? However this I assert: if our July had not been so drye and hot also, My management would have appeared more conspicuous than that of others; for I dare bet anything that none of the Tobacco tended as they have done can be thick as mine. And this is one cause of it firing. It was never so workt as to keep the plant in growth, and rain upon such plants must make them fire. . . .

Buckland went yesterday into my Tobacco ground, and said it was by far the thickest and finest he had ever seen.

He laughed and told me peoples' tones were vastly changed. One while he heard I should make no crop and now people were fancying I should not find house soon for my crop. But here I said they were as much mistaken as they were before; for I did not tend Crops without calculating where to put them; although what we had as yet cut would not do more than fill three good rooms.

Eliza Lucas on Love and Business, 1740, 1741

March [?] 1740

[To Colonel Lucas]
Hond. Sir

Your letter by way of Philadelphia which I duly received was an additional proof of that paternal tenderness which I have always Experienced from the most Indulgent of Parents from my Cradle to this time, and the subject of it is of the utmost importance to my peace and happiness.

As you propose Mr. L. to me I am sorry I can't have Sentiments favourable enough of him to take time to think on the Subject, as your Indulgence to me will ever add weight to the duty that obliges me to consult what best pleases you, for so much Generosity on your part claims all my Obedience, but as I know tis my happiness you consult [I] must beg the favour of you to pay my thanks to the old Gentleman for his Generosity and favourable sentiments of me and let him know my thoughts on the affair in such civil terms as you know much better than any I can dictate; and beg leave to say to you that the riches of Peru and Chili if he had them put together could not purchase a sufficient Esteem for him to make him my husband.

As to the other Gentleman you mention, Mr. Walsh, you know, Sir, I have so slight a knowledge of him I can form no judgment of him, and a Case of such consiquence requires the Nicest distinction of humours and Sentiments. But give me leave to assure you, my dear Sir, that a single life is my only Choice and if it were not as I am yet but Eighteen, hope you will [put] aside the thoughts of my marrying yet these 2 or 3 years at least.

You are so good to say you have too great an Opinion of my prudence to think I would entertain an indiscreet passion for any one, and I hope heaven will always direct me that I may never disappoint you; and what indeed could induce me to make a secret of my Inclination to my best friend, as I am well aware you would not disaprove it to make me a Sacrifice to Wealth, and I am as certain I would indulge no passion that had not your aprobation, as I truly am

> Dr. Sir, Your most dutiful and affecte. Daughter
> E. Lucas

To my Father.
Hon'd Sir   June the 4th, 1741
. . . We expect the boat dayly from Garden Hill when I shall be able to give you an account of affairs there. The Cotton, Guiney corn, and most of the Ginger planted here was cutt off by a frost. I wrote you in [a] former letter we had a fine Crop of Indigo Seed upon the ground, and since informed you the frost took it before it was dry. I picked out the best of it and had it planted, but there is not more than a hundred bushes of it come up— which proves the more unluckey as you have sent a man to make it. I make no doubt Indigo will prove a very valuable Commodity in time if we could have the seed from the west Indias [in] time enough to plant the latter end of March, that the seed might be dry enough to gather before our frost. I am sorry we lost this season. We can do nothing towards it now but make the works ready for next year. The Lucern is yet but dwindlering, but Mr. Hunt tells me 'tis always so here the first year.

Reverend Charles Woodmason on the "Wild Peoples" of the Carolina Backcountry, 1768

Sunday, August 7 It is impossible that any Gentleman not season'd to the Clime, could sustain this—It would kill 99 out of 100—Nor is this a Country, or place where I would wish any Gentleman to travel, or settle, altho' Religion and the State requires a Number of Ministers—Their Ignorance and Impudence is so very high, as to be past bearing—Very few can read—fewer write—Out of 5000 that have attended Sermon this last Month, I have not got 50 to sign a Petition to the Assembly. They are very Poor—owing to their extreme Indolence for they possess the finest Country in America, and could raise but ev'ry thing. They delight in their present low, lazy, sluttish, heathenish, hellish Life, and seem not desirous of changing it. Both Men and Women will do any thing to come at Liquor, Cloaths, furniture, &c. &c. rather than work for it—Hence their many Vices—their gross Licentiousness Wantonness, Lasciviousness, Rudeness, Lewdness, and Profligacy they will commit the grossest Enormities, before my face, and laugh at all Admonition.

Last Sunday I distributed the last Parcel of Mr. Warings Tracts on Prayer. It is very few families whom I can bring to join in Prayer, because most of them are of various Opinions the Husband a Churchman, Wife, a Dissenter, Children nothing at all. My Bibles and Common Prayers have been long gone, and I have given away to amount of £20 of Practical Books, besides those I received of the Society—Few or no Books are to be found in all this vast Country, beside the Assembly, Catechism, Watts Hymns, Bunyans Pilgrims Progress—Russells—Whitefields and Erskines Sermons. Nor do they delight in Historical Books or in having them read to them, as do our Vulgar in England for these People despise Knowledge. . . .

Saturday, September 3 Many of these People walk 10 or 12 Miles with their Children in the burning Sun—Ought such to be without the Word of God, when so earnest, so desirous of hearing it and becoming Good Christians, and good Subjects! How lamentable to think, that the Legislature of this Province will make no Provision—so rich, so luxurious, polite a People! Yet they are deaf to all Solicitations, and look on the poor White People in a Meaner Light than their Black Slaves, and care less for them. Withal there is such a Republican Spirit still left, so much of the Old Leaven of Lord Shaftsbury and other the 1st principal Settlers still remains, that they seem not at all disposed to promote the Interest of the Church of England—Hence it is that above 30,000£ Sterling have lately been expended to bring over 5 or 6000 Ignorant, mean, worthless, beggarly Irish Presbyterians, the Scum of the Earth, and Refuse of Mankind, and this, solely to ballance the Emigrations of People from Virginia, who are all of the Established Church. . . .

It will require much Time and Pains to New Model and form the Carriage and Manners, as well as Morals of these wild Peoples—Among this Congregation not one had a Bible or Common Prayer—or could join a Person or hardly repeat the Creed or Lords Prayer—Yet all of 'em had been educated in the Principles of our Church. . . .

It would be (as I once observ'd before) a Great Novelty to a Londoner to see one of these Congregations—The Men with only a thin Shirt and pair of Breeches or Trousers on—barelegged and barefooted—The Women bareheaded, barelegged and barefoot with only a thin Shift and under Petticoat—Yet I cannot break [them?] of this—for the heat of the Weather admits not of any [but] thin Cloathing—I can hardly bear the Weight of my Whig and Gown, during Service. The Young Women have a most uncommon Practise, which I cannot break them off. They draw their Shift as tight as possible to the Body, and pin it close, to shew the roundness of their Breasts, and slender Waists (for they are generally finely shaped) and draw their Petticoat close to their Hips to shew the fineness of their Limbs—so that they might as well be in Puri Naturalibus—Indeed Nakedness is not censurable or indecent here, and they expose themselves often quite Naked, without Ceremony—Rubbing themselves and their Hair with Bears Oil and tying it up behind in a Bunch like the Indians—being hardly one degree removed from them—In few Years, I hope to bring about a Reformation, as I already have done in several Parts of the Country.

"We Are *Free-Men* . . . Not Born Slaves": Grievances from the Backcountry, 1767

Thus situated and unreliev'd by Government, many among Us have been obliged to punish some of these Banditti and their Accomplices, in a proper Manner—Necessity (that first Principle) compelling them to Do, what was expected that the Executive Branch of the Legislature would *long ago*, have Done.

We are *Free-Men*—British Subjects—Not Born *Slaves*—We contribute our Proportion in all Public Taxations, and discharge our Duty to the Public, equally with our Fellow Provincials Ye[t] We do not participate with them in the Rights and Benefits which they Enjoy, tho' equally Entituled to them.

Property is of no Value, except it be secure: How Ours is secured, appears from the foremention'd Circumstances, and from our now being obliged to defend our Families, by *our own Strength:* As *Legal Methods* are beyond our Reach—or not as yet *extended* to Us.

We may be deem'd too bold in saying *"That the present Constitution of this Province is very defective, and become a Burden, rather than being beneficial to the Back-Inhabitants"*—For Instance—To have but *One* Place of Judicature in this Large and Growing Colony—And that seated *not Central*, but *In a Nook* by the SeaSide—The Back Inhabitants to travel Two, three hundred Miles to carry down Criminals, prosecute Offenders appear as Witnesses (tho' secluded to serve as Jurors) attend the Courts and Suits of Law—The Governour and Court of Ordinary—All Land Matters, and on ev[e]ry Public Occasion are Great Grievances, and call loudly for *Redress* For 'tis not only *Loss of Time* which the poor Settlers sustain therefrom, but the *Toil of Travelling,* and *Heavy-Expences* therefrom arising. Poor Suitors are often driven to Great Distresses, Even to the spending their Last Shilling or to sell their *Only* Horse for to defray their traveling and Town Costs; After which, they are oblig'd to trudge home on foot, and beg for Subsistence by the Way. . . .

Nor can We be said to possess our Legal Rights as Freeholders, when We are so unequally represented in *Assembly*—The South Side of Santee River, electing 44 Members, and the North Side, with these Upper Parts of the Province (containing 2/3 of the White Inhabitants) returning but Six—It is to this Great Disproportion of Representatives on our Part, that our Interests have been so long neglected, and the Back Country disregarded. But it is the Number of *Free Men,* not *Black Slaves,* that constitute the Strength and Riches of a State.

The not laying out the Back Country into Parishes, is another most sensible Greivance. This Evil We apprehend to arise from the Selfish Views of those, whose Fortune and Estates, are in or near *Charlestown*—which makes them endeavour, That all Matters and Things shall center there, however detrimental to the Body Politic, Hence it arises, That Assemblies are kept setting for six Months, when the Business brought before them might be dispatch'd in six Weeks—to oblige us (against Inclination) to chuse such Persons for Representatives, who live in or contiguous to *Charlestown;* and to render a Seat in the Assembly too heavy a Burden, for any Country Planter, of a small Estate, for to bear. From this our Non-Representation in the House, We conceive it is; That Sixty thousand Pounds Public Money, (of which we must pay the Greater Part, as being levy'd on the Consumer) hath lately been voted, for to build an *Exchange* for the Merchants, and a *Ball-Room* for the Ladies of Charlestown; while near *Sixty thousand* of Us Back Settlers, have not a Minister, or a place of Worship to repair too! As if We were not worth even the Thought off, or deem'd as *Savages,* and not *Christians!*

To leave our Native Countries, Friends, and Relations—the Service of God—the Enjoyment of our Civil and Religious Rights for to breathe here (as We hop'd) a Purer Air of Freedom, and possess the *utmost Enjoyment* of *Liberty,* and *Independency*—And instead hereof, to be set adrift in the Wild Woods among *Indians,* and *Out Casts*—To live in a State of Heathenism—without Law, or Government or even, the *Appearance of Religion*—Expos'd to the Insults of Lawless and Impudent Persons—To the Depredations of *Theives* and *Robbers*—and to be treated by our Fellow Provincials who hold the Reins of Things, as Persons hardly worthy the Public Attention, Not so much as their Negroes:—These Sufferings have broken the Hearts of Hundreds of our New Settlers—Made others quit the Province, some return to *Europe* (and therefrom prevent others coming this Way) and deterr'd Numbers of Persons of Fortune and Character (both at Home, and in *America*) from taking up of Lands here, and settling this our Back Country, as otherwise they would have done.

ㅅ *E S S A Y S*

The changing demography of Chesapeake society in the eighteenth century gave rise to what historian Allan Kulikoff of Northern Illinois University has called domestic patriarchy. The dominance of white elite fathers had implications not only for family relations but for the economic and social development of the area, as the first essay demonstrates. In South Carolina, the "country ideal," according to University of South Carolina historian Robert M. Weir, emerged during the eighteenth century as a series of shared assumptions about the responsibilities and rights of government and the governed. Weir argues in the second essay that country ideology was in place well before the Revolution and helped to mold South Carolina's response to the conflict with the British. The final selection, by Rhys Isaac, a historian at La Trobe University in Australia, focuses on a major challenge to Virginia's established political and social structure in the mid-eighteenth century: a wave of religious enthusiasm, provoked particularly by Baptists filtering into the interior of the colony from the North, attacked the easy life-styles and the authority of secular and clerical elites.

A Man's World: Family Life in the Chesapeake

ALLAN KULIKOFF

In March 1729 Ann Thomas urged the Prince George's County court in Maryland to permit her "to tend such a Quantity of Tobacco for herself, her labouring girls and her [sickly] slave as may be Sufficient for a maintenance for herself and them." Her request ran counter to current law— meant to improve tobacco prices—which permitted slaves and white men and boys to tend tobacco plants but forbade white women to tend them. In support of her petition to waive the law, Thomas recounted her attempts to provide for her family. Her husband's "Several Mismanagements and ill Conduct" had "reduced [her] to so great want and necessity that for some time she had relief by a pension from the Court." About ten years before, her husband left her, but she was "a Constant hard Labourer in Tobacco" and had "made an honest shift to Maintain herself and family of Several Small children without putting the County to charge of a pension." She purchased a slave, but he was too sick to work and drained her resources. Despite her husband's departure, she "had frequently done the part of wife by him in his Sickness and been at great expense on his account and never has had any benefit of his Labour for many years." The new law, however, prevented her from making a crop and supporting her three daughters, ages eleven, thirteen, and fifteen, and she would soon require county assistance again.

The justices refused Thomas's request. They probably investigated her claim and discovered that the family had greater resources than Thomas admitted. In the first place, she owned a healthy slave woman who could work in the ground. Two sons, both in their late teens, worked as laborers on nearby plantations and could assist their mother, and a married son resided with his family nearby and might take in his mother and sister. Families as poor as Thomas's survived on similar allotments of tobacco plants, the justices may have reasoned, and there was little reason that Thomas could not emulate them.

Although Thomas and the justices agreed in principle about the fundamentals of family government—that women should nurture children and comfort their husbands in sickness and health while men supported their families by growing tobacco for the market—Thomas's independence challenged the subservient behavior that the justices expected of women. While Thomas explained that her husband's incompetence and departure from the home and her slave's illness forced her into the fields, the justices wanted her husband and sons to return home and fulfill their obligations. To gain these ends, the justices refused to waive the rarely enforced stinting law.

This case suggests the acceptance of a kind of patriarchalism as the ideal form of family government by some early eighteenth-century Chesapeake planters. Although these planters rejected the connection between male supremacy in the family and royal absolutism in government that lay at the heart of European patriarchal theory, they sought to retain patriarchal control over their families. This *domestic patriarchalism* was both a set of beliefs about power relations within families and households and a description of behavior within the family. The ideology of domestic patriarchalism placed husbands over wives within the family, asserted that women were legally inferior to men, and separated the economic roles of men and women into distinct spheres, with men responsible for the economic well-being of the family and for civic participation outside it and women responsible for child nurture and household management. In a patriarchal family system, one would expect to find husbands controlling the distribution of family assets (and preferring sons over daughters), the separation of public and private roles, distinctive economic roles for men, women, and children, and paternal control of their children's marriage decisions. Children and wives willing to accept their place could expect affectionate and even companionate fathers and husbands, especially in wealthy families where servants and slaves lightened the workload of both women and men. This domestic patriarchy was very different from the kind of bourgeois family government that slowly developed in England and the American North. Although both systems of family government ensured male supremacy by keeping women out of public life and by enforcing a sexual division of labor, the equality of husbands and wives in domestic relations and the elevation of women's roles of child nurture and family management to a position of great ideological importance never occurred in the eighteenth-century Chesapeake region.

Although some white immigrants brought patriarchal ideals with them when they came to the Chesapeake, they found the practice of domestic patriarchalism difficult. Since adult life expectancy was quite low in the

Chesapeake colonies during the seventeenth century and generational continuity was difficult to maintain, few men lived long enough to impose their will upon their children. Planters' wives, moreover, often had to work in the fields beside their husbands because of the growing shortage of labor during the middle and late seventeenth century, a practice that reduced the economic differentiation of men and women at the heart of patriarchal theory.

When demographic conditions improved at the end of the seventeenth century and the growing slave trade eased the labor shortage, many more families took on patriarchal characteristics. Since men lived together, they could more readily impose their will upon their wives and children, and the acquisition of slaves permitted them to take their wives out of the tobacco fields and set them to domestic tasks. Men who owned slaves not only could afford this division of labor but knew they should not debase their wives by setting them to do slaves' work. Poor families, in contrast, still needed the wives' labor and probably continued the system of family labor common in the seventeenth century throughout the succeeding generations.

The Demographic Basis of Domestic Patriarchy

Immigrant men and women, who constituted a majority of the white adult population until the end of the seventeenth century, married late, died young, and left numerous orphans to the care of their heirs and the community at large. After English men and women left home, about age twenty, and came to the Chesapeake, they worked four or five years as servants; and those who survived their seasoning could expect to live only about twenty years after completion of their term. Since at least two men migrated for every woman, men had to postpone marriage until nearly age thirty, well after they had become freedmen, and they often married women ten or more years younger than themselves.

In such a demographic environment, a woman could anticipate little long-term support from her first husband, nor could a husband expect to maintain lengthy patriarchal authority over his wife. Very few immigrant marriages were long: in two Maryland counties, for instance, marriages lasted, on average, only eleven to thirteen years before one spouse died. Since widows and widowers soon remarried, several husbands exercised authority sequentially over a woman who lived to age fifty. Because men married much younger women, a wife was likely to become a widow; she probably learned the tobacco business while her husband was alive so she could take over once he died. During the interval between marriages, a widow gained some independent power and sometimes retained control over her first husband's property even after she remarried.

The high ratios of men to women among immigrants and the shortage of labor in the region after 1660 accelerated the development of more egalitarian relations between husbands and wives than were common in rural English families. With so many men clamoring for wives among the few women in the region, women could choose their spouses. Women and men, moreover, performed similar tasks and worked together growing tobacco because there was insufficient labor on most plantations to meet European demand for tobacco.

Although women on the tobacco coast thus had some advantages over their English counterparts, they lost the paternal protection common in the mother country. Native-born women commonly married in their middle to late teens during the seventeenth century, often as soon as they reached menarche. Some of these girls may have been forced into marriage by fathers or guardians before they were willing to begin their own families, and they had to bear the risk of reduced immunity to disease that each pregnancy brought. Setting up a household with a new husband did not offer a woman any remission of exploitation. Not only was she expected to work in the fields, but she had to maintain the cabins, bear and nurse infants, and take care of children.

Short marriages and frequent parental death meant great uncertainty for children. Children born in the Chesapeake region during the seventeenth century could anticipate that one or both parents would die before they could fend for themselves. Step-parents, siblings, uncles, and neighbors often succeeded to parental authority before children reached adolescence: the proportion of children in seventeenth-century Middlesex County, Virginia, who lost at least one parent rose from a quarter of the five-year-olds to more than half of the thirteen-year-olds. Guardians on occasion despoiled the estates of orphans (in law, those without fathers), deprived their charges of necessities, or even physically abused them. Children who lost one or both of their parents must have matured early and learned to accept responsibility for their own sustenance at an early age.

The legislators of the Chesapeake colonies understood well the risks that orphans faced and accordingly passed laws giving local justices of the peace, sitting as an orphans' court, greater authority over the estates and lives of orphans than was usual in England. The orphans' court, in both Chesapeake colonies, bound out poor children, appointed or registered the names of guardians of freeholders, oversaw the operation of orphans' plantations, and adjudicated disputes between orphans and their guardians. Justices took these responsibilities seriously. The children of more than four-fifths of the men who died in Prince George's County, Maryland, for instance, came under the jurisdiction of the orphans' court of the county: security was taken from guardians of children with landed estates, and the children of tenants were bound out to local planters. More than one-sixth of the children in neighboring Anne Arundel County—246 in all—were under the jurisdiction of the orphans' court in 1706 and probably accounted for nearly nine of every ten children who had lost their fathers in the county.

The demographic conditions that prevented the development of patriarchal family government disappeared at the end of the seventeenth century. As white immigration declined, the proportion of native-born adults in the white population rose, reaching half by 1700. These natives lived longer and married at younger ages than their immigrant parents. Family life in the eighteenth century therefore became more secure than it had been previously. Women could expect economic support for many years, since the marriages that natives contracted lasted longer than those of immigrants. Fathers could more readily control the economic destiny of their children because they more often lived to see them married. And children could expect more sustained parental care and were less likely to live in families with step-parents and step-siblings than their ancestors.

Marriages celebrated by native-born couples often lasted twice as long as those of immigrants. In Somerset County, Maryland, for instance, marriages between two native-born spouses lasted twenty-six years on average, nearly twice as long as those between two immigrants and a third longer than those between an immigrant and a native. In Prince George's County during the eighteenth century, these longer marriages became typical, lasting, on average, from twenty-two to twenty-five years, with first marriages probably continuing another ten years. One in three recorded marriages was extraordinarily long, lasting more than thirty years—forty-one years on average.

The increased duration of marriage substantially altered the lives of women. A husband could, if he desired, establish and maintain continuous authority over his wife and children, and his wife could count on his economic support for many years. Many wives died before their husbands, and women who lost their husbands tended to be older than forty and, since the surplus of men had disappeared, found remarriage increasingly difficult. Although widows in their twenties and thirties who lived in Prince George's in the 1770s remarried as frequently as widowers of the same age, widowers in their forties and fifties remarried four to seven times more frequently than widows.

When the duration of marriages rose during the first third of the eighteenth century, the probability that children would lose their parents declined substantially. There were both fewer orphans and more children with both parents alive at every age in eighteenth-century Prince George's than in seventeenth-century Middlesex. Two-thirds of the eighteen-year-old youths in Middlesex, but only half in Prince George's, for instance, had lost at least one parent; and nearly a third of that group in Middlesex, but only a tenth in Prince George's, had lost both parents. The proportion of fathers who lived to see their sons reach twenty-one increased from less than half in seventeenth-century Middlesex to nearly two-thirds in Prince George's during the eighteenth century.

Children of native-born parents lived more secure lives than earlier generations in the Chesapeake region. Even though a child still usually lost a parent before maturity, he was older when that event occurred than his ancestors had been, and he probably had adult siblings willing to protect his interests. As the number of orphans declined and their ages increased, the orphans' courts lost much of their importance. The number of poor, fatherless orphans bound out by the Prince George's orphans' court declined from 8.5 per year during the 1720s to 4.6 a year during the 1730s and 1740s, and the number of children brought to court to choose their guardians barely rose from 1720 to 1750, despite a doubling of the number of white children in the county. Parents relied less on the courts and more on informal arrangements with kin and neighbors to care for their orphaned children, and mothers uniformly retained custody of children when their husbands died. The orphans' court became a last resort to adjudicate disputes rather than a pervasive influence over orphan children.

Not only did parents live longer, but fathers retained control over both land and slaves, valuable property that their children needed to prosper. During the seventeenth century, life expectancy was so low that most sons of freeholders inherited land in their early twenties, but as life expectancy rose in the eighteenth century, sons waited longer for their portions. Two-fifths of the fathers of freeholders in Prince George's County, for instance, maintained plantations long after their sons had married. Though fathers often set up their sons on family land when they married, older sons of long-lived fathers usually waited ten or fifteen years after marriage before gaining title to their farms: fewer than a fifth of fathers under seventy gave any land to their sons, and only half of those over seventy began to distribute it. Older planters held on to their land to support their families, to ensure their maintenance if they fell ill, and to strengthen paternal authority over their sons. About half of tidewater planters owned fewer than two hundred acres and had to retain title to their farms to support their families, but even the largest landowners, who could well afford to give land to their children, usually kept title to most of it until they died, perhaps wishing to ensure the continued deference of their sons. The increase in slaveholding added to the power planters held over their children, for slaveholders could offer their offspring (both sons and daughters) the added capital and prosperity that title to slaves would yield, in return for good behavior.

The increased length of marriage, with the reduction in the number of remarriages it brought, helped streamline authority in plantation households. Conflicts within families, between step-children and step-parents, or between guardians and their charges may have been common in the seventeenth century, when most households contained a wide variety of kin, including step-parents, step-siblings, and half-siblings. These conflicts probably diminished, and the authority of fathers probably increased during the eighteenth century because most planter households contained only parents and their own children. The composition of households in Prince George's County in 1776 may have been representative. Although about half the planters owned slaves, these chattels rarely lived in the master's house. Only one-seventh of all householders owned servants, hired laborers, or boarded guests. Nearly half of all county households included only husband, wife, and their own children, and another tenth were headed by widows or widowers and housed the surviving spouse and the children. A third of the households included people other than parents and children, but even these were not particularly complex, with most adding a laborer or two, step-children, or an orphan assigned to the family by the county. Only a tenth of the families were extended generationally or laterally, mostly by widowed mothers of the husband or wife.

Husbands and Wives in the Domestic Economy

Although many unmarried men started households in the Chesapeake region during the seventeenth century, married couples were the center of plantation businesses and of family government during the eighteenth century. Unmarried men headed only one household in fourteen in Prince George's County in 1776, and only a tenth of the single men in their twenties ran farms that year. Once a new couple married, they set up a plantation almost immediately, only rarely living with the bride's or groom's family. Husbands increasingly ran these domestic commonwealths in ways consistent with the principles of domestic patriarchalism, sometimes responding violently when wives challenged their authority.

Planters and their wives realized that a prosperous farm business and a successful marriage supported each other. "Two young persons who marry without a reasonable prospect of an income to support them and their family," a Virginia essayist wrote in 1770, "are in a condition as wretched as any I know of." As soon as a couple decided to wed, negotiations between their fathers ensued to ensure that the couple would have a good chance to succeed. These negotiations were the most protracted among the gentry class, where parents wished to be certain that bride and groom would bring equal wealth into the marriage, but yeoman families also insisted that portions and dowries be paid to the new couple. Ignatious Doyne of Calvert County followed this custom in 1749 when James Brooke asked for one of Doyne's "Daughters in Marriage." Since he had no objection to the match, he "went to Madame [Sarah] Brooke to know what she would give her Son." Widow Brooke insisted that she did not have "anything in the world," but Doyne persisted and complained that James Brooke had "but one Negro." "I hope you will contrive to give him one at least." She refused and even asked to use the Negro girl she had given to James as her servant. Joseph Wheat of Montgomery County had better luck when his daughter married Zephaniah Prather, son of William, in 1761. After the wedding, Wheat visited Prather and told him "what he intended to give his said Daughter." Prather "appeared well Satisfied" and in turn took Wheat to a "small plantation" near his home, "and said this place I intend to give unto my son Zephaniah Prather Together with my Negro Boy Tobey."

A man and a woman should not contemplate marriage unless they loved and respected each other, for "mutual love and esteem" were "the very cement of matrimonial happiness." This writer would have approved the 1759 marriage of Sarah Lee and Philip Fendall, both members of the Maryland gentry, for they not only possessed "every natural Endowment, and needful Accomplishment to . . . promise them Happiness in private Life," but they were sure to reap "the Benefit of their early and Constant Affection for each other."

Since men and women possessed different sensibilities and performed different roles within marriage, they brought contrasting social qualities into their new homes. Men should enjoy the esteem of other men of their station, possess an upright character and be fair and honest in all their economic dealings, be careful and industrious in their daily tasks, and be courteous in their relationships with both men and women. The *Maryland Gazette* eulogized Robert Boone of Anne Arundel County when he died in 1759, for instance, because he was "an honest and industrious Planter, who Died on the same Plantation where he was Born in 1680, . . . and has left a Widow, to whom he was married 57 Years." While men were expected to possess qualities that prepared them for the marketplace, wives were encouraged to practice submissiveness to authority. A well-accomplished woman should above all be agreeable, affable, amenable, and amiable; she should practice charity and benevolence to her neighbors and the poor; and she should always behave virtuously. A woman who possessed these attributes was "endow'd with every Qualification to render a man happy in the Conjugal State."

Gentlemen insisted that wives be submissive to their husbands, and women tolerated, and even on occasion supported, a subordinate role within the family because that was the only way they could gain status as an adult. Marriage reduced the legal rights a single woman enjoyed but, at the same time, made her mistress over her husband's home, permitted her to bear legitimate children, and entitled her to economic support from her husband. An essay published in the *Virginia Gazette* in 1738 urged a wife to be "a faithful Friend, one who has no Views or Interest different from his, and makes his Joys and Sorrows all her own." Edith Cobb, the wife of the county clerk of Amelia County, Virginia, followed this advice during her long marriage, and her husband Samuel showed his appreciation by bequeathing her most of his estate in 1757. He gave "a very considerable Power" to her because "she has been my Wife near Forty Years during which Time hath always been kind, loving, and obedient to me without affectation."

English common law and the statute law of Maryland and Virginia legitimated the subservience of wives by granting husbands legal dominion over them. They controlled their wives' property (unless a premarital agreement was signed), and the wife could rarely sell property, buy goods, sign contracts, or make a will while her husband lived. Even though wives—to protect their dower rights to a third of the family land—had to give their consent before their husbands could sell land, husbands often informed their wives of land sales only after the transaction was completed. In Louisa County, Virginia, between 1765 and 1812, for instance, women gave their consent to land transfers more than seven days after the sale in half of the transactions. Women in Louisa had few choices and always agreed to the sale. One wife, when presented with a completed deed, wished that "the land . . . mentioned not be sold, but since it is the case she is entirely willing that the conveyance . . . should be recorded."

Ideally, the division of labor within marriage was supposed to sustain the authority of men in the family. A husband's most important responsibility was to provide food, clothing, and other necessities for his wife and children to the limit of his ability and economic station. That Chesapeake planters considered this task the very essence of manhood is suggested by the sad case of John Jackson. He had rented "a plantation at a very dear rate" in Prince George's County from 1724 to 1731 and had used "his honest Endeavours to maintain himself his Wife and a small Child now but eight years old" despite an illness that had left his wife lame and "altogether helpless" since 1727. Now, in 1731, Jackson found himself and his family destitute, and his "Endeavours fruitless," and begged of the county court to grant him "such relief as your Worships Compassion and charity shall think fit." If Jackson—a tenant who owned no slaves and hired no labor— was ashamed of his predicament, the court was hostile and rejected his petition and waited three years before it granted him a pension.

Not only did planters cultivate tobacco to support their families, but they sold the crop, did all the shopping and marketing, and kept the plantation's books. Husbands, who could expect long marriages in the eighteenth century, refused to share responsibility for plantation management with their wives. From time to time, husbands therefore tried to instruct their wives about plantation work in their wills. In 1758 Thomas Bowie, a wealthy planter with three small children, bequeathed land to his wife "Provided she does not Clear or Cutt down above twenty thousand Tobacco Hills in any one year"; similarly, in 1740 Capt. Charles Beall told his wife "not to Sel or Destroy any timber of . . . moor than what may bee for the Plantations Use and the Mill."

Planters usually worked in the ground as well as directed the labor of their mature sons, slaves, and white hired men in the cultivation of tobacco and in the maintenance of the farm. Although most planters could muster two or three workers to help them, many newly married men, tenants, and small freeholders relied only on their own efforts to support their families. A small proportion of planters owned or hired enough workers to stand back and oversee farm operations, and only the richest gentlemen could afford to hire overseers and manage their plantations from afar. Most slaveholders found themselves in circumstances similar to those of Jeremiah Pattison's, who complained in 1737 that he had labor enough to "enable him with a good deal of pain and Industry to support himself and Family by making Tobacco Corn and Other grain having no more than three taxable Slaves of which Two are almost past their Labour . . . and six young Slaves some of which do Jobs and the rest are but a . . . Burthen."

While the great majority of men living in counties like Prince George's continued to labor in their fields throughout the eighteenth century, the economic position of planters slowly improved as more of them used slaves to increase the standard of living of their families. The proportion of planters in Prince George's who toiled alone declined from two-fifths in 1733 to a third in 1776. At the same time, the number of householders who could direct a gang of five to nine workers rose from a tenth to a seventh, and the proportion of men who worked ten or more laborers grew from one in twenty-five to one in fourteen.

While men managed the plantation, women took care of their homes. They prepared the family's food, washed clothes, tended gardens, made clothes, spun thread, wove cloth, milked cows, and churned butter. Though a few wives of wealthy gentlemen directed a retinue of slave women in these tasks, most planters kept slave women in the field, leaving their wives to complete household chores by themselves until their daughters were old enough to help them. Each of these tasks had to be repeated week after week, and wives sometimes envied the more varied jobs their husbands performed.

Cloth and clothes production was the wife's most important economic contribution to the household economy. Although women infrequently spun thread, carded wool, or wove cloth from fiber during the seventeenth century, planters responded to recurring depressions in the tobacco trade by purchasing sheep, cards, and spinning wheels for their wives, and cloth-making became a very important domestic activity during the first half of the eighteenth century. Women universally made clothes from imported cloth, knitted bulky items, and repaired damaged wearing apparel, thereby saving the household from the great expense of importing ready-made clothing. Cloth production from scratch or, more commonly, local trade of wool, flax, thread, and cloth among farms possessing one part of the production process further added to the value of the wife's production.

Seventeenth-century wives served their families and occasional guests at crude tables or barrels, and the family ate from wooden (or sometimes earthen) bowls with fingers or spoons and knives. Housewives added more formal meal preparation and service to their numerous chores during the eighteenth century, when meals became far more ceremonial and hospitality more common. This change is most clearly documented in St. Mary's County, the poorest county on Maryland's tobacco coast. Planters there began purchasing earthenware plates and bowls and table linen during the seventeenth century, and all but the poorest householders owned all of those items by the 1720s. Knives and forks reached a majority of substantial planters in the 1720s and 1730s and less prosperous folk by the 1750s and 1760s. Finally, county families increasingly livened their meals with spices and tea. Though none but the wealthiest families added spices to their food early in the century, a majority of middling planters and a third of poorer freeholders used them by the 1750s and 1760s. And while fewer than a tenth of the planters' wives served tea before 1740, the proportion who used it thereafter rose steadily, reaching nearly three-quarters of the households by the 1770s.

Child care was the most time-consuming task assigned to Chesapeake wives. A woman could expect to give birth once every two to three years from marriage to menopause, and she assumed the burdens of childbearing, nursing, weaning, and child care with little assistance from her husband. This division of labor tied younger women to their homes, although it freed men to work in the fields or visit neighbors and nearby villages without concern for the safety or care of their offspring.

No Chesapeake family could possibly attain the harmony and complete separation of tasks that the domestic patriarchal ideal demanded. Husbands and wives bickered, argued, and occasionally even separated. From time to time, husbands and wives brought their difficulties to local or provincial courts. The two cases examined below paint a vivid picture of marital expectations and roles and suggest the limits of patriarchal domestic economy.

When John Abington, a wealthy Prince George's merchant, died in 1739, he left his widow Mary and their six children an estate of two thousand pounds sterling and several thousand acres of land. Unable to manage this fortune, she soon married Dr. Andrew Scott, a man of high status but small fortune. The couple paid almost all of Abington's personal estate to his creditors but collected few debts owed to him. They soon began bickering, and in 1746 Mary Scott sued her husband in Maryland's chancery court for separate maintenance. She claimed that she had behaved properly to-ward her husband; when he "prevailed upon" her to "joyne in a Deed" to break entail on some of Abington's land and have it assigned to him, she "had in all things . . . Complyed with the Request . . . and had thereby put every thing out of her Power." After he received the land, he treated her "with so much Cruilty and Inhumanity" that she "could not live or Cohabit with him without running a Manifest hazard of her Life." Finally, he turned her "out of Doors almost naked and quite Destitute of all the Necessaries of Life," forced her to turn to neighbors, and refused to give her the thirty pounds he promised her for her support.

Dr. Scott painted a far different picture. While he admitted taking the land, he claimed the estate was otherwise too small to support her and added that he had given Abington's children the land bequeathed to them. He denied treating her "with any Cruielty" but claimed he had suffered from her "indecent, Disorderly, Abusefull and Turbulent" behavior caused by her "common and frequent Drunkedness" until he had to leave the house and stay with neighbors. They urged him to "Seperate from her," but he "was Resolved to bear with her as Long as he could and to endeavour by all easy and Moderate means to Reclaim and reform her." When he learned that "she had been guilty of the worst and most Scandalous of Crimes which a Wife could be guilty of to a husband," of bringing "a Disease upon him which for Decency and the Shamefullness of it he forbears to give a name," he finally forced her from the house. After listening to both sides, the court ordered Scott to pay his wife thirty pounds as long as she lived apart from him.

A decade before the Scotts separated, Jane Pattison of Calvert County sued her second husband, Jeremiah, a middling planter, for separate main-tenance in chancery court. From the start of her marriage, she had "behaved herself in a virtuous and respectful manner toward" him despite his ap-propriation of "a considerable Estate" left by her first husband to her and her children. Notwithstanding her good behavior, within a year of the wedding he "conceived so very great Dislike and Aversion to" her that "not only he used her very cruelly by beating her with Tongs . . . without any just or reasonable provocation . . . but also turned her out of Doors about Six years ago destitute of Cloaths and almost naked" and cut off her credit when she tried to replace them. Friends witnessed repeated beatings before the couple separated and later helped find her clothing, but Pattison still refused to support her "suitable to what he could afford." And Mrs. Pattison therefore sued for an annual allowance.

Jeremiah Pattison vehemently disagreed with his estranged wife. While he "was not wealthy" when he married her, he lived "in a comfortable and decent manner." After he paid her first husband's debts and distributed part of the remainder of the estate to her children, little was left. Mrs. Pattison "treated him not only with the greatest . . . Contempt" but even threw firebrands and iron candlesticks at him, all the while shouting "the most horrid and shocking Imprecations" at him. He responded with "the most gentle and persuasive Means he could think of to reclaim" her, and when that did not work, he "corrected her in a very moderate Manner." She abandoned him voluntarily, despite his attempts to "prevail on her to stay at home and manage her household Affairs which she absolutely refused to do." After she left home a second time, he urged her to return, writing: "My Dear I am Sorry that you should be so ill advised to desert your Habitation and send this to desire you would return home and behave Yourself as a loving Wife ought if you'l do that you shall always by me be used Lovingly. I am your Loving Husband." Mrs. Pattison refused to return, and the court ordered him to pay her thirty pounds a year.

Disagreement over the financial operation of the plantation lay at the root of Pattison's unhappiness. Samuel Abbot, her first husband, left a small personal estate with no taxable slaves but farmed four hundred acres of excellent land. Pattison lived on the edge of respectability, working as an itinerant carpenter before his marriage in 1724, but he too owned land. After the marriage, Pattison supported his family on his wife's land and rented his property to tenants, netting about two thousand pounds of tobacco each year. He used the profits from his two estates to buy five adult slaves by 1733. Mrs. Pattison, who wanted this bounty for her children, asked him to "dispose of all that he had at his Death to her Children" and was "much dissatisfied" when he refused. The couple argued repeatedly over this, calling each other vile names and usually concluding with Mrs. Pattison's throwing household implements at him and Pattison's beating his wife so severely that she left home to recover. Finally, since he would not bequeath his property to her children or stop beating her, she resolved to "take no Care of his Affairs but would make all she Could for her Children." She made good on her threat, forcing him to "put out" his linen "to be washed, his Stockings to be knit and his Negroes Cloaths to be made," and refused to serve him when he "asked for victuals," insisting that if he "was above taking it himself he might go without" and at the same time feeding "some very good meat" to a male neighbor.

Although the behavior reported by these two cases may have become increasingly unrepresentative as the number of second marriages diminished, the cross section of ordinary and wealthier planters and their wives who testified in court agreed about the principles of family government. They agreed, for instance, that wives owed their husbands obedience and smooth operation of the household in return for the financial support needed to purchase the necessities of life. The litigants claimed to follow these norms. While Scott and Pattison insisted that they properly supported their wives, their wives claimed fidelity and obedience. Mrs. Pattison even asked her witnesses about her first marriage, and they all agreed that she had been "a very dutiful good wife." Since the husband ruled the household, he had the right to correct his wife moderately when she went astray and punish her more harshly if necessary. Even the wives agreed with this idea, insisting that they gave their husbands no provocation but implying that clear reason would justify punishment.

Landed families generally accepted these principles of family government and the power relations they entailed throughout the eighteenth century. The emotional sensibilities of relations between gentry husbands and wives, however, probably began to soften during the last quarter of the eighteenth century. The slaves owned by these wealthy families performed all the plantation's heavy labor, thus freeing gentlemen and their wives from much of the work of ordinary white women and men. Freed from servile labor, these wealthy women and men increasingly emphasized emotion, love, individual feelings, and companionship within their marriages. Child rearing took on a heightened importance, especially for women. A new and highly charged emotional and possessive language began to appear in family correspondence. These new sensibilities were incorporated into patriarchal family government. Plantations remained units of production. Gentry women did not create a new, semiautonomous sphere dominated by child nurture for themselves. Even the wealthiest women retained important productive functions, for they directed and participated in gardening, cloth production, and candlemaking.

The Family Life Cycle in the Domestic Economy, 1720–1800

Unlike the Scotts and Pattisons, nearly every Chesapeake couple had children soon after marriage, who modified relations between husbands and wives, gave each spouse added responsibilities, and created new layers of authority in the household. Since women bore children regularly until menopause, some children remained at home throughout their parents' lives. Variations within family government probably hinged upon the ages of spouses and their children: young parents with small children, middle-aged couples with adolescents, and widows and widowers with their unmarried children faced varying problems. This life-cycle approach sheds light on the economy of the family and the changing nature of domestic patriarchy within it.

The birth of children during the early years of marriage increased the work load wives sustained. A woman, age thirty-three, who had married when she was twenty-one, would probably be pregnant with her sixth child. She had spent 4 of her first 12 years of marriage pregnant and perhaps another 4.5 years nursing the surviving children, a task which sometimes made her ill. Each new child, moreover, forced her to make more clothing for her growing family. Few women could call on any help in these tasks in the early years of marriage. Daughters were too young to help with child care and sewing, and only the wealthiest planters owned enough slaves to put one or two to work as domestics. Even the wealthiest wives, furthermore, nursed their own children, sometimes refusing to send them out to wet nurse, even if in delicate health themselves.

The work of all but the wealthiest slaveholders intensified when children began to arrive. Whatever help their wives had provided in the fields was reduced when their domestic duties increased, and infants had to be fed and clothed without providing compensating field work. Poorer men struggled to maintain their standard of living, but might fail during the periodic depressions that hit the tobacco trade. Men who owned slaves possessed greater resources, but unless their labor force grew when their children were born, they probably had to push their slaves harder to sustain the same standard of living.

While women in their thirties and early forties continued to bear and nurse children, their maturing daughters assumed some responsibilities for child care and domestic industry. Parents sometimes left young children with older siblings when they went out. John Hatherly and his wife, for instance, allowed their fourteen-year-old daughter to watch her nine-year-old brother while they attended a funeral in Anne Arundel County in 1751. Daughters copied their mothers' household chores even before they learned the necessary skills. . . .

Sons joined their fathers in cultivating tobacco and grain at the age of ten to twelve. . . .

Parents enjoyed their children's help on the plantation until the children left home to marry, set up a household, or work on a nearby farm. Few adolescents lived with or worked for neighbors or kin; in Prince George's in 1733, for instance, three-quarters of sons whose fathers were alive lived at home, and nearly every youth waited until he reached his majority at twenty-one before leaving home. Similar numbers of sons remained at home in southside Virginia in the 1750s and 1760s, and the proportion of sons living at home until marriage in Prince George's probably increased in the 1770s.

The birth of children modified the distribution of authority in the household. Fathers expected sons and daughters to obey them while at home, insisted upon the right to approve marriage partners they chose, and demanded their respect even after they matured. Mothers shared parental authority with their husbands and gained sole authority over minor children if their husbands died. Siblings also sustained mutual obligations to each other. Peter Dent, a gentleman and justice, suggested the power of this family hierarchy when he wrote his will in Prince George's County in 1757. He urged of his "Dear Children that they be Dutifull to their Mother During her Life and Loving and Obligeing to Each other the youngest always Submitting to the Eldest in reason and the Eldest bearing with the Infirmitys of the youngest and advising them in the best manner they can that they may Live in Concord all their Lives."

As children were born and matured, the bundle of mutual duties and responsibilities that tied the family together grew more complex. Since few children in Prince George's in 1776 left home before marriage, the number of children directed by parents grew, reaching a peak of five or six when the mother was in her early forties and her husband was near fifty, and declined slowly thereafter, diminishing to four children when mothers were in their mid-fifties and fathers were sixty. Older children may have eased the burdens of child nurture. Although only three or four children lived in a typical household in the county in 1776, the typical child grew up with four or five siblings.

Children's obligations to parents and siblings sometimes dictated financial sacrifice. Fathers often insisted that sons allow their mothers full use of the land they would ultimately inherit. Francis Waring, a gentleman of great wealth who died in Prince George's in 1769, bequeathed his home farm to his son Leonard, "provided he Suffers his Mother to Enjoy the Land which I have Alloted her." Similarly, Thomas Wilson gave son Josiah the home plantation only if he did not interrupt "his Mother during her Life for making use of the Land as she shall think proper." Reciprocal obligations between siblings became especially important after both parents died. Edward Willett, a pewterer, gave all his pewterer's molds and tools to his son William when he died in Prince George's in 1744, "provided he Doth make what necessary pewter the rest of my Children shall want." William Young especially wanted to ensure that his son William find a home after he died. He knew that William was "not Capable of himself to Act soe in the world as to Gitt a Liveing," and accordingly he gave William's part of the estate to his son John in his 1760 will, with the request that John "Assist the Said William," his brother.

Fathers held a potent lever over their children. They rarely turned over ownership of land or slaves to their children before they died, even if they permitted use of this capital during their lifetime. If children failed to obey their fathers, they might find themselves cut out of the parental estate. Robert White, of Prince George's County, refused to bequeath land to his son James in 1768 that he had let him farm for thirty years, because the two argued about religion. James had converted to Anglicanism from Catholicism and served as a vestryman and considered his father an "Ignorant Illerate man wholy Biggotted to all the Follies and Superstitions of the Roman Church." Thirteen years earlier John Anderson of Charles County told his daughter Mary Burch that "his Son James and Daughter Caty were running about and took no Care of him," and though "they expected a great Deal when he died, . . . they should find little of it."

Although couples farmed their land together as long as the marriage lasted, the number of children remaining at home diminished greatly when the couple grew older. In Prince George's in 1776, fewer than two children lived at home with mothers over sixty years old, and between two and three children lived with fathers (who had more often remarried) of the same age. Most of the children in these households were adolescents and young adults, well able to take care of themselves and help provide their parents with a comfortable living in their old age.

Married men and widowers, even those of advanced ages, maintained a household and continued working the ground. Only one of every seven men above sixty in Prince George's in 1776 lived as a dependent in the home of kin or neighbors. Two-thirds resided with their wives, and the rest, only a seventh of the total, were widowers. These proud men usually refused to seek aid from loved ones. Ninian Beall of Thomas, a widower of eighty, headed a household on a small plantation near Bladensburg town but worked no slaves. Two children still lived with him, including a daughter and her husband, but whatever help they provided for him was under his direction as the master of the family. . . .

Women faced far greater problems when their husbands died, because of their inferior social status and lack of experience in operating a plantation. Though widows possessed the legal right of the feme sole to buy and sell property and act for themselves, most widows in their twenties and thirties probably remarried, thereby losing their legal rights. Older women, whose numbers increased as the century progressed, usually did not remarry but remained widows the rest of their lives. However long a widow stayed single, she needed more than legal rights to support her children. Husbands recognized the economic problems their widows would have and tried to ease their burdens in two ways. First, they often appointed their wives executors of their estate, thereby guaranteeing that they would control all the familial property while the estate passed through probate. And, second, they bequeathed their wives sufficient property to ensure that profitable farming would continue.

Although planters almost always named wives as executors of their estates during the first half of the eighteenth century, they began to question their wives' ability to administer their property as the century progressed. Between 1710 and 1760, planters in tidewater York, St. Mary's, and Prince George's counties sometimes appointed a mature son or, less frequently, another kinsman or friend as coexecutor, but men excluded widows from executorships in only a tenth of the wills in the three counties. In the 1760s and 1770s, however, the proportion of planters in St. Mary's County who appointed adult sons or kinsmen to help wives administer their estates doubled. . . .

Eighteenth-century tidewater planters usually gave their wives sufficient property to support their children and live comfortably after the children left home. Despite the increasing age of widows (and the growing number of adult sons), there was remarkable continuity in the powers tidewater planters gave their widows throughout the colonial era. Widows, by law, were entitled to a third of the husband's estate, and they could reject any smaller bequest and demand to receive their thirds. Only about a third of the planters in tidewater Maryland during the colonial period limited their wives to their dower rights or attempted to have them accept less, and only a tenth granted them property on the condition that they remained widows. Six of every ten married testate decedents used their wills to increase their widows' rights beyond the dower third, either by granting them control of the dwelling plantation and all its stock, labor, and implements during their natural life or by giving them the equivalent in land, slaves, and movable property. Though widows could operate the farms as they saw fit, their husbands often limited their control by bequeathing the property to a particular child or children after the death of their mother. . . .

Although widows usually possessed legal authority over the husband's estate, any widow's actual power depended more upon the age of her sons than on the legal terms of her husband's will. As long as all the children remained minors, the widow as executor controlled most of her husband's estate, but as sons came of age, they took their portions with them or stayed at home uneasily waiting for their mothers to die so they could inherit the home plantation. Tensions between widows and their adult sons over the use of property occurred because of unresolved tensions within domestic patriarchalism between the authority of mothers (whom sons were bound to obey) and the dominance of adult men over women.

Wealthy planters in Prince George's County sometimes tried to prevent this discord between widows and sons by provisions in their wills. In 1751 Daniel Carroll, a wealthy merchant and gentleman planter, urged his wife and children to consult several neighboring kinsmen and friends "In case any Difference or Dispute shou'd hereafter unfortunately happen Between my said loving Wife and any of my Dear Children, either about the management or Division of any part of the Estate." Other planters admonished widows and sons to allow each other to live peaceably on their allotted plantations. . . .

Adult sons usually gained control of property from their widowed mothers in Prince George's. Fathers often permitted their sons to work for themselves when they reached their middle or late teens and allowed them to inherit property at age twenty-one. As sons took their portions and daughters married and depleted the estate yet further, widows found themselves unable to earn a subsistence and dependent upon their children for their bread. Only a quarter of the widows in the county in 1776 over the age of fifty-seven maintained their own households. The rest lived with sons or neighbors. Widows frequently lost control even over their own plantation when the son who would inherit the property came of age. Unmarried sons as young as twenty or twenty-one who lived at home assumed the position of head of household from their widowed mothers nearly two-thirds of the time.

Some women, ill prepared to operate plantations, gladly turned over the farm to their sons in return for support. When Thomas Richardson of Prince George's came "of age to receive his fortune by his Fathers Will," his mother Susannah said "that she did not care to put herself to the Trouble of paying him his Fortune" but "had agreed to go Equally halfs in every thing." She was apparently satisfied with the arrangement: not only did Thomas reopen the family tavern, but his mother felt that "her son Thomas Richardson was very Carefull and that if he continued to be so and took care of the House, she would take care in the House and would not begrudge him the half of every thing that should be made and raised on the plantation."

A son's assertion of authority might, however, leave his mother resentful and force her to find ways to maintain some autonomy. Sarah Brooke, widow of John of Calvert County, lived with her son Roger in the 1740s and 1750s, when she was in her fifties and sixties. Though Roger operated the plantation, his mother still nominally owned much of it. When he complained that "she did not give his two Negroes Meat enough," she replied that he should "kill Meat of his own as he had Hoggs and then he might give them what he pleased as he was not contented with what She gave them." She wanted "to keep the Staff in her own Hand better her Children should come to her than she to go to them," but her attempts at autonomy were not very successful. She distributed all her property to her sons James and Roger, and Roger "made use of all the crops every Year . . . without any Division and disposed of it as he thought proper for his own use" despite the desires of his mother. She depended upon him for subsistence, and without him would have to "beg my Bread from Door to Door," yet even this minimal care was given only grudgingly, for she complained that she had "no Body to do anything for me not so much as to bring me a Coal of Fire to light my Pipe."

Morality, Virtue, and the Family Economy

Parents in the eighteenth-century Chesapeake were responsible for training their children to take their proper place in adult society and teaching them the reciprocal responsibilities of parents and children, husbands and wives, masters and slaves, and magistrates and citizens. All education in the region, whether formal literacy training in schools or informal instruction in the home, aimed at this end. Sons who learned proper behavior in this society were ultimately rewarded with sufficient property from their fathers' estates to permit them to start their own patriarchal families.

Although tidewater planters infrequently expressed emotional religious commitments, they understood the necessity of strong moral education. The Reverend Thomas Craddock of Baltimore County probably expressed the common Anglican view on moral training in a sermon in 1752 on a murder in his parish. The murderers both ignored moral education *and* deprived the victim's children of that training by killing a nurturing parent. If the murderers had "been trained up in the ways of religion and virtue, they wou'd never have been guilty of this wickedness," Craddock told his congregation. But the deed was done, and "a young, defenseless tribe of children" lost "the care and assistance of their father or mother," the adults responsible "for their *spiritual,* as well as temporal interest," and reduced them "to a state of indigence, who, had their parents liv'd, might have had a sufficient competency." To prevent similar acts in the future, masters and fathers ought to be "conspicuous in the worship of God, in acts of justice and charity to man; in a *Spiritual* care of your families . . . ; and such a conduct, with the blessing of God, may have a happy influence o'er many of them."

Planters and their wives shared and on occasion expressed this concern.

The *Maryland Gazette* eulogized Rebeccah Sanders, when she died at seventy-five in 1752 in Anne Arundel County, not only because she had "a just Sense of Religion herself" but also because "she instilled the Principles of it thro' her numerous Family; and having educated her Children in the Paths of Virtue and Piety, had the inexpressible satisfaction . . . to reflect that they were each an Honour to her." Several planters in Prince George's County admonished their wives in similar tones in their wills. In 1734, Archibald Edmonston asked his widow and son James to "inspect into the behavior and deportment of my Son Thomas Edmonston," who was to be under their control during his minority. . . .

In an ideal society, each person knows how to behave in the presence of social inferiors and superiors. The children of slaveholders—a majority of the white populace—saw their parents deprive slaves of freedom, expropriate their labor, and barter them from hand to hand and learned thereby that they could treat black people with contempt they should never use on their white peers. Thomas Jefferson best captured the consequences of this training in a well-known passage: "The whole commerce between master and slave is a perpetual exercise in the most boisterous passions, the most unremitting despotism on the one part, and degrading submissions, on the other." As "the parent storms," Jefferson insisted, "the child looks on, catches the lineaments of wrath, puts on the same airs in the circle of smaller slaves, gives a loose to the worst of passions, and thus . . . educated and daily exercised in tyranny, cannot but be stamped by it."

Parents instructed their children to take their proper place in white society by training them to perform tasks appropriate to their sex. Fathers took their sons with them when they went abroad from the plantation and sent them on errands to nearby farms or to the general store as soon as they could ride horses and accept responsibilities. Most important, they introduced them to the world of male work by teaching them how to cultivate tobacco and grains and instilled in them the male ethic of aggressive behavior by taking them hunting.

Daughters stayed closer to home and learned both housewifery and their inferior place in the family order from their mothers. The daughters of Robert Carter of Nomini Hall, one of Virginia's richest gentlemen, imitated woman's work at a young age, and Philip Fithian, their tutor, even discovered them one day "stuffing rags and other Lumber under their Gowns just below their Apron-Strings, . . . prodigiously charmed at their resemblance to Pregnant Women!" Mothers were particularly responsible for training their daughters to sew, knit, and spin so they could engage in necessary plantation labor. When Margaret Gough of Calvert County charged her guardians with improperly maintaining her, she considered the fact that she "never was taught to sew and would not have known how to make her own Shifts had her [step-]sister not taught her" to be potent evidence of neglect.

White children learned to identify themselves not only by race and gender but by their position in the social hierarchy. . . .

Children learned to read and write in order to understand their moral obligations and to help them perform the work demanded of them. Substantial planters sometimes reflected upon these twin goals of formal education. Samuel Pottinger, who died in Prince George's in 1742, directed that his son "be taught to Read write and cast Accompts and my Daughter to Read." Before he died in 1730, Thomas Brooke, a gentleman with many children, similarly requested that his "two youngest Sons . . . be well educated in reading writing and arithmetick and That they shall be brought up in the doctrine and principles of the Church of England."

Since most Chesapeake planters and their wives were barely literate, they had to send their children to school to learn how to read, write, and cipher. Before the middle of the eighteenth century, there were few free schools in Virginia, and private schoolmasters, paid by parents, were in short supply. There was but one schoolteacher for every hundred white families in eight tidewater Virginia parishes in 1724, a figure that implies that each child might attend one short school term. At the same time, only four teachers, each responsible for more than four hundred families, ran schools in two piedmont parishes, and at best they reached a quarter of the children entrusted to their care.

As areas developed, more schools sprang up. In Elizabeth City County, one of Virginia's original shires, the number of schoolmasters grew from two in 1670, to three in 1724, and five in 1782; and at the same time, the number of families each teacher had to serve declined from about eighty-five to sixty-five. The parish schools, furthermore, included an academy where boys might study Latin as well as English. Though Prince George's County was not founded until 1697, there were already several private schools within its borders in 1724, and a free parish school joined them in the 1740s. By 1755, there were between ten and fourteen schoolmasters in the county, each responsible for eighty-five to a hundred families. County schools at that date attracted various kinds of students: although most teachers ran reading schools, one operated a Latin school, another taught practical and advanced mathematics as well as reading and writing, and two women instructed girls in French, sewing, and knitting.

Educational resources were unevenly spread through the white population. Wealthier parents, who could better afford to pay for schooling, more frequently wished to educate their children, and planters, no matter what their economic condition, educated sons more thoroughly than they did daughters. Parents and magistrates in Prince George's followed these expectations. The wealthier the father with young children, the more likely he was to mention education in his will. While only one planter in ten in the county whose wealth totaled less than four hundred pounds directed that his children be educated, more than one in three with more than one thousand pounds included a similar provision.

The schooling that the Prince George's orphans' court required masters or guardians to provide orphans and apprentices suggests the minimal educational expectations of ordinary planters. The court ordered some education for three-quarters of the girls and seven-eighths of the boys brought before it between 1720 and 1750. However, the justices differentiated the content of education by gender, insisting that more than half the boys given an education be taught to read and write (and the rest just to read), while asking that only one girl in sixteen be taught to read and to write. Orphans' courts in Lancaster County, Virginia, in the 1720s and Anne Arundel County, Maryland, 1770–1779, ordered similar training, but added ciphering to the boys' education.

The educational experience of most planters' children closely followed these prescriptions. Orphans of middling and substantial planters in three Virginia counties between 1731 and 1808 enjoyed one or two years of formal education after their fathers died. While boys received two years of training, more than half the girls probably had none, and girls who attended a reading school usually went for only one year. Since school terms lasted only a few weeks to a few months, boys probably learned to read and write during their attendance, while girls learned only to read.

Schools in colonial Virginia did teach their more privileged male students to read and write. About two-thirds of the men born in three tidewater Virginia counties and three-fifths born in five piedmont counties during the first half of the eighteenth century could sign their names as adults. Men with wealthy parents were more likely to learn to sign. Although literacy was nearly universal among planters who owned land and slaves, only two of every five poor tenants could read and write.

Once children learned to read, they had access to a few books. Nearly six of every ten householders living in Prince George's between 1730 and 1769 owned at least one book. Literate parents not only sent their children to school more frequently than their less wealthy, illiterate neighbors, but they also owned books with far greater regularity. Although only a third of the tenant nonslaveholders and about half of the planters who owned land or slaves possessed books, three-quarters of freeholders who worked slaves on their own land owned a book or two.

A majority of literate parents owned a few edifying or practical volumes that they used to teach morality and farm management to their children. Anglican parents used the Bible and the Book of Common Prayer, supplemented by such patriarchal tomes as Richard Allestree's seventeenth-century *Whole Duty of Man* as guides for proper behavior. The Bible was the most important book in most plantation libraries; nearly all literate families owned one, and sometimes they possessed no other book. Parents and schoolmasters commonly taught children to read "distinctly in the Bible," because the Bible was God's literal word and, moreover, no other book contained so many edifying stories and moral principles or had such a prominent role (along with the prayer book and psalter) in divine services.

Planter families commonly counted an almanac among their small bundle of books. Nearly two-thirds of the ten thousand volumes sold in the 1750s and 1760s at the *Virginia Gazette* office in Williamsburg were almanacs. Almanacs contained a broad collection of information useful to planters, including monthly calendars, data on the time of sunrise and sunset, weather predictions, the distance between the colony's villages and towns, and essays on scientific and medical topics. Moreover, planters could jot down their thoughts or farm accounts in the volume's margins and blank pages. And finally, a Virginia almanac cost only 7.5 pennies each year— a cheap price every planter could afford!

Since most boys received only a brief introduction to literacy, and girls often none, few people in the Chesapeake region read for pleasure or intellectual stimulation. Only sons of the wealthy gentlemen, many of whom attended Latin schools or the College of William and Mary, could participate in a high literary culture or understand the political and philosophical articles found in the region's two newspapers. (Less-educated men, of course, read almanacs, Bibles, and newspaper advertisements.) This lack of childhood training and the subsequent minimal adult interest were reflected in planters' libraries: only magistrates owned law books, and only one literate planter in six possessed a Latin classic, political tract, or volume of history.

White children in the Chesapeake were trained to take their place in society through repeated instruction by adults. Parents taught their children patriarchal principles at home and sent them to school and church to reinforce the lesson. When preachers alluded to biblical passages to sustain a moral principle, parish children understood what they meant; when parents wished to explain the social hierarchy of the Chesapeake to their offspring, they chose to read the Bible or the *Whole Duty of Man*. Children observed and learned to emulate the fundamentals of proper deportment every day at home, in the tobacco fields, at school and church, and in visiting kindred.

Children needed property as well as moral lessons to be able to take their appropriate place in white society. The ownership of land and slaves buttressed the moral order of the region by making the perpetuation of domestic patriarchy possible. Parents therefore tried to ensure that all their children possessed enough property to replicate the family government of their childhood, a goal that led some planters to reject primogeniture (still a part of the law of intestacy) in their wills. In societies where patriarchy and political order were strongly connected, primogeniture maintained the social and political hierarchy that linked king and father, but chattel slavery helped sever that link by making each person a potential master as well as parent. Since servile work and dependence were identified with slaves, all men ideally should have owned land, the hallmark of independence. Planters who lived in frontier areas could readily distribute land to all their sons, and sometimes to their daughters. Wealthy planters gave each of their sons a fully stocked plantation, thereby maximizing the number of men able to behave like patriarchs in their own families. Poorer men favored one or two of their sons, hoping thereby that at least one son could emulate his father, but, of course, thereby reducing the total number of men who could play patriarchal roles in the future. Increased population density reduced the size of landholdings so much that primogeniture began to rise even among middling yeomen. This increased favoritism in the redistribution of resources to eldest sons created a gap between the expectation that all children ought to form their own domestic patriarchies and their ability to do so.

From the outset of colonization, planters favored older sons over their sisters and younger brothers, but most planters who made wills owned enough land to give each son a plantation. About three-quarters of the testators in St. Mary's County during the seventeenth century, and in Prince George's and Albemarle counties during the next century, gave some land to all their sons; only a third of these men, however, bequeathed land to any of their daughters. The rest of the testators, more than a quarter of the total, owned so little land that they had to favor several sons or give all their land to their oldest son.

As population density increased in tidewater during the eighteenth century, the typical size of landholdings diminished, and more and more planters excluded one or more of their sons from land distribution in order to give working plantations to the remaining sons. Only one testator in seven in Prince George's County favored one or two sons or practiced primogeniture during the 1730s, when frontier land was still available; but after 1740, nearly all the lands were soon taken, and the proportion of men who favored older sons doubled. Planters who gave all their land to their oldest son owned an average of only 180 acres; and if they had divided their land equally among all their sons, each son would have received only 54 acres, about half the minimum needed to make tobacco. Similarly, planters who gave land to their two or three oldest sons, excluding the rest, bequeathed an average of only 101 acres to each favored son. If they had given all their sons an equal share, each son would have farmed 57 acres. Since the price of land increased more rapidly than any other commodity during the 1760s and 1770s, sons of a small freeholder who inherited land enjoyed a great advantage over their landless brothers, no matter how equitably the rest of their father's assets were disbursed.

Fathers gave each daughter and son a portion of their personal estate sufficient to set up housekeeping, sometimes specifically granting each some livestock, kitchen utensils, bedding, and slaves. While sons received a stocked plantation, daughters took personal goods bequeathed to them as a dowry. Most testators in Prince George's County attempted an equitable distribution of their personal goods: more than half of them divided their movable property equally among all their children, including those who inherited land; another quarter granted landless children a larger share than children with land; and the remaining planters favored some sons at the expense of other children. An equal distribution of movable goods often favored older sons over their siblings because much of the personal property, but not the land, could be used to pay debts the decedent owed. . . .

Domestic Patriarchy within Chesapeake Society

Although seventeenth-century immigrants to the Chesapeake colonies found the practice of domestic patriarchy difficult, by the early eighteenth century landed families in the tidewater region had developed a distinctive patriarchal form of family government and refined it as the century progressed. In these landed and slaveholding families, women obeyed their husbands and kept to their proper place, and children deferred to both parents, but especially to their fathers. Planters educated their children to behave respectfully and used their control of property that adult children wanted to reinforce this lesson.

Even though patriarchal behavior was limited to the family, it did restrain the competitive way that men behaved in informal groups and in political discourse. Although political relations between gentlemen and yeomen were based upon principles of reciprocity rather than upon any analogies with paternal power in the family, when men associated, they replicated the hierarchy of the family by dividing themselves into groups based upon wealth, status, and education. Yeomen learned the habit of deference in their own families and therefore understood the superior place of gentlemen in the political order.

The influence of domestic patriarchy was most strongly felt by freeholding families in tidewater, where resources were becoming scarce. Tidewater slaveholders, whose families stayed on the land for generations, wielded a substantial influence over the behavior of wives and children. But men needed land and slaves in order to follow patriarchal norms. Poor tenants had too few resources to hold their children to the ancestral home and needed all the labor they could muster, including that of their wives, to survive economically, and the poorest freeholders were not much better situated. Migrants to piedmont Virginia, in contrast, lived in a raw society with abundant resources, where a son could always find cheap land just beyond his father's plantation, and he therefore had less incentive to defer to his father.

Since patriarchal norms were not always clear, conflicts between members of patriarchal families sometimes occurred. Three kinds of conflict may have been particularly common. Because patriarchalism only weakly proscribed violence against wives, husbands sometimes tried to whip their wives into submission, a practice that eventually could lead even the most deferential wife to run away from home. Second, fathers who wanted to hold on to their land may have fought with sons who wished to be fully independent. And third, patriarchal norms did not rank the authority of widowed mothers and adult sons in the family—and once the patriarch had died, the struggle for authority that ensued sometimes led to conflict between mothers and sons.

Patriarchalism, finally, weakened the bonds between slave and master. Fathers distributed slaves among all their children when they died, much like other kinds of personal property. Since few men owned enough slaves to bequeath entire families to each child, they inevitably separated black husbands from wives and parents from children. Those masters who separated families broke one of the primary rules of a paternalistic relationship by arbitrarily breaking up families and thereby lost some of the power they had over the personal lives of their slaves.

"The Harmony We Were Famous For": South Carolina Politics Before the Revolution

ROBERT M. WEIR

I

By the mid-eighteenth century South Carolinians shared a coherent body of ideals, assumptions, and beliefs concerning politics. The foundation of all their political assumptions was their conception of human nature: they deeply distrusted it. Although man was a social being, he was hardly fit for society. The daily experiences of life demonstrated that he was unreliable, subject to his passions, and motivated by self-interest. But man's capacity for rational action made him more than a mere animal; therefore freedom, defined as the ability to act in conformity with the dictates of one's own reason, was the greatest of human values. As the quality that distinguished a man from a beast or a slave, liberty was the source of human dignity.

Thus, the central problem of human existence was the maintenance of freedom in the face of the manifold threats posed by man's own frailties; unless limits were placed on the exercise of passions and power, life was chaos and liberty impossible. At all times the prudent individual would therefore endeavor to order his life in such a way as to preserve his liberty. Aided by Christian virtue, education, and concern for his honor, he could practice self-discipline to avoid becoming a slave to his own passions. If wise, he did not trust even himself with the possession of excessive power, lest it be a temptation to its abuse. Above all, constant exposure to the realities of slavery reminded him never to allow another man to assume uncontrolled power over him. Personal independence therefore became a nearly obsessive concern, and the absolute necessity of maintaining it meant that the possession of property was of prime importance. Economic independence was the bulwark of personal liberty. The resources of the individual alone, however, were insufficient to secure the social order necessary to freedom. Therefore governments had been established to aid him by protecting his property, his freedom, and his life from the aggressions of his fellow creatures. When a government discharged its responsibility its citizens were obligated to support and obey it. But when it threatened liberty by exceeding the limits of its authority, the people had not only the right but also the duty to resist.

Frequent recourse to such drastic measures was dangerous because it threatened to create the chaos that governments were instituted to avoid; therefore continuous effective checks on the power of government were necessary. Under the English system the constitution performed this func-

From Robert M. Weir, "The Harmony We Were Famous For: An Interpretation of Pre-Revolutionary South Carolina Politics," 3rd Series, 26 (1969), *William and Mary Quarterly.* Reprinted by permission of the author.

tion, and South Carolinians invoked the hallowed term frequently but ambiguously. Often they used it to refer to the limits that society placed on its rulers; power and authority were different attributes. The former represented absolute force; the latter was power sanctioned by right, and the authority of government did not include the power to invade fundamental human rights. At other times the constitution denoted the spirit and principles that men believed ought to animate government; these included the idea that free men were bound only by laws to which they had consented, that private interests ought not to be set in competition with public good, and that the welfare of the whole was the supreme law. Finally, the constitution also referred to the existing composition of government.

To South Carolinians the glory of the British constitutional system was that it included institutional means to limit government and insure—as far as humanly possible—that it would act according to the principles which ought to animate it. Because the freedom of a citizen depended on the security of his property, taxes were considered voluntary though necessary gifts toward the support of government. To facilitate the grant of taxes property holders of the nation chose representatives whose primary control over the public purse gave them an effective means to check the executive power and obtain a redress of grievances. In practice, therefore, the chief historical role of the British House of Commons had been the protection of the people. Considering their own Commons House of Assembly to be a small counterpart, South Carolinians looked upon their local representatives as the natural guardians of the liberties and properties of the people.

The discharge of such important responsibilities required ability and the freedom to use it; therefore a member of the Commons was expected to be a relatively free agent. Theoretically he did not solicit but accepted a duty which imposed upon him an almost professional obligation to use his political expertise in behalf of his constituents, the whole people. He should therefore be able, independent, courageous, virtuous, and public-spirited. Although riches did not insure that a man would exhibit these qualities, it was assumed that they made it more likely. Economic independence promoted courage and material possessions fostered rational behavior. In addition a large stake in society tied a man's interest to the welfare of the whole. Wealth enabled him to acquire the education believed necessary for statecraft. Finally, the influence and prestige of a rich man helped to add stature and effectiveness to government. Thus a series of interrelated assumptions about the virtues thought to be associated with wealth helped to maintain the belief that members of the elite should rule.

Nevertheless, no matter how qualified and how public-spirited an individual seemed, appearances might be deceiving and human nature was prone to corruption. It was therefore necessary for a representative's constituents to retain due checks upon him. The most effective means was to harness his own self-interests to theirs. In theory this usually meant that he should hold property where they did. Over a period of time, however, the interests of a representative and his constituents might diverge; to prevent such a development, the election law stipulated a maximum term of three years for each assembly. Moreover, the entire process of representation was a sham without free elections. South Carolinians therefore prided themselves on using the secret ballot which provided a convenient means to undermine the efficacy of coercion and bribery. In addition, collective bodies of men should be checked against each other. Everyone therefore gave at least habitual allegiance to the ideal of balanced government. Governor Lord Charles Montagu prized it as the "Palladium" of liberty, and the popular patriot Christopher Gadsden declared that he no more wished to see the power of the Commons enlarged beyond its proper limits than vice versa. Not surprisingly, however, most local leaders considered those limits very wide.

The efficacy of balanced government, indeed the validity of the whole concept of checks and balances, appeared to be predicated on the discreet identity of each element in the system. Parties or factions, by definition combinations of men acting together for selfish purposes, were dangerous. In the absence of factions the self-interested politician found himself checkmated at every turn by individuals whose common attributes were personal independence and a concern for the public welfare. Factional politics, however, provided a context which allowed private interests to flourish at the expense of the public and which permitted the executive to build centers of support in the other branches of government, thereby weakening their will and subverting their ability to check the encroachments of executive power. Factionalism and corruption, especially when associated with the executive, presaged the demise of freedom.

Elitist in its assumptions, this ideology envisioned the existence of a society in which the clash of economic and class interests played no role. Instead, a struggle between the executive and the united representatives of the people appeared to supply the dynamics of politics. The idealized political figure was therefore the individualistic patriot who exhibited his disinterested concern for the public welfare by rejecting factional ties while remaining ready to join with like-minded individuals in curbing arbitrary exercises of executive power.

II

The country ideal, at least in part, figured in the political life of the colony from its founding, but its dominant role represented a delayed development. Lord Shaftesbury, the man most responsible for the Fundamental Constitutions of Carolina, was also one of the progenitors of country ideology; as a result that document sought to structure society and government so that rule by an elite composed of public-spirited men of independent property would be the natural result. Often attacked as anachronistic, the Fundamental Constitutions were ahead of their time in this aspect. Of diverse origins, linked together chiefly by their common residence and economic ambitions, South Carolinians spent most of the first seventy years squabbling over religious differences and contending for the perquisites of power.

A degree of order, stability, and prosperity, as well as a fairly strong sense of community, were necessary before a sophisticated and basically altruistic political ethic could have much relevance to local politics—something that eighteenth-century writers apparently realized when they assumed that chaotic factionalism was normal in small, immature colonial societies. Gradually, however, during the first four decades of the eighteenth century economic and social developments provided the prerequisites necessary for the growth of Shaftesbury's ideals.

Prosperity was the most important factor. Until the 1730's the economic history of the colony was a checkered one; thereafter, except for a relatively brief period during King George's War, ever-increasing prosperity seems to have been the rule. From 1730 to 1760 rice production almost doubled; indigo production catapulted from nothing to more than one-half million pounds per year. Annual returns on invested capital are difficult to calculate, but they may have ranged as high as 30 per cent for planters and perhaps 50 per cent for the luckiest merchants. Given returns such as these, it is no wonder that by the 1760's travelers marveled at the wealth to be seen in Charleston. Not surprisingly, South Carolinians were soon convinced that theirs would be the richest province in America.

Economic plenty bound the community together in several ways. It not only lessened competition among groups for a portion of its benefits but it also fostered upward social mobility by individuals. As a result, the distance between social classes was never very wide, though the contemporary historian Alexander Hewatt doubtless exaggerated when he reported that "in respect of rank, all men regarded their neighbour as their equal. . . ." In addition, prosperity and social mobility homogenized interest groups. Although merchants if rich were considered eminently respectable, possession of land tended to connote high social status. Wealthy merchants therefore purchased plantations and in the process acquired an understanding of the planters' economic interests and problems. Significantly, by the end of the colonial period almost all of the prominent leaders among the professional men and merchants in the Assembly owned plantations. Intermarriage between planting and mercantile families also blurred distinctions. In addition, as every planter was well aware, the economic health of the province depended upon the export trade. Thus consanguinity and a consciousness of shared economic interests helped to bind together potentially disparate segments of society.

The passage of time and waning religious zeal also contributed to a growing sense of community. Ethnic diversity and religious antagonisms had been major causes of factional strife in the early 1700's. By mid-century, the Huguenots had been completely assimilated and a broad religious toleration had replaced narrow sectarianism. Lieutenant Governor William Bull reflected the prevailing spirit when, speaking as a public official, he wrote, "I charitably hope every sect of Christians will find their way to the Kingdom of heaven," but for political reasons he thought "the Church of England the best adapted to the Kingdom of England." Thomas Smith, a merchant member of the Assembly, was even more tolerant when he privately noted that if an Anglican church were not available, he would be just as willing to take communion in a dissenting one.

Geographic and demographic features of the society also unified it. In the first place, Charleston was the economic, political, social, and cultural center of the colony. As a result, urban values permeated the culture of even the most remote low country parishes, giving substance to the common saying that as the town went, so went the country. In addition, society was remarkably small, and as late as 1790 most of the low country parishes contained less than 200 white families. In 1770 there were only 1,292 dwellings, housing about 5,030 white persons, in Charleston. The central position of the city in the life of the colony, coupled with the relatively small population, meant that members of the elite had the opportunity to know each other, communicate, and develop a community of shared values. A prominent figure like Speaker of the House Peter Manigault could realistically assert that "I am well acquainted with the Circumstances of most of our Inhabitants." In short, low country society possessed many of the characteristics of a primary group and its mores much of the power of those enforced by the family. Perhaps this fact helps to account for much of the harmony and politeness which visitors observed in the community.

In addition, strategic considerations related to geographic location and the composition of the population produced community solidarity. Even after Georgia was established as a buffer between South Carolina and Spanish Florida, Charleston remained open to assault from the sea, and throughout the colonial period South Carolinians were periodically convinced that they were the target of imminent attack. Moreover, until the Revolution, the Creek and Cherokee Indians represented a real threat to the safety of the backcountry. But what tied all of these dangers together into a source of constant, deep concern was the growing slave population. Huge importations of slaves accompanied the rising prosperity; in 1710 Negroes represented less than 40 per cent of the population; by 1730 they outnumbered whites 2 to 1, and by the end of the colonial period the ratio in some low country parishes was more than 7 to 1. Whether in the nineteenth century Sambo was real or a figment of wishful thinking is an open question, but South Carolinians of the eighteenth century certainly failed to recognize him. To them, the African represented "a fierce, hardy and strong race," a "Domestic Enemy" who was ever ready to revolt or join any outside attackers. His presence meant that any lapse in vigilance, any failure of government, appeared to threaten the white community with annihilation. South Carolinians were therefore notoriously leery of any disorders. Indeed, the prevailing atmosphere approached that of a garrison state. Unity among the defenders was essential, divided command dangerous, and momentary lapse an invitation to disaster. In part this is no doubt why prominent leaders like Henry Laurens considered internal political discord "more awful and more distressing than Fire Pestilence or Foreign Wars." In short, disruptive factionalism was regarded as a potentially fatal luxury and, significantly, panics over insurrection often coincided with political turmoil in the white community, notably in the Stamp Act crisis and the outbreak of the Revolution.

By the 1730's this growing Negrophobia, as well as the social and economic changes which contributed to it, began to mute political discord. Planters who were dependent on the export trade and merchants who had sought the prestige of plantation ownership cooperated to facilitate final settlement of a long disruptive controversy over paper currency—the last major factional battle in South Carolina politics. This compromise signalized the emergence of an increasingly well-integrated society, knit together by a community of economic interests and social values. Thus the controversies associated with the land boom during Governor Robert Johnson's administration did not prove permanently divisive. In fact, the heavy acquisition of land in the 1730's satiated the appetite of a generation and thereby helped to remove land as a future source of serious contention. More important, between 1738 and 1742 South Carolinians confronted a crisis in Indian affairs, the most serious slave rebellion of the colonial period, a very destructive fire in Charleston, a real possibility of Spanish invasion, and the apparent threat to order and stability posed by the Great Awakening. The result was an unprecedented willingness by local leaders to compromise and cooperate with each other. In short, the crises of the late 1730's and early 1740's tended to produce political unity at the same time that potentially divisive issues were losing much of their sense of urgency. Significantly, many of the leading planters, whose social status was already assured, soon found politics boring, and in increasing numbers they refused to accept election to the Commons House.

Not everyone, however, succumbed to the prevailing political apathy. Increasing prosperity and the accompanying growth in population led to the development of a relatively large class of merchants and professional men. The departure of the leading planters created a void in political leadership which members of this group could fill. Their residence in Charleston made it convenient for them to attend sessions of the legislature and their technical knowledge proved useful when the House considered commercial and legal matters. They in turn undoubtedly hoped to realize benefits from their service. For the less affluent, economic and professional advancement might be one hope; for the wealthier, prestige and high social status might be more important goals; for some—and their numbers increased over the years—the feeling that one had discharged his duty to society became the chief reward. These were the devotees of country ideology, and at least in the beginning they came chiefly from the ranks of the merchants and lawyers. Relatively well-educated, often maintaining contacts in Great Britain, the permanent residents of Charleston were able to stay abreast of intellectual developments in the mother country; they were importers of culture as well as material goods and technical skills; they made the *South Carolina Gazette*, established in 1732, a success; they patronized the booksellers, formed discussion groups, and founded the Charleston Library Society.

At the same time that Charleston was emerging as something of a center of intellectual activity, the works of two British journalists, John Trenchard and Thomas Gordon, were enjoying remarkable popularity in Great Britain and especially in America. *Cato's Letters*, as Clinton Rossiter first noted, soon became the "most popular, quotable, esteemed source of political ideas" in the colonies, and *The Independent Whig* was not far behind. Like other Americans, South Carolinians found these works attractive. The *South Carolina Gazette* reprinted many of *Cato's Letters* during the first two decades of its existence, while individuals as well as the Charleston Library Society purchased collected editions. This was not a temporary fad; for more than fifty years the works of these two journalists continued to be staple reading for South Carolinians. In 1772 Laurens made a special present to a chance acquaintance of *The Independent Whig*, which he noted was to be found "in almost every Gentleman's Library." Trenchard and Gordon presented a version of country ideology in particularly readable form, but booksellers' advertisements, inventories of personal estates, and the records of the Charleston Library Society indicate that the Whig historians of the eighteenth century and the classical republicans of the seventeenth century, as well as Henry St. John, Viscount Bolingbroke, and the members of his literary circle, were also popular writers. Content rather than form was obviously the basic cause of the popularity of the works embodying the lexicon of country ideology.

There were several reasons for the appeal of these ideas. First, many of them reflected the orientation of religious dissenters, and the dissenting tradition was strong in Charleston, not only among persons of Huguenot descent but also in the large Baptist, Presbyterian, and Congregational population. Second, country ideology was the product of a group at the periphery of political power; being in the same situation, Americans found it congenial. It justified an increasing degree of local autonomy and South Carolinians had long felt themselves better informed about and more capable of handling local problems than imperial authorities. Moreover, South Carolinians sought to emulate the English gentry in every way they could. Some retired to English country estates; others built English country houses in the swamps of Carolina, traced their genealogies, and attempted to found families. The adoption of country ideology was one more step by which they could play what they believed to be the role of the independent English country gentleman. In addition it has been suggested that Americans adopted this ideology in part because they discovered it to be a handy weapon against factional opponents. South Carolinians found a different but related utility in these ideas.

The implications of country ideology made it particularly attractive to local leaders who were unable to become councilors. Following institution of royal authority in 1721, the Council was at its height, and its prestige, if not its power, considerably overshadowed that of the Commons. Men coveted membership and gladly gave up a seat in the lower house to accept one in the upper. But only twelve men could sit in the Council at one time. To be one of the twelve required luck and influence. For those who failed to achieve appointment the implications of country ideology proved to be soothing to wounded egos. Obviously councilors holding office at the pleasure of the Crown could not be independent. Election to the Commons could therefore be interpreted as being more prestigious. Certainly, it represented public recognition that a man had reached a social status which entitled him to a position of public leadership.

Moreover, country ideology told him how to discharge his duties with honor. In blunting the antagonisms of the earlier period, prosperity and increasing social integration had made it less appropriate for a representative to be the champion of a particular interest group. Collectively, the Commons could model its conduct on that of the British House of Commons, and it had tried to do so at least from the 1690's. But for the individual member the problem was potentially acute. How was he to conduct himself under the changing conditions of political life? Because country ideology provided a particularly satisfactory answer, it became the contemporary *Book of the Governor*. Its precepts delimited an honorable role; by following them an aspiring politician could justify his leadership.

In the final analysis, however, what gave country ideology its overwhelming power over political behavior was its ability to satisfy rather than thwart the needs and desires of local leaders. Its precepts—which made sense in the light of their experience—helped to give purpose to their lives, justified their conduct, rationalized their freedom of action, supported their position of leadership, and brought them honor, while depriving them of little except the pursuit of private gain at public expense. But prosperity, their own increasing wealth, and the relative lack of lucrative patronage in the hands of either the governor or the lower house made it fairly easy to forego the lesser for the greater reward. Perhaps if the society had been larger and the turnover in membership in the Commons smaller, the pursuit of status and power might have taken forms condemned by country ideology. As it was, a man could satisfy his ambitions without denying the same satisfaction to others.

III

Country ideology therefore transformed the character of local politics well before the Revolution. . . .

. . . Nowhere is the effect of [country ideology] more apparent than in the link they provided between internal changes within the Commons and its changing relationship with the Council.

Theoretically, only a house composed of independent men of property could be counted upon to fulfill its role in checking the other agencies of government. Beginning in the mid-1730's the Commons, under the leadership of Speaker Charles Pinckney, began vigorous efforts to make the reality coincide with the theoretical ideal. Thereafter the lower house repeatedly attempted to insure that its own membership would conform to the ideals of country ideology by revising the election laws to require higher property qualifications and to exclude placemen. Imperial authorities refused to permit the exclusion of Crown officials and repeatedly disallowed these laws for various other reasons. Nevertheless the passage of time achieved what the law could not; by the end of the colonial period electors usually agreed with "A Native," who noted that "men in public employments are not the properest for your choice." In the meantime both the caliber and wealth of the average member rose, in part because the leading planters who had formerly refused to sit in the House gradually returned as they assimilated the new ideals and viewed the rising prestige of the lower house. In contrast, the status of the upper house declined. To the Commons it appeared that councilors, lacking the independence necessary to qualify them as members of a separate house of the legislature, were in reality nothing more than appendages of the executive. Temporarily discarding the British Parliament as a model, the members of the Commons dropped the name Commons House of Assembly in 1744 and arrogated to themselves alone the title of General Assembly. In the following year they attempted to give real substance to this symbolic gesture by denying the Council any role whatever in the passage of legislation. Both force of habit and the opposition of Governor James Glen barred success; most persons continued to call the lower house the Commons and Glen refused to sign legislation that had not been passed by the Council.

Later, however, Governor Lyttelton and the Board of Trade unwittingly played into the hands of the Commons. In 1756 Lyttelton ousted William Wragg from the Council without publicly giving his reasons for the action. The Board of Trade then gave the coup de grace to the already dwindling prestige of the Council by confirming Wragg's suspension and adopting a deliberate policy of appointing placemen in the hopes of obtaining a more pliant upper house. Then, when the ministry belatedly realized that the Council needed strengthening, they could find few South Carolinians of stature who would accept appointments; obviously a position held by so precarious a tenure was not compatible with the status of an independent country gentleman. By the end of the colonial period the Council had become a cipher, its real power practically nonexistent and most of its members virtual incompetents, not only in the estimation of many South Carolinians, but also in that of a capable Crown investigator, Captain Alexander Innes.

The results of the Council's actual decline, in the context of a political culture suffused with the ideals of country ideology, were far reaching. On one level, it appeared that the Crown had subverted the constitution by capturing control of a second branch of government—the upper house— as well as the executive. Moreover, its action reversed the natural order of things: councilors occupied their official position not because they belonged to the class whose right and responsibility it was to govern; rather they sought entree to that class because of their official position. As a result, the status of the Council became a tangible symbol of other imperial measures which frequently appeared to be unnatural and subversive of good government. More important yet, the increasing identification of the governor with these measures and the declining position of the Council apparently vitiated the ideal of balanced government. Everyone recognized that the composition of the upper house did not reflect a separate stratum of society comparable to that of the British Lords. The habit of thinking in terms of old concepts nevertheless tended to persist, and members of the Council such as William Henry Drayton and Egerton Leigh frequently advocated permanent appointment of councilors in order to add dignity and weight to the upper house. Outside the Council, however, men were less enthusiastic about bolstering it, and Christopher Gadsden even noted that the power of the American councils was a kind of "politico-Meter" which varied inversely with the liberty of the people. By the end of the colonial period everyone recognized that the lower house dominated local government and most local leaders believed its position fully justified. By 1772 Speaker Manigault revealed a willing acceptance of the realities that undermined the ideal of balanced government when he noted, "I . . . Love to have a weak Governor"; had he added a weak Council as well, probably few persons would have disagreed.

Nevertheless, even in its decline, the Council maintained sufficient weight to serve as a foil to the lower house. The more attached to the prerogative the upper house appeared, the more concerned the lower became about preserving the rights and liberties of the people; the more irresponsible the Council seemed to become, the more members of the Commons felt their responsibility for the public welfare, because they alone appeared to have it at heart. Moreover, rivalry between the houses contributed to the esprit which unified the lower house. By the early 1740's members were finding it politically expedient to join in supporting claims to rights and privileges whether or not they privately considered these claims justified. By the early 1770's both Governor Montagu and Lieutenant Governor Bull noted that members who singly disagreed with steps taken by the House would jointly approve them; moreover, Bull reported that because members felt honor bound to support the Commons it was practically impossible to induce one house to reverse the actions of another.

The solid front which the Commons was able to present reflected the lack of factions within the House. . . . The testimony of local leaders is even more conclusive. Sorrowfully viewing the political struggles of the 1780's, Gadsden lamented the apparent loss of that "harmony we were famous for," and Laurens, horrified at the factional alignments within the Continental Congress, noted that he "discovered parties within parties, divisions and Sub-divisions" which he compared unfavorably with the situation in South Carolina.

The absence of factionalism did not mean that local leaders never differed over men and measures; it did mean that these differences, even when they involved strong personal animosities or clashes of opinion, did not lead to permanent alignments that fractured the unity of the Commons House. Potentially the most disruptive and politically significant personal quarrel was between successive speakers Rawlins Lowndes and Manigault who cordially disliked each other and gave vent to their feelings in a series of newspaper polemics in which Lowndes professed to believe that he had been ousted from the speakership by a clique surrounding Manigault. Yet after Manigault resigned because of ill health, a house led by substantially the same men reelected Lowndes to the post. Moreover, there is no evidence that there was any important difference in the way the two men handled the Commons. The general policy pursued under the leadership of each was the same and committee assignments did not change significantly. From the beginning of the century it had been customary to elect the speaker unanimously; by mid-century what began as a symbol of wished-for unity became the expression of real unanimity.

Paradoxically, however, this unanimity concealed—even in large measure arose from—the independence upon which each member of the Commons prided himself. In essence the House remained an aggregate of individuals. [William] Wragg, a universally admired but cantankerous figure who was unable to cooperate with anyone, nevertheless voiced a sentiment to which everyone subscribed when he declared, "He must be a very weak or a very wicked man, and know very little of me, who thinks me capable of surrendering my judgment, my honor and my conscience upon any consideration whatever." Drayton declared that he had made it a "first principle not to proceed any farther with any party, than I thought they travelled in the Constitutional highway." Laurens phrased the same sentiment only slightly differently: "I am for no Man nor for any Party—you see—one Minute after they depart from Principles of Honesty." This spirit—the epitome of the local version of country ideology, altruistic yet intensely individualistic—suffocated factions. It even put strict limits on the influence of family connections. In contrast to contemporary British politics and later conditions in South Carolina, family relationships apparently counted for surprisingly little on the local scene. British placemen thought in terms of connections and frequently claimed to see their operations; by mid-century South Carolinians seldom did. Indeed, Laurens could effectively refute a charge of being disloyal to his family by noting that so meager a consideration as family connection alone would never influence him where the public welfare was concerned.

Because local leaders shared similar interests and a common code of political behavior, their hypertensive individualism did not prevent cooperation with one another. Like Manigault, they preferred "to sail with the Stream, when no Danger or Dishonour, can attend it. . . ." Under the prevailing circumstances neither honor nor fear often prompted them to take singular positions, even in matters pertaining to their own constituents. Members of the Commons took seriously the admonition to remember that though they were elected as representatives of a particular area or group, once they took their seats, their responsibility was to the welfare of the whole. Thus on the one hand, except in matters of unusual importance, it was of no great consequence whether an elected representative actually owned property or resided in the parish that elected him, and prominent members of the Commons frequently represented constituents with whom they had no direct material connection. On the other hand, in matters of more importance or where different geographical areas or interest groups could be presumed to be unequally affected by public measures, equity required that each entity be separately represented. Perhaps it was only coincidence, but the twelve men who performed most of the committee business in the Commons in the early 1760's included four lawyers, four merchants, and four planters, and the three delegates to the Stamp Act Congress represented the same three economic groups. In 1769 the committee that drafted and enforced the nonimportation agreements included thirteen mechanics, thirteen planters, and thirteen merchants. In addition, local representatives consistently discharged most of the business of the Commons that affected their constituents. Ideological consensus and social homogeneity made localism and particularism compatible with the unity of the whole. . . .

During the thirty years before the Revolution in South Carolina, ideas had increasingly become the dominant force in local politics; by the end of the colonial period the intangible ideal had found expression in the realities of everyday politics. The majority of political leaders actually were the independent men of property revered in country ideology and, to an amazing extent, generally accepted ideals, assumptions, and normative expectations about political conduct governed their behavior. Upholders of the prerogative excepted, there was virtually unanimous agreement that social and political harmony prevailed in what was an unusually well governed colony. Perhaps one of the reasons for the proverbial pride of South Carolinians and the high esteem which they have traditionally accorded to politicians can be found here. Certainly, colonial South Carolinians believed that they had achieved an unusually successful political system that safeguarded a freedom which they were morally obligated to bequeath to posterity.

The Baptist Counterculture

RHYS ISAAC

An intense struggle for allegiance had developed in the Virginia countryside during the decade before the Revolution. Two eyewitness accounts may open to us the nature of the conflict. First, a scene vividly remembered and described by the Reverend James Ireland etches in profile the postures of the contestants. As a young man Ireland, who was a propertyless schoolmaster of genteel origin, had cut a considerable figure in Frederick County society. His success had arisen largely from his prowess at dancing and his exuberant facility as a satiric wit. Then, like many other young men at this time (*ca.* 1768), he became "awakened to a sense of [his] guilty state" and withdrew from the convivialities of gentry society. An older friend and patron of Ireland's, hearing that his young protégé could not be expected at a forthcoming assembly, sensed the challenge to his way of life that was implicit in Ireland's withdrawal. He swore instantly that "there could not

From *The Transformation of Virginia, 1740–1790*, by Rhys Isaac, pp. 161–174, 175–177. © 1982 The University of North Carolina Press. Published for the Institute of Early American Literature and Culture. Reprinted by permission.

be a dance in the settlement without [their young friend] being there, and if they would leave it to him, he would convert [him], and that to the dance, on Monday; and they would see [Jemmy] lead the ball that day." Frederick County, for all its geographical spread, was a close community. Young James learned that his patron would call, and dreaded the coming test of strength:

> When I viewed him riding up, I never beheld such a display of pride in any man, . . . arising from his deportment, attitude and jesture; he rode a lofty elegant horse . . . his countenance appeared to me as bold and daring as satan himself, and with a commanding authority [he] called upon me, if I were there to come out, which I accordingly did, with a fearful and timorous heart. But O! how quickly can God level pride. . . . For no sooner did he behold my disconsolate looks, emaciated countenance and solemn aspect, than he . . . was riveted to the beast he rode on. . . . As soon as he could articulate a little his eyes fixed upon me, and his first address was this; "In the name of the Lord, what is the matter with you?"

The evident overdramatization in this account is most revealing for it displays the tormented convert's heightened awareness of the contrast between the social world he was leaving and the one he was entering.

The confrontation between evangelicalism and the traditional order in Virginia had begun with the Hanover Awakening in the 1740s, but it entered into its fiercest and most bitter phase as the New Light Separate Baptists moved into the longer-settled parts of Virginia in the years after 1765. The social conflict was not over the distribution of political power or of economic wealth, but over the ways of men and the ways of God. By the postures of the antagonists we may see how the sides were drawn. On the one hand there was a mounted gentleman of the world with "commanding authority," and on the other hand there was a guilt-humbled God-possessed youth with "disconsolate looks . . . and solemn aspect."

A second scene—this time in the Tidewater—reveals the characteristic responses of the forces arrayed. A 1771 diary entry gives a description of the disturbance of a Baptist meeting by some gentlemen and their followers intent on upholding the cause of the Established Church:

> Brother Waller Informed us . . . [that] about 2 Weeks ago on the Sabbath day Down in Caroline County he Introduced the Worship of God by Singing[.] . . . While he was Singing the Parson of the Parish [who had ridden up with his clerk, the sheriff, and some others] would Keep Running the End of his Horsewhip in [Waller's] Mouth, Laying his Whip across the Hym Book, &c. When done Singing [Waller] proceeded to Prayer. In it he was Violently Jerked off of the Stage, [they] Caught him by the Back part of his Neck[,] Beat his head against the ground, some Times Up[,] Sometimes down, they Carried him through a Gate that stood some Considerable Distance, where a Gentleman [the sheriff] Give him . . . Twenty Lashes with his Horse Whip. . . . Then B[rother] Waller was Released, Went Back Singing praise to God, Mounted the Stage & preached with a Great Deal of Liberty.

Violence of this kind had become a recurrent feature of social and religious life in Tidewater and Piedmont. The questions that arise are: What kind of conflict was this? What was it that aroused such antagonism? What manner of man, what manner of movement, was it that found liberty in endurance under the lash?

The remainder of the narrative gives fuller understanding of the meaning of "liberty" and of the true character of this encounter. Asked "if his Nature did not Interfere in the time of the Violent persecution, when whiping, &c.," Waller "answer'd that the Lord stood by him . . . & pour'd his Love into his Soul without measure, & the Bretheren & Sisters Round him Singing praises . . . so that he Could Scarcely feel the stripes . . . Rejoicing . . . that he was Worthy to Suffer for his Dear Lord & Master."

Again contrasted postures appear: on the one hand there was forceful, indeed brutal, response to the implicit challenge of religious dissidence; while on the other hand can be seen an acceptance of suffering sustained by shared emotions that gave release—"liberty." Both sides were, of course, engaged in combat, yet their modes of conducting themselves were diametrically opposite. If we are to understand the struggle that had developed within Virginia society, we must look as deeply as possible into the divergent styles of life—at the conflicting visions of what life should be—that are reflected in this episode.

Opposites are intimately linked not only by the societal context in which they occur but also by the very antagonism that orients them to each other. The strength of the fascination that accompanied hostility to the New Lights is evident from the numerous accounts of men who were at first drawn to Baptist meetings to make violent opposition, and at a later time, or even then and there, came "under conviction" and experienced conversion.

The Appearance of a Counterculture

The social world of the Baptists seems so striking a negative image of gentry-dominated milieus that it must be considered to have been shaped to a large extent in reaction to the dominant culture. Of course evangelical counterculture was no more exclusively the growth of Virginia soil than was the style of life of the country gentleman. . . . It was from New England that the first Separate Baptist missionaries came to Virginia, bringing their vision of an austere way of life that eschewed the refinements of gentility and the customary indulgences of traditional popular culture. Significantly, the intrusive movement of radical religious dissent did not initially take hold in places where it would have had to oppose a mature establishment in full strength. The first Separate Baptist churches were formed in southern and Piedmont Virginia where institutions, although present as patterns of expected development, were not yet underpinned by generations of great-family dominance, as they were in the Tidewater. Nevertheless, during the tumultuous 1760s and 1770s the values and organization of the rebels in religion were inexorably carried from the peripheral to the longer-settled regions.

Contemporaries were struck by the contrast between the challenging gaiety of traditional Virginia formal exchange and the solemn fellowship of the Baptists, who addressed each other as "Brother" and "Sister" and were perceived as "the most melancholy people" who "cannot meet a man upon the road, but they must ram a text of Scripture down his throat." The finery of a gentleman who might ride forth in a gold-laced hat, sporting a gleaming Masonic medal, must be contrasted with the strict dress of the Separate Baptist, who "cut off" his hair and explicitly renounced such "superfluous forms and Modes of Dressing . . . [as] cock't hatts."

The Baptists' appearance was austere, to be sure, but we shall not understand the deep appeal of the evangelical movement, or the nature and full extent of its pointed negation of the style and vision of the gentry-oriented social world, unless we look into the rich offerings beneath this somber exterior. Converts were proffered some escape from the harsh realities of disease, debt, overindulgence and deprivation, violence and fear of sudden death, that were the common lot of small farmers. They could seek refuge in a close, supportive, and orderly community, "a congregation of faithful persons, called out of the world by divine grace, who mutually agree to live together, and execute gospel discipline among them." To obtain entrance into this fellowship, a candidate related experiences of profound personal importance, which would certainly be heard with respect, however humble the candidate's station. There was community resonance for deep feelings, since despite their sober face to the outside world, the Baptists encouraged in their religious practice a sharing of emotion to an extent that would have elicited crushing ridicule in gentry-dominated society. Personal testimonies of the experiences of simple folk have not come down to us from that time, but the records clearly show the central importance given to narrations of the workings of grace upon the souls of the candidates for admission. A communal reliving of conversion, the decisive event in the lives of all the members, is evoked by such recurrent phrases in the church books as: "And a Doore was opened to receive Experiances." The Baptist search for deep fellow feeling must be set in contrast to the formal distance and rivalry in the social exchanges of the traditional system.

The supportive relationship that fellowship in faith and experience could engender appears to have played an important part in the spread of the movement. For example, about the year 1760 Peter Cornwell of Fauquier County sought out in the backcountry one Hays of pious repute, whom he settled on his own land for the sake of godly companionship. "Interviews between these two families were frequent, and their conversation religious and devout; in so much that it began to be talked of abroad as a very strange thing. Many came to see them, to whom they related what God did for their souls . . . to the spreading of seriousness through the whole neighbourhood."

A concomitant of fellowship in deep emotions was comparative equality. Democracy is an ideal, and nothing suggests that the pre-Revolutionary

Baptists espoused it as such. Yet it is certain that these people, who called one another brothers and sisters, believed that the only authority in their church was the meeting together of those in fellowship. They conducted their affairs on a footing of equality so different from the explicit preoccupation with rank and precedence that characterized the world from which they had been called. Important Baptist church elections generally required unanimity and might be held up by the doubts of a few. The number of preachers who were raised from obscurity to play an epic role in the Virginia of their day is a clear indication of the opportunities for personal fulfillment that the movement opened up to men who would otherwise have found no avenue for public achievement. The following of the early Virginia Separate Baptist movement was accurately reputed to be composed of the poor and unlearned. Only isolated converts were made among the gentry, but many among the slaves.

The cohesive brotherhood of the Baptists must be understood as an explicit rejection of the formalism of traditional community organization. Fithian's diary contains an account of an Anglican parish congregation that dispersed without any act of worship when a storm prevented the attendance of both parson and clerk. This stands in contrast to the report of the Baptist David Thomas that "when no minister . . . is expected, our people meet notwithstanding, and spend . . . time in praying, singing, reading, and in religious conversation."

The popular style and appeal of the Baptist church found its most powerful and visible expression in the richness of its rituals, again a total contrast to the Prayer Book reading of the colonial Church of England, where even congregational singing appears to have been rare. The most prominent and moving rite practiced by the sect was the adult baptism by which candidates were publicly sealed into fellowship. A scrap of Daniel Fristoe's journal for June 15–16, 1771, survives as a singular contemporary description of a participant's experience:

> (Being sunday) about 2000 people came together; after preaching, [I] heard others that proposed to be baptized. . . . Then went to the water where I preached and baptized 29 persons. . . . When I had finished we went to a field and making a circle in the center, there laid hands on the persons baptized. The multitude stood round weeping, but when we sang *Come we that love the lord* & they were so affected that they lifted up their hands and faces towards heaven and discovered such chearful countenances in the midst of flowing tears as I had never seen before.

The emotional appeal at a popular level can even now be sensed in Fristoe's account, but it must be noted that the scene was also a vivid representation of *a* community within and apart from *the* community. One must try to see the closed circle for the laying on of hands through the eyes of persons who had been raised in Tidewater or Piedmont Virginia with the expectation that they would always have a monistic parish community that encompassed all the inhabitants within its measured liturgical celebrations. The antagonism and violence that the Baptists aroused then also become intelligible.

The celebration of the Lord's Supper frequently followed baptism and was a further open enactment of closed community. An idea of the importance attached to such public display is given by David Thomas's justification of it:

> Should we forbid even the worst of men, from viewing the solemn representation of his [the LORD JESUS CHRIST's] dying agonies? May not the sight of this mournful tragedy, have a tendency to alarm stupid creatures . . . when GOD himself is held forth . . . trembling, falling, bleeding, yea, expiring under the intollerable pressure of that wrath due to [sin]. . . . And therefore, this ordinance should not be put under a bushel, but on a candlestick, that all may enjoy the illumination.

More intimate, and evidently vital for these tight little religious associations, were the rites of fellowship. The forms are elusive, but a ritual abundance is suggested in the brief note made by Morgan Edwards concerning Falls Creek: "In this church are admitted, Evangelists, Ruling Elders, deaconesses, laying on of hands, feasts of charity, anointing the sick, kiss of charity, washing feet, right hand of fellowship, and devoting children." Far from being mere formal observances, these and other rites, such as the ordaining of "apostles" to "pervade the churches," were keenly experimented with to determine their efficacy.

Preaching itself was as much a form of ritual as a means of verbal instruction. Persons commonly came under conviction or obtained ecstatic release "under preaching," thus establishing a special relationship between the neophyte and his or her "father in the Gospel." Nowhere was the incantatory character of the preaching more apparent than in the mass assemblies of the Virginia Separate Baptist Association. The pastors would preach to the people along the way to the meeting place and back; thousands would gather for the Sunday specially set aside for worship and preaching. Then the close, independent congregational communities found themselves merged in a great and swelling collective. The varieties of physical manifestations, such as crying out and falling down, that were frequently brought on by the stylized emotionalism of popular evangelical preaching are too well known to require description.

Virginia Baptist sermons from the 1770s have not survived, perhaps another sign that the preachers did not consider their purely verbal content to be of the first importance. The Reverend James Ireland's account of his early ministry (he was ordained in 1769) reveals the recurrence of the dominant themes expected to lead those who were not hardened into repentance: "I began first to preach . . . our awful apostacy by the fall; the necessity of repentance unto life, and of faith in the Lord Jesus Christ. . . . Our helpless incapacity to extricate ourselves therefrom I stated and urged."

As "seriousness" spread, with fear of hellfire and concern for salvation, it was small wonder that a gentleman from Loudoun County should find to his alarm "that the *Anabaptists* . . . growing very numerous . . . seem to be increasing in afluence [influence?]; and . . . quite destroying pleasure in the Country; for they encourage ardent Pray'r; strong & constant faith, & an intire Banishment of *Gaming, Dancing,* & Sabbath-Day Diversions.'' That the Baptists were drawing increasing numbers away from the dominant to the insurgent culture was radical enough, but the implications of solemnity, austerity, and stern sobriety were more radical still, for such demeanor called into question the propriety of the occasions and modes of display and association traditionally so important in maintaining the bonds of Virginia's geographically diffuse society. Against the system in which proud men were joined in rivalry and convivial excess was set a reproachful model of an order in which God-humbled men would seek a deep sharing of emotion while repudiating indulgence of the flesh. Yet the Baptist movement, although it must be understood as a revolt against the traditional system, was not primarily negative. Behind it can be discerned an impulse toward a tighter, more effective system of values to be established and maintained within the ranks of the common folk. Evangelicalism can be seen as a popular response to a mounting sense of social disorder. Whether alarm at encroaching evil was expressed in the moralization of gentlemen patriots or in the thundering of Baptist preachers against sin, it was directed against those forms of conviviality that provided such an important medium for customary definition and assertion of the self.

As the conversion experience was at the heart of the popular evangelical movement, so a sense of a great burden of guilt was at the heart of the conversion experience. Popular perceptions of disorder in society—and hence by individuals in themselves—came now to be articulated in the metaphor of "sin." The movement was largely spread by revolt from within, not by "agitators" from without. Commonly the first visit of itinerant preachers to a neighborhood was brought about through the invitation of a group of penitents already formed and actively meeting together. Thus the "spread of seriousness" and alarm at the sinful hurly-burly of the traditional world tended to precede the creation of an emotional mass movement "under preaching." A further indication of the importance of order/disorder preoccupations as the ruling idea behind the spread of the new vision was the insistence on "works." Conversion could ultimately be validated among church members only by a radical reform of conduct. The Baptist church books reveal close concern for the disciplinary supervision of such changes. Censure, ritual excommunication, and moving expressions of penitence were invoked as means to deal with persistent problems like drunkenness. Quarreling, slandering, and disputes over property were other endemic transgressions that the churches patiently and endlessly sought to control within their own communities.

With its base in slavery, the plantation world was one in which contest readily turned into unruly aggression. An episode in the life of one of the great Baptist preachers, John Waller (formerly "Swearing Jack"), illustrates the prevailing violence and the relationship between classes. Waller and some gentry companions were riding on the road when a drunken butcher addressed them in a manner they considered insolent. One of the gentlemen had a horse trained to rear and "paw what was before him," which he then had it do to frighten the butcher. The man was struck by the hooves and died soon after. Tried for manslaughter, the company of gentlemen were acquitted because the court declared itself uncertain whether the injury had indeed caused the butcher's death. The episode may have helped prepare Waller for conversion into a radically opposed social world.

The new sect's concern for ordered self-control revealed itself most clearly in its members' attitude toward physical aggression. Traditional society expected a free man to "resent" insult and showed approval if he did. Yet in the Baptist community a man might even come forward to confess and ask forgiveness for "Geting angry Tho in Just Defence of himself in Despute." The monthly meeting of one church was informed of an incident involving its clerk, Rawley Hazard. He had been approached on his own land, addressed in "Very Scurrilous language," and then assaulted. When the church members heard that he "did defend himself against this sd Violence, that both the Assailant and Defendent was much hurt," they voted, seeming to make no allowances for the provocation, that the minister "do Admonish Brother Rawley Hazard in the presents of the Church . . . saying that his defence was Irregular."

The recurrent use of the words "order," "orderly," and "disorderly" in the Baptist records reveals a preoccupation with establishing a tighter regulation of everyday life. "Is it orderly?" was the usual introduction to the queries concerning right conduct that were frequently brought forward for resolution at monthly meetings.

The evangelicals' determination to impose controls within the "loose" society that they sensed around them was supremely expressed in their strict Sabbath-day observance. This concern is constantly manifested in autobiographies, apologetics, and church books. It appears that the Virginia method of keeping the Sabbath with "sport, merriment, and dissipation" readily served to symbolize the general disorder perceived in society. Conversely, cosmic order was affirmed and held up as a model for society by setting aside all worldly pursuits on the Lord's Day while men expressed their reverence for their Maker and Redeemer.

By their "seriousness"; by their abstinence from convivial pastimes; and by the discipline with which these observances were maintained—in a word, by their insistence on strict purity—the Baptists marked out sharp boundaries segregating themselves as individuals and as church groups from the world. Yet their ways combined opposite aspirations regarding social relations. On the one hand they were heedless of how they disrupted traditional society, acknowledging that they not only sowed discord among neighbors but also turned slaves from their masters, children from their parents, wives from their husbands, since "our SAVIOUR told his disciples, that, he 'came not to send peace on earth but rather division.'" On the other hand, they created tight supportive communities "of persons, called by the Gospel out of the world," seeking "to live together as brethren." Bound up with the Baptists' urge to break down community at one level and rebuild it at another were the contrasting experiences through which many of the white converts passed. In the first place they underwent radical individualization as each was "awakened" to a sense of his or her sinfulness and faced alone the meaning of God's judgment. After "conviction" of sin, segregation of the self from "the world," and the lone ecstasy of conversion, however, the initiates received the comfort of close fellowship. Only the social validation of the individual works of grace, brought about through acceptance of testimony in the meetings, preserved converts (and then only partially) from being beset by doubts about the validity of the assurances of salvation they had received in solitude. Experiences polarized between individual isolation and intimate togetherness were replicated in the double character that Baptist church societies assumed. On the one hand each society was a divinely ordained corporate community fostering the work of grace. Yet, on the other hand, according to individualistic principles, each was "a voluntary assembly, or company . . . associated, or connected of their own accord for the exercises of religion."

It was a particular mark of the Baptists' radicalism, and without doubt the most significant aspect of their quest for means of moral regulation located among the people, that they included the slaves as "brothers" and "sisters" in their close communities. When the Baptists sealed the slaves unto eternal life, leading them in white robes into the water and then back to receive the bread and wine, the white preachers were also laying upon their black converts a responsibility to maintain godly conduct, and demanding that they internalize strict Protestant Christian values and norms. The dissenters were seeking to extend orderly moral community to the quarters, where hitherto there had seemed to be none. The slaves were members and therefore subject to church discipline. The incidence of excommunication of slaves for the sin of adultery points to the desire of the Baptists to introduce among the slaves their own ideal standards of conduct concerning marital relationships. The white Baptist perception of the slaves' mores can be sensed in the recurrent phrase that was often given as the sole reason for excommunication: "disorderly walk."

Cultural differences between white and black converts, however, could not be removed merely by discipline. The success of the Baptists among the slaves was spectacular and inspired a good deal of the hostility of gentlemen in the legislature who sought to curb the expansion of the movement. It is nevertheless misleading to refer to this success in terms that imply that whites simply brought evangelicalism to blacks. We know that "a large number of blacks, belonging chiefly to the large estate of Colonel [William] Byrd," near the North Carolina border, were among the first converts that the Separate Baptists made in Virginia, and that "the breaking up of Byrd's quarters scattered these blacks into various parts." The result was that "through their labors in the different neighborhoods into which they fell many persons were brought to the knowledge of the truth." Perhaps the receptiveness of slaves to the new conception of religion helped open the whole society for its propagation. That is not to say, however, that "conversion" had the same meaning for blacks as for whites. It seems that Afro-American evangelicalism, taking root in the profoundly communal ethos of the quarter, did not typically involve its adherents in an isolating experience of awakening to a deep sense of guilt and sinfulness. Black religion, unlike its white counterpart, was not polarized between individualism and communitarianism but was centered much more unambiguously in collective celebration.

Confrontations

When the Virginia Baptist movement is understood as a rejection of the style of life for which the gentry set the pattern and as a search for different models of proper conduct, it can be seen why the main battleground was not the estate or the great house, but the small planter's house and the slave quarter. It was generally charged that the Baptists were "continual fomenters of discord." Similarly, the only reported complaint against the first preachers to be imprisoned was that they entered "private houses . . . making dissensions." It was in lowly dwellings that the most intense struggles took place between a style of life modeled on that of the leisured gentry and the style embodied in evangelicalism. In humbler, more straitened households a popular culture oriented to proud self-assertion and almost hedonistic values was necessarily less securely established than among the more affluent gentry. For this reason, an anxious aggressiveness was manifest in anti–New Light feeling and action among the common planters.

With the rise of the Separate Baptists, the effrontery of the New Side Presbyterian itinerants in preaching without licenses seemed as nothing compared to the overturning of deference and respect that was proclaimed in the evangelicals' readiness to send out the humblest of men, including slaves, to expound Scripture, declaring them qualified by a "gift" of the Holy Spirit. The Baptist following may have amounted to as much as 10 percent of the population by 1772. More alarming for those wedded to the traditional system was the movement's rate of growth. In 1769 only seven Separate Baptist churches were constituted in Virginia, with no more than three of them located in the longer-settled regions north of the James. By October 1774 the number had climbed to fifty-four in all—twenty-four north of the river.

Even during their most rapid advance the Baptists did not make a bid for control of the political system—still less did they seek a leveling of society or redistribution of worldly wealth. It was clearly a mark of the strength of the gentry's hegemony and of the rigidities of the social hierarchy that had slavery at its base that the evangelical revolt should have been so restricted in scope. Yet the Baptists' Sabbatarianism and anxiety over individual salvation effectively redefined morality and human relationships. Among the lesser folk, Baptist church leaders and organization introduced more popular focuses of authority and sought to impose a radically different and more inclusive model for the maintenance of order in society. Within the context of traditional conceptions of community and the forms of deference expected to sustain it, such a regrouping necessarily constituted a genuine challenge.

The beginnings of a cultural disjunction between gentry and sections of the lower orders where hitherto there had been a continuum, posed a serious threat to the traditional leaders of the community. Their response was characteristic. The popular emotional style, the encouragement given to men of little learning to "exercise their gifts" in preaching, and the preponderance of humble folk in the movement gave the proud gentry their readiest defense—contempt and ridicule. The stereotype of the Baptists as "an ignorant" and "contemptible class of the people," a "poor and illiterate sect" that "none of the rich or learned ever join," became generally accepted. References in the *Virginia Gazette* to "ignorant enthusiasts" were common. It even published, without protest, a heartless satire detailing "A Receipt to make an ANABAPTIST PREACHER": Take the Herbs of Hypocrisy and Ambition, . . . of the Seed of Dissention and Discord one Ounce, . . . [and] one Pint of the Spirit of Self-Conceitedness." . . .

The class of folk who filled the Baptist churches were a great obstacle to gentry participation. Behind their ridicule and contempt lay incomprehension, and behind that, fear of this menacing, unintelligible movement. The only firsthand account we have of a meeting broken up by the arrest of the preachers tells how they "were carried before the . . . magistrate," who took them "one by one into a room and examined [their] pockets and wallets for firearms." He accused them of "carrying on a mutiny against the authority of the land." This sort of dark suspicion impelled David Thomas, in his printed defense of the Baptists, to protest several times that "we concern not ourselves with the government . . . we form no intrigues . . . nor make any attempts to alter the constitution of the kingdom to which as men we belong."

Fear breeds fantasy. So it was that alarmed observers put a very crude interpretation on the emotional and even physical intimacy of this intrusive new society. Its members were associated with German Anabaptists, and a "historical" account of the erotic indulgences of that sect was published on the front page of the *Virginia Gazette*.

Driven by uneasiness, although toughened by their instinctive contempt, some members of the establishment made direct moves to assert proper social authority and to outface the upstarts. Denunciations from parish pulpits were frequent. Debates were not uncommon, being sought by both sides. Ireland recalled vividly a clash that reveals the pride and presumption of the gentlemen who came forward in defense of the Church of England. Captain McClanagan's place was thronged with people, some of whom had come forty miles to hear John Pickett, a Baptist preacher of Fauquier County. The rector of a neighboring parish attended with some leading parishioners "who were as much prejudiced . . . as he was." "The parson had a chair brought for himself, which he placed three or four yards in front of Mr. Pickett . . . taking out his pen, ink and paper, to take down notes of what he conceived to be false doctrine." When Pickett had finished, "the Parson called him a schismatick, a broacher of false doctrines . . . [who] held up damnable errors that day." Pickett answered adequately (according to Ireland), but "when contradicted it would in a measure confuse him." So Ireland, who had been raised a gentleman, took it upon himself to sustain the Baptist cause. The parson immediately "wheeled about on his chair . . . and let out a broadside of his eloquence, with an expectation, no doubt, that he would confound me with the first fire." However, Ireland "gently laid hold of a chair, and placed . . . it close by him, determined to argue the point with him from end to end." The contest was long, and "both gentlemen and ladies," who had evidently seated themselves near the parson, "would repeatedly help him to scripture, in order to support his arguments." When the debate ended (as the narrator recalled) in the refutation of the clergyman, Ireland "addressed one of the gentlemen who had been so officious in helping his teacher; he was a magistrate. . . . 'Sir, as the dispute between the Parson and myself is ended, if you are disposed to argue the subject over again, I am willing to enter upon it with you.' He stretched out his arm straight before him, at that instant, and declared that I should not come nigher than that length." Ireland "concluded what the consequence would be [and] therefore made a peaceable retreat." Such scenes of action speak for themselves. They are the stuff of social structure, as of social conflict.

Great popular movements cannot be outfaced, nor can they be stemmed by the ridicule, scorn, or scurrility of incomprehension. Moreover, they draw into themselves members of all sections of society. Although the milieus most open to the Baptists' proselytizing were the poor whites' plantations and the slaves' quarters, there were converts from the great houses too. Some of the gentry defectors, such as Samuel Harris, played a leading role in the movement. Members of the squirearchy were particularly disturbed by the realization that the contemptible sect was making inroads among themselves. Exchanges between Baptist minister Morgan Edwards and the gentlemen in the Goochland inn were confused by the breakdown of the stereotype of ignorance and poverty. Edwards's cultured facility reminded the squires that "there are some clever fellows among [the Baptists]. I heard one Jery Walker support a petition of theirs at the assembly in such a manner as surprised us all, and [made] our witts draw in their horns." The pride and assurance of the gentry were threatened by awareness that their own members might withdraw from their ranks and choose the other way. The vigorous response of Ireland's patron to the challenge implicit in his defection provides a striking example.

The intensity of the conflict among the people and, increasingly, among the gentry, makes intelligible the growing frequency of violent clashes of the kind already illustrated. The violence was, however, one-sided and self-defeating. The episode of April 1771, when the parson brutally interfered with the devotions of the preacher who was then horsewhipped by the sheriff, must have produced a widespread shock of revulsion. Those who took part in such actions were not typical of either the Anglican clergy or the country gentlemen. The extreme responses of some, however, show the anxieties to which all were subject, and the excesses in question could only heighten the tension.

The continuing upsurge of the New Lights rendered the social challenge increasingly urgent. The gentry were forced to maneuver between a partial revolution in values and organization among the common planters and their own unshaken attachment to the Established Church—an institution that had served to affirm and legitimate their dominance over the whole community.

FURTHER READING

Warren M. Billings, John E. Selby, and Thad W. Tate, *Colonial Virginia: A History* (1986)

T. H. Breen, *Tobacco Culture: The Mentality of the Great Tidewater Planters on the Eve of Revolution* (1985)

Carl Bridenbaugh, *Myths and Realities: Societies of the Colonial South* (1952)

Robert E. Brown and B. Katherine Brown, *Virginia, 1705–1786: Democracy or Aristocracy?* (1964)

Lois G. Carr and Lorena S. Walsh, "The Planter's Wife: The Experience of White Women in Seventeenth-Century Maryland," *William and Mary Quarterly*, 3d ser., 24 (1977), 542–71

Paul G. E. Clemens, *The Atlantic Economy and Colonial Maryland's Eastern Shore: From Tobacco to Grain* (1980)

Peter A. Coclanis, *The Shadow of a Dream: Economic Life and Death in the South Carolina Low Country, 1670–1920* (1989)

Kenneth Coleman, *Colonial Georgia: A History* (1976)

Verner W. Crane, *The Southern Frontier, 1670–1732* (1929)

Richard Beale Davis, *Intellectual Life in the Colonial South, 1585–1763*, 3 vols. (1978)

Carville Earle and Ronald Hoffman, "The Urban South: The First Two Centuries," in Blaine A. Brownell and David R. Goldfield, eds., *The City in Southern History: The Growth of Urban Civilization in the South* (1977)

A. Roger Ekirch, *"Poor Carolina": Politics and Society in Colonial North Carolina, 1729–1776* (1981)

Jack P. Greene, *The Quest for Power: The Lower Houses of Assembly in the Southern Royal Colonies, 1689–1776* (1963)

Aubrey C. Land, "Economic Behavior in a Planting Society: The Eighteenth-Century Chesapeake," *Journal of Southern History* 33 (1967), 469–85

————, *Colonial Maryland: A History* (1981)

Kenneth A. Lockridge, *The Diary, and Life, of William Byrd of Virginia, 1674–1744* (1987)

D. W. Meinig, *The Shaping of America: A Geographical Perspective on 500 Years of History*, vol. 1: *Atlantic America, 1492–1800* (1986)

H. Roy Merrens, *Colonial North Carolina in the Eighteenth Century: A Study in Historical Geography* (1964)

Jacob M. Price, *Capital and Credit in British Overseas Trade: The View from the Chesapeake, 1700–1776* (1980)

Darrett B. Rutman and Anita H. Rutman, *A Place in Time: Middlesex County, Virginia, 1650–1750* (1984)

Daniel Blake Smith, *Inside the Great House: Planter Family Life in Eighteenth-Century Chesapeake Society* (1980)

Julia Cherry Spruill, *Women's Life and Work in the Southern Colonies* (1938)

Charles S. Sydnor, *Gentlemen Freeholders: Political Practices in Washington's Virginia* (1952)

Wilcomb E. Washburn, *The Governor and the Rebel: A History of Bacon's Rebellion in Virginia* (1957)

Robert M. Weir, *Colonial South Carolina—A History* (1983)

————, *"The Last of American Freemen": Studies in the Political Culture of the Colonial and Revolutionary South* (1986)

CHAPTER
4

The American Revolution

⅄

Early in this century, historian Carl Becker suggested that the American Revolution involved two conflicts—home rule and who should rule at home. This was an especially accurate characterization of the Revolution in the South, where colonists fought against both the British and each other. As the selections in the previous chapter illustrate, challenges to the established order in the southern colonies occurred prior to the Revolution. The British provided opportunities for reconciliation (as in Virginia) and for expansion of intracolonial conflicts (as in the Carolinas). Pre-Revolutionary attitudes obviously played a role in determining loyalty to either crown or colony, but additional factors loomed large. In fact, the issue of what and who determined whether an individual became a Tory or a patriot remains an important question.

Was the American Revolution revolutionary in the South? Were the new state governments merely continuations of prior administrations, with the notable exception that British officeholders were gone? Did the respective state constitutions reflect the oft-stated Revolutionary ideals? Though a significant turnover in officeholders assuredly did not occur, debates in the state legislatures reveal a genuine concern for putting the ideal into practice. Suffrage requirements, the established church, and executive privileges usually underwent some modifications in the South during and immediately after the Revolution. Slavery persisted, of course, but patriots displayed ambivalence toward the institution. While Virginians openly discussed eventual emancipation, for example, they were furious when Governor Dunmore issued an emancipation proclamation to blacks in exchange for British military service. And white South Carolinians worried about the loyalty of the black population in their midst.

What happened to domestic patriarchy, country ideology, and other common elements that had served to hold a maturing colonial society together? Did they survive the Revolution intact? Or did new common themes emerge? Historians are demonstrating that the American Revolution in the South was much more than a war of independence. It was another—and very important—event on the way toward defining a distinctive region, the South.

⚔ D O C U M E N T S

The first document concerns South Carolinians' early preparations for war, scarcely ten days after the first shots were fired at Lexington and Concord. John Drayton, a scholar, attorney, and patriot political leader from that colony, wrote a memoir of these early days, capturing the open defiance, ribald humor, and optimism of the times. Only a few months later, a more serious mood arose with respect to the situation in the Carolina backcountry. The South Carolina Assembly dispatched three men, including two ministers, Baptist Oliver Hart and Presbyterian William Tennent, to use their powers of persuasion among key individuals to ensure support, or at least neutrality, in the war. The accounts of Hart and Tennent in the second document paint a picture of a troubled region where the animosities noted by the Reverend Woodmason in the previous chapter had evidently spilled over into the Revolution. Few measures infuriated southern colonists, especially Virginians, more than Royal Governor Lord Dunmore's emancipation proclamation in November 1775. The proclamation, reprinted in the third selection, served to unite Dunmore's opponents, who easily conjured up images of rapacious blacks roaming from plantation to plantation, wreaking vengeance. Although no wholesale defections occurred, as whites had feared, enough blacks took up the proclamation to participate in a few military campaigns. However, most of the blacks who ran away to the British served as informers or laborers. Slaves scarcely required an official document to recognize the opportunities for independence themselves, or at least to escape to the British in response to implied or explicit promises of freedom as the fourth excerpt shows. Thomas Jefferson listed in his Farm Book, amid notations of crops and livestock, the names of his slaves who escaped to the British. During this period, Jefferson was also very active in the Virginia state assembly, sponsoring numerous measures designed to put the Revolution's ideals into practice. His bill on religious freedom, reprinted in the fifth document, was drafted in 1777 but not passed until 1786 (the italicized words in the selection were not included in the final version). The exhilarating and terrifying impact of the war on civilians is evident from the next document, an excerpt from the letters of Eliza Wilkinson, a young widow who resided on Yonge's Island, some thirty miles south of Charleston. While the Revolution brought danger into the relatively placid lives of elite women such as Wilkinson, it also offered them an opportunity to diverge from their accustomed roles. Colonel David Fanning, a prominent North Carolina loyalist who singlemindedly pursued patriots for seven years before he was forced into exile in Canada, offers a soldier's perspective of the war in the final document.

John Drayton on South Carolina's Preparation
for Revolution, 1775

Mr. Speaker and Gentlemen,
    Mr. Poaug, the Ordnance Store-Keeper, informed me last Saturday morning, that upon examining the public arms and stores in the armoury, about eight hundred stands of arms, two hundred cutlasses, all the cartouch boxes, with some bundles of matches, and some flints, belonging to the public, had been taken out of the State-House the preceding night: and Mr. Cochran, Deputy Powder Receiver, who has the charge of the public

Magazine on the town Neck, about four miles from town, informed me, that on his visiting the Magazine last Saturday morning, he found the doors broken open; and that all the gun-powder, about five hundred pounds weight, was carried away, the preceding night, by persons unknown. I have published a proclamation, offering a reward for discovering the persons concerned in such daring acts of violence, against the property, of the public, of this Province.

I have also been informed, by Mr. Prince, who has charge of the public Magazine at Hobcaw; that it was broken open the beginning of this month, and seventy-five pounds weight of gun-powder then taken out: and, that it was again broken open on the 21st instant, and one thousand and twenty-five pounds of gun-powder, being all that was in the Magazine, was carried away.

Upon so very extraordinary, and alarming an occasion; it becomes my indispensable duty, to acquaint you therewith, without loss of time; and earnestly to recommend this important matter to your investigation, and most serious consideration.

WILLIAM BULL

April 24th, 1775.

The Assembly, laughed at this act of Government. However, to carry on the farce, it was referred to the Committee who had been appointed to examine the public arms: and Mr. Bee, Dr. Olyphant, Mr. Izard, and Col. Gaillard were added to the Committee. On the 27th of April, Mr. Bee brought in a report to the House on the subject, which being agreed to, was in the following words: "That with all the inquiry your Committee have made, they are not able to obtain any certain intelligence relative to the removal of the public arms, and gun-powder, as mentioned in his Honour's Message; but, think there is reason to suppose, that some of the inhabitants of this Colony, may have been induced to take so extraordinary and uncommon a step, in consequence of the late alarming accounts from Great Britain:" and, a copy of the same, was sent by the House to the Lieutenant-Governor, with the following Message:

May it please your Honour,
Your Message dated the 24th instant, which you sent to this House the next day, was referred to a Committee: and their report, as agreed to, by the House, we herewith send you.
By order of the House.

RAWLINS LOWNDES, Speaker.

April 27th, 1775.

After the first efficient act, of the Secret Committee; by which, in hazarding their persons in a treasonable affair, they had proved themselves deserving of the high confidence which had been placed, in their ability, firmness, and patriotism; they privately went about, borrowing money for the public service. And so successful were they on this occasion, that on the first day of their progress, they procured one thousand guineas: so ready were the citizens, to meet the call of their country.

During this time, a report had been made in the General Committee, on the 26th day of April, that since the 8th day of March, there had been collected for the relief of the poor in Boston,

From St. Philip's Parish, £1,400 in cash, and 66 barrels Rice.

St. Michael's do.   700 in cash, and 14 barrels Rice.

St. Stephen's do.   600

St. Paul's   do.   600

£3,300

All of which, was remitted to Boston. And, on the same day, a Committee was raised and appointed by the General Committee, denominated *"The Committee of Intelligence:"* which was particularly charged, with obtaining and receiving information, both public and private; and forthwith communicating the same to the Secret Committee, or the General Committee; as might be most proper, and advantageous, for the public service.

With all these occurrences, men's minds had become agitated; and it was deemed proper to bring forth something, calculated to arrest the public attention; to throw odium on the British Administration; to put down the Crown officers in the Province; and to invigorate the ardor of the people. And nothing was deemed more likely to effect the same, than some public exhibition, which might speak to the sight and senses, of the multitude. For this purpose, effigies were brought forward; supposed to be by the authority or connivance, of the Secret Committee. They were executed under the direction of Mr. Poyas, in the Masonic Lodge room, in Lodge-alley; and represented the Pope, Lord Grenville, Lord North [two especially odious British prime ministers], and the Devil. They were placed on the top of a frame, capable of containing one or two persons within it: and the frame was covered over with thick canvass, so that those within, could not be distinguished. In the front of the frame of the top, the Pope was seated in a chair of state, in his pontifical dress; and at a distance immediately behind him, the Devil was placed in a standing position, holding a barbed dart in his right hand; between the Pope and the Devil on each side, Lords Grenville and North were stationed. Thus finished, the frame and effigies were fixed on four wheels; and early in the morning, this uncommon spectacle, was stationed between the Market and St. Michael's Church in Broad-street, to the gaze of the citizens. Many were the surmises respecting it; but at length by its evolutions, it soon began to explain the purposes, for which it was constructed. For no sooner, did any of the Crown officers, Placemen, Counsellors, or persons known to be disaffected to the common cause pass by, than the Pope immediately bowed with proportioned respect to them; and the Devil at the same moment, striking his dart at the head of the Pope, convulsed the populace, with bursts of laughter. While on the other hand, the immoveable effigies of Lords Grenville and North, appearing like attendants on the Pope, or Criminals; moved the people with sentiments of disgust, and contempt against them and the whole British Administration: for the many oppressive acts, which they had been instrumental in procuring to be passed, through both Houses of Parliament. In this manner, the machine was exposed; after which it was paraded through the town the whole day, by the mob: and in the evening they carried it beyond the town: where, surrounding it with tar barrels, the whole was committed to the flames. Nor did the idea or influence of the thing, end here—for, boys forsook their customary sports, to make models like it: with which, having amused themselves, and roused their youthful spirits into a detestation of oppression; they also committed them to the flames. And many of those very boys, supported with their services and blood; the rights, and liberties, of their country.

Two Attempts at Converting the Carolina Backcountry

Reverend William Tennent Records Some Difficult Conversions, 1775

[August] 6th.— . . . Finding some disaffected among the soldiers, Mr. Drayton harangued them and was followed by myself; until all seemed well satisfied, and we returned to Mr. Chestnut's, about two miles. About midnight were alarmed by an officer from the camp, who, informed us that they had mutinied and were determined to go off in the morning. We agreed to let matters rest until then. Ordered the companies to come to us.

7th.—Discovered that the mutiny arose from some words dropped by some officers concerning their pay and tents.

We dealt plainly with the corps of officers, and addressed the men at the head of the Regiment in such a manner as that they all went away happy. . . .

[8th.] Crossed Congaree river and rode five miles to an election for the Congress, where they refused to proceed unless we should enlighten them. We found persons had come a great way to oppose the election. Harangued the meeting in turns until every man was convinced, and the greatest opposer signed the Association and begged pardon for the words he had spoken to the people. . . .

[14th.] . . . It seems as though nothing could be done here, as they have industriously taught the people that no man from Charleston can speak the truth, and that all the papers are full of lies. . . .

20th.— . . . Set off at half after eight for King creek, to a muster of Capt. Robert McAfee's company, after a hard and rough ride of twenty miles, in which crossed King creek at a beautiful rocky ford; found about one hundred people assembled, among whom were some of the most obstinate opposers of the Congress. Spoke to the people at large on the state of America. They seemed much affected towards the close, but afterwards aided by two gainsaying Baptist preachers, they all refused to sign the Association except ten. After their refusal which proceeded from the grossest ignorance and prejudice, spoke again to their heads, who, upon renewing the charge, seemed quite softened, and only asked a little time.

They proposed to obtain some powder to defend themselves from the Indians who are troublesome; told them it was impossible; knew they would not use it properly; told them as soon as they would associate and let us know it, we would try to do something for them. This I hope will have its influence.

Reverend Oliver Hart Encounters Resentment and Failure, 1775

[Thurs. Aug. 10] . . . Upon discoursing wth Mr. Mulkey, found that He rather sides with ministerial Measures, and is agt. those adopted by the Country. Altho' He profess Himself difficulted about these Things; The People, in general, are certainly (as they say) for the King; ie, for the Minister, & his Measures; one Man, with whom we conversed, fairly trembled through Madness. Friday Augt. ye 11th: Rose in Health, but somewhat fatigued; Some of the Neighbors came to see us, with whom we had much Conversation about the present States of the Times; found them so fixed on the Side of the Ministry, that no argument on the contrary Side seemed to have any Weight with them. . . . One of them wish'd 1000 Bostonians might be kill'd in Battle—One wish'd there was not a grain of Salt in any of the sea Coast Towns on the Continent. On the whole they appear to be obstinate and irritated to an Extreme. Saturday Augt. 12th: . . . After Sermon had some Conversation with Col: Fletchal, who declar'd that He had no Intention of fighting against his Country Men, but at the same Time highly disapproved of the Measures fallen upon to preserve our Rights, and complain'd of sundry Threats which He says are given out against Himself, and the Inhabitants of the Frontiers. A number of People gathered round us while we were conversing together, who seem'd almost universally, by Words & actions to applaud every Thing the Col: said. Upon the Whole there appears but little Reason, as yet, to hope that these People will be brought to have a suitable Regard to ye interest of America. . . . Lords Day Augt: 13th: . . . Went home with Mr: Mulkey, Mr: Newton in Company, who gave us an account of the distracted State of the frontier Inhabitants, which at present wears the most alarming Face; insomuch that there is the greatest appearance of a civil War; unless God, by some remarkable Interposition of Providence prevent.

Lord Dunmore's Proclamation Freeing
Virginia's Slaves, 1775

As I have ever entertained Hopes that an Accommodation might have taken Place between *Great Britain* and this Colony, without being compelled, by my Duty, to this most disagreeable, but now absolutely necessary Step, rendered so by a Body of armed Men, unlawfully assembled, firing on his Majesty's Tenders, and the Formation of an Army, and that Army now on their March to attack his Majesty's Troops, and destroy the well-disposed Subjects of this Colony: To defeat such treasonable Purposes, and that all such Traitors, and their Abetters, may be brought to Justice, and that the Peace and good Order of this Colony may be again restored, which the ordinary Course of the civil Law is unable to effect, I have thought fit to issue this my Proclamation, hereby declaring, that until the aforesaid good Purposes can be obtained, I do, in Virtue of the Power and Authority to me given, by his Majesty, determine to execute martial Law, and cause the same to be executed throughout this Colony; and to the End that Peace and good Order may the sooner be restored, I do require every Person capable of bearing Arms to resort to his Majesty's STANDARD, or be looked upon as Traitors to his Majesty's Crown and Government, and thereby become liable to the Penalty the Law inflicts upon such Offences, such as Forfeiture of Life, Confiscation of Lands, &c. &c. And I do hereby farther declare all indented Servants, Negroes, or others (appertaining to Rebels) free, that are able and willing to bear Arms, they joining his Majesty's Troops, as soon as may be, for the more speedily reducing this Colony to a proper Sense of their Duty, to his Majesty's Crown and Dignity. I do farther order, and require, all his Majesty's liege Subjects to retain their Quitrents, or any other Taxes due, or that may become due, in their own Custody, till such Time as Peace may be again restored to this at present most unhappy Country, or demanded of them for their former salutary Purposes, by Officers properly authorized to receive the same,

Thomas Jefferson on the Defection of His Slaves to the British, 1781

Slaves who went off with the British & died

Hannibal	Nanny
Patty	Fanny
Prince	Nancy
Sam 9. years old	Flora
Sally	Quomina

Went off with the British & was never more heard of.
Sam.

Went off with the British, returned & died of the camp fever Lucy. Black Sall. Jane 10. years old.

Lost for want of cultivation by loss of the hands
    about 80 barrels of corn
        130. lb of cotton
        7. hogshead of tobacco

Thomas Jefferson's Bill for Establishing Religious Freedom in Virginia, 1777

Well aware that the opinions and belief of men depend not on their own will, but follow involuntarily the evidence proposed to their minds; that Almighty God hath created the mind free, *and manifested his supreme will that free it shall remain by masking it altogether insusceptible of restraint;*

that all attempts to influence it by temporal punishments, or burthens, or by civil incapacitations, tend only to beget habits of hypocrisy and meanness, and are a departure from the plan of the holy author of our religion, who being lord both of body and mind, yet chose not to propagate it by coercions on either, as was in his Almighty power to do, *but to extend it by its influence on reason alone;* that the impious presumption of legislators and rulers, civil as well as ecclesiastical, who, being themselves but fallible and uninspired men, have assumed dominion over the faith of others, setting up their own opinions and modes of thinking as the only true and infallible, and as such endeavoring to impose them on others, hath established and maintained false religions over the greatest part of the world and through all time: That to compel a man to furnish contributions of money for the propagation of opinions which he disbelieves *and abhors,* is sinful and tyrannical: that even the forcing him to support this or that teacher of his own religious persuasion, is depriving him of the comfortable liberty of giving his contributions to the particular pastor whose morals he would make his pattern, and whose powers he feels most persuasive to righteousness; and is withdrawing from the ministry those temporary rewards, which proceeding from an approbation of their personal conduct, are an additional incitement to earnest and unremitting labours for the instruction of mankind; that our civil rights have no dependance on our religious opinions, any more than our opinions in physics or geometry; that therefore the proscribing any citizen as unworthy the public confidence by laying upon him an incapacity of being called to offices of trust and emolument, unless he profess or renounce this or that religious opinion, is depriving him injuriously of those privileges and advantages to which, in common with his fellow citizens, he has a natural right; that it tends also to corrupt the principles of that *very* religion it is meant to encourage, by bribing, with a monopoly of worldly honours and emoluments, those who will externally profess and conform to it; that though indeed these are criminal who do not withstand such temptation, yet neither are those innocent who lay the bait in their way; *that the opinions of men are not the object of civil government, nor under its jurisdiction;* that to suffer the civil magistrate to intrude his powers into the field of opinion and to restrain the profession or propagation of principles on supposition of their ill tendency is a dangerous falacy, which at once destroys all religious liberty, because he being of course judge of that tendency will make his opinions the rule of judgment, and approve or condemn the sentiments of others only as they shall square with or differ from his own; that it is time enough for the rightful purposes of civil government for its officers to interfere when principles break out into overt acts against peace and good order; and finally, that truth is great and will prevail if left to herself; that she is the proper and sufficient antagonist to error, and has nothing to fear from the conflict unless by human interposition disarmed of her natural weapons, free argument and debate; errors ceasing to be dangerous when it is permitted freely to contradict them.

We the General Assembly of Virginia do enact that no man shall be compelled to frequent or support any religious worship, place, or ministry whatsoever, nor shall be enforced, restrained, molested, or burthened in his body or goods, nor shall otherwise suffer, on account of his religious opinions or belief; but that all men shall be free to profess, and by argument to maintain, their opinions in matters of religion, and that the same shall in no wise diminish, enlarge, or affect their civil capacities.

And though we well know that this assembly, elected by the people for the ordinary purposes of legislation only, have no power to restrain the acts of succeeding Assemblies, constituted with powers equal to our own, and that therefore to declare this act irrevocable would be of no effect in law; yet we are free to declare, and do declare, that the rights hereby asserted are of the natural rights of mankind, and that if any act shall be hereafter passed to repeal the present or to narrow its operation, such act will be an infringement of natural right.

Eliza Wilkinson's Thoughts on Women and War, 1779

Never were greater politicians than the several knots of ladies, who met together. All trifling discourse of fashions, and such low little chat was thrown by, and we commenced perfect statesmen. Indeed, I don't know but if we had taken a little pains, we should have been qualified for prime ministers, so well could we discuss several important matters in hand. . . .

Well, now comes the day of terror—the 3d of June. (I shall never love the anniversary of that day.) In the morning, fifteen or sixteen horsemen rode up to the house; we were greatly terrified, thinking them the enemy, but from their behavior, were agreeably deceived, and found them friends. They sat a while on their horses, talking to us; and then rode off, except two, who tarried a minute or two longer, and then followed the rest, who had nearly reached the gate. One of the said two must needs jump a ditch— to show his activity I suppose; for he might as well, and better, have gone in the road. However, he got a sad fall; we saw him, and sent a boy to tell him, if he was hurt, to come up to the house, and we would endeavor to do something for him. He and his companion accordingly came up; he look'd very pale, and bled much; his gun somehow in the fall, had given him a bad wound behind the ear, from whence the blood flowed down his neck and bosom plentifully: we were greatly alarmed on seeing him in this situation, and had gathered around him, some with one thing, some with another, in order to give him assistance. We were very busy examining the wound, when a negro girl ran in, exclaiming—"O! the king's people are coming, it must be them, for they are all in red." Upon this cry, the two men that were with us snatched up their guns, mounted their horses, and made off; but had not got many yards from the house, before the enemy discharged a pistol at them. Terrified almost to death as I was, I was still anxious for my friends' safety; I tremblingly flew to the window, to see if the shot had proved fatal: when, seeing them both safe, "Thank heaven," said I, "they've got off without hurt!" I'd hardly utter'd this, when I heard the horses of the inhuman Britons coming in such a furious manner, that they seemed to tear up the earth, and the riders at the same time bellowing out the most horrid curses imaginable; oaths and imprecations, which chilled my whole frame. Surely, thought I, such horrid language denotes nothing less than death; but I'd no time for thought—they were up to the house—entered with drawn swords and pistols in their hands; indeed, they rushed in, in the most furious manner, crying out, "Where're these women rebels?" (pretty language to ladies from the *once famed Britons!*) That was the first salutation! The moment they espied us, off went our caps, (I always heard say none but women pulled caps!) And for what, think you? why, only to get a paltry stone and wax pin, which kept them on our heads; at the same time uttering the most abusive language imaginable, and making as if they'd hew us to pieces with their swords. But it's not in my power to describe the scene: it was terrible to the last degree; and, what augmented it, they had several armed negroes with them, who threatened and abused us greatly. They then began to plunder the house of every thing they thought valuable or worth taking; our trunks were split to pieces, and each mean, pitiful wretch crammed his bosom with the contents, which were our apparel, &c. &c. &c.

I ventured to speak to the inhuman monster who had my clothes. I represented to him the times were such we could not replace what they'd taken from us, and begged him to spare me only a suit or two; but I got nothing but a hearty curse for my pains; nay, so far was his callous heart from relenting, that, casting his eyes towards my shoes, "I want them buckles," said he, and immediately knelt at my feet to take them out, which, while he was busy about, a brother villain, whose enormous mouth extended from ear to ear, bawled out "Shares there, I say; shares." So they divided my buckles between them. The other wretches were employed in the same manner; they took my sister's ear-rings from her ears; hers, and Miss Samuells's buckles; they demanded her ring from her finger; she pleaded for it, told them it was her wedding ring, and begged they'd let her keep it; but they still demanded it, and, presenting a pistol at her, swore if she did not deliver it immediately, they'd fire. She gave it to them, and, after bundling up all their booty, they mounted their horses. But such despicable figures! Each wretch's bosom stuffed so full, they appeared to be all afflicted with some dropsical disorder; had a party of rebels (as they called us) appeared, we should soon have seen their circumference lessen.

They took care to tell us, when they were going away, that they had favored us a great deal—that we might thank our stars it was no worse. But I had forgot to tell you, that, upon their first entering the house, one of them gave my arm such a violent grasp, that he left the print of his thumb and three fingers, in black and blue, which was to be seen, very plainly, for several days after. I showed it to one of our officers, who dined with us, as a specimen of British cruelty. If they call this *favor*, what must their cruelties be? It must want a name. To be brief; after a few words more, they rode off, and glad was I. "Good riddance of bad rubbish," and indeed such rubbish was I never in company with before. One of them was an officer too! a sergeant, or some such, for he had the *badge of honor*

on his shoulders! After they were gone, I began to be sensible of the danger
I'd been in, and the thoughts of the vile men seemed worse (if possible)
than their presence; for they came so suddenly up to the house, that I'd
no time for thought; and while they staid, I seemed in amaze! Quite stupid!
I cannot describe it. But when they were gone, and I had time to consider,
I trembled so with terror, that I could not support myself. I went into the
room, threw myself on the bed, and gave way to a violent burst of grief,
which seemed to be some relief to my full-swollen heart. . . .

I do not love to meddle with political matters; the men say we have
no business with them, it is not in our sphere! and Homer . . . gives us
two or three broad hints to mind our domestic concerns, spinning, weaving,
&c. and leave affairs of higher nature to the men; but I must beg his
pardon—I won't have it thought, that because we are the weaker sex as
to *bodily* strength, my dear, we are capable of nothing more than minding
the dairy, visiting the poultry-house, and all such domestic concerns; our
thoughts can soar aloft, we can form conceptions of things of higher nature;
and have as just a sense of honor, glory, and great actions, as these "Lords
of the Creation." What contemptible *earth worms* these authors make us!
They won't even allow us the liberty of thought, and that is all I want. I
would not wish that we should meddle in what is unbecoming female delicacy, but surely we may have sense enough to give our opinions to commend or discommend such actions as we may approve or disapprove;
without being reminded of our spinning and household affairs as the only
matters we are capable of thinking or speaking of with justness or propriety.
I won't allow it, positively won't.

Colonel David Fanning's Memoirs of a Loyalist, 1781

In the 19th year of my age, I entered into the War; and proceeded from
one step to another, as is herein mentioned, and at the conclusion thereof,
was forced to leave the place of my nativity for my adherence to the British
Constitution; and after my sore fatigues, I arrived at St. John River; and
there with the blessing of God, I have hitherto enjoyed the sweets of peace,
and freedom under the benevolent auspices of the British Government. . . .

 King's County,
  Long Beach,
   New Brunswick.
 June 24th, 1790.

. . . After a little while some of us had assembled at a friend's house, where
we were surrounded by a party of 14 Rebels under the command of Capt.
John Hinds; we perceived their approach and prepared for to receive them;
when they got quite near us, we run out of the door of the house, fired
upon them, and killed one of them; on which we took three of their horses,
and some firelocks—we then took to the woods and unfortunately had two
of our little company taken, one of which the Rebels shot in cold blood,

and the other they hung on the spot where we killed the man a few days before. We were exasperated at this, that we determined to have satisfaction, and in a few days I collected 17 men well armed, and formed an ambuscade on Deep River at Coxe's Mills, and sent out my spies. In the course of two hours, one of my spies gave me information of a party of Rebels plundering his house, which was about three miles off. I instantly marched to the place and discovered them in a field near the house. I attacked them immediately, and kept up a smart fire for half an hour, during which time we killed their Captain, and one private, on the spot—wounded three of them, and took two prisoners besides eight of their horses well appointed, and several swords. This happened on the 11th of May, 1781. The same day, we persued another party of Rebels, and came up with them the morning following; we attacked them smartly and killed four of them on the spot, wounded 3 dangerously and took one prisoner with all their horses, and appointments. In about an hour after that, we took two men of the same party, and killed one more of them; the same evening we had intelligence of another party of Rebels, which were assembling about 30 miles off in order for to attack us; as I thought it best to surprise them where they were collecting, I marched all night and about 10 o'clock next morning, we came up with them; we commenced a fire upon each other, which continued for about 10 minutes when they retreated; we killed two of them, and wounded 7, and took 18 horses well appointed; we then returned to Deep River again. . . .

. . . One evening, I had assembled thirty men, at a friend's house, and sent out spies. They soon returned with the account of a party of rebels within four miles of us, distressing and plundering our friends. We immediately set forward to render our assistance, and got within a half a mile of them; I, then, sent out to get information how they were situated, and by break of day came upon them. We retook seven horses which they had carried off, with a large quantity of baggage. We wounded two of them mortally, and several of them slightly; we came off without injury except two horses wounded. The day following, we pursued them, to Cumberland county, and on my way, I burnt Capt. Coxe's house, and his Father's. I had also two skirmishes and killed two of the rebel party. On my return to Little River, I heard of a Capt. Golson; who had been distressing the Loyalists; and went in search of him, myself; but unfortunately I did not meet him; but fell in, with one of his men, who had been very assiduous, in assisting the rebels. I killed him. I mounted a man of my own on his horse, and returned back. I then took Capt. Currie and the man of my own before mentioned, and I went with a design of burning Capt. Golson's house; which I did; and also two others. In my way, I fell in, with a man, who had been very anxious for to have some of my men executed. I sent him word for to moderate and he should have nothing to fear, but if he persisted, I would certainly kill him. He took no notice of this; but persisted, for several months, and on observing me that day, he attempted to escape; but I shot him.

人 *E S S A Y S*

The lapse in time between the introduction of Thomas Jefferson's bill for religious freedom and its passage indicates that not all Virginia lawmakers shared
the sage of Monticello's republican ideals. The first essay, by former University
of Virginia historian and Jefferson biographer Merrill D. Peterson, demonstrates
Jefferson's dominant role in the new state legislative body, as well as the difficulty he encountered in persuading his colleagues to put Revolutionary ideals
into practice. Women were not part of Jefferson's scheme, however, as Mary
Beth Norton, a Cornell University historian, makes clear in her essay on the
Revolution's meaning for southern women. The Revolution caused some southern white women to question their social role, but little came of such thoughts,
and, in fact, Norton implies that the Revolution may have even contracted the
already-narrow sphere of southern women. The conflicts among patriots Peterson
noted and the internal conflicts southern women experienced underscore the
point that the American Revolution in the South was far more than a war of
independence from Great Britain. Nowhere was this more evident than in the
backcountry. Rachel N. Klein, a historian at the University of California, San
Diego, explores in the final selection the complexities of backcountry affiliations,
stressing the importance of local leaders and the misfiring of British strategies.

Thomas Jefferson, Revolutionist

MERRILL D. PETERSON

Jefferson was more interested in revolution than in union. . . . The time
was ripe for revolutionizing the colonial governments. It was, as [John]
Adams said, "a time when the greatest lawgivers of antiquity would have
wished to live." Jefferson, with a sense of history and of his place in it
no less acute than Adams's, wished to be a lawgiver to the new age. He
was determined to seize the opportunity while the Revolutionary spirit
flamed in every patriot breast. It would not last. "From the conclusion of
the war we shall be going down hill," he later reflected. "It will not then
be necessary to resort every moment to the people for support. They will
be forgotten, therefore, and their rights disregarded. They will forget themselves, but in the sole faculty of making money, and will never think of
uniting to effect a due respect for their rights."

So he must return to Virginia. There the work of reformation was under
way, and Jefferson, three hundred miles from the scene, was deeply disturbed by the conservative course it was taking. In the opinion of many
Virginians, the work was finished and done with upon the adoption of a
constitution some days before Congress proclaimed independence. Such
men were separationists—rebels against Britain but conservatives at home.
Jefferson was a revolutionist. He had hoped that the Virginia delegates

Excerpted from *Thomas Jefferson and the New Nation: A Biography* by Merrill D. Peterson.
Copyright © 1970 by Oxford University Press, Inc. Reprinted by permission.

might have been recalled from Congress for a short time in order to have a voice in the making of the constitution. "In truth," he wrote to a friend in Williamsburg, "it is the whole object of the present controversy; for should a bad government be instituted for us in future it had been as well to have accepted the bad one offered to us from beyond the water without the risk and expense of contest." But in the momentous spring of 1776 Virginia could not be without a delegation in Congress. And had Jefferson got his wish he would not, in all probability, have become the author of the Declaration of Independence. He had to content himself with submitting a proposed constitution from afar, relying on his old teacher, George Wythe, to carry it to Williamsburg. It was late June when Wythe arrived at the convention. The weather was hot, the delegates were tired, and they had so far agreed on a plan of government widely at variance with this fresh proposal from Jefferson that they had not the patience to discuss it. They found it convenient, nevertheless, to tack on Jefferson's preamble, the parent of his arraignment of George III in the Declaration of Independence, and to incorporate two or three propositions of his in the finished document.

The constitution fell far below Jefferson's expectations, thus deepening his anxiety to return home. He was anxious in any event. Martha [Jefferson's wife] was not well; and the desire to be near his family was as strong as the spur of public responsibility. Against his declared will, the convention had re-elected him to another term in Congress. No sooner was he notified than he resigned, vaguely begging "the situation of my domestic affairs." But his correspondence with friends at home during the same months makes it abundantly clear that he was eager to take up the work of reformation where the convention had left off. He retired from Congress on September 2, and after a month at Monticello, took his seat in the House of Delegates, the old Burgesses, at Williamsburg.

The Virginia Constitution

The constitution Jefferson drafted and placed in Wythe's hands in Philadelphia was an epitome of his political science in 1776. Actually, this was the third draft. As one who believed the framing of new republican constitutions "the whole object of the present controversy," he probably gave to the task more time and thought than ever he did to the drafting of the immortal Declaration. There he boldly sketched the philosophy of the new nation; here, in planning a government for his countrymen, he endeavored to implement that philosophy and to secure the rights declared in the fundamental law of the new commonwealth. While some of his patriot friends looked upon the achievement of independence as the end toward which the Revolution aimed, it was for Jefferson only the beginning. The ultimate justification of American independence was moral: in the obligation to conform all conduct to the standard of right raised in the Declaration. Rhetoric was cheap, as Jefferson knew. Philosophers had talked of "natural rights" and "self-government" for centuries, but when had these theories been reduced to practice? Where had a government been instituted by "the consent of the governed"? Where had the rights of "life, liberty, and the pursuit of happiness" been held sacred? This was the harder part. And while it could not be finished in a day, a year, or a century, while it could never be accomplished with the nicety of abstract theory, the strongest possible beginning ought to be made lest the noble principles of 1776 be hooted down the corridors of time.

The constitution adopted at Williamsburg was undoubtedly more representative of Virginia political opinion than Jefferson's draft. Mainly the work of George Mason, a Fairfax planter close to the Lees, it steered a middle course between the conservatism of Edmund Pendleton, Carter Braxton, and the old guard generally, and the liberalism of Jefferson, Wythe, and many young Virginians. It did not in any way alter the distribution of power in Virginia society. It continued the freehold suffrage qualification under which one-third or more of the adult white males were disfranchised. It continued a system of representation in the legislature favorable to the smaller eastern counties. It actually increased the oligarchical power of the fountainheads of local justice and administration, the county courts. The most conspicuous change was in the executive office. Stripped of the vestments of monarchy, the Governor was annually elected by the General Assembly, and required to act with the consent of an eight-man Council of State, also elected by the assembly. Judges too, except for the self-perpetuating county courts, received their appointments from the assembly. All powers thus resided in the legislative body. . . . The Virginia convention's originality lay not in the constitution but in Mason's Declaration of Rights appended to it. This was a magnificent achievement, even if its authority was uncertain. There were distressing disparities between the Declaration and the constitution, between the equalitarian phrases of the one and the aristocratic features of the other. The Virginia Declaration of Rights nevertheless set a model for governments of free men the world over.

Jefferson at once became the Virginia constitution's severest critic. His lifelong quarrel with it picked up more and more democratic accents in progress with his political opinions. He argued, first of all, that the constitution was illegitimate—a mere ordinance or statute with no permanent and binding power on the government. The convention that framed the constitution was, as he correctly observed, the Revolutionary successor of the House of Burgesses, its members elected in April 1776 to perform the *ordinary* business of government. "They could not, therefore, pass an act transcendent to the power of other legislatures." The term "convention" as then employed in Virginia in no way conveyed the idea, still nebulous, of a constitutional convention: an especially elected body of delegates to draw the fundamental law of the state. This is what was necessary, Jefferson thought, for without it succeeding legislatures might freely alter the constitution to please themselves. Jefferson stated his objection through Edmund Randolph at the time of the convention's meeting. But Pendleton, Mason, and Patrick Henry, to whom Randolph talked, "saw no distinction between the conceded power to declare independence"—a more than or-

dinary power the convention had exercised—"and its necessary consequence, the fencing of society by the institution of government." The fact
that Jefferson went ahead and submitted his own proposal to the body
whose rightful authority he denied suggested that his objection was captious
and might not have occurred to him had he been in Williamsburg.

But Jefferson was not being frivolous. He was attempting to work out
the practical means whereby a people, taking sovereignty to themselves,
may create a government of their own choosing. There was, in his opinion,
a vast difference between the revolutionary act of independence and the
institution of government according to principles that alone justified the
act. "Necessities which dissolve a government, do not convey its authority
to an oligarchy or to a monarchy. They throw the authority back, into the
hands of the people . . . and leave them to shift for themselves." . . .

As finally and fully developed, the process included three elements: a
convention emanating from the people for the purpose of framing a constitution, popular ratification of the document, and provision for its periodic
amendment and revision. None of the first constitutions, hastily framed in
the face of the enemy, exhibited all these cardinal elements, nor did Jefferson or anyone grasp the finished theory in 1776. He had a good idea of
it, however. . . .

The fact is that Jefferson, with many others, at first fumbled and groped
in searching out a practical means of implementing the principles of the
Revolution. "In truth," he reflected years later, "the abuses of monarchy
had so much filled all the space of political contemplation, that we imagined
everything republican which was not monarchy. We had not yet penetrated
to the mother principle, that governments are republican only in proportion
as they embody the will of the people, and execute it." If this can be said
with respect to the foundations of authority, it can also be said with respect
to the structure of government. . . .

Jefferson was farthest at odds with his compatriots in Virginia and
elsewhere on the related issues of suffrage and representation. His unhes-
itating advocacy of a broadly popular suffrage and of equal representation
of the people in the legislature held the promise of making his constitution
a vital instrument of democratic government. Although he did not entirely
abandon the freehold suffrage qualification, he reduced it by more than
one-half and, further, extended the suffrage to all taxpayers. Moreover, he
ensured the enfranchisement of still other Virginians by a unique measure
of both economic and political democracy: every person of full age who
did not own fifty acres of land was entitled to a government appropriation
of so many acres as necessary to make up that amount. Jefferson thus
revived the old colonial importation or headright system, under which a
fifty-acre grant was awarded to the person responsible for settling an immigrant in Virginia, and turned it toward democratic ends. But if he hoped
to overcome the resistance of the planter class to universal white male
suffrage by, in effect, making every man a freeholder, he was quickly
disappointed. Young Randolph could not recall that any delegate in the
convention uttered a word against the traditional freehold suffrage. It re-

mained the rock of conservative influence for decades to come. Jefferson's reform would also eliminate special property qualifications for officeholders. Public office would be thrown open to a large electorate virtually identical with the community. Jefferson proposed to achieve fair and equal representation geographically by proportioning the legislature to the rule of numbers. Under the county-unit system of representation which the convention perpetuated, the tidewater counties controlled one-half the Senate and nearly one-half the House, though they possessed well under half the population and were steadily losing ground to the interior sections. The question was one of interest as well as of principle. The wealth and privilege of the state centered in the east. Jefferson identified himself with the aspirations of the west. But the point of equal representation struck him as "capital and fundamental" on whatever ground it was put, and he would not rest easy until it could be obtained.

Most of the remaining differences between Jefferson's plan and the one adopted at Williamsburg fall into the general category "rights and liberties." In view of his staunch advocacy of a federal Bill of Rights in 1788, it is surprising he did not add a similar document to the proposed Virginia constitution. He endeavored, he later said, "to reach all the great objects of public liberty" in the constitution itself. In fact, he reached only a few of them. The Virginia Declaration of Rights contained guarantees of the right against self-incrimination, the right of *habeas corpus,* and freedom from unwarranted searches and seizures, none of which were to be found in Jefferson's drafts. He upheld these rights, of course. They were in the common law. But in 1776 he evidently did not think it essential to give them constitutional protection. On the other hand, he incorporated in his constitution a number of liberal reforms—on religion, slavery, descent of lands, punishment of crimes—that were strangers to the Virginia constitution.

That frame of government proved utterly recalcitrant to change. Several times during the next fifty years Jefferson rode full tilt against it, each charge more democratic than the last, and each time he retired in defeat. But if he could not revamp the Constitution, he might, for the present, turn one of its vicious principles, the unfettered power of the assembly, to virtuous ends, and endeavor to achieve by ordinary legislation those fundamental reforms in Virginia law and institutions he had hoped to accomplish at one stroke by a liberal constitution.

In the House of Delegates

The House of Delegates Jefferson entered in October 1776 was, with the exception of several members like himself, the same body as formed the constitution. He took his seat, occupied by an alternate in his absence, by virtue of his election to the convention in April. Soon after he arrived in Williamsburg, a messenger from Congress notified him of his election as a joint commissioner, with Benjamin Franklin and Silas Deane, to negotiate a treaty of alliance at the Court of Louis XVI. Duty, the pleasures of

France, the delightful company of Dr. Franklin—all inclined him to accept the charge. Although more sanguine than most men about the prospects of American arms, he knew the capital importance of the French mission, and he was honored by so distinguished an appointment. For three days he groped toward a decision; finally, on October 11, he dismissed the messenger with a letter politely declining the commission. The circumstances of his family, he explained, neither permitted him to leave them behind nor to expose them to the dangers of the crossing. "I saw, too," he later reflected, "that the laboring oar was really at home, where much was to be done, of the most permanent interest, in new modeling our governments. . . ." No task seemed more urgent to him, or more agreeable, since it permitted him to live as he was accustomed and be near his ailing wife. She joined him in Williamsburg. During [George] Wythe's absence in Philadelphia, the Jeffersons occupied his modest house, which still stands facing the Palace green, a monument to an age of gentle simplicity.

A revolution had come, but the only noticeable change in the old capital was the new face in the Governor's Palace. Patrick Henry had been elected first Governor of the Commonwealth. The conservatives had put up an opposition in the person of Thomas Nelson, Sr., long-time secretary of the colony; but the popular orator drew support from both moderate and liberal men, and thus carried the election handily. It was a tribute owing to his unrivaled leadership in the Revolutionary movement. Despite his reputation as a "radical," Henry was satisfied with the new frame of government. The conservatives had nothing to fear from him. His powers were forensic; he was amiable and pliable; he was a Virginian to the core of his being, no less attached to the old ways than his arch-antagonist Edmund Pendleton. In 1776 Henry's great work was done; the work of his young friend and comrade Thomas Jefferson was just beginning. Henry led Virginia to the Revolution, but lacking either talent or zeal for constructive reform, he could not consolidate it. This was to be Jefferson's role. Elevated to the governorship, jealously guarded as it was, Henry lost much of the influence he formerly had. The vacuum he left in the legislative chamber, Jefferson hastened to fill. The delegate from Albermarle was one of the half-dozen most popular figures in the assembly. While this counted for much, the fact that he knew what he wanted, that he had a program for correcting abuses, righting wrongs, and expanding liberty, counted for more. Developing this line of politics, Jefferson did not displace Henry in the affections of the people—no one could do that—but made his brand of demagogical politics unnecessary to successful leadership in a republic of free men.

In the House of Delegates most of the faces were familiar. In the Speaker's chair sat Edmund Pendleton, one of Jefferson's prized friends among the elder statesmen of Virginia. The two men heartily liked and respected each other, though their political swords were usually crossed. Genial, unaffected, and judicious, Pendleton embodied the virtues of the ruling class without either its wealth or its vices. Jefferson did not feel the same esteem for other leaders on the conservative side, such as opulent Benjamin Harrison, of Berkeley, with whom he had served in Congress, and Robert Carter Nicholas, the former treasurer and guardian of the Church. He was perhaps not yet well acquainted with George Mason, who best represented the moderate element in the assembly and whose authorship of the Declaration of Rights commended him to Jefferson. The master of Potomac's Gunston Hall was a man of marvelous force and presence. A successful planter with a large family and a distinct preference for private life, he shied away from the leadership that might have been his. During the next several years, when he served in the assembly, Jefferson found him to be perhaps his "most steadfast, able and zealous" colleague. Looking back on the time from the perspective of nearly half a century, Jefferson also remembered the assistance of two other men, more eager and more advanced in their opinions than Mason but lacking his influence. One was George Wythe, who returned from Congress in 1777, the other the new delegate from Orange, James Madison. A delicate little man, reserved, always garbed in black, and without surface brilliance of any kind, Madison was wise and learned beyond his twenty-five years. He had been educated at the College of New Jersey, in Princeton, where he acquired clear ideas of civil and religious liberty from its Scottish Presbyterian president, John Witherspoon. Several months earlier, in the convention, he had posted his liberal colors by proposing a crucial amendment to the article on religion in the Declaration of Rights. But Madison was not a man to invite instant attention or friendship. Jefferson came to know and respect his abilities during the first session of the assembly. Not until three years later, however, when he was Governor and Madison a member of the Council, did they become intimate. In the years ahead Jefferson drew long and well on "the rich resources of his luminious and discriminating mind."

There were, of course, factions and followings in the government, and Henry was even accused of leading a party. Jefferson carefully skirted these political entanglements, with the personal animosities they often involved. The cordiality of his relations with men who were notorious enemies of each other—Henry and Pendleton, Lee and Harrison—bespeaks a mild temperament, a studied courtesy, and a revulsion from the dubious glories of political gladiators. This fact, combined with his forwardness in legislative business and the force of his ideas, ensured his ascendancy in the House of Delegates. Given the convenience of political labels, it is tempting to label Jefferson a "radical." A committed revolutionist, even if a gentle one, could hardly be anything else. And so he seemed to many Virginians of the old order. He was, certainly, more advanced in his thinking and objectives than the great host of his contemporaries in and out of Virginia. Yet he had none of the typical radical's rage against the past, intolerance of opposition, and perfectionist aspirations. With other philosophers of the time, he made a god of nature; yet, without idealizing the past, he embodied history in the cause of the future. He did not compromise his political convictions; but he recognized that they were *his* convictions, to be enjoyed with the same confidence he accorded to others, that perfect agreement was as unnecessary as it was unattainable, and that force could never substitute for reason and persuasion in republican government. He had no blueprint for a new society. He was, at bottom, attached to Virginia society, wishing only to reform its abuses—its feudal holdovers, unnatural privileges, its slavery, and massive ignorance. He would not go to radical lengths to achieve his objectives. And even his most progressive reforms were streaked with conservatism. . . .

Religion

The Church of England was established in the infancy of the Old Dominion and reigned virtually free of challenge for more than a century. Buttressed and safeguarded by many laws both local and English, aided by a long tradition, the Anglican Church functioned as an arm of the government. Its clergy, creed, and worship held a privileged status, while all others were subject to varying degrees of restraint, and it exacted support from believers and non-believers alike. The principles of the Revolution rendered this state of affairs intolerable. Jefferson at once set himself the task of tearing up the establishment by its roots. His draft constitution contained this sweeping clause: "All persons shall have full and free liberty of religious opinion, nor shall any be compelled to frequent or maintain any religious institution." This was too big a step for the Virginia convention. The constitution of 1776 pleaded mute. The Declaration of Rights, however, stated the true principle: "all men are equally entitled to the free exercise of religion according to the dictates of conscience." If the realization of this right became an object of legislation, the establishment was doomed.

The dissenting sects and others, secular liberals like Jefferson, who opposed the "spiritual tyranny" of the Anglican Church were alert to the opportunity. The first legislative assembly was crowded with petitions calling for disestablishment. "These brought on the severest contest in which I have ever been engaged," Jefferson reflected many years later. Soon after taking his seat, he was appointed to a nineteen-member committee on religion charged with the responsibility of reporting on these numerous petitions. The conflict must have been intense, resulting in stalemate, for after a month's deliberation the committee was discharged and the matter thrown into the House. On November 19 the House agreed to a set of six resolutions, all but one of which supported the liberal position as formulated in resolutions Jefferson had drafted. A new committee was now appointed, Jefferson again a member, to bring in a bill founded on the resolutions. Before this could be accomplished, the House drew back and instructed the committee to report a moderate bill. The upshot of these maneuvers was the act of December 1776 repealing oppressive acts of Parliament and exempting dissenters from taxes to support the Church. While this was an advance, it did not disestablish the Church or secure full freedom of religious conscience. Virginians might still be punished for heretical opinions, either under common law or Virginia statutes. Parish levies on members of the Church were suspended but not abolished. Finally, the act expressly reserved decision on the question, "Whether a general assessment should not be established by law, on every one, to the support of the pastor of his choice, or whether all should be left to voluntary contributions." This was a new issue going beyond the fate of the Established Church. It rapidly became the crucial issue in the long campaign for religious freedom. The climax came a decade later, when Jefferson was in France, with the enactment of his remarkable Bill for Establishing Religious Freedom.

When late in life Jefferson penned his epitaph, he named the Virginia Statute for Religious Freedom one of the three achievements for which he wished to be remembered. More than a statute, it was an eloquent manifesto of the sanctity of the human mind and spirit. It gave mature expression to convictions that, though they might have been reached wholly along the untroubled path of reason, were, in fact, tempered and formed in the crucible of religious controversy in Virginia. In denouncing the establishment and in advocating the fullest freedom in religious concerns, Jefferson drew on his experience as well as his philosophy.

Theological differences played a part in Jefferson's early alienation from the Virginia Church; but the Church was notably indifferent to theology in any case, so it could not have contributed materially to his growing disaffection. He came to oppose the union of Church and State in any form or dogma; and as the abuses of the Anglican connection more and more pressed upon him, he targeted it for dissolution in the holy cause of the Revolution. A pernicious colonial survival, the establishment in his eyes served neither religion nor liberty. The clergy, weak, indolent, and ineffectual, shared the worst vices of the community. "It is a melancholy fact," recalled a leading churchman of the next generation, "that many of them had been addicted to the race-field, the card-table, the ball room, the theatre—nay, more, to the drunken revel." The Church had failed in its moral and spiritual mission. Largely for that reason, and despite its privileged status, as Jefferson observed, a majority of Virginians were dissenters on the eve of the Revolution. The offices of some of the parishes had actually been taken over by dissenters. Such anomalies made a mockery of the establishment. Possessing little intrinsic strength, the Church depended all the more on the support of civil authority, which was extrinsic in its nature. First, on the faintly aristocratic governing bodies of the parishes, the vestries, which levied tithes, looked after church property, cared for the poor, and so on. Second, on protective statutes such as required religious services according to the articles of the Church of England, restricted marriage to its forms, and punished heresy. Finally, and ultimately, on the ecclesiastical authority of the Crown. Independence abolished the latter. Practically, it had never been important. The establishment had always been essentially colonial rather than imperial, and not even Jefferson made it one of the grounds of revolt against Britain. Yet political independence was a calamity for the Church. At least one-third of the Anglican ministers affirmed their loyalty to Britain, while still others silently opposed the patriots. In New England, on the other hand, the Congregational clergy enlisted in the cause of liberty. What subtracted from the Church's strength added to the power and prestige of the strangely allied forces marshaled under the banner of religious freedom.

The Baptists, numbering in excess of five thousand, formed the spearhead of sectarian opposition. Whether in spite of persecution or because of it, they had grown remarkably during the previous decade. Writing to a friend in Pennsylvania in 1774, the young Madison bemoaned "the state and liberty of my country," citing the imprisonment of five or six Baptist preachers in neighboring Culpeper. "That diabolical Hell conceived principle of persecution rages among some and to their eternal infamy the Clergy can furnish their quota of imps for such business." These preachers were of a particularly enthusiastic Baptist sect, the Separates. Their revivalistic style of preaching, their coarse and provocative manners, their itinerant ministry, their appeal to the poor and ignorant combined to make them obnoxious not only to easygoing Virginians of the Anglican faith but to the less zealous, better-educated Presbyterians and old-style Baptists as well. "They cannot meet a man upon the road but they must ram a text of Scripture down his throat," said a prosecutor of these evangelists. The invariable charge against them was "disturbance of the peace." Under the English Act of Toleration, which legally extended to Virginia, dissenting Protestants were permitted to hold religious services provided their ministers and places of worship were registered. Most dissenters were content to work within the generous limits of the Act of Toleration. But the Separate Baptists, not finding them convenient, willfully violated the regulations society thought necessary for its peace and order, thereby furnishing the civil magistrates, prodded by the Anglican clergy, the handle of their persecution. In 1772 they began petitioning the House of Burgesses for religious freedom.

Jefferson became an outright champion of this cause in 1776. Prior to independence he had followed with concern the developments in the religious life of Virginia and unquestionably given a good deal of thought and study to the relationship between civil and ecclesiastical authority. His little essay on the fraudulent incorporation of Christianity into the common law has been noted. "We might as well say that the Newtonian system of philosophy is a part of the common law, as that the Christian religion is," he declared. As usual with him, history proved a convenient handmaid of his convictions. When he came to advocate the cause in the assembly he drew upon formidable legal and historical knowledge. Among his papers are several of the "scraps" he worked from: a list of the acts of Parliament and of the Virginia assembly concerning religion, a series of notes and observations on these acts, notes on episcopacy, on heresy, and so on. These notes, together with an abstract of Locke's views, formed the basis of a speech, probably delivered in November 1776, which compressed his whole philosophy of the subject.

Jefferson did not often rise to address the House, nor was he an eloquent speaker; but when the principle was as important as this one, he wished to expose it thoroughly to view, and the known strength of his ideas assured him a careful hearing. He first discussed the injuries of the establishment, with a detailed accounting of the statutory oppressions inseparable from it. Heresy might be punished by death; denial of the Trinity was punishable, on the third offense, by three years' imprisonment; Unitarians and free-thinkers might be declared unfit parents and have their children taken from them; Roman Catholics were excluded from the mantle of toleration and burdened with legal disabilities; periodic church attendance was compulsory; profanity carried a fine of ten pounds for each offense; and so on. Yet, Jefferson observed, "most men imagine that persecution is unknown to our laws." He conceded that the statutes were dead letters for the most part. There were a few Virginians—Catholics, Unitarians, heretics—on whom the penalties might fall. "Happily, the spirit of the times is in favor of the rights of conscience." But when was this ever a sufficient reliance? "Everyone should know under what law he lives, and should not be obliged to recur to the spirit of the times for protection." Now, while the spirit was sound and union against the common enemy a necessity, now was the time to fix every right on firm foundations. Over one-half the inhabitants were dissenters from the Church they were nevertheless taxed to support, and despite the voluntary support many gave to the ministries of their choice. This, too, was a form of persecution. What kind of attachment might these people feel toward a government that so flagrantly, and in the face of declared principle, discriminated against them? Political realism as well as abstract right demanded that all religions be placed on a footing of freedom and equality.

Jefferson then posed this fundamental question: "Has the state a right to adopt an opinion in matters of religion?" His answer was an unequivocal no. The conclusion followed logically from the contract theory of government. Men unite in government to secure those rights they cannot secure themselves. The rights of conscience are not submitted to civil authority, first, because men are answerable for them solely to God, and second, because their exercise does no injury to others. Jefferson later gave memorable statement to the principle in the *Notes on Virginia*: "The legitimate powers of government extend to such acts only as are injurious to others. But it does me no injury for my neighbor to say there are twenty gods or no god. It neither picks my pocket, nor breaks my leg." In all this and more he simply followed Locke, particularly the first *Letter Concerning Toleration*. But as Jefferson observed in his "Notes on Locke," the great Whig failed to push his principles to conclusion, declining to extend freedom to Catholics, atheists, and some others. "It was a great thing to go so far . . . but where he stopped short, we may go on." Significantly, Jefferson, with Madison and others of the liberal persuasion, dropped the term *toleration*, which implied an official and preferred religion, in favor of the term *liberty*. The religious liberty advocated in 1776 involved both freedom *from* the privileges and oppressions of a state church and freedom *to* worship according to the dictates of conscience without legal hindrance or discrimination of any kind.

Irrespective of the question of right, as Jefferson went on to show, the intervention of government in the affairs of religion was neither necessary nor advantageous to either one. Some men feared the consequences of government showing religion to the door, turning it out like a pauper to struggle in the world of ideas, both sacred and profane, for a place in the minds of men. Such men hungered for Truth infallible and absolute. But it would forever elude them, Jefferson warned. "Millions of innocent men, women and children, since the introduction of Christianity, have been burnt, tortured, fined, and imprisoned; yet we have not advanced one inch towards uniformity. What has been the effect of coercion? To make one half the world fools, and the other half hypocrites." The history of progress in religion as in philosophy was the history of the march of free inquiry and private judgment against the coercion and error of public authority. "It is error alone which needs the support of government," Jefferson declared. "Truth can stand by itself." Religious differences were beneficial to the peace and order of society: "The several sects perform the office of a *censor morum* over each other." They were equally beneficial to religion, setting up a virtuous competition among the sects and forcing them to develop their own resources rather than to depend on external support.

. . . The first contest in the assembly ended in a halfway measure. Dissenters of every description declined to stop there. During the next several years they kept the initiative and, propelled increasingly by the force of an idea, pressed the assembly to finish the work. The next victory came in 1779; repeal of the laws requiring members of the Anglican Church to contribute to its support. This pushed the establishment into irretrievable ruin, though vestiges of its exclusive status remained for a time. An act of the assembly in 1780 legalized marriages performed by non-Anglican clergy, and it was later liberalized in 1784 to overcome Baptist objections. The vestries continued for some years yet to discharge civil functions, such as the care of the poor. Not until 1802 were the parishes deprived of glebe lands for the support of the clergy.

These were details. Much more important was the new ground of contest: government support of Christianity as the established religion of the Commonwealth. Religious freedom being extended to all citizens, all sects and persuasions being put on an equal footing, churchmen and some other religionists, with strong political backing, called for a general assessment of all citizens for the support of all Christian ministers. The act of 1776 had specifically reserved this question for later decision. And in 1779, after the doom of the old establishment, its friends introduced the first general assessment bill. They sought thereby to prop up the decaying edifice of the Anglican Church, but the scheme committed them to a principle of far greater import. Historically, in America and throughout the Christian world, "the establishment of religion" meant official sanction and support of a single state church. In the course of religious controversy in Virginia, however, the concept acquired a new meaning: state encouragement and support of Christianity without preference as to sect.

The position staked out by liberals and dissenters in the early stages of the controversy was sufficient to meet the new challenge. Of course, their arguments had been directed against the existing establishment, and none of Jefferson's statements on record emphatically barred simple tax support of different faiths without discrimination. Yet this was the whole tone and tenor of his doctrine. If required to be more explicit about it, he certainly would be, and without revising anything. He believed with Locke that religion consists in "the *inward* persuasion of the mind," that a church is "a *voluntary* society of men," and that the jurisdiction of civil government cannot extend to either. He was far too sophisticated in his views of government, far too convinced of the tenderness of the private conscience, to believe that religious liberty, so conceived, could be secured under the patronage of the state. He would have been equally opposed to the introduction of government support for all religions—the Jewish, the Mohammedan, the Hindu with the Christian—though such a program would have overcome powerful objections of another kind. "Hands off" was the only acceptable policy. Thus Jefferson's doctrine necessarily involved *the separation of church and state,* even if none of the reformers had yet uttered that doctrine.

Still, men who conceded the injustice of a state church might see nothing unjust or illogical in a general establishment of religion, all supporting the minister or church of their choice. It was partly to close off this fortuitous development that Jefferson drafted his Bill for Religious Freedom. Drawn in 1777 as part of the Revision of the Laws, it was not introduced in the House until two years later. The delay was probably a question of timing. The first protests against the "general assessment" plan reached the Assembly in the spring of 1777, and it was discussed in subsequent sessions, but the time grew ripe for it only after the old establishment was disposed of. Neither Jefferson's bill nor the first version of the plan to establish the Christian religion could command a majority in 1779 or for several years to come. The issue was well understood by the people. The contending principles and measures were identified with the two giants of Virginia politics, Jefferson and Henry. Starting as a champion against the Church, the famous orator came around to the cause of churchmen and conservatives like Pendleton and Nicholas without, in his opinion, the least change of principle. In 1784 the assembly entered upon the climactic stage of the long controversy. It called up a bill, principally sponsored by Henry, to levy "a moderate tax or contribution annually for the support of the Christian religion, or for some Christian church, denomination or communion of Churches, or for some form of Christian worship." The bill, somewhat more liberal than its predecessor, justified government support of religion not on any grounds of ecclesiastical authority but on the recognized power of the state to diffuse knowledge (Christian knowledge in this case), restrain vice, and preserve the peace of society. The idea that the state might thus, in the name of peace and morals, do what it could not do in the name of religion seemed to underscore the need to raise a wall of separation between church and state. The old dissenter coalition of rationalists and sectarians— the Presbyterians alone wavering for a time—blocked passage of the bill in 1784 and, under Madison's vigorous leadership, defeated it in 1785.

Seeking to cap the climax, Madison then brought forward Jefferson's Bill for Religious Freedom.

As Jefferson reflected in his autobiography, he had drawn the bill "in all the latitude of reason and right" regardless of principles that might already have been established in law. Like the Declaration of Independence, to which it was a corollary, the great statute had more importance as an eloquent manifesto than as substantive legislation. But while the Declaration might be criticized for want of passion, the Statute for Religious Freedom burned with an ardor that belied mere rationality. Jefferson poured into the preamble—four times the length of the act itself—all his rage against the cant, the falsehood, the hypocrisy, the self-righteousness, the corruption, and the tyranny associated with the history of the alliance between Church and State. He did not stop with the assertion that it is "sinful and tyrannical" to compel a man to support opinions he disbelieves, but argued, no doubt with the assessment plan in mind, "that even the forcing him to support this or that teacher of his own religious persuasion" deprives him of liberty and the ministry of "incitement to earnest and unremitting labours for the instruction of mankind." He condemned religious tests and discriminations. He roundly declared "that the opinions of men are not the object of civil government, nor under its jurisdiction." The assembly struck this clause, but the statute in its entirety made evident how far the general cause of intellectual liberty—freedom of mind—was involved in Jefferson's argument for religious liberty. Of all men's convictions those of a religious nature were the most tender, most subjective, most private, and therefore, Jefferson believed, the least subject to authority or compulsion of any degree.

After several amendments which Madison termed "frivolous," the bill passed into law on January 16, 1786. Apparently no objection was raised to the enacting clause, only to the radical preamble. The legal effect of the statute was to make positive and unambiguous what had heretofore been the result of essentially negative actions, such as repeal laws and the defeat of the general assessment scheme. Never satisfied to leave fundamental rights to the hazard of statute, Jefferson had added an unusual final clause declaring that, though the act could not bind succeeding legislatures, nevertheless "if any act shall be hereafter passed to repeal the present or to narrow its operation, such act will be an infringement of natural right." Succeeding assemblies heeded the admonition. Reporting the conclusion of the campaign in which he shared equal honors with his friend in France, Madison grandly announced that the statute "extinguished forever the ambitious hope of making laws for the human mind."

The fame of the Virginia Statute for Religious Freedom rapidly spread beyond American shores. No other act of legislation so pointedly enforced the reality of the American Revolution on the enlightened heads of Europe. . . .

Churchmen then and for generations after openly, charged that Jefferson was motivated by hostility to the Episcopal Church and, indeed, to all Christian profession or religious life of any kind. Nothing could be more mistaken. As a philosopher has said, "The power and eloquence of Jefferson's writings on religious freedom is due largely to his evident religious devotion." Unlike the anti-clericalism of the Old world, his hatred of establishments and priesthoods did not involve him in hatred of religion. He wished for himself, for all his countrymen, not freedom from religion but freedom to pursue religion wherever reason and conscience led, and the more sensitive and upright the pursuit the more respect it won from him. He attempted to say as much but, of course, the onus of his public work and utterance was on the side of tearing down, so he must appear to many as a mere destroyer of religion. His own deepest convictions he kept to himself, nor did the public know of the generous support he gave to various churches throughout his life. In 1777, for example, he subscribed six pounds to the annual support of the Reverend Charles Clay, St. Anne's Parish, Charlottesville. Jefferson may have had no personal call for the Reverend Mr. Clay's services but his neighbors did. His contribution—nearly twice the amount subscribed by any other parishioner—proved Jefferson's readiness to accept the consequences of his own principle: the voluntary support of churches and ministers.

In the liberality of his mind, as in his entire personality and background, Jefferson obviously had more in common with the mild and genial Episcopalians than with the evangelical Baptists and "New Light" Presbyterians who furnished the battalions for the campaign generaled by Madison and himself. It was a strange alliance: rationalists and enthusiasts, secularists and sectarians, skeptics and believers united by their common opposition to the established order. They were able to co-operate, in part, because they were so far apart, appeals to reason giving no practical trouble to sectaries who relied on the converting presence of the Holy Spirit. Thus by the unique logic of American history the seekers after God and the seekers after enlightenment were allies in liberty. Some of Jefferson's friends, like his boyhood chum John Page, were stunned by his stubborn support of the "bigoted and illiberal" folk after they had stolen the flocks and disrobed the shepherds of the "rational sect." "Nothing but a general assessment can prevent the State from being divided between immorality and enthusiastic bigotry," Page told Jefferson. The warning carried a partial truth, as Jefferson would discover in the course of time. Whatever the long-run effect of the newer sects on Virginia piety and morality, they were to do irreparable injury to the state's reputation for liberality and enlightenment. Yet even had Jefferson calculated this loss, it could have had no weight with him. "Reason and free inquiry are the only effectual agents against error." What he shared with Baptist ranters was more fundamental than his intellectual distaste for them. He looked to schools, not to churches, to improve the mass of people. Moreover, while Page with so many others thought the old church would go steadily downhill without public support, Jefferson's belief in the salubrity of freedom promised a better future for the Episcopalians. Viewing the progress several decades later, Bishop William Meade observed that "nothing could have been more injurious to the cause of true religion in the Episcopal Church, or to its growth in any way, than the continuance of either stipend or glebes." The revival of the Church commenced, Meade thought, when she was "thrown upon her own resources."

Jefferson's motives on the side of religion were entirely creditable, yet it would be quite erroneous to imply that he was motivated primarily by concern for religion. Religious freedom absorbed him most earnestly where it intersected intellectual freedom. The martyrs of science and philosophy, rather than the martyrs of religion, won his highest admiration. Both sectarian religionists and secular liberals sought separation of church and state; but the former feared most the power of the state to corrupt and tyrannize the church, while the latter feared, above all, the inquisitorial tendencies of the church. Religion and philosophy in all their amplitude do not comprehend the earnestness of Jefferson's purpose, however. A republican statesman who had made "the pursuit of happiness" his creed, he believed that the "voluntary system" would tend to produce loyalty in the state, moderation in the government, and peace and harmony in the society. The circumstances of war and revolution and nation-building gave an urgency to considerations of this kind. Writing to Jefferson in 1779 the Reverend John Todd, a leader of the famed Hanover Presbytery, stated the shared conviction "that people of different sentiments in religion will be all one in their love and fidelity to the State which secures to them everything dear and valuable: and the more catholic and friendly one to another, and free from *pride* and *envy* when the State rewards all men according to their merit." Two years later Jefferson thought the experiment had proved itself in New York and Pennsylvania, more varied religiously than Virginia. Unparalleled harmony prevailed amidst widest diversity. "They have made the happy discovery, that the way to silence religious disputes, is to take no notice of them." It would not prove quite so simple, but the history of American society justified his optimism.

Education

The backbone of Jefferson's republic was a system of public education. "If a nation expects to be ignorant and free in a state of civilization, it expects what never was and never will be," he once observed. The state of civilization being one of organization and power, of progress and improvement, it demanded commensurate means of enlightenment. Without the diffusion of knowledge through all the ranks of society, adapted to its different degrees and conditions, individuals could neither attend to their own happiness nor, as citizens, secure the freedom and the welfare of the state. It was axiomatic with Jefferson that the people were the only safe depository of their rights and liberties, always provided, however, that they were adequately informed and instructed. Education was too important a matter to be left to chance. It must be planned and carried out as a paramount responsibility of republican government.

Jefferson's "quixotism for the diffusion of knowledge," as he styled it, thus sprang from his political principles. The men of his class, favored by wealth and family, educated at private hands, had brought the country to freedom and self-government amidst colossal ignorance. There were no schools for children of the common people. Too many were raised up in the ignorance in which they were born. Much of Virginia was but a step or two removed from the reckless, brawling frontier, where education was a luxury and communal responsibility unformed, while the settled eastern portion was dominated by an haughty aristocracy notably more conscious of its rights than of its social obligations. Except for slavery, which added to the problem but raised peculiar dangers of its own, the ignorance and torpor of the people presented the main obstacle to the success of the republican experiment. . . .

. . . He projected three distinct grades of education—elementary, middle, and higher—the whole rising like a pyramid from the local communities. The latter, unfortunately, had almost no existence in Virginia. Jefferson proposed to create them. Counties would be laid off into *hundreds,* or *wards,* each of a size and population suitable for the maintenance of an elementary school. "At these schools all the free children, male and female, resident within the respective hundred, shall be entitled to receive tuition gratis, for a term of three years, and as much longer, at their private expense, as their parents, guardians or friends, shall think proper." Of course, the schools would teach reading, writing, and arithmetic. The aims of primary education included moral improvement, the acquisition of skills necessary for the common personal and business transactions of life, and instruction in the rights and duties of citizens. The last of these particularly absorbed his attention in 1778; and he specifically directed instruction in the history and experience of other ages and nations so that young citizens may come to recognize tyranny in embryo and exert themselves to crush it. Instead of drawing their moral lessons from the Bible, the children were to take the histories of Greece, Rome, Europe, and America as their texts. The Bible called for more mature judgment than children possessed, and was precluded in any event in a secular state. History furnished a secular guide to morality and promised to be even more useful as a monitor of the civil polity. "History, by apprizing them [the children] of the past, will enable them to judge of the future . . . it will qualify them as judges of the actions and designs of men; it will enable them to know ambition under every disguise it may assume; and knowing it, to defeat its views." This was expecting a good deal of the judgment of children! Jefferson was no Rousseau. His knowledge of the psychology and the learning pocesses of children was never very great. The design of an educational system deeply interested him; the theory of teaching it embodied clearly did not. He simply assumed with Locke that young minds were formed by the impressions passed before them, hence the right curriculum could make the right kind of citizens. Children were but incipient adults to him. . . .

Above the hundred schools, freely educating all children, were the grammar schools, twenty in all, laid off in districts embracing several counties. These schools were also to be maintained by the state; however, most of the pupils coming from homes "in easy circumstances," they would be charged tuition and board. The exceptions were the "public foundationers," perhaps sixty or seventy of the most promising geniuses, who, being also from poor families, would be annually chosen after rigorous examinations in the lower schools and awarded, in effect, state scholarships. One-third of these scholars would be eliminated after the first year's instruction, the remainder after two years, excepting the best scholar of each school, who would be at liberty to continue four more years. "By this means," Jefferson wrote of his ingenious selection system, "twenty of the best geniuses will be raked from the rubbish annually, and be instructed, at the public expense, so far as grammar schools go." And they would go to the teaching of the classical languages, English grammar, geography, and the higher branches of mathematics. At the top of the pyramid stood the College of William and Mary, which Jefferson sought by a companion bill to convert into a state university offering instruction in all the sciences. Every year ten seniors "of the best learning and most hopeful genius and disposition" would be chosen from the grammar schools of the state to be sent to the university, "there to be educated, boarded, and clothed, three years" on the public account. . . .

Nothing came of this bill, but in 1779, when he became Governor, Jefferson was elected a visitor of the College, and he attempted in this capacity to make some limited progress toward his objectives. Restrained by the charter to six professorships, he succeeded in replacing three of them, in Divinity, Oriental Languages, and Greek and Latin, with professorships in Law and Government, Anatomy and Medicine, and Modern Languages. (Jefferson favored instruction in the ancient languages but felt it belonged to the academy or grammar school.) One of the professorships, called the Brafferton after the estate of its English donor, would be transformed from its stated mission, the conversion of the Indians to Christianity, into a kind of anthropological chair for the study of the American Indians. These changes struck very advanced secular and utilitarian notes in keeping with the idea of a university rather than a college. Their actual effect was small, however, and the assembly never got around to revising the charter or acting on other parts of Jefferson's bill. Nothing could erase the College's reputation as a Church institution. "The religious jealousies, therefore, of all the dissenters, took alarm lest this [the bill] might give an ascendancy to the Anglican sect . . . ," Jefferson accurately reported. "Its local eccentricity, too, and the unhealthy outward climate, lessened the general inclination toward it." Finally, the success of his own measure for removing the capital from Williamsburg hurt the College by severing its connections with the seat of government. Decades later, when Jefferson revived his dream of a university, he brushed aside the claims of his alma mater and built from the ground up.

. . . The leading objections to the plan were "1. the expense, which was alleged to exceed the ability of the people. 2. the difficulty of executing it in the present sparse settlement of the Country." The objections mortgaged the future to exigencies of the present. Virginia *was* poor. But she would grow poorer still without the education of her people. The plan *was* impractical for large parts of the state. Each hundred was supposed to cover an area of five or six square miles at most—children could not be expected to traverse a greater distance daily—but many such areas had but a scattering of people. Yet the bill might have been revised to take account of this problem. There were still other objections, for the plan reached deep into the society and touched a number of sensitive interests. Religionists generally distrusted its secularism, while the Presbyterians in particular opposed the influence of William and Mary over the schools. The bill posed a threat to the country courts by the creation of potentially new units of local government, the hundreds or wards, with popularly elected officials called aldermen to administer the schools and perform other duties, such as poor relief and tax assessment, which were assigned to them by other bills of the revisal. Taxation to support the schools would fall most heavily on the propertied class, and from a purely selfish viewpoint the rich felt no interest in paying for the education of the poor. Whatever the reasons for the defeat of the plan, it was a terrible disappointment to Jefferson. ''I think by far the most important bill in our whole code is that for the diffusion of knowledge among the people,'' he wrote to Wythe from France, which he thought the best school in the universe to cure Americans of the folly of seeking public happiness without public enlightenment. ''Preach, my dear Sir, a crusade against ignorance; establish and improve the law for educating the common people,'' he implored. ''Let our countrymen know . . . that the tax which will be paid for this purpose is not more than the thousandth part of what will be paid to kings, priests and nobles who will rise up among us if we leave the people in ignorance.''

Regardless of defeat, Jefferson's Bill for the More General Diffusion of Knowledge was a landmark in the history of American education. The principle of public education was not new: common schools had existed in New England for generations. In fact, the principal difficulty of Jefferson's plan was the attempt to introduce a system borrowed from the close-knit town environment of New England into the spread-out rural environment of Virginia. But the plan broke sharply with the essentially religious ideal of New England education, substituting for it the citizen-republicanism of the new nation. Public responsibility for the enlightenment of the people was founded in the interest all men felt in freedom and self-government. Also significant was the conception of a complete and unified educational system, from the common schools at the bottom to the university at the top. There were no models for this, and whatever the possible literary sources of the idea—John Knox's sixteenth-century Scottish Presbyterian *Book of Discipline* has been suggested—it appears to have been an independent product of Jefferson's republican imagination. Three years of elementary education—all that Jefferson's plan guaranteed—seems very niggardly by modern standards, which must also condemn omission of the compulsory principle. But that principle was unheard of for many years yet, and a larger commitment to common schooling would have been hopelessly unrealistic. Jefferson perhaps would not have advocated it in any event. He did not believe the mass of citizens either required or were susceptible to education at advanced levels. But nature had sown talent and energy as liberally among the poor as the rich. As Sir William Perry had observed a century earlier, "many are now holding the plough which might have been made fit to steer the state." The state had an obligation both to nature and to itself to prevent these abilities from running to waste. Jefferson's selection scheme aimed to scale education to merit; and he unreservedly placed the state on the side of talent by proposing to tax the entire community for the education of its most promising offspring of adversity. An audacious experiment indeed! It carried elitist overtones, though it was no part of Jefferson's purpose to establish an elite, even a natural one. Unfortunately, the current neologism of the educators, "meritocracy," did not occur to him, for that is precisely what he had in mind when he spoke of "natural aristocracy." The ideal could find no place in the democratic ideology of public education in nineteenth-century America, and only recently have educators begun to catch up with it.

[Slavery]

Next to education as a means of improving the lot of his countrymen, Jefferson set his heart on the eradication of slavery. But he never underestimated the resistance he would meet on this question, and he would let it lie rather than risk the loss of all power of accomplishment by untimely advocacy of so arduous a cause. He had warmly denounced the African slave trade in his draft of the Declaration of Independence. His proposed constitution for Virginia prohibited holding in slavery any person henceforth coming into the country. In 1778 the assembly, while not going this far, slammed the door on the foreign slave trade. Although Jefferson's authorship of the statute cannot be definitely established, he claimed responsibility for it and there is no one else to whom it can be as fairly assigned. The original bill sought to encourage the private manumission of slaves, which existing law made virtually impossible, and firmly declared an anti-slavery position. As enacted the statute simply raised a bar to foreign importation.

The greater question of emancipation came before the revisers in connection with the codification of colonial slave laws. The bill they reported, and the assembly enacted after several amendments in 1785, contained no provision for emancipation and was for the most part "a mere digest" of the old laws. The principal difference lay in the limits set to the increase of slaves by confining this status henceforth to the descendants of female slaves currently in Virginia. The provision alone, by limiting the source of replenishment, would have gone some way toward eliminating slavery. As finally enacted, the bill did not have this effect. The revisers, according to Jefferson, prepared a plan of gradual emancipation under which all the slaves born after the passage of the act would become free at the age of adulthood and be colonized outside the limits of Virginia. "It was thought better that this should be kept back," Jefferson later wrote, "and attempted only by way of amendment, whenever the bill should be brought up." But, of course, he was abroad when the bill came up, and the amendment was never offered, perhaps because, as he observed, "the public mind would not yet bear the proposition." While he continued to favor the plan of gradual emancipation, first published in the *Notes on Virginia* in 1785, neither he nor any other prominent Virginian was ever willing to risk friends, position, and influence to fight for it. . . .

Perhaps he attempted too much too soon. Disappointed by mindless and selfish opposition to reform, he had need of the philosophy commended to an impatient cohort a dozen years later: "the ground of liberty is to be gained by inches . . . we must be contented to secure what we can get from time to time, and eternally press forward for what is yet to get. It takes time to persuade men to do even what is for their own good." What he sought, most of all, was to create a more favorable public climate for the freedom and happiness of his countrymen. In order to create, it was first necessary to destroy—feudal holdovers, aristocratic privileges, the religious establishment. But Jefferson was not a happy destroyer and the balance of his effort was on the constructive side. Freedom was many things—suffrage and representation, land and mobility, education and learning—all interwoven in his republican design. . . .

. . . It may be misleading to label him liberal or conservative, democratic or aristocratic, radical or moderate, for he was all these things in degrees and in different contexts. He called himself a Whig, which is the historical term, in America, that best describes his political outlook. He was a Whig, however, in a revolutionary situation, when there was both the opportunity and the determination to embody principles in the foundations of a new experiment. Embarked in this way, exalting reason, striking at privilege, opening rights, and releasing talents, Jefferson's direction was inescapably democratic in the line of American progress.

Southern Women and the Revolution

MARY BETH NORTON

I

Before one can assess the impact of the Revolution on southern women, one must begin by outlining the patterns of women's lives in the South in the years prior to the war. Those lives centered largely upon the household. Without today's—or even the nineteenth century's—labor-saving devices, female colonists had to spend the vast majority of their time caring for the needs of their families. But just as the economic conditions, geographic locations, and sizes of colonial households varied, so, too, did the duties and roles of the women within those households. For the purposes of this

From "What an Alarming Crisis Is This?" by Mary Beth Norton in *The Southern Experience in the American Revolution*, ed. by Jeffrey Crow and Larry Tise, pp. 204–219, 220–227. Reprinted by permission of the author.

analysis, it is best to distinguish three separate types of households in which southern women led quite different lives: first, the rural homes of the poorer and "middling" parts of the white population; second, the urban households inhabited by members of the same group; and third, the large, multiracial households (whether rural or urban) that contained both the wealthiest whites and the black Americans who served them, the latter usually constituting a numerical majority of the family.

Because poorer and middling southern women frequently were illiterate, or, if able to write, rarely were called upon to do so, historians seeking to study their lives must turn to the accounts of observers and to the records of their dealings with governments to gain insight into the conditions of their existence. In rural areas, such an investigation shows, white women worked in the fields or tended livestock in addition to caring for their houses and children. When Oliver Hart, a lonely South Carolinian separated from his wife by the war, daydreamed about her, he told her he saw her "on my Farm, busying yourself with your Poultry, traveling the Fields, admiring the Flocks and Herds, or within, managing the Dairy." That his characterization of his wife's role was accurate is revealed not only by the statements of such persons as the tutor Philip Vickers Fithian, who noticed white women planting corn in Virginia fields, but also by the contents of claims submitted by female refugees after the war to the loyalist claims commission in London. Rural women demonstrated a wide-ranging knowledge of farm tools and livestock, while admitting their ignorance of many aspects of their husbands' financial affairs. Their knowledge, in effect, revealed the dimensions of their lives. The Georgian Janet Russell, for example, mentioned that she regularly milked thirty-two cows and noted that she had counted the sheep on her farm "a few days before she came away." She and other rural southern loyalist women submitted claims documents that included long lists of the dishes and utensils they handled daily, of the spinning wheels and looms they occasionally operated, of the foodstuffs they prepared and stored, of the livestock they helped to feed, and of the clothing, linens, and furniture that were their prize possessions.

The lives they led were hard and exhausting, with little respite or relief. The Reverend Charles Woodmason, an itinerant Anglican clergyman who traveled extensively in the Carolina backcountry, commented that the people there ate "fat rusty Bacon" and corn bread; lived in "open Logg Cabbins with hardly a Blanket to cover them"; and wore but scanty clothing and no shoes or stockings. He noted that the women were "so burthen'd with Young Children" that they could not "attend both House and Field," thus confirming the work demands made on rural women and recognizing that in many cases they were unable to meet them. One wonders how many rural white women were like the mother of a boy (the fourth of eight children) born on a Shenandoah Valley farm in 1769, whom he described thus: she "from my earliest recollection was weak & sickly . . . confined principally to her bed for the last two or three years of her life."

In the towns, there were no crops to plant, no herds of livestock to attend (though there might be a cow or a few chickens), and as a result the lives of women of the "middling sort" who resided in urban areas were somewhat different. They prepared the food, but instead of cultivating crops in the fields they raised produce in small kitchen gardens or purchased it at city markets. They cared for numerous children, but the children might attend small schools run by women much like themselves for part of the day. They spun some wool and linen thread, but were more likely to buy their cloth at local stores. They also were more likely to engage in business activities on their on. In rural areas, the only way women could make money was by taking in travelers or by doing some spinning or weaving for wealthier neighbors, but in towns women could work alongside their husbands in taverns or shops or run independent businesses. In Charleston, for example, William Brockie sold "Fruit & Garden stuff" and his wife Mary was a mantua maker; Katherine Williamson ran a grocery store while her husband Robert "worked at his Trade as a Bricklayer"; the widowed Janet Cumming made £400 annually as the most respected midwife in town; Eleanor Lestor took over her husband's liquor store after his death; and Mary and Robert Miller together kept a tavern. Most of these women were "in low life" (to use the phrase with which the claims commission described Mrs. Lestor), and they represented only a small proportion of the overall female population, but they led quite independent lives. When all the women just described became loyalist refugees, their experience in coping with manifold business problems stood them in good stead. . . .

The lives of the wealthiest group of southern white women differed markedly from those of the poorer and middling sort. Foreigners and northerners almost invariably described well-to-do southern women as "indolent" because of the combined effect of "their living in so warm a climate and being surrounded by such a multitude of slaves." But appearances were deceiving to a certain extent. Such women were freed from the more monotonous and onerous household duties by the labor of female slaves, but in exchange they had to superintend large and complex families. One Virginia wife, complaining of how she and her husband could not leave home, told a friend that she and her female neighbors were "almost in a State of vegitation" because they constantly had to "attend to the innumerable wants" of their multiracial households. Appropriately, these women commonly were described as "good managers" or "remarkable Economists." The skills they developed were those of command and of personnel management rather than of handwork and of "making do" with less than ample supplies of food or clothes.

They learned the habit of command early. In her diary, one little Virginia girl complained about the laziness of her black washerwoman and raged about a male slave who killed a cat: "a vile wretch of new negrows, if he was mine I would cut him to pieces, a son of a gun, a nice negrow, he should be kild himself by rites." A four-year-old North Carolina girl was described by a doting cousin as "strutting about in the yard after Susanna (whom she had ordered to do something) with her work in her hand & an Air of as much importance as if she had been Mistress of the family." As adults, such women were entirely capable of directing the many-faceted activities of a plantation household. Eliza Lucas's 1742 description of how she spent her days is instructive here. Arising at five o'clock, she read till seven, saw "that the Servants are at their respective business," then ate breakfast. Afterward she practiced music, studied, and taught her younger sister until dinner time. She again turned to her music, then to needlework, and finally in the evening once again read or wrote. Although Eliza Lucas may have been more insistent on early rising than her female contemporaries (she recorded that at least one woman neighbor warned that the practice would age her unnecessarily), the diaries and letters of other wealthy southern women show a similar daily pattern: giving orders to servants in the morning, doing needlework in the afternoons, and reading, writing, or playing music at various times during the day.

The labor of blacks allowed Eliza Lucas Pinckney and her counterparts to spend a good deal of time with their children. Unlike the poorer southern females, whose time had to be divided among a number of physically demanding tasks, well-to-do mothers (and fathers, too) could devote large amounts of their days to the care and education of their offspring. Mrs. Pinckney described the care of her daughter Harriott as "one of the greatest Businesses of my life," and she remarked upon the "pleasure it certainly is to cultivate the tender mind, to teach the young Idea how to shoot." Her attention to her eldest son Charles Cotesworth is well documented: by the time he was four months old she had decided "to teach him according to Mr. Locks method (which I have carefully studied) to play him self into learning." Her husband Charles made his son "a set of toys to teach him his letters," and by the age of twenty-two months Charles Cotesworth was so precocious that he "can tell all his letters in any book without hesitation and begins to spell." . . .

And what of the black women whose labor made all of this possible? Their lives differed in obvious ways from those of the whites, most notably, of course, in the inescapable fact of their servitude. But married women of all descriptions in the colonial South were, in a legal sense, "slaves" to their husbands, and white female servants sometimes worked alongside black women in both house and field. The tasks female slaves performed were equivalent to, if not exactly the same as, those done by the poorer and middling whites: they worked in the fields, prepared food, cared for children, and spun thread. But, significantly, specific individuals did not do all of these tasks, for the sheer size of plantation households meant that the work of slave women could be specialized in a way that that of poor white women could not. During her lifetime, a slave woman probably would serve her master and mistress in several capacities: as a youngster, she might spin or mind smaller children; as an able-bodied woman, she might work in the fields; as an older woman she might again spin, work as a house servant, or be a nurse or a midwife to both blacks and whites. But she would not engage in these tasks simultaneously. And on occasion a young girl would be singled out "to bring up in the House," or would show such aptitude for a particular job that she would be assigned to that task alone (as was Mulatto Milly, the "principal spinner" on John Hatley Norton's quarter in Fauquier County, Virginia). As a result, slave women living on large plantations had opportunities to acquire a level of skill that their white mistresses did not, and this may have contributed to the development of such self-confidence as that exhibited by "Miss Charlotte," an East Florida slave who in 1769 reacted to a dispute between two whites over who owned her, one of them reported, by "living with neither of us," but instead going "about from house to house," saying "now she's a free woman."

Slave women in the mid-eighteenth-century South, unlike the vast majority of female whites, lived in truly extended families, in which they, their siblings, parents, children, cousins, and more distant relatives daily worked alongside each other, and, moreover, often shared tasks and divided responsibilities. White women rarely had large kinship networks so readily available to them. That family ties played a major role in the lives of slave women is demonstrated by the records of planters and overseers, in which a constantly recurring theme is that of black females' unwillingness to be parted permanently from their relatives. Historians have demonstrated that runaway slaves often were seeking to reunite themselves with their families, and kinship ties also motivated many other movements of slaves. One Virginia planter, for example, told another that "Darby wants to Cum to liv with me and as his wife is not sattisfyed with out him" he would hire him. Similarly, there are numerous documented cases of slave mothers refusing to move unless they could be accompanied by their children and of husbands and wives being moved together, though the presence of only one of them was required at the new location.

Whether black or white, rich or poor, however, the lives of most colonial southern women can be summed up in one word: "circumscribed." All were tied down by the care of their families. The nature of that care varied, as did the size and racial composition of the households, but the women bore responsibility for the day-to-day familial routine. They rarely traveled, and the demands of their regular duties seldom allowed them to venture outside their domestic sphere, though the shape of that sphere varied according to their race, place of residence, and economic status. Foreign travelers noted this quality in southern white women: Maryland females, observed an Englishman in 1745, had "an Air of Reserve and somewhat that looks at first to a Stranger like Unsociableness," but was rather the "effect of living at a great Distance from frequent Society and their Thorough Attention to the Duties of their Stations." A Venezuelan commented nearly forty years later on North Carolinians that the "married women maintain a monastic seclusion and a submission to their husbands such as I have never seen; . . . their entire lives are domestic. Once married, they . . . devote themselves completely to the care of home and family."

It does not take much imagination to realize that women with little experience outside the confines of their households would find being in the midst of a disruptive civil war an unnerving experience. In the years after 1775, and especially in 1778 and thereafter, southern women had to cope with a myriad of unprecedented problems: armies on the march, guerrilla bands, runaway inflation, shortages of food and other supplies, epidemics spread by the military movements—all in the absence of the husbands, fathers, brothers, and sons they long had been told to look to for guidance. It was not an easy time.

II

Paradoxically, in light of the reputed paucity of sources for black history, it is easier to assess the impact of the Revolution on southern black women than on their white counterparts. This is essentially because to slaves the war brought a chance—a slim one, admittedly, but still a chance—for freedom. The Revolution, furthermore, by depriving planters of the British manufactured goods on which they previously had depended, also caused a significant rise in the production of cloth within plantation households. Thus some slave women were afforded the opportunity to develop new skills of spinning and weaving, and, by implication, perhaps gained somewhat greater independence and self-confidence.

Before the nonimportation movements of the 1760s and 1770s, most planters of the tidewater regions seem to have purchased "negro cloth" as well as fancier goods from British sources, using the labor of their female slaves in the fields instead of in textile production. But when cloth no longer could be obtained from England, many planters established "wool and linen manufactories." In October 1775, John Harrower, an indentured servant in Virginia, commented that for the first time "coarse linnen for Shirts to the Nigers" was being made on the plantation where he lived. Several months previously, Robert Carter had begun planning for what was to become a large "Linnen and Woolen Factory" at his Aries plantation, ordering an overseer to "sett a part, Ten black Females the most Expert spinners belonging to me—they to be Employed in Spinning, solely." By spring 1776, Carter had discovered that this work force was not sufficient to supply his needs, and he told another overseer to hire a woman to teach six more slave girls to spin, if his wife could not take on that task herself. In April 1782, Carter was employing twelve spinners at Aries under the direction of a female overseer, and in August 1791, even though English goods had long since again become available, he still had seven female spinners working at Aries, along with three male weavers.

Far more dramatic than the opening of this skilled occupation to slave women were the direct consequences of the war itself and, in particular, the results of British military policy regarding blacks. In November 1775, in an attempt to bolster his sagging cause, Lord Dunmore, the last royal governor of Virginia, issued a proclamation offering freedom to all blacks and indentured servants who would join him to fight the rebellion. Although only an estimated eight hundred slaves responded to Dunmore's call immediately, southern whites were terrified by the implications of the offer. One commented, "Hell itself could not have vomitted any thing more black than his design of emancipating our slaves." In July 1776, Robert Carter called together the black residents of his Coles Point plantation (which was dangerously situated on the Potomac) and suggested that Dunmore intended to sell those who joined him to West Indian planters. Carter's argument apparently dissuaded potential runaways at that time, but when the British army returned to Virginia in 1781 thirty-two of the Coles Point Negroes absconded during one nine-day period. Throughout the South, the story was the same: everywhere, the redcoats attracted slaves "in great numbers," according to the contemporary historian David Ramsay.

Although a majority of runaways were male, women apparently sought freedom in greater numbers during the war than in peacetime. Jefferson noted twenty-three who "joined British" in his farm book, twelve of whom were women, and one of whom took her three children with her. The South Carolinian John Ball listed the names of fifty-three runaways to the redcoats in his plantation accounts; of these, only fifteen were adult women (many of whom left with their children), but none returned voluntarily, whereas at leat ten of the men did. A woman named Charlotte may have instigated a mass escape. She originally fled on 10 May 1780, but "was brought home." A week later, however, she left again in company with fourteen other slaves, none of whom appears to have returned. That the sex ratios among runaways from the Jefferson and Ball plantations were not unusual is suggested by the lists of black evacuees prepared by British authorities at the end of the war. One Savannah list of 1,956 slaves is 41 percent male, 36 percent female, the remainder being children; and of the 3,000 blacks recorded as leaving New York City in 1783, 914 (or approximately 30 percent) were women.

Even when the blacks did not run off, all was not well from the owner's point of view. Thomas Pinckney reported to his mother Eliza that the only slaves left on his Ashepoo plantation after a British raid in May 1779 were pregnant women and small children, who "pay no Attention" to the overseer's orders and "who are now perfectly free & live upon the best produce of the Plantation." Mrs. Pinckney had similar problems with her slaves at Belmont: she wanted them to come to her daughter Harriott's Santee plantation, she told Tom, but they were "attached to their homes and the little they have there [and so] have refused to remove." She concluded that if the blacks wished to join the British, neither she nor anyone else could stop them, "for they all do now as they please everywhere." More than a year later she complained of how she had been "Rob'd and deserted" by her slaves, remarking that it was impossible even to raise money by selling them because the "slaves in this country in genl, have behaved so infamously and even those that remain'd at home so Insolent and quite their own masters that there are very few purchasers" who would take them.

Not all of the slaves who joined the British found freedom. Smallpox and camp fever were endemic in the British encampments, and many thousands of southern blacks died from those and other diseases. Of the runaways from Jefferson's plantations, only three (two men and a woman) seem to have joined the enemy and survived in freedom. Five more initially fled to the British, "returned & lived." The other fifteen died with the British or after they returned home, and Jefferson recorded the deaths of eleven more slaves as a result of disease caught from the returnees. Blacks who were the property of loyalists also ran the risk of being returned to their masters, and after the war it appears that some of the Negroes who were evacuated with the British army to the West Indies were sold as slaves. But although the British formally agreed at the evacuation of Charleston and in the provisional peace treaty of November 1782 that they would not carry slaves away belonging to Americans, the army proved extremely reluctant to return to servitude blacks who had sought its protection. One South Carolina planter, all of whose slaves were in Charleston with the redcoats, was reduced in autumn 1782 to the futile hope that "they will not have transports enough to carry the negroes off." In all, the British carried with them approximately four thousand from Savannah, six thousand from Charleston, and four thousand from New York City. After the war, white southerners estimated their total losses in slaves at more than fifty-five thousand.

If the British army attracted black Americans like a magnet, it repelled white Americans with similar force and efficiency. Everywhere the army went, fighting followed, and wherever there was fighting civilians, rebel and loyalist alike, left their homes to find places of greater safety. In January 1779, a South Carolinian told his brother, "the poor Georgians are flying over into this State, by Hundreds; many of them leaving their All behind." A few months later, as the British advanced northward, the people of his own state were experiencing "ravaging" and "Havoc." That year the revolutionaries successfully resisted the British invasion, but Charleston and much of South Carolina fell to royal forces in 1780. The victory did not bring peace to the province; quite the contrary. David Ramsay later recalled that after the surrender of Charleston," political hatred raged with uncommon fury, and the calamities of civil war desolated the State." Then it was North Carolina's turn, and Virginia's. In 1781, Cornwallis's incursion into the latter state sent "every body scampering," to use the words of the young Yorktown girl Betsy Ambler. "What an alarming crisis is this," she wrote to a friend as she and her family fled before the advancing redcoats. "War in itself, however distant, is indeed terrible, but when brought to our very doors . . . the reflection is indeed overwhelming."

In later years Betsy described her mother as having been especially "afflicted" by the family's repeated moves during the war; throughout the South white women had to endure similar hardships. Not only were many widowed by the war (reputedly there were 1,200 to 1,400 widows in the sparsely populated Ninety-Six district of South Carolina alone), but also they frequently had to face marauding troops and irregulars by themselves, since their husbands, fathers, and brothers were absent serving with one army or the other. Isolated in the countryside, groups of women and children gathered together for protection: at least twice during the war, for example, female friends of the Pinckney family sought refuge at Daniel and Harriott Horry's Santee plantation, and the wealthy widow Eliza Wilkinson, who lived in the sea islands south of Charleston, wrote of seeing "crowds of helpless, distressed women, weeping for husbands, brothers, or other near relations and friends, who were they knew not where, whether dead or alive." According to Mrs. Wilkinson, when the British moved through her neighborhood en route to Charleston in 1779, there were "nothing but women, a few aged gentlemen, and (shame to tell) a few skulking varlets" to oppose them. . . .

For most well-to-do slaveholding whites like Mrs. Wilkinson, such troubles were unprecedented. Raised in luxury, accustomed to the constant attention and service of slaves, many were unprepared to cope with the situation in which they found themselves, and they recognized their own lack of resiliency. After the war, once-wealthy southern loyalist women frequently referred to the fact that they had been "accustomed to the Indulgence of Fashion & Fortune," had been "nurtured in the Lap of Affluence," or had been "born and breed to Affluence and indulgences of the tenderst Nature," when each explained her lack of success in handling "difficultys of which she had no experience in her former life."

Contrast to this the behavior of southern women who had had previous experience in handling "difficultys," many of whom were of the poorer or middling sorts. They, too, encountered problems of unprecedented magnitude, but they—especially the urban businesswomen—seemed to land on their feet more often than their wealthier neighbors, and they were more willing to take the initiative and to act positively instead of sitting back passively waiting for the worst to happen.

Thus in 1780 a rural North Carolina woman impulsively followed her husband's militia unit to a battlefield, where she cared for the wounded of both sides until she learned he was unhurt. A Maryland carpenter's wife, whose drunken husband had enlisted on a privateer, physically resisted the marines who came for him and caused such an uproar by calling the recruiting officer "every vile name she could think of" that her husband was allowed to remain at home. Eleanor Lestor, the widowed Charleston shopkeeper, hid British sailors in her house and spoke "freely" against the rebel cause, and another "she-merchant" from Charleston, Elizabeth Thompson, assisted British prisoners of war, carried letters through the lines, and drove a disguised British spy through the American camp in her own chaise. Other women like these followed their husbands to the armies of both sides and, though they lost many of their meager possessions, managed to surmount innumerable difficulties. The amazing saga of Susannah Marshall is a case in point. She and her loyalist husband William ran a tavern and boarding house in Baltimore before the war, until the rebels forced him to flee to the West Indies. She continued to operate their business, though the rebels looted the house, quartered troops in it, and prevented her from collecting from her debtors. In 1776 she chartered a ship to sail to Norfolk to join Lord Dunmore, but he had left the area by the time she arrived. Sailing back up Chesapeake Bay to Head of Elk, she there acquired another tavern and the local ferry concession. Allowed to leave the state in 1777, Mrs. Marshall invested her money in a cargo of foodstuffs, chartered another ship, and once again set sail. En route to the West Indies her ship was captured by the Americans, then recaptured by a royal cruiser. Since the cargo had been in the possession of rebels, it was forfeited under British law, and Mrs. Marshall salvaged nothing. Finally, she made her way to England, only to learn that her husband had died and to have her petition for a loyalist pension rejected by the authorities. Undaunted, she went to work as a nurse to support her family and in 1789 at last was awarded a permanent annual allowance by the British government.

Susannah Marshall's tale doubtless was unique. But southern loyalist and patriot women alike saw their husbands murdered before their eyes, traveled hundreds of miles to escape one set of partisans or the other, endured repeated plunderings of their homes and farms, and survived physical ordeals. . . . At the end of the war many were left with little more than the knowledge that they had managed to live through it all. Mrs. Wilkinson wrote, "It is some degree of satisfaction to look back on our sufferings, and congratulate ourselves on their being past, and that they were no *worse* when present." Eliza Lucas Pinckney wondered at the fate that had "so intirely deprived" her of a "Fortune sufficient to live Genteely in any part of the world," and a Georgia woman found her memories of wartime experiences so bitter that she absolutely refused to return to her former home.

It is hardly surprising that in later years Betsy Ambler Brent . . . entertained mixed feelings about the Revolution. The same event that had brought "independence and prosperity to my country," she mused in 1809, had involved "my immediate family in poverty and perplexity of every kind." Striving to discover the beneficial effects of the war, she found them not in public occurrences but rather in her own personal development: speaking of herself and her younger sister, she commented, "The only possible good from the entire change in our circumstances was that we were made acquainted with the manners and situation of our own Country, which we otherwise should never have known; added to this, necessity taught us to use exertions which our girls of the present day know nothing of, We Were forced to industry to appear genteely, to study Manners to supply the place of Education, and to endeavor by amiable and agreeable conduct to make amends for the loss of fortune."

Surely Mrs. Brent's characterization of the war as requiring "exertions which our girls of the present day know nothing of" could have come from the pen of any other southern woman who had lived through the Revolution. Less wealthy families did not find their circumstances as greatly altered by the war as did the Amblers, but other southern women had had similar experiences. Accordingly, during and after the war the more highly educated and reflective among the white women began to raise questions about the social role to which they and their northern counterparts long had been confined. The fact that they did so constitutes an important consequence of the Revolution for American women; when coupled with the opportunity for freedom that the war offered to black females, it shows that, contrary to what historians usually have maintained, women did not simply "quietly sink back in their places and take up the old endless routine of their existence" after the war. . . .

III

. . . [Some] southern white women began to express dissatisfaction with certain of the proscriptions that defined their lives. Two aspects of this trend stemmed directly from wartime experiences. Under the common law, man and wife were one person; a woman lost her independent legal identity when she married. This meant, in terms of the Revolution, that a wife could suffer as a result of her husband's actions and political beliefs, whether or not she shared them. Thus Anne Hart, a resident of Charleston during the British occupation, feared she would be banished from her home because her husband Oliver had been a revolutionary activist early in the war. David Ramsay later declared that such women had borne their banishment with uniform "cheerfulness" and "resolution," but Anne Hart's letters indicate otherwise. Explaining her forthrightness by commenting, "I can speak free to my dearest," she wrote her husband of her "Anxiety" at the prospect of having to leave Charleston. She did not "condemn" him for what he had done, she said, but she was distressed because she was "liable to Banishment to transportation for Actions not her own." Of the other women in similar circumstances, she inquired, "What must those Wives expect from their Husbands, for whom they will suffer so much, what can they render to recompense for the Trouble they give?" The Revolution clearly had taught Mrs. Hart a lesson about women's inferior status before the law. One indication of her subsequent independence of mind was the fact that she was extremely reluctant to leave South Carolina to rejoin her husband in New Jersey after the war.

The second example relates not to legal disabilities but to social limitations on the female role. With woman's sphere sharply defined to encompass only the household, the subject of politics was universally regarded as outside a woman's competence during the prewar years. And so in the 1760s and early 1770s when women discussed political matters in their letters, they invariably added a disclaimer: for instance, after making an acute loyalist analysis of America's current troubles, the wife of a Virginia Anglican cleric wrote in 1776, "Dont think I am engaging in politics. no; I assure you its a subject for which I have not either Talents or Inclination to enter upon." As the war continued, however, and women realized how important military and political events were in their lives, the formal disclaimers disappeared. A North Carolina woman, importuning her brother-in-law for more news in 1780, exuberantly declared, "you know I am a great politician." . . .

Such sentiments were not unusual, if not exactly commonplace, in the writings of American women in the 1780s. But, strikingly, only north of the Mason-Dixon line did they have a significant impact. There men began to respond to the women's concerns and to expand their notions of what constituted women's sphere, to provide increased educational opportunities for women, and to publish (if not always to agree with) women's statements on their own behalf. In the South no comparable developments occurred. There women expressed their sentiments privately, to each other and to their husbands, but they did not find men responsive to the issues they raised. The key question is why, and to find the answer it is necessary to return to a discussion of the impact of the war in the South.

By all accounts, the South suffered more from the Revolution than did the northern and middle states. The phases of the war fought on southern soil were both more destructive and more prolonged than those experienced by any northern region other than the immediate vicinity of New York City. The war in the North (with the same exception) largely concluded with the evacuation of Philadelphia in summer 1778, and so by the time the peace treaty was signed in autumn 1782 even the hardest-hit northern area had had time to recover. Not so the South. Long after Yorktown, guerrilla warfare continued throughout the Carolinas in particular, and not until after peace was officially proclaimed could recovery begin. And then it proved to be a long, slow process. Plantations had been laid waste, farms neglected, houses and fences left in disrepair, for far too long a time. Naval stores and indigo, two of the South's most important prewar exports, were now denied the bounties they had received when America was part of the British empire. Britain began to tax American rice and tobacco, thus necessitating a search for new markets and subjecting those products to increased competition in Britain itself.

But most of all the South lacked labor. Those fifty-five thousand or more slaves lost during the war had been vital to the functioning of the southern agricultural economy. And so those planters who could afford it—and many who could not—began pouring their resources into the purchase of Negroes in order to bring their labor supply to prewar levels. Between 1783 and 1785, some seven thousand slaves were imported into South Carolina alone, and, because too many planters had gone deeply into debt to British traders, the South Carolina legislature in 1787 banned the further importation of slaves. In Georgia, the 1790 census recorded the presence of nearly thirty thousand blacks, where just seven years earlier slavery had "well-nigh disappeared," according to the leading historian of that state. And in both Virginia and South Carolina the 1790 census figures, when compared with 1782 estimates of the size of the black population, suggest a far higher rate of growth than would be expected from natural increase alone.

Southerners frequently commented on the distressed economic conditions in the region during the postwar period. A Virginian in 1782 noted the "extreme poverty of our Country"; Eliza Lucas Pinckney described South Carolina as "greatly impoverished" by the loss of slaves; and a

North Carolina woman recognized that her remaining blacks were now "va[lua]bel, . . . Chef of my Intrast." A Savannah resident observed in 1786 that "this place is far from having repaired the ruins of the late warr," and as late as 1799 an English visitor to Charleston remarked that the "people of this State tho' wealthy & very luxurious, have not yet got over the baleful effects of the revolutionary war. Their independance cost the Carolinians, much blood & treasure."

The impact of this devastation upon society and social attitudes was incalculable. In the less-affected North, the postwar period could be one of experimentation with new ideas and social forms. Slaves could be emancipated, women could be educated, egalitarianism could be instituted in theory, if not in practice. But not in the South. There efforts were directed simply at rebuilding what had been lost, at conservatively reconstituting colonial society rather than at creating a new republican way of life. And so a Virginia planter in 1780 refused even to pay lip service to egalitarian rhetoric when he criticized the "little people": "Do they not know that a Gentleman is as necessary in a State, as a poor Man, and the poor as necessary as the Gentleman"? he asked. "So it must be! through all generations—for if we were all equall, one hour, nay one minute, wou'd make a difference according to mens Genious & Capacity." A Carolina boy born in 1785 recalled his youth as a time "when every nerve was strained to repair the broken fortunes of the Planters by the severest thrift and patient industry." It was not, his son concluded, "a good time to be born, for all the social relations of life had been badly disrupted." David Ramsay appropriately summed up the postwar years: "In such a condition of public affairs, to re-produce a state of things favorable to social happiness, required all the energies of the well disposed inhabitants."

And what was the southern white woman's contribution to this rebuilding effort? According to Ramsay, "they aided by their economy and retirement from the world to repair the losses." In other words, they retreated to the households that had shaped their lives before the war and to their standard prerevolutionary roles. Whether Ramsay's statement was factually accurate as far as the white women were concerned is questionable—indeed, the examples of Anne Hart and Eliza Wilkinson would seem to suggest otherwise—but it undoubtedly represented the wishes of their husbands, of whom Ramsay, of course, was one. For in rebuilding colonial society, in putting their resources into reconstructing an agricultural economy based on slavery, white southern males were ensuring, consciously or not, that the lives of their wives and daughters would continue to be determined by the nature of their households. Southern men were reinforcing a patriarchal society centered on an expanded household economy. In the North, the household became progressively less important in the economy as the years passed, as factories began to produce items formerly manufactured within the household, and as men increasingly worked outside the home. But in the South the household retained, perhaps even in certain areas expanded, its significance, as slavery gained an ever-tighter grip on the southern economy. Where the optimal family continued to be large and multiracial, and where the husband continued as the head of the increasingly important household, the wife's role necessarily contracted or remained the same. In the North, the family was left for the wife to supervise and eventually to control, at least theoretically. . . .

This observation can be illustrated by an examination of the changes, or the lack of such, in the image of women during the revolutionary era. Before the war, few or no regional differences can be discerned in the delineation of the ideal to which white women were expected to conform. Genteel colonial women in both the North and South read the same books and were told the same things: they were to be modest, pious, and submissive to their husbands; they must cultivate the feminine qualities of dependence, delicacy, and sensibility; and their chief accomplishments must be ornamental rather than useful. In the 1780s, although some northern writers continued to compose their didactic literature in this vein, a new theme appeared, and indeed soon became dominant. As Linda Kerber has pointed out, the northern republican woman, though domestic, was characterized as "competent and confident," as one who ignored the "vagaries of fashion," as one who was "rational, benevolent, independent, self-reliant." And she was a woman who, moreover, had an important contribution to make to society at large. Yet in the South the image of women remained enmired in the colonial pattern. In 1789, when Charles Cotesworth Pinckney delivered a Fourth of July oration in Charleston, he described southern white women as having demonstrated "a sensibility so exquisitely delicate, a constancy so heroically firm" during the war that "admiration & delight are cold & inadequate terms to express the effect it had upon their enraptured Countrymen." Seeking a proper metaphor to express his admiration, Pinckney hit upon the following, a passive, stylized depiction if there ever was one: among the "massy ruins" of warfare were "a number of slender Columns, the most beauteous models of elegance & taste, erect & unimpaired notwithstanding the violence that occasioned the desolation which surrounds them." In sharp contrast, a northern orator in a similar speech just a year later emphasized the active and important role that republican women played in American society. Noting that the "female parent is considered of greatest importance" in raising children, that women's "thoughts and opinions are of the utmost consequence to the public," and that the influence of "female benevolence, candor and justice" would contribute to the "heightning of every improvement in political society," he reached the conclusion, startling for the eighteenth century, that women's control over manners was "of equal importance" in the republic to men's control of laws. Despite the fact that in the years after 1800 progressively fewer northern authors seem to have approved an active role for women in politics and society, nevertheless the change in the years of the early republic was real. And there are few if any signs of a similar change in the South—a result, as has been argued, of the differential impact of the war.

Who Should Rule at Home?
The Revolution in the Carolina Backcountry

RACHEL N. KLEIN

Nearly a year before the colonies declared their independence from Great Britain, the South Carolina backcountry was already embroiled in a violent conflict between whigs and loyalists. Estimates of loyalist strength varied throughout the war, but several observers believed that the inhabitants of Ninety-Six District were about evenly divided and that tories may have outnumbered whigs in the fork between the Broad and Saluda rivers. As early as 1774 coastal radicals were concerned about inland allegiances and struggled, with only mixed success, to win frontier support. In September 1775 the British governor William Campbell could write with confidence that "the loyalty of those poor, honest, industrious people in the back part of this and neighboring provinces discontents them [the Charleston whigs] greatly." By November of that year the two sides had come to blows, and not until winter did whig forces finally gain a temporary ascendancy by rounding up the "most leading and active" tories whom they carried to jail in Charleston. Sporadic fighting persisted through the later 1770s, and in 1780, with the arrival of the British, the frontier exploded into a virtual civil war.

Historians have generally recognized a connection between frontier loyalism and sectional hostilities. On the eve of the Revolution the backcountry had only three seats allotted in the colonial assembly even though the region contained about three-fourths of the colony's white population. Before hundreds—perhaps thousands—of self-proclaimed Regulators drew attention to backcountry grievances, inland settlers had lacked local courts and jails. During the 1760s the growing colonial struggle had drawn legislative attention away from the backcountry, giving South Carolina frontiersmen added cause to resent coastal whigs. Finally, backcountry settlers, particularly those in the western piedmont, complained that lowcountry leaders had provided insufficient protection against the Indians. When the Revolution came, they had ample reason to resent requests for support from Charleston rebels.

This sectional interpretation of backcountry loyalism provides an insufficient explanation of frontier allegiances during the Revolution because it cannot account for the many frontier settlers who supported the Americans. Richard Maxwell Brown's discovery that only 6 of the 120 known Regulators actively supported the loyalists, while 55 joined the Americans, compounded the problem. Brown's research demonstrated that the most outspoken proponents of frontier demands for courts, schools, churches, and legislative representation tended to join the whig cause. Regulators

Rachel N. Klein, "Frontier Planters and the American Revolution: The South Carolina Backcountry, 1775–1782," in Ronald Hoffman, Thad W. Tate, and Peter J. Albert, eds., *An Uncivil War: The Southern Backcountry During the American Revolution,* 1985, pp. 37–55, 57–58, 61–69. Reprinted by permission of the University Press of Virginia.

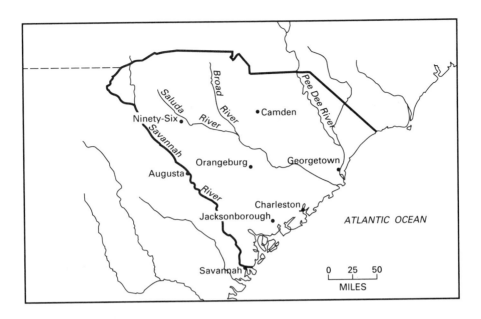

resented the neglectful assembly, but their concern for the protection of property, their growing involvement in slavery, and their increasing interest in commercial agriculture tied them in fundamental ways to the wealthier planters and merchants of the coast. We can thus understand how Regulators managed to overcome their sectional animosity and join with low-country whigs, but the loyalty to the crown of many other inland settlers remains a mystery.

Nor is there evidence to suggest that ideology distinguished backcountry whigs from loyalists. Charles Woodmason, the Anglican minister who became the Regulators' leading spokesman, demonstrated how easily republican rhetoric could be turned against Charleston radicals. Woodmason was one of the few former Regulators who remained a staunch loyalist, and he admonished lowcountry rebels who made "such a noise about Liberty! Liberty! Freedom! Property! Rights! Privileges! and what not; And at the same time keep half their fellow subjects in a State of Slavery." Woodmason was not referring to black slaves but to the thousands of white frontiersmen who remained all but unrepresented in the South Carolina assembly. Inland and coastal leaders spoke the same political language, but on the frontier republican rhetoric could accommodate the loyalist as well as the whig position.

Finally, ethnic and simplistic economic interpretations can provide little additional help in distinguishing frontier whigs from tories. Wallace Brown, in his analysis of South Carolina's 320 loyalist claimants, found that foreign-born were more likely than native-born colonists to have sided with the loyalists, and contemporaries believed that the German origin of many settlers at the lower Broad and Saluda fork was largely responsible for loyalism in that region. But many Irish, English-born, and German South

Carolinians joined the rebels. Similarly, Camden-area Quakers and New Light Baptists of latter-day Union County inclined to loyalism, and Regular Baptists of Charleston and Cheraw supported the Americans, but Presbyterians and Anglicans, who formed the majority of the inland population, were divided. Neither wealth nor occupation provides additional clues as to divisions on the frontier. Storekeepers, planters, slaveholders, and non-slaveholders were found in both rebel and loyalist camps.

If, however, the Revolutionary backcountry failed to divide along clearly defined class lines, the frontier struggle did have an important class dimension. Although ambitious planters and merchants chose one side or the other for a variety of reasons, the whigs more consistently represented the broad class interests of rising backcountry slaveholders. Those inland leaders who joined the whig side extended a process begun during the 1760s and gradually became the vanguard of an emerging planter class.

During the decade preceding the outbreak of the Revolution, South Carolina's backcountry had erupted into violence as Regulators struggled to suppress the bandit gangs that had been robbing and torturing frontier settlers and attracting slave runaways into their ranks. Leading Regulators were ambitious entrepreneurs. They were millowners, surveyors, distillers, and storekeepers who were in the process of acquiring slaves for the production of cash crops and were contributing to a growing backcountry demand for black labor. Their primary concern was to make the frontier safe for property holders, and they were especially concerned about property in slaves.

Regulators were also angered by those frontier hunters whose hunting practices, tendency to pilfer from planters, and inclination to support the more aggressive bandits ran counter to the interests of the more settled population. Referred to by their contemporaries as "white Indians," some of these hunters were squatters or even landowners, but they were simply unable or unwilling to plant enough for a subsistence. Regulators demanded various measures designed to restrict this hunting population.

Impelled to action by the immediate threat to their lives and property, Regulators took the opportunity to enumerate a series of smoldering backcountry grievances. In addition to calling for local courts, jails, schools, churches, and a vagrancy act, they expressed outrage that the backcountry had only two representatives in the assembly.

As the Regulator uprising progressed, a number of prosperous frontiersmen became alarmed by the violence of Regulator methods and urged the council to authorize an all-out offensive against the insurgents. They chose a man named Joseph Scoffel (also spelled "Scophol," "Scovil," or "Coffel") to lead the anti-Regulator forces. Apparently they saw Scoffel as a man who would attract precisely those people who had fallen victim to Regulator attacks. Scoffel himself was later convicted of hog stealing, and Gen. William Moultrie recalled him as "a man of some influence in the backcountry, but a stupid, ignorant blockhead."

Scoffel, assuming the title of "Colonel," succeeded very well in attracting followers who, not surprisingly, began to behave like bandits. According to one correspondent, Scoffel had "many returned horsethieves and banditti in his midst." Another insisted that Scoffel's party were impressing "provisions and horses" wherever they went, "leaving whole families destitute of both." These and other reports prompted the council to withdraw all support. Violence between the Regulators and Scoffel's people was narrowly averted.

With the passage of the South Carolina Circuit Court Act in 1769, the Regulators finally dispersed, but resentment persisted. Although Regulators had, by marching to places of election in 1768, elected six of their candidates to the assembly, the backcountry remained grossly underrepresented. Regulators had prompted coastal leaders to pass a law restricting hunters, but as the assembly became increasingly preoccupied by the broader colonial struggle, it failed to follow through on a proposed vagrancy act. The grievances and social divisions that had erupted in the Regulator uprising would influence the configuration and outcome of the longer struggle on the Revolutionary frontier.

As the Revolution approached, coastal whigs rightly feared that sectional animosities would incline South Carolina frontiersmen to support the loyalists. They sought to offset the loyalist threat not only by increasing backcountry legislative representation but by dispatching a three-man committee on a stump-speaking tour through loyalist strongholds. The committee, consisting of the Baptist minister Oliver Hart, the Presbyterian minister William Tennent, and the Charleston radical William Henry Drayton, struggled to win the support of certain prominent "men of influence." They recognized that the primary divisions within the Carolina backcountry were by neighborhoods or communities that tended to coalesce around such key individuals. The committee had only mixed success, but the record of their mission serves as a window onto the process by which backcountry settlers chose one side or the other during the first phase of the Revolution.

The committee concentrated its efforts on Thomas Fletchall, a militia colonel in the area between the Broad and Saluda rivers. Though he appears not to have joined the Regulation, Fletchall had publicly supported several Regulator demands. His defection to the loyalist side caused considerable alarm among lowcountry whigs. As one observer later wrote, Fletchall's position as colonel "of course gave him great influence in that part of the country." At a stump meeting held near Fletchall's home at Fairforest Creek, Oliver Hart observed "with Sorrow . . . that Col. Fletchall has all those people at his beck, and reigns amongst them like a little King." Not surprisingly, those areas in which Drayton, Tennent, and Hart enjoyed greatest success were neighborhoods in which militia captains were sympathetic to the whig cause.

There were other such loyalist men of influence who helped to make that region a persistent problem for South Carolina whigs. Among these were two former Regulators, Moses Kirkland and Robert Cunningham. The American militia general Andrew Pickens later testified to Cunningham's local prestige when he insisted that "there would not have been so virulent an opposition to our cause in this country'' had Cunningham joined the rebels. Evan McLaurin, a prosperous storeowner at the lower Broad and Saluda fork, was also successful in attracting surrounding settlers to the loyalist cause. When Drayton visited the area in August 1775, he found that McLaurin was able to throw such "a damp on the people" that no one signed the Continental Association. McLaurin managed to put a stop to one meeting "only by his presence."

The very term *man of influence,* so frequently used by contemporaries, is revealing. In communities where settlers depended upon stores and mills for a variety of services, it is not surprising that merchants and millers, many of whom were also magistrates or militia officers, should have wielded extensive political influence. Drayton recognized the power of such men when, in the course of his journey, he declared that "no miller who was a subscriber [to the Continental Association] should grind wheat for a non-subscriber." It is no coincidence that such prominent backcountry loyalists as Cunningham, McLaurin, and Kirkland were all involved in local trade and that Fletchall owned and operated large gristmills.

Influence could and apparently did work two ways. Thomas Fletchall lived on lands adjoining those of the pacifist and tory minister Philip Mulkey and presumably serviced the Mulkey community with his mills. One cannot help but wonder to what extent Mulkey and Mulkey's followers influenced Fletchall. Similarly, Evan McLaurin operated his store in the lower Broad and Saluda fork, where Germans predominated. According to contemporary reports, these "Dutch" settlers became tories because they feared that coastal rebels would retract all royal land grants. McLaurin's proximity to the German settlement may have encouraged him to remain loyal.

Whatever the interaction between various inland areas and their leading men, it worked to divide the Revolutionary backcountry by neighborhood. When persuasion failed, communities had ways of enforcing or trying to enforce unanimity. One loyalist refugee from the Camden area admitted to having taken the "Rebel Oath," but insisted that "the millers and black-smiths would not work for any one who did not take the oath." That families and common ethnic groups often lived on adjoining lands only reinforced the tendency for clusters of population to act as whig or tory units. Following the British occupation, one loyalist officer could observe that "the whole province resembled a piece of patch work, the inhabitants of every settlement when united in sentiment being in arms for the side they liked best and making continual inroads into one another's settlements."

Not surprisingly, the storeowners, millers, magistrates, and officers most likely to wield local influence were also those most likely to entertain statewide political and military ambitions. For some, the decisive consideration in choosing sides was status. In January 1775 both Robert Cunningham and Moses Kirkland were, by all appearances, sympathetic to the American cause. Yet by the following summer, the two were among the staunchest opponents of the provincial government. Many years later Andrew Pickens offered what seems a plausible explanation. When the Council of Safety established a backcountry regiment, the candidates for colonel were Cunningham, Kirkland, and James Mayson—all former Regulators. The position went to Mayson which, according to Pickens, "so exasperated the others that they immediately took the other side of the Question." Pickens was not concerned with bad-mouthing tory leaders, for he also pointed out that he "never had any doubt but that . . . [Cunningham] . . . would have made the best officer." Henry Laurens, president of the Council of Safety, suspected that Thomas Fletchall had been motivated by similar concerns. "It has been said," wrote Laurens in a letter to Fletchall, "that you were in some measure disposed to unite with the friends of America, but that you were deterred partly . . . by the dread of losing your commission of Colonel and your rank of Justice of the Peace."

Recognizing both the ambition and the local authority of backcountry men of influence, lowcountry whigs sought to win support by offering access to political and military positions. In July 1775 Henry Laurens was eager to prevent the defection of a Captain Whitfield to the loyalists. It occurred to Laurens "that Captn. Whitfield however chearfully he may shew an inclination to serve the colony by resignation, may not be content with a subcommand," and he suggested that the captain petition the council for a higher rank. Also in 1775 the provincial congress established three regular regiments, one of which was to consist of backcountry mounted rangers. As the Revolutionary general William Moultrie later recalled, "It was thought not only useful, but political to raise them, because the most influential gentlemen in the backcountry were appointed officers which interested them in the cause."

As the Revolution progressed—as people lost friends and family in the fighting—the war assumed greater meaning for many of those involved. Some undoubtedly fought to preserve liberty as they conceived it. As one frontier officer wrote to his son from headquarters at Ninety-Six: "I feel myself distracted on both hands by this thought, that in my old age I should be obliged to take field in defense of my rights and liberties, and that of my children. God only knows that it is not by choice, but of necessity, and from the consideration that I had rather suffer anything than lose my birthright and that of my children." Experience on the frontier may well have made some such men particularly sensitive to colonial complaints about Parliament.

But during the early phase of the struggle most backcountry settlers were less concerned about Britain than their own local grievances and personal aspirations. Coastal whigs were able to win inland support precisely because they recognized and helped fulfill the political and military ambition of leading frontiersmen. In so doing, they extended the statewide political power of backcountry settlers and thereby furthered the political goals expressed by Regulators during the preceding decade. Following roughly the system of apportionment established for the provincial congress, the state constitution of 1776 allowed the backcountry 76 out of 202 seats in the assembly. Although the new constitution did not establish anything approximating proportional representation of the white population, it greatly increased the political influence of frontier settlers. For Moses Kirkland and Robert Cunningham, the whig offer was not good enough; but for others with similar ambitions, opportunities opened by the Revolution must have been very welcome.

Like their whig counterparts, many backcountry loyalists were ambitious slaveholders, storekeepers, millowners, and rising planters, but in their effort to attract followers they played on widespread resentments against the wealthier planters and merchants of the coast. Writing of his unsuccessful labors between the Broad and Saluda rivers, William Tennent complained that leading loyalists "blind the people and fill them with bitterness against the gentlemen as they are called." Settlers believed that "no man that comes from below, and that no paper printed there can speak the truth." At a meeting held near Fairforest Creek, Colonel Fletchall addressed the nonslaveholding population by intimating that "the people below wanted them to go down and assist them against the Negroes." Only a "Fool," suggested Fletchall, would agree to go. . . .

Although resentment against lowcountry planters proved a powerful weapon in the hands of backcountry loyalists, it also involved them in the first of a series of inconsistencies. Such prominent tories as Evan McLaurin, Moses Kirkland, and Robert Cunningham had various business connections with the coastal elite and, as slaveowners, had fundamental interests in common with them. They also had statewide political ambitions. By fueling antagonism toward the "gentlemen of fortune and ambition on the seacoast," loyalist leaders worked against the broad class interests of wealthy inland settlers who were seeking greater participation in statewide political and economic affairs. Although many backcountry whigs also felt personally suspicious of seacoast gentlemen, their participation in the American cause helped to accelerate a pre-Revolutionary trend toward growing political and economic association between the elites of both sections.

A far greater advantage for South Carolina whigs was their own inability to win support from the western Indians, a failure that actually strengthened the whig position among frontier settlers who lived in constant fear of Cherokee attack. As inland men of influence were drawing their local communities toward one side or the other during the first months of the Revolutionary conflict, many settlers were unwilling to become actively involved on either side. They were suspicious of coastal whigs, but apart from those areas in which loyalist men of influence held sway, they tended not to join the tories. Some of these previously uninvolved people—particularly those living in the western piedmont—became sympathetic to the American cause only after the broader colonial struggle became identified with a frontier war against the Indians.

During the summer and fall of 1775, many inland families had their attention focused not on the growing colonial crisis but on the growing threat from the western Indians. Both loyalists and whigs attempted to capitalize on the situation by accusing each other of trying to foment a Cherokee war. The accusations were probably groundless on both sides, but the ensuing rumors caused great alarm among western settlers, who had borne the brunt of the Indian conflicts of the 1760s. Writing from the backcountry in July 1775, the American officer Andrew Williamson told of "considerable confusion . . . on account of the expected danger from the Cherokees."

Although neither side wanted to instigate an Indian war, both whigs and tories were trying to win the allegiance of the Cherokee to prevent the Indians from joining the opposition. The British sent the deputy Indian agent, Alexander Cameron, to negotiate with the Cherokee, while the Council of Safety, in a last effort at conciliation, agreed to send a gift of ammunition. On November 3, 1775, a band of loyalists intercepted the shipment of powder and used it as evidence that the whigs were, in fact, attempting to provoke a conflict. Andrew Williamson's militiamen were able to retake the ammunition, but in late November two thousand loyalist troops laid siege to Fort Ninety-Six, where the powder was held. That Williamson had fewer than six hundred recruits for defense of the fort is itself testimony to the unpopularity of whig efforts at appeasement.

Recognizing the seriousness of the situation, the provincial congress tried to defend its actions by issuing a declaration claiming that "nothing could in the least degree satisfy them [the Cherokee] but a promise of some ammunition." Although the gift was "the only probable means of preserving the frontiers from the inroads of the Indians," it had been "by some non-associators made an instrument for the most diabolical purposes." The whigs, by their very efforts to win the allegiance of the western Indians, were alienating backcountry settlers, particularly those in the vulnerable area of Ninety-Six District.

What finally decided the question of Cherokee allegiance and brought on an Indian war had little to do with whig or loyalist efforts. The Cherokee had good reason to be less suspicious of British officials than of the rebel government because the former had at least tried to restrict western migration onto Indian lands. By spring of 1776 the Cherokee were on the brink of war with South Carolina settlers over the familiar problem, and in April they attacked a community in latter-day York County.

With the Cherokee veering toward the British side, whig leaders abandoned their policy of conciliation and called for an all-out offensive against the Indians. This time Williamson had no problem in raising troops. By July 1776 he had approximately one thousand militiamen from Ninety-Six District who virtually burned their way through the Cherokee nation. William Henry Drayton, who had negotiated the gift of ammunition less than a year before, now called for the total destruction of the western Indians. "It is expected," wrote Drayton to a backcountry officer, "that you make smooth work as you go—that is, you cut up every Indian corn-field and burn every Indian town."

Though the whigs adopted an aggressive policy only after failing at conciliation, their new strategy was far more consistent with the experience and aspirations of backcountry settlers. Many, particularly in Ninety-Six District, had lost friends and relatives during the Cherokee War and other clashes of the 1760s. The threat of Indian attack had been a perpetual source of terror. By their all-out anti-Cherokee campaign, whig forces inevitably won some support from previously neutral settlers. That several active loyalists admitted to having served under Williamson during the summer of 1776 suggests the broad consensus that underlay the newly aggressive whig strategy.

Although greed for land was not an immediate motive behind Williamson's Cherokee campaign, the connection between land hunger and Indian war was obvious. Land hunger had been the source of the initial conflict. Even while Williamson was raising his troops, Drayton urged that the Cherokee nation "be extirpated, the lands become the property of the public." He promised never to support a treaty with the Indians "upon any other terms than their removal beyond the mountains." As it turned out, Drayton had his way. In the ensuing treaty, the Cherokee ceded the entire area of latter-day Pendleton County. From those lands South Carolina's militia and Continental soldiers would receive their bounty payments after the war.

Evan McLaurin, who eventually became a loyalist officer, inadvertently identified the tory dilemma. "The Indians," he wrote, "God knows they are good for Little." McLaurin believed that they could be used only as a "Bug Bear" to annoy whig settlements and interrupt communications. For that purpose he proposed the building of a frontier fort in order to protect the Indians' northern townships. But in return for a negligible military advantage, McLaurin found himself advocating a measure that could only have antagonized western settlers. All in all, the Indians did the Americans far more good as enemies than they could have done as allies. It was whigs, rather than loyalists, who found themselves in a position to continue the struggle for land and security begun during the preceding decade.

Loyalists attracted others as allies who, like the Indians, did them more harm than good. If, as seems to have been the case, the whigs had best success in winning allegiance from former Regulators, loyalists attracted the hunters and bandits who had inspired Regulator wrath. With the outbreak of Revolution, Joseph Scoffel, formerly the leader of anti-Regulator forces, reappeared in the backcountry, this time as a British supporter. The Council of Safety was alarmed in July 1775 by the appearance of "one Coffel" at Fort Charlotte, and Henry Laurens ordered that the fort be immediately taken. Later that year the council received information that "the Scoffel Lights were coming down from the backcountry in great force" to take public records and ammunition being held by whig forces at Dorchester. According to South Carolina's first historian, David Ramsay, "The names of scovilites and regulators were insensibly exchanged for the appellation of tories and whigs, or the friends of the old and new order of things." Many, he thought, had actually followed Scoffel, though the name "was applied to others as a term of reproach on the alleged similarity of their principles." . . .

By associating with well-known bandits, the British gave their opponents a moral advantage among backcountry settlers. In fighting the Revolution, whigs were also continuing the struggle against South Carolina's bandit and wandering population. They were better able than loyalists to present themselves as protectors of inland farmers. Thus William Thomson ordered another whig officer to "keep the inhabitants secure from the depredations of such unlawful banditty as may cross Savannah River . . . and protect those citizens who are well affected in their Persons and Properties." A whig militia colonel near Peedee requested aid for his regiment which was trying to protect neighboring settlements from "every murder, plundering, every cruelty, that could be perpetrated by a banditti of the most desperate villains and mulattoes, immediately bordering in our settlements." In characteristic fashion David Ramsay was able to pinpoint the British and loyalist dilemma. Referring to "horse thieves" and other "banditti" who attached themselves to parties of the British, he observed that "the necessity which their indiscriminate plundering imposed on all good men of defending themselves, did infinitely more damage to the royal cause than was compensated by all the advantages resulting from their friendship."

The British made matters worse by participating themselves in plundering raids, thereby failing to conciliate settlers who otherwise might have been willing to accept British protection. The British officer Banastre Tarleton, whose "Loyal Legion" moved into the backcountry during the spring of 1780, became infamous among back settlers for his pillaging raids. Writing to his cousin in 1782, a settler from Ninety-Six District described his personal experience of the British occupation in the following terms: "Our own true Colonels & head officers fled into the North State & a grat many of the young men went also. We being left like sheep among wolves, were obliged to give up to them our Arms & take purtection. But no sooner we had yielded to them but set to Rob us taking all our living things, horses, Cows, Sheep, Clothing, of all Sorts, money pewter, tins, knives, in fine Everything that sooted them. Untill we were Stript Naked." . . .

Despite complaints of plundered backcountrymen, the British general Cornwallis was less than sympathetic to the problems of frontier settlers. Writing from a backcountry post in November 1780, he observed that "if those who say they are our friends will not stir, I cannot defend every man's house from being plundered; and I must say that when I see a whole settlement running away from twenty or thirty robbers, I think they deserve to be robbed." By the following month Nathanael Greene could write that many tories were giving themselves up to the whigs, "being tired of such a wretched life & not finding the Support, Respect or attention which they expected from the British army."

Torn between policies of terrorizing and attracting the backcountry population, the British were never able to make the most of loyalist sympathies. They compounded their problems by issuing a series of orders that further alienated active whigs. Gen. Henry Clinton's proclamation of June 3, 1780, stated that all paroled prisoners, excepting those who had been in Charleston or Fort Moultrie at the time the city surrendered, were subject to British military service. In Camden the British Lord Rawdon attempted to enforce the order by imprisoning about 160 people, including John Chesnut and Joseph Kershaw, for refusing to join the royal militia. The result of this rigid policy was that many whig officers resumed active opposition to the invading army. To make matters worse, in August 1780 Lord Cornwallis ordered that the property of anyone refusing to take up arms with the British be confiscated. According to one prominent South Carolinian, it was "notorious that he [Cornwallis] has no abilities as a politician, or he would have endeavored to conciliate the affections of those he had subdued."

Plundering and banditry were not, of course, the exclusive province of British and loyalist forces. By the later years of the Revolution, South Carolina rebels and tories were, with considerable justification, accusing each other of behaving like bandits. Parties from both sides were plundering their opponents (and sometimes their allies) with impunity. Thomas Sumter, who solemnly urged the American general Francis Marion to "suppress every species of plundering," personally took the entire library of a wealthy backcountry loyalist. Officers who were genuinely concerned that at least whig settlements be protected still had considerable difficulty controlling their men. A chronic shortage of supplies exacerbated the problem. Through their repeated injunctions against plundering, Nathanael Greene, his generals, and even Gov. John Rutledge suggest that the practice was widespread.

But if whigs engaged in plunder along with their opponents, the behavior and policy of the two sides was far from identical. Whigs escaped the stigma of association with Scoffel's people, and their commanders were far more consistent in refusing to sanction plundering raids. General Greene understood what the British would never quite grasp: that the country would be "inevitably ruined" and the inhabitants "universally disgusted, if, instead of protection, they are exposed to the ravages of every party." Finally, it was whigs, rather than loyalists, who found themselves in a position to reestablish order. As rebel militiamen retook posts once held by the British, they, along with the government in Charleston, set about trying to suppress plundering parties. During the spring of 1781, Governor Rutledge issued a proclamation ordering an end to plunder and appointing magistrates in all parts of the state recovered from the British. In August 1782 Andrew Pickens requested twenty-five horsemen to suppress "such parties of men, as lost to every sense of justice or principle of honesty or humanity, make it their sole study to ruin and distress . . . every man who shews the least attachment to honesty, regular order and civil government." Also in 1782 the legislature passed a militia law establishing severe penalties for officers and men found guilty of plundering. It was whigs who, like the Regulators before them, became the champions of social order and defenders of private property.

The British attracted other allies, who, like Indians, hunters, and bandits, did them more harm than good. In June 1780 General Clinton issued a proclamation promising freedom to all rebel-owned slaves on the condition that they agree to serve the British throughout the war. Thousands of slaves followed Clinton's troops in the belief that the invading army was an army of liberation. Many died in disease-ridden camps or were shipped to the West Indies for sale. But some made their way to East Florida and others became foragers, spies, workmen, or even soldiers for the British. Toward the close of the war, the whig major Henry Hampton attacked a black British regiment in the backcountry, and in 1782 British commanders created a black cavalry unit.

The problem for British and loyalist forces was obvious. By using slaves as soldiers with the promise of freedom in payment, they simultaneously threatened the slave system and evoked the specter of insurrection. In so doing, the British could only have alienated people from whose support they might have benefited. Writing to General Marion from a backcountry whig encampment, Sumter observed that "the Enemy oblige the negroes they have to make frequent sallies. This circumstance alone is sufficient to rouse and fix the resentment and detestation of every American who possesses common feeling."

Had the British been a true army of liberation for South Carolina's slave population, they might have gained considerable military advantage from their natural allies. The irony was that British leaders could not wholeheartedly embrace the notion of having large numbers of armed slave recruits. The prominent South Carolina loyalist William Bull was alarmed even by the formation of the small black cavalry unit that, he insisted, was committing the sort of "outrages" to which "their savage nature prompts them." In 1781 British commanders rejected or ignored proposals calling for the creation of two black regiments. Instead they followed a halfhearted policy. Clinton encouraged slaves to follow his armies, and he used some runaways as soldiers. But, ultimately, leading loyalists were as dependent on slavery as their whig opponents. They could not, without having threatened their own interests, exploit the potential military strength of the thousands of slaves who flocked to their camps.

By contrast, whig policies were consistent with the interests and attitudes of both actual and aspiring slave owners. Despite a serious problem in raising recruits, South Carolina's leadership continually resisted attempts to employ slaves as soldiers. In 1779 the legislature decisively rejected a proposal by Congress to recruit slave troops. According to David Ramsay, the plan was "received with horror by the planters [in the House], who figured to themselves terrible consequences." Subsequent efforts by Nathanael Greene and others to use slaves as soldiers fared no better in the legislature. Instead, the whig government chose to deal with the recruitment problem by appealing to the burgeoning backcountry demand for slaves.

That greed for slaves could become a motive for Revolutionary service was apparent as early as 1776 when Andrew Williamson asked the legislature whether he might tell his men that "such of those Indians as should be taken Prisoners would become slaves and the Property of the Captors." According to Governor Rutledge, that expectation already "prevailed in his [Williamson's] Camp insomuch that an Indian woman who had been taken prisoner was sold as a slave." William Drayton probably helped to encourage the notion by suggesting that "every Indian taken shall be the slave and property of the taker." The assembly refused to grant Williamson's request, insisting that Indians should be regarded as prisoners of war because enslavement might "give the Indians a precedent which may be fatal to our own people who may unfortunately fall into their Hands." Williamson's troops had to settle for indents issued in return for Indian scalps.

When it came to black slaves, South Carolina's legislature had no such reservations. Members sanctioned efforts by militia generals to raise recruits by providing a bounty payment not only in land, but in slaves taken from tory estates. Thomas Sumter set a precedent for other generals when, in April 1781, he sought to raise six regiments by offering a slave bonus to each militiaman who would serve for ten months. Even privates were to receive "one grown negro," and the numbers increased with rank. Sumter promised each lieutenant colonel "three large and one small negro." Other militia generals followed suit, with slight variations in their pay scales. The legislature also established a slave bonus for Continental troops.

So great was the demand for slaves among backcountry troops that Greene and others had considerable difficulty preventing soldiers and officers from taking slaves, without discrimination, from whigs and loyalists alike. After the war, numerous petitions requested that slaves taken by Sumter's troops be returned or that compensation be provided by the state.

Once again the British managed to act in opposition to the broad class interest of South Carolina's planters without incurring to themselves any significant military advantage. By serving as a magnet for runaway slaves, and by using such slaves as armed fighters, the British could hardly have endeared themselves to South Carolina's slave-owning population. Meanwhile, whigs not only avoided the contradictions of British policy, they also exploited and encouraged a growing backcountry demand for slaves.

The Revolution in South Carolina's backcountry cannot be called a class struggle in any simple sense. Rather than wealth or occupation, it was neighborhood affiliation reinforced by ethnic, religious, and familial ties that influenced the initial division between whigs and loyalists. Considerations of status more than ideological disagreements moved many leading men to choose one side or the other during the early phase of Revolutionary conflict. But if whig and loyalist forces failed to divide along clear-cut class lines, the British did attract groups that had fundamental grievances against the elites of both sections. The Cherokee, hunters, bandits, and slaves all gravitated to the British in opposition to an emerging social order more clearly represented by the whigs. Had the British been able fully to accept their "disaffected" allies, those groups might have done them considerable military service. As it was, leading loyalists were involved in a series of contradictions. By their various associations they alienated potential supporters and sealed the fate of the British war effort in the South.

It was finally the whigs who were best able to represent the interests and aspirations of those rising planters and merchants previously represented in the Regulator movement. The Revolution had forced lowcountry whigs to make political concessions to their inland counterparts. By joining the whig cause, leading frontiersmen could pursue their struggle for greater access into statewide political affairs. In fighting the war, whigs were also continuing a pre-Revolutionary struggle for Indian lands and security from Indian attack. By opposing backcountry loyalists, they were simultaneously working to suppress the bandits and "low" population previously opposed by the Regulators. And while South Carolina whigs may not have fought for anything so abstract as American slavery in general, many did, particularly in the backcountry, fight the Revolution for slaves.

人 *F U R T H E R*   *R E A D I N G*

John Richard Alden, *The South in the Revolution, 1763–1789* (1957)

Bernard Bailyn, *The Ideological Origins of the American Revolution* (1967)

Richard R. Beeman, *Patrick Henry: A Biography* (1975)

Richard R. Beeman and Rhys Isaac, "Cultural Conflict and Social Change in the Revolutionary South: Lunenburg County, Virginia," *Journal of Southern History* 46 (1980), 525–50

Ira Berlin and Ronald Hoffman, ed., *Slavery and Freedom in the Age of the American Revolution* (1983)

Irving Brant, *James Madison, the Virginia Revolutionist* (1941)

Richard Maxwell Brown, *The South Carolina Regulators* (1963)

Edward J. Cashin and Heard Robertson, *Augusta and the American Revolution: Events in the Georgia Back Country, 1773–1783* (1975)

Jeffrey J. Crow, "Slave Rebelliousness and Social Conflict in North Carolina, 1775 to 1802," *William and Mary Quarterly*, 3d ser., 37 (1980), 79–102

Jack P. Greene, "The Social Origins of the American Revolution: An Evaluation and an Interpretation," *Political Science Quarterly* 88 (1973), 1–22

————, " 'Slavery or Independence': Some Reflections on the Relationship Among Liberty, Black Bondage, and Equality in Revolutionary South Carolina," *South Carolina Historical Magazine* 80 (1979), 193–214

Don Higginbotham, *War and Society in Revolutionary America: The Wider Dimensions of Conflict* (1988)

W. Robert Higgins, ed., *The Revolutionary War in the South: Power, Conflict, and Leadership: Essays in Honor of John Richard Alden* (1979)

Ronald Hoffman et al., eds., *The Economy of Early America: The Revolutionary Period, 1763–1790* (1988)

Harvey H. Jackson, "Consensus and Conflict: Factional Politics in Revolutionary Georgia, 1774–1777," *Georgia Historical Quarterly* 59 (1975), 388–401

Pauline Maier, "The Charleston Mob and the Evolution of Popular Politics in Revolutionary South Carolina, 1765–1784," *Perspectives in American History* 4 (1970), 173–96

Jackson Turner Main, *The Social Structure of Revolutionary America* (1965)

Dumas Malone, *Jefferson the Virginian* (1948)

Robert D. Mitchell, *Commercialism and Frontier: Perspectives on the Early Shenandoah Valley* (1977)

Mary Beth Norton, *Liberty's Daughters: The Revolutionary Experience of American Women, 1750–1800* (1980)

James H. O'Donnell III, *Southern Indians in the American Revolution* (1973)

Benjamin Quarles, *The Negro in the American Revolution* (1961)

John E. Selby, *The Revolution in Virginia, 1775–1783* (1988)

Russell F. Weigley, *The Partisan War: The South Carolina Campaign of 1780–1782* (1970)

Gordon S. Wood, *The Creation of the American Republic, 1776–1787* (1969)

CHAPTER
5

The South in the New Nation

⋏

Despite the presence of slavery and the separate course of development on which the South had embarked, there was little national consciousness of regional distinction before the American Revolution. Few northerners thought about a "South"—or a "North" for that matter—and southerners had not developed a strong sense of their region as different or separate from the other American colonies.

With the Revolution and the founding of a new American nation, however, the first signs of regional consciousness and self-consciousness appeared. The South continued to grow and develop in the decades after independence and did so in distinctively southern ways. The population rose, the area of settlement advanced, and slavery expanded, growing rapidly in Georgia and South Carolina and becoming more deeply entrenched throughout the entire region. Moreover, as time passed, slavery's influence spread throughout upcountry society (the settlements in piedmont or hilly regions farther inland) as well as in coastal plantation districts.

How and why did southerners become aware of their region as a separate entity with separate interests? What issues spurred this awareness? What changes occurred in the institution of slavery as it expanded in the coastal districts of South Carolina, and how did these changes affect the slaves? What were the emerging characteristics of society in the backcountry—the South's more western piedmont regions? To what extent did slavery bind the different subregions of the South together?

⋏ *D O C U M E N T S*

During the Revolution and under the Confederation, well before the constitutional convention met in Philadelphia, the American colonies had begun to discover their separate interests. In the federal convention, on July 14, 1787, James Madison of Virginia referred to what he had learned about the differences between the sections. His remarks, which are contained in the first document, came as part of an argument against giving all states equal representation in the Senate. Little more than a decade later, the Alien and Sedition Acts provoked a

208

protest with sectional overtones; the legislatures of Virginia and Kentucky advanced constitutional theories, reprinted in part in the second selection, that would support later sectional defiance. Slavery's influence on southerners is evident in different guises. Richard Randolph's will, the third document, illustrates the kind of antislavery feeling that Revolutionary ideology could foster, but other reactions to slavery and blacks, contained in the fourth document, show the desire of whites to control that separate population in their midst. Crosscurrents of thought continued in the 1810s and 1820s, first as some southerners shared John C. Calhoun's early nationalism, evident in the fifth document, and later as many began to feel the anxieties awakened by the Missouri controversy. The battle over whether to admit Missouri as a free state or a slave state revealed the great divisiveness of the slavery issue. The last document contains speeches by Congressman Benjamin Hardin of Kentucky and Senator Nathaniel Macon of North Carolina, who were among many southerners who reacted sharply to efforts to bar slavery from Missouri.

James Madison on the Importance of Slavery, 1787

Mr Madison expressed his apprehensions that if the proper foundation of Governmt. was destroyed, by substituting an equal in place of a proportional Representation, no proper superstructure would be raised. If the small States really wish for a Government armed with the powers necessary to secure their liberties, and to enforce obedience on the larger members as well as on themselves he could not help thinking them extremely mistaken in their means. He reminded them of the consequences of laying the existing confederation on improper principles. All the principal parties to its compilation, joined immediately in mutilating & fettering the Governmt. in such a manner that it has disappointed every hope placed on it. He appealed to the doctrine & arguments used by themselves on a former occasion. It had been very properly observed by (Mr. William Patterson) that Representation was an expedient by which the meeting of the people themselves was rendered unnecessary; and that the representatives ought therefore to bear a proportion to the votes which their constituents if convened, would respectively have. Was not this remark as applicable to one branch of the Representation as to the other? But it had been said that the Govert. would in its operation be partly federal, partly national; that altho' in the latter respect the Representatives of the people ought to be in proportion to the people: yet in the former it ought to be according to the number of States. If there was any solidity in this distinction he was ready to abide by it, if there was none it ought to be abandoned. In all cases where the Genl. Governmt. is to act on the people, let the people be represented and the votes be proportional. In all cases where the Govert. is to act on the States as such, in like manner as Congs. now act on them, let the States be represented & the votes be equal. This was the true ground of compromise if there was any ground at all. But he denied that there was any ground. He called for a single instance in which the Genl. Govt. was not to operate on the people individually. The practicability of making laws, with coercive sanctions, for the States as Political bodies, had been exploded on all hands. He observed that the people of the large States would in some way or other secure to themselves a weight proportioned to the importance accruing from their superior numbers. If they could not effect it by a proportional representation in the Govt. they would probably accede to no Govt. which did not in great measure depend for its efficacy on their voluntary cooperation, in which case they would indirectly secure their object. The existing confederacy proved that where the Acts of the Genl. Govt. were to be executed by the particular Govts. the latter had a weight in proportion to their importance. No one would say that either in Congs. or out of Congs. Delaware had equal weight with Pensylva. If the latter was to supply ten times as much money as the former, and no compulsion could be used, it was of ten times more importance, that she should voluntarily furnish the supply. In the Dutch confederacy the votes of the Provinces were equal. But Holland, which supplies about half the money, governs the whole republic. He enumerated the objections agst. an equality of votes in the 2d. branch, notwithstanding the proportional representation in the first. 1 the minority could negative the will of the majority of the people. 2. they could extort measures by making them a condition of their assent to other necessary measures. 3. they could obtrude measures on the majority by virtue of the peculiar powers which would be vested in the Senate. 4. the evil instead of being cured by time, would increase with every new State that should be admitted, as they must all be admitted on the principle of equality. 5. the perpetuity it would give to the preponderance of the Northn. agst. the Southn. Scale was a serious consideration. It seemed now to be pretty well understood that the real difference of interests lay, not between the large & small but between the N. & Southn. States. The institution of slavery & its consequences formed the line of discrimination. There were 5 States on the South, 8 on the Northn. side of this line. Should a proportl. representation take place it was true, the N. side would still outnumber the other: but not in the same degree, at this time; and every day would tend towards an equilibrium.

The Virginia and Kentucky Resolutions, 1798, 1799

Virginia Resolutions

Resolved, That the General Assembly of Virginia doth unequivocally express a firm resolution to maintain and defend the Constitution of the United States, and the Constitution of this state, against every aggression either foreign or domestic; and that they will support the Government of the United States in all measures warranted by the former.

That this Assembly most solemnly declares a warm attachment to the union of the states, to maintain which it pledges all its powers; and that, for this end, it is their duty to watch over and oppose every infraction of those principles which constitute the only basis of that Union, because a faithful observance of them can alone secure its existence and the public happiness.

That this Assembly doth explicitly and peremptorily declare that it views the powers of the Federal Government as resulting from the compact to which the states are parties, as limited by the plain sense and intention of the instrument constituting that compact; as no further valid than they are authorized by the grants enumerated in that compact; and that, in case of a deliberate, palpable, and dangerous exercise of other powers not granted by the said compact, the states, who are parties thereto, have the right and are in duty bound to interpose for arresting the progress of the evil, and for maintaining within their respective limits the authorities, rights, and liberties appertaining to them.

That the General Assembly doth also express its deep regret, that a spirit has in sundry instances been manifested by the Federal Government to enlarge its powers by forced constructions of the constitutional charter which defines them; and that indications have appeared of a design to expound certain general phrases (which, having been copied from the very limited grant of powers in the former Articles of Confederation, were the less liable to be misconstrued) so as to destroy the meaning and effect of the particular enumeration which necessarily explains and limits the general phrases; and so as to consolidate the states, by degrees, into one sovereignty, the obvious tendency and inevitable consequence of which would be to transform the present republican system of the United States into an absolute, or, at best, a mixed monarchy.

That the General Assembly doth particularly PROTEST *against the palpable and alarming infractions of the Constitution in the two late cases of the "Alien and Sedition Acts," passed at the last session of Congress; the first of which exercises a power nowhere delegated to the Federal Government, and which, by uniting legislative and judicial powers to those of [the] executive, subverts the general principles of free government, as well as the particular organization and positive provisions of the Federal Constitution: and the other of which acts exercises, in like manner, a power not delegated by the Constitution, but, on the contrary, expressly and positively forbidden by one of the amendments thereto,—a power which, more than any other, ought to produce universal alarm, because it is levelled against the right of freely examining public characters and measures, and of free communication among the people thereon, which has ever been justly deemed the only effectual guardian of every other right.*

That this state having, by its Convention which ratified the Federal Constitution, expressly declared that, among other essential rights, "the liberty of conscience and of the press cannot be cancelled, abridged, restrained or modified by any authority of the United States," and from its extreme anxiety to guard these rights from every possible attack of sophistry or ambition, having, with other states, recommended an amendment for that purpose, which amendment was in due time annexed to the Constitution,—it would mark a reproachful inconsistency and criminal degeneracy, if an indifference were now shown to the palpable violation of one of the rights thus declared and secured, and to the establishment of a precedent which may be fatal to the other.

That the good people of this commonwealth, having ever felt and continuing to feel the most sincere affection for their brethren of the other states, the truest anxiety for establishing and perpetuating the union of all and the most scrupulous fidelity to that Constitution, which is the pledge of mutual friendship, and the instrument of mutual happiness, the General Assembly doth solemnly appeal to the like dispositions of the other states, in confidence that they will concur with this Commonwealth in declaring, as it does hereby declare, that the acts aforesaid are unconstitutional; and that the necessary and proper measures will be taken by each for cooperating with this state, in maintaining unimpaired the authorities, rights, and liberties reserved to the states respectively, or to the people.

The Kentucky Resolutions of 1799

Resolved, That this commonwealth considers the federal Union, upon the terms and for the purposes specified in the late compact, conducive to the liberty and happiness of the several states: That it does now unequivocally declare its attachment to the Union, and to that compact, agreeably to its obvious and real intention, and will be among the last to seek its dissolution: That if those who administer the general government be permitted to transgress the limits fixed by that compact, by a total disregard to the special delegations of power therein contained, an annihilation of the state governments, and the creation upon their ruins of a general consolidated government, will be the inevitable consequence: That the principle and construction contended for by sundry of the state legislatures, that the general government is the exclusive judge of the extent of the powers delegated to it, stop not short of *despotism*—since the discretion of those who administer the government, and not the *Constitution*, would be the measure of their powers: That the several states who formed that instrument being sovereign and independent, have the unquestionable right to judge of the infraction; and, *That a nullification of those sovereignties, of all unauthorized acts done under color of that instrument is the rightful remedy:* That this commonwealth does, under the most deliberate reconsideration, declare, that the said Alien and Sedition Laws are, in their opinion, palpable violations of the said Constitution; and, however cheerfully it may be disposed to surrender its opinion to a majority of its sister states, in matters of ordinary or doubtful policy, yet, in momentous regulations like the present, which so vitally wound the best rights of the citizen, it would consider a silent acquiescence as highly criminal: That although this commonwealth, as a party to the federal compact, will bow to the laws of the Union, yet, it does, at the same time declare, that it will not now, or ever hereafter, cease to oppose in a constitutional manner, every attempt at what quarter soever offered, to violate that compact. And, finally, in order that no pretext or arguments may be drawn from a supposed acquiescence, on the part of this commonwealth in the constitutionality of those laws, and be thereby used as precedents for similar future violations of the federal compact—this commonwealth does now enter against them its solemn PROTEST.

Last Will and Testament of Richard Randolph, 1797

To make retribution, as far as I am able, to an unfortunate race of bondmen, over whom my ancestors have usurped and exercised the most lawless and monstrous tyranny, and in whom my countrymen (by their iniquitous laws, in contradiction of their own declaration of rights, and in violation of every sacred law of nature; of the inherent, inalienable and imprescriptible rights of man, and of every principle of moral and political honesty) have vested me with absolute property; to express my abhorrence of the theory as well as infamous practice of usurping the rights of our fellow creatures, equally entitled with ourselves to the enjoyment of liberty and happiness; to exculpate myself to those, who may perchance think or hear of me after death, from the black crime which might otherwise be imputed to me of voluntarily holding the above mentioned miserable beings in the same state of abject slavery in which I found them on receiving my patrimony at lawful age; to impress my children with just horror at a crime so enormous and indelible; to conjure them, in the last words of a fond father, never to participate in it in any the remotest degree, however sanctioned by laws (framed by the tyrants themselves who oppress them), or supported by false reasoning; used always to veil the sordid views of avarice and the lust of power; to declare to them and to the world that nothing but uncontrollable necessity, forced on me by my father (who wrongfully bound over them to satisfy the rapacious creditors of a brother who, for this purpose, which he falsely believed to be generous, mortgaged all his slaves to British harpies for money to gratify pride and pamper sensuality; by which mortgage, the said slaves being bound, I could not exercise the right of ownership necessary to their emancipation, and, being obliged to keep them on my land, was driven reluctantly to violate them in a great degree) (though I trust far less than others have done) in order to maintain them . . . ; for the aforesaid purposes and, with an indignation, too great for utterance, at the tyrants of the earth, from the throned despot of a whole nation to the most despicable, but not less infamous, petty tormentors of single wretched slaves, whose torture constitutes his wealth and enjoyment, I do hereby declare that it is my will and desire, nay most anxious wish that my negroes, all of them, be liberated, and I do declare them by this writing free and emancipated to all intents and purposes whatsoever.

The *Richmond Virginian* Calls for Tighter Control of Blacks, 1808

The benefits to be derived from the establishment of a military corps cannot be denied: nor can it be pretended, that under the actual state of society, some provision of that sort is not absolutely necessary.

And why absolutely necessary? it is because the state of slavery which exists, added to recent events, impresses it on the mind of every man of reflection, that some effectual and permanent means ought to be employed to guard against actual danger, as well as to ensure public tranquility.

If this be so; if the necessity of incurring a heavy public expence, proceeds altogether from the situation of society as relates to the slaves—then nothing can be more reasonable, than that the whole expense ought to be borne by the holders of that particular species of property.

It is foreseen that this will be immediately opposed upon the allegation of partiality and inequality—It will be alledged [*sic*] that all the expenses of government ought to be mutually borne by all descriptions of people, and that every tax calculated to serve one portion of society, from the burthens which are imposed on others, is not only in itself unjust and oppressive, but will trench upon the established principles of a free government. All that can be now said in relation to this objection, is to deny it. The design of the writer is merely to bring into notice those opinions which prevail in his own mind. He believes that a public guard is absolutely necessary; that the system which he has recommended is far superior to that which exists; and that a tax on slaves is not only just and reasonable in itself, but by no means inconsistent with the equal principles of our constitution, and he would willingly afford aids to widows, orphans, and other cases of extreme hardship.

With respect to the slaves, it is likely that a general change of policy would be productive of greater benefits, than could have been expected from the public guard—In order to invite the attention of the public to the subject, the following remarks are submitted to notice.

Two opposing opinions now distract the state. One set of men, with honest, generous, but imprudent zeal, aim at a general and unconditional emancipation—Others influenced by motives equally pure, not only thwart and oppose these humane innovators, but seem to take delight in oppressing and embittering the fate of the unfortunates. In both of these cases perhaps true policy is neglected. The general weight and influence of public harmony is lost; the energies of the state are paralyzed; and men of equal respectability, of equal claims to public favour are arrayed against each other. Another course ought then to be adopted, promising not only to guard against general emancipation, but an amelioration of the condition of slaves.

Every slave ought to have some means of protection against the cruelty, injustice, and systematical oppressions of inhuman and flinty hearted masters; this may be done by competent tribunals, and upon terms dictated by justice and benevolence.

Indiscriminate and general emancipation at this time ought not to be countenanced, so far from it, the privilege ought to be extended, with care and caution, only to such as deserve so great a boon, by eminent service, or by a general course of a meritorious deportment.

Slaves ought to be solely employed in agricultural or other occupations of plain labour. It is also worthy of enquiry whether mechanics, house servants, waiters, waggoners, draymen, and water-men ought not to pay a higher tax, than those who are employed in agriculture, and whether in future, and by degrees the blacks should not be excluded from mechanical employments, and from being public carriers.

Innovations of this sort, would be at first attended with some inconvenience, but as soon as the regulations were known to be firmly settled and established, the labourers and industrious poor would very readily embrace those occupations, which are now, for the most part discharged by slaves—By this change alone, society would receive a much greater security than can result from the establishment of guards, even though their numbers and organization, should be equal to those ideas which have been partially unfolded. The dangers to be apprehended from slaves depend upon several causes; one is, they are the common carriers of the lower country—they have under their immediate care all the horses and accoutrements for horses—they are almost without exception good riders, and drivers, and among them may be found almost every kind of artist; Smiths and Carpenters without number. From these causes they have the means, without much exertion[,] of doing a great deal of mischief.

Now as the object of writing these sentences, is not to render the condition of the good and virtuous slave worse than heretofore, but to prevent the wicked from forming plots and conspiracies, the benevolent reader must not condemn what has been, or what may be said, before he looks through the vista of futurity, and impartially considers the different prospects which may be afforded. Peace, quiet industry on one hand—robbery, scourging, hanging, alarms and insurrections on the other.

If these or similar innovations are adopted, all the various duties now performed by slaves as carriers, artists, &c. will be performed by whites. The military strength of the city of Richmond alone, will be immediately doubled, and instead of danger from the black population, requiring a constant guard and patrol, there would be no other danger than that which is to be apprehended from the general depravity of mankind. The number of cultivators would be accordingly increased, and the general improvement of the country of course would be promoted.

Many other benefits would be obtained by this city. At present, there are at least one thousand black men, who are solely employed, some in bringing the produce to the city, by the means of the canal, and others in conveying it to tide water by the means of the drays. It is believed that at least every other boat which comes into the Basin, brings in it some articles which have been stolen—these are either sold or exchanged with draymen, or others in league with them; and although the boats may be pursued, the articles stolen will seldom be found. So likewise the plunder of Richmond is disposed of and conveyed away so as to escape detection. Besides these evils, there are in the city many retail shops, whose entire trade is with the dray-men and boat-men—Many of whom are always ready to receive stolen articles in exchange for ardent spirits, or perhaps a small pecuniary compensation. It is true that these dealers are frequently detected—but the means of proof is equally defective; because the testimony of a black man or mulatto cannot be received against a white man.

The complaint is as general as the wickedness is notorious—the inhabitants look to the magistrates, and the magistrates in vain try to check the evil; a few punishments to be sure are inflicted; but they bear no proportion to the extent of the mischief, and rather tend to irritate and harden the offenders, than to reclaim or deter them.

The notorious existence of such growing evils, ought of themselves, to excite the attention of the Legislature; but when they are coupled with the other, when the existence of so many black men in the city, in the employments which ought to be confided alone to whites, increase the common danger, these double inducements ought to exist for banishing them, not only from the city, but to employ them in future in agricultural or other occupations where the chances to commit depredations, and engage in conspiracies will be less frequent.

John C. Calhoun's Early Nationalism, 1816

Speech Introducing the Bank Bill

February 26, 1816

Mr. Calhoun rose to explain his views of a subject so interesting to the Republic, and so necessary to be correctly understood, as that of the bill now before the committee. He proposed at this time only to discuss general principles, without reference to details. He was aware, he said, that principle and detail might be united; but he should at present keep them distinct. He did not propose to comprehend in this discussion, the power of Congress to grant bank charters; nor the question whether the general tendency of banks was favorable or unfavorable to the liberty and prosperity of the country; nor the question whether a National Bank would be favorable to the operations of the government. To discuss these questions, he conceived, would be an useless consumption of time. The constitutional question had been already so freely and frequently discussed, that all had made up their minds on it. The question whether banks were favorable to public liberty and prosperity, was one purely speculative. The fact of the existence of banks, and their incorporation with the commercial concerns and industry of the nation, proved that enquiry to come too late. The only question was, on this hand, under what modifications were banks most useful, and whether the United States ought or ought not to exercise the power to establish a bank. As to the question whether a National Bank would be favorable to the administration of the finances of the government, it was one on which there was so little doubt, that gentlemen would excuse him if he did not enter into it. Leaving all these questions then, Mr. C. said, he proposed to examine the cause and state of the disorders of the national currency, and the question whether it was in the power of Congress, by establishing a National Bank, to remove those disorders. This, he observed, was a question of novelty and vital importance; a question which greatly affected the character and prosperity of the country.

As to the state of the currency of the nation, Mr. C. proceeded to remark—that it was extremely depreciated, and in degrees varying according to the different sections of the country, all would assent. That this state of the currency was a stain on public and private credit, and injurious to the morals of the community, was so clear a position as to require no proof. There were, however, other considerations arising from the state of the currency not so distinctly felt, not so generally assented to. The state of our circulating medium was, he said, opposed to the principles of the Federal Constitution. The power was given to Congress by that instrument in express terms to regulate the currency of the United States. In point of fact, he said, that power, though given to Congress, is not in their hands. The power is exercised by banking institutions, no longer responsible for the correctness with which they manage it. Gold and silver have disappeared entirely; there is no money but paper money, and that money is beyond the control of Congress. No one, he said, who referred to the Constitution, could doubt that the money of the United States was intended to be placed entirely under the control of Congress. The only object the framers of the Constitution could have in view in giving to Congress the power "to coin money, regulate the value thereof and of foreign coin," must have been to give a steadiness and fixed value to the currency of the United States. The state of things at the time of the adoption of the Constitution, afforded Mr. C. an argument in support of his construction. There then existed, he said, a depreciated paper currency, which could only be regulated and made uniform by giving a power for that purpose to the general government. The states could not do it. He argued, therefore, taking into view the prohibition against the states issuing bills of credit, that there was a strong presumption this power was intended to be exclusively given to Congress. . . .

Remarks on the Need for a National Bank

March 6, 1816

Mr. Calhoun . . . almost despaired of the passage of the bill [to establish a national bank], after some of the indications which he had witnessed, and began to doubt whether any bill would pass at all on the subject. For himself, Mr. C. said, his anxiety for the measure was not extreme—but as long as there was a lingering hope of its success, he should omit no effort to make it an efficient remedy for the evils of the present currency. If, after making it suit, as far as possible, the taste of every one, gentlemen determined to oppose it, it was time for them to look out for some other remedy. Mr. C. said, he felt deeply the evil of the disordered state of our currency, and the necessity of a cure. In devising that cure, difficulties were to be expected. The direction of the bank he knew had been made a *sine qua non* by some gentlemen on one side of the House, and he was sorry to find it was one also with some on the other. It was a fate peculiar to great measures, to fall in their details. The obstinacy of gentlemen in matters of what they deemed principle, was honorable to them, but he feared it would be fatal to the bill. He lamented it—the disorders were so deep, so great, that justice to the country called for a remedy at the hands of the government. If gentlemen would seriously consider the character and power and nature of the evil—two hundred and sixty banks issuing almost as many millions of depreciated paper—they must see the necessity of co-operating in the measure of relief. The necessity for union was great and urgent, for the disease was almost incurable—it was a leprosy on the body politic—&c.

Speech on the Tariff Bill

April 4, 1816

The debate heretofore on this subject, has been on the degree of protection which ought to be afforded to our cotton and woollen manufactures; all professing to be friendly to those infant establishments, and to be willing to extend to them adequate encouragement. The present motion assumes a new aspect. It is introduced professedly on the ground, that manufactures ought not to receive any encouragement; and will, in its operation, leave our cotton establishments exposed to the competition of the cotton goods of the East Indies, which, it is acknowledged on all sides, they are not capable of meeting with success, without the proviso proposed to be stricken out by the motion now under discussion. Till the debate assumed this new form, he had determined to be silent; participating, as he largely did, in that general anxiety which is felt, after so long and laborious a session, to return to the bosom of our families. But on a subject of such vital importance, touching, as it does, the security and permanent prosperity of our country, he hoped that the House would indulge him in a few observations. He regretted much his want of preparation—he meant not a verbal preparation, for he had ever despised such, but that due and mature meditation and arrangement of thought, which the House is entitled to on the part of those who occupy any portion of their time. But whatever his arguments might want on that account in weight, he hoped might be made up in the disinterestedness of his situation. He was no manufacturer; he was not from that portion of our country supposed to be peculiarly interested. Coming, as he did, from the South, having, in common with his immediate constituents, no interest, but in the cultivation of the soil, in selling its products high, and buying cheap the wants and conveniencies of life, no motive could be attributed to him, but such as were disinterested.

He had asserted, that the subject before them was connected with the security of the country. It would, doubtless, by some be considered a rash assertion; but he conceived it to be susceptible of the clearest proof; and he hoped, with due attention, to establish it to the satisfaction of the House.

The security of a country mainly depends on its spirit and its means; and the latter principally on its monied resources. Modified as the industry of this country now is, combined with our peculiar situation and want of a naval ascendancy; whenever we have the misfortune to be involved in a war with a nation dominant on the ocean, and it is almost only with such we can at present be, the monied resources of the country, to a great extent, must fail. He took it for granted, that it was the duty of this body to adopt those measures of prudent foresight, which the event of war made necessary. We cannot, he presumed, be indifferent to dangers from abroad, unless, indeed, the House is prepared to indulge in the phantom of eternal peace, which seemed to possess the dream of some of its members. Could such a state exist, no foresight or fortitude would be necessary to conduct the affairs of the Republic; but as it is the mere illusion of the imagination, as every people that ever has or ever will exist, are subjected to the vicissitudes of peace and war, it must ever be considered as the plain dictate of wisdom, in peace to prepare for war. What, then, let us consider constitute the resources of this country, and what are the effects of war on them? Commerce and agriculture, till lately, almost the only, still constitute the principal sources of our wealth. So long as these remain uninterrupted, the country prospers; but war, as we are now circumstanced, is equally destructive to both. They both depend on foreign markets; and our country is placed, as it regards them, in a situation strictly insular; a wide ocean rolls between. Our commerce neither is or can be protected, by the present means of the country. What, then, are the effects of a war with a maritime power—with England? Our commerce annihilated, spreading individual misery, and producing national poverty; our agriculture cut off from its accustomed markets, the surplus product of the farmer perishes on his hands; and he ceases to produce, because he cannot sell. His resources are dried up, while his expences are greatly increased; as all manufactured articles, the necessaries, as well as the conveniences of life, rise to an extravagant price. The recent war fell with peculiar pressure on the growers of cotton and tobacco, and other great staples of the country; and the same state of things will recur in the event of another, unless prevented by the foresight of this body.

If the mere statement of facts did not carry conviction to any mind, as he conceives it is calculated to do, additional arguments might be drawn from the general nature of wealth. Neither agriculture, manufactures or commerce, taken separately, is the cause of wealth; it flows from the three combined; and cannot exist without each. The wealth of any single nation or an individual, it is true, may not *immediately* depend on the three, but such wealth always presupposes their existence. He viewed the words in the most enlarged sense. Without commerce, industry would have no stimulus; without manufactures, it would be without the means of production; and without agriculture, neither of the others can subsist. When separated entirely and permanently, they perish. War in this country produces, to a great extent, that effect; and hence, the great embarrassment which follows in its train. The failure of the wealth and resources of the nation necessarily involved the ruin of its finances and its currency. It is admitted by the most strenuous advocates, on the other side, that no country ought to be dependent on another for its means of defence; that, at least, our musket and bayonet, our cannon and ball, ought to be of domestic manufacture. But what, he asked, is more necessary to the defence of a country than its currency and finance? Circumstanced as our country is, can these stand the shock of war? Behold the effect of the late war on them. When our manufactures are grown to a certain perfection, as they soon will under the fostering care of government, we will no longer experience these evils.

The farmer will find a ready market for his surplus produce; and what is almost of equal consequence, a certain and cheap supply of all his wants. His prosperity will diffuse itself to every class in the community; and instead of that languor of industry and individual distress now incident to a state of war, and suspended commerce, the wealth and vigor of the community will not be materially impaired. The arm of government will be nerved, and taxes in the hour of danger, when essential to the independence of the nation, may be greatly increased; loans, so uncertain and hazardous, may be less relied on; thus situated, the storm may beat without, but within all will be quiet and safe.

To give perfection to this state of things, it will be necessary to add, as soon as possible, a system of internal improvements, and at least such an extension of our navy, as will prevent the cutting off our coasting trade. The advantage of each is so striking, as not to require illustration, especially after the experience of the recent war. . . .

Other objections of a political character were made to the encouragement of manufactures. It is said they destroy the moral and physical power of the people. This might formerly have been true to a considerable extent, before the perfection of machinery, and when the success of the manufactures depended on the minute sub-division of labor. At that time it required a large portion of the population of a country to be engaged in them; and every minute sub-division of labor is undoubtedly unfavorable to the intellect; but the great perfection of machinery has in a considerable degree obviated these objections. In fact it has been stated that the manufacturing districts in England furnish the greatest number of recruits to her army, and that, as soldiers, they are not materially inferior to the rest of her population. It has been further asserted that manufactures are the fruitful cause of pauperism; and England has been referred to as furnishing conclusive evidence of its truth. For his part, he could perceive no such tendency in them, but the exact contrary, as they furnished new stimulus and means of subsistence to the laboring classes of the community. We ought not to look to the cotton and woollen establishments of Great Britain for the prodigious numbers of poor with which her population was disgraced. Causes much more efficient exist. Her poor laws and statutes regulating the price of labor with heavy taxes, were the real causes. But if it must be so, if the mere fact that England manufactured more than any other country, explained the cause of her having more beggars, it is just as reasonable to refer her courage, spirit, and all her masculine virtues, in which she excels all other nations, with a single exception; he meant our own; in which we might without vanity challenge a pre-eminence.

Another objection had been made, which he must acknowledge was better founded, that capital employed in manufacturing produced a greater dependance on the part of the employed, than in commerce, navigation or agriculture. It is certainly an evil and to be regretted; but he did not think it a decisive objection to the system; especially when it had incidental political advantages which in his opinion more than counterpoised it. It produced an interest strictly American, as much so as agriculture; in which it had the decided advantage of commerce or navigation. The country will from this derive much advantage. Again, it is calculated to bind together more closely our widely-spread Republic. It will greatly increase our mutual dependence and intercourse; and will as a necessary consequence, excite an increased attention to internal improvement, a subject every way so intimately connected with the ultimate attainment of national strength and the perfection of our political institutions. He regarded the fact that it would make the parts adhere more closely, that it would form a new and most powerful cement, far out-weighing any political objections that might be urged against the system. In his opinion the *liberty* and the *union* of this country were inseparably united! That as the destruction of the latter would most certainly involve the former; so its maintenance will with equal certainty preserve it. He did not speak lightly. He had often and long revolved it in his mind.

Southern Congressmen Defend Slavery in Missouri

*Speech of Benjamin Hardin of Kentucky to the House
of Representatives, February 4, 1820*

Sir, the manner in which this nation seems divided upon this subject [the admission of Missouri] convinces me of one thing that I have long suspected to be true, that our opinions, upon all that variety of subjects upon which we in the course of our lives are called upon to decide, are the result of affections and passions, and that judgment has no concern therein. Upon this occasion, we see this opinion fully illustrated; because men, distinguished both for integrity and talents, are to be found on each side; and the line that divides the parties is a local one. But, sir, the unwillingness manifested by the opposite side of the house to adjust and settle this dispute, and prevent an explosion that must shake the American world to its centre, induces me to believe that their judgments are warped by a passion, in this case, which may be denominated an unsatiable thirst after power, an unwarrantable lust of domination.

We now, Mr. Chairman, come to the last question I proposed to discuss. It is this: If there be no impediment to the powers of Congress from the constitution, and the national faith will not be violated by adopting the present amendment [providing for the emancipation of future descendents of slaves presently in Missouri], does policy dictate the measure? I do verily believe, that, instead of its being expedient to impose the proposed restriction upon the people of Missouri, that it would be unwise and impolitic, as it respects the nation; it would be unjust as it relates to the slave holding states; it would be iniquitous towards those who have been invited to settle there, and purchase our land at a high price; and a most aggravated and flagrant breach of public and national faith to those who lived there at the time of the ratification of the treaty between the United States and France. . . .

. . . This dispute is like no other that ever came into this house, that was ever before the legislative body of this nation. Party spirit, I know, has at times run high, but the great danger from this question as it relates to the safety and integrity of the Union, is this, that it is not the same state divided into parties; it is not the states in the same section of the Union divided against each other. It is the north and east against the south and west. It is a great geographical line that separates the contending parties. And those parties, when so equally divided, shake mighty empires to their centre, and break up the foundations of the great deep, that sooner or later, if not settled, will rend in twain this temple of liberty, from the top to the bottom. My friends reply to me, and say, how can you compromise? how can you surrender principle?

It strikes me, Sir, that this matter can be settled with great facility, if each party be so disposed, and neither give up any point in this question which may be called principle. Can it not be done by permitting Missouri to go into the Union without the restriction, and then draw a line from the western boundary of the proposed state of Missouri, due west, to the Pacific? North of the line prohibit slavery, and south admit it?

The principle we contend for is, first, that Congress cannot demand a surrender of any sovereignty from a new state which is retained by the old states. In the proposed compromise this principle will not be violated. Next, we say that the faith of the nation is pledged to the people of that territory. Neither will this principle be given up, for the territory upon which the compromise, as contemplated, is intended to operate, is a wilderness, no inhabitants, citizens of the United States, living thereon. As it respects the gentlemen who are in favor of the present proposed restriction, it is no sacrifice of principle if they, finding that they cannot gain all they contend for, are content with partial success. I beg them to beware of one thing, as they love and revere this Union, not to push matters to extremities; for, although they may have a majority on this floor, we will never submit at discretion. I call on them to recollect the old proverb, "beware of the desperation of a peaceable man." No, Mr. Chairman, sooner than be delivered over, not to our brethren, either in politics or affection, but a federal party in the north, bound hand and foot, and to have no voice, no lot, no part, in this Union, we will burst all the ties and bonds that unite us together, and stand erect in our own majesty, as did that mighty man of old, when Delilah said, "the Philistines be upon thee, Sampson."

Speech of Nathaniel Macon of North Carolina to the Senate, January 20, 1820

The character of the present excitement is such, that no man can foresee what consequences may grow out of it.

But why depart from the good old way, which has kept us in quiet, peace, and harmony—every one living under his own vine and fig tree, and none to make him afraid? Why leave the road of experience, which has satisfied all, and made all happy, to take this new way, of which we have no experience? The way leads to universal emancipation, of which we have no experience. The eastern and middle states furnish none. For years before they emancipated they had but few, and of these a part were sold to the south, before they emancipated. We have not more experience or book learning on this subject than the French Convention had which turned the slaves of St. Domingo loose. Nor can we foresee the consequences which may result from this motion, more than the Convention did their decree. A clause in the Declaration of Independence has been read, declaring "that all men are created equal:" follow that sentiment, and does it not lead to universal emancipation? If it will justify putting an end to slavery in Missouri, will it not justify it in the old states? Suppose the plan followed, and all the slaves turned loose, and the Union to continue, is it certain that the present constitution would last long? Because the rich would, in such circumstances, want titles and hereditary distinctions; the negro food and raiment, and they would be as much, or more degraded, than in their present condition. The rich might hire these wretched people, and with them attempt to change the government, by trampling on the rights of those who have only property enough to live comfortably.

Opinions have greatly changed in some of the states, in a few years. The time has been when those now called slave-holding states, were thought to be the firm and stedfast friends of the people and of liberty. Then they were opposing an administration and a majority in Congress, supported by a sedition law; then there was not a word heard, at least from one side, about those who actually did most towards changing the administration and the majority in Congress, and they were from slave-holding states. And now it would be curious to know how many members of Congress actually hold seats in consequence of their exertions at the time alluded to. Past services are always forgot when new principles are to be introduced.

It is a fact, that the people who move from the non-slave-holding to the slave-holding states, when they become slave-holders by purchase or marriage, expect more labor from them than those do who are brought up among them. To the gentleman from Rhode Island (Mr. Burrill) I tender my hearty thanks for his liberal and true statement of the treatment of slaves in the Southern states. His observations leave but little for me to add, which is this, that the slaves gained as much by independence as the free. The old ones are better taken care of than any poor in the world, and treated with decent respect by all their white acquaintants. I sincerely wish that he and the gentleman from Pennsylvania, (Mr. Roberts,) would go home with me, or some other southern member, and witness the meeting between the slaves and the owner, and see the glad faces and the hearty shaking of hands. . . .

. . . Can it be thought that the Convention which framed the constitution would have given the power to emancipate in so indirect a way that it was never discovered till the last session, when they were so particular as even to prohibit an interference with the slave trade until 1808? The following words in the constitution are chiefly relied on for the authority: "Congress shall have power to dispose of, and make all needful rules and regulations respecting the territory and other property belonging to the United States." The fair and only meaning of these words is, that Congress may sell and manage their own property, but not the property of the people. The power over the territories is very different from that over the District of Columbia, where exclusive legislation is granted. "New states may be admitted by the Congress into this Union." Under these words, a power is claimed to declare what shall be property in a new state. As well might a power be claimed to fix the age when people shall marry in the state. The ordinance so often referred to declares, that the new states shall be admitted on an equal footing with the original states. And so all the new states have been. It seems to be authority for every one but Missouri. . . .

It is to be regretted, that, notwithstanding the compromise made in the constitution about slaves, gentlemen had thought proper, at almost every session, to bring the subject before Congress, in some shape or other, and that they regularly, in their arguments, claim new power over them. What have the people of the southern states done, that such a strong desire should be manifested to pen them up? It cannot be because their representatives have uniformly opposed the African slave trade, or because they as uniformly opposed the impressment of American sailors by British officers; or because their banks are drained of specie to supply other places, and the revenue collected from them is not spent among them; or because they have been so tolerant in politics that when Mr. Jefferson came into office, their opponents, who had every office, were not turned out—a proof that they did not oppose them for their places of honor or profit; or because they have been willing to admit new states into the Union without regard to the number of people;—Ohio will remember, that the speeches of southern members were printed to induce her citizens to become a state—or because they have never requested Congress to tax others for their benefit; or because they have not abused the late pension law, but have at all times been obedient to the laws of the United States and of the states, never giving cause for uneasiness or alarm to the United States or the neighboring states, and, at all times which tried men's souls, have been found good and true; or because, in old times, they opposed the shutting of the Mississippi for 25 years.

If the decision be in favor of the amendment, it may ruin us and our children after us; if against it, no injury will result to any part of the United States.

⅄ *E S S A Y S*

John R. Alden, formerly professor of history at Duke University, traced the origins of regional self-consciousness in the South to the Revolutionary period and to early attempts to form a national government. In the first essay, notice how conflicts over economic issues, the costs and powers of the central government, and slavery made southerners aware of their regional interests and identity. Historian Philip D. Morgan of Florida State University focuses in the second essay on the lowcountry of South Carolina and Georgia, where slavery was dominant and growing in importance. Yet he shows that blacks there had an unusual degree of control over their daily lives. Richard R. Beeman, professor of history at the University of Pennsylvania, studied Virginia as an example of the evolution of the southern backcountry. The excerpts reprinted here as the third selection describe both increasing social diversity and growing unity around the institution of slavery in Lunenburg County, Virginia.

The Rise of Southern Self-Awareness

JOHN R. ALDEN

This First South existed during the years 1775–1789. It appeared with the American nation; it was christened as early as 1778; and it clashed ever more sharply with a First North during and immediately after the War of Independence. This First South did not hasten under the Federal Roof with swift and certain steps, but haltingly and uncertainly. Many of her people feared that the Federal cover would offer greater protection north of the Susquehanna than it would south of that river. It should not be said that their alarm was without cause, that they saw troubles which the future did not bring. They feared lest they become a minority in an American union dominated by a Northern majority, lest they suffer in consequence. Whatever may be the merits of measures since imposed upon the South by the North—and the West—it will not be denied that the South has felt the power of external American forces, especially since the middle of the nineteenth century. . . .

. . . The word Southern was acquiring a more restrictive meaning, the phrase "Middle states" being used more and more to describe New York, New Jersey, Pennsylvania, and Delaware. These "Middle states" with the "Eastern states" were increasingly put together as the "Northern states," another usage which long endured.

Quickly shorn of the Middle states, the Southern states became a South and a section. The limits of that section were, of course, only gradually established in the minds of men; indeed, they cannot now be firmly laid down between it and the Middle states. There was disagreement about its northern boundaries at the time, although no one doubted that the Carolinas and Georgia were part of it.

Strange to say, none other than George Washington, until the adoption of the Constitution, was reluctant to include Virginia within the First South. In 1787 and again in 1788 he refers in his correspondence to the Carolinas and Georgia as the "Southern states." In 1786 he invited Don Diego de Gardoqui, the official emissary of Spain to the United States, to pay a visit to Mount Vernon "if you should ever feel an inclination to make an excursion into the middle states." It is apparent that Washington, a stout nationalist even before the close of the War of Independence, wished to minimize the South and its special interests. But he was forced to recognize

---

John Richard Alden, *The First South* (Baton Rouge: Louisiana State University Press, 1961), pp. 4–9, 22–24, 40–49. Reprinted by permission of the publisher.

that they existed, and he too began to refer to the region between Pennsylvania and the Floridas as the "Southern states." Not until his first term as president did he fully realize the vitality of a Southern section that included Virginia. Becoming genuinely and even gravely alarmed, he urged his countrymen, in his Farewell Address, to soften their sectional antagonisms.

Except for Washington, I have found no Revolutionary worthy who would have drawn a line between Virginia and the South. And I have discovered only one other Founding Father who did not include Maryland in the "Southern states." That person was William Henry Drayton of South Carolina, who declared most emphatically in the winter of 1777–1778 that Virginia, the Carolinas, and Georgia formed "the body of the southern interest." Almost invariably, men in public life perplexed by North-South contests said or assumed that Maryland belonged to the Southern connection. Frequently politicians referred to difficulties between the eight Northern states and the five Southern ones. Others indicated that the North and the South were set apart by the Susquehanna River. The prevailing view was put flatly in 1787 by Charles Pinckney of South Carolina, who declared, "When I say Southern, I mean Maryland, and the states to the southward of her." . . .

The contest between South and North began even before the Declaration of Independence. In the first general American assembly—in the First Continental Congress in 1774—came the first quarrel. It was, as were most of such struggles before 1789, economic in nature. When that body considered measures to compel Parliament and Crown to change their course to American wishes, it decided to use a weapon which had become familiar, a boycott of British goods. There was no sectional disagreement regarding the use of this boycott, even though the importation of Negro slaves was also forbidden. Nor was there any difficulty between North and South because the Congress decreed nonconsumption of British goods, this measure being calculated to prevent merchants from pulling profits out of scarcities. It was otherwise when the delegates decided to use the club of nonexportation to Britain and the British West Indies, in case of need, the date for cessation being set at September 10, 1775. The delegates from South Carolina, except for Christopher Gadsden, asked that rice and indigo be excepted from the embargo, and so raised a controversy.

In this clash varying economic interests were basic. On the surface, the South Carolina men in the Congress were asking a special favor for the Low Country; from their point of view they were merely requesting equal sacrifice from all sections. Because of British law and other circumstances rice and indigo markets in England and the British West Indies were very important to South Carolina. Were exportation of those products to those markets forbidden, the Low Country planters, almost utterly dependent upon sales of rice and dye stuffs, must suffer grievously. The Northern colonies would be able to sell outside Britain and the islands, as they had in the past; and even the Chesapeake colonies, their tobacco going largely to London, Bristol, and Liverpool because of Parliamentary law, could escape the worst effects of the self-inflicted punishment of embargo by turning to wheat-growing. Even so, the attitude of the South Carolina delegation was not generous, especially with respect to their fellow planters of the Chesapeake; and Gadsden was prepared to offer a total sacrifice. When Northerners in Congress cried favoritism, the dominant Carolinians withdrew their request for excepting indigo; and for the sake of creating a solid front against Britain, the free sending of South Carolina's rice to sea was permitted. Thus the quarrel was resolved by concession on the part of the others to the Low Country planters. . . .

The most serious sectional controversy during the War of Independence, and one which continued after the bullets had ceased to whistle, arose, inevitably, when the Patriots undertook to make a national constitution. The provisions of such a basic document might have the most profound effects into the most distant future, consequences far greater than those which could proceed from Congressional resolutions. Because there was a widespread fear of central tyranny in the Northern states as well as the Southern ones, the first constitution of the United States, the Articles of Confederation, provided for a weak central government. Since neither section then wanted a powerful one, clash between them regarding its powers, methods of representation, and appointment of financial burdens was reduced. Nevertheless, the making of the Articles during the years 1776–1777 and attempts to revise them which continued for a decade created much sectional ill feeling within Congress and without. Peculiarly sharp were debates over distribution of the cost of the central regime. But other issues were raised and squabbled about; and in South Carolina the need for constitutional protection of Southern interests against Northern tyranny was raised in startling fashion.

When the men at Philadelphia began in 1776 to go into the business of constitution-making, Edward Rutledge was already distrustful of national power. Said Rutledge: "The idea of destroying all provincial distinctions and making everything of the most minute kind bend to what they call the good of the whole, is in other terms to say that these [Southern] colonies must be subject to the government of the Eastern provinces." His concern could not have been allayed by the terms of a draft of the Articles of Confederation which was submitted to the delegates by a special committee on July 12. This document, apparently because of the influence of John Dickinson of Pennsylvania, would have created a national legislature wielding great authority, except that its funds were to be supplied by requisitions upon the states. But that authority was sharply reduced by the body of delegates, with men from the South taking the lead in the making of the most significant change, the addition of a statement, "Each state retains its sovereignty, freedom, and independence, and every power, jurisdiction and right, which is not by this confederation expressly delegated to the United States in Congress assembled." North Carolinian Thomas Burke moved its inclusion, and the representatives of South Carolina seconded. Virginia gave the only vote against the change. Burke was apparently swayed principally by state allegiance, as were the deputies from the North.

It may reasonably be guessed that the South Carolinians were moved by larger considerations. Many other alterations were made which, taken together, lessened the powers of Congress until they were little more than those then exercised by the United States in the Pennsylvania State House.

Joining with their Northern colleagues in reforming the Articles so that the national assembly became feeble rather than potentially tyrannical, the delegates from the South fought bitterly with those from the North over the apportionment of the costs of the central government among the states. The Congress had created a precedent in July, 1775, when it had declared that its paper currency was to be made good by the colonies in ratio to their respective numbers, including Negroes. The general committee's draft of the Articles similarly provided that the states would contribute to the national funds in proportion to inhabitants, Indians not taxed being not counted.

But the Southern delegates, realizing that their country was relatively much poorer, and that by this arrangement they would pay nearly half of the national expenses, demanded that it be modified; and a hot debate concerning apportionment began toward the close of July, 1776, and continued intermittently for several years. Samuel Chase of Maryland denounced the arrangement because, as he said, Negroes were property rather than persons—hence they should not be included in population. He offered an amending motion to that effect. John Adams, a Yankee satisfied with the system, tried to answer the Marylander. He said that a slave produced as much wealth as a white man—which was certainly not the fact—hence the Negroes should not be omitted. He was supported, more cogently, by James Wilson of Pennsylvania, who asserted that Chase's amendment would enable the Southerners to reap profit from slaves and would impose too heavy a burden upon the Northerners. Pointing out that Adams erred remarkably when he equated slave with white labor, Benjamin Harrison of Virginia declared that the labor of a white man was worth twice as much as that of a slave. Accordingly, he offered a compromise: that two Negroes should be counted as one white. This solution was acceptable to the Southerners, not to the Northerners. John Witherspoon of New Jersey, who saw that the Southerners had a case, then urged that the basis of apportionment be shifted from numbers to the value of private lands, together with improvements upon them. This scheme would have placed a relatively heavy burden upon the Northern states, especially those of New England, with its small and well kept farms. The Northern deputies insisted that donations be calculated according to the general committee's formula. Southerners more and more vigorously attacked it. It was useless to talk further about union, said Thomas Lynch of South Carolina, if it were not admitted that slaves were property. They were, and they were so taxed in South Carolina, said Lynch and Edward Rutledge. Rutledge, refusing to defend slavery as an institution, claimed it would be unfair to include Negroes in the formula, for their owners would be forced to contribute, while the proprietors of Northern merchant shipping, which must make great profits in carrying American goods as a result of union, would not be taxed therefor. William

Hooper, a Yankee transplanted to North Carolina, properly pointed out that the formula was unfair to his state, which had a large population and relatively little wealth. All these arguments availed the Southerners nothing at the time. The Chase amendment was defeated, the sections lining up almost solidly in the balloting. New England and the Middle states, save for Delaware, voted nay; Georgia was divided, but the remainder of the South, with Delaware, voted aye.

This decision could not stand. Samuel Chase and other delegates from Maryland openly declared that their state would never ratify the Articles of Confederation if it were not rescinded; and we may properly conclude that still other deputies from the Far South harbored similar sentiments. In 1777 the problem of dividing the burden of national expenses among the states was again debated. John Witherspoon's substitute formula calling for the use of lands and improvements thereupon was warmly discussed. The New Englanders were, as before, vigorously opposed to it. They wanted the Negroes included in any formula that might be adopted; and they had a new argument for doing so. A provision had been placed in the Articles calling for a Continental army with the states contributing men in ratio to their white inhabitants. The Yankees believed that recognition of the principle that the Negro was merely property would force them both to pay and to fight more than they equitably should. There was a belief among the Middle state delegates, however, that the South must be satisfied; and Witherspoon's formula was sanctioned by the Congress, Maryland, Virginia, the Carolinas, and New Jersey voting for it; Pennsylvania and New York splitting; and New England solidly voting in the negative.

The Witherspoon arrangement, endorsed by so narrow a margin, remained in the Articles of Confederation so long as that constitution endured. But Northern assaults upon it continued. The legislature of Connecticut, when the Articles were presented to the states for action in 1777, proposed an amendment which called for a return to the numbers-and-Negroes formula. It was promptly rejected by Congress, and Connecticut ratified the Articles without it. However, Southern and Northern states were equally remiss when it came to paying their quotas under the Witherspoon plan, for dollars were equally valued and difficult to secure on both sides of the Mason-Dixon line. The requisition system, as we all know, was a failure. Only too well aware that it must have substantial and reliable funds to operate, Congress in 1781 proposed an amendment which would have given it power to levy import duties. It failed to secure the unanimous approval of the states required by the Articles.

In 1783 the Congress again attacked its money problem, reviving the sectional quarrel over state contributions. On March 7, a Congressional committee on revenue brought before the delegates a proposed amendment which would have given Congress authority to impose import duties for a period of twenty-five years—such duties being the most obvious and the simplest means of securing money. But the committee also called for the continuance of requisitions upon the states—contributing in ratio to numbers, including Negroes. The old quarrel was then resumed, with the Southerners again denouncing that scheme. Nor would they approve another, one offered by Pennsylvanian James Wilson, a $.25 per 100 acres tax on land—Southern soil was still less valuable than Northern. The committee on revenue revised its proposal: two Negroes should be counted as one white. This suggested compromise opened up a game of fractions on the floor of the house. Oliver Wolcott of Connecticut and Stephen Higginson of Massachusetts said four Negroes should be considered equal to three whites. Marylander Daniel Carroll would have it 4:1. John Rutledge thought 3:1 proper, but offered to accept 2:1. Other New Englanders supported 4:3. A motion for 3:2 was lost because all the Southern states voted against it. When solution seemed almost impossible, James Madison suggested 5:3, which Rutledge supported. Reconsidering, some Northern delegates then brought up 3:2, which was rejected. Madison had found the magic middle, and the amendment was framed accordingly. All the Southern states then represented, voted for it, and it was approved by the assemblies of Virginia and Maryland. But a majority of the states gave their consent only with clogging reservations; four of them did not even bother to reply yes or no; and it was accordingly defeated.

The Expansion of Slavery in the Lowcountry

PHILIP D. MORGAN

The Revolutionary era saw slaves gain formal freedom in the North and "considerably greater independence, mobility and opportunity" in the upper Chesapeake. In lowcountry South Carolina and Georgia, change was much less dramatic; in one sense, the opposite occurred, for slavery became more rather than less entrenched. Indeed, lowcountry planters developed a deeper commitment to slavery than did those in the lower Chesapeake. At the same time, however, black autonomy in the lowcountry assumed dimensions unparalleled elsewhere in mainland North America. The growing entrenchment of slavery and the growing autonomy of the black community constitute the central themes of black life in the lowcountry during the Revolutionary era. This seeming paradox will be explored in two ways: first, through an analysis of the long-term development of black society— a *"longue durée"* stretching from 1760 to 1810—and, second, through an investigation of the disruptions that accompanied the Revolutionary War.

Many of the changes in lowcountry black life during the Revolutionary era had been well underway before the war began and, indeed, had little to do with the conflict. The development of the backcountry had been shifting the distribution of South Carolina's slave population for several decades. Less than one-tenth of the colony's slaves resided outside the lowcountry

Philip D. Morgan, "Black Society in the Lowcountry, 1760–1810," from Ira Berlin and Ronald Hoffman, eds., *Slavery and Freedom in the Age of the American Revolution*, originally published by the University Press of Virginia.

in 1760; by 1810 almost one-half lived in the backcountry. Although the Revolution did not cause the upcountry migration, the shift in population intensified in the post-Revolutionary years. Similarly, within the lowcountry itself the slave population had been growing most rapidly in those districts to the extreme north and south of Charleston during the late colonial period, and that trend continued in the late eighteenth and early nineteenth centuries. Furthermore, planters in post-Revolutionary South Carolina had as voracious an appetite for slaves as had those in colonial South Carolina. But if the demand for slaves remained high, important differences in the pattern of importation emerged. Postwar South Carolina imported slaves from other North American states as well as from Africa, and most slaves were destined for the backcountry rather than the lowcountry. In the first decade of the nineteenth century, however, the overland traffic came to a virtual halt as South Carolina reaffirmed its colonial heritage: indeed, in one period of four years (1804–7) South Carolina imported almost twice as many Africans as in any previous five-year period in its history.

Long-term developments in the structure of the slave population matched long-term developments in the movement of slaves into and within the state. For example, the transition from a period of negative to one of positive natural increase occurred among South Carolina's slave population in the early 1750s. The Revolutionary era maintained that pattern, although the massive influx of Africans in the first decade of the nineteenth century temporarily slowed the upward trend. This development can be explored in a number of ways. For example, the sex ratio among inventoried adult lowcountry slaves moved in a uniform way from a high point of 133 males for every 100 females in the 1760s to equality by the 1790s. The adult-child ratio followed a similar pattern: in the 1760s there were 120 children for every 100 adult females; by the 1790s that ratio had increased to 150 children for every 100 adult females. Admittedly fragmentary information further suggests that birth-spacing intervals decreased between the late colonial and early national periods, while the mean age of slave mothers at the birth of their first child rose. Furthermore, the range of ages at which slave mothers gave birth to their first child seems to have increased. Finally, the proportion of Africans in the adult slave population declined fairly steadily from about 45 percent in the 1760s to under 20 percent in the 1790s.

Although ignorant of the details of these demographic developments, contemporaries sensed an improvement in the conditions of slave life. In 1798 one planter pointed out that his tidal swamp plantation was "in a very healthy situation, evinced by the great increase which the present proprietor has had of his Negroes since they have been on it." Another lowcountry planter, when offering his gang of fifty slaves for sale in 1796, singled out the "wenches" as "young and improving." Furthermore, he claimed, these fifty slaves were "not Negroes selected out of a larger gang for the purpose of sale, but are prime[.] Their present Owner, with great trouble and expence selected them out of many for several years past. They were purchased for stock, and breeding Negroes, and to any Planter who particularly wanted them for that purpose, they are a very choice and desirable gang." By 1788 the Reverend James Stuart could testify to antislavery forces in Britain that he had been a "Rector of a Parish in Carolina, and was ready to advance that many Estates in that District, though more unhealthy than the West Indies, supported Themselves, by proper Treatment, independently of the Slave-Trade."

Like the structure of the slave population, the environment in which most lowcountry slaves found themselves also changed in the latter half of the eighteenth century. Most lowcountry slaves resided in parishes where they increasingly outnumbered whites. It is not possible to calculate this trend from mid-century, but between 1790 and 1810 the slave population increased more rapidly than that of whites in most lowcountry parishes, so that in 1810 all lowcountry rural parishes were over 80 percent black, and in at least five, blacks numbered over 90 percent of the total. Furthermore, as time passed, more slaves resided on large plantations than ever before. In the 1760s, 40 percent of inventoried lowcountry slaves resided on plantations of fifty or more slaves; by the 1780s that proportion had risen to 52 percent. In some regions the late eighteenth and early nineteenth centuries witnessed a staggering degree of concentration. In the rice-growing parishes of All Saints and St. James Santee, for example, about half the slaves in 1790 belonged to planters who owned 100 or more; by 1810 that proportion had risen to 81 and 61 percent, respectively. Although the degree of concentration was less marked in sea island cotton-producing areas, it remained significant. While in St. Helena the proportion of slaves in units of fifty or more increased by just under 10 percent between 1800 and 1810, in St. John Colleton the proportion almost doubled between 1790 and 1810. Lowcountry parishes, then, generally witnessed greater and greater concentration of blacks, both in terms of their distribution in the total population and the size of slaveholding units.

The increasing size of plantations reflected other changing economic realities. One of the most significant components of the slaves' economic world was their opportunity to do specialized work. The late colonial period saw a slight but significant upward trend in the skill levels of slaves. By the 1770s about 18 percent of inventoried adult slave men had been exempted from field labor; this upward trend accelerated markedly in the late eighteenth century, when over a quarter held specialized positions. Occupational opportunities for slave women also expanded in the late eighteenth century, but they remained extremely limited: even in the 1790s, nine of every ten adult women worked in the fields. Most of the increase in skills apparently resulted from an expansion in the number of domestic servants, although the continued expansion in the size of plantation estates also buttressed the trend. A slight decline in the proportion of skilled slaves about the turn of the century probably reflected in part the beginning of the cotton boom, which pulled some skilled slaves out of the lowcountry along with thousands of field hands. And among those skilled blacks who remained in the lowcountry, some were pushed into the fields by the resulting shortage of labor. When Charles Ball's slave coffle arrived at a South Carolina inn just after the turn of the century, there was no stableman to tend to the trader's horse, and the landlord explained apologetically "that at this season of the year, the planters were so hurried by their crops . . . that for his part, he had been compelled to put his coachman, and even the waiting-maids of his daughters into the cotton fields, and that at this time, his family were without servants, a circumstance that had never happened before!"

Still, most slaves remained unaffected by expanding or contracting opportunities for skilled work; they continued to labor in the fields as had most adult slaves throughout the eighteenth century. Rice remained South Carolina's premier crop, . . .

. . . The task system remained the norm. . . . As throughout the eighteenth century, tasking allowed slaves to appropriate a portion of the day for themselves by working intensively to complete a task. As one Georgian put it, after a slave completed his task, "his master feels no right to call on him." . . .

Compared to the powerful effect of long-term demographic and economic changes, the impact of the Revolution on lowcountry black life was—in one sense—minimal. Moses Kirkland, a backcountry loyalist, predicted that "the instant that The Kings Troops are put in motion in those colonies, these poor Slaves would be ready to rise upon their Rebel Masters"; unfortunately for his cause, this prediction proved groundless. As one historian has recently put it, "South Carolina blacks apparently did not take advantage of their owners' predicament during the Revolution, nor did lowcountry planters exhibit the anxiety about their slaves' loyalty manifested by Maryland and Virginia slaveholders." Given the intensive preparations of fearful lowcountry slaveholders, it would have been difficult for slaves to do otherwise. According to one newspaper report, militia companies regularly patrolled as early as the summer of 1775; Charleston had to be defended, one patriot general was instructed in the spring of 1776, because "in slave counties so much depends on opinion, and the opinion which the slave will entertain of our superiority or inferiority will naturally keep pace with our maintaining or giving ground." That white South Carolinians would give no ground can be gauged by an admission by one of the state's representatives to the Continental Congress: his state could not defend itself, he claimed, "by reason of the great proportion of citizens necessary to remain at home to prevent insurrection among the Negroes, and to prevent the desertion of them to the enemy." Moreover, even though the British army briefly assumed the mantle of an army of liberation through Clinton's 1779 proclamation, once in control of territory that same army worked for the racial status quo. As one British officer ruefully noted, "The Bandittis of Negroes who flock to the conquerors . . . do ten thousand times more Mischief than the whole Army put together." Before long, the administrative arm of the British occupation, the Charleston Board of Police, sent parties of soldiers to outlying plantations so that, for example, "the ill behavior and insurrectious conduct of Mr. Isard's Negroes towards their Overseer" could be quelled.

But in another sense the Revolution had a far-reaching impact. Some slaves, of course, stood by their masters. One slave driver demonstrated such fidelity that "during the invasion of the country, [he] never went off with the British, and had the address to prevent any going who were under his care." But many others cared more for their own liberty than for their master's property. For example, driver Andrew "when the British were in possession of Savannah . . . carried off all Mrs. Graeme's negroes that were then in Prince William's Parish; and Mrs. Graeme could not get them back, until she made terms with Andrew." Moreover, the lowcountry's raging civil war and military occupation created unprecedented opportunities for slaves to widen their own freedom within bondage and, occasionally, outside of it. Although planters eventually regained their place in lowcountry society, wartime anarchy created a power vacuum in the countryside that allowed slaves to expand their liberty. Even those who remained at home became, as one South Carolina mistress observed of her slaves, "insolent and quite their own masters." If few followed Andrew's dramatic example, many slaves could, like those on one Ashepoo plantation, ignore their overseer's orders and be "perfectly free [to] live upon the best produce on the Plantation" or, as on "Watboo" plantation, act "under little or no subjection to the Overseers." As William Bull observed in 1781, since the commencement of the rebellion, the slaves had become "ungovernable."

Lowcountry blacks did not readily surrender their wartime gains. Even after the war many continued to flaunt their increased autonomy. If slavemasters desired to recreate the status quo ante bellum, slaves did not easily return to the old way of life. Many used their wartime experience to win still greater independence. Driver Andrew . . . put his wartime experience to good effect some fifteen years after the event. One boatman and pilot presumably treasured the "pass he received from the British during the war," because he used it in 1796 to pass as a free man. Another South Carolina slave, located in St. Augustine in 1784, told his master's envoy that he was prepared to return "willingly . . . but not at present"; the envoy was reduced to hoping that he might "be able to persuade him" to return earlier than the slave intended. These incidental increments in the power of individual slaves suggest a much broader process by which slaves increased governance of their daily affairs in the overwhelmingly black countryside.

The Maturation of the Southern Backcountry

RICHARD R. BEEMAN

The forces of economic and demographic growth that gave most Lunenburg households an increased level of agricultural output and a slightly enhanced standard of physical comfort appear to have cut across the religious and ethnic lines that had worked to divide the white citizens of the county

From *The Evolution of the Southern Backcountry* by Richard R. Beeman. © 1984 by the University of Pennsylvania Press.

during the prerevolutionary period. While growing similarities in economic circumstance did not eliminate the cultural differences that separated evangelicals, Episcopalians, and unbelievers, they did, in combination with a revised institutional structure that removed the privileges and powers of sanction from the Episcopal church, greatly reduce the conflicts those differences had previously generated.

Toward Religious Pluralism

The unequal distribution of economic and political power which gave disproportionate advantage to the members of the Anglican gentry elite in the prerevolutionary period did not disappear completely after the war, but there was a marked trend toward an evening of those imbalances. The formal power of the Protestant Episcopal Church had declined markedly; most obvious, it no longer possessed the legal power to command attendance at its weekly services, and it could not command the taxpayers to support either its doctrines or its ministers. And in a display not so much of militant repudiation as of unconcern and apathy, many of Lunenburg's citizens—both well-to-do and middling—simply ceased to take an interest in the affairs of the church once compulsory support had been eliminated.

The members of the church vestry, who in the decade before the Revolution constituted a group nearly synonymous with wealth and political power in the county, were by the end of the eighteenth century steadily losing their claim to preeminence. By 1795 fewer than half the members of the county court had also served the Episcopal church as vestrymen, and only five of the twenty wealthiest men in the county had held that post. By 1815 the separation of secular authority and the old church was even more marked. Only three of the eighteen justices and only five of the twenty wealthiest men in the county had served as vestrymen. As might be expected, certain prominent family names closely associated with positions of leadership in the economic, political, and religious life of the county in earlier years (Chambers, Billups, Stokes, and Taylor) continued to appear on the lists of court justices and of the affluent, but in many cases those sons and relations of the pillars of the prerevolutionary Anglican church did not choose to follow the example of their elders and devote their time to serving the Episcopal church. Disestablishment facilitated the movement of at least a few prominent Lunenburg citizens out of the ranks of the Episcopal church altogether and into the ranks of what previously had been defined as "dissenting" religions. The most prominent example of this trend was the Rev. Clement Read, the grandson of the great patriarch of Lunenburg and one of the pillars of the Anglican church during the formative years of the county. The younger Read, after completing a course of study at the newly established Presbyterian college of Hampden-Sydney in neighboring Prince Edward County, was received as a candidate in the Presbyterian ministry in 1788. Ultimately Read spurned Presbyterianism, becoming instead one of the leaders in the emergent Republican Methodist Church. The growth of the Republican Methodists, just one of the variants of Methodism that was making its influence felt in the Southside by the turn of the century, was itself another sign of the growing acceptance within the county of a pluralistic cultural-religious standard. The Republican Methodists, like the Presbyterians, constituted a thoroughly "respectable" group within Lunenburg, and while Episcopalians continued to enjoy a slight preponderance among the economic and political elite of the county, members of other denominations increasingly appeared in the ranks of the wealthy and powerful. Even the Separate Baptists, who in Lunenburg continued to represent the most radical and numerically significant alternative to the values of traditional religion, had by 1815 managed to place four of their members on the county court; one, Joseph Yarborough, could be counted among the fifteen wealthiest men in the county, and several other members could boast of landholdings and slaveholdings that placed them in the upper 10 percent of the county's population.

Those members of the Baptist rank and file who continued to live in Lunenburg through both the pre- and postrevolutionary eras also showed a tendency to improve their fortunes in the years following their decision to join the church. They were men like Benjamin Evans, who owned neither land nor slaves when he first joined the Baptist church in 1769, but who by 1782 owned 660 acres and five slaves and by the time of his death in 1806 possessed eight slaves, five horses, and an estate worth over $3,000. Similarly, Benjamin Hawkins, who like Evans owned no land or slaves when he joined the Meherrin church in 1771, had become a solid member of Lunenburg's middling planter class at his death in 1802, leaving an estate of 100 acres and four slaves. Other Baptist converts also indicated the growing appeal of the Baptists to men and women endowed with more substantial material advantages. William Stone, who was listed as a tithable on his father's medium-sized plantation in 1769, deserted the Anglicans for the Meherrin church in 1776. By the time of his death in 1802, he had accumulated an estate of nearly 1,000 acres and six slaves worth over $2,000.

The narrowing of the gap between Episcopalians and dissenters was perhaps best symbolized, though not typified, by the estates of the two leading religious figures in the county's eighteenth-century history, those of James Craig, Anglican minister of Cumberland Parish, and John Williams, minister of the Meherrin church and spiritual leader of perhaps a dozen other Baptist congregations within and outside the county. Antagonists for over a quarter of a century, Craig and Williams died within a few months of one another in 1795. Craig, who presided first over the move toward respectability and subsequently the spiritual and financial decline of the Episcopal church in Lunenburg, had over the course of his thirty-five-year tenure as minister acquired virtually all the trappings of a Virginia gentleman. His estate, valued at £2,744, contained forty-two slaves, eight feather beds, a variety of walnut furniture, an eight-day clock, a substantial quantity of silver plate, and all the equipment—stills, boilers, hydrometers—to run a distillery! The quantity of slaves, horses, cattle, hogs, and farm implements in Craig's estate indicates that his was a working plantation designed to produce an income substantially above that which he received as minister of his flock. His inventory listed over 10,000 pounds of tobacco in his possession at the time of his death, and his gristmill, probably the busiest in the county, served not only his own needs but also those of many of his parishioners and neighbors. All in all, Craig's estate suggests the life not only of a genteel and learned parson but of a country gentleman as well.

Although far more modest than Craig's estate, the estate of John Williams was not that of a man shut off from worldly concerns. Williams had earlier attempted, apparently without success, to persuade the Meherrin church to provide him with an independent income that would allow him to pursue his ministerial duties free from the distractions of the tobacco fields or the marketplace, but when that support proved inadequate, he evidently devoted his own efforts to those concerns, with results that left him a comfortable if not opulent estate at his death. Valued at £902, Williams's estate included sixteen slaves, a walnut chest, a library of nearly one hundred books, and the usual farm implements found on a plantation devoted to the raising of wheat and tobacco. Williams's accumulation of slaves, which had increased steadily, coincided both with the growing reliance of many of his Baptist congregants on unfree labor and with the noticeable quieting of Baptist opposition to the peculiar institution. Williams himself appears to have fallen into a mode of antislavery sentiment that stressed amelioration rather than abolition. In his will he provided that any of his legatees found guilty of mistreating the slaves in their possession be disinherited, and he stipulated "that if any of the Negroes are sold, it should be at a private sale, and to only those that are of indisputable Human characters, or Such if possible, that the Negroes should choose to serve."

Lunenburg's Baptists had always been ambivalent about the institution of slavery, and even during the fervent years of evangelical awakening in the 1760s and early 1770s the church stopped short of outright condemnation of slavery. The evangelical Baptists were not premillennialists; their primary concern was the redemption of individual sinners and not the radical change of a whole social system. Slavery had always been a part of the social system in which they had lived, and while the Baptists of the prerevolutionary period showed far more concern for both the material and spiritual condition of individual slaves, they never meant their stewardship of black laborers to be transformed into a crusade against the institution itself.

Yet the tenor of the Baptists' attitudes toward their own black bondsmen and bondswomen and those of their neighbors had changed unmistakably between the time when they were a distinct, countercultural force in the prerevolutionary years and the early nineteenth century, when Lunenburg's Baptists began to approach the standard of the county's other citizens in economic circumstances and social station. For example, the Meherrin congregation remained much more active than any other religious group in encouraging slaves to become members, but the records show both a marked decrease in efforts to prevent cruelty at the hands of white Baptist masters and an increased tendency to use the doctrines of the church as a means of oppression. Whereas in 1772 the church went on record as opposing excessive cruelty in the whipping of slaves and in that same year moved against a member for mistreating his slaves, by the late 1790s the record is silent with respect to censures directed at white masters for cruel treatment and more abundant in its chronicle of punishments of black members such as "Robertson's George," who was disciplined for "several elopements from his master . . . and of sundry other evils which circumstances are well known," or Winn's Ben, who was excommunicated "for attempting to bead with a white woman."

The wavering of moral concern about the institution of slavery was not confined to the Meherrin Baptists. By the early 1790s, John Leland, one of the Virginia Baptist leaders whose abhorrence of slavery was stern and consistent, found to his dismay that fellow Baptists in the state were growing decidedly touchy about his efforts to make antislavery ideology a central part of Baptist church policy. Leland was able to use his considerable influence to persuade the Virginia Baptist General Committee to pass a resolution denouncing slavery as a moral evil, but when that resolution was transmitted to individual congregations, he discovered that the combination of a growing defensiveness about their own ownership of slaves and a continuing determination to defend congregational autonomy produced a chilly reaction among his brethren. The Roanoke Association, a group of separate Baptist churches immediately to the west of Lunenburg in Pittsylvania County, responded that they were "not unanimously clear" about either the morality or immorality of slavery, but then asserted that "neither the General Committee nor any Religious Society whatever has the least right to concern therein." The message was much the same from the churches within the Strawberry Association, serving Bedford, Botetourt, and Franklin counties; they answered in 1792 with the injunction "We advise them not to interfere with it."

We cannot discount those feelings of humanitarianism and limited egalitarianism which continued to evoke in the Baptists a greater concern for the spiritual life of their black bondsmen and bondswomen than that evinced by most other white citizens of the region. Yet the increased dependence of the rank and file of the church on slave labor may have contributed to a decline in antislavery zeal among the evangelicals. As a disillusioned Baptist leader, Richard Dozier, put it in 1783: "They have taken themselves out of the world, and at the same time [are] following the world." To follow the world of the late-eighteenth-century Virginia Southside meant to avert one's eyes from the moral dilemma of slavery. . . .

Racial Solidarity

As early as the mid-1780s, it was beginning to become apparent that black slavery served as the basis for the joining of interests between the well-established, eastern regions of Virginia and the Southside. Reacting to the efforts of a few Quakers and Methodist ministers (Thomas Coke and Francis Asbury in particular) to arouse sentiment within Virginia in favor of a legislative bill for the general emancipation of slaves, the Southside counties of Amelia, Mecklenburg, Pittsylvania, Brunswick, Halifax, and Lunenburg each sent petitions to the legislature defending their right to own slaves and, what is more striking, defending the benevolence of the institution itself. The Virginia House of Delegates rejected the arguments of the antislavery activists out of hand. Indeed, it was so hostile to any talk of emancipation that it nearly went so far as to repeal an existing act allowing for private manumission of slaves. Judging from the hysterical tone of the Southside proslavery petitions, however, one would think that the abolitionist threat within Virginia had reached dangerous proportions. The rhetoric of the 1785 petitions suggests that the traditional assumption that the South aggressively advocated slavery only in reaction to Northern abolitionist agitation in the 1830s requires some revision. Most of those Methodists who preached in the Southside in the 1780s had long been associated with the region, yet such was the uneasiness of Southsiders about their growing dependence on slavery that they were quick to lash out at anyone who seemed to threaten either their physical security or their economic security.

Like their counterparts from the other Southside counties, the Lunenburg petitioners attempted to bend revolutionary principles to defend their right to own human property, reminding the members of the legislature that "in order . . . to Fix a Tenure on our property on a Basis of Security not to be shaken in the future, we dissolved our union with our parent County." They viewed the agitation for general emancipation as "flagrant Contempt of the constitutional powers of the Commonwealth" and predicted that it would result in

> Want, Poverty, Distress & Ruin to the free Citizens; the Horrors of all the Rapes, Robberies, Murderers, and Outrages, which an innumerable Host of unprincipled, unpropertied, vindictive, and remorseless Banditti are capable of perpetrating; Neglect, Famine and Death to the abandoned black infant and superannuated Parent; inevitable Bankruptcy to the Revenue; Desperation and revolt to the disappointed, oppressed Citizen, and sure and final ruin to this happy, free and flourishing Country.

All in all, it was seen as quite a despicable scheme, and one that in the petitioners' view was consistent "with the principles and Designs of a Bute or a North" but that was in this case perpetrated by a cabal of those evil tyrants working in unison "with a proscribed Coke, and imperious Asb[ur]y, and other contemptible Emissaries and Hirelings of Britain."

The 161 Lunenburg freeholders who signed the petition not only went on record opposing the principle of general emancipation; they also enjoined the delegates to repeal the act allowing for voluntary manumission and "to provide effectively for the good Government and due restraint of those already set free, whose disorderly conduct and thefts and outrages are so generally the just subject of Complaint." The Lunenburg citizens concluded their petition with what to them was the most powerful example of those "just subjects of complaint" provoked by the free black community, namely, the "Insolences and Violences so frequently of late committed to and on our respectable Maids and Matrons.'' This concern about the dangers posed by free blacks, a concern that is strikingly apparent in all the 1785 proslavery petitions, is difficult to penetrate. By 1790, free blacks in Lunenburg numbered eighty, less than 1 percent of the population, and the court records indicate only minor incidences of crime by either slaves or free blacks. But the mere possibility of such crime, even before the black rebellion in Santo Domingo became part of the public consciousness in 1792–94, was plainly enough to cause the white population of Lunenburg to raise the alarm.

All the proslavery petitions from the Southside were nearly identical, indicating perhaps that only a few people had taken a hand in drafting and then circulating them more widely throughout the region. The only item missing from the Lunenburg petition that was a standard part of the arguments of virtually all the others was a lengthy religious and moral justification of the institution itself. That justification was generally based on biblical texts, the most common from chapter 9 of Genesis, reciting the story of God's curse on Canaan, and that from chapter 25 of Leviticus, in which the right to hold ''Bond-men and Bond-maids'' was asserted. Those biblical references, designed (in the words of the Brunswick County petitioners) to prove ''that it was ordained by the Great and Wise Disposer of all things, that some Nations should serve others; and that all Nations have not been equally free,'' seem to carry the Southside defenders of slavery well beyond the confused and apologetic defenses that most historians have seen as typical of the late-eighteenth-century Virginia attitude toward slavery. Rather, as early as the mid-1780s we can perceive a notable combativeness and aggressiveness in the Southside Virginia defense. It was not that white Virginians were assuming a burden laid on them by the prerevolutionary British policies respecting the slave trade, nor was it merely that the right to own chattel slaves was an important ingredient in the Southside economy, although that fact was readily observable and readily acknowledged. Rather, in the eyes of the Southside petitioners,

> It hath been the practice and custom for above 3500 Years, down to the present time, for one Nation to buy and keep Slaves of another Nation: That God so particularly (as above recited) Licensed or Commanded his People, to buy of other Nations and to keep them for Slaves: And that Christ and his Apostles hath in the mean time come into the World, and past out of it again, leaving behind them the New Testament, full of all instructions necessary to our Salvation; and hath not forbid it: But left that matter as they found it, giving exhortations to Masters and Servants how to conduct themselves to each other.

It is not surprising that the 161 signers of the Lunenburg petition were predominantly those whose own economic and social position would incline them toward a defense of slavery. Men like Christopher Billups, Edward Brodnax, virtually all the members of the prominent Ragsdale and Garland families, and James Craig were featured prominently at the head of the list of signatories. Indeed, every resident of the county owning thirty or more slaves signed the petition, as did about two-thirds of the county court and Episcopal vestry. Members of dissenting religious groups were not as enthusiastic in their support of the peculiar institution. It is difficult to trace the names of individual Methodists who lived within the county in 1785, but given the involvement of prominent Southside Methodists in the antislavery movement, it seems probable that the few Methodists in Lunenburg refrained from signing the petition. The Baptists, far more numerous than the Methodists in Lunenburg, were conspicuous by their absence among the signatories of the petition. Most of the Baptists were still not slave owners and were engaged in a bitter political struggle with an Anglican slave-owning class over the issue of separation of church and state at precisely the time that the proslavery petition was circulated. In subsequent decades, however, as the mild, antislavery ideology of the Baptist church waned still further and as Baptist congregants themselves joined the ranks of the slave owners, the consensus within the Southside on a militant defense of slavery would become nearly complete. . . .

The Afro-American Community

The black population of Lunenburg, so vitally important to the county's improved position in the tobacco economy of the Old Dominion, remains only barely visible in our survey of the expansion of economic opportunity and proliferation of religious and community institutions in the county. That population, which by 1820 accounted for 64 percent of the people living in the county, probably experienced as substantial a change in circumstance between the mid-eighteenth century and the early nineteenth century as any other part of the population, yet the very looseness of the bonds of social organization in places like Lunenburg makes the history of those changes extraordinarily difficult to reconstruct. In the earliest years of the county's history, when blacks were a distinct minority and when most of the slaveowning households possessed just one or two slaves, the material condition of most slaves was probably not drastically different from that of most whites. If blacks lived in crude housing and possessed only the scantest material comforts, then so too did most whites, freeholders and dependent laborers alike. And for better and for worse, those blacks living on small plantations could not have experienced too much separation from their white masters; the demands of an intensive agricultural system and the constraints imposed by the modest housing stock of the region made it necessary for most blacks and whites to live and work closely together.

Even as the slave population of Lunenburg increased, the pattern of concentration of those slaves remained essentially different from that prevailing in eastern Virginia. At no point in the county's history did anyone accumulate the amount of capital that enabled a Robert Carter or a William Byrd to assemble nearly complete villages of bondsmen and bondswomen, many with highly specialized skills, on their plantations. The smaller scale of plantation life in Lunenburg permitted a degree of personal interaction between white and black that was not possible on more elaborately structured plantations, but at the same time the dispersion of blacks among many relatively isolated farmsteads worked to inhibit the development of the slave family life and community institutions that came into being in areas of Virginia where the concentration of slaves was greater.

The one community institution that seemed to reach out most aggressively to include blacks within its ranks was the Baptist church meeting. Much of the early suspicion and distrust that Anglican gentry felt toward the Baptists was provoked by those open-air meetings for exhortation and baptism in which large numbers of blacks and whites alike came together, confessed their sins, and accepted in common God's gift of the new birth. For a brief time in the late 1750s and early 1760s, a portion of the black community around Lunenburg was given an even stronger and more distinctive sense of its own religious identity through its affiliation with the Bluestone Baptist church. A substantial portion of the membership of that church was composed of blacks from one of William Byrd's plantations in the area, one of the few plantations to support more than just a handful of slaves. For a time the church had a black preacher and some fifty black members who could be counted "bright and shining Christians." When Byrd sold his holdings in the region and the slaves were dispersed, the Bluestone church itself faded from existence, weakening still further the bonds of community that those black slaves had once enjoyed.

. . . By the postrevolutionary period the attitude of white Baptists toward their black brethren had begun to harden. More solidly connected to the county, with substantial holdings in slaves themselves, white Baptist leaders tended increasingly to use the religious doctrines of their church as a means of social control over the slave population rather than as a requirement of mutual submission. As slaves came to outnumber whites in the county, the need for control over blacks was perceived to be much greater. By the time of the Methodist insurgence in the first decade of the nineteenth century, evangelical religion was still an important spiritual and social gathering point for Lunenburg's black residents, but the Southside Methodists, even more than the Baptists, were committed to a society in which blacks were kept under close surveillance.

In some senses, then, slave life in early-nineteenth-century Lunenburg may have combined all the worst features of chattel slavery across the antebellum South. The black men and women who lived under the slave regimen were part of an economic system dependent on the continued expansion of production of a single crop, tobacco, without much of the diversification of skills that marked the Tidewater economy even during the years of its most concerted commitment to that same crop. Few if any of the plantation owners who controlled those slaves had either the economic resources or the inclination to indulge the instincts toward patriarchy that motivated some of the Tidewater's principal planters; and, living on plantations lacking the scale of Westover, Nomini Hall, or Mount Airy, Lunenburg's slaves were generally denied the benefit of numbers that permitted creation of alternative modes of community life on larger plantations.

FURTHER READING

Thomas P. Abernethy, *The South in the New Nation, 1789–1819* (1961)

John Richard Alden, *The First South* (1961)

Richard R. Beeman, *The Evolution of the Southern Backcountry: A Case Study of Lunenburg County, Virginia, 1746–1832* (1984)

Ira Berlin and Ronald Hoffman, eds., *Slavery and Freedom in the Age of the American Revolution* (1983)

James Broussard, *Southern Federalists, 1800–1816* (1978)

Rhys Isaac, *The Transformation of Virginia, 1740–1790* (1982)

Jan Lewis, *The Pursuit of Happiness: Family and Values in Jefferson's Virginia* (1983)

Robert McColley, *Slavery and Jeffersonian Virginia* (1964)

Norman K. Risjord, *The Old Republicans: Southern Conservatism in the Age of Jefferson* (1965)

Marshall Smelser, *The Democratic Republic, 1801–1815* (1968)

Charles Snydor, *Gentlemen Freeholders: Political Practices in Washington's Virginia* (1952)

The Old South

⅄

Students of American history have long been fascinated by the nature and character of the Old South—that is, the South after the early national period but before the Civil War. Compared to the colonial South, this was a much larger, trans-Appalachian region. It relied on slave labor to grow cotton, sugar, tobacco, and rice as major staple crops, and it profited greatly from a sustained cotton boom based on demand from the British textile industry. As the most extensive slaveholding region in the Western Hemisphere and as the region that ultimately seceded from the Union, the Old South would deserve much attention.

Several interpretive issues have stimulated widespread interest in the Old South. Were the planters grasping, ambitious, American men on the make, or were they cut from different cloth—impressive and influential citizens who held prebourgeois values and paternalistic beliefs? How did the region's rapid growth affect society? What place was there in the Old South for industrial development? Did prebourgeois planters dominate the social system and create a seigneurial, precapitalist society; or was the South vigorously capitalistic, with more than a touch of the frontier in its character? How did slavery affect the South and white southerners? Did it make the region essentially different from the American mainstream or merely give it a special interest to defend? These and other questions generate lively debates among scholars and have produced an abundance of fine historical literature.

⅄ *D O C U M E N T S*

A Virginian named Joseph G. Baldwin moved in 1836 to what was then the Southwest and became a lawyer and writer. His sketches, published as *The Flush Times of Alabama and Mississippi* and contained in the first selection, describe southwestern society during the late 1830s. The second document, the journal of Bennet Barrow of Louisiana, serves as a fine example of a cotton planter's diary. Barrow represented fairly new wealth, since the rich lands around his Louisiana homestead were settled by whites primarily between 1800 and 1830. His diary reveals much about his attitudes and values, as well as the daily routine and commercial problems facing cotton planters. In December 1852 a northerner, Frederick Law Olmsted, embarked on a fourteen-month southern tour, the object of which was to produce articles for the *New York Daily Times*, whose editor was an antislavery Whig. The excerpts in the third document describe parts of Virginia and Mississippi he visited. The status of free blacks was always controversial in the Old South, as the petitions in the fourth and fifth documents, from Virginia and South Carolina, illustrate. In general, free blacks were regarded as a dangerous class and many states had laws requiring them to leave shortly after their emancipation. The fourth document shows that Arthur Lee received considerable white support for his plea to be allowed to remain in Virginia, but white artisans in the fifth document complained strongly about competition from free blacks. One successful free black was William Ellison of South Carolina, whose profits from the sale of cotton gins enabled him to become a substantial slaveholder. Some advertisements for his wares are reproduced in the sixth selection. Another area of controversy centered on the question of industrial development, which is discussed in the last excerpt by one of its advocates, the South Carolina textile manufacturer William Gregg.

Joseph Baldwin on Society in Alabama and Mississippi, 1835–1837

In trying to arrive at the character of the South-Western bar, its opportunities and advantages for improvement are to be considered. It is not too much to say that, in the United States at least, no bar ever had such, or so many: it might be doubted if they were *ever* enjoyed to the same extent before. Consider that the South-West was the focus of an emigration greater than any portion of the country ever attracted, at least, until the golden magnet drew its thousands to the Pacific coast. But the character of emigrants was not the same. Most of the gold-seekers were mere gold-diggers—not bringing property, but coming to take it away. Most of those coming to the South-West brought property—many of them a great deal. Nearly every man was a speculator; at any rate, a trader. The treaties with the Indians had brought large portions of the States of Alabama, Mississippi and Louisiana into market; and these portions, comprising some of the most fertile lands in the world, were settled up in a hurry. The Indians claimed lands under these treaties—the laws granting preemption rights to settlers on the public lands, were to be construed, and the litigation growing out of them settled, the public lands afforded a field for unlimited speculation, and combinations of purchasers, partnerships, land companies, agencies, and the like, gave occasion to much difficult litigation in after times. Negroes were brought into the country in large numbers and sold mostly upon credit, and bills of exchange taken for the price; the negroes in many instances were unsound—some as to which there was no title; some falsely pretended to be unsound, and various questions as to the liability of parties on the warranties and the bills, furnished an important addition to the litigation: many land titles were defective; property was brought from other States clogged with trusts, limitations, and uses, to be construed according to the laws of the State from which it was brought: claims and contracts made elsewhere to be enforced here: universal indebtedness, which the hardness of the times succeeding made it impossible for many men to pay, and desirable for all to escape paying: hard and ruinous bargains, securityships, judicial sales; a general looseness, ignorance, and carelessness in the public officers in doing business; new statutes to be construed; official liabilities, especially those of sheriffs, to be enforced; banks, the laws governing their contracts, proceedings against them for forfeiture of charter; trials of right of property; an elegant assortment of frauds constructive and actual; and the whole system of chancery law, admiralty proceedings; in short, all the flood-gates of litigation were opened and the pent-up tide let loose upon the country. And such a criminal docket! What country could boast more largely of its crimes? What more splendid rôle of felonies! What more terrific murders! What more gorgeous bank robberies! What more magnificent operations in the land offices! Such . . . levies of black mail, individual and corporate! Such superb forays on the treasuries, State and National! Such expert transfers of balances to undiscovered bournes! Such august defalcations! Such flourishes of rhetoric on ledgers auspicious of gold which had departed for ever from the vault! And in INDIAN affairs!— the very mention is suggestive of the poetry of theft—the romance of a wild and weird larceny! What sublime conceptions of super-Spartan roguery! Swindling Indians by the nation! (*Spirit of Falstaff, rap!*) Stealing their land by the township! (*Dick Turpin and Jonathan Wild! tip the table!*) Conducting the nation to the Mississippi river, stripping them to the flap, and bidding them God speed as they went howling into the Western wilderness to the friendly agency of some sheltering Suggs duly empowered to receive their coming annuities and back rations? What's Hounslow heath to this? Who Carvajal? Who Count Boulbon?

And all these merely forerunners, ushering in the Millennium of an accredited, official Repudiation; and IT but vaguely suggestive of what men could do when opportunity and capacity met—as shortly afterwards they did—under the Upas-shade of a perjury-breathing bankrupt law!—But we forbear. The contemplation of such hyperboles of mendacity stretches the imagination to a dangerous tension. There was no end to the amount and variety of lawsuits, and interests involved in every complication and of enormous value were to be adjudicated. The lawyers were compelled to work, and were forced to learn the rules that were involved in all this litigation.

Many members of the bar, of standing and character, from the other States, flocked in to put their sickles into this abundant harvest. Virginia, Kentucky, North Carolina and Tennessee contributed more of these than any other four States; but every State had its representatives.

Consider, too, that the country was not so new as the practice. Every State has its peculiar tone or physiognomy, so to speak, of jurisprudence imparted to it, more or less, by the character and temper of its bar. That had yet to be given. Many questions decided in older States, and differently decided in different States, were to be settled here; and a new state of things, peculiar in their nature, called for new rules or a modification of old ones. The members of the bar from different States had brought their various notions, impressions and knowledge of their own judicature along with them; and thus all the points, dicta, rulings, offshoots, quirks and quiddities of all the law, and lawing, and law-mooting of all the various judicatories and their satellites, were imported into the new country and tried on the new jurisprudence.

After the crash [a sharp recession] came in 1837—(there were some *premonitory fits* before, but *then* the *great convulsion* came on)—all the assets of the country were marshalled, and the suing material of all sorts, as fast as it could be got out, put into the hands of the workmen. Some idea of the business may be got from a fact or two: in the county of Sumpter, Alabama, in one year, some four or five thousand suits, in the common-law courts alone, were brought; but in some other counties the number was larger; while in the lower or river counties of Mississippi, the number was at least double. The United States Courts were equally well patronized in proportion—indeed, rather more so. The white *suable* population of Sumpter was then some 2,400 men. It was a merry time for us craftsmen; and we brightened up mightily, and shook our quills joyously, like goslings in the midst of a shower. We look back to that good time, "now past and gone," with the pious gratitude and serene satisfaction with which the wreckers near the Florida Keys contemplate the last fine storm.

It was a pleasant sight to profesional eyes to see a whole people let go all holds and meaner business, and move off to court, like the Californians and Australians to the mines: the "pockets" were picked in both cases. As law and lawing soon got to be the staple productions of the country, the people, as a whole the most intelligent—in the wealthy counties—of the rural population of the United States, and, as a part, the *keenest* in all creation, got very well "up to trap" in law matters; indeed, they soon knew more about the delicate mysteries of the law, than it behooves an honest man to know.

Bennet Barrow's Diary, 1838, 1839, 1841

1838

January 1 Com'ced work Hands appear in fine spirits—. . . one weakes picking 3 weakes Gining verry trashy—Joshuas leg cut—Isaac Erwin sent his Bob Oakley colt up to have trained—and a present of two young hounds

2 Cloudy wind East. Went to Town great distress through country for money stopping of the Banks. Merchants Failing &c. no Silver in circulation

From *Plantation Life in the Florida Parishes of Louisiana, 1836–1846*, edited by Edwin Adams Davis, Copyright © 1967. Reprinted by permission of the editor.

3 raining from the South. George Joor and Family came down yesterday

4 Cloudy pleasant wind South—heavy rain and lightning afternoon half Bale scattering cotten to pick

5 Foggy cool Men getting rails and pressing—started Gin Gns—women spinning and trashing Cotten

6 Cloudy hauling Cotten—went to the race best 3 in 5. Louisa Bascome one

7 Heavy rain this evening from the North.

9 Some clouds. 4 hands in swamp getting out pickets—two preparing to plough the Quarter and Orchard all women trashing Cotten—Caught my Brother boy Henry in the Quarter last night—kept him untill to day—better than Whipping

11 Hailing Sleeting and snowing

12 ice and Hail remaining since yesterday Emily left for her mother to remain some time—"on the 9th"

13 Clear verry cold—knocking down Stalks

14 Appearance of rain—pressed 7 B. last Sunday—pressing to day at Gibsons—Will ship on Tuesday next 66 B. in 384 in No 50 to Gin—On selling from 5 to 11½ cts.—The times are seriously hard—all most impossible to raise one dollars. and that in shin plasters—great Excitement in Congress. Northern States medling with slavery—first they com'ced by petition—now by openly speaking of the sin of Slavery in the southern states—on the floor of congress—must eventually cause a separation of the Union

20 returned from Woodvill—verry cold. and bad weather—I have a verry bad cold—pressed 8 B. last Sunday.

21 Cloudy verry cold. pressed 9 Bales

22 Making plough lines—threatened with Rheumatism

23 White Frost pleasant day—during my stay at Mr Joors last week my House servants Jane Lavenia & E. jim broke into my store room—and helped themselves verry liberally to every thing—Center—Anica—& Peter had some of the good drink "as they say"—I Whiped the three first worse than I ever Whiped any one before

24 Showery day. Finished Ginning yesterday started 15 ploughs for oats near 450 Bales—putting up stalles for work horses—my House boy E. Jim the meanest, dirtiest boy I ever had about me—women and trash gang cleaning up

26 ploughing for corn since yesterday warm—too wet to plough

27 Mistey morning. Cleared beautifull Put up the Tombstone over my Father—removed from Washington City Fall of 1836

28 Cloudy cool morning left Home for Woodvill—took with me Eleven Fox hounds shall com'ce hauling my last lot Cotten to morrow . . .

September 18 Cloudy damp morning—some rain at noon. picking cotten since Breakfast—went driving with james Leak Dr Desmont and

Sidney Flower. started two Fawns in my field, ran some time. dogs quit them.

19 Clear pleasant morning—62 Bales pressed last night—Cotten bend down verry much from wind on Sunday—between 90 & 100 Bales out in No—Went hunting in my field started 3 Deer. Killed a fine young Buck—Several joined me afterwards—went driving on the swamp—started a Deer dogs ran off—in coming out of the drive started a Bear. only one dog—he became too much frightened to do any thing

20 Clear pleasant picking P. Rice bottom—hands pick well considering the storm—several sick

21 Verry Foggy morning—Com'enced hauling Cotten this morning—1st shipment—Bales will avreage 470 lbs upwards of 100 out in No 100 & 15 of 400. this time last year had out 125—25 behind last year. owing to the season—cotten more backward in opening—at first picking—never had Cotten picked more trashy than yesterday. And to day by dinner—some few picked badly—5 sick & 2 children

22 Considerable rain before Breakfast, Appearance of a bad day—pressing—4 sick—Caught Darcas with dirt in cotton bag last night. weighed 15 pounds—Tom Beauf picked badly yesterday morning Whiped him. few Cuts—left the field some time in the evening without his Cotten and have not seen him since—He is in the habit of doing so yearly. except last year Heavy rains during the day women spinning—trashing Cotten men & children—Tom B. showed himself—"sick"—Cotten picked since the storm looks verry badly—Cotten market opened this year at 13 & 13¾ cts—Bagging & *cordage* 20 & 24 and 8½ & 9 cts—Porke from $16 to $24 a Barrel—Never com'ence hauling Cotten that it did'ent rain— . . .

October 7 raining—as usual Whenever I hault Cotten—Caught one of Mr Howells negros stealing Chickens last night—some stealing Potatoes. Escaped took him home this evening Howell absent

8 Clear pleasant. Went Fox hunting this morning missing trail—Hands picked well to day—223 lbs—each

9 Clear cold morning—picking Cotten upper new ground—the 50 Acres will make 75 Bales—Went to Town—Turnbull & family called here yesterday evening

10 Clear cool morning heavy dews. went Fox hunting started on ¼ past 6. caught it one hour & Quarter Beautifull run

11 Clear cold morning. Frost Gave the negros shoes last night hands picked worse to day by dinner than they have done this year. Owens excepted, 146 Bales shiped—205 out last night

12 Clear verry cold morning—hands picked worse yesterday than they have done this year. lowest avreage 157—picked in the morning—in the bottom on L creek—rotten open long time—the same this morning—Whiped near half *the* hands to day for picking badly & trashy Tom Beauf came up and put his Basket down at the scales and it is the last I've seen of him—will Whip him more than I ever Whip one, I think he deserves more—the second time he has done so this year—light Frost yesterday and to day

13   Clear. Weather moderated verry much—Hands picked badly yesterday   no more bottom, never saw more Cotten open at this Season—would make 550 Bales if nicely saved

14   Clear   pleasant. Went Driving in the swamp yesterday   Killed one Deer—threatning rain this evening

15   Cloudy   cool wind from the North. light sprinkle of rain last night. hands got Potatoes yesterday—215 B. 400 lbs   205 in No yesterday—220 to night—Cloudy   cool wind from the North. Cleared off at 12 Oclock—fine day for picking Cotten—Caroline Joor has been with us for two weeks past & has reced considerable Flattery from the negros   LA miss you so pretty. Fills Jerry ran off this afternoon—weighed Cotten twice to day in the field—averaged 185 at the second weighing—223 at night

16   Cool East wind   verry disagreeable—picking Cotten Gns   picked Cleaner Cotten than they have done for the last 4 weeks

17   raining this morning—appearance of bad weather—Wind from the East. Two hundred and thirty Bales out last night—of 400 lbs—215 or 20 in No   Heavy rains during the day

18   raining this morning—verry warm   no appearance of weather breaking—at least 100 Bales open in the field—places from 8 to 1200 weight to the Acre—4 sick yesterday—spinning   pressing, trashing Cotten & shelling corn—Candis child very ill. week old—rainey day—shelled all old corn to day for Race Horses—20 Barrels

19   Cloudy   cold wind from the North—gathering Pond cut of corn—332930 picked—now out 230 of 400 lbs & 200 pressed in No—Cotten turns out better than last year

20   Cloudy   cool—picking Cotten   appearance of rain—gathered 12 Loads corn yesterday—turns out poorley—Son James went out Fox hunting with me this morning—bids fair to be a first rate Horseman—beautifull chase of ½ hour & caught it—G. Jerry did not weigh Cotten at 12   I think he has run off—Whiped about half to day.   highest picked 115. wet at that—heavy rain till night

21   Cloudy   cool. great deal of rain Fallen since yesterday noon—Mrs Joor & Jno. Mayrant came down yesterday in the rain

23   Cloudy morning   cool—Cleared off at noon—fresh wind from the North—245 Bales of 400 lbs out. 235 of 400 lbs pressed or 230 out in No or more—yesterday & to day the best days for picking we have had for two weaks past. Emily went to See Mrs Joor at the plantation to day—avreaged yesterday 211. today 182

24   Cloudy   spring looking day—Jno-Mayrant drawing off my Acct with Mrs Joor. went to Town

25   Clear   pleasant. Sold 158 Bales of 400 lbs at 13¼ & 13¢. 265 Bales out to night of 400 lbs

26   Clear pleasant weather—Cotten picks verry trashy—Whiped 8 or 10 for weight to day—those that pick least weights generally most trash

27   Clear   warm—picking Gns—Dennis ran off yesterday—& after

I had Whiped him—hands picked verry light weight by dinner—complaint picking in Rank & Rotten Cotten—4 sick—have out 270 Bales or upward of 400. certain 250 or upwards out in No by 1st of November. Will [be] at least 30 Bales ahead of last year

28 Cloudy cool wind from the North. Misty—Ruffins overseer was over here this evening and informed me that his Home place hands avreaged 353 never heard any thing to Eaquel it—trashy as could be—my hands picked verry trashy yesterday evening. had a settlement with Mrs Joor & *Estate*—275 B. out of 400—232 pressed in No 255 of 400 pressed

29 Clear cold—Mrs Joor returned to Woodvill—Mrs Joor owes me \$13387.73. her notes payable in 5 years from Oct. 29, 1838

30 Clear.cool—Frost—hands picked badly and Trashy—yesterday

31 Clear pleasant. Mr Warfield my Cotten merchant or "Factor" came home with me last night. looking through the Country for buisness—Com'enced as comn merchant this Fall—as Finley & Co. Verry much pleased with him. . . .

1839

January 1 Cloudy wind from the East—went driving against my wish

2 rainny morning—wind East. Gathering corn since dinner

3 Raining—raining—The worst winter & latter part Fall I have recollection of—365 Bales shiped & sold from 12 cts to 13¼—never made as Bad Cotten, 60 more to send—News came to day of the Last weakes racing in N. Orleans—the Brag—race Horse Wagner was Beaten the 4 mile day by Zelina—Belong to Taylor. she beat Pressure the last race he ran

4 Cloudy cold—Finished gathering corn yesterday—hauling to day—3 cribs Full—2 smaller ones & one Large one. one Large one two 3ds full—Whiped evry hand in the field this evening comencing with the driver

5 Cloudy appearance of rain—went to Town

6 Clear pleasant. best & most pleasant day in 6 Weeks

7 Cloudy Warm Wind South—hands picked well to day 235 highest . . .

April 18 Foggy morning—warm Times harder than Ever meet from \$17 to \$22—Cotten selling from 10 cts to 18½

19 Cloudy verry warm—Went to Town.

20 Cloudy verry warm—Emily taken Sick last night—sent for me in Town—returned Home after 2 O. in the night—brought Dr McKelney out with me—Com'encd scraping Cotten yesterday—ground verry dry—Every thing wants rain

21 Cloudy warm—Emily quit well this morning

22 Clear verry warm—ground verry dry bad scraping

23 Cloudy morning—went to Town verry dusty—want rain verry much

24 Clear cool morning—Races com'ence to day—Laurent 2 yrs old

ran two mile Heats—against the nag horse Threshley—1st Heat a dead
Heat—Laurent lost the 2d & we drew him   distanced some colt from
Tnnes

25   Clear   verry warm   Guy Doe won to day 3 mile Heats beating
Dr Ira Smiths Filly   no race

26   Clear   Hot—Jos Bell started to day 4 mile Heats against Kave-
naugh & won the 1st Heat in a gallop—2d Heat broke down in running a
mile   & in a gallop a head—ruined for Ever

27   Cloudy   Hot—Guy Doe walked for the purse to day—best 3 in
5—my Hands worked verry badly—so far   general Whipping yesterday—
made a race to day   mile Heats against Clinton—with my bay Filley by
Luzborough won it Easey

29   Cloudy   verry warm—Finished   scraping cotten above—320
acres—by Dinner—half over—looks well   corn verry good   half leg to
knee high

30   Cloudy   verry warm—sprinkle rain in the night—13 ploughs running—light shower at Eleven—appearance of rain . . .

August 8 . . . do not recollect of ever seeing better picking in August
than at this time   trash gang avreaged 80 at dinner—170 the highest at
night

9   Few clouds. never knew or felt warmer weather than has been for
two weeks past—hoeing Gns since 10 oclock—new land cotten verry fine
opening   good picking

11   Clear cool morning—Appearance of Fall—Gave Dave Bartley &
Atean a suit. I bought them in N. O. for their fine conduct   picking cotten
&c.

12   Morning Clear & cool—last night quit Cool—fine Picking. Making
a push to get to Picking on Wednesday—never saw as many mawking
Birds together as I saw this morning in coming from the Gns place

13   Morning cloudy—Bartley was not to be found last night 'till late,
was not seen after 12. taken sick at Gns   found in the night—& never saw
hands in better spirits. worked finely—Ginny Jerry has not been seen since
Friday morning last—has been shirkin for some time   came to me Friday
morning sick—suspecting him   Examined him   found nothing the matter
complaining of pains &c. told him to go & work it off—he has concluded
to woods it off—cotten in Lower part Gns place improved verry much
new land still doing well old Land past recovery—owing I am certain to
its having been broke up wet—both an injury to the land Horses & negros
to work in the mud & wet

14   Cloudy—Com'enced working the road this morning from Wades
to the river—verry bad—women & children picking cotten

15   Morning cloudy   sprinkle of rain this evening, started 5 scrapers
old Land above

16   Cloudy morning—Finished the roade last night—well done—
never finished as soon   part or most of it worse than usual—negros . . .
at the rascal in giving them Whiskey &c.   5 scrapers running—2 putting

up scaffolds—all others picking cotten—was taken yesterday with violent pain in my right side in going to swamp—had to stop & get a blister at Ruffins &c. I Bennet H. Barrow do certify that I the said Bennet have got the meanest crop in this neighborhood & the meanest by far I ever had—been absent too often—would not care how mean it was if I was not in Debt—& last accounts from England verry unfavorable—two thirds of the people must be ruined—should the times continue beyond this season

17 Morning Clear   pleasant—wind from the East for some days past—cause some sickness—sprinkle of rain at 2. appearance of Heavy rain this evening—Hands do not appear as lively picking as I expected to see them

18 Cloudy warm morning—I have 20 Bales *out*. "last night"

20 Damp cloudy morning   started Gins at Home yesterday picking to day at Gns   avreaged yesterday 176—picking as clean cotten as I ever saw—Dr Desmont an Englishman has left here. verry strangely   a villian no doubt—& left me to pay between 10.000 & 16.000 for him—his uncommonly gentlemanly manners—modesty & chastity caused me to be discerned by him—I've allways been opposed to Yankey speculators coming out here to seek their fortunes. by marrying or any thing else that suits their purpose—particular the D———proffessional Preachers—stragling foreigners, are no better—sister Eliza here to day

21 Foggy morning—Hands picked well yesterday   highest 265   clean cotten

22 Clear   verry warm—B S Joor came down yesterday. Went out last night to have a Fox hunt. could'ent start—Son Bat threatened to be sick again—well digger repairing my well—more water &c.

23 Clear   verry warm—hands picking well—Avreaged 201 day before yesterday—picked 3 days at Gns 15 Bales—most ever picked there in Augst—Want rain very much—ground as dry as can be—cotten com'-enced forming in the last 8 days verry fast. rain now & a late fall would make a verry fair crop—attempting to Learn James & John their book—had rather drive a Team of Mules—James 8 years old John 6—Johns looks one way & thinks another—more sickness for week past than I've had this season, bowel complaints &c.

24 Some clouds—Morning cool   Fine picking to day—averaged yesterday 187—the avreage every day this week will be 190

25 Clear warm morning—wind from the East—Fifty Bales out last night—between 60 & 100 Bales open at this time Hands look to day as if they were determined to try themselves lively & happy

26 Clear pleasant morning—two children quit sick   Cealys & Leahs Adiline—worms—hands picked the worst cotten picked this year

27 Clear   verry warm day   went to Town—better news from cotten market

28 Clear cool morning—more sickness yesterday & to day than I've had this season—avreaged two day 203—never saw a better crop than Turnbulls Home crop—my crop injured as much "I think" from being too thick *as the drought*

29 Cool wind from the North   two negros verry sick (*child & boy*) suffering for rain verry much. Com'enced pressing 1st time

30 Clear morning   verry cool. caught Ben with stollen cotten in his Basket last night—My Lauderdale has the scratchers verry bad. running in corn field

31 Nights & mornings verry cool—never saw as much cotten open in August by 3 fourths—White every Where—dry as can be—picks verry trashy . . .

November 6 . . . Mrs Joor owes me from the 1st of this month $14727.23   not paying me the interest yearly—& nothing 'till the End of 5 years—I will loose $1500 thus—interest—Each year added to the principle for 5 yrs   will make 21559.30—upon the Amount she owes me dated 29 Oct. 1838 $13387.73, I wish all young persons knew What I've learnt of this world in the last 3 years—one thing marry a Daughter against the mothers will—hatred or dislike remains with her forever, & 99 out of a 100 think of nothing but self—corruption appears the order of the day— a corrupt govement makes corrupt people—Gnl Jackson 1st destroying the United S. Bank & then distributing the revenue among the State Bank inducing them to over issue—& this creating a spirit of speculation—not with the people but by the Banks themselves—through their agents buying up large bodies of Land & he then issued his Specie circular—that nothing but Gold & Silver would be taken for dues to the Government. caused a rush for Metals—Banks having over issued people borrowed largely— everything rose to an enormous price—& altogether fictitious—the consequence was the Banks were forced to stop specie paying—curtail money greatly depreciating—has caused the Whole country to be Bankrupt. We are forced in buying any thing not to give What it is worth in Gold & Silver—or What our money is worth here—but What it is worth to the trader in his country—an Excuse for them to add from 25 to 100 pr. ct above the usual rates   you cannot buy a decent horse for less $200. 5 yr ago $200 bought the finest saddle horse &c. turning verry cold. . . .

1841

July 17 Clear   verry warm   Returned from Woodville this morning, Caroline B. Joor was Married on 15th to James Flower jur, Received a note from Ruffin stating that several of my negros were implicated in an intended insurection on the 1st of August next. It seems from What he writes me, it was to have taken place Last March—mine are O Fill   O Ben   Jack   Dennis & Demps—will go up to Robert J. B to have them examined &c. six negros were found guilty in the first degree, it appears they were to meet at jno. Towles Gate and at Mr Turnbulls inheritance place, Leaders one of Robert J. Barrow   one Bennet J. B.   one of Towles one of C. Perceys   one W. J. Forts & one of D. Turnbulls, none of mine were implicated farther than one of Robert J. B boys said he heard the names of the above mentioned &c. intend having an examination of the Whole plantation & the neighbourhood

19   Clear   Verry Hot—Examined Mrs Stirlings negros   Courtneys & my own yesterday   found none of them concerned in the Expected insurection, Went to Judge Wades this morning, found several of his men concerned it. Dave Bonner the most & he was the Leder, Sent to Jail for trial

20   Clear   Verry warm. Thermometer Lower this morning than it has been in 3 weeks, fine shower

21   Cloudy   Verry warm—Examined Robt. H. Barrows negros yesterday. one or two deeply concerned. Sit last night for negros on the road, good many runaways about.

22   Clear   Verry warm, Examined Ruffins negros yesterday   they pretended more ignorance than any Negros I've met with—one of his Old Pete deeply concerned

23   Clear   verry warm—Examined A. Barrows & Mrs Joors negros couldent find out any thing of importance. . . .

August 13   Clear cool morning. all hands on the road. hard work

14   Clear morn   night quit cool—Son John & Clifford sick—several negros quit sick yesterday

15   Clear pleasant morning. Finished working the road yesterday,   our District Attorney, (W. D. Boyle) made a beggininng towards enforcing the Law, in removing free negros from the Parish,   came to old Greys family, saw the Law in a different Light, no doubt Bribed

16   Cloudy   warm—Several of my negros in returning off of the road Saturday night came through Ruffins Quarter. he having the measles forbid their Returning that way. had them staked down all yesterday, several of them had killed a hog, found out the right ones. gave them all a severe Whipping, Ginney Jerry has been sherking about ever since Began to pick cotten. after Whipping him yesterday told him if ever he dodged about from me again would certainly shoot him. this morning at Breakfast time Charles came & told me that Jerry was about to run off. took my Gun found him in the Bayou behind the Quarter, shot him in his thigh—&c. raining all around

17   Cloudy   verry warm, hands picked well yesterday. Avd 203½, 60 picking. none at the scaffold, hard rain in sight. ground here verry hot to the negros feet

18   Clear pleasant morning, Hands Avd verry high yesterday, 246. picked at Gibson place—Caroline Came down this morning   Light rain

19   Cloudy   verry warm, hands would have avd over 250 had it not of rained—as hard a rain as could or ever fall fell this evening, great many sick, Mr. Thuer horse ran off with his sulkey yesterday in the Lot. Broke it

20   Clear   verry warm, Light shower at noon—picking cotten since Eleven ok

Frederick Law Olmsted's Observations on the South, 1852–1854

The Wilderness

I have described, perhaps with tedious prolixity, what adventures befell me, and what scenes I passed through in my first day's random riding, for the purpose of giving an idea of the uncultivated and unimproved—rather, sadly worn and misused—condition of some parts, and I judge, of a very large part, of all Eastern Virginia, and of the isolated, lonely and dissociable aspect of the dwelling places of a large part of the people.

Much the same general characteristics pervade the Slave States everywhere, except in certain rich regions, or on the banks of some rivers, or in the vicinity of some great routes of travel and transportation, which have occasioned closer settlement or stimulated public spirit. For hours and hours one has to ride through the unlimited, continual, all-shadowing, all-embracing forest, following roads in the making of which no more labor has been given than was necessary to remove the timber which would obstruct the passage of wagons; and even for days and days he may sometimes travel and see never two dwellings of mankind within sight of each other, only at long distances often several miles asunder these isolated plantation patriarchates. If a traveler leaves the main road to go any distance, it is not to be imagined how difficult it is for him to find his way from one house to any other in particular; his only safety is in the fact that, unless there are mountains or swamps in the way, he is not likely to go many miles upon any wagon or horse track without coming to some white man's habitation.

The Meeting-House

The country passed through, in the early part of my second day's ride, was very similar in general characteristics to that I have already described, only that a rather larger portion of it was cleared, and plantations were more frequent. About eleven o'clock I crossed a bridge and came to the meeting-house I had been expecting to reach by that hour the previous day. It was in the midst of the woods, and the small clearing around it was still dotted with the stumps of the trees out of whose trunks it had been built; for it was a log structure. In one end there was a single square port, closed by a sliding shutter; in the other end were two doors, both standing open. In front of the doors, a rude scaffolding had been made of poles and saplings, extending out twenty feet from the wall of the house, and this had been covered with boughs of trees, the leaves now withered; a few benches, made of split trunks of trees, slightly hewn with the axe, were

From Frederick Law Olmsted, *The Slave States*, edited by Harvey Wish. New York: Capricorn Books, 1959.

arranged under this arbor, as if the religious service was sometimes conducted on the outside in preference to the interior of the edifice. Looking
in, I saw that a gallery or loft extended from over the doors, across about
one-third the length of the house, access to which was had by a ladder.
At the opposite end was a square, unpainted pulpit, and on the floor were
rows of rude benches. The house was sufficiently lighted by crevices between the upperlogs.

A Tobacco Plantation

Half an hour after this I arrived at the negro-quarters—a little hamlet of
ten or twelve small and dilapidated cabins. Just beyond them was a plain
farm-gate, at which several negroes were standing; one of them, a well-
made man, with an intelligent countenance and prompt manner, directed
me how to find my way to his owner's house. It was still nearly a mile
distant; and yet, until I arrived in its immediate vicinity, I saw no cultivated
field, and but one clearing. In the edge of this clearing, a number of negroes,
male and female, lay stretched out upon the grounds near a small smoking
charcoal pit. Their master afterwards informed me that they were burning
charcoal for the plantation blacksmith, using the time allowed them for
holidays—from Christmas to New Year's—to earn a little money for themselves in this way. He paid them by the bushel for it. When I said that I
supposed he allowed them to take what wood they chose for this purpose,
he replied that he had five hundred acres covered with wood, which he
would be very glad to have any one burn, or clear off in any way. Cannot
some Yankee contrive a method of concentrating some of the valuable
properties of this old-field pine, so that they may be profitably brought into
use in more cultivated regions? Charcoal is now brought to New York from
Virginia; but when made from pine it is not very valuable, and will only
bear transportation from the banks of the navigable rivers, whence it can
be shipped, at one movement, to New York. Turpentine does not flow in
sufficient quantity from this variety of the pine to be profitably collected,
and for lumber it is of very small value.

　　Mr. W.'s house was an old family mansion, which he had himself
remodeled in the Grecian style, and furnished with a large wooden portico.
An oak forest had originally occupied the ground where it stood; but this
having been cleared and the soil worn out in cultivation by the previous
proprietors, pine woods now surrounded it in every direction, a square of
a few acres only being kept clear immediately about it. A number of the
old oaks still stood in the rear of the house, and, until Mr. W. commenced
his improvements, there had been some in its front. These, however, he
had cut away, as interfering with the symmetry of his grounds, and in place
of them had planted ailanthus trees in parallel rows.

　　On three sides of the outer part of the cleared square there was a row
of large and comfortable-looking negro-quarters, stables, tobacco-houses,
and other offices, built of logs.

　　Mr. W. was one of the few large planters, of his vicinity who still made the culture of tobacco their principal business. He said there was a general prejudice against tobacco in all the tidewater region of the State, because it was through the culture of tobacco that the once fertile soils had been impoverished; but he did not believe that, at the present value of negroes, their labor could be applied to the culture of grain with any profit, except under peculiarly favorable circumstances. Possibly, the use of guano might make wheat a paying crop, but he still doubted. He had not used it, himself. Tobacco required fresh land, and was rapidly exhausting, but it returned more money for the labor used upon it than anything else, enough more, in his opinion, to pay for the wearing out of the land. If he was well paid for it, he did not know why he should not wear out his land.

His tobacco-fields were nearly all in a distant and lower part of his plantation; land which had been neglected before his time in a great measure, because it had been sometimes flooded, and was, much of the year, too wet for cultivation. He was draining and clearing it, and it now brought good crops.

He had had an Irish gang draining for him, by contract. He thought a negro could do twice as much work in a day as an Irishman. He had not stood over them and seen them at work, but judged entirely from the amount they accomplished: he thought a good gang of negroes would have got on twice as fast. He was sure they must have "trifled" a great deal, or they would have accomplished more than they had. He complained much, also, of their sprees and quarrels. I asked why he should employ Irishmen, in preference to doing the work with his own hands. "It's dangerous work [unhealthy?], and a negro's life is too valuable to be risked at it. If a negro dies, it's a considerable loss, you know."

He afterwards said that his negroes never worked so hard as to tire themselves—always were lively, and ready to go off on a frolic at night. He did not think they ever did half a fair day's work. They could not be made to work hard: they never would lay out their strength freely, and it was impossible to make them do it.

This is just what I have thought when I have seen slaves at work—they seem to go through the motions of labor without putting strength into them. They keep their powers in reserve for their own use at night perhaps.

Mr. W. also said that he cultivated only the coarser and lower-priced sorts of tobacco, because the finer sorts required more pains-taking and discretion than it was possible to make a large gang of negroes use. "You can make a nigger work," he said, "*but you cannot make him think.*"

Although Mr. W. was very wealthy (or, at least, would be considered so anywhere at the North), and was a gentleman of education, his style of living was very farmerlike, and thoroughly Southern. On their plantations, generally, the Virginia gentlemen seem to drop their full-dress and constrained town-habits, and to live a free, rustic, shooting-jacket life. We dined in a room that extended out, rearwardly, from the house, and which, in a Northern establishment, would have been the kitchen. The cooking was done in a detached log-cabin, and the dishes brought some distance, through the open air, by the servants. The outer door was left constantly open, though there was a fire in an enormous old fire-place, large enough, if it could have been distributed sufficiently, to have lasted a New York seamstress the best part of the winter. By the door, there was indiscriminate admittance to negro-children and fox-hounds, and, on an average, there were four of these, grinning or licking their chops, on either side of my chair, all the time I was at the table. A stout woman acted as head waitress, employing two handsome little mulatto boys as her aids in communicating with the kitchen, from which relays of hot corn-bread, of an excellence quite new to me, were brought at frequent intervals. There was no other bread, and but one vegetable served—sweet potato, roasted in ashes, and this, I thought, was the best sweet potato, also, that I ever had eaten; but there were four preparations of swine's flesh, besides fried fowls, fried eggs, cold roast turkey, and opossum, cooked I know not how, but it somewhat resembled baked sucking-pig. The only beverages on the table were milk and whisky.

I was pressed to stay several days with Mr. W., and should have been glad to have accepted such hospitality, had not another engagement prevented. . . .

"Swell-heads"

. . . The farce of the vulgar-rich has its foundation in Mississippi, as in New York and in Manchester, in the rapidity with which certain values have advanced, especially that of cotton, and, simultaneously, that of cotton lands and negroes. Of course, there are men of refinement and cultivation among the rich planters of Mississippi, and many highly estimable and intelligent persons outside of the wealthy class, but the number of such is smaller in proportion to that of the immoral, vulgar, and ignorant newly-rich, than in any other part of the United States. And herein is a radical difference between the social condition of this region and that of the sea-board slave States, where there are fewer wealthy families, but where, among the people of wealth, refinement and education are much more general.

I asked how rich the sort of men were of whom he spoke.

"Why, sir, from a hundred thousand to ten million."

"Do you mean that between here and Natchez there are none worth less than a hundred thousand dollars?"

"No, sir, not beyond the ferry. Why, any sort of a plantation is worth a hundred thousand dollars; the niggers would sell for that."

"How many negroes are there on these plantations?"

"From fifty to a hundred."

"Never over one hundred?"

"No; when they've increased to a hundred they always divide them; stock another plantation. There are sometimes three or four plantations adjoining one another, with an overseer for each, belonging to the same man; but that isn't general—in general, they have to strike off for new land."

"How many acres will a hand tend here?"

"About fifteen—ten of cotton, and five of corn; some pretend to make them tend twenty."

"And what is the usual crop?"

"A bale and a half to the acre on fresh land and in the bottom. From four to eight bales to a hand they generally get; sometimes ten and better, when they are lucky."

"A bale and a half on fresh land? How much on old?"

"Well, you can't tell—depends on how much it's worn and what the season is, so much. Old land, after a while, isn't worth bothering with."

"Do most of these large planters who live so freely anticipate their crops as the sugar planters are said to—spend the money, I mean, before the crop is sold?"

"Yes, sir, and three and four crops ahead generally."

"Are most of them the sons of rich men? are they old estates?"

"No, sir; many of them were overseers themselves once."

"Well, have you noticed whether it is a fact that these large properties seldom continue long in the same family? Do the grandsons of wealthy planters often become poor men?"

"Generally the sons do; almost always their sons are fools, and soon go through with it."

"If they don't kill themselves before their fathers die," said the other.

"Yes; they drink hard and gamble, and of course that brings them into fights."

This was while they were smoking on the gallery after supper. I walked to the stable to see how my horse was provided for; when I returned they were talking of negroes who had died of yellow fever while confined in the jail at Natchez. Two of them were spoken of as having been thus "happily released," being under sentence of death, and unjustly so, in their opinion. . . .

Review of a First-Rate Cotton Plantation

We had a good breakfast in the morning, and immediately afterward mounted and rode to a very large cottonfield, where the whole field-force of the plantation was engaged.

It was a first-rate plantation. On the highest ground stood a large and handsome mansion, but it had not been occupied for several years, and it was more than two years since the overseer had seen the owner. He lived several hundred miles away, and the overseer would not believe that I did not know him, for he was a rich man and an honorable, and had several times been where I came from—New York.

The whole plantation, including the swamp land around it, and owned with it, covered several square miles. It was four miles from the settlement to the nearest neighbor's house. There were between thirteen and fourteen hundred acres under cultivation with cotton, corn, and other hoed crops, and two hundred hogs running at large in the swamp. It was the intention that corn and pork enough should be raised to keep the slaves and cattle. This year, however, it has been found necessary to purchase largely, and such was probably usually the case, though the overseer intimated the owner had been displeased, and he "did not mean to be caught so bad again."

There were 135 slaves, big and little, of which 67 went to field regularly—equal, the overseer thought, to 60 able-bodied hands. Beside the field-hands, there were 3 mechanics (blacksmith, carpenter and wheelwright), 2 seamstresses, 1 cook, 1 stable servant, 1 cattle-tender, 1 hog-tender, 1 teamster, 1 house servant (overseer's cook), and one midwife and nurse. These were all first-class hands; most of them would be worth more, if they were for sale, the overseer said, than the best of field-hands. There was also a driver of the hoe-gang who did not labor personally, and a foreman of the plow-gang. These two acted as petty officers in the field, and alternately in the quarters.

There was a nursery for sucklings at the quarters, and twenty women at this time who left their work four times each day, for half an hour, to nurse their young ones, and whom the overseer counted as half-hands— that is, expected to do half an ordinary day's work.

Deserters and Detectives

He had no runaways out at this time, but had just sold a bad one to go to Texas. He was whipping the fellow, when he turned and tried to stab him— then broke from him and ran away. He had him caught almost immediately by the dogs. After catching him, he kept him in irons till he had a chance to sell him. His niggers did not very often run away, he said, because they were almost sure to be caught. As soon as he saw that one was gone he put the dogs on, and if rain had not just fallen, they would soon find him. Sometimes, though, they would outwit the dogs, but if they did they almost always kept in the neighborhood, because they did not like to go where they could not sometimes get back and see their families, and he would soon get wind of where they had been; they would come round their quarters to see their families and to get food, and as soon as he knew it, he would find their tracks and put the dogs on again. Two months was the longest time any of them ever kept out. They had dogs trained on purpose to run after niggers, and never let out for any thing else.

Driving

We found in the field thirty plows, moving together, turning the earth from the cotton plants, and from thirty to forty hoers, the latter mainly women, with a black driver walking about among them with a whip, which he often cracked at them, sometimes allowing the lash to fall lightly upon their shoulders. He was constantly urging them also with his voice. All worked very steadily, and though the presence of a stranger on the plantation must have been rare, I saw none raise or turn their heads to look at me. Each gang was attended by a "water-toter," that of the hoe-gang being a straight, sprightly, plump little black girl, whose picture, as she stood balancing the bucket upon her head, shading her bright eyes with one hand, and holding out a calabash with the other to maintain her poise, would have been a worthy study for Murillo.

Days and Hours of Labor

I asked at what time they began to work in the morning. "Well," said the overseer, "I do better by my niggers than most. I keep 'em right smart at their work while they do work, but I generally knock 'em off at 8 o'clock in the morning Saturdays, and give 'em all the rest of the day to themselves, and I always gives 'em Sundays, the whole day. Pickin' time, and when the crap's bad in grass, I sometimes keep 'em to it till about sunset, Satudays, but I never work 'em Sundays."

"How early do you start them out in the morning, usually?"

"Well, I don't never start my niggers 'fore daylight except 'tis in pickin' time, then maybe I got 'em out a quarter of an hour before. But I keep 'em right smart to work through the day." He showed an evident pride in the vigilance of his driver, and called my attention to the large area of ground already hoed over that morning; well hoed, too, as he said.

"At what time do they eat?" I asked. They ate "their snacks" in their cabins, he said, before they came out in the morning (that is before day-light—the sun rising at this time at a little before five, and the day dawning, probably, an hour earlier); then at 12 o'clock their dinner was brought to them in a cart—one cart for the plow-gang and one for the hoe-gang. The hoe-gang ate its dinner in the field, and only stopped work long enough to eat it. The plow-gang drove its teams to the "weather houses"—open sheds erected for the purpose in different parts of the plantation, under which were cisterns filled with rain water, from which the water-toters carried drink to those at work. The mules were fed as much oats (in straw), corn and fodder as they would eat in two hours; this forage having been brought to the weather houses by another cart. The plowmen had nothing to do but eat their dinner in all this time. All worked as late as they could see to work well, and had no more food nor rest until they returned to their cabin. At half past nine o'clock the drivers, each on an alternate night, blew a horn, and at ten visited every cabin to see that its occupants were at rest, and not lurking about and spending their strength in fooleries, and that the fires were safe—a very unusual precaution; the negroes are gen-erally at liberty after their day's work is done till they are called in the morning. When washing and patching were done, wood hauled and cut for the fires, corn ground, etc., I did not learn: probably all chores not of daily necessity, were reserved for Saturday. Custom varies in this respect. In general, with regard to fuel for the cabins, the negroes are left to look out for themselves, and they often have to go to "the swamp" for it, or at least, if it has been hauled, to cut it to a convenient size, after their day's work is done. The allowance of food was a peck of corn and four pounds of pork per week, each. When they could not get "greens" (any vegetables) he generally gave them five pounds of pork. They had gardens, and raised a good deal for themselves; they also had fowls, and usually plenty of eggs. He added, "the man who owns this plantation does more for his niggers than any other man I know. Every Christmas he sends me up a thousand or fifteen hundred dollars' [equal to eight or ten dollars each] worth of molasses and coffee, and tobacco, and calico, and Sunday tricks for 'em. Every family on this plantation gets a barrel of molasses at Christmas." (Not an uncommon practice in Mississippi, though the quantity is very rarely so generous. It is usually made somewhat proportionate to the value of the last crop sold.)

Beside which, the overseer added, they are able, if they choose, to buy certain comforts for themselves—tobacco for instance—with money earned by Saturday and Sunday work. Some of them went into the swamps on Sunday and made boards—"puncheons" made with the ax. One man sold last year as much as fifty dollars' worth.

Petitions Concerning Free Blacks

Petition of Arthur Lee, Freeman, 1835

To the General Assembly of Virginia: The Petition of Arthur [Lee] a free man of colour, of the County of Alleghany, respectfully represents,

That he was purchased as a slave by Dr. John McDowell of the Hot Springs in Virginia, of [from] Dr. Charles Lewis of Botetourt. That his former master Dr. McDowell, was for many years confined to his bed at the Hot Springs, unable to use any of his limbs, in which situation he continued until his death, a period of more than twenty years. That yr petitioner during that time served him faithfully as a Blacksmith, besides rendering him important and valuable service, as a body servant. That for these services, and the fidelity of your petitioner, the s[ai]d McDowell promised to set free yr petitioner, at his death. This honour he omitted to do, and yr petitioner became the property of Colonel Hamilton Brown of North Carolina. That Colonel Brown hearing the services and character of yr petitioner and the relations that had subsisted between yr petitioner and his former master, would not remove him from Virginia, but permitted him to remain in the State, and pay him $100 per year as a hire. That he had paid Colonel Brown about 1600 $ for hire and $500 for his freedom, and has moreover purchased his wife and one child of Mr. Henry Massie; and since the purchase has had born to him 3 other children. All this he has done by great industry and good conduct, and is now anxious to remain in the State as a freeman. Your petitioner begs leave further to state to yr Honorable body that such has been his good conduct in the County in

Petition of Arthur Lee, Freeman, 1835 from The Petitions of Allegheny 1835 (collection of documents). Reprinted by permission of Virginia State Library and Archives, Richmond, Virginia 23219.

which he has lived for the last twenty years that the whole County are not only willing but desirous that the Legislature should grant the permission he asks to remain with his wife and children in the State of Virginia. This he will make appear to your Honorable body. He therefore most respectfully and earnestly prays that you will pass a law permitting him on the score of long and meritorious service to remain in the State, together with his wife and four children, and not force him in his old age to seek a livelihood in a new Country. For his good character, conduct, and industry he begs leave to refer yr Honorable body to the subjoined statements of those that have long known him, and as in duty bound he will ever pray.

Samuel B. Lowry	Wm Bolinger	Archibald J. Mann
James H. Leet	Philip Bolinger	Earel W. Sawyers
Joseph Dickson	Augustin Luck	James T. Robeson
Th Rogers	Jesse Carter	John Lockhart
John Mastin	Lemuel Hanes	Jno. Handy
John Crow	Dr. M. Frankling	Churchill T. Breedlove
John Teadrow	James W. Hanley	George W. Rogers

We citizens of the Counties of Alleghany [and] Bath take pleasure in testifying to the good character and conduct of Arthur Lee, Petitioner. He is a first rate Blacksmith; very industrious and well behaved; and it would afford us satisfaction that he should be allowed to remain in the State. He would be a loss to the County as a workman, and no one we believe would wish him to be forced to leave the State.

John Shumate	R. O. B. Menius	Wm Scott
Geo. H. Dayne	Isaac W. Lockitt	John Callaghan
Alfred Plumb	Isaac Wolf	John Monroe
Isaac Steele	Hamilton Bess	Elizabeth Williams
Isaac Moore	Jacob Dysart	John Pessinger
Chas Callahan	John Allen	Archibald M. Kincaid
O. Callaghan	Noah W. Kendall	William Dickson
Wm. H. Plumb	Sampson Sawyers	Sam Carpenter, Jr.
Chs. L. Francisco	Harvey Pessinger	Lee Pessinger
of Bath	William P. Herin	Andrew Sawyer
Jeramiah Moore	Samuel Kean, Jr.	Hosiah Pevey
Wm Skeen	John W. Bright	William Eagan
Wm. H. Terrill	William Kyle	Michael Barnes

Petition of William J. Grayson, James R. Verdier, and 62 Other Citizens of St. Helena Parish to the Senate of South Carolina, c. 1831

To the Honorbl the President and other members of the Senate, The undersigned inhabitances of St. Hellena Parish convinced of the perniceous consequences resulting to the State of So Car from the number of free persons of colour within her limits beg leave respectfully to bring the subject before you. The State not only derives no strength from the class of wich we complain, but is essentially injured, the example of indolence and vice exhibited by the coloured free persons is perpetually before the Slaves. They encourage insubordination by pricept as well as example. They are rapidly drawing from the country the valuable class of industrious mechanics, on whose intelegence and hardihood the safety of S° C^{ar} must mainly depend. What will be the condition of the State when your carpenters and painters and Blacksmiths, and the occupants of all the departments of mechanical industry are free men of colour. Yet such must be the consequences of the competition which the white mechanic encounters from the coloured labourer, the latter is able to work at a less price from obvious causes. He has very often no family to support, his wife and children are Slaves. He lives on the premises of their owner. He has no house rent to pay no clothing or food but his own to purchase. His expences are almost nothing, and he can therefore labour for almost nothing. Your petitioners cannot believe that you will permit a class so useless, perniceous, and degrading, to the character of the State, to Supplant the intellegent industrious and vigorous freemen, who in the various mechanical departments would so essentially increase her physical and moral strength. Your petitioners therefore pray that you will take the whole subject into consideration, and make such provisions for the removal of the free coloured persons as to your wisdom may seem meet—and as in duty bound they will ever pray.—

William Ellison Advertises His Cotton Gins, 1848, 1851

Sumter [*S.C.*] Banner, *December 13, 1848*

IMPROVED COTTON GINS.

Thankful for past favors, the subscriber wishes to inform the public, that he still *Manufactures Cotton Gins* at his establishment in *Stateburg* on the most improved and approved plan, of the most simple construction, of the finest finish, and of the best materials; to wit: *Steel Saws and steel plated Ribs, case hardened*, in which he will sell for Two Dollars per Saw. He also repairs old Gins and puts them in complete order, at the shortest notice. All orders for Gins will be promptly and punctually attended to.

WILLIAM ELLISON.

Stateburg, May 1, 1848.

Sumter [*S.C.*] Banner, *April 23, 1851*

IMPROVED COTTON GINS.

Thankful for past favours the subscriber wishes to inform the public that he still manufactures Cotton Gins at his establishment in Stateburg, on the most improved and approved plan, which he thinks that the cotton ginned on one of those gins of the late improvement is worth at least a quarter of a cent more than the cotton ginned on the ordinary gin. He also manufactures them on the most simple construction, of the finest finish and of the best materials; to wit, Steel Saws and Steel Plated Ribs, Case hardened which he will sell for $2 per Saw.—He also repairs old gins and puts them in complete order at the shortest notice. All orders for Gins will be promptly and punctually attended to.

WILLIAM ELLISON.

Stateburg, Sumter Dist, S.C. April 23, 26

William Gregg Advocates Manufacturing, 1845

It must be apparent to all men of discernment that whether a tariff for protection is continued or not, our only safety, in this State, lies in a change of our industrial pursuits. The United States is destined to be a great manufacturing country, and a few years, even without a protective Tariff, will place her on a footing with, if not ahead of the most skilful nations, and all who have any knowledge of the subject admit that South-Carolina and Georgia possess advantages, which only need to be fostered to lead to success in Cotton Manufacturing. We already see North-Carolina on the one side, and Georgia on the other, making rapid strides in these pursuits, and shall we stand with our arms folded, crying save us from our oppressors, until we are awakened to compete with those neighboring States, skilled in the arts! It is only necessary for us to turn our faces to the South-West to behold the people who are to take the very bread from our mouths, if we continue to place our reliance on the culture of Cotton, and the time is at hand when we shall set about, in good earnest, changing our pursuits. It would indeed be well for us, if we were not so refined in politics—if the talent, which has been, for years past, and is now engaged in embittering our indolent people against their industrious neighbors of the North, had been with the same zeal engaged in promoting domestic industry and the encouragement of the mechanical arts. If so, we should now see a far different state of things in South-Carolina. It is only necessary to travel over the sterile mountains of Connecticut, Massachusetts, Vermont, and New-Hampshire, to learn the true secret of our difficulties, (Mr. McDuffie to the contrary notwithstanding) to learn the difference between indolence and industry, extravagance and economy. [George McDuffie, formerly Governor and in 1845 Senator from S.C., blamed the protective tariff for South Carolina's ills.] We there see the scenery which would take the place of our unpainted mansions,—dilapidated cabins with mud chimneys and no windows,—broken down rail fences,—fields overgrown with weeds, and thrown away, half exhausted, to be taken up by pine thickets,—beef cattle unprotected from the inclemency of winter, and so poor as barely to preserve life. In fact, every evidence that can possibly be exhibited to satisfy a stranger, that we are, to say the least, destitute of every feature which characterises an industrious people, may be seen among us. Laying aside the vexed question of a Tariff for Protection, which I don't pretend to advocate, I cannot see how we are to look with a reasonable hope for relief, even from its abandonment, without a total change of our habits. My recent visit to the Northern States has fully satisfied me that the true secret of our difficulties, lies in the want of energy on the part of our capitalists, and ignorance and laziness on the part of those who *ought* to labour. We need never look for thrift while we permit our immense timber forests, granite quaries and mines, to lie idle, and supply ourselves with hewn granite, pine boards, laths and shingles, &c., furnished by the *lazy* dogs at the North—ah, worse than this, we see our back country farmers, many of whom are too lazy to mend a broken gate, or repair the fences, to protect their crops from the neighbouring stock, actually supplied with their axe, hoe and broom handles, pitch forks, rakes, &c., by the *indolent* mountaineers of New-Hampshire and Massachusetts. The time was, when every old woman in the country had her gourd, from which, the country gardens were supplied with seeds. We now find it more convenient to permit this duty to devolve on our careful friends, the Yankees. Even our boat-oars, and hand-spikes for rolling logs, are furnished, ready made, to our hand, and what jim-crack can possibly be invented of which we are not the purchasers? These are the drains which are impoverishing the South— these are the true sources of all our difficulties. . . .

Surely there is nothing in cotton spinning that can poison the atmosphere of South-Carolina. Why not spin as well as plant cotton? The same hand that attends the gin may work a carding machine. The girl who is capable of making thread, on a country spinning wheel, may do the same with equal facility, on the *throstlé frame*. The woman who can warp the thread and weave it, on a common loom, may soon be taught to do the same, on the *power loom;* and so with all the departments, from the raw cotton to the cloth, experience has proved that any child, white, or black, of ordinary capacity, may be taught, in a few weeks, to be expert in any part of a cotton factory; moreover, all overseers who have experience in the matter, give a decided preference to blacks as operatives.

There are many reasons why blacks should be preferred: two of which may be adduced. First—You are not under the necessity of educating them, and have, therefore, their uninterrupted services from the age of eight years. The second is, that when you have your mill filled with expert hands, you are not subjected to the change which is constantly taking place with whites. In the Northern States, these are inconveniences of no small moment. In Massachusetts, the laws forbid the employment of persons under *fourteen* years of age, unless the employer can show a certificate from a school master, stating that the individual has been at school three months in the year. The teaching of new hands and the constant change of operatives, are evils seriously felt; and in the summer season, when it is desirable to ramble in the country, many eastern factories have one-third of their machinery standing idle for the want of hands. While on this part of my subject, I would ask, shall we stop at the effort to prove the capacity of blacks for manufacturing? Shall we pass unnoticed the thousands of poor, ignorant, degraded white people among us, who, in this land of plenty, live in comparative nakedness and starvation? Many a one is reared in *proud* South-Carolina, from birth to manhood, who has never passed a month, in which he has not some part of the time, been stinted for meat. Many a mother is there, who will tell you that her children are but scantily supplied with bread, and much more scantily with meat, and if they be clad with comfortable raiment, it is at the expense of their scanty allowance of food. These may be startling statements, but they are nevertheless true, and if not believed in Charleston, the members of our Legislature, who have traversed the State, in electioneering campaigns, can attest their truth.

It is only necessary to build a manufacturing village of shanties, in a healthy location in any part of the State, to have crowds of these poor people around you, seeking employment at half the compensation given to operatives at the North. It is indeed painful to be brought in contact with such ignorance and degradation; but on the other hand, it is pleasant to witness the change, which soon takes place in the condition of those, who obtain employment. The emaciated, pale-faced children, soon assume the appearance of robust health, and their tattered garments are exchanged for those suited to a better condition; if you visit their dwellings, you will find their tables supplied with wholesome food; and on the Sabbath, when the females turn out in their gay colored gowns, you will imagine yourself surrounded by groups of city belles. How easy would it be for the proprietors of such establishments, with only a small share of philanthropy, to make good use of the school fund in ameliorating the condition of this class of our population, now but little elevated above the Indian of the forest. The cause of this degradation and poverty will hereafter be noticed; it is an interesting subject, and one that ought to engage the attention of every philanthropist and christian. It is, perhaps, not generally known, that there are *twenty-nine thousand* white persons in this State, above the age of twelve years, who can neither read nor write—this is about one in every five of the white population.

That we are behind the age in agriculture, the mechanic arts, industry and enterprise, is apparent to all who pass through our State.

Clement Eaton, formerly professor of history at the University of Kentucky, wrote widely and knowledgeably about the Old South. In the selection reprinted here, he describes the expansion of the Cotton Kingdom and the cycles associated with its settlement. Historian Eugene Genovese of the College of William and Mary has advanced provocative Marxist interpretations of southern society. In the second essay, he questions whether the Old South was capitalist and argues for the predominance of the slaveholding planter and his values in southern society. A contrasting interpretation is advanced by historian James Oakes of Northwestern University in the last essay. His view that middle-class slaveholders, rather than great planters, were the predominant and influential class in the South leads to different conclusions about the region's character.

Expansion of the Cotton Kingdom

CLEMENT EATON

The sundials in quiet Southern gardens registered the passage of time in an unhurried civilization—until the rise of the Cotton Kingdom. After the invention of the cotton gin in 1793, the tempo of life in the South quickened. The Whitney gin was a technological break-through that affected nearly every phase of Southern life, stimulating the growth of the materialistic spirit, a vast westward migration, an unbalanced economy, and, most unfortunate of all, the revitalization of the moribund institution of slavery. It resulted in a King Cotton psychology, which James H. Hammond of South Carolina expressed flamboyantly in the Senate in 1858: "What would happen if no cotton was furnished for three years . . . England would topple headlong and carry the whole civilized world with her save the South. No, you dare not make war on cotton. No power on earth dares to make war on it. Cotton is king."

Hammond was speaking primarily of short-staple cotton, but the first commercial cotton produced in the South was the long-staple or sea-island variety. This variety had been introduced into Georgia in 1786 from seed sent by Loyalist refugees in the Bahama islands. Possessing a staple of two inches in length, approximately twice as long as that of upland cotton, it was used principally in delicate laces and superfine cloth of a silky luster. The seeds were glossy and black and could be easily ginned or separated from the fibers by rollers. Upland cotton, on the other hand, had green seed to which the fibers tightly adhered, so that it took a slave a whole day to gin a pound of lint by hand. Consequently, before the invention of the Whitney gin, little upland cotton was grown in the American colonies and hardly any was exported. Sea-island cotton was always much more valuable than the upland variety, bringing in 1803 fifty cents a pound, while short staple cotton sold for approximately half that amount. The high price of sea-island cotton was owing partly to the excessive amount of labor involved in its production, which required ten or twelve pickings, while the short-staple variety could be harvested in three. Furthermore, sea-island cotton could be grown commercially only on the sea islands off the coast of Georgia and South Carolina and the adjacent littoral. After an enormous spurt in production during the latter part of the eighteenth century, sea-island cotton exports remained stabilized between eight or nine million pounds from 1805 to 1850, when production increased greatly because it was found that this prized variety could be grown successfully in the interior of Florida. In 1860 over fifteen million pounds were exported from the Southern states.

By the close of the eighteenth century a great potential market for cotton fiber had been created by English inventions of spinning and weaving machinery. Only a practicable gin was needed, and this was supplied by the invention of young Eli Whitney, who after graduating from Yale College in 1793 took passage on a ship bound for Savannah, Georgia, to accept a position as tutor on a South Carolina plantation. On board ship he met the vivacious and warmhearted widow of the Revolutionary general Nathanael Greene, who was returning to her plantation near Savannah. Mrs. Greene invited Whitney to visit Mulberry Grove, and here he heard planters talking about the need for a cotton gin to separate the fiber from the green seed of upland cotton. He set to work to design a model, which he completed in ten days. It was a simple machine consisting of a roller equipped with wire teeth which tore the fiber from the seed as the spikes revolved between the slats of a hopper. The original Whitney gin, which was patented in 1794, was operated by a hand crank and could gin fifty pounds of cotton a day, as contrasted with one a day by the old method.

Whitney formed a partnership with Phineas Miller, Mrs. Greene's manager and tutor, to manufacture gins in New Haven. They tried to maintain a monopoly on the use of the invention, but it was of such simple construction that a blacksmith could make it, and soon many gins were built that infringed the patent rights. Moreover, improvements were made by others, notably Hodgen Holmes of Augusta, Georgia, who in 1796 substituted circular iron saws for wooden rollers with wire teeth. Whitney and his partner prosecuted many suits against infringers, but with little success before Southern juries. Finally Judge Johnson of the Supreme Court of Georgia upheld Whitney's patent rights in the year before they expired. The South Carolina legislature appropriated a lump sum of $50,000 to pay Whitney and Miller for their rights in that state, and North Carolina and Tennessee levied a tax on each gin using the Whitney patent and paid the proceeds to the inventor. But having spent large sums in court litigation, the partners realized little from the epoch-making invention.

Short-staple cotton was almost ideally suited for cultivation in the South with its warm climate and its slave labor system. Early in the spring the seeds were planted in rows; as the plants grew, the grass grew too, and had to be kept down by frequent plowing and hoeing. Horace Holley, the Northern-born president of Transylvania University, described the flowering of the plant on Andrew Jackson's plantation near Nashville in a letter to his father: "The flower of this plant is white the first day of blooming, red the second, and falls the third." Then green bolls developed, bursting open when the plants matured in August. Forty or fifty bolls grew on the ante-bellum plant; some luxuriant specimens contained as many as a hundred and fifty. After they burst, a good cotton field was a white carpet on the land.

Cotton was well adapted to the slave-gang system. The height of the plant was low enough not to hide the workers; they could be kept like an army marching across the wide fields in plowing, hoeing, and picking gangs. Since the slaves could cultivate twice as much cotton as they could pick, the acreage planted was limited by the picking capacity of the plantation force. Usually ten acres, together with eight or ten acres of corn, were as much as could be cultivated by a hand. Under favorable weather conditions, good soil produced a 500-pound bale or a bale and a half of ginned cotton per acre.

The picking lasted from the latter part of August to early January. Women and small children as well as the male hands were used in this operation. Dragging a long sack tied to their waists to deposit the cotton in, they employed both hands to pluck the fleece from the open bolls. Since the bolls ripened unevenly, it was necessary for the field to be picked over at least three times. This unequal ripening was the most important reason for the failure until the 1930's to develop a successful mechanical picker. The yield of cotton was greatly increased after 1815 by the introduction into the lower South of the Mexican variety, whose bolls opened more widely and could be picked more easily than the upland cotton. Consequently the amount of cotton picked by a slave in a day doubled during the ante-bellum period. Full-grown hands were required to pick from 150 to 200 pounds of seed cotton per day. The seed cotton was taken to the planter's gin, which was usually driven by mules attached to a long sweep. After ginning, it was pressed into bales by means of a screw and covered with hemp cloth, or bagging, tied by ropes. In the ports it was reduced by steam presses into smaller bulk for shipment to Europe.

Three-fourths of the world's supply of cotton came from the Southern states, and the remainder from India, Egypt, and Brazil. From the beginning of the cotton trade until the Civil War, the great port to which Southern cotton was shipped was Liverpool, the port of entry for Manchester, the textile center of Great Britain. The destination of Southern cotton exports in 1859–60 was divided as follows: Great Britain, 2,344,000 bales; continental Europe, 1,069,000; and the United States, 943,000.

Liverpool determined the world market price for cotton; consequently the Southern planters anxiously awaited the news from there of the varying prices paid for different grades of their staple. The main determinant in its price was whether there was a short crop or a bonanza yield in the Southern states, but other factors, such as disturbed conditions in Europe or a panic, also influenced the market. In the first decade after the invention of the gin, prices of short-staple cotton rose as high as 23 cents a pound, but the increased production that resulted from high prices led to a rapid decline; in 1812, largely because of the outbreak of war, the price in New Orleans descended to 7 or 8 cents a pound. After the conclusion of peace with Great Britain in 1815, prices became phenomenally good, rising in 1818 to 33 cents a pound. The panic of 1819 depressed prices to 8 cents, but in 1835 cotton rose spectacularly to 15 cents, then began a long decline, reaching a low point of 4 cents in January, 1844. The last five years of the ante-bellum period were a time of prosperity for the cotton planters, who in 1860 produced their greatest crop of over four and a half million bales. Yet the future for both cotton and slavery was clouded by the prospect of overproduction of this staple.

The Whitney gin opened up a vast kingdom for cotton. Upland cotton could be grown wherever there were two hundred frostless days. The western limit of cultivation was the ninety-eighth meridian of longitude, beyond which the minimum requirement of twenty-three inches of annual rainfall was not met. The northern limit excluded Virginia and Kentucky except for the western tip of the latter; before 1826, cotton was grown enthusiastically in the southeastern corner of Virginia and in Piedmont North Carolina, but crop failures caused both states to reduce their planting drastically after that date. In the decade of the 1850's, however, cotton brought such a high price that these states started growing it again.

In the Atlantic seaboard states the center of the production of short-staple cotton soon moved from the coastal plain to the Piedmont. Here in 1799 Wade Hampton I of Millwood, near Columbia, South Carolina, the first great cotton planter of the region, with his eighty-six slaves made a crop of six hundred bales worth $90,000. Thereafter he prospered so greatly from his cotton planting in South Carolina and his absentee sugar plantation in Louisiana (acquired in 1811) that when he died in 1835 he was reputed to have been the richest planter in the United States. The expansion of cotton culture into the Piedmont tended to unify the people of the state economically and politically.

At the same time a decline took place in the economy of the coastal plain. The competition of the fresh lands of the Piedmont and even more of the virgin soil of the Southwest drained population, both white and black, from this old region. When Edmund Ruffin made his agricultural survey of South Carolina in 1843, he was saddened by seeing the decay and desolation of the plantations of the tidewater. Goose Creek Parish, for example, once the seat of many wealthy planters, was now a scene of dilapidation and abandonment. Beautiful old houses, standing in groves of noble and venerable live oaks, such as Oak Forest, the former home of Sir James Wright, were deserted and falling into decay. Land values in the low country had declined enormously, and instead of producing crops some of the old plantations were valuable chiefly for their lumber, which was floated in rafts to Charleston. The countryside gave Ruffin the impression of "the former residence of a people who have all gone away, leaving the land tenantless."

Even more melancholy was the sight of the deserted towns of the low country, Dorchester, Jacksonborough, Pineville, and Purysburg; Beaufort, Ruffin remarked, was sustained by malaria, which drove people to it for refuge.

The typical cotton planter of the Piedmont was not the owner of many slaves and a large estate but rather a small planter, such as Moses Waddel. Waddel owned a cotton plantation near Abbeville in upcountry South Carolina, on which he had twenty-three slaves. Cotton planting was only one of his interests, for he was a preacher and a famous schoolmaster of the Old South. His diary shows that he visited his plantation often and was much concerned with the practical details of its operation and the management of the Negroes. The largest amount of cotton picked by his slaves was twenty bales. He had his own gin, operated by mules attached to a long sweep, and a press which compressed the cotton into bales by means of a screw. The market for his cotton was Augusta, to which he sent his crop by boat, paying freight of one dollar a bale. He received good prices of 15 to 16 cents a pound, and his expenses were slight, chiefly the cost of shoes, cloth, and blankets. Besides cotton he raised oats, wheat, and corn. During the winter he kept his Negroes employed clearing new ground, splitting rails for fences, and pulling fodder. His slave women performed various tasks, including picking peaches and apples, cutting them into pieces, and preserving them by drying them in the sun.

Waddel's diary gives many interesting details of slave management on a small cotton plantation. He employed an overseer, who whipped the slaves for delinquent conduct, at the same time Waddel, the schoolmaster, was flogging his pupils. During the picking season, he "encouraged his hands much & sincerely with the promise of hats, blankets, etc." He recorded with satisfaction that two hands picked 836 pounds in one day, a fine performance. Waddel was apparently as strict a master of his slaves as of his pupils. He reproved his slaves for absence from prayers, for want of industry, and for untruthfulness. On July 8, 1834, he wrote that Dick had rebelled against the hard work of clearing new ground and that the other Negroes had refused to aid the overseer in subduing him. The recalcitrant slave then ran away, but, after being absent twelve days, was captured and whipped. Waddel seems to have been much more concerned than the average planter with the religious condition of his bondsmen, for his diary contains frequent references to his praying with them, catechizing them, and rebuking them for derelictions from virtue.

The expansion of the Cotton Kingdom into the Gulf region was facilitated by the passage of the Harrison Frontier Land Act of 1800, which fixed the minimum price of government land at two dollars an acre and permitted payment to be made in four annual installments. As early as 1804, cotton was cultivated in the wild territory of Mississippi, for in that year Abram Mordecai erected a cotton gin at the junction of the Coosa and Tallapoosa rivers. Cotton planters began settling the rich Tennessee Valley of northern Alabama around Huntsville between 1805 and 1809, and a large migration to Alabama occurred after the war with England. James

A. Graham of the Piedmont village of Hillsborough, North Carolina, wrote in 1817: "The *Alabama Fever* rages here with great violence and has carried off vast numbers of our citizens. I am apprehensive if it continues to spread as it has done, it will almost depopulate the country." The Treaty of Fort Jackson in 1816 had made available much agricultural land, but the full exploitation of the arable land of the state was not possible until the removal of the Creek Indians west of the Mississippi twenty years later.

The purchase of cotton lands in Tennessee and the Southwest was not confined to bona fide settlers but was eagerly made by speculators and land sharks. The acquisition by the federal government of rich cotton lands in western Tennessee from the Chickasaw Indians, the so-called Jackson Purchase of 1818, was a signal for North Carolina and Virginia farmers and speculators to rush to that area. Among the speculators were Andrew Jackson, Marcus Winchester, and John Overton, who in 1819 founded the town of Memphis. Jackson and his friend General John Coffee also speculated in the lands of the Tennessee Valley in the Huntsville area. Coffee organized the Cyprus Land Company before 1819, acquired coveted land around Muscle Shoals, and founded Florence in northern Alabama. Federal land offices were opened at Cahaba, which became the early capital of Alabama, and at St. Stephens, where spirited bidding at auctions ran the price of fertile bottom lands far above the minimum of $2 per acre. Settlers flowed into Alabama lands not occupied by Indians by way of the Upper Federal Road, opened in 1811, which led from Athens, Georgia, through Columbus and Montgomery to St. Stephens (north of Mobile), or else by the Natchez Trace from Nashville to Muscle Shoals and then to St. Stephens. Many settlers, too poor to buy federal lands, squatted upon them. Cotton lands were also available to poor men in Georgia if they were lucky enough to win a farm in the Georgia land lottery, which was started in 1803 to dispose of the lands from which the Indians had been removed. Any man who had resided in the state for three years was entitled to a lottery ticket for himself as well as one for his wife and another for his children. . . .

Tyrone Power, the Irish actor, during his travels in the Gulf states in 1835 was impressed by the restless energy and acquisitive spirit of the recent settlers. They displayed much the same desire for quick wealth, the feverish energy, the speculative urge, the desire for change, that motivates the real estate developers of our era. Neither the climate nor the hard conditions of pioneer living slowed them down:

> These frontier tamers of the swamp and forest are hardy, indefatigable and enterprising to a degree; despising and condemning luxury and refinement, courting labour, and even making a pride of the privation, which they, without any necessity, continue to endure with their families. . . .
> Their pride does not consist in fine houses, fine raiment, costly services of plate or refined cookery; they live in humble dwellings of wood, wear the coarsest habits, and live on the plainest fare. It is their pride to have planted an additional acre of cane-brake, to have won a few feet from the river, or cleared a thousand trees from the forest; to have added a couple of slaves to their family, or a horse of high blood to their stable.

Emigration to the Southwest followed a time pattern that throws doubt on the validity of Frederick Jackson Turner's safety-valve theory. The heaviest emigration occurred during boom times, 1819, 1830–37, and 1853–57. During hard times there was a notable diminution of westward migration—one must have cash or good credit to buy land even at the low prices of the public domain. The settler also required money for the trip and to finance himself until a crop could be grown and sold. Nevertheless, there were numerous poor people who emigrated to the Southwest like Ike and Betsy in the old ballad "Sweet Betsy from Pike."

> Oh, dont you remember Sweet Betsy from Pike,
> Who crossed the big mountains with her lover Ike,
> With two yoke of oxen, a large yaller dog,
> A tall Shanghai rooster and one spotted hog.

Thousands of these poor people became squatters on the public land.

The period of the 1830's until the panic of 1837 was what one of the Virginia emigrants called "flush times in Alabama and Mississippi." It was a time of great inflation of bank notes, when it was easy to borrow paper money to pay for land. The new settlers endorsed one another's notes freely and grandly, for it was regarded as an insult not to do so. When James D. Davidson left his native Virginia for the lower South in 1836, he wrote from Vicksburg that the people were mad with speculation. "They do business," he reported, "in a kind of frenzy, largely on credit." The most frequent question asked was what was the price of cotton and the next was the price of "niggers." In the 1830's settlers flocked to the Black Belt of Alabama, a strip of rich black soil, twenty to fifty miles wide, running across the south central part of the state into northeastern Mississippi. This region had been avoided by the early settlers because of its lack of trees, its thick canebrake, and its stiff soil. Yet it contained the richest soil of the state and became the seat of the finest plantations.

The spirit of the times in the Black Belt was reflected in the letters of Henry Watson, a young Northern tutor who settled in the village of Greensboro, Alabama, in 1834. He noted that the country in his neighborhood had been settled by people from Virginia and the Carolinas who brought their Negroes with them and bought lands from the original settlers at an advance of price. "They are," he wrote, "some of the nobility of the old states, the Randolph family, the Taylors, and the Bollings—first rate & intelligent men." Nevertheless the settlers lived altogether in log houses, had no tea, all commodities were outrageously high—corn four dollars a bushel, eggs 37 cents a dozen, $5 clocks sold for $40—everybody was in debt for land and Negroes, and materialism prevailed. So strong was the democratic spirit among the people that the politicians running for office sought to ascertain public sentiment and follow it—"the candidates would consider it madness to attempt to lead."

The westward and southern flow of Southerners followed in general along isothermal lines. Emigrating farmers liked to settle in areas where there would be no abrupt changes in their mode of life. As a rule, if they were used to growing tobacco and had acquired skill in producing it, they had no desire to try a new crop. Grain and cattle farmers usually moved into regions like their old homes, where they could continue to raise wheat, corn, and livestock. They were even influenced in their selection of a site by whether the drinking water was like that of their old home, limestone or freestone. The women, with clothes of the family to wash, hated to move to an area where they had to contend with hard water. The emigrants also preferred a soil that was similar to but richer than the land to which they had been accustomed. They preferred, moreover, to locate, not on the fertile river bottoms, which were unhealthy, hard to clear, and subject to floods, but on the higher lands. . . .

The cotton planters who emigrated to the virgin lands of the Southwest carried on the same wasteful type of agriculture that had exhausted their old plantations. As a consequence, in the 1840's and 1850's farms in Alabama and Mississippi were being abandoned for fresher lands in Texas and Arkansas. Robinson found in 1845 that lands in Mississippi were being eroded because the farmers "skinned" the soil, or scratched the surface only two inches deep with their plows. He discovered that many of the farmers in Mississippi were not "fixed" but ready to sell out and move to Texas. In the fertile counties of Madison and Hinds in the delta country, he passed what he called "Gone to Texas" farms, abandoned and desolate-looking.

Notwithstanding the youth of society in Alabama in the 1850's, there was constant and extensive emigration from the state. Part of this movement was caused by prosperous planters' buying the adjacent farms of poor men, who would then leave for land farther west. Senator Clement C. Clay, Jr., of Alabama explained this flow of population from the state: "Our small planters, after taking the cream off their lands, unable to restore them by rest, manures, or otherwise, are going farther west and south, in search of other virgin lands, which they may and will despoil and impoverish in like manner." He pointed out that numerous farmhouses once occupied by yeoman farmers were at the time abandoned or occupied by Negroes, and that the once fertile fields were unfenced and covered with broomsedge and foxtail. Counties of Alabama were exhibiting the same signs of decay and exhaustion that had characterized Virginia and the Carolinas. He cited one county which in 1825 had cast 3,000 votes, but thirty years later cast only 2,300. In crossing Louisiana into Texas, Olmsted passed many abandoned farms on both sides of the Sabine River. Numerous emigrant trains going to Texas presented a melancholy picture: jaded cattle, spiritless and ragged slaves, the men in homespun, silent and surly, the women bedraggled and forlorn.

Of all the classes of Southern society, the nonslaveholding farmers were the most migratory, and many were propelled westward by the advance of the plantation. Jefferson County, Mississippi, was an example of an area where the emigration of the lower classes of the population was striking. Located on the lower Mississippi River, the county was one of the earliest settled areas of the state, but by 1850 its hilly lands of loess soil had become badly eroded. Partly because of this fact, between 1850 and 1860, 85 per cent of the nonslaveholders left the county. Indeed, the number of small farms in the delta-loess area of Mississippi declined sharply in the decade, those having less than 50 acres of improved land from 17 to 7 per cent of the farms, and those having 50 to 99 acres from 13 to 8 per cent, while the percentage of plantations having over 500 acres of improved land rose from 11 to 22 per cent. . . .

The rapid advance of the Cotton Kingdom was registered in the admission of new states into the Union: Louisiana in 1812; Mississippi, 1817; Alabama, 1819; Missouri, 1821; Arkansas, 1836; Florida and Texas, 1845. The drain of population from the older Southern states was indicated by the fact that North Carolina, despite having one of the largest birth rates in the nation, remained virtually stationary in population during the decade 1830–40, and Virginia increased only 7 per cent. During the same decade the population of Alabama increased 76 per cent and that of Mississippi 154 per cent. The growth of the slave population in these states was even more spectacular, 114 and 197 per cent respectively. By 1830 the Gulf states had surpassed the Atlantic seaboard states in the production of cotton, and at the outbreak of the Civil War were raising three-fourths of the cotton grown in the South. In 1850 the leading cotton-growing state was Alabama, but by 1860 it was surpassed by Mississippi. The last frontier of the Cotton Kingdom was the rich soils of eastern Texas and the alluvial lands of Arkansas.

The Shaping of a Unique Society

EUGENE D. GENOVESE

The uniqueness of the antebellum South continues to challenge the imagination of Americans, who, despite persistent attempts, cannot divert their attention from slavery. Nor should they, for slavery provided the foundation on which the South rose and grew. The master-slave relationship permeated Southern life and influenced relationships among free men. A full history would have to treat the impact of the Negro slave and of slaveless as well as slaveholding whites, but a first approximation, necessarily concerned with essentials, must focus on the slaveholders, who most directly exercised power over men and events. The hegemony of the slaveholders, presupposing the social and economic preponderance of great slave plantations, determined the character of the South. These men rose to power in a region embedded in a capitalist country, and their social system emerged as part of a capitalist world. Yet, a nonslaveholding European past and a shared experience in a new republic notwithstanding, they imparted to Southern life a special social, economic, political, ideological, and psychological content.

To dissolve that special content into an ill-defined agrarianism or an elusive planter capitalism would mean to sacrifice concern with the essential

From *The Political Economy of Slavery* by Eugene D. Genovese. Copyright © 1961, 1963 by Eugene Genovese. Reprinted by permission of Pantheon Books, a division of Random House, Inc.

for concern with the transitional and peripheral. Neither of the two leading interpretations, which for many years have contended in a hazy and unreal battle, offers consistent and plausible answers to recurring questions, especially those bearing on the origins of the War for Southern Independence. The first of these interpretations considers the antebellum South an agrarian society fighting against the encroachments of industrial capitalism; the second considers the slave plantation merely a form of capitalist enterprise and suggests that the material differences between Northern and Southern capitalism were more apparent than real. These two views, which one would think contradictory, sometimes combine in the thesis that the agrarian nature of planter capitalism, for some reason, made coexistence with industrial capitalism difficult.

The first view cannot explain why some agrarian societies give rise to industrialization and some do not. A prosperous agricultural hinterland has generally served as a basis for industrial development by providing a home market for manufactures and a source of capital accumulation, and the prosperity of farmers has largely depended on the growth of industrial centers as markets for foodstuffs. In a capitalist society agriculture is one industry, or one set of industries, among many, and its conflict with manufacturing is one of many competitive rivalries. There must have been something unusual about an agriculture that generated violent opposition to the agrarian West as well as the industrial Northeast.

The second view, which is the more widely held, emphasizes that the plantation system produced for a distant market, responded to supply and demand, invested capital in land and slaves, and operated with funds borrowed from banks and factors. This, the more sophisticated of the two interpretations, cannot begin to explain the origins of the conflict with the North and does violence to elementary facts of antebellum Southern history. . . .

Capitalist and Pseudo-Capitalist Features of the Slave Economy

The slave economy developed within, and was in a sense exploited by, the capitalist world market; consequently, slavery developed many ostensibly capitalist features, such as banking, commerce, and credit. These played a fundamentally different role in the South than in the North. Capitalism has absorbed and even encouraged many kinds of precapitalist social systems: serfdom, slavery, Oriental state enterprises, and others. It has introduced credit, finance, banking, and similar institutions where they did not previously exist. It is pointless to suggest that therefore nineteenth-century India and twentieth-century Saudi Arabia should be classified as capitalist countries. We need to analyze a few of the more important capitalist and pseudo-capitalist features of Southern slavery and especially to review the barriers to industrialization in order to appreciate the peculiar qualities of this remarkable and anachronistic society.

The defenders of the "planter-capitalism" thesis have noted the extensive commercial links between the plantation and the world market and the modest commercial bourgeoisie in the South and have concluded that there is no reason to predicate an antagonism between cotton producers and cotton merchants. However valid as a reply to the naive arguments of the proponents of the agrarianism-versus-industrialism thesis, this criticism has unjustifiably been twisted to suggest that the presence of commercial activity proves the predominance of capitalism in the South. Many pre-capitalist economic systems have had well-developed commercial relations, but if every commercial society is to be considered capitalist, the word loses all meaning. In general, commercial classes have supported the existing system of production. As Maurice Dobb observes, their fortunes are bound up with those of the dominant producers, and merchants are more likely to seek an extension of their middlemen's profits than to try to reshape the economic order.

We must concern ourselves primarily with capitalism as a social system, not merely with evidence of typically capitalistic economic practices. In the South extensive and complicated commercial relations with the world market permitted the growth of a small commercial bourgeoisie. The resultant fortunes flowed into slaveholding, which offered prestige and economic and social security in a planter-dominated society. Independent merchants found their businesses dependent on the patronage of the slaveholders. The merchants either became planters themselves or assumed a servile attitude toward the planters. The commercial bourgeoisie, such as it was, remained tied to the slaveholding interest, had little desire or opportunity to invest capital in industrial expansion, and adopted the prevailing aristocratic attitudes.

The Southern industrialists were in an analogous position, although one that was potentially subversive of the political power and ideological unity of the planters. The preponderance of planters and slaves on the countryside retarded the home market. The Southern yeomanry, unlike the Western, lacked the purchasing power to sustain rapid industrial development. The planters spent much of their money abroad for luxuries. The plantation market consisted primarily of the demand for cheap slave clothing and cheap agricultural implements for use or misuse by the slaves. Southern industrialism needed a sweeping agrarian revolution to provide it with cheap labor and a substantial rural market, but the Southern industrialists depended on the existing, limited, plantation market. Leading industrialists like William Gregg and Daniel Pratt were plantation-oriented and proslavery. They could hardly have been other.

The banking system of the South serves as an excellent illustration of an ostensibly capitalist institution that worked to augment the power of the planters and retard the development of the bourgeoisie. Southern banks functioned much as did those which the British introduced into Latin America, India, and Egypt during the nineteenth century. Although the British banks fostered dependence on British capital, they did not directly and willingly generate internal capitalist development. They were not sources of industrial capital but "large-scale clearing houses of mercantile finance vying in their interest charges with the local usurers."

The difference between the banking practices of the South and those of the West reflects the difference between slavery and agrarian capitalism.

In the West, as in the Northeast, banks and credit facilities promoted a vigorous economic expansion. During the period of loose Western banking (1830–1844) credit flowed liberally into industrial development as well as into land purchases and internal improvements. Manufacturers and merchants dominated the boards of directors of Western banks, and landowners played a minor role. Undoubtedly, many urban businessmen speculated in land and had special interests in underwriting agricultural exports, but they gave attention to building up agricultural processing industries and urban enterprises, which guaranteed the region a many-sided economy.

The slave states paid considerable attention to the development of a conservative, stable banking system, which could guarantee the movement of staple crops and the extension of credit to the planters. Southern banks were primarily designed to lend the planters money for outlays that were economically feasible and socially acceptable in a slave society: the movement of crops, the purchase of land and slaves, and little else.

Whenever Southerners pursued easy-credit policies, the damage done outweighed the advantages of increased production. This imbalance probably did not occur in the West, for easy credit made possible agricultural and industrial expansion of a diverse nature and, despite acute crises, established a firm basis for long-range prosperity. Easy credit in the South led to expansion of cotton production with concomitant overproduction and low prices; simultaneously, it increased the price of slaves.

Planters wanted their banks only to facilitate cotton shipments and maintain sound money. They purchased large quantities of foodstuffs from the West and, since they shipped little in return, had to pay in bank notes. For five years following the bank failures of 1837 the bank notes of New Orleans moved at a discount of from 10 to 25 per cent. This disaster could not be allowed to recur. Sound money and sound banking became the cries of the slaveholders as a class.

Southern banking tied the planters to the banks, but more important, tied the bankers to the plantations. The banks often found it necessary to add prominent planters to their boards of directors and were closely supervised by the planter-dominated state legislatures. In this relationship the bankers could not emerge as a middle-class counterweight to the planters but could merely serve as their auxiliaries.

The bankers of the free states also allied themselves closely with the dominant producers, but society and economy took on a bourgeois quality provided by the rising industrialists, the urban middle classes, and the farmers who increasingly depended on urban markets. The expansion of credit, which in the West financed manufacturing, mining, transportation, agricultural diversification, and the numerous branches of a capitalist economy, in the South bolstered the economic position of the planters, inhibited the rise of alternative industries, and guaranteed the extension and consolidation of the plantation system.

If for a moment we accept the designation of the planters as capitalists and the slave system as a form of capitalism, we are then confronted by a capitalist society that impeded the development of every normal feature of capitalism. The planters were not mere capitalists; they were precapitalist, quasi-aristocratic landowners who had to adjust their economy and ways of thinking to a capitalist world market. Their society, in its spirit and fundamental direction, represented the antithesis of capitalism, however many compromises it had to make. The fact of slave ownership is central to our problem. This seemingly formal question of whether the owners of the means of production command labor or purchase the labor power of free workers contains in itself the content of Southern life. The essential features of Southern particularity, as well as of Southern backwardness, can be traced to the relationship of master to slave.

The Barriers to Industrialization

If the planters were losing their economic and political cold war with Northern capitalism, the failure of the South to develop sufficient industry provided the most striking immediate cause. Its inability to develop adequate manufactures is usually attributed to the inefficiency of its labor force. No doubt slaves did not easily adjust to industrial employment, and the indirect effects of the slave system impeded the employment of whites. Slaves did work effectively in hemp, tobacco, iron, and cotton factories but only under socially dangerous conditions. They received a wide variety of privileges and approached an elite status. Planters generally appreciated the potentially subversive quality of these arrangements and looked askance at their extension.

Slavery concentrated economic and political power in the hands of a slaveholding class hostile to industrialism. The slaveholders feared a strong urban bourgeoisie, which might make common cause with its Northern counterpart. They feared a white urban working class of unpredictable social tendencies. In general, they distrusted the city and saw in it something incongruous with their local power and status arrangements. The small slaveholders, as well as the planters, resisted the assumption of a heavy tax burden to assist manufacturers, and as the South fell further behind the North in industrial development more state aid was required to help industry offset the Northern advantages of scale, efficiency, credit relations, and business reputation.

Slavery led to the rapid concentration of land and wealth and prevented the expansion of a Southern home market. Instead of providing a basis for industrial growth, the Southern countryside, economically dominated by a few large estates, provided only a limited market for industry. . . .

The Ideology of the Master Class

The planters commanded Southern politics and set the tone of social life. Theirs was an aristocratic, antibourgeois spirit with values and mores emphasizing family and status, a strong code of honor, and aspirations to luxury, ease, and accomplishment. In the planters' community, paternalism provided the standard of human relationships, and politics and statecraft were the duties and responsibilities of gentlemen. The gentleman lived for politics, not, like the bourgeois politician, off politics.

The planter typically recoiled at the notions that profit should be the goal of life; that the approach to production and exchange should be internally rational and uncomplicated by social values; that thrift and hard work should be the great virtues; and that the test of the wholesomeness of a community should be the vigor with which its citizens expand the economy. The planter was no less acquisitive than the bourgeois, but an acquisitive spirit is compatible with values antithetical to capitalism. The aristocratic spirit of the planters absorbed acquisitiveness and directed it into channels that were socially desirable to a slave society: the accumulation of slaves and land and the achievement of military and political honors. Whereas in the North people followed the lure of business and money for their own sake, in the South specific forms of property carried the badges of honor, prestige, and power. Even the rough parvenu planters of the Southwestern frontier—the "Southern Yankees"—strove to accumulate wealth in the modes acceptable to plantation society. Only in their crudeness and naked avarice did they differ from the Virginia gentlemen. They were a generation removed from the refinement that follows accumulation.

Slavery established the basis of the planter's position and power. It measured his affluence, marked his status, and supplied leisure for social graces and aristocratic duties. The older bourgeoisie of New England in its own way struck an aristocratic pose, but its wealth was rooted in commercial and industrial enterprises that were being pushed into the background by the newer heavy industries arising in the West, where upstarts took advantage of the more lucrative ventures like the iron industry. In the South few such opportunities were opening. The parvenu differed from the established planter only in being cruder and perhaps sharper in his business dealings. The road to power lay through the plantation. The older aristocracy kept its leadership or made room for men following the same road. An aristocratic stance was no mere compensation for a decline in power; it was the soul and content of a rising power.

Many travelers commented on the difference in material conditions from one side of the Ohio River to the other, but the difference in sentiment was seen most clearly by Tocqueville. Writing before the slavery issue had inflamed the nation, he remarked that slavery was attacking the Union "indirectly in its manners." The Ohioan "was tormented by wealth," and would turn to any kind of enterprise or endeavor to make a fortune. The Kentuckian coveted wealth "much less than pleasure or excitement," and money had "lost a portion of its value in his eyes."

Achille Murat joined Tocqueville in admiration for Southern ways. Compared with Northerners, Southerners were frank, clever, charming, generous, and liberal. They paid a price for these advantages. As one Southerner put it, the North led the South in almost everything because the Yankees had quiet perseverance over the long haul, whereas the Southerners had talent and brilliance but no taste for sustained labor. Southern projects came with a flash and died just as suddenly. Despite such criticisms from within the ranks, the leaders of the South clung to their ideals, their faults, and their conviction of superiority. Farmers, said Edmund Ruffin, could not expect to achieve a cultural level above that of the "boors who reap rich harvests from the fat soil of Belgium." In the Northern states, he added with some justification, a farmer could rarely achieve the ease, culture, intellect, and refinement that slavery made possible. The prevailing attitude of the aristocratic South toward itself and its Northern rival was ably summed up by William Henry Holcombe of Natchez: "The Northerner loves to make money, the Southerner to spend it."

At their best, Southern ideals constituted a rejection of the crass, vulgar, inhumane elements of capitalist society. The slaveholders simply could not accept the idea that the cash nexus offered a permissible basis for human relations. Even the vulgar parvenu of the Southwest embraced the plantation myth and refused to make a virtue of necessity by glorifying the competitive side of slavery as civilization's highest achievement. The slaveholders generally, and the planters in particular, did identify their own ideals with the essence of civilization and, given their sense of honor, were prepared to defend them at any cost.

This civilization and its ideals were antinational in a double sense. The plantation offered virtually the only market for the small nonstaple-producing farmers and provided the center of necessary services for the small cotton growers. Thus, the paternalism of the planters toward their slaves was reinforced by the semipaternal relationship between the planters and their neighbors. The planters, in truth, grew into the closest thing to feudal lords imaginable in a nineteenth-century bourgeois republic. The planters' protestations of love for the Union were not so much a desire to use the Union to protect slavery as a strong commitment to localism as the highest form of liberty. They genuinely loved the Union so long as it alone among the great states of the world recognized that localism had a wide variety of rights. The Southerners' source of pride was not the Union, nor the nonexistent Southern nation; it was the plantation, which they raised to a political principle.

Slaveholders in Legend and Reality

JAMES OAKES

The patterns of slaveholding that emerged in colonial America were not profoundly altered in the nineteenth century. Long before the Revolution, the cash-crop economy had encompassed small slaveholding farms and large plantations alike. Cotton technology did not yet dominate southern agriculture, nor was there a workable marketing system that could service the cotton economy. But if the specific crops changed, if the South's physical boundaries expanded, most of the fundamental aspects of the slave system were in place by 1800, and they remained virtually intact through the antebellum years. Nearly a century before the United States officially withdrew from participation in the Atlantic slave trade, American blacks had begun to distinguish themselves among New World slave populations by achieving a birthrate that permitted southern bondsmen not only to reproduce but to expand their numbers at an unparalleled rate. Thus the debate over the closing of the slave trade followed rather than precipitated this major demographic development.

By that time most slaveholders had rejected the paternalistic ideology and allied themselves with the revolutionaries who upheld the principle of human equality. But they could do so only after they had incorporated into their thinking the assumption that blacks were a "wretched Race" enslaved by virtue of their color. "White people were unequal to the Burthen in this Climate," James Habersham wrote from Georgia in 1768, "and therefore it was absolutely necessary to allow us the free use of slaves." Having rejected paternalism, revolutionary slaveholders developed an entirely new defense of bondage, which was at base racial, and which took form in the great political controversies of the nineteenth century. . . .

The slaveholders of legend were men bound by tradition. Attached to family and community, they lived lives of stability and comfort. If they were hedonistic, the needs of their black and white dependents were nevertheless chief among their concerns. Solidly agrarian, they resisted the hectic materialism of the more urban and industrial North. The society they established was unique, marked by its gentility, its reverence for the established ways, and an admirable blend of self-discipline and civility. But this legend has served the purposes of proslavery ideologues and post-Civil War romantics more than the cause of historical accuracy. It distorts the past by dismissing almost entirely the experience of the vast majority of slaveholders who were not planters and who rarely lived in bucolic relaxation. It further distorts by presenting an idealized image of the plantation divorced from the mundane and oppressive realities of everyday life. Most slaveholders, including the planters, would have recognized little in the legend that conformed to their own lives.

To own twenty slaves in 1860 was to be among the wealthiest men in America, easily within the top five percent of southern white families. Barely one in twenty slaveholders owned that many bondsmen, and not one in a hundred southern white families was headed by such a man. Yet southern white society is frequently analyzed from the perspective of this tiny elite. Similarly, the distinction between "slaveholders" and "planters" has often disappeared, despite numerous efforts to establish precise statistical definitions.

Arbitrary numerical boundaries serve well the needs of individual scholars whose differing definitions impel the exclusion or addition of large numbers of slaveholders from the planter class. In each case the specific definition may be justified, but in their very proliferation simple numerical boundaries reveal their own limitations. In reality, the slaveholding class was fluid. Most slaveholders spent their lives defying the statistical boundaries historians so emphatically establish. Masters commonly entered the slaveholding class from the yeomanry; they moved from the ranks of small slaveholders into the middle class, and if they were lucky, they crossed from one definition of planter to the next in predictable patterns.

This is not to say that there were no class divisions among slaveholders. Rather, it is to suggest that of all the ways of marking those divisions, numbers may be the least useful. Even in the Old South the term "planter" did not simply mean a large slaveholder. The distribution of slaves among those who defined themselves as "planters" in the 1850 census did not differ substantially from that of "farmers." In some counties nearly all slaveholders were called planters, while in others all were farmers. Nevertheless, there were patterns in the lives of small slaveholders, middle-class masters, and planters that separate each group from the other. And there is historical significance in their differing experiences.

Small slaveholders were particularly mobile. Among them shifting jobs was common, and movement into and out of the slaveholding class was widespread. Under the circumstances, the master-slave relationship varied enormously from one small slaveholder to the next. Walter Overton, for example, was born in Virginia in 1830, and after graduating from Mercer College moved to Georgia, where he married and settled down. He does not appear to have suffered any severe economic setbacks in his life before the war broke out, yet Overton was not really a stable member of his community if his employment record is any indication. He moved from job to job, working at various times as a brickmaker, plasterer, teacher, magistrate, and post office assistant. In 1860, he owned one slave, John, a skilled brickmason with whom he worked closely. The slave's value to Overton was consequently high. In one instance he withdrew from the job of helping to raise a neighbor's house rather than "run the risk of getting hurt or having John crippled [even] for a good sum of money."

In contrast was Samuel Edward Burges. His home was a small farm in Cheraw, South Carolina, where his single slave, Tom, worked virtually alone. Before the war, Burges spent most of his time on the road collecting subscription fees for his employer, the Charleston *Mercury*. His travels allowed Burges to see his relatives and friends more often than his slave. A pleasant and helpful man by nature, Burges could always be counted on for a favor. On one occasion he drove an incorrigible slave to Bennetville and sold him "for Aunt Mary." Another time he helped a friend find a runaway slave hiding in an old house. "We tied her hands behind her back and locked her up in the smokehouse," Burges wrote, whereupon she "pretended to be very sick."

For the thousands of small slaveholders whose jobs kept them away from their farms, indifference to the slaves was probably the rule rather than the exception. Certainly this was the case with James Buckner Barry's slaves. Born in Onslow County, North Carolina, in 1821, Barry left for

Texas when he was twenty-three. He joined the army for two years before returning to his father's home in North Carolina. In 1847, after his marriage, Barry, his wife, her brother, and two slaves set out for Texas. They settled in recently organized Bosque County, where they raised livestock. But conditions on the Texas frontier, as well as Barry's apparent love of army life, kept him from his home a good deal of the time. He spent most of his days hunting or patrolling the frontier in search of Indians. Whatever else Barry's slaves did while he was away, they did not grow crops sufficient to feed his family. Thirteen years after settling in Texas, Barry revealed in his diary that he was still obsessed with fighting Indians, while at home bread was "scarce" and his crops "blighted by the drought."

Conditions varied over time as well, making the master-slave relationship even less predictable among small slaveholders. W. J. Simpson worked his two slaves on a small cotton farm near Henderson, South Carolina, in the mid-1840's. After ten years of struggling and stagnation, Simpson hired out one of his two slaves and became his father's overseer on a farm with about seven bondsmen. As the manager of a larger group of slaves, he faced new problems. At the beginning of the cotton season in 1855, for example, several of the slaves took sick, others were away or busy elsewhere, and "Jack, Leah & Ned not being field hands just work when it suits them." In January 1856, Simpson estimated his worth at just over four thousand dollars. He still owned two slaves: a "boy," Joe, whom he rented out yearly for $175, and a female worth $700. His father's farm produced about ten bales of cotton each year, and although it prospered, it did not grow. In late 1860 Simpson's father died, and his slave holdings reached an all-time high of ten. In January 1861, one year before he volunteered his services to the Confederate Army, Simpson estimated his worth at over $15,000. Just when it no longer really mattered, Simpson had achieved the kind of economic security that eluded most small slaveholders.

If there is a pattern in the treatment of bondsmen by small slaveholders, it cannot be derived from the imperatives of the master-slave relationship. As on the largest plantations, the interracial relations on the smallest farms depended on the personalities of individual owners, their immediate economic circumstances, the economic structure of slavery itself, and the willingness of the slaves to cooperate. Walter Overton and W. J. Simpson worked closely with their bondsmen, but where Overton and his slave labored together as skilled artisans and regularly attended the same church services, Simpson hired out his one male slave and worked with his father's bondsmen as a frustrated overseer. Samuel Burges and James B. Barry, by contrast, saw their slaves only occasionally, and if Burges's attitude toward bondsmen other than his own is any indication, he treated his slave with callous indifference at best.

Among small slaveholders such variation was the inevitable product of a way of life marked by constant struggle, spurts of progress and occasional setbacks, and seemingly endless physical movement. These were the forces that shaped several generations of the Lincecum family. Hezekiah Lincecum was the only surviving son of a small slaveholding family that had fled Georgia during the American Revolution. His father and two brothers died in the war, and all of the Lincecums' slaves ran away. With little reason to remain at home, and "being of a restless spirit," Hezekiah stayed only two seasons on his mother's farm, just long enough to court and marry his fourteen-year-old wife, before moving out to the Georgia frontier. Chased back to Hancock County by Indians, the still restless Hezekiah was impressed by the repeated urgings of his Tennessee relations. After three prosperous years in Georgia, he "sold everything he could not carry with him." He and his wife left for Tennessee with four children, four slaves, and his eighty-eight-year-old mother, whose sickness prevented them from completing the trip. They rented a farm for a year, grew a good cotton crop, then packed up and headed for Tennessee.

Once again the Lincecum family did not reach its destination. Instead, Hezekiah decided to buy a farm in Abbeville District, South Carolina, where he planted cotton for a year, after which he bought another farm in Athens, Georgia. The following year, 1805, they left again for Tennessee, this time with only one slave. But an accident along the way caused the family to settle on a farm in Pendleton District, South Carolina, until pressure from relatives brought them back to Georgia. There Hezekiah sent his children to school for five months before moving again to the booming frontier town of Eatonton, Georgia. The Lincecum family stayed there during the War of 1812, while the eldest son, Gideon, left home, worked for some local merchants, joined the armed forces, served as a local tax collector, got married, and moved back home to help out on his father's farm for a year before going to work on someone else's farm. Gideon was soon pressured to move by his restless father and his well-born wife, whose relatives "had been mean enough to cast little slurs at her and her poverty." They moved out of Georgia onto Indian land. . . .

The Lincecum family is more prototypical than representative. Few slaveholding families moved that much; still fewer slaveholders had that many different jobs. Although economic insecurity was common among small slaveholders, few experienced such radical and recurrent shifts of fortune. Still, by comparison with the image of the stable planter, born and reared on his father's estate and never wandering far from his place of birth, the experiences of the Lincecum family are considerably closer to the historical record. Gideon Lincecum was nearly sixty years old when he finally settled on his Texas farm, and it is fair to say that his world view was shaped by forces quite unrelated to plantation life. So it was for the vast majority of small slaveholders, who neither grew up on plantations nor achieved planter status. More typically, their lives were shaped by restlessness, drift, and economic insecurity.

. . . What separated small slaveholders from middle-class masters was something more than just the number of slaves but something less than the plantation experience. The behavior of middle-class slaveholders whose success could well have permitted them the leisurely life so widely associated with the plantation South indicates that such an existence was neither common nor commonly sought. It was the rare master who ceased his quest for more land and slaves, and it was precisely this grasping materialism which stands out in the collective biographies of middle-class slaveholders. They tended to be well educated; they frequently were trained in the professions or began their careers as businessmen. They usually started life with all the advantages that small slaveholders struggled to achieve. Even when not career-oriented, they could generally rely on a small patrimony allowing them to skip altogether the roughest years when the price of a single slave seemed an impossible expense.

Yet, their lives were hardly those of princely heirs. Their earliest years were difficult; they usually left home in young adulthood and were expected to make it on their own. Like most slaveholders, they were migratory, especially in their twenties and thirties. They often sought their success in frontier towns where the amenities of their childhood years, however limited, were nowhere to be found. But they were not frontiersmen by temperament. After several years of search, struggle, and accumulation, they began to purchase land and slaves in small parcels, slowly building on the profit of their careers. Those who made agriculture their only source of income traveled the same slow, arduous road to prosperity.

Traveling through the backcountry in the 1850's, Frederick Olmsted noticed that the slaveholders were "chiefly professional men, shop-keepers, and men in office, who are also land owners, and give a divided attention to farming." In 1850, one out of five masters was employed in an occupation unrelated to agriculture, making the slaveholders the least "landed" of all classes in the antebellum South. Ten years earlier the United States census had reported that seventy-eight percent of the northern workers were employed in agriculture, a breakdown almost identical to that of southern slaveholders in 1850. But while the North was only beginning to feel the effects of the immigration, industrialization, and urbanization that would transform its work force dramatically in the twenty years before the Civil War, there is no evidence that the occupational structure of the slaveholding class underwent any similar change. Indeed it had always been one of the defining characteristics of middle-class slaveholders that they combined careers to enhance their prospects for upward mobility.

Artisan's skills or professional educations protected the slaveholding middle-class from the most severe instabilities of the agricultural economy. The flexibility of a dual career was thus invaluable to the aspiring slaveholder. The profits of a trade or a profession were invested in the slave economy while the effects of economic dislocation in one sphere were softened by the middle-class master's ability to fall back on the other. In sum, the lives of middle-class slaveholders, who constituted perhaps a fourth of all masters, were shaped by a few significant historical experiences: struggle in the early years, migration, and upward mobility, often founded on a dual career.

Olmsted estimated that "of the class properly termed 'the planters,'" middle-class slaveholders "constituted probably nine-tenths." Indeed, middle-class masters held the majority of all the slaves in the South. For while most slaveholders held five slaves or fewer, most slaves were owned by masters with more than five bondsmen. The significance of middle-class slaveholders derived not from their numerical preponderance but from their economic power, their broad control of the slave labor force, and their political activity. In Alabama, for example, nearly all the antebellum congressmen and most of the state legislators had dual careers or had begun their adult lives in non-agricultural jobs that served to propel their later success. If there was any single class of men that set the tone of life in the antebellum South, surely this was it. . . .

What distinguished the planter aristocracy from the slaveholding middle class was not any lack of accumulation but a lack of struggle. Only a small fraction of the slaveholders, less than two and a half percent, ever owned fifty slaves or more. Their relatively small number alone suggests the difficulty of achieving such heights of wealth. However, these richest of planters rarely had to rely on an alternative career to reach their positions. If the middle-class master began his adult life where most small slaveholders ended theirs, so too did the wealthiest planters start out with all the advantages middle-class slaveholders struggled to achieve. Yet comfortable beginnings did little to stem the acquisitiveness of the planter aristocracy.

Even small patrimonial gifts could be of considerably more substance than they might otherwise seem. In 1850, Dugal McCall was just setting up his plantation in Rodney, Mississippi, and he borrowed slaves from his father to clear his land, selling the lumber for profit. At first McCall grew only corn, potatoes, and a few other staples, to which he soon added peaches. His wife and child did not yet live on the plantation, residing instead in a nearby town. After a year, McCall began building slave quarters and smokehouses. In 1851 he fenced in his property and constructed his own home. By 1852, when he first planted cotton, he already owned sixteen slaves, and his first crop was huge for a beginner, fifty bales. The following year McCall doubled the number of plows he owned, and in 1854, with thirty slaves, his plantation made 165 bales of cotton—an astonishing increase. If McCall's unusually swift entry into the planter class confirms the complaint that a lack of money at the outset of a career could be crucial, it is his unrepresentativeness that is most significant. It was the rare slaveholder, even among the sons of planters, who could count on so much initial support that within five years his farm could produce over 75,000 pounds of cotton a year.

Rapid growth from lucrative beginnings was one of the outstanding traits of the planter aristocracy. The most significant indication of a slaveholder's growing wealth was neither the increasing size of successive harvests nor the steady accumulation of land, but the increase in the number of slaves. In this the planter aristocracy was not alone. Where many middle-class masters remained in nonagricultural careers and so bought little land, the accumulation of slaves was a lifelong occupation for virtually all masters.

But only the wealthiest planters had the means to accumulate slaves swiftly and in great numbers. Even so well-born a planter as George J. Kollock, who inherited large numbers of slaves and owned several plantations near Savannah, Georgia, never ceased adding to his holdings. In the dozen years following his acquisition of Rosedew Plantation, Kollock's force of fifteen and one-half full hands grew to fifty-six slaves in all. From 1849 to 1861, Kollock's slave force at Ossabaw Island grew from fifty-six to seventy-two. John Houston Bills never stopped buying slaves either. In 1845 he counted forty-five bondsmen on his Tennessee farm. With his remarriage the following year, Bills stepped up his interest in accumulating more lands, larger harvests, and a bigger slave force. The growing concern with his own economic advancement seemed to coincide with an increasing interest in his legacy to his heirs. Whatever the reason, he began to attend slave auctions regularly and watched more closely his annual profits. He complained that from his 1853 cotton crop he "got 78 bales only." By 1858, his slaves numbered eighty-four, and in 1860 the value of Bills's eighty-seven bondsmen was $79,950, a nearly five-fold increase in fifteen years.

The habit of accumulation passed through the generations and did not stop with the achievement of planter status. John Arrington, who paid forty pounds for a slave boy in 1789, continued to purchase bondsmen in small parcels throughout his lifetime. By 1830 he was able to bequeath substantial holdings to his children, including twenty slaves to his son, Archibald. Archibald, however, was not content with his huge inheritance. He became a lawyer and used his experience with conflicting property claims of other slaveholders to enhance his own wealth. With the combined profits of his plantation and law practice, Archibald Arrington continued to buy slaves throughout the 1840's and 1850's, long after he had established himself as one of the wealthiest planters in both North Carolina and Alabama.

The zealous pursuit of wealth by Arrington and others like him was far too commonplace to be considered the holding action of a planter aristocracy digging in its heels to maintain its power. For most slaveholders acquisition was a way of life. If there was any tendency for the acquisitiveness of the slaveholding class to wane over the generations in the most successful families, it was slight at best. The sons of slaveholders, as much as any other group, were products of their upbringing.

Between 1830 and 1860, in all the southern states, at least 170,000 people entered the slaveholding class. Between 1790 and 1860, there was no increase in the concentration of wealth within that class. As time went on, in other words, the percentage of the slave population controlled by the wealthiest masters did not significantly increase. If upward mobility was not the norm, if slaves were simply controlled by the richest planters who passed on their property from generation to generation, there would not have been such a substantial growth in the number of slaveholders. Neither would the statistics indicate as they do that the older southern men got, the more likely they were to become slaveholders, and the more slaves they were likely to own.

Wealth, particularly slaveholding wealth, was never equally distributed in the South. But there was always substantial mobility into and out of the slaveholding class. If marriage patterns are any indication, it appears that white Southerners paid little attention to class distinctions in choosing mates. Thus, despite huge disparities of wealth, it is futile to locate clearly delineated boundaries between slaveholders and non-slaveholders, just as it is difficult to draw simple numerical distinctions between small slaveholders and planters. How many slaves did a small farmer need to acquire before he ceased to behave like a yeoman? Or an artisan? At which point in his career did a lawyer begin to act like a planter? Did a merchant's life become "agrarian" when he bought a farm but kept his business? There is, in fact, no convincing body of evidence to demonstrate that the mere ownership of slaves, even in large numbers, automatically entailed the embrace of a distinctive world view.

This is not to say that no slaveholding culture emerged in the Old South. It did. But that culture developed from historical conditions that were only in part related to the ownership of slaves and only minimally associated with plantation agriculture. The dominant slaveholding culture grew out of the colonial experience in America and embraced the diversity of southern society. It took form in the rapidly expanding slave economy of the antebellum period and so produced a world view that equated upward mobility with westward migration. For unlike plantation life, physical movement, upward mobility, and social fluidity shaped the destinies of the vast majority of American slaveholders.

人 F U R T H E R   R E A D I N G

Edward L. Ayers, *Vengeance and Justice* (1984)
Dickson D. Bruce, Jr., *And They All Sang Hallelujah: Plain Folk Camp-Meeting Religion, 1800–1845* (1974)
——, *Violence and Culture in the Antebellum South* (1979)
Orville Vernon Burton and Robert C. McMath, Jr., eds., *Class, Conflict and Consensus: Antebellum Southern Community Studies* (1982)
Randolph B. Campbell, *An Empire for Slavery: The Peculiar Institution in Texas, 1821–1865* (1989)
W. J. Cash, *The Mind of the South* (1941)
Bruce Collins, *White Society in the Antebellum South* (1985)
Clement Eaton, *Freedom of Thought in the Old South* (1940)
——, *The Growth of Southern Civilization, 1790–1860* (1961)
John Hope Franklin, *The Militant South* (1956)
Eugene D. Genovese, *The Political Economy of Slavery* (1965)
J. William Harris, *Plain Folk and Gentry in a Slave Society: White Liberty and Black Slavery in Augusta's Hinterlands* (1985)
William Sumner Jenkins, *Pro-Slavery Thought in the Old South* (1935)
Donald G. Mathews, *Religion in the Old South* (1977)
John Hebron Moore, *The Emergence of the Cotton Kingdom in the Old Southwest: Mississippi, 1770–1860* (1987)
James Oakes, *The Ruling Race: A History of American Slaveholders* (1982)
Frederick Law Olmsted, *The Slave States*, ed. Harvey Wish (1959)
Frank L. Owsley, *Plain Folk of the Old South* (1949)
Larry E. Tise, *Proslavery: A History of the Defense of Slavery in America, 1701–1840* (1987)
Bertram Wyatt-Brown, *Southern Honor* (1982)

Slavery and Southern Blacks

火

Modern scholarship has focused a great amount of attention on the important subject of slavery, probing its economics, legal structure, disease environments, and many other topics. The outpouring of literature on southern slavery is vast, and the work of high quality.

At the core of the most widely read studies has been a concern with the psychological realities of slavery. What was it like to be a slave? How did America's slaves cope with their oppression? Numerous scholars have examined the life of the slaves and the master-slave relationship, seeking to understand the motives and dynamics in this complex situation. The nature of the slave experience and the character of slave culture have been the major subjects of research and interpretation.

A variety of viewpoints has emerged. All agree that slaves were not psychologically helpless before their masters; they had a body of culture and the support of the slave community on which they could draw for strength and support. But within that broad consensus, substantial differences remain. How independent of white control was slave culture and thought? How effectively did the masters shape the outlook of the slaves? What were the conditions of black southerners who were not enslaved? How much independence and freedom did they have in a society that increasingly defined itself in relation to slavery?

火 D O C U M E N T S

Opportunities for frank testimony by slaves about their bondage were rare, but one such opportunity arose during the Civil War. The American Freedmen's Inquiry Commission was established in 1863 to gather information and report to the secretary of war with recommendations on the future of the slaves. The frank accounts that Harry McMillan and Alexander Kenner gave the commission about their differing experiences of bondage appear in the first selection. Many decades later, in the 1930s, the Federal Writers' Project interviewed former slaves. The recollections of the men and women interviewed, who were then quite elderly, provide valuable insights into the slave's experience. Two of these accounts are provided in the second document. Talented and trusted slaves sometimes were permitted to manage their owner's plantation in his absence, as the third document shows. The slave George Skipwith did so on an Alabama plantation of John Hartwell Cocke, an absentee landlord who resided at his Virginia plantation, Bremo. Letters to Cocke from Lucy Skipwith, George's daughter, reveal her intensely religious nature, which developed in adulthood. The photograph from the Library of Congress in the fourth selection shows five generations of a South Carolina slave family and suggests the importance of family ties to those in bondage. R. Henry Gaston was a white man who agreed to assume the duties of overseer on a farm in the North Carolina piedmont. His letter to a relative, reprinted as the fifth document, lays bare the type of contests that frequently ensued between slaves and their overseers. Additional insight on what was known as the "management" of slaves, and the daily realities of slavery, can be gained from the advice that planters gave to one another in southern agricultural journals and other periodicals. A number of these appear in the sixth selection. Successful free blacks in Charleston, South Carolina, did not have to deal with overseers, but they faced a different threat on the eve of the Civil War. Affluent and frequently well known to a few high-status whites, these free people suddenly confronted a rising popular demand that free blacks be reenslaved or made to furnish strict legal proof (often difficult to obtain) of their free status. James M. Johnson, a tailor, describes these frightening developments to his brother-in-law, Henry Ellison. (Henry's father, William Ellison, was the successful manufacturer of high-quality cotton gins; see Chapter 6.)

Freedmen Describe Their Bondage, 1863

Harry McMillan, South Carolina

I am about 40 years of age, and was born in Georgia but came to Beaufort when a small boy. I was owned by General Eustis and lived upon his plantation.

Q. Tell me about the tasks colored men had to do?

A. In old secesh times each man had to do two tasks, which are 42 rows or half an acre, in "breaking" the land, and in "listing" each person had to do a task and a half. In planting every hand had to do an acre a day; in hoeing your first hoeing where you hoe flat was two tasks, and your second hoeing, which is done across the beds, was also two tasks. After going through those two operations you had a third which was two and a half tasks, when you had to go over the cotton to thin out the plants leaving two in each hill.

Q. How many hours a day did you work?

A. Under the old secesh times every morning till night—beginning at daylight and continuing till 5 or 6 at night.

Q. But you stopped for your meals?

A. You had to get your victuals standing at your hoe; you cooked it over night yourself or else an old woman was assigned to cook for all the hands, and she or your children brought the food to the field.

Q. You never sat down and took your food together as families?

A. No, sir; never had time for it.

Q. The women had the same day's work as the men; but suppose a woman was in the family way was her task less?

A. No, sir; most of times she had to do the same work. Sometimes the wife of the planter learned the condition of the woman and said to her husband you must cut down her day's work. Sometimes the women had their children in the field.

Q. Had the women any doctor?

A. No, sir; There is a nurse on the plantation sometimes—an old midwife who attended them. If a woman was taken in labor in the field some of her sisters would help her home and then come back to the field.

Q. Did they nurse their children?

A. Yes, sir; the best masters gave three months for that purpose.

Q. If a man did not do his task what happened?

A. He was stripped off, tied up and whipped.

Q. What other punishments were used?

A. The punishments were whipping, putting you in the stocks and making you wear irons and a chain at work. Then they had a collar to put round your neck with two horns, like cows' horns, so that you could not lie down on your back or belly. This also kept you from running away for the horns would catch in the bushes. Sometimes they dug a hole like a well with a door on top. This they called a dungeon keeping you in it two or three weeks or a month, and sometimes till you died in there. This hole was just big enough to receive the body; the hands down by the sides. I have seen this thing in Georgia but never here. I know how they whip in the Prisons. They stretch out your arms and legs as far as they can to ring bolts in the floor and lash you till they open the skin and the blood trickles down. . . .

Q. Suppose a son of the Master wanted to have intercourse with the colored women was he at liberty?

A. No, not at liberty, because it was considered a stain on the family, but the young men did it. There was a good deal of it. They often kept one girl steady and sometimes two on different places; men who had wives did it too sometimes, if they could get it on their own place it was easier but they would go wherever they could get it.

Q. Do the colored people like to go to Church?

A. Yes, Sir; They are fond of that; they sing psalms, put up prayers, and sing their religious songs.

Q. Did your Masters ever see you learning to read?

A. No, Sir; You could not let your Masters see you read; but now the colored people are fond of sending their children to school.

Q. What is the reason of that?

A. Because the children in after years will be able to tell us ignorant ones how to do for ourselves.

Q. How many children have you known one woman to have?

A. I know one woman who had 20 children. I know too a woman named Jenny, the wife of Dagos, a slave of John Pope, who has had 23 children.

In general the women have a great many children[;] they often have a child once a year.

Q. Are the children usually obedient?

A. There are some good and some bad, but in general the children love their parents and are obedient. They like their parents most but they stand up for all their relations.

Q. Suppose a boy is struck by another boy what does he do?

A. If he is injured bad the relations come in and give the boy who injured him the same hurt. I would tell my boy to strike back and defend himself.

Q. How about bearing pain—do you teach your children to bear pain?

A. Yes, sir.

Q. When a colored man was whipped did he cry out?

A. He would halloa out and beg, but not cry for pain but for vexation.

Q. Did they try to conceal their whippings and think it a disgrace?

A. Yes, sir; they tried to conceal it; a great many are marked all over and have not a piece of skin they were born with.

Alexander Kenner, Kentucky

Mr. Kenner said he was born in Louisiana. His father was the Hon. George R. Kenner. His father had seven children by his mother, and then married a white woman, but told his mother she might go away. She went away, and took with her four of her children. Another was subsequently born. Mr. Kenner intended to make her free, but did not give her free papers. They went to St. Louis, and the mother worked for several years at washing, and he (Alexander) carried out the clothes. She throve exceedingly well. After seven years, Mr. George Kenner sold out the plantation, with all its rights, to his brother, Hon. Duncan F. Kenner, and his mother bought three of her children, including Alexander, for $1800. The oldest brother had remained on the plantation, and became valuable to Mr. Kenner as a rider of his race horses, and he would not let him go. They were very anxious indeed to buy him, and having prospered, they offered Mr. Kenner $2000 for him, which he refused to take. The mother, in the mean time, had rented some apartments and furnished them, and let them out to single men, and made a good deal of money. When she died, she was 53 years old, & her property was appraised at $7000. He and his brothers wanted Mr. Kenner to sell their oldest brother to them, but he had become valuable to him there as a trainer of race horses, & therefore he said he would not sell him unless they would give him the whole of the mother's property. Alexander would not consent to this, but the other brothers were exceedingly anxious to have their oldest brother, and they offered to give their shares, amounting to $2500, for his freedom; but the master insisted that besides this, the brother should serve three years, at $15 a month, to pay the balance, so that the whole amount would be $3400—and he a millionaire. When the mother died, this Kenner got himself made executor, and the three children being under age, he received the property. When Alexander became of age, he demanded his share, but Kenner refused it to him, then Alexander sued him in the court, and recovered the amount. Alexander had gone before this to the plantation, and offered to give Mr. Kenner all his share if he would free William, but he wouldn't do so. Besides, William was very much devoted to his master. He lingered on the plantation, and felt himself bound to remain until he had paid all the money which he had agreed to. When the war broke out, Alexander came away; William is still on the plantation.

On most of the plantations, the blacks have small patches of land, which they fence in, and take a great deal of care of. They raise poultry and hogs, and take the money they get from the sale of these to buy themselves tea, clothes and little comforts, and are very fond of dressing out in their clothes to go to the log churches. They are so anxious to make money that they work upon their little patches at night. On the plantation where he lived, he has known them to raise a thousand dozen chickens in a year; but their master obliged them to sell the chickens to him, instead of selling them to the hucksters, because he wanted to know how much money they had, and didn't want them to have too much; and besides, he wanted to get the advanced price from the hucksters. He would give them twenty cents a pair, and sell them to the hucksters for thirty cents. The masters didn't wish the slaves to accumulate any property, but to spend whatever money they got. Sometimes, however, they did accumulate property. He knew one man, old Cudjo, on a neighboring plantation, who used to get him (Alexander) to come and count his dollars. He stated that he had counted for him over five hundred silver dollars. Cudjo himself couldn't count over thirty or forty, but nobody could take any of the money without his knowing it, for he knew by the appearance or weight whether it was all right or not, but he wanted to know the exact number. His (Alexander's) mother, although an intelligent woman, could never count over one hundred, & certainly did not know how many hundred there were in a thousand. The negroes on the river, he thinks, are intelligent, and certainly take care of themselves. Those in the interior, away from the river, are stupid; they see nothing, know nothing, and are very like cattle. The negroes in Mississippi are more stupid than those in Louisiana, on account of the masters being more cruel and oppressive. The masters in Mississippi are sometimes bloody and cruel; they may kill their negroes, and there is no law to punish them.

Ex-Slaves Recall Slavery, 1936, 1937

Nancy Boudry, Thomson, Georgia

"If I ain't a hunnerd," said Nancy, nodding her white-turbaned head, "I sho' is close to it, 'cause I got a grandson 50 years old."

Nancy's silky white hair showed long and wavy under her headband. Her gingham dress was clean, and her wrinkled skin was a reddish-yellow color, showing a large proportion of Indian and white blood. Her eyes were a faded blue.

"I speck I is mos' white," acknowledged Nancy, "but I ain't never knowed who my father was. My mother was a dark color."

The cottage faced the pine grove behind an old church. Pink ramblers grew everywhere, and the sandy yard was neatly kept. Nancy's paralyzed granddaughter-in-law hovered in the doorway, her long smooth braids hanging over Indian-brown shoulders, a loose wrapper of dark blue denim flowing around her tall unsteady figure. She was eager to take part in the conversation but hampered by a thick tongue induced, as Nancy put it, "by a bad sore throat she ain't got over."

Nancy's recollections of plantation days were colored to a somber hue by overwork, childbearing, poor food and long working hours.

"Master was a hard taskmaster," said Nancy. "My husband didn' live on de same plantation where I was, de Jerrell place in Columbia County. He never did have nuthin' to give me 'cause he never got nuthin'. He had to come and ask my white folks for me. Dey had to carry passes everywhar dey went, if dey didn't, dey'd git in trouble.

"I had to work hard, plow and go and split wood jus' like a man. Sometimes dey whup me. Dey whup me bad, pull de cloes off down to de wais'—my master did it, our folks didn' have overseer.

"We had to ask 'em to let us go to church. Went to white folks church, 'tell de black folks got one of dere own. No'm, I dunno how to read. Never had no schools at all, didn't 'low us to pick up a piece of paper and look at it."

"Nancy, wasn't your mistress kind to you?"

"Mistis was sorta kin' to me, sometimes. But dey only give me meat and bread, didn' give me nothin' good—I ain' gwine tell no story. I had a heap to undergo wid. I had to scour at night at de Big House—two planks one night, two more de nex'. De women peoples spun at night and reeled, so many outs a night. Us had to git up befo' daybreak be ready to go to de fiel's.

"My master didn' have but three cullud people, dis yuh man what I stayed wid, my young master, had not been long married and dus' de han's dey give him when he marry was all he had.

"Didn' have no such house as dis," Nancy looked into the open door of the comfortable cottage, "sometimes dey have a house built, it would be daubed. Dus' one family, didn' no two families double up."

"But the children had a good time, didn't they? They played games?"

"Maybe dey did play ring games, I never had no time to see what games my chillun play, I work so hard. Heap o' little chillun slep' on de flo'. Never had no frolics neither, no ma'm, and didn' go to none. We would have prayer meetings on Saturday nights, and one night in de week us had a chairback preacher, and sometimes a regular preacher would come in."

Nancy did not remember ever having seen the Patterollers [patrollers].

"I hearn talk of 'em you know, heap o' times dey come out and make out like dey gwine shoot you at night, dey mus' been Patterollers, dey was gettin' hold of a heap of 'em."

"What did you do about funerals, Nancy?"

"Dey let us knock off for funerals, I tell de truth. Us stay up all night, singin' and prayin'. Dey make de coffin outter pine boards."

"Did you suffer during the war?"

"We done de bes' we could, we et what we could get, sometimes didn' have nothin' to eat but piece of cornbread, but de white folks allus had chicken."

"But you had clothes to wear?"

"Us had clothes 'cause we spun de thread and weaved 'em. Dey bought dem dere great big ole brogans where you couldn' hardly walk in 'em. Not like dese shoes I got on." Nancy thrust out her foot, easy in "Old Ladies' Comforts."

"When they told you were free, Nancy, did the master appear to be angry?"

"No'm, white folks didn' 'pear to be mad. My master dus' tole us we was free. Us moved right off, but not so far I couldn' go backwards and forwards to see 'um." (So it was evident that even if Nancy's life had been hard, there was a bond between her and her former owners.) "I didn' do no mo' work for 'um, I work for somebody else. Us rented land and made what we could, so we could have little somethin' to eat. I scoured and waited on white people in town, got little piece of money, and was dus' as proud!"

Nancy savored the recollection of her first earned money a moment, thinking back to the old days.

"I had a preacher for my second marriage," she continued. "Fo' chillun died on me—one girl, de yuthers was babies. White doctor tended me."

Asked about midwifery, Nancy smiled.

"I was a midwife myself, to black and white, after freedom. De Thomson doctors all liked me and tole people to 'git Nancy.' I used 'tansy tea'— heap o' little root—made black pepper tea, fotch de pains on 'em. When I would git to de place where I had a hard case, I would send for de doctor, and he would help me out, yes, doctor holp me out of all of 'em."

Asked about signs and superstitions, Nancy nodded.

"I have seed things. Dey look dus' like a person, walkin' in de woods. I would look off and look back to see it again and it be gone." Nancy lowered her voice mysteriously, and looked back into the little room where Vanna's [her paralyzed granddaughter-in-law] unsteady figure moved from bed to chair. "I seed a coffin floatin' in de air in dat room . . ." she shivered, "and I heard a heap o' knockings. I dunno what it bees—but de sounds come in de house. I runs ev'y squeech owl away what comes close, too." Nancy clasped her hands, right thumb over left thumb, "does dat—and it goes on away—dey quite hollerin', you chokin' 'em when you does dat."

"Do you plant by the moon, Nancy?"

"Plant when de moon change, my garden, corn, beans. I planted some

beans once on de wrong time of de moon and dey didn' bear nothin'—I
hated it so bad, I didn' know what to do, so I been mindful ever since
when I plant. Women peoples come down on de moon, too. I ain't know
no signs to raise chillun. I whup mine when dey didn' do right, I sho' did.
I didn' 'low my chillun to take nothin'—no aigs and nothin' 'tall and bring
'em to my house. I say 'put dem right whar you git 'em.' "

"Did you sing spirituals, Nancy?"

"I sang regular meetin' songs," she said, "like 'lay dis body down' and
'let yo' joys be known'—but I can't sing now, not any mo'."

Nancy was proud of her quilt-making ability.

"Git 'um, Vanna, let de ladies see 'um," she said; and when Vanna
brought the gay pieces made up in a "double-burst" (sunburst) pattern,
Nancy fingered the squares with loving fingers. "Hit's pooty, ain't it?" she
asked wistfully, "I made one for a white lady two years ago, but dey hurts
my fingers now—makes 'em stiff."

Delia Garlic, Montgomery, Alabama

Delia Garlic lives at 43 Stone Street, Montgomery, and insists she is 100
years old. Unlike many of the old Negroes of the South, she has no good
words for slavery days or the old masters, declaring: "Dem days was hell."

She sat on her front porch and assailed the taking of young children
from mothers and selling them in different parts of the country.

"I was growed up when de war come," she said, "an' I was a mother
befo' it closed. Babies was snatched from dere mother's breas' an' sold to
speculators. Chilluns was separated from sisters an' brothers an' never saw
each other ag'in.

"Course dey cry; you think dey not cry when dey was sold lak cattle?
I could tell you 'bout it all day, but even den you couldn't guess de awfulness
of it.

"It's bad to belong to folks dat own you soul an' body; dat can tie you
up to a tree, wid yo' face to de tree an' yo' arms fastened tight aroun' it;
who take a long curlin' whip an' cut de blood ever' lick.

"Folks a mile away could hear dem awful whippings. Dey was a turrible
part of livin'."

Delia said she was born at Powhatan, Virginia, and was the youngest
of thirteen children.

"I never seed none of my brothers an' sisters 'cept brother William,"
she said. "Him an' my mother an' me was brought in a speculator's drove
to Richmon' an' put in a warehouse wid a drove of other niggers. Den we
was all put on a block an' sol' to de highes' bidder.

"I never seed brother William ag'in. Mammy an' me was sold to a man
by de name of Carter, who was de sheriff of de county.

"No'm, dey warn't no good times at his house. He was a widower an'
his daughter kept house for him. I nursed for her, an' one day I was playin'
wid de baby. It hurt its li'l han' an' commenced to cry, an' she whirl on
me, pick up a hot iron an' run it all down my arm an' han'. It took off de
flesh when she done it.

"Atter awhile, marster married ag'in; but things warn't no better. I seed his wife blackin' her eybrows wid smut one day, so I thought I'd black mine jes' for fun. I rubbed some smut on my eyebrows an' forgot to rub it off, an' she kotched me. She was powerful mad an' yelled: 'You black devil, I'll show you how to mock your betters.'

"Den she pick up a stick of stovewood an' flails it ag'in' my head. I didn't know nothin' more 'till I come to, lyin' on de floor. I heard de mistus say to one of de girls: 'I thought her thick skull and cap of wool could take it better than that.'

"I kept on stayin' dere, an' one night de marster come in drunk an' set at de table wid his head lollin' aroun'. I was waitin' on de table, an' he look up an' see me. I was skeered, an' dat made him awful mad. He called an overseer an' tol' him: 'Take her out an' beat some sense in her.'

"I begin to cry an' run an' run in de night; but finally I run back by de quarters an' heard mammy callin' me. I went in, an' raght away dey come for me. A horse was standin' in front of de house, an' I was took dat very night to Richmon' an' sold to a speculator ag'in. I never seed my mammy any more.

"I has thought many times through all dese years how mammy looked dat night. She pressed my han' in bofe of hers an' said: 'Be good an' trus' in de Lawd.'

"Trustin' was de only hope of de pore black critters in dem days. Us jest prayed for strength to endure it to de end. We didn't 'spect nothin' but to stay in bondage 'till we died.

"I was sol' by de speculator to a man in McDonough, Ga. I don't ricolleck his name, but he was openin' a big hotel at McDonough an' bought me to wait on tables. But when de time come aroun' to pay for me, his hotel done fail. Den de Atlanta man dat bought de hotel bought me, too. 'Fo' long, dough, I was sol' to a man by de name of Garlic, down in Louisiana, an' I stayed wid him 'till I was freed. I was a regular fiel' han', plowin' an' hoein' an' choppin' cotton.

"Us heard talk 'bout de war, but us didn't pay no 'tention. Us never dreamed dat freedom would ever come."

Delia was asked if the slaves ever had any parties or dances on her plantation.

"No'm," she replied, "us didn't have no parties; nothin' lak dat. Us didn't have no clothes for goin' 'roun. I never had a undershirt until jest befo' my first chil' was borned. I never had nothin' but a shimmy an' a slip for a dress, an' it was made out'en de cheapes' cloth dat could be bought; unbleached cloth, coarse, but made to las'.

"Us didn't know nothin' 'cept to work. Us was up by three or four in de mornin' an' everybody got dey somethin' to eat in de kitchen. Dey didn't give us no way to cook, nor nothin' to cook in our cabins. Soon as us dressed us went by de kitchen an' got our piece of cornbread. Dey wan't even no salt in dem las' years. Dat piece of cornbread was all us had for breakfus', an' for supper, us had de same.

"For dinner us had boiled vittles; greens, peas an' sometimes beans. Coffee? No'm, us never knowed nothin' 'bout coffee.

"One mornin' I 'members I had started to de fiel', an' on de way I los' my piece of bread. I didn't know what to do. I started back to try to fin' it, an' it was too dark to see. But I walk back raght slow, an' had a dog dat walked wid me. He went on ahead, an' atter awhile I come on him lyin' dere guardin' dat piece of bread. He never touched it, so I gived him some of it.

"Jus' befo' de war I married a man named Chatfield from another plantation; but he was took off to war an' I never seed him ag'in. Atter awhile I married a boy on de plantation named Miles Garlic.

"Yas'm, Massa Garlic had two boys in de war. When dey went off de Massa an' missis cried, but it made us glad to see dem cry. Dey made us cry so much.

"When we knowed we was free, everybody wanted to git out. De rule was dat if you stayed in yo' cabin you could keep it, but if you lef', you los' it. Miles was workin' at Wetumpka, an' he slipped in an' out so us could keep on livin' in de cabin.

"My secon' baby soon come, an' raght den I made up my min' to go to Wetumpka where Miles was workin' for de railroad. I went on down dere an' us settled down.

"Atter Miles died, I lived dere long as I could an' den come to Montgomery to live wid my son. I'se eatin' white bread now an' havin' de best time of my life. But when de Lawd say, 'Delia, well done; come up higher,' I'll be glad to go."

George and Lucy Skipwith Write Their Master, 1847, 1857, 1859

may the 11 [1847] green County Ala

Sir

I imbrace this oppertunity to write you a few lines. I Reseved your letter and should have anserd it before now but master John was from home on busness and I could not write untel he returned wich was last Sunday. You told me in your letter that you was glad that I had the management of the farm my self, and you said that you noed that I was able to do as you and master John wish providing that I would not make use of ardent spirits, but I am convinced that it has been my greatest enemy and I shall consider it so as long as I live. We have not been able to do any thing towards marling our land   our team could not be spared from farming except wet spells and it would be too wet for hauling, and master

Cocke Family Papers (#2433-b, #5685, #1480), Manuscripts Division, Special Collections Department, University of Virginia Library.

John thougt we could do as good busines by toating leaves to put on the poorest partes of the land by the spare hands and we put down two thousand and five hndred baskets full weighing from thirty five to forty, and thirty cart load out of the farm pen, and ninety out of the horse lot. We have a very good stand of cotton, but it has been so cold that it does not grow but our corn cannot be beaten and about three days from now we will finish plowing our corn the second time and our peas. we will be then reddy to commence plowing our cotton the second time. it has been about a week since the hoes started over the second time. our oats crop hav been somwhat backward but we had a very fine rane and I am in hopes they will start to growing again. Lee and archa hav been working with us for sum time building a screw whiat looks very fine   I have not herd any thing from brother peyton sence you was out here   I should be very glad to hear when you herd from him   We are all well and hav had no call for a docter this year and I hope that you will reseve this letter in good helth   my self and master John gets on very smooth together   he have not given me a cross worde this year. give my love to every boddy boath white and black and beleave me to be your umble servant

George Skipwith

June the 17 1847

Sir

I would hav written to you a few days suner but i was wating to see if you found any fault in my letter or not   I hav nothing perticulerly to say more than how we have spent our time sence i wrote to you. I mentioned in my letter that i could not write untel mas John returned but i signed no reason. I will now sign my reason   I wanted mas John to see my letters so that you may knoe that what I write is so. I hav ploued my cotten over the second time putting four furrows in a roe with the sweeps and we will finish in three days from to day   the hoes will also finish the last of this week or the first of next the third time in the cotten. then you may considder your cotten crop out of the danger of grass, tho we have had grass and a plenty of it and so has every boddy in green County for grass hav never growed so before. the Lice hav ingured the cotten cropes in our naberhood very much. they hav been very plentyful with us but hav not done us no great damage. mas John told me to chop it out in large bunches and that was all that saved it. it is now growing and ses it is the best cotten he has seen. I hav also ploued my corn the third time and hav laid it by and i dont see any thing to pervent us from makine an elogent crop of corn for it [is] much such a crop as we made the first year that we come into the country and it is praised by every boddy that speakes about it. there was about thirty acers of sandy land corn that was too thick, and mas John told me to thin it out and give it the second working over with the hoes and i hav don so and it is improveing every day. we expect rane every day and if we can get it in eight or ten days I shall not dought it for a moment. I Thought at one time that our oats would not be worth cutting but they mend very fast and I think that we will make a pretty good crope. I think that our last years crope will last us untel the new crope comes. our potatoes looks better this year than any we hav had since we hav been into this country our muls stands well after hard driven and i can shoe them all with second sholders except too. I hav ten regelar worke muls but I hav been oblige to worke the three mares and the horse utill, but i can spell them in a few days. we hav six young coalts amonge them are four horse coalts two of them which will be three years old this coming spring they are boath very likely coalts. the other too, one is about ten days old and the other about a year old. we also hav two filies among them one is two years old and the other is one year old, and the one at one year old is the finest colt I ever saw. I hav sixty hogs for this years killing. our fouls hav failed this year we have hatched hundreds of turkeys and chickins but the Rats destroied them all so that we have not raised none. we are all well and hav had no sickness since i wrote except Spencer he is got a risen hand, and i am in hopes that this letter will fine them all as well there as they are here. Lee and Archa are done ther Job at home (haveing Quitt cotton Prep) and are hierd out. Remember me to the family boath black and white a[nd] Beleave me your servant

George Skipwith

hopewell   July the 8 1847

Sir

on the forth day of July I reseved your letter dated may the 25. I wrote to yo the 15 of June the second time giveing you a true statement of the crops, horses, hogs, and chickeins but I am sorry that I shall have to write yo princerble about other matters. I hav a good crop on hand for you, boath of cotten and corn. this you knoe could not be don without hard worke. I have worked the people but not out of reason, and I have whiped none without a caus the persons whome I have correct I will tell you thir name and thir faults.

Suky who I put to plant som corn and after she had been there long anuf to hav been done I went there and she had hardly began it I gave her som four or five licks over her clothes I gave isham too licks over his clothes for covering up cotton with the plow.

I put frank, isham, violly, Dinah Jinny evealine and Charlott to Sweeping cotten going twice in a roe, and at a Reasonable days worke they aught to hav plowed seven accers a peice, and they had been at it a half of a day, and they had not done more than one accer and a half and I gave them ten licks a peace upon thir skins I gave Julyann eight or ten licks for misplacing her hoe. that was all the whiping I hav done from the time that I pitched the crop untell we comenced cutting oats.

Hopewell   Aug the 31st 1857

my Dear Master

I would have writen to you before this but for eight or ten days I have been sick. I feels better at this time tho not well. Maria also has been very sick but is up again. mrs Carters Baby also has been very sick but it is now a little better. it has fallen off a great deal. mrs Carters health is not very good. the Children all seem to be suffering with very bad Colds. the old ones seem to stand very well. we have two very fine young Babies. one is Jinneys, and the other Bettias. Matilda also had one but it died. I do not think that our sweet potatoe patch will make us many potatoes. they were planted so late I think that the frost will catch them. the Cotton seem to be opening very fast   they will start to picking it out before very long. the Carpenters are still workeing at the low place   mr Powell told Archa to try to get the Buildeings done by the first of November any how. mr Powell left this place on the 27th. he wrote to you from this place. you have heard I supose of his wifes sickness   he expects to be here again the middle of November   Mr Bendon visited him while he was here. mrs Avery and miss mary was here a few days ago   they were well. miss Fanny has not yet returned from North Carolina. mr Ben Carter is still liveing with them, and expect to live there next year. the Topp mare has a very fine horse colt. it is a very pretty Male. I am in hopes that you will soon be makeing ready to start out here and spend a longer time than ever with us, and should any thing pervent you comeing I hope that master Charles will come. I send you these verses which I have taken from the 10 Commandments. I wish you would have them printed for me in a small track. I will now bring my letter to a close   hopeing soon to hear from you I remane your servant

Lucy Skipwith

The 10 Commandments

1st

Thou no god shalt have but me
This Command I give to Thee
love me then with all thy heart
Never from my words depart

2nd

Thou no golden gods shalt have
gods of silver do not love
Seek the true the liveing Lord
For I am a Jealous god

3rd

Thou shalt not take my name in vain
Sinful words thou shalt disdain
guiltless live before my face
And I will be thy hideing place

4th

Remember thou the Sabbath day
Never work nor even play
The god of Heaven will ever bless
The man who keeps the day of rest

5th

Honour thou thy Mothers words
Never break they Fathers laws
They who does their Parents will
Long upon this earth shall live

6th

Thou no murder shall commit
With the murders do not set
Lest thou learn his wicked ways
And live in Sorrow all thy days

7th

Thou no wicked deed shall do
Righteousness shalt thou persue
Let your actions all be right
And like the morning star be bright

8th

Thou shalt see by this Command
Honesty do I demand
Every human being should feel
That it is a sin to steal

9th

Thou shalt always speak the truth
To the aged and the youth
False witnesses do I despise
Ile drag them downwards from the sky

10th

Covetousness here thou see
Is a great offence to me
Thy neighbours goods thou shalt not crave
Thy neighbours goods thou shalt not have

Hopewell   June the 9th 1859

my Dear Master

I received your message by mr Powell, also the one by mr Lawrence about not writeing to you, and I am sorry that you had to remind me of it. I would have writen to you before this but I have been waiteing to hear of your safe arival at home. as we had not heard a word from you we did not know but what you was sick on the road. we are much releaved by hearing from you and will try to let you hear from us as often as necessary, and keep you informed of our movements here.

I knoe that you will be mortified to hear of the troble that my little girl Betsey has got into at mr Joe Bordens by being perswaded by one of their servants to steal money for him, and I lear[ne]d that this is the second time that he has made her do it. she says that she had no thought of it being so much monney neither did he. he saw that she did not dress up like the other girls did and he tempted her with such things as he knew she wanted. I do not know what master Joe will do with the man. he belongs to mr Ben Borden but he lives with master Joe. he has a wife and four Children at master Joes. he also has Brothers and Sisters there, and I heard mas Joe say to day that they were good hands to work, but they would steal, and that girl is growing up among them and if she continue there they will bring her to everlasting destruction. her mistress has taken very little pains to bring her up right. the girl has had the raising of her self up. she has been left down there among those people four and six weeks at a time with not as much as a little sewing to do, and now they complains of her being so lazy. It seems to be almost Imposeing upon you to ask the faver of you to let the Child come home, but I would thank you a thousand time If you would do so. I want to give her religious instructions and try to be the means of saving her soul from death. master Joe says he rather that she would come home. mr Powell says he thinks she had better come home and work in Williams place and let him work out. I hope that you will not sell her if you can posuble do any thing else with her. if you do sell her, have you any objection of my trying to get mr Powell to bye her, providing he is willing to do so, as I think that he could make a woman of her. let me hear from you on the Subject by the first of July. if it was not for the grace of god I would sink beneath such a load as this, but I have a preasant help in the time of troble. I have not seen the girl but once in twelve months. We are all geting along very well at this time. the people are all well, and in good Spirits, and I hope that we may continue to do well. mr Lawrence still holds family Prayers with us every Sunday morning, and explains the scriptures to us. we have had preaching at the Chapple three times this year. we have mr Duboise and Dr Mears the school teacher from greensboro. they will preach every second and fourth sunday in the month. we have Just received a letter from mr Crains sister. she wants his things to be sent to her by mr Powells wagon when it comes down after his goats next monts. we have seven beautiful little kids since you went away, and two very pretty Coalts. we have a very nice garden but every thing is suffering very much for rain.

I have seen nothing of the Japan plum seed in the flower pots nor the garden. only one of the Chessnuts have come up. I will write to you again soon. the people Joines me in love to you. nothing more at preasant from your servant

Lucy Skipwith

To Gen John H Cocke

Five Generations of a South Carolina Slave Family

R. Henry Gaston on His Contests with Slaves, 1850

I have scarcely enough to write to make a letter but I will write all I can think of and "praps" I can fill up.

First I must tell you of a "criminary" I got into with those negroes. On the Monday morning after I came here [Gibsons Quarter, Concord, North Carolina] I called them all up (the men of them) and told them how I intended to be governed here and allotted off their work they would have to do of evenings and mornings feeding + c. and told one of them named Rob to make a fire for me at night and morning.

But instead of coming to make my fire he goes to Concord (where his master lives) to know of him if he should make fires for me. Gibson told him he must do what I told him. The next day I Rec^d. a note from Gibson

Letter from R. Henry Gaston reprinted with permission of Rachel Kirksey Abernathy.

directing me to whip all that disobeyed me. Next morning I call up Rob + commence on him with my cowhide (wich I intended to do any how). I give him a stripe or two + he run saying I shouldn't whip him a dam lick.

I concluded I would wait until he thought I would forget it before I would attack him again. On Saturday following I told Aaron (a young lad just grown) to make fire for me + he also failed to do it. I spoke to Gen. Means who lives ¼ mile of here to assist me to whip them. He said if he came they would suspicion something at once. I got Dr. Gibson here on Monday morning last + we went to the clearing where they were all choping + I called Rob + Aaron up and made them take their coats off + I thrashed them in good style. This I thought would make them obey me but the same evening Rob failed again. (I told him when I whiped him that he had to make a fire for me that week out + then I intended to make Aaron do it as Rob has a house of his own + 2 sisters to attend to). I went down where Rob was choping his wood and asked him if he intended making my fire. Says he "didn't master say I had to curry the mules" (This was mentioned when I whiped them but he got no such orders). I told him to lay down his axe + go make me a fire on. He sidled around the wood pile + didn't seem like he was going to do it.

I then drew my Pistol with a full determination to shoot him let the consequences have been as they may. As soon as he saw what was coming he dashed off like lightning + fell over some gullies. I could have caught him easily when he fell but I knew it wouldn't do to shoot.

After my passion cooled a little I came to the House without saying a word. The following morning he was sick (or pretended to be). I went to his bed + told him in as determined a tone as I could that he could have his choice either to make my fire or be beaten to death because I was determined to make him do it or take his life. Also that he or any of them need not expect to trifle with me.

That evening he was up here in due time + made the fire and has been doing it ever since.

You can Judge from this what kind of Negroes I have to deal with. I don't blame the negroes as much as I do the former overseers for from all I can learn they have had their own way all the while and the overseer had to knock under.

I don't think I will have much more trouble with them for they are beginning to find that they cant get over me. I put it on one to make a fire for me because there is more of them than has any thing to do of evenings + mornings + I thought they may as well do that as nothing and I havent time to do it myself. There is a great many Negroes about here the most I ever saw in any neighbourhood + they think themselves about as good as any common poor people if not better.

There is nine grown men here and about the same no. of women + 3 boys and lots of children

Enough about Negroes.

Slaveowners on the Management of Blacks, 1828–1860

Good Management

South Carolina, 1838, Young Planter

There is no employment I am acquainted with that requires more constant and unremitted attention than a plantation when profitably managed. The master must have a thorough knowledge of every part of his business. It is not alone his duty to plan every thing, but he must see that every plan is executed properly, and as he intended it; no profits can be obtained without it. I care not what may be said to the contrary. The first thing that presents itself to his most serious consideration is the management of his negroes; and upon this depends every thing, but how wretchedly is it often neglected! I will readily acknowledge the difficulties to be encountered in reducing to a system and order the complicated operations of a plantation where nothing like system or order ever prevailed. But the difficulties are at the beginning alone, and you are soon remunerated ten fold. Where negroes have been well fed and clothed and strict, even-handed justice has been meted out both to them and their master, tempered with kindness and humanity, you will as surely obtain the two great principles in their government, *fear and love,* as effect follows cause. Their attachment frequently reaches enthusiasm, and I am inclined to repose much confidence in it. To effect so desirable a state of things, the master should make himself thoroughly acquainted with their habits, character and disposition. He should invariably give a willing ear to all their complaints, put them to the test of investigation and apply an efficient remedy. They will then look up to him as their great arbiter and protector in all their difficulties, which will inspire both respect and confidence, and he will find them much more true to his interest than they are generally supposed to be. He should never suffer them to be degraded either in the manner of inflicting punishment or in any other way. They should be punished in moderation and without passion. The overseer should be a man of fair moral character, of good sense, mild temper and great firmness. What difficulty could be found in introducing the strictest order and discipline in a plantation that had been so managed? Not the least. But, when they have been treated with injustice and falsehood, and a deaf ear turned to their complaints, the master knowing nothing except through the medium of an overseer, probably as trifling and contemptible as the negroes, the worst consequences must be anticipated, and it would be a Herculean task to introduce any thing like system or order. Nothing is more common or more pernicious than to invest your overseer with discretionary powers in inflicting punishment. Passion, prejudice, or ignorance often makes him grossly abuse it. The negro does not go to his master for protection, for he will find none there, but must quietly submit to the despotic will of one but little his superior. It would be almost impossible to organize any regular system under such government. The laws necessary for the regular and proper management of a plantation should be few and simple, operating alike upon overseer and negro, and as immutable and inviolable as those of the Medes and Persians. There should be a certain and definite penalty imposed upon both immediately following their violation. The penalty imposed upon the overseer should be pecuniary, that upon the negro corporeal. The overseer that would not submit to this is not worth having, for if he has intelligence and honesty enough efficiently and faithfully to discharge his duty the advantages both to himself and employer would be presented in so strong a light that they could not be misunderstood.

South Carolina, 1840, Young Planter

There are, in all concerns of life, extremes much to be regretted and avoided, and to an alarming extent is this the case in not using a proper, close, uncompromising discipline over negroes, keeping in mind at all times the line of distinction between master and servant and prohibiting entirely the association of any and all white persons from intercourse with them who do not observe the same rule rigidly, and all innovations to said rule should be fearlessly, instantly, and promptly punished. Upon the other hand, however, there are many, very many, weighty responsibilities due from masters to slaves—and it is a source of just satisfaction to the exalted citizens of our own State, and the South generally, to know that many of these obligations they daily acquit themselves of most honourably, as in the daily allowance of food, clothing, and comfortable cabins—and of at least paramount importance only a moderate service is required; all of which, in the eye of the humane, or even judicious owner, are necessary, scrupulously so, for his own advancement, if not to satisfy the risings of a benevolent heart—which is, with but few exceptions, the prompter to good deeds. But there are exceptions to this rule of conduct which deserve our attention and action from its source being diametrically opposed to both the laws of God, and man, and to reason, common sense, and self-interest. The more to be regretted, too, from the fact that such inhuman owners of slaves frequently perturb whole neighborhoods and inflict, measureably, disgrace upon whole districts, yea States.

Plantation Order

Mississippi, 1851, Planter, 150 slaves

"Rules and Regulations for the Government of a Southern Plantation"

1. THERE SHALL BE A PLACE FOR EVERY THING, AND EVERY THING SHALL BE KEPT IN ITS PLACE.

2. On the first days of January and July, there shall be an account taken of the number and condition of all the negroes, stock, and farming utensils of every description on the premises, and the same shall be entered in the plantation book.

3. It shall be the duty of the overseer to call upon the stockminder once each day to know if the cattle, sheep, and hogs have been seen and counted, and to find out if any are dead, missing, or lost.

4. It shall be the duty of the overseer, at least once in every week, to see and count the stock himself, and to inspect the fences, gates, and water-gaps on the plantation and see that they are in good order.

5. The wagons, carts, and all other implements are to be kept under the sheds and in the houses where they belong, except when in use.

6. Each negro man will be permitted to keep his own axe, and shall have it forthcoming when required by the overseer. No tools shall be taken or used by any negro without the permission of the overseer. . . .

12. It shall be the duty of the driver, at such hours of the night as the overseer may designate, to blow his horn and go around and see that every negro is at his proper place, and to report to the overseer any that may be absent; and it shall be the duty of the overseer, at some hour between that time and daybreak, to patrol the quarters himself and see that every negro is where he should be.

Workdays

Georgia, 1860, Farmer

EDITORS *SOUTHERN CULTIVATOR*—As I am a new beginner, and a *small farmer,* and am disposed to do my own overseeing, I find it very inconvenient and troublesome on account of not knowing the amount of work a hand ought to do per day, and am consequently often much imposed on. Will you, or some one of your many subscribers, be so kind as to answer the following questions:

1. What is a task, in hoeing or hilling Corn?
2. Chopping out Cotton?
3. Hoeing and bringing Cotton to a stand?
4. Hoeing Rice (not subject to irrigation) in its different stages?
5. Hoeing Potatoes, &c.?
6. Ditching?
7. Turning up land with a hoe?
8. Listing ground?
9. Bedding up with a hoe?
10. Trenching for Rice?
11. Splitting Pine Rails, &c.?

Adapted to Pine and Bay Lands.
Yours, very respectfully,   SMALL FARMER
                              Scriven Co., Ga., June, 1860.

REPLY.—We find answers to most of the above inquiries in Holmes' "Southern Farmer," and proceed to give them in order—

1. From one half to a full acre.
2. Half an acre.
3. From half an acre to an acre.
4. On inland from 1/4 to 1/2 acre.
5. From 1/2 an acre to an acre.
6. About 600 square feet.
7. Say 1/4 of an acre.
8. From 1/4 to 1/2 acre.
9. From 1/4 to 1/2 acre.
10. A square of 150 feet each way, or about 1/2 an acre.
11. From 100 to 125 heavy rails, 12 feet long.

It will be necessary to modify these tasks in accordance with the nature of the soil, obstructions by stumps, rocks, &c., but in the main they will be found nearly correct.—EDS. *So. Cult.*

Discipline

South Carolina, 1828, Overseer

More punishment is inflicted on every plantation by the men in power from private pique than from a neglect of duty. This I assert as a fact; I have detected it often. . . . When I pass sentence myself, various modes of punishment are adopted; the lash least of all.—Digging stumps or clearing away trash about the settlements in their own time; but the most severe is confinement at home six months to twelve months, or longer. . . . The lash is, unfortunately, too much used; every mode of punishment should be devised in preference to that, and when used, never to lacerate—all young persons will offend. A Negro at twenty-five years old, who finds he has the marks of a rogue inflicted when a boy (even if disposed to be orderly) has very little or no inducement to be otherwise.

South Carolina, 1830, Planter

The proper management and discipline of slaves subjects the man of care and feeling to more dilemmas than perhaps any other vocation he could follow. To keep a diary of their conduct would be a record nothing short of a series of violations of the laws of God and man. To moralize and induce the slave to assimilate with the master and his interest has been and is the great desideratum aimed at; but I am sorry to say that I have long since desponded in the completion of this task. But, however true this picture may be, of those servile creatures, we are bound under many sacred obligations to treat them with humanity at all times and under all circumstances. Although compelled to use coercive measures for their good discipline, yet we should never lose sight of humanity in its strictest sense. Under all these considerations, it requires for the good management and discipline of those people a man of steady habits, connected with sobriety, fortitude, energy, and humanity, and a passion for enterprise. To clothe the naked, feed the hungry, and soothe the sick should be our ceaseless duty toward the slave; and to compel them to theirs should be the order of the day.

Virginia, 1834, Planter

In the management of negroes there should always be perfect uniformity of conduct toward them; that is, you should not be too rigid in your discipline at one time and too lax at another. They should understand that real faults will not go unpunished; but at the same time, moderate punishment, with a certainty of its succeeding a fault, is much more efficient in producing good conduct than severe punishment irregularly inflicted—that is, sometimes inflicted for an offence and at others omitted when the same or a worse [one] is committed; for the ill disposed will always risk the chances of escaping punishment altogether. It is the certainty of punishment, and not its severity, which deters from misconduct and, in fact, after awhile, on a well regulated plantation, that certainty will prevent the necessity of inflicting punishments almost entirely. The best evidence of the good management of slaves is the impartiality of treatment to be used towards them all, unless for particular good conduct, and then it should be understood as such.

South Carolina, 1836, Overseer

For the breach of every rule, *certainty of punishment* is every thing. If a negro is permitted to go once unpunished for a fault, he will at any time afterwards do the same and risk being flogged. I have always discovered that where the overseer is positive that the negroes are better disciplined, more mildly treated, and consequently more happy; once, however, a negro has been punished, the fault should be overlooked, and his spirits should not be broken down by continually reminding him of his past misconduct. Not observing this rule has very often ruined some of the very best negroes. I have frequently met with negroes, whom the whip would ruin, with whom a little flattery could do everything.

Tennessee and Arkansas, 1860, Planter

Allow me [A. T. Goodloe] to place before your readers a few important facts in reference to the management of negroes. When I was a boy (and it has not been many years since) negroes, as far as my knowledge extends, were kept under strict discipline. But since Mrs. [Harriet Beecher] Stowe and others of a like stripe have, from pecuniary motives (for I have no idea they fancy black more than any other color), sent out their vile publications to the world, many at the South have thought proper, perhaps from similar motives, to write books and newspaper articles in answer to those abolition works. Most of these Southern writers have, in my opinion, done more injury than good to the institution which they pretend to defend, for the plan of management which they generally lay down is such as to render a slave unhappy and very unprofitable property.

The general published opinion seems to be that negroes should be managed with great lenity and encouraged to labor by kind words.

Now, I speak what I know when I say it is like "casting pearls before swine" to try to *persuade* a negro to work. He must be *made* to work, and should always be given to understand that if he fails to perform his duty he will be punished for it.

There was an article published last fall in the Nashville *Christian Advocate* on this subject, and the writer tried to prove that the only humane and profitable way to manage negroes was to allow them to have patches of such sizes as they wished, and be permitted to work them every time they worked over their master's crop. To prove that to be the right way, some Senator from Georgia I believe (who has devoted his life to the study of politics) owning a great many slaves let them have patches, and the annual income of their crops was good wages for a white man. Can such stuff be called management? No sir. What do slaves want with money? What good can it possibly do them? I can tell you what becomes of most of it. The proprietors of road-side groceries get it. There are several such filthy institutions in the country, and they are considered by the good neighbors to be great nuisances; but these neighbors, with scarcely an exception, allow their negroes to make what money they can for themselves, and give them the privilege of going wherever their inclinations may lead them at night and on Sunday. Tell me, if you please, who is responsible for the existence of whiskey-venders on the road-side in a moral neighborhood? I will take the liberty of saying that, if the negroes were kept at home, as they should be, such characters would go somewhere else to seek a support. Every managing farmer can well afford to buy such things for their negroes as he wishes them to have. Take his negroes to the nearest dry goods store, or send the overseer with them (do not let them go alone), and let them select such things as suit their fancies, within a certain limit, and pay for the goods himself, always rewarding more liberally those that have performed their duty best.

I read an article in the *Southern Cultivator* some time last year (I don't recollect now what number it was in) written by a rich Southern planter, in which he said he always took negro evidence against an overseer. Negroes are weak-minded, unprincipled creatures, and at the same time will frequently evince a great deal of shrewdness in fixing up a "tale" on an overseer they do not like. I had an evidence of that on my plantation last year. The negroes had become tired of the overseer, and concluded to fix up a plan to have him turned off [fired]. They assembled in counsel near the cabins one night, after they thought he had gone to bed and was asleep;

but he, ever on the watch, as an overseer should be who regards the interests of his employer, concealed himself near where they were, and learned all they said. He told me of it next morning and requested that I should hear it all from their own lips before I punished them, for it has always been a rule with me to whip any negro that tries to tell me anything about the overseer. I think I can find out without their assistance whether he is a gentleman or not. Their plans were well laid, and they, no doubt, would have succeeded in their measures if they had belonged to such a man as the rich Southern planter. In compliance with the request of my overseer, I heard them with my own ears, and they acknowledged their "tale" was entirely false, that their only object was to get the overseer turned off. The impropriety and absurdity of listening to what negroes have to say about their overseer is perfectly evident to any one who will reflect a minute on the subject.

Abolitionists and their books can never affect the institution of slavery, but managing negroes in the way I have referred to will. It will make them a reckless, dissatisfied population and expense to their owners. People adopting such government with their negroes are laboring against their own interests, the interests of their slaves, and the interests of the South.

I have a plantation in Arkansas on which I have been living six years and have been quite successful for a beginner. In order to gain information, when I first went out, I observed very closely and made many inquiries about the management of negroes. Most of the neighbors (clever people) allowed their negroes to visit about through the country, and cultivated small crops to the land. The land was rich and they always made enough to live on, which was all they cared for. I went there to make money, and soon found out that I could not make anything by following their example. I, therefore, after consulting the most successful planters, arrived at the following conclusions, viz: Negroes should have as much as they can eat and a sufficient quantity of comfortable clothing. They should be made to go to bed early at night and be up in time next morning to get breakfast and be at their places in the field as soon as it is light enough to see to work, and remain diligently at work till dark. They should not be permitted to visit away from the plantation, nor negroes from the neighborhood allowed to visit them. Rigid discipline should always be observed with them, for it is the only way to make them contented and profitable.

Charleston's Free Blacks on Fear of Reenslavement, 1859–1860

Charleston, Decr 23d/59

Dear Henry,

I hope this will find you relieved from your cold. I am annoyed with one. The wedding came off in style. Nat Fuller was the caterer. He had

From *No Chariot Let Down: Charleston's Free People on the Eve of the Civil War*, edited by Michael P. Johnson and James L. Roark, pp. 41, 101–102. © 1984 The University of North Carolina Press.

oysters served for E Ann at 9 o'clock. We left soon after. We had two bottles of champagne broached before leaving & did not even eat a piece of cake. The crowd was a large & respectable one. Mr Gadsden performed the ceremony, Dr Hanckel being sick. There were 10 attending of each sex. Some of the bridesmaids left before we did for Savannah. Beard went down with them but took care to get back before supper. The bride & groom are gone on a Tour in the country.

Matilda was at Home today for the first time. She is well. Mrs Bonneau is quite feeble. R Kinloch gets married shortly, also Miss Gourdin, an apprentice of Mrs. Lee.

Do tender my congratulations to your Father on the adjournment of the Legislature. He ought to read Col Memminger's speech against Moore's bill. It is in the Courier of 16th. I prophesied from the onset that nothing would be done affecting our position.

We have sent some little nick nacks for the children, not having room for the grown folks. You must come down & follow the fashion. I heard a few days ago my cotton was sold, but did not learn the rates. I will be able to settle up with your Father for Bagging, Rope, &c. Do see that Sarah behaves herself & salts the creatures regularly. We have not heard from Charley for some days. Father, Mother, Gabriella, & E Ann unite with me in wishing you & all at Wisdom Hall a Merry Christmas. As ever, I am yrs truly

J M J

Charleston Aug 28th 1860

Dear Henry,

Yours is recd. I am sorry to hear of Wm & Charlotte's indisposition. We are not very well. The heat is oppressive.

The stir has subsided, but arrests are still made & the people are leaving. It is vain for us to hope that if it is not the *will* of God he will not permit it. The bible tells us He is not the minister of Sin, & again the wicked shall flourish &c. In that model prayer we are taught to pray that His will may be done on earth as it is in heaven, & yet as free agents we are free to obey or reject. Hence it is that on earth wicked rule prevails, while in Heaven His will is done by the Just. I have implicit Faith in Providence & recognize its doing in directing those who seek His guidance, by over-ruling what is a present calamity to the future good of the virtuous. But I very much doubt that He wills or sanctions unrighteous acts, although in answer to prayer He often overthrows them & converts them into an engine of good provided we will act in accordance with His will as suggested by His Spirit & not supinely wait for the working of a miracle by having a Chariot let down to convey us away.

The magistrates boast of the good it has done them & Trusted that they did not know they were so rich. Slaves have come by magic. It is evident that the movement is intended for their emolument. On the other hand it must prove the Death of many & the loss of earthly goods, the hard earnings of a life time, to others. And yet those who put their trust in God may derive benefits spiritually & temporally.

Our Friends sympathise & express indignation which has checked it, but they are not in power & cant put down the majority. Nothing more is heard of the suits. Fordham had to comply with the Law. Gen. Schnierlie placed himself in the stead of a Man he holds & defied them to touch him. He would beat the one to Death who did. And Col. Whaley says he will stand a lawsuit before complying, but the majority has succumbed. The money has to come out of the purses of those held in Trust.

Hicks had his watch & chain taken from him in a Mob raised in Market St.

Col. Seymour stood in front of our House speaking to an Irish carter on the subject & pointed to No 7 & 9 as being for sale. And you can see Hand bills on property held by cold. people in every quarter, which will have the effect of depreciation. The action of the people has taken them by surprise & the originators blame the Mayor for being so rash. They say All must leave but they did not want them ran off thus.

As it regards the Miss D's I expected you to select for yourself first, which would be a good recommendation. They wont leave before their Father except entrusted to better hands. He is not disposed to move quick enough for them.

Father has been to Niagara Falls with Charley & to Love Feast & class meetings with Marshall & R. Clark & to pic nics with Gabriella & Charlotte & is enjoying the sights with a zest. Charley begs to join with Father in Love to you & to assure you that you have never been forgotten.

Jas Glover was taken to the Guard House at the instance of Dr Dessausure for standing in a Drug store with his Hat on. I have not heard the sentence. Beard has closed his school & is about to leave before he is pounced upon.

Dr. Dereef is flourishing in Washington yet. He has written about 30 Letters home since he left. They come daily. If the one I saw is a sample he must have more constant employment than the Secry of State.

I cant write your Father for the present. I suppose the H & G affair has attained the result. I fancy I see them in a Fond embrace.

W. P. Dacoster appears to be circumspect. De Large has got back to fret a few. Sasportas has Returned from Aiken with his daughter. They tried to prevail on him to make his abode there. The Family joins me in Love.

Yours,
J M J

⅄ *E S S A Y S*

Historian Eugene D. Genovese of the College of William and Mary has written widely about slave culture and the hegemonic power of the masters. In the first essay, he discusses paternalism, arguing that it controlled and contained slave resistance, and also describes certain slave religious beliefs that were independent of white religion and embraced African elements. The late Herbert Gutman, who taught history at the City College of New York, challenged Genovese's views of white control over black thought. The excerpt from his work on the black family, reprinted in the second essay, advances a theory of biculturalism that implies a greater degree of mental independence among the slaves than Genovese's interpretation suggests. The most comprehensive work to date on free blacks has been done by historian Ira Berlin of the University of Maryland. In the third selection, he explains the origins and composition of the differing groups of free blacks in the Upper and Lower South, presents a demographic profile of free blacks in the period 1820–1860, and probes white southerners' fear and dislike of free blacks.

Paternalism and Slave Culture

EUGENE D. GENOVESE

The Old South, black and white, created a historically unique kind of paternalist society. To insist upon the centrality of class relations as manifested in paternalism is not to slight the inherent racism or to deny the intolerable contradictions at the heart of paternalism itself. Imamu Amiri Baraka captures the tragic irony of paternalist social relations when he writes that slavery "was, most of all, a paternal institution" and yet refers to "the filthy paternalism and cruelty of slavery." Southern paternalism, like every other paternalism, had little to do with Ole Massa's ostensible benevolence, kindness, and good cheer. It grew out of the necessity to discipline and morally justify a system of exploitation. It did encourage kindness and affection, but it simultaneously encouraged cruelty and hatred. The racial distinction between master and slave heightened the tension inherent in an unjust social order.

Southern slave society grew out of the same general historical conditions that produced the other slave regimes of the modern world. The rise of a world market—the development of new tastes and of manufactures dependent upon non-European sources of raw materials—encouraged the rationalization of colonial agriculture under the ferocious domination of a few Europeans. African labor provided the human power to fuel the new system of production in all the New World slave societies, which, however, had roots in different European experiences and emerged in different geographical, economic, and cultural conditions. They had much in common, but each was unique.

Theoretically, modern slavery rested, as had ancient slavery, on the idea of a slave as *instrumentum vocale*—a chattel, a possession, a thing, a mere extension of his master's will. But the vacuousness of such pretensions had been exposed long before the growth of New World slave societies. The closing of ancient slave trade, the political crisis of the ancient civilization, and the subtle moral pressure of an ascendant Christianity had converged in the early centuries of the new era to shape a seigneurial world in which lords and serfs (not slaves) faced each other with reciprocal demands and expectations. This land-oriented world of medieval Europe slowly forged the traditional paternalist ideology to which the southern slaveholders fell heir.

The slaveholders of the South, unlike those of the Caribbean, increasingly resided on their own plantations and by the end of the eighteenth century had become an entrenched regional ruling class. The paternalism encouraged by the close living of masters and slaves was enormously reinforced by the closing of the African slave trade, which compelled masters to pay greater attention to the reproduction of their labor force. Of all the slave societies in the New World, that of the Old South alone maintained a slave force that reproduced itself. Less than 400,000 imported Africans had, by 1860, become an American black population of more than 4,000,000.

A paternalism accepted by both masters and slaves—but with radically different interpretations—afforded a fragile bridge across the intolerable contradictions inherent in a society based on racism, slavery, and class exploitation that had to depend on the willing reproduction and productivity of its victims. For the slaveholders paternalism represented an attempt to overcome the fundamental contradiction in slavery: the impossibility of the slaves' ever becoming the things they were supposed to be. Paternalism defined the involuntary labor of the slaves as a legitimate return to their masters for protection and direction. But, the masters' need to see their slaves as acquiescent human beings constituted a moral victory for the slaves themselves. Paternalism's insistence upon mutual obligations—duties, responsibilities, and ultimately even rights—implicitly recognized the slaves' humanity.

Wherever paternalism exists, it undermines solidarity among the oppressed by linking them as individuals to their oppressors. A lord (master, *padrone, patron, padrón, patrão*) functions as a direct provider and protector to each individual or family, as well as to the community as a whole. The slaves of the Old South displayed impressive solidarity and collective resistance to their masters, but in a web of paternalistic relationships their action tended to become defensive and to aim at protecting the individuals against aggression and abuse; it could not readily pass into an effective weapon for liberation. Black leaders, especially the preachers, won loyalty and respect and fought heroically to defend their people. But despite their will and considerable ability, they could not lead their people over to the attack against the paternalist ideology itself.

In the Old South the tendencies inherent in all paternalistic class systems intersected with and acquired enormous reinforcement from the tendencies inherent in an analytically distinct system of racial subordination. The two appeared to be a single system. Paternalism created a tendency for the slaves to identify with a particular community through identification with its master; it reduced the possibilities for their identification with each other as a class. Racism undermined the slaves' sense of worth as black people and reinforced their dependence on white masters. But these were tendencies, not absolute laws, and the slaves forged weapons of defense, the most important of which was a religion that taught them to love and value each other, to take a critical view of their masters, and to reject the ideological rationales for their own enslavement.

The slaveholders had to establish a stable regime with which their slaves could live. Slaves remained slaves. They could be bought and sold like any other property and were subject to despotic personal power. And blacks remained rigidly subordinated to whites. But masters and slaves, whites and blacks, lived as well as worked together. The existence of the community required that all find some measure of self-interest and self-respect. Southern paternalism developed as a way of mediating irreconcilable class and racial conflicts; it was an anomaly even at the moment of its greatest apparent strength. But, for about a century, it protected both masters and slaves from the worst tendencies inherent in their respective conditions. It mediated, however unfairly and even cruelly, between masters and slaves, and it disguised, however imperfectly, the appropriation of one man's labor power by another. Paternalism in any historical setting defines relations of superordination and subordination. Its strength as a prevailing ethos increases as the members of the community accept—or feel compelled to accept—these relations as legitimate. Brutality lies inherent in this acceptance of patronage and dependence, no matter how organic the paternalistic order. But southern paternalism necessarily recognized the slaves' humanity—not only their free will but the very talent and ability without which their acceptance of a doctrine of reciprocal obligations would have made no sense. Thus, the slaves found an opportunity to translate paternalism itself into a doctrine different from that understood by their masters and to forge it into a weapon of resistance to assertions that slavery was a natural condition for blacks, that blacks were racially inferior, and that black slaves had no rights or legitimate claims of their own.

Thus, the slaves, by accepting a paternalistic ethos and legitimizing class rule, developed their most powerful defense against the dehumanization implicit in slavery. Southern paternalism may have reinforced racism as well as class exploitation, but it also unwittingly invited its victims to fashion their own interpretation of the social order it was intended to justify. And the slaves, drawing on a religion that was supposed to assure their compliance and docility, rejected the essence of slavery by projecting their own rights and value as human beings. . . .

On the plantations and farms the slaves met for services apart from the whites whenever they could. Weekly services on Sunday evenings were common. Where masters were indulgent, additional meetings might take place during the week, and where they were not, they might take place anyway. Masters and overseers often accepted the Sunday meetings but not the others, for the slaves would stay up much of the night praying, singing, and dancing. The next day being a workday, the meetings were bad for business.

The slaves' religious meetings would be held in secret when their masters forbade all such; or when their masters forbade all except Sunday meetings; or when rumors of rebellion or disaffection led even indulgent masters to forbid them so as to protect the people from trigger-happy patrollers; or when the slaves wanted to make sure that no white would hear them. Only during insurrection scares or tense moments occasioned by political turmoil could the laws against such meetings be enforced. Too many planters did not want them enforced. They regarded their slaves as peaceful, respected their religious sensibilities, and considered such interference dangerous to plantation morale and productivity. Others agreed that the slaves presented no threat of rising and did not care about their meetings. Had the slaves been less determined, the regime probably would have been far more stringent; but so long as they avoided conspiracies and accepted harsh punishment as the price for getting caught by patrols, they raised the price of suppression much too high to make it seem worthwhile to planters with steady nerves.

When the meetings had to be held in secret, the slaves confronted a security problem. They would announce the event by such devices as that of singing "Steal Away to Jesus" at work. To protect the meeting itself, they had an infallible method. They would turn over a pot "to catch the sound" and keep it in the cabin or immediate area of the woods. Almost infallible: "Of course, sometimes they might happen to slip up on them on suspicion." George P. Rawick suggests that the practice of turning over a pot probably had African origins, and John F. Szwed links it to rituals designed to sanctify the ground. The slaves' belief in its efficacy gave them additional confidence to brave the risks, and their success in avoiding detection led some whites to think that there might just be something to the pot technique.

The desire of the slaves for religious privacy took a limited as well as a general form. Eliza Frances Andrews went down to the plantation praisehouse after dinner one night to hear the slaves sing. "At their 'praise meetings,' " she commented, "they go through all sorts of motions in connection with their songs, but they won't give way to their wildest gesticulations or engage in their sacred dances before white people for fear of being laughed at." But the slaves had no objection to pleasing curious whites when they expected an appreciative response. They took enormous pride in their singing and in the depth of their religious expression. They resisted being laughed at, but they responded to expressions of respect. Gus Feaster, an ex-slave from Union County, South Carolina, proudly told of such instances:

> At night when the meeting done busted till next day was when the darkies really did have they freedom of spirit. As the wagon be creeping along in the late hours of moonlight, the darkies would raise a tune. Then the air soon be filled with the sweetest tune as us rid on home and sung all the old hymns that us loved. It was always some big black nigger with a deep bass voice like a frog that'd start up the tune. Then the other mens jine in, followed up by the fine little voices of the gals and the cracked voices of the old womens and the grannies. When us reach near the big house

us soften down to a deep hum that the missus like! Sometimes she hist up the window and tell us sing "Swing Low, Sweet Chariot" for her and the visiting guests. That all us want to hear. Us open up, and the niggers near the big house that hadn't been to church would wake up and come out to the cabin door and jine in the refrain. From that we'd swing on into all the old spirituals that us love so well and that us knowed how to sing. Missus often 'low that her darkies could sing with heaven's inspiration.

This pride, this self-respect, this astonishing confidence in their own spiritual quality, explain the slaves' willingness to spend so much of their day of leisure at prayer meetings. Often they would hear the white preacher or the master himself on Sunday morning, but the "real meeting' " and the "real preachin' " came later, among themselves. Richard Carruthers, an ex-slave from Texas, explained another feature of the concern with prayer. "Us niggers," he said, "used to have a prayin' ground down in the hollow and some time we come out of the field, between eleven and twelve at night, scorchin' and burnin' up with nothin' to eat, and we wants to ask the good Lord to have mercy."

The meetings gave the slaves strength derived from direct communion with God and each other. When not monitored, they allowed the message of promised deliverance to be heard. If the slaves had received false information or had been misled by the whites, they provided an opportunity for correction, as when the white preachers led them in prayers for the Confederacy, and their black preachers, in secret session, led them in prayers for the Union. But above all, the meetings provided a sense of autonomy—of constituting not merely a community unto themselves but a community with leaders of their own choice.

The slaves' religious frenzy startled white onlookers, although few ever saw it fully unleashed. The more austere masters tried to curb it but usually had little success. Emoline Glasgow of South Carolina had a Methodist master who took one of his slaves to church and determined to keep him in line by bribery if necessary. He offered to give the slave a new pair of boots if he behaved himself. All went well until about the middle of the service, when the slave let go: "Boots or no boots, I gwine to shout today." The slaves took their letting-go seriously and condemned those who simulated emotion. When the Catholic priests forbade shouting in Louisiana, Catherine Cornelius spoke for the slaves in insisting that "the angels shout in heaven" and in doggedly proclaiming, "The Lawd said you gotta shout if you want to be saved. That's in the Bible." Sincerity meant everything. Emma Fraser, an ex-slave from South Carolina, talked about her singing in church in the way that others talked about shouting. "But ef I sing an' it doan move me any, den dat a sin on de Holy Ghost; I be tell a lie on de Lord." The frenzy, as W. E. B. Du Bois called it, brought the slaves together in a special kind of communion, which brought out the most individual expressions and yet disciplined the collective. The people protected each other against the excesses of their release and encouraged each other to shed inhibitions. Everyone responded according to his own spirit but ended in a spiritual union with everyone else.

Possession appeared much less often among the slaves of the Old South than among those of Saint-Domingue or Brazil, where the practice of Vodûn and the rites of the African cults ran high. Yet ecstatic seizures, however defined, appeared frequently and submit to differing interpretations. Critics have recognized in them a form of hysteria, and Frantz Fanon even speaks of a kind of madness. Roger Bastide has suggested that they are vehicles by which repressed personalities surface in symbolic form. Many anthropologists, however, have remained skeptical of psychoanalytic explanations and have pointed out that no genuine schizophrenic could possibly adjust to the firm system of control that the rituals demand. No matter how wild and disorderly they look to the uninitiated, they are in fact tightly controlled; certain things must be done and others not done. They thus require, according to Alfred Métraux, social, not psychological, explanation. Yet, schizophrenia aside, a psychoanalytic explanation is compatible with a social one. The question may be left for experts, if any. Two things are clear. First, the slaves' wildest emotionalism, even when it passed into actual possession, formed part of a system of collective behavior, which the slaves themselves controlled. The slaves may have been driven wild with ecstasy when dancing during their services, but never so wild that their feet would cross without evoking sharp rebuke. And second, the slaves' behavior brought out a determination to assert their power and the freedom of their spirit, for, as Max Weber says, ecstasy may become an instrument of salvation or self-deification.

If emotional fervor alone had distinguished black religion, the usual interpretations would take on greater credibility—that no great difference existed between the religion of the slaves and that of the lower-class whites who followed the frontier Baptist and Methodist preachers. The frequently heard assertion that the blacks merely copied the whites may be left aside as unworthy of discussion. If one must choose between the two separate tendencies, the view of Dr. Du Bois, according to which the style of the poor whites has been a "plain copy" of the style of the blacks, easily holds the field. White and black responses reinforced each other, as they had to in an interracial setting. Their blending reflected a common frontier Christian character and no doubt contributed something toward bringing together two antagonistic peoples. But there were differences that illuminate the special quality of the black experience.

Neither a common body of belief—to the extent that it was in fact common—nor even common rites could guarantee a common spiritual experience. Rites reflect, and in turn reshape, the communities that practice them. Slaves and poorer rural whites (that is, small farmers and actual "poor whites") brought fundamentally different community settings to their common rites, and they therefore brought fundamentally different spiritual needs, responses, and values. When slaves from small farms shared religious meetings and churchgoing with their white yeomen and poor white neighbors, they no doubt drew closer to their inner experience, but even then some distance was inevitable. For plantation blacks, the distance had to be much greater.

The blacks did not hide their disdain for white shouters, whom they regarded, as Dr. Du Bois did later, as a plain copy of themselves. Even in the early camp meetings the blacks notoriously outshouted the whites and stayed up singing and praying long after the whites had retired. They made up their own hymns, which drew protests from orthodox whites because they were their own and because they came too close to sounding like plantation jubilee melodies. Viewing a meeting in Georgia, which attracted even more blacks than whites, Olmsted observed: "The Negroes kept their place during all the tumult; there may have been a sympathetic groan or exclamation uttered by one or two of them, but generally they expressed only the interest of curiosity. . . . There was generally a self-satisfied smile upon their faces; and I have no doubt they felt they could do it with a great deal more energy and abandon, if they were called upon." Beneath the similarities and differences of style lay a divergence of meanings, including some divergence in the very meaning of God.

The slaves drew their call-and-response pattern from their African heritage, however important the reinforcing elements from the Europeans. Europeans had also used something like a song-style of preaching and responding, which had somewhat different qualities. Blacks and whites in the South performed in distinct ways. The content of the white responses to a preacher—undoubtedly with many exceptions—consisted of "Amens" and the like. The whites cheered their preacher on or let him know they were moved. The preacher needed that response, craved it, even demanded it. But the black preacher had to evoke it, not for his own satisfaction, subjectively important as that may have been, but because without it the service had no relationship to God. This difference in style betrayed a difference in theological tendency. The whites were fundamentalists to the core, the blacks only apparently so. Both preached the Bible in fiery style, but as the Reverend Henry H. Mitchell suggests, the whites were fiery mad, while the blacks were fiery glad. Or as Martin Ruffin, an ex-slave from Texas, said of a black preacher, Sam Jones, he "preached Hell-fire and judgment like the white preachers." . . .

Original sin does not appear in African religions, and the problem of freedom and order therefore assumes radically different forms. Without such a doctrine the delicate balance between the two tips toward the claims of the collective against those of the individual. Much as the doctrine of original sin reflects the class divisions in Western society, whatever its deeper insight into human nature, it also creates greater possibilities for individual freedom, particularly since the cause of individual freedom has historically been inseparable from the use of private property. When the Christian faith took its stand on the doctrine of original sin, it constructed a defense of the individual personality on which the most secularized ideologies of liberalism came to be built. But Christianity's world-shaking achievement also rested on guilt and self-contempt, without which its doctrine of freedom could not have been theologically and socially disciplined. This particular tension between freedom and order provided the driving force of Western culture, as well as the basis for its pessimism.

The African legacy to Afro-America—that celebrated joy in life which is so often denigrated or explained away—represented a life-affirming faith that stressed shame and minimized guilt. Enslavement might be shameful and an expression of weakness, but it could not easily produce a sense of guilt—of getting what you deserved and of being punished for having offended God. Christianity might have transformed the slaves into the slavish robots of Nietzsche's polemic or the Sambos of Stanley Elkins's model, if they had not virtually reshaped it to fit their own psychic needs and their own sensibility.

A Bicultural Model of Slave Behavior

HERBERT G. GUTMAN

Philip D. Curtin's very important study *The Atlantic Slave Trade: A Census* (1969) reinforces the need to study slave behavior in an enlarged time perspective. Curtin estimates the number of Africans imported into the United States at slightly less than half a million. By the emancipation, the Afro-American population had increased to more than nine times the number imported, a rapid natural increase that started in the first half of the eighteenth century and continued throughout the period of enslavement. Such population growth contrasted sharply with that of other New World slave populations and, as C. Vann Woodward writes, remains "a neglected historical experience," one that "has gone virtually unnoticed or has been taken for granted by historians of the United States." Curtin's study, moreover, demonstrates that of the fewer than half million Africans brought to the North American continent, nearly half (about 46 percent) came between 1741 and 1780 and about another 25 percent between 1781 and the abolition of the legal slave trade in 1808.

A period of between eighty and one hundred twenty years separated nearly half of the enslaved Africans brought to the North American mainland from their Afro-American slave descendants at the moment of the general emancipation. Only a few slave generations connect these two moments in time. But a social process of "creolization" (the transformation of the African into the Afro-American) was already well under way by the time the federal Constitution was adopted and before the invention of the cotton gin. Culture formation among the slaves, which began before the War for Independence and well before the plantation system spread from the Upper to the Lower South, blended together African and Anglo-American cultural beliefs and social practices, mediated through the harsh institution of enslavement. Most slaves involved in the spread of the plantation system and of the developing Afro-American culture over the entire South in the six decades prior to the Civil War were the children and the

From *The Black Family in Slavery and Freedom, 1750–1925* by Herbert Gutman. Reprinted by permission of Pantheon Books, a division of Random House, Inc.

grandchildren of that adaptive eighteenth-century slave culture, a culture neither African nor American but genuinely Afro-American. . . .

. . . Slave belief and behavior at the emancipation were the consequence of a recurrent interaction between accumulating slave historical experiences (culture) as transmitted over time through an adaptive slave-family and kinship system and the changing slave society in which the slaves lived. Radical external changes regularly tested the adaptive capacities of several different slave generations. There was first the adaptation associated with initial enslavement, then the adaptation associated with the spread of plantation slavery from the Upper to the Lower South (1815 to 1860), and finally the adaptation associated with the Civil War and emancipation. How the slaves dealt with these changes in external circumstance—and with other changes which they could not affect such as the development of a farm into a plantation, the sale of a child, and the death or sale of a spouse—depended at all times upon the accumulated experiences and beliefs of the slave men and women who had lived before them. . . .

. . . Common Afro-American beliefs and behavior developed in quite different slave communities. . . . The developing Afro-American culture had at its core common adaptive slave domestic arrangements and kin networks and [the] enlarged slave communities emerged over time out of these adaptive kin arrangements. . . .

The slaves studied in the present work—those whose behavior has been reconstructed from diverse plantation records—allow us to redefine some of the important questions that deserve study by students of slave and ex-slave belief and behavior. Despite variations in their treatment, these slaves acted on common beliefs. It did not matter whether they had resident or absentee owners, whether they lived on plantations their entire lives or lived on farms that became plantations, or whether they lived near or had been separated from their families of origin. Such behavior therefore means that the question posed by Fredrickson and Lasch—*what did slavery do to the slave?*—requires first knowing *who the slave was*. How owners treated their slaves affected how individual slaves behaved. But how slaves behaved depended upon far more than their "treatment." Slave naming practices and marital rules (as well as the length of slave marriages in settings where slaves could remarry) are unmistakable evidence of the importance of interior slave beliefs and experiences in shaping their behavior. But these beliefs and the developing culture that sustained them could not have regularly revealed themselves over time if they were no more than free-floating slave beliefs. That would be expecting the impossible from the slaves.

Institutional arrangements—especially among slaves—had to exist for such beliefs to be acted upon over time, and that is why the inter- and intragenerational linkages between slave families are so important. The significance of this evidence, however, should not be misinterpreted. The immediate family and the enlarged kin group were among the central binding institutions within developing slave communities. In themselves, however, these familial linkages do not explain either the full range of slave beliefs and behavior or their origins. Instead, the presence of these linkages makes it possible to re-examine the development of and changes in slave beliefs and behavior over time.

A cluster of slave beliefs—many of which await study—was sustained by these linkages and defined individual slaves with whom owners dealt. In other words, the *context* which shaped slave behavior was far more subtle than the setting emphasized by those whose primary concern remains the treatment of slaves. Talcott Parsons describes "institutions" as "normative patterns which define what are felt to be . . . proper, legitimate, or expected modes of action or of social relationship." Such norms pervade all areas of social life, and individual behavior usually reflects the presence of some accepted standards of behavior learned from others and shared with others. It is inconceivable that the beliefs and behavior of slaves living on such different places as the Good Hope, Cedar Vale, and Stirling plantations could have existed in the absence of what Stanley M. Elkins describes as "alternative social bases." Their presence, however fragile their structure, is the reason why "treatment" is an inadequate explanation of slave behavior and why the mimetic theories of Afro-American culture that dominated much of the mid-twentieth-century conceptualization of the Afro-American historical experience (and which shaped the influential writings of such able scholars as E. Franklin Frazier and Gunnar Myrdal) are erroneous. The "force of circumstance," Frazier believed, caused the slaves to "take over, however imperfectly, the folkways of the American environment," finding "within the patterns of the white man's culture a purpose in life." Myrdal made a similar point, insisting that "American Negro culture is not something independent of general American culture. It is a distorted development, or a pathological condition, of the general American culture."

Slaves always were affected by the decisions of their owners, and the developing Afro-American culture included beliefs and practices derived from "the folkways of the American environment." But the slave behavior revealed in this study shows the inadequacy of such a conceptual framework and is strong evidence supporting the appropriateness of a bicultural model for studying all aspects of slave and ex-slave belief and behavior over time. That "model," as the anthropologist Charles A. Valentine points out, makes it possible to put aside the "deficit model" that shaped the works of Frazier and Myrdal as well as the oversimplified "difference model," with its "implicit assumption that different culture systems are necessarily competitive alternatives, that distinct culture systems can enter human experience only as mutually exclusive alternatives, never as intertwined and simultaneously available repertoires." Biculturation "helps explain how people learn and practice both mainstream culture and ethnic culture at the same time. Much intragroup socialization is conditioned by ethnically distinct experiences . . . but at the same time members of all subgroups are thoroughly enculturated in the dominant culture patterns by mainstream institutions." What Valentine describes as "ethnic cultural socialization" occurs mostly "within family units and primary groups, with much mainstream enculturation coming from wider sources." Viewed in this perspective, the slave bicultural experience was never a static one. It differed in 1740 from what it became in 1790, 1820, and 1860. But it was shaped over time by the development of expanded slave kin and quasi-kin networks and by the presence of intra- and intergenerational slave family linkages.

What a slave child learned always depended upon how that child was taught and who taught that child. A bicultural analysis of slave socialization together with an awareness of the relationship between the slave family and the enlarged slave kin group allows us to view the slave family as far more than an owner-sponsored device to reproduce the labor force and to maintain "social control," a view emphasized in the writings of John Blassingame, Robert Fogel and Stanley Engerman, and Eugene D. Genovese. That emphasis focuses primarily on its utility in disciplining the slave husband and father, a far too narrow perspective. If owners encouraged family formation for that reason (and many did), such decisions had profound, if unanticipated, social and cultural consequences among the slaves and their children. Intergenerational family linkages developed. Passageways for a developing slave culture shaped the interior fabric of developing slave communities, and also served to socialize the slave child. "If a master wished to keep his plantation going," Genovese observes, "he had to learn the limits of his slaves' endurance." How slaves defined those limits resulted primarily from what they had learned as children and young adults from parents, other kin, and older non-kin. Slave-rearing—essential to the economic welfare of most slaveowners—therefore posed a contradiction for all slaveowners. The plantation pyramid developed at its base significant slave familial and kin networks that shaped slave behavior over more than one generation. If most plantation owners found it cheaper to rear than to purchase slaves and more efficient and orderly to permit such rearing to occur in settled slave families, such decisions reinforced the essential slave bicultural experience and became the social basis for developing alternative and sometimes even oppositional forces within slave society.

Two examples illustrate the interplay between family, kinship, and slave belief and behavior. Patience was purchased as a four-year-old in 1828 by the North Carolina Pettigrews and thereby separated from her family of origin. By that time, slaves on the two Pettigrew plantations had developed families and kin networks similar to those on the other plantations studied. The young girl joined a slave community increasingly bound together by expanding affinal and consanguinal ties. She matured within that community, absorbing beliefs about correct behavior from long-time Pettigrew slaves. When a seventeen-year-old, Patience had a child by Dick Buck. She married him two years later, and they lived in a conventional slave family, becoming the parents, in all, of seven children. Dick Buck's sixty-four-year-old father, William, died in 1844, and Patience and Dick named their first son for him. (Dick Buck's brother Glasgow married Amy, and they named a daughter for Dick Buck and Glasgow's mother Abagail. Amy's husband, Demps, had been named for his father.) Theirs was conventional slave behavior. But that is no reason to assume that such familial and kin behavior integrated Patience and Dick Buck efficiently into their owner's code of proper plantation behavior. In 1857, Patience (and quite possibly her twelve-year-old son William) was one of five slaves who made false keys, robbed their owner of $160 in gold and silver, and ran away. Captured, they were flogged and locked up for a time. The next year, Dick Buck was caught carrying flour at night, beaten by a slave patrol, later whipped by the black overseer Moses, and finally put into the Pettigrew "penitentiary." The same year that Patience and the others robbed their owner, the planter David Gavin complained bitterly after the slave team returned: "[H]e is a mean fellow. I bought him to keep him with his wife and this is the 2d or 3d time he has run away, and lost nearly a years work, I cannot afford to keep him at this rate, he will spoil the rest of my people by his bad example, besides the loss I sustain."

Unproductive slave "habits" rooted in generational family ties also revealed themselves in other ways. The cost efficiencies that came from rearing a labor force in families made for later costly inefficiencies. That was learned by the Louisiana cotton planter Bennet H. Barrow. "What is essentially necessary for his happiness," Barrow said of the slave, "you must provide for him Yourself and by that means create in him a habit of perfect dependence on you—Allow it ounce to be understood by a negro that he is to provide for himself, and you that moment give him an undeniable claim on you for a portion of his time to make for this provision." "Get your negroes ounce disciplined and planting is a pleasure," he wrote in his diary. "A H[ell] without it." A serious obstacle to that discipline, Barrow's records reveal, was what younger slaves learned from older slaves. "Social control" on his and other plantations meant much more than manipulating or satisfying the familial sensibilities of adult male slaves. It also concerned the relations between slave parents and their children, between slave generations. The median age of cotton pickers whipped by Barrow in 1840–1841 was about twenty-three. Most were whipped for inefficient labor. Their age indicates that these men and women had grandparents born in the 1760s and greatgrandparents who may have been Africans. Barrow also complained in his diary: ". . . there never was a more rascally set of old negroes about any lot than this. Big Lucy Anica Center & cook Jane, the better you treat them the worse they are, Big Lucy the leader, corrupts every young negro in her power. . . . " The older slaves embittered Barrow, and he regularly whipped the younger slaves. Slaves born in the late eighteenth or early nineteenth century had "improperly" socialized slaves born a generation or two later. Far too many young slaves listened to Big Lucy, and her message was not one that Barrow wanted them to hear. Rearing slaves had some advantages for owners but also resulted in important costs. Big Lucy was not a slave driver. She was a slave "aunt" and grandmother.

Frederick Olmsted shared many of the biases of so many mid-nineteenth-century northern and southern white observers of the slaves. Nevertheless his were among the most astute comments of that time. "I begin to suspect," Olmsted concluded, "that the great trouble and anxiety of Southern gentlemen is—How, without quite destroying the capabilities of the negro for any work at all, to prevent him from learning to take care of himself." On the eve of their emancipation, most slaves learned how to "take care" of themselves from kin and quasi-kin.

The World of Free Blacks

IRA BERLIN

The American Revolution swelled the ranks of the tiny Southern free Negro population. Few whites desired to enlarge the number of black freemen; even those who opposed slavery and hoped for its eventual abolition could not conceive of living with blacks who were free. But the events of the Revolutionary era moved in directions few could predict and none could control. If whites tried to seal the cracks in the door to freedom, blacks pushed all the harder. In the years following the Revolution, the number of free Negroes increased manyfold, so that by the end of the first decade of the nineteenth century there were over 100,000 free Negroes in the Southern states and they composed almost 5 percent of the free population and nearly 9 percent of the black population. The free Negro caste had grown from a fragment of the colonial population to a sizable minority throughout the South.

The War of Independence propelled large numbers of blacks from slavery to freedom. The desperate need for troops and laborers forced both belligerents to muster blacks into their service with the promise of liberty. Given the chance, most blacks gladly traded the chains of bondage for military service and eventual freedom. . . .

The spectacular increase in manumissions and runaways and the influx of West Indian people of color altered the size and character of the Southern free Negro caste. The change can best be viewed in Maryland. Between 1755 and 1790 the free Negro population of Maryland grew over 300 percent to about 8,000, and in the following ten years it more than doubled. By 1810, almost one-quarter of Maryland's Negroes were free, and they numbered nearly 34,000; this was the largest free Negro population of any state in the nation.

Free Negroes registered similar gains throughout the Upper South. In 1782, the year Virginia legalized private manumission, St. George Tucker estimated the number of Virginia free Negroes to be about 2,000. By 1790, when the first federal census was taken, the number of Virginia free Negroes had grown to 12,000. Ten years later, the caste numbered 20,000 and by 1810 it stood at over 30,000. During the twenty years between 1790 and 1810, the free Negro population of Virginia more than doubled. In all, the number of Negro freemen in the Upper South grew almost 90 percent between 1790 and 1800 and another 65 percent in the following decade, so

From *Slaves Without Masters: The Free Negro in the Antebellum South* by Ira Berlin. Reprinted by permission of Pantheon Books, a division of Random House, Inc.

that freemen composed more than 10 percent of the region's Negro population.

In Georgia and South Carolina, which sternly refused to enlist blacks in the Revolutionary cause and stifled the development of antislavery sentiment, considerably fewer masters freed their slaves and fewer fugitives found freedom. But the arrival of light-skinned refugees from Saint-Domingue expanded the free Negro population in the Lower South well beyond the bounds of natural increase. Georgia's tiny free Negro population of 400 in 1790, probably all but nonexistent before the Revolution, totaled 1,800 in 1810, a gain of well over 300 percent. Likewise, the number of Negro freemen in South Carolina more than doubled during those twenty years to total over 4,500. Nevertheless, these states lagged far behind the Upper South. In 1800, free Negroes from Georgia and South Carolina composed a mere 7 percent of the Southern free Negro population. Even after the purchase of Louisiana with its large free Negro caste, only 13 percent of Southern free Negroes resided in the Lower South. Moreover, while the free Negro population of the Upper South grew darker through indiscriminate manumission and the addition of many black fugitives, that of the Lower South remained light-skinned. A crack, which would widen during the antebellum years, appeared in the ranks of the growing free Negro caste.

By 1810, the 108,000 free Negroes were the fastest-growing element in the Southern population. Although the number of Southern whites and slaves also increased rapidly during the early years of the Republic, the growth of the free Negro population outstripped both. In Virginia, for example, the free Negro caste doubled between 1790 and 1810, while whites increased 24 percent and slaves 31 percent. In Maryland during the same period, the comparison was even more startling. Maryland free Negroes increased fourfold, while the white population grew 12 percent and the slave population a paltry 8 percent. In Delaware, the expansion of freedom undermined slavery. In 1790, the Delaware free Negro caste of about 4,000 was less than the state's slave population. Twenty years later its 13,000 free Negroes outnumbered slaves more than three to one, and Delaware slavery was permanently impaired. Even South Carolina and Georgia free Negroes multiplied more rapidly than whites and slaves in their respective states. Moreover, since the law presumed all blacks to be slaves and some free Negroes had been illegally freed if not outright fugitives, many free Negroes doubtless avoided census marshals, and the census substantially underenumerated the free Negro caste.

The increase in size also altered the character of the free Negro caste. Large-scale indiscriminate manumission and the successful escape of many black fugitives darkened the free Negro population. In the Upper South, where the manumission movement had its greatest impact, the balance between mulatto and black freemen may have been shifted to the blacks. Furthermore, since most of the runaways were young men and women, the increased number of successful fugitives infused the free Negro caste with a large group of restless youth. By the beginning of the nineteenth century, the free Negro caste was no longer the tiny group of mulattoes and cripples it had been before the Revolution. It included blacks as well as mixed-bloods, vigorous young as well as elderly former slaves. Throughout the South, the greatly enlarged caste was an important and, in some areas, an indispensable part of the labor force, an ever-present example to slaves, and a direct contradiction to the white man's racial ideal. . . .

The diverse defenses of slavery pointed to a split in Southern ranks which would grow steadily throughout the antebellum years. Yet both the necessary-evil and the positive-good arguments arose from a common fear and hatred of blacks who were free and the implicit threat free Negroes posed to slavery. Whether the Negro was culturally or innately inferior, whites would not tolerate free Negroes living among them. Once freed, Negroes degenerated into unproductive, irresponsible vagrants and quickly became a burden on the white community. To stay alive, they stole uncontrollably from plantations and became the "agents, factors, and carriers" of slave-pilfered goods. Free Negroes refused to work, maliciously destroyed property, stirred unrest among the slaves, and depreciated the value of all property. Emancipation, predicted a group of some eighty Virginians in 1782, would be "productive of Want, Poverty, Distress and Ruin to the Free Citizens; Neglect, Famine, and Death to the helpless black infants and superannuated Parents; Horrors of all the Rapes, Murders, and Outrages, which a vast Multitude of unprincipled, unpropertied, vindictive, and remorseless Banditti are capable of perpetrating . . . and lastly Ruin to this now free and flourishing Country."

In a slave society, the free Negro was an incorrigible subversive. "If blacks see all of their color slaves," observed a Virginia lawmaker, "it will seem to them a disposition of Providence, and they will be content. But if they see others like themselves free, and enjoying rights they are deprived of, they will repine." Events on Saint-Domingue magnified the fear of free Negro subversion inherited from the colonial years. Southern whites were well aware that unrest among the free people of color had triggered the revolt which eventually established the Haitian Republic, and they worried about restlessness among their own growing free black population. Already well-informed free Negroes, observed the citizens of Petersburg, were complaining, "What is liberty . . . without social intercourse?" In an age of revolutions, these remarks needed no interpretation, for "with such language among the free people of color a train was laid, a mine sprung in St. Domingo that totally annihilated the white population." The growth of African churches and the willingness of free Negroes to aid fugitive slaves pointed to a growing sense of black self-esteem which was plainly contagious. During Dunmore's rebellion [1775–1776], noted one Virginian in the aftermath of the Gabriel conspiracy [1800], blacks "sought freedom merely as a good; now they also claim it as a right."

The free Negroes' fervent attempt to shake off the habits of slavery, purchase property, build churches and schools, and establish an identity as a free people heightened white fears. Ironically, the more the free Negro became like them, the more enraged whites became. It was easy for a people who professed to love freedom to despise a slave; whites needed reasons to hate blacks who were free. The growth of the free Negro caste and the development of Afro-American culture as manifested in the independent black churches and schools forced whites to define more carefully than ever the differences between free and slave, white and black. It was no accident that an articulate defense of slavery appeared with the emergence of the free Negro caste. . . .

The peculiar pattern of growth resulting from manumissions, successful escapes, and natural increase, from kidnapping and passing, and from in- and outmigration gave the free Negro caste a unique demographic profile [in the period 1820–1860]. Unlike whites or slaves, free Negroes shunned the rich agricultural interior and lived on the periphery of the South. Wherever the plantation culture held sway, few free Negroes could be found.

The cities that ringed the South were centers of free Negro population. The propensity of urban masters to free their slaves, the ability of fugitives to find freedom within municipal limits, the steady influx of rural free Negroes, and the abandonment of enfeebled bondsmen in the cities swelled the number of urban free Negroes. Although the majority of free Negroes, like the vast majority of Southern people, resided in the countryside, free Negroes were the most urban caste in the South. In 1860, better than a third of the Southern free Negro population dwelled in cities or towns, while barely 15 percent of the whites and about 5 percent of the slaves lived in urban centers. Free Negroes were more than twice as urban as whites and seven times as urban as slaves. Urban freemen also tended to congregate in the larger cities for the same reasons they preferred urban to rural life. More than two-thirds of the urban free Negroes lived in cities of ten thousand or more.

Negro freemen were also generally older than slaves or whites. Delays in manumission and the difficulties of self-purchase or escape meant that many blacks did not achieve their liberty until maturity. This, combined with the dumping of elderly slaves and the comparatively low rate of natural increase among free Negroes, resulted in an older free Negro population. In 1860, about 28 percent of the free Negro caste was under ten years of age, while slave and white children of the same age composed over 30 percent of their respective populations. On the other hand, better than 20 percent of the free Negroes were over forty years old, while about 15 percent of the slaves and whites had reached that age. Compared with whites and other blacks, there were fewer free Negro youngsters and many more old folks. The free Negro caste was a top-heavy group.

In contrast to the white and slave populations, there were many more free Negro women than men in the South. The great preponderance of free Negro women was confined almost entirely to the cities. There the combined effects of manumission and migratory patterns played havoc with the sexual balance. Urban emancipators tended to bestow favors on women, partly because slave women outnumbered slave men in the cities and partly because close intermingling encouraged sexual liaisons which sometimes led to manumission. While emancipated women increased the urban free Negro

population, the greater mobility of free Negro men allowed a disproportionate number of them to leave the South. Although the slaveholding states
had an excess of free Negro women, the Northern border states had a
surplus of free Negro men. But the sexual imbalance generally stopped at
the city line. In most settled rural areas, the number of free Negro men
and women was roughly the same. On the frontier, where free Negro men,
like white men, pioneered alone and later brought their families, the sexual
balance usually favored men.

As a general rule, freemen were lighter in color than slaves. Although
some of the fairest free Negroes passed out of the caste, the manumission
of the children of slaveholders and other privileged bondsmen and the free
status accorded the offspring of white and Indian women by black men
made free Negroes a disproportionately mulatto caste. In 1860 fully 40
percent of the Southern free Negro population were classified as mulattoes,
while only one slave in ten had some white ancestry. Urban free Negroes,
as usual, were an exception to the rule. The intermingling of whites and
blacks in Southern cities produced a free Negro population that was generally lighter that that of the countryside. But throughout the South, a light
skin was the freeman's distinguishing characteristic.

The tawny color of many free Negroes suggests other characteristics
which distinguished Negro freemen from the mass of slaves. The slaveholder's increasingly selective liberation of favored bondsmen and the difficulties slaves had running away or purchasing their liberty meant that free
Negroes were generally more skilled, literate, and well connected with
whites than the mass of slaves. Even before they were emancipated, most
free Negroes had enjoyed a privileged position within the slave hierarchy.

The distinctions between whites and slaves and free Negroes hid the
major cleavage within the Southern free Negro caste. The great mass of
Negro freemen lived in the tidewater of the Upper South between Delaware
and North Carolina, where the post-Revolutionary manumission movement
had flourished. Better than half the free Negroes in the South resided in
Delaware, Maryland, and Virginia. To the south and the west, the free
Negro population thinned. Proportional to total population, Maryland had
more free Negroes than Virginia, Virginia than North Carolina or Kentucky,
Kentucky than Tennessee or Missouri. By 1860, more than 85 percent of
the Southern free Negro caste resided in the Upper South.

A second but considerably smaller group of free Negroes lived in the
Lower South. As in the Upper South, the greatest proportion of free Negroes dwelled on the periphery in the port cities that stretched from Charleston on the Atlantic to New Orleans on the Gulf of Mexico and up the
Mississippi River past Natchez to Memphis. The older states of the Lower
South had resisted the post-Revolutionary manumission movement, and the
newer states had either been unsettled or under foreign domination during
the Revolutionary era. From the first, the free Negro population of the
Lower South was largely the product of illicit sexual relations between
black slave women and white men which led directly to manumission or

to privileged positions from which elite slaves could buy their way out of bondage.

The distinctly different origins of free Negroes in the Upper and Lower South were reflected in other characteristics as well. The free Negro population of the Lower South was much lighter than that of the Upper South. While the post-Revolutionary manumission movement and the continued decline of slavery in the border states encouraged slaveholders to emancipate black as well as mulatto slaves, miscegenation and selective emancipation produced a light-skinned population in the Lower South. The influx of brown émigrés from Saint-Domingue and elsewhere in the West Indies into the ports of the Lower South further widened the somatic gap between Lower and Upper South free Negroes. Ideological emancipation waned in the Upper South during the nineteenth century, and emancipators (except in the border states) adopted the pattern of manumission that had always been present in the Lower South. But a large free black—as opposed to mulatto—population had already established itself, and the comparatively small increment of mixed-bloods lightened the free Negro caste of the Upper South but did not alter its black majority. On the eve of the Civil War, mixed-bloods composed only a third of the free Negro population in the Upper South, while fully three-quarters of Lower South free Negroes had some white ancestry. In some of the port cities of the Lower South, mulattoes made up nearly 90 percent of the free Negro caste. Whites, recognizing the distinction between these light-skinned freemen and those of a darker hue, designated them "free people of color," a term used frequently in the Lower South but rarely in the Upper South.

The free people of color of the Lower South were also more urban than those of the Upper South. Ideologically inspired manumission by the Revolutionary generation had created a large free black peasantry throughout the Upper South, and most stayed in the countryside. In 1860, barely a third of Upper South free Negroes lived in cities. Even Baltimore, which had the largest urban black population in the nation, contained less than a third of Maryland's free Negro population. On the other hand, better than half the free Negroes in the Lower South resided in urban areas.

Free Negroes were an even more anomalous group than their name suggests. Drawn from the slave elite, they were generally older and more urban than whites or slaves. A largely mulatto caste with ties of blood and kinship with black and white, they were clearly distinct from both. But the characteristics that distinguished free Negroes from whites and slaves were magnified in the free people of color of the Lower South. As a general rule, Lower South free Negroes were not only more urban and light-skinned, but better educated, more skilled, and more closely connected with whites than those of the Upper South. The South, in short, spawned two distinct groups of free Negroes. Their differences as well as their similarities reflected and influenced white racial attitudes. Those attitudes determined, in large measure, the free Negro's place in Southern society. The South was, after all, a white man's country. . . .

In the white mind, the free Negro was considerably more dangerous than the slave. Although free Negroes, with the exception of Denmark Vesey [a free black who headed an extensive conspiracy in Charleston in 1822], rarely had anything to do with slave insurrections, whites uniformly identified them as the most rebellious. Following the Nat Turner rebellion of 1831, whites directed their frenzied outrage not so much against slaves as against free Negroes. In Southside Virginia, near the scene of the rebellion, white mobs roamed the countryside, assaulting free Negroes and forcing them to take refuge in the woods for months after. Townspeople in Raleigh, North Carolina, fearing that the rebellion would spread, clapped every free Negro into jail. Perhaps that was for the best, for in a nearby county a gang of white toughs kicked down the door to one free Negro's home and murdered the entire family. Officials captured one of the killers, but there seemed little chance that he would be brought to justice. "The mere imprisonment of this man has already aroused considerable excitement among the nonslaveholding population," observed a local white. These assaults were more than outrages by poor whites. From all over Virginia and Maryland poured demands for the physical removal of free Negroes. In isolated Northampton County on the Eastern Shore of Virginia, leading citizens met and decided it was "absolutely necessary" to rid the county of Negro freemen. They agreed not to employ free Negroes or rent them land or houses, and eventually borrowed $15,000 from the state to facilitate deportation. Yet only a handful of free Negroes were implicated in the Nat Turner rebellion, and after the postinsurrection hysteria subsided, most of the free Negroes arrested in Southampton County were quietly released.

As far as free Negroes were concerned, Southampton was no isolated incident. Whenever the South felt threatened, free Negroes suffered hard times. The success of Toussaint L'Ouverture, the Missouri Crisis, the Vesey conspiracy, the advent of Garrisonian abolition, all stimulated assaults on the free Negroes' liberty and often their persons. In part, free Negroes simply provided the handiest scapegoats. It made no sense to cripple valuable slave property or to limit the liberty of those who had none. The slaves' position, which sheltered them from white vigilantism, seemed to intensify the abuse heaped on the free Negroes. Their presence reminded a people who professed, above all, to value liberty and despise tyranny that they themselves were tyrants. And it told them that the Negro— however fawning and servile in appearance—would ever be a foe. The free Negro, in short, personified the dangers and guilt inherent in owning slaves.

Given these beliefs, whites did not need to degrade free Negroes on the scale of being to deprive them of their rights. Characteristically, the 1834 Tennessee and the 1835 North Carolina constitutional conventions disfranchised the free Negro without discussing the nature of the Negro at all. Questions of *"policy and expediency,"* as one Tennessee delegate emphasized, provided reason enough to take away the freemen's suffrage in states where property-holding free Negroes had long voted according to the same requirements as whites. When the opponents of Negro disfranchisement suggested that suffrage was the natural right of all free men, restrictionists did not feel compelled to counter, as many later would, that Negroes were not men. They denied free Negroes the right to vote for the same reason they barred women from the polls: it contradicted the "manners and habits" of the country. Circumstances and beliefs, not divine strictures or natural law, made disfranchisement necessary.

⅄ *F U R T H E R   R E A D I N G*

Herbert Aptheker, *American Negro Slave Revolts* (1943)

Ira Berlin, *Slaves Without Masters* (1974)

John W. Blassingame, *The Slave Community* (1972)

John B. Boles, ed., *Masters and Slaves in the House of the Lord: Race and Religion in the American South, 1740–1870* (1988)

Judith Wragg Chase, *Afro-American Art and Craft* (1971)

Dena J. Epstein, *Sinful Tunes and Spirituals* (1977)

Paul D. Escott, *Slavery Remembered: A Record of Twentieth-Century Slave Narratives* (1979)

Eric Foner, ed., *Nat Turner* (1971)

John Hope Franklin, *The Free Negro in North Carolina, 1790–1860* (1943)

Eugene D. Genovese, *Roll, Jordan, Roll* (1974)

Herbert Gutman, *The Black Family in Slavery and in Freedom, 1750–1925* (1976)

Vincent Harding, *There Is a River* (1981)

Luther P. Jackson, *Free Negro Labor and Property Holding in Virginia, 1830–1860* (1942)

Michael P. Johnson and James L. Roark, *Black Masters* (1984)

Charles Joyner, *Down by the Riverside* (1984)

Lawrence W. Levine, *Black Culture and Black Consciousness* (1977)

Ronald L. Lewis, *Coal, Iron, and Slaves* (1970)

Stephen B. Oates, *The Fires of Jubilee* (1975)

Leslie Howard Owens, *This Species of Property* (1976)

Albert J. Raboteau, *Slave Religion* (1978)

George P. Rawick, *From Sundown to Sunup: The Making of the Black Community* (1972)

Todd L. Savitt, *Medicine and Slavery: The Health Care of Blacks in Antebellum Virginia* (1978)

Kenneth M. Stampp, *The Peculiar Institution* (1956)

Robert S. Starobin, *Denmark Vesey* (1970)

———, *Industrial Slavery in the Old South* (1970)

Sterling Stuckey, *Slave Culture* (1987)

The Nonslaveholding Whites

⋏

Although wealthy planters and black slaves figure most prominently in popular images of the South, nonslaveholding whites formed a larger group than either. In terms of numbers, they might be considered the "typical" southerners in the antebellum period. Their experiences as small farmers were familiar to almost all free families at some point in the agrarian South. Accordingly, historians are endeavoring to learn more about this large and important group, despite the comparative lack of surviving letters, diaries, wills, and other manuscript sources from these southerners.

More than a generation ago, the late historian Frank Lawrence Owsley called attention to the "plain folk" and pointed out that most of them were landowning agriculturalists, often called yeoman farmers. Following his lead, other scholars are trying to discover more about their values, attitudes, way of life, and relationship to both slaves and slaveowning whites. What goals and values were important to the southern yeomen? How did they view their place in society and the racial and class systems of which they were a part? Were they subject to the planter class's hegemony or dominance? Or did they hold separate, distinctive views on the southern social system?

⋏ D O C U M E N T S

In 1860, southern writer D. R. Hundley described the yeomen and their attitudes in a passage from his book, *Social Relations in Our Southern States*. This passage appears as the first document. In the 1940s, Frank L. Owsley demonstrated that the records of the U.S. Census Bureau are a vital source of information for historians on the nonslaveholding yeoman farmers. The page from an 1850 manuscript schedule, reproduced as the second document, shows some of the information that can be gathered about the yeomen and suggests some of the difficulties researchers face in using census data. Ferdinand L. Steel was one southern yeoman whose diary has survived. The entries contained in the third document describe his daily routine as a small farmer in Mississippi in the 1830s and 1840s. He worked the land with the help of his brother Samuel and was deeply religious. The minutes of North Carolina's Mount Zion Baptist Church, which appear in the fourth selection, illustrate the importance of churches to the community life of small farmers, white and black. The Mount Zion congregation adjudicated disputes among its members, punished wrongdoers by excluding them from the church's fellowship, and received blacks into its membership. Although some southern writers discounted the likelihood of collisions between slaveholders and nonslaveholders, the work of Hinton Rowan Helper, excerpted in the fifth selection, demonstrates the real possibility of overt class conflict. Documents revealing the nonslaveholders' attitudes toward slavery are of interest to historians. In the last selection, artisans and mechanics of Wake County, North Carolina (the county surrounding the state capital, Raleigh), speak for themselves, protesting the low rates of taxation on slave property.

D. R. Hundley Describes Nonslaveholders, 1860

Of all the hardy sons of toil, in all free lands the Yeomen are most deserving of our esteem. With hearts of oak and thews of steel, crouching to no man and fearing no danger, these are equally bold to handle a musket on the field of battle or to swing their reapers in times of peace among the waving stalks of yellow grain. For, in the language of the poet:

———Each boasts his hearth
And field as free as the best lord his barony,
Owing subjection to no human vassalage
Save to their king and law. Hence are they resolute,
Leading the van on every day of battle,
As men who know the blessings they defend.
Hence are they frank and generous in peace,
As men who have their portion in its plenty.

But you have no Yeomen in the South, my dear Sir? Beg your pardon, our dear Sir, but we have—hosts of them. *I thought you had only poor White Trash?* Yes, we dare say as much—and that the moon is made of green cheese! You have fully as much right or reason to think the one thing as the other. *Do tell, now; want to know?* Is that so, our good friend? do you really desire to learn the truth about this matter? If so, to the extent of our poor ability, we shall endeavor to enlighten you upon a subject, which not one Yankee in ten thousand in the least understands.

Know, then, that the Poor Whites of the South constitute a separate class to themselves; the Southern Yeomen are as distinct from them as the Southern Gentleman is from the Cotton Snob. Certainly the Southern Yeomen are nearly always poor, at least so far as this world's goods are to be taken into the account. As a general thing they own no slaves; and even in case they do, the wealthiest of them rarely possess more than from ten to fifteen. But even when they are slaveholders, they seem to exercise but few of the rights of ownership over their human chattels, making so little distinction between master and man, that their negroes invariably become spoiled, like so many rude children who have been unwisely spared the rod by their foolish guardians. . . .

In his origin, aside from the German settlers in Western Virginia, the Southern Yeoman is almost purely English. He nearly always bears some good old Anglo-Saxon name, and will tell you, if interrogated about his ancestors, that "grandfather so and so came over from the Old Country"— by which familiar and endearing phrase he always designates Great Britain. He is thorough English in fact, in both physical heartiness and dogged perseverance. Very seldom is he troubled with dyspepsia, or melancholy, or discontent with his humble lot—evils which in most cases have their origin in a disordered stomach. Just so rarely, too, will you ever meet a Southern Yeoman who has learned to fear mortal man, or who would under any circumstances humiliate himself to curry favor with the rich or those in authority. He always possesses a manly independence of character, and though not so impetuous as the gentry of the South usually are, still, in the midst of the dangers and carnage of the battlefield, and in the thickest of the fray, his eye never quails; but with steady tramp and unflinching nerve he marches right on to where duty and honor call, and with un-blanched cheek meets death face to face. His wounds, like the scars of the old Roman, themselves bespeak his praise, for they are ever received from the front and never from behind.

The usual weapon of the Southern Yeoman is the deadly rifle—even in his sports—and this he handles with such skill as few possess, even in America. He likes the quick sharp report which announces in a clear tongue when the leaden messenger is *sent home;* and affects to despise the rattling fowling piece, the peculiar sporting gun of the Southern Gentleman. With his rifle the Yeoman shoots squirrels, ducks, turkeys, deer, bear, buffalo, and whatever else he pleases. The best riflemen are found in Georgia, Mississippi, Tennessee, and Kentucky—*the* best, perhaps, in the last-named brave and chivalrous Commonwealth. Herein turkey-shooting is practised by all classes, but chiefly by the yeomen. A live turkey is securely fastened to a stake at the distance of one hundred paces, and you pay five or ten cents for the privilege of each shot; if you hit the fowl in the head the carcass is yours, but any other *hit* is considered *foul,* and so passes for nothing. This is the kind of school in which were trained the hunting-shirt heroes of King's Mountain, and those unerring riflemen who, at the memorable battle of New-Orleans, made such havoc in the ranks of Pack-enham's veterans. So also were trained those brave defenders of Texan independence—Crockett, Travis, and their compeers, who buried them-selves beneath the countless heaps of Mexicans slain at the heroic defense of the Alamo. And it was because of a similar schooling that Col. Jeff. Davis was enabled to say to the retreating Indianians at the battle of Buena Vista, pointing proudly to the gallant yeomanry of Mississippi: "Stay, and re-form behind that wall!" For well the brave Colonel knew the rifles in the hands of his favorite regiment would soon with their iron hail beat down the advancing foe, and cause them to rush back in disorderly rout to their tents and entrenchments. Indeed, take them all in all, and we doubt if the world can produce a more reliable citizen soldiery than the yeomanry of our Southern States. They only require the right sort of leaders—officers under whom they are willing to fight, and in whose mettle and abilities they have perfect confidence. General Taylor was such a man, and in this regard no American General of late years has been his peer. Southern born himself, and Southern bred, plain and unostentatious in his manners, and at all times cool and determined in the hour of danger; his soldiers loved the *man*, while they respected and trusted the *general*. Noble old Soldier! no true heart can fail to regret, that the exigencies of politics forced you to lay aside the sword for our republican sceptre, and thus with the weighty cares and perplexities of a station which you never were fitted to adorn, too soon consigned you to the grave and deprived the Union of one of her most able and patriotic defenders. Green be the turf above you, honest Roman, and may your successors in office learn to emulate your virtues!

The Southern Yeoman much resembles in his speech, religious opinions, household arrangements, indoor sports, and family traditions, the middle class farmers of the Northern States. He is fully as intelligent as the latter, and is on the whole much better versed in the lore of politics and the provisions of our Federal and State Constitutions. This is chiefly owing to the public barbecues, court-house-day gatherings, and other holiday occasions, which are more numerous in the South than in the North, and in the former are nearly always devoted in part to political discussions of one kind or another. Heard from the lips of their neighbors and friends, and having the matter impressed upon their minds by the presentation of both sides of every disputed question at the same time, it is not strange that poor men in the South should possess a more comprehensive knowledge of the fundamental principles of our artificial and complex system of government, or should retain a clearer perception of the respective merits of every leading political issue, than if they derived their information solely from books or newspapers; which always furnish but one view of the matter in dispute, and which they must painfully peruse after a long day of toil, being more exercised meanwhile (aside from the drawback of physical weariness) in laboring to interpret the meaning of the "dictionary words," than in attempting to follow the facts or the argument of the writer, be he never so lucid and perspicuous. . . .

Besides being given to hospitality, although in a very primitive way, . . . the Yeomen of the South are also quite social and gregarious in their instincts, and delight much in having all kinds of frolics and family gatherings during the long winter evenings. On all such occasions, nearly, something serviceable is the ostensible cause of their assembling, though the time is devoted almost wholly to social pleasures: sometimes, 'tis true, there is a wedding, or a birth-day party, or a candy-pulling; but much more frequently it is a corn-husking, or the everlasting quilting—this last being the most frequent and most in favor of all the merrymakings which call the young people together. There is, indeed, nothing to compare to a country quilting for the simple and unaffected happiness which it affords all parties. The old women and old men sit demurely beside the blazing kitchen fire, and frighten one another with long-winded ghost stories; thus leaving the young folks all to themselves in the "big room," wherein is also the quilt-frame, which is either suspended at the corners by ropes attached to the ceiling, or else rests on the tops of four chairs. Around this assemble the young men and the young maidens, robust with honest toil and honestly ruby-cheeked with genuine good health. The former know nothing of your *dolce far niente* or dyspepsia, and the latter are not troubled with crinoline or consumption, but all are merry as larks and happy as it is possible for men and women to be in this lower world. No debts, nor duns, nor panics, nor poverty, nor wealth disturbs their thoughts or mars the joyousness of the hour. Serene as a summer's day, and cloudless as the skies in June, the moments hurry by, as they ply their nimble needles and sing their simple songs, or whisper their tales of love, heedless of the great world and all the thoughtless worldlings who live only to win the smiles of "our best society." Meanwhile the children play hide and seek, in-doors and out, whooping, laughing, and chattering like so many magpies; and, in the snug chimney-corner, Old Bose, the faithful watch-dog, stretches himself out to his full length and dozes comfortably in the genial warmth of the fire, in his dreams chasing after imaginary hares, or baying the moon; while, as the poet sings:

> Around in sympathetic mirth
> Its tricks the kitten tries;
> The cricket chirrups in the hearth,
> The crackling fagot flies.

In their religious convictions and practices, the Southern Yeomen very much resemble the Middle Classes; are prone to shout at camp-meetings, and to see visions and dream dreams. Although generally moral in their conduct and punctilious in all religious observances, they do yet often entertain many very absurd ideas in regard to Christianity, ideas wholly at variance with any rational interpretation of the Sacred Scriptures; and hence they are led not infrequently, to mistake animal excitement for holy ecstasy, and seem to think, indeed, with the old-time priests of Baal, that God is not to be entreated save with *loud* prayers, and much beating of the breasts, and clapping of the hands, accompanied with audible groans and sighs. For all which, however, their officiating clergy are more to blame than themselves; for they are often ignorant men of the Whang Doodle description, illiterate and dogmatic, and blessed with a nasal twang which would do no discredit to New-England. . . .

As to the Vital Question of the Day, to make use of the cant phrase so greatly in vogue at the present writing, although not as a class pecuniarily interested in slave property, the Southern Yeomanry are almost unanimously pro-slavery in sentiment. Nor do we see how any honest, thoughtful person can reasonably find fault with them on this account. Only consider their circumstances, negrophilist of the North, and answer truthfully; were you so situated would you dare to advocate emancipation? Were you situated as the Southern Yeomen are—humble in worldly position, patient delvers in the soil, daily earning your bread by the toilsome sweat of your own brows—would you be pleased to see four millions of inferior blacks suddenly raised from a position of vassalage, and placed upon an equality with yourselves? made the sharers of your toil, the equals and associates of your wives and children? You know you would not. Despite your maudlin affectation of sympathy in behalf of the Negro, you are yet inwardly conscious that you heartily despise the sooty African, and that you deny to even the few living in your own midst an equality of rights and immunities with yourselves. You well know that you entertain a natural repugnance to coming in contact with Sambo—a repugnance so great that you slam your church doors in his face, shut him out of the theatres, refuse him a seat in your public conveyances, and, so fearful are you of the contamination of a black man's presence any where, in nine tenths of your States drive him away from the ballot-box, thus making your statute-books even belie your professions of philanthropy. And yet you seek to turn loose upon your white brethren of the South *four millions of these same despised Africans,* congratulating yourselves meanwhile that you would be doing a most disinterested act of benevolence! Shame on your consistency, gentlemen. Judged by your own acts, were you situated as the Southern people are to-day, stronger pro-slavery men than yourselves would not be found in the world. Hence we ask you again, did you occupy the position of the Southern Yeomanry in particular, is there a man in your midst who would favor emancipation? You know there is not. By the love you owe your race—by all the sacred ties of family and home—by every instinct of a superior nature—you would be restrained from perpetrating so iniquitous an act; an act which would sweep away in one overwhelming flood of anarchy and barbarism every trace of civilization, as well as every semblance of law and order. And do you suppose the Yeomen of our Southern States are not rational and reflecting beings like yourselves? Although not so learned as some others, they yet possess the hearts of men, of fathers and husbands, and they know as well as any political economist of you all, that their own class, in the event of emancipation, would suffer the most of all classes in the South, unless we except the negroes themselves. For the Southern Gentleman would soon convert his property into cash, as did the wealthier planters of Jamaica, and immediately retire to some more congenial soil to enjoy his *otium cum dignitate.* So, too, the thrifty Middle Classes would retire to the present Free States, and begin business in a different line; but the Yeomen would be forced to remain and single-handed do battle with Cuffee, who, no longer forced to labor, and resorting again to toad-eating and cannibalism for the food necessary to sustain life, would in a few years reproduce on the shores of the New World a second Africa, all except the lions and elephants, the sandy deserts, and the anacondas.

Census Record of Guilford County, North Carolina, 1850

SCHEDULE I. Free Inhabitants in *Northern Division* in the County of *Guilford* State of *North Car* enumerated by me, on the *3rd* day of *Sept* 1850. *Arch Wilson Ass't Marshal.*

1 Dwelling-houses numbered in the order of visitation.	2 Families numbered in the order of visitation.	3 The Name of every Person whose usual place of abode on the first day of June, 1850, was in this family.	4 Age.	5 Sex.	6 Color (White, black, or mulatto).	7 Profession, Occupation, or Trade of each Male Person over 15 years of Age.	8 Value of Real Estate Owned.	9 Place of Birth Naming the State, Territory, or Country.	10 Married within the year.	11 Attended School within the year.	12 Persons over 20 y'rs of age who cannot read & write.	13 Whether deaf and dumb, blind, insane, idiotic, pauper, or convict.
728	728	Thomas McMichal	34	M		Blacksmith	100	Guilford NC				
		Margaret McMichal	22	F				do* NC				
		James M McMichal	8	M				do NC				
		William L McMichal	7	M				do NC		✓		
		Mary J McMichal	4	F				do NC		✓		
		Sarah McMichal	5/12	F				do NC				
		George Colman	19	M		B. Smith		do NC				
		Sarah Colman	21	F				do NC				
		Adison Smith	15	M				do NC				
729	729	Vincent P Russum	31	M		Farmer	425	Guilford NC				
		Margaret Russum	37	F				do NC				
		Morandy Russum	9	M				Rockingham NC		✓		
		Vincent E Russum	6	M				do NC				
		Wellise Abigal	3	F				do NC				
		John T Russum	1	M				Guilford NC				

No.	Dwelling	Family	Name	Age	Sex		Occupation	Value	Birthplace
16	730	730	Branch Gorden	63	M		Farmer	700	Virginia
17			Martha Gorden	24	F				Guilford NC
18			Eunice Gorden	3	F				do NC
19	731	731	Thomas Case	28	M		Farmer	300	Guilford NC
20			Armisted Ellington	21	M				do NC
21	732	732	William Donnell	27	M		Farmer	550	Guilford NC
22			Mary Donnell	25	F				Washington NC
23			Milton Ross	21	M	M	Carpenter		Guilford NC
24	733	733	James Hobbs	50	M		Farmer	300	Guilford NC
25			Anna F Hobbs	44	F				do NC
26			Alfred F Hobbs	27	M				do NC
27			Amanda C Hobbs	19	F				do NC
28			M V Hobbs	21	M		Farming		do NC
29			Olivir T Hobbs	17	M				do NC
30			William T Hobbs	14	M				do NC
31			John W Hobbs	11	M				do NC
32			Emma V. Hobbs	7	F				do NC
33			Edward Hobbs	5	M				do NC
34			Thomas Hobbs	3	M				do NC
35	734	734	Thomas S. Holt	49	M		Black Smith		Orange NC
36			Elizabeth Holt	46	F				Guilford NC
37			Letha M Holt	22	F				do NC
38			Eliza Holt	19	F				do NC
39			Henry Holt	16	M				do NC
40			Sarah Holt	7	F				do NC
41			Thomas Holt	4	M				do NC
42			James Long	16	M		Hireling		do NC

* Ditto.

345

Ferdinand L. Steel's Diary, 1838–1841

Sunday, June 3d, 1838

Went to Meeting Mr. Fitzgerald preach a fine sermon.

Monday, June 4th, 1838

We run around cotton with both ploughs.

Tuesday, June 5th, 1838

finished running around cotton and commenced to work in corn. Sam'l chopped through cotton. We have been something like a month almost exclusively [in] the cotton. And I find it has hurt our corn very much. I do not think that it is a good plan to depend so much on cotton; it takes up all our time; we can find no time scarcly to do the smallest business. I at this time think that we had better raise corn and let cotton alone. We are to[o] weak handed; we had better raise small grain and corn and let cotton alone; raise corn and keep out of debt and we will have no necessity of raising cotton. Another thing it makes us work to excess as well as do many other things to excess. Look at this by and by.

Monday, September 17, 1838

We went to work on the road; rained very hard. I got very wet. This day is my birthday; this day closes my 25th year. My life is thus prolonged. Bless the Lord, may I set out afresh this coming year to love & serve the Lord more faithfully.

Monday, September 24, 1838

I picked out 107 lbs. Cotton. Sam'l went to mill, returned and picked out some cotton.

Tuesday, September 25, 1838

I picked out 103 lbs. of Cotton. Sam'l picked out 100 lbs. Fine weather.

Wednesday, September 26, 1838

I picked out 105 lbs. of cotton; Sam'l 105.

Thursday, September 27, 1838

We picked out cotton; 106 lbs. each

Friday, September 28, 1838

We picked out cotton. S 122 lbs., F. 110.

Saturday, September 29, 1838

We gathered some corn, about 20 bushels; hauled wood. I went to Grenada & bought 2 pr. of fine shoes. One pair for Mar & the other for myself. Bought also 2 dols worth coffee, $1 worth nails.

Sunday, September 30, 1838

We had Sunday school & class meeting.

Excerpts from Ferdinand L. Steel's Diary, 1838–1841, from the Southern Historical Collection, Library of the University of North Carolina at Chapel Hill.

Friday, March 22, 1839

A few Remarks on my Present manner of life, which will do for me to look at in after days. I arise regularly at 5 o'clock in the morning. After the rest of the family have arisen we have Prayers. I then feed 2 horses and with the assitance of m[y] Brother milk 3 cows. From then to Breakfast I jenerally do some little job about the house. After breakfast I go to my regular work which is cultivating the soil, and work untill 12 o'clock at which time I come into dinner. Rest jennerally 2 hours, during which time I dine, then Pray to God and endeavor to improve my mind by some useful study. At 2 o'clock I again repair to work, and work untill sun down. I then come in, feed horses, milk Cows, and the days work is done. I sup and then I have a few hours for study. At 9 o'clock we have Prayers, and then we all retire to Rest. This is the manner in which my time is spent. My life is one of toil, but blessed be God that it is as well with me as it is. I confess with shame, that when I look ahead, I am prone to give way to anxiety. But I truly desire and humbly Pray that I may be anxious for nothing. I cannot add one cubit to my statu[r]e by taking thought. When I look back on my past life I can see great cause of Gratitude to my heavenly father. He hath hitherto helped me, and I will endeavor hearafter to trust in him.

Wednesday, July 28, 1841

It is, undoubtedly, the Dryest time of any I have ever seen, Cotton suffering greatly for the want of rain, Corn crops will be cut short, in this neighborhood. What would now be my case, if I had no other Comfort, but that which is derived from the acquisition of Temporal good? It would be a pitiful case. But blessed be God, I am enabled to believe, that he does all things Well, and although I suffer loss in temporal things; I believe my soul prospers, & grows in the love of God.

Wednesday, August 4, 1841

Our Camp Meeting Commenced, and continued until Tuesday 10th. We had a Blessed Time from the presence of the Lord. The Merciful Giver of all Good, not only blessed us spiritually, But he also Blessed us temporily. During the time, the long needed showers of Rain, were poured out on our thirsty land. A goodly number of Persons proffessed Religion, among which was one Sullivan who was reported to have been the most ungodly man in Yalobusha County. He had (contrary to the Rules of the meeting), brought two bottles of ardent Spirits. After he obtained Religion, on Some of his Companions saying, now he had got Religion [he] give them the liquor. He declared (It is said) I will never touch it again.

A Baptist Church Meets in Conference, 1859

The [Baptist] Church of Mt. Zion [in Alamance County, North Carolina] met in Conference on Saturday before the 2nd Sunday in January 1859 and the way opened for Complaints. There being a Difficulty existing betwixt

---

A Baptist Church Meets in Conference, 1859 taken from minutes of Mt. Zion Baptist Church, reprinted courtesy of North Carolina Division of Archives and History.

some of the Brethren of this church, on motion the church agreed to apoint a Committee to investigate the Difficulty, the Committee to wit Brother H. Kevitt, Brother Teague, Brother Brothers, and Brother Foster & Brother Burgess to act and make Report at next meeting at this place; the Difficulty between Semour Alred and Enoch Crutchfield about some unmarked hogs which Alred Claims as his which hogs Crutchfield also claims.

The Church of Mt. Zion met in Conference on Saturday before the 2nd Sabath in February. . . . The Committee was Call on to report and the report Rec'd. Brother Crutchfield made satisfactory acknowledgements for what he said on that occation & Brother Alred was laid under Censure of the church until next Church meeting for not Confessing that he had Charged Crutchfield wrongfully.

Committee Report   Whereas a serious difficulty exists between Brother Elder Enoch Crutchfield and Semour Alred in regard to some unmarked hogs which the said Crutchfield has in his possession, the said Alred Claiming the same, & We the Committee appointed by the Church By the Request of the parties at the last meeting to [inqu]ire into & investigate the above named Difficulty Proceeded immediately to hear the Claims and examine witnesses for each; & after mature deliberation we the committee unanimously decided that the hogs in Dispute were the property of Enoch Crutchfield and he is inocent of the Charge Confered against him by the said Alred & as the Charge against Brother Enoch Crutchfield has Bin Circulated greatly to his injury as a man & as a Cristian & more particularly a minister of the gospel

We suggest that the church Require Brother Alred to take back the charge against Elder Crutchfield and repent of the wrong done him & repair the injury as much as in his power hath & that the said Crutchfield render unto the Church all nessessary acknowledgements for any thing he has said or done inconsistant with the Christian Character.

The Church of Mt. Zion met in Conference on Saturday before the 2nd Sabath in March. . . . On motion the case of Brother Alred Continued until next church meeting. . . . On motion the church agreed to set apart a Day for the particular Benefit of the Coloured people to be on to morrow. . . . Also the same priviledge for the Coloured people to be Continued indeffinately.

The Church of Mt. Zion met in Conference on Saturday before the 2nd Sabath in April. . . . On motion the case of Brother Alred taken up & on motion at his request Continued until next Saturday at Mount Pleasant. . . .

The Church of Mount Zion met at Mount Pleasant on Saturday night before the 3d Sunday in April acording to Previous appointment and on motion the Case of Brother Alred taken up, he being absent, and after some deliberation [he] was Excluded from the fellowship of this Church, for not makeing acknowledgements that he had charged Crutchfield wrongfully, until he gives satisfaction.

The Church of Mt. Zion met in Conference on Saturday before the 2nd Sabath in May. . . . On Sunday after preaching an invitation was given to the Coloured people & Samuel a man of Colour formerly belonged to Enoch Crutchfield Came forward and was Rec'd by Experience & baptised. Also Nathan a man of Colour belonging to Robt Letha Rec'd at a former meeting was baptised as members of our body.

The Church of Mt. Zion met in Conference on Saturday before the 2nd Sunday in June. . . . On Sunday the door of the church was opened for the Reception of Colloured members and James a man of Colour belonging to Dr. B. A. Sellars came forward and Related his Experience and was Rec'd as a Candidate for Baptism to be baptised at next meeting in Course on Sunday at 2 o'clock.

The Church of Mt. Zion met in Conference on Saturday before the 2nd Sunday in July. . . . The Door of the church was opened for the Reception of Member[s] and Sam a man of Coluor Belonging to Wm Patterson Came forward and Related a very good Experience & was Rec'd as a Candidate for baptism to be baptised to morow at 9 o'clock.

Hinton Rowan Helper Attacks Slavery, 1857

The causes which have impeded the progress and prosperity of the South, which have dwindled our commerce, and other similar pursuits, into the most contemptible insignificance; sunk a large majority of our people in galling poverty and ignorance, rendered a small minority conceited and tyrannical, and driven the rest away from their homes; entailed upon us a humiliating dependence on the Free States; disgraced us in the recesses of our own souls, and brought us under reproach in the eyes of all civilized and enlightened nations—may all be traced to one common source, and there find solution in the most hateful and horrible word, that was ever incorporated into the vocabulary of human economy—*Slavery!*

Reared amidst the institution of slavery, believing it to be wrong both in principle and in practice, and having seen and felt its evil influences upon individuals, communities and states, we deem it a duty, no less than a privilege, to enter our protest against it, and to use our most strenuous efforts to overturn and abolish it! Then we are an abolitionist? Yes! not merely a freesoiler, but an abolitionist, in the fullest sense of the term. We are not only in favor of keeping slavery out of the territories, but, carrying our opposition to the institution a step further, we here unhesitatingly declare ourself in favor of its immediate and unconditional abolition, in every state in this confederacy, where it now exists! Patriotism makes us a freesoiler; state pride makes us an emancipationist; a profound sense of duty to the South makes us an abolitionist; a reasonable degree of fellow feeling for the negro, makes us a colonizationist. . . .

The first and most sacred duty of every Southerner, who has the honor and the interest of his country at heart, is to declare himself an unqualified and uncompromising abolitionist. No conditional or half-way declaration will avail; no mere threatening demonstration will succeed. With those who desire to be instrumental in bringing about the triumph of liberty over slavery, there should be neither evasion vacillation, nor equivocation. We should listen to no modifying terms or compromises that may be proposed by the proprietors of the unprofitable and ungodly institution. Nothing short of the complete abolition of slavery can save the South from falling into the vortex of utter ruin. Too long have we yielded a submissive obedience to the tyrannical domination of an inflated oligarchy; too long have we tolerated their arrogance and self-conceit; too long have we submitted to their unjust and savage exactions. Let us now wrest from them the sceptre of power, establish liberty and equal rights throughout the land, and henceforth and forever guard our legislative halls from the pollutions and usurpations of proslavery demagogues. . . .

. . . It is not so much in its moral and religious aspects that we propose to discuss the question of slavery, as in its social and political character and influences. To say nothing of the sin and the shame of slavery, we believe it is a most expensive and unprofitable institution; and if our brethren of the South will but throw aside their unfounded prejudices and preconceived opinions, and give us a fair and patient hearing, we feel confident that we can bring them to the same conclusion. Indeed, we believe we shall be enabled—not alone by our own contributions, but with the aid of incontestable facts and arguments which we shall introduce from other sources—to convince all true-hearted, candid and intelligent Southerners, who may chance to read our book, (and we hope their name may be legion) that slavery, and nothing but slavery, has retarded the progress and prosperity of our portion of the Union; depopulated and impoverished our cities by forcing the more industrious and enterprising natives of the soil to emigrate to the free states; brought our domain under a sparse and inert population by preventing foreign immigration; made us tributary to the North, and reduced us to the humiliating condition of mere provincial subjects in fact, though not in name. We believe, moreover, that every patriotic Southerner thus convinced will feel it a duty he owes to himself, to his country, and to his God, to become a thorough, inflexible, practical abolitionist. So mote it be! . . .

. . . Agriculture, it is well known, is the sole boast of the South; and, strange to say, many pro-slavery Southerners, who, in our latitude, pass for intelligent men, are so puffed up with the idea of our importance in this respect, that they speak of the North as a sterile region, unfit for cultivation, and quite dependent on the South for the necessaries of life! Such rampant ignorance ought to be knocked in the head! We can prove that the North produces greater quantities of bread-stuffs than the South! Figures shall show the facts. Properly, the South has nothing left to boast of; the North has surpassed her in everything, and is going farther and farther ahead of her every day. We ask the reader's careful attention to the following tables, which we have prepared at no little cost of time and trouble, and which, when duly considered in connection with the foregoing and subsequent portions of our work, will, we believe, carry conviction to the mind that the downward tendency of the South can be arrested only by the abolition of slavery. . . .

RECAPITULATION—FREE STATES.

Wheat	72,157,486 bush.	@	1.50	....	$108,236,229
Oats	96,590,371	"	" 40	....	38,636,148
Indian Corn	242,618,650	"	" 60	....	145,571,190
Potatoes (I. & S.)	59,033,170	"	" 38	....	22,432,604
Rye	12,574,623	"	" 1.00	....	12,574,623
Barley	5,002,013	"	" 90	....	4,501,811
Buckwheat	8,550,245	"	" 50	....	4,275,122
Beans & Peas	1,542,295	"	" 1.75	....	2,699,015
Clov. & Grass seeds	762,265	"	" 3.00	....	2,286,795
Flax Seeds	358,923	"	" 1.25	....	448,647
Garden Products				....	3,714,605
Orchard Products				....	6,332,914

Total, ... 499,190,041 bushels, valued as above, at $351,709,703

RECAPITULATION—SLAVE STATES.

Wheat	27,904,476 bush.	@	1.50	....	$ 41,856,714
Oats	49,882,799	"	" 40	....	19,953,191
Indian Corn	348,992,282	"	" 60	....	209,395,369
Potatoes (I. & S.)	44,847,420	"	" 38	....	17,042,019
Rye	1,608,240	"	" 1.00	....	1,608,240
Barley	161,907	"	" 90	....	145,716
Buckwheat	405,357	"	" 50	....	202,678
Beans & Peas	7,637,227	"	" 1.75	....	13,365,147
Clov. & Grass seeds	123,517	"	" 3.00	....	370,551
Flax Seeds	203,484	"	" 1.25	....	254,355
Garden Products				....	1,377,260
Orchard Products				....	1,355,827

Total .... 481,766,889 bushels, valued as above, at $306,927,067

TOTAL DIFFERENCE—BUSHEL-MEASURE PRODUCTS.

	Bushels.		Value.
Free States	499,190,041	....	$351,709,703
Slave States	481,766,889	....	306,927,067
Balance in bushels	17,423,152	Difference in value ..	$44,782,636

So much for the boasted agricultural superiority of the South! Mark well the balance in bushels, and the difference in value! Is either in favor of the South? No! Are both in favor of the North? Yes! Here we have unquestionable proof that of all the bushel-measure products of the nation, the free states produce far more than one-half; and it is worthy of particular mention, that *the excess of Northern products is of the most valuable kind.* The account shows a balance against the South, in favor of the North, of *seventeen million four hundred and twenty-three thousand one hundred and fifty-two bushels,* and a difference in value of *forty-four million seven hundred and eighty-two thousand six hundred and thirty-six dollars.* Please bear these facts in mind, for, in order to show positively how the free and slave States do stand upon the great and important subject of rural economy, we intend to take an account of all the other products of the soil, of the live-stock upon farms, of the animals slaughtered, and, in fact, of every item of husbandry of the two sections; and if, in bringing our tabular exercises to a close, we find slavery gaining upon freedom—a thing it has never yet been known to do—we shall, as a matter of course, see that the above amount is transferred to the credit of the side to which it of right belongs.

In making up these tables we have two objects in view; the first is to open the eyes of the non-slaveholders of the South, to the system of deception, that has so long been practiced upon them, and the second is to show slaveholders themselves—we have reference only to those who are not too perverse, or ignorant, to perceive naked truths—that free labor is far more respectable, profitable, and productive, than slave labor. In the South, unfortunately, no kind of labor is either free or respectable. Every white man who is under the necessity of earning his bread, by the sweat of his brow, or by manual labor, in any capacity, no matter how unassuming in deportment, or exemplary in morals, is treated as if he was a loathsome beast, and shunned with the utmost disdain. His soul may be the very seat of honor and integrity, yet without slaves—himself a slave—he is accounted as nobody, and would be deemed intolerably presumptuous, if he dared to open his mouth, even so wide as to give faint utterance to a three-lettered monosyllable, like yea or nay, in the presence of an august knight of the whip and the lash. . . .

. . . Notwithstanding the fact that the white non-slaveholders of the South, are in the majority, as five to one, they have never yet had any part or lot in framing the laws under which they live. There is no legislation except for the benefit of slavery, and slaveholders. As a general rule, poor white persons are regarded with less esteem and attention than negroes, and though the condition of the latter is wretched beyond description, vast numbers of the former are infinitely worse off. A cunningly devised mockery of freedom is guarantied to them, and that is all. To all intents and purposes they are disfranchised, and outlawed, and the only privilege extended to them, is a shallow and circumscribed participation in the political movements that usher slaveholders into office.

We have not breathed away seven and twenty years in the South, without becoming acquainted with the demagogical manœuverings of the oligarchy. Their intrigues and tricks of legerdemain are as familiar to us as household words; in vain might the world be ransacked for a more precious junto of flatterers and cajolers. It is amusing to ignorance, amazing to credulity, and insulting to intelligence, to hear them in their blattering efforts to mystify and pervert the sacred principles of liberty, and turn the curse of slavery into a blessing. To the illiterate poor whites—made poor and ignorant by the system of slavery—they hold out the idea that slavery is the very bulwark of our liberties, and the foundation of American independence! For hours at a time, day after day, will they expatiate upon the inexpressible beauties and excellencies of this great, *free* and *independent* nation; and finally, with the most extravagant gesticulations and rhetorical flourishes, conclude their nonsensical ravings, by attributing all the glory and prosperity of the country, from Maine to Texas, and from Georgia to California, to the "invaluable institutions of the South!" With what patience we could command, we have frequently listened to the incoherent and truth-murdering declamations of these champions of slavery, and, in the absence of a more politic method of giving vent to our disgust and indignation, have involuntarily bit our lips into blisters.

The lords of the lash are not only absolute masters of the blacks, who are bought and sold, and driven about like so many cattle, but they are also the oracles and arbiters of all non-slaveholding whites, whose freedom is merely nominal, and whose unparalleled illiteracy and degradation is purposely and fiendishly perpetuated. How little the "poor white trash," the great majority of the Southern people, know of the real condition of the country is, indeed, sadly astonishing. The truth is, they know nothing of public measures, and little of private affairs, except what their imperious masters, the slave-drivers, condescend to tell, and that is but precious little. . . .

It is expected that the stupid and sequacious masses, the white victims of slavery, will believe, and, as a general thing, they do believe, whatever the slaveholders tell them; and thus it is that they are cajoled into the notion that they are the freest, happiest and most intelligent people in the world, and are taught to look with prejudice and disapprobation upon every new principle or progressive movement. Thus it is that the South, woefully inert and inventionless, has lagged behind the North, and is now weltering in the cesspool of ignorance and degradation.

A Challenge to Low Taxes on Slaves, 1859

Resolutions

At a meeting held in the Court House, on the 10th of October, 1859, the following Resolutions [of the Wake County, North Carolina, Working-Men's Association] were offered and adopted:

Resolved, That it is the opinion of the Mechanics and Working-Men here assembled, that the Revenue Laws of this State are not framed in accordance with the principles of justice and equality; that said laws discriminate against, and operate most heavily upon those who are least able to bear the burthens of the State; and whilst we are ready and willing, as

---

From Perkins Library, Duke University "A Challenge to Low Taxes on Slaves".

faithful and loyal citizens, to meet and defray, at all times, our due *proportion* of the public charge and expenditure, we nevertheless have a right to insist, and we do respectfully insist, that these laws shall be so altered as to tax every citizen according to what he is worth.

Address

Slave property in the State [is worth] $248,567,800. This amount of property paid into the State Treasury in 1858, for the protection *it enjoys,* which, in our opinion, in its duplicate capacity of property and persons, far exceeds that thrown around any other species of property by our laws, the sum of $75,462, a little more than *half* the amount paid by $97,842,481 worth of real estate. Is there any reason why such a discrimination should be made between these two species of property? Why is it that $1,000 worth of land should pay, as it did under the tax bill of 1856–'7, $1 50, while $1,000 worth of slave property paid only 50 cents? In our opinion there is no just and good reason for such inequality. . . .

Is there any cause why $1,000 in money at interest, *restricted by our law in its productiveness to $60 per annum,* should be made to pay $2,40 for the protection it enjoys, while $1,000 in slave property, unrestricted in its production, paid 50 cents, and $1,000 in land paid $1,50? Under our Bill of Rights, no man or set of men are entitled to exclusive or separate emoluments or privileges from their neighbors, except for *good and just* reasons. Why cannot this just, fundamental principle be extended in its application likewise to property? . . .

Under the tax bill of 1856–'7

$1,000 worth of land paid	$1 50
1,000 " slaves "	50
1,000 in money loaned paid	2 40
1,000 of dividend and profit paid	2 40
1,000 [earned] in labor and industry paid	10 00
1,000 in goods purchased [by merchants] paid	3 33
1,000 " clothing " "	10 00
1,000 " liquors " "	55 00
1,000 of capital in buying slaves, paid	3 33
1,000 " other trade, "	2 00
1,000 worth of buggies, carriages, &c., paid	10 00
1,000 " pianos paid	7 50

Such are some of the inequalities of our existing revenue system. We ask you, can it be defended?

E S S A Y S

The late Frank Lawrence Owsley, who taught at Vanderbilt University, pioneered in the modern study of nonslaveholding white southerners. His book *Plain Folk of the Old South* remains a classic. The excerpts from it reprinted in the first essay discuss the importance of nonslaveholding yeoman farmers in southern society and describe some typical folk customs of rural yeomen. Elizabeth Fox-Genovese and Eugene D. Genovese of Emory University and the College of William and Mary, respectively, argue that the yeomen, despite their attitudes of independence, fell under the hegemonic control of the planter class. In the second essay, they explore the place of yeomen in southern society and the means and extent of planter control over them. Paul D. Escott of Wake Forest University has studied the rebellious behavior of many yeomen farmers during the Civil War. In the final selection, which deals with North Carolina yeomen, he describes the sources of their independence in a hierarchical society and then examines the circumstances under which they challenged established authority.

The Property and Culture of the Plain Folk

FRANK LAWRENCE OWSLEY

Most travelers and critics who wrote about the South during the late antebellum period were of the opinion that the white inhabitants of the South generally fell into two categories, namely, the slaveholders and the "poor whites." Moreover, whether or not they intended to do so, they created the impression in the popular mind that the slaveholder was a great planter living in a white-columned mansion, attended by a squad of Negro slaves who obsequiously attended his every want and whim. According to the opinion of such writers, these "cavaliers" were the great monopolists of their day; they crowded everyone not possessed of considerable wealth off the good lands and even the lands from which modest profits might be realized; they dominated politics, religion, and all phases of public life. The six or seven million nonslaveholders who comprised the remainder of the white population and were, with minor exceptions, considered "poor whites" or "poor white trash" were visualized as a sorry lot indeed. They had been pushed off by the planters into the pine barrens and sterile sand hills and mountains. Here as squatters upon abandoned lands and government tracts they dwelt in squalid log huts and kept alive by hunting and fishing, and by growing patches of corn, sweet potatoes, collards, and pumpkins in the small "deadenings" or clearings they had made in the all-engulfing wilderness. They were illiterate, shiftless, irresponsible, frequently vicious, and nearly always addicted to the use of "rot gut" whiskey and to dirt eating. Many, perhaps nearly all, according to later writers, had malaria, hookworm, and pellagra. Between the Great Unwashed and the slaveholders there was a chasm that could not be bridged. The nonslaveholders were six or seven million supernumeraries in a slaveholding society. . . .

Upon reading page after page of tax lists and census returns, both of which give the landholdings and much of the personal property of all individuals, the picture of the economic structure of the Old South gradually

From *Plain Folk of the Old South* by Frank Lawrence Owsley, Quadrangle Books, 1949. Reprinted by permission.

takes form. These sources reveal the existence of a society of great complexity. Instead of the simple, two-fold division of the agricultural population into slaveholders and nonslaveholding poor whites, many economic groups appear. Among the slaveholders there were great planters possessed of thousands of acres of land and hundreds of slaves, planters owning a thousand or fewer acres and two score slaves, small planters with five hundred acres and ten or fifteen slaves, large farmers with three or four hundred acres and five to ten slaves, small farmers with two hundred or fewer acres and one or two slaves. Among the nonslaveholders were large farmers employing hired labor who owned from two hundred to a thousand acres; a middle group which owned from one hundred to two hundred acres; "one horse farmers" with less than one hundred acres; and landless renters, squatters, farm laborers, and a "leisure class" whose means of support does not appear on the record. But the core of the social structure was a massive body of plain folk who were neither rich nor very poor. These were employed in numerous occupations; but the great majority secured their food, clothing, and shelter from some rural pursuit, chiefly farming and livestock grazing. It is the plain country folk with whom I am most concerned here—that great mass of several millions who were not part of the plantation economy. The group included the small slaveholding farmers; the nonslaveholders who owned the land which they cultivated; the numerous herdsmen on the frontier, pine barrens, and mountains; and those tenant farmers whose agricultural production, as recorded in the census, indicated thrift, energy, and self-respect. . . .

The slaveholding families composed nearly one third of the white population of the South, and most of them were small slaveowners and small landowners. As estimated, 60 per cent owned from one to five slaves, and another large group held from five to ten. Most slaveholders whose chief occupation was agriculture owned their farms, and the small slaveholders, as would be expected, were small landowners. At least 60 per cent of the small slaveholders had farms ranging in size from fifty to three hundred acres. Over 60 per cent of the nonslaveholders outside the upper seaboard states—who . . . were classed as poor white trash—were also landowners. In the lower South and in portions of the upper south central states an estimated 70 per cent owned farms. The sizes of their holdings differed very little from those of the small slaveholders. About 75 per cent ranged from a few to two hundred acres, and the other 25 per cent were above two hundred acres in size. . . .

. . . Rural Southerners did not divide their lives into well-separated compartments as do their urban and even rural descendants. They often made little distinction between work and play, for all co-operative work was accompanied by play and was almost invariably followed by a party. A few examples of this co-operative work will be described, such as house-raisings, logrollings, the burning of the woods, and corn shuckings.

When a new family moved into a community and purchased land on which there was no house, or when a home burned or a couple married, it was the custom for the neighbors to gather and build a house for the homeless family or the newly wed couple. This was not just a frontier custom, though it doubtless originated on the frontier, but a rural folkway practiced in many parts of the South as late as World War I. Nor were the houses thus co-operatively raised necessarily of logs as they had been in the frontier days. On the contrary, in a country where the vast pine forests were considered encumbrances and there were numerous small sawmills, plank houses were as often put up as log. If the houses were to be built of planks, the co-operative task would consist chiefly of constructing what was called "the shell"—the framework, the flooring, roof, and weatherboarding. The shell could usually be built in one or two days; and then the family could move in. After that, individual neighbors might contribute two or three days each as the time could be spared, for putting in ceiling, windows, doors, and for the general finishing. More often than not, perhaps, the finishing process was done by the owner of the house, and might extend over a number of years. One room would be ceiled one year and another later. Frequently in the warmer parts of the South nothing but doors, window shutters, a chimney, and stove flue were added after the shell was built.

Every day we see frame houses in the various stages of construction; but few if any of us have ever seen a bona fide log house being built. There are numerous contemporary descriptions of house-raisings. I will quote from one written by a man who saw log houses raised—perhaps helped raise them—many of which are standing today. This is the account that the Reverend George Brewer gives in his unpublished History of Coosa County, Alabama. Brewer lived in and near this county from the 1830's until his death, about 1922.

"The county [he writes] settled rapidly and houses were needed. At first there were no saw mills, and for sometime but few, so that sawed lumber could not be gotten at all, or only by long and expensive hauls. The consequence was that log houses were the rule. To 1850 frame houses were scarce. . . . Houses of course varied in size from the single room log hut, to the large two storied houses made of large hewn logs with verandas or awnings. The most common, however, for the average man who looked after comfort and not too much expense, was what was called the two room or double log house, with a hall [dog run] of ten or twelve feet between. The rooms were usually from 18 to 20 feet square. The walls were made of skinned poles five or six inches through, or logs of ten or twelve inches split in two in the center. After the walls were raised the split side which was inward, was hewed comparatively smooth, and the outside likewise well skelped with the broad axe. The cracks were usually lined with long boards rived from good splitting timber, and drawn to smoothness with the drawing knife. Some times if the house was desired to be very tight the cracks were chinked on the outside with split pieces of timber, and this daubed with mortar. These houses usually had shed rooms, thus making four rooms to the house; and if more room was needed, two sheds on the front some less [in length] than the main rooms [were added] so as to have a sort of open court in front of the hallway [in which a porch was built later]. These sheds were made either of poles or boards rived in long strips. The houses were covered with two- or three-foot boards rived out of blocks of these lengths sawed from good splitting trees.

"There were generally built in the back yard, some distance from the main building, separate houses for cook and dining rooms, smoke or meat houses, store room, and dairy. Stables, cribs, and barns were made in like manner, nearby, but with less care usually to appearance.

"When the logs for a house were cut and put on the ground near where the house was to be built the neighbors were invited to come to the house raising on a specified day. They would assemble by seven or eight o'clock, and after the sills had been properly placed on their pillars of sawed light-wood blocks, or rocks, four men, skillful with an axe, were chosen as corner men, and each took possession of a corner. If the house was double eight corner men were required. The other men brought the logs and hoisted them to the corner men who would proceed at once to cutting a notch so as to fit the log below after the first had been fitted to the sill, so as to keep the wall both perpendicular and steady. Often a good fit would be secured at the first cutting. If not, the corner men turned the log up, and remoddled [*sic*] the notch until a fit was secured. These men had for scaffolding on which to stand while cutting and fitting these notches only the cracks between the logs, or . . . [the] top of the turned up log or pole. . . . A constant run of social chat, hunting feats, stirring incidents, interesting exploits, or political matters made the time pass pleasantly, and more like a good natured social gathering than the hard work it was."

The midday dinner would be a feast, for the smokehouse, pantry, chicken yard, and garden would be called on for their choice products. If the family did not own a good Negro cook, one would be hired, perhaps, and in any case the women folks of the neighborhood would co-operate in the preparation of the meal. Usually, too, the ladies would have a quilting while the men were raising the house. The men sat "around a long, improvised table," says Brewer, "made gay with the jest, the joke, or lively talk." Then the ladies, who had waited upon the men's table, would eat while the men rested, smoked, chewed their tobacco, and cracked jokes. After a short rest the men resumed their work, and "usually by night the house would be raised and the rafters (commonly skinned poles) were properly set upon the plates, as the flattened top log was called. Another bountiful meal for supper was eaten, and then all would break off for home, unless a party had been decided on in connection with the house raising, in which [case] the younger members of the families would come in and share in the social function. If the 'raising' was not completed, they would come back next day and finish up."

Perhaps the next co-operative jobs would be a series of logrollings. These affairs usually took place in the late winter and early spring just before spring plowing was begun. In the South, the farmers never cleared their lands by cutting the trees down and removing them, but girdled them with an ax, which would cause them to die very quickly. A crop would then be grown in this "deadening" or "new ground" with no further clearing, for there was seldom any underbrush, because of the habit, first of the Indians and then of the farmers, of burning the woods annually. During the fall and winter the deadened trees would be set on fire and many would burn in two, where they had been girdled, and would fall; others would be weakened at this point by fire and would be blown down during the year. In the spring the farmer and his boys and two or three slaves, if he owned any, would cut the branches from the fallen trees and pile them in what was nearly always called a "bresh heap." The logs were then cut into ten- or twelve-foot lengths and the neighbors were invited to a logrolling which would usually be a few days after the invitation was sent out.

On the appointed day the neighbors would gather and proceed to the field. Here they paired off, each pair having a hand stick or hand spike between them. This hand stick, made of a hickory sapling, was about five feet long and three inches in diameter and was tapered at the ends to make it easy to grasp. It was flattened on top to prevent it from turning. From two to four pairs of men with hand sticks were assigned to each piece of log or "cut." The hand sticks were then thrust under the log so that it would rest on the center of the sticks, and at a signal the men stooped down and grasped the ends firmly. Then, at the signal "ready," the men in a squatting position braced themselves, keeping their bodies erect and alert; and at the next signal, such as "heave," "up," or "go," they all lifted in unison, planted their feet firmly, and then walked slowly and often in step, as if marching, to the place designated for the log heap. Here they lowered the log to the ground by squatting, but taking care to keep their backs as erect as possible. The log was then rolled from the hand sticks and the men returned for another log. These men were skilled weight lifters, for it will be observed that the log was actually raised and lowered primarily by leg power. Among these people size and heft and symmetry of muscle made no impression. A man's strength was judged by his lifting power; and ofttimes a man of 140 pounds with no bulging muscles, but with sinews like steel cables, would bring up his end of the hand stick under the "butt cut" of a huge pine, while his 200-pound partner, unable to rise, would have his knuckles buried in the ground under his end of the hand stick. Such feats were called "pulling down," and no logrolling was a success in which some champion did not thus go down.

When the log pile was waist high another would be started, and in this way hundreds of such heaps would be made in a day.

While the men were thus "toting" the logs—not rolling them except to get them off the hand sticks onto the log heap—the mothers and their daughters were cooking dinner and quilting. Ward in his *History of Coffee County, Georgia*, gives some of the chief items of one of these dinners: A sixty-gallon sugar boiler filled with rice, chicken, and fresh pork backbone— a sort of camp stew; a large pot of turnip greens and corn-meal dumplings, served with a boiled ham sliced and laid on top; crackling or shortening bread; Irish potatoes; sweet potatoes; a variety of cakes; two-story biscuits; and, of course, the huge pot of coffee, so strong that it could walk, or float an iron wedge, as these folk would have expressed it. When dinnertime came, a loud and long blast or two on a hunting horn would make the announcement; whereupon all hands would lay aside their hand sticks, dispose of their tobacco cuds, take a few gulps from the jug, and lose no time in getting to the dinner table. The logrolling was usually followed by a square dance, the music for which would be furnished by a fiddler and banjo picker who played such tunes as "One Eyed Gopher" and "Squirrel Gravey" until bribed to play some other dance tune such as the "Arkansas Traveller" and "Turkey in the Straw." . . .

Another interesting and exciting custom was the corn shucking. On an appointed night the neighbors gathered in the barn lot and shucked a quantity of corn, sometimes as much as one hundred bushels in an evening. There were evidently several ways of conducting a corn shucking, most of which contained some element of rivalry. Often two captains would be appointed by the host, and each would choose a team. The corn would then be divided into two piles of equal size. Then came the race, the shouting and the singing of corn songs, long ago forgotten. Soon the bottle of brandy or whiskey would be put into circulation, and the tempo of the corn shucking and of the corn songs would be increased. During the evening a few would show their liquor to some extent, though it was considered disgraceful to become intoxicated. The winning team would march around their pile of corn, carrying their captain on their shoulders, singing a corn song of triumph. Sometimes but not often, some disgruntled member of the losing team, who had had too much to drink, would send a well-aimed ear of corn at the exposed head of a member of the rival team, and a fight would promptly follow, in which most would enthusiastically participate. After the corn was shucked came the shucking supper. The following is a partial list of the dishes served at a corn shucking in Rowen County, North Carolina: loaf bread, biscuits, ham, fresh pork, chicken pie, pumpkin custard or pie, apple pie, grape pie, cakes, coffee, sweet milk, buttermilk, and preserves. One type of corn shucking was that in which the young men and girls were the chief participants. The prize went to the boy or girl who found the largest number of red or multicolored ears of corn. The lucky boy could kiss any girl he chose—which would, for policy's sake and other reasons, be the girl he brought to the party. The girl who won the prize could kiss any boy she chose or make any other demand, which had to be fulfilled, even to having some silly oaf jump into a cattle pool. This kind of corn shucking was usually a very hilarious occasion. A great deal of hard work was performed with little feeling of weariness. After the corn was shucked, the supper and dance would inevitably follow, and the party would hardly break up before dawn.

Another type of corn shucking apparently had no element of rivalry in it, but was a co-operative task lightened by corn songs and rhythmic potations of corn liquor. The Reverend George Brewer, who participated in these affairs, has left a description of such a corn shucking. The portion dealing with the corn songs is worth quoting: "There were usually two or more recognized leaders in singing the corn songs, and as they would chant or shout their couplet, all the rest would join in the chorus. There was no poetry or metre, to these songs, but there was a thrill from the melody welling up with such earnestness from the singers that it was so inspiring that the hands would fly with rapidity in tearing off the shucks, and the feet [would] kick back the shucks with equal vigor. The leader would shout:

'Pull off the shucks boys, pull off the shucks,' the crowd [would] shout out in a singing chorus:

'Round up the corn boys, round up the corn'

The leader would then chant:

'The night's getting off boys, the night's getting off'

The crowd would again sing the chorus:

'Round up the corn boys, Round up the corn.'

The leader would chant:

'Give me a dram, sir, Give me a dram.'

The chorus:

'Round up the corn boys, Round up the corn' "

"This singing," says Brewer, "could be heard on a still night 2 miles."

The Reverend further recalled that when the corn was shucked, "The leaders would pick up the owner on their shoulders and carry him several times around the house, followed closely by all the others singing some of their most stirring corn songs, and praising him in their songs. After thus carrying him around in triumph, they would enter the hallway with him on their shoulders, and seat him in a chair, and with a shuffling dance, go out into the yard. A hearty dram was then given them and they were seated to a rich supper around an improvised table. Negroes and whites enjoyed these shuckings very much . . . [and] there was the best of feeling mutually among them."

The most noteworthy of all co-operative undertakings was the folk custom of taking over and working or gathering the crops of a neighbor who was handicapped by his own illness or that of a member of his family. The fields would be plowed and hoed, and, in the fall, fodder would be pulled and cotton picked or tobacco cut and stripped. The women and girls ofttimes shared equally with the men in such work. Indeed, in stripping tobacco and picking cotton, the girls often excelled the men. This relief work would be done usually by the neighbors contributing hoe hands, teams, and plow hands for a certain number of days each. Another method of extending this kind of relief was what was called "swapping work," a custom that still lingers in some communities. The number of days work contributed by each neighbor would be paid back hand for hand, team for team, and day for day at a suitable time. It is probable that most farmers preferred to repay in this fashion rather than accept as a gift the aid which they had received during their illness. It should be observed, however, that "swapping work" was also a community custom practiced as a matter of economy and sociability and in no way connected with illness or hardship cases. For example when a farmer had fully hoed and plowed all his fields, and had several days of idleness in prospect, he and his sons—and his slaves if he had a few—would ofttimes go into a neighbor's fields and "catch him up with his work" as the phrase went. Later, when needed, this work would be repaid. This was putting not money, but work in the bank to be drawn on when it was required.

The Yeomen and Planter Hegemony

ELIZABETH FOX-GENOVESE AND EUGENE D. GENOVESE

In 1861, enough nonslaveholders hurled themselves into a prolonged blood-bath to enable a proudly proclaimed slave republic to sustain itself for four ghastly years. These "plain folks" suffered terrible casualties and privations on behalf of a social order within which they were oppressed in a variety of well-known ways. Many contemporary northerners and indeed even some southerners expressed wonder, as many subsequent historians would do, at the nonslaveholders' gullibility, ignorance, and docility. Slavery, it has long been asserted, had numbed the lower-class whites quite as much as it had ostensibly numbed the enslaved blacks. Abolitionists, for under-standable reasons, became the bitterest proponents of this argument and railed in frustration at the nonslaveholders' groveling before the aristocratic pretensions of the haughty planters.

Yet, we know very well that those nonslaveholders were touchy, proud people who hardly specialized in groveling and who were as quick as the planters to shed blood over questions of honor. We know also that they seized and maintained substantial political rights and were largely respon-sible for some of the most democratic state constitutions in the United States. . . .

In a variety of ways, the upcountry made the slaveholders and especially the secessionist politicians nervous. Upcountry farmers ostentatiously sneered at the aristocratic pretensions of the planters. In many instances, they took the plantation counties as a "negative reference point" for their own voting behavior. And many defiantly opposed extremist and anti-Union measures.

Yet, we might also note that some of these counties went for secession and many others split or tamely acquiesced. The fire-eating Albert Gallatin Brown built much of his power on such districts in Mississippi. Those who try to correlate upcountry districts with a specific behavior pattern are usually driven to distraction by the apparent ideological inconsistencies, quite as much as by the methodological difficulties.

These quasi-autonomous social worlds showed limited concern for the great questions of southern and national politics. Some of the same up-country districts in Mississippi that followed Brown into support of pro-slavery extremism and secession ended by deserting the Confederate cause. This apparent inconsistency was expressed less dramatically in more typical upcountry counties of the Lower South, which moved from moderate

Unionism to acceptance of secession and then to defection from the Confederacy. Initially, they may well have been motivated by allegiance to particular local leaders whom they had come to trust to defend their regional autonomy against the plantation belt and indeed against all outsiders.

The upcountry, notwithstanding its manifest hatred for the pretensions of the black-belt planters, benefited from and reinforced the slaveholders' commitment to state rights—or rather to opposition to the centralization of political power. So long as the slaveholders made few demands on these regions, their claims to being champions of local freedom and autonomy against all meddling outsiders appeared perfectly legitimate. Northern abolitionists and free-soilers appeared as outsiders who claimed the right to determine local institutions. Conversely, the provincialism of the upcountry held to a minimum demands on the slaveholders for extensive expenditure for an infrastructure capable of "developing" the nonplantation areas. The great majority of the upcountry yeomen showed little desire to exchange a proud isolation and regional way of life for integration into the commercial economy of the despised plantation belt. Certainly, things were different in West Virginia, East Tennessee, and some other areas, but they were slowly becoming an extension of the economy of the neighboring free states.

The extent to which the upcountry yeomen resisted the penetration of merchant capital and even of railroads requires further study and no doubt varied considerably across the South. The contrast with the behavior of the yeomen of the free states nonetheless remains striking. The behavior of the upcountry southern yeomen, however much manifested as a defense of local cultural autonomy, had its roots in the political economy of slavery, broadly understood. In the free states, cheap transportation could rapidly transform the family farm into a paying enterprise, as it could do in those portions of the Upper South that could be linked with markets to the north. In the Lower South, however, cheap transportation would draw the yeomen into the cotton economy at high economic and social risk without offering much in the way of financial returns in the absence of slave labor, which could be obtained only at generally prohibitive prices.

In the Lower South, at least, those upcountry farmers who swore loyalty to the Union and those who swore loyalty to their state were generally of a piece. Their first loyalty remained to their own local community, and either the Union or the state might respect or threaten that community autonomy. Hence, the Confederacy suffered a soaring upcountry desertion rate, and outright treason accompanied the imposition of necessary war measures. The exigencies of war had forced the Confederacy to do to the upcountry the very things it had sworn to oppose. The whole point of secession, after all, was to defend local rights against the pressures of centralization. Confederate conscription, taxation, requisitioning, in a word, outside domination, had to be perceived in the upcountry as a betrayal of trust.

The slave South held the allegiance of its second society not because the yeomen farmers and herdsmen outside the plantation belt had been duped, or even because they were ignorant. Rather, their alleged ignorance was an ignorance on principle—a provincial rejection of an outside world that threatened to impinge on the culture as well as the material interests of the local community. The slaveholders could abide the autonomy of the upcountry not because they necessarily respected its moral foundations but because they could be—and indeed had to be—indifferent to its development. The last thing the slaveholders of the plantation belt wanted was an additional tax burden to finance the opening of areas regarded as potentially competitive or simply irrelevant to the plantation economy. Much less did they wish to promote the development of areas that might have to proceed with free labor and might, therefore, develop a marked hostility not merely to slaveholding aristocrats but to slavery itself. The solution lay in a mutually desired silence and limited intercourse, nothwithstanding occasional struggles over a few more roads and schools and, perhaps even more important, demands for ritualistic respect and recognition. This type of silent understanding has had many parallels elsewhere—in Sicily, for example.

The yeomen of the plantation belt present a more difficult problem. Antebellum dissent, such as it was, and wartime desertion centered in the upcountry. The commitment of the farmers of the plantation belt to the regime, by normal political standards, proved much firmer. Why? The answer of race will not, by itself, do. The upcountry yeomen hated and feared the blacks and wanted them under tight racial control. But the upcountry yeomen also were quick to identify slaveholders with slaves—to perceive the organic connection between the two, not only materially but culturally. To the upcountry yeomen, slaveholders and slaves were two peas in the same pod. The plantation-belt yeomen also saw the master-slave relation as organic, but they judged the effects differently and yielded much more easily to planter leadership.

Those who wonder at the plantation-belt yeomen's support of slavery might well begin by asking themselves a question: Why should the non-slaveholders not have supported slavery? After all, men and women normally accept, more or less uncritically, the world into which they are born. Something must drive them to reject and resist the social order that, at the least, offers them the security of a known world.

Let us imagine Joshua Venable, dirt farmer of Hinds County, Mississippi. Josh owned no slaves, worked forty acres of so-so land more or less competently, and struggled to keep his head above water. Fortunately for him, he was kin to Jefferson Venable, owner of the district's finest Big House, Ole Massa to a hundred slaves, and patron to the local judge as well as the sheriff. Josh Venable's wife was kin to John Mercer, himself "massa" to only ten or twelve slaves but decidedly a man on the make. The marriage, in fact, brought the Venables and the Mercers into an uneasy conviviality. Massa Jefferson Venable had to swallow a bit to tolerate his parvenu relatives at table, especially since John Mercer could not be broken of the habit of spitting on the floor in the presence of the ladies. But, business is business, and kinfolk are kinfolk—even those by marriage.

Now, poor Josh Venable rarely got invited to Cousin Jeff's home and virtually never to his dining-room table. Rather, he was usually invited to an outdoor affair—a barbecue to which many of the nonslaveholders of the neighborhood were also invited to celebrate lay-by or the Fourth of July. Josh also had to notice that he was invited only when many neighboring slaveholders were urged not only to come but to bring all their "niggers." Still, kin was kin, and Josh got an effusive welcome as a member of the family. Ole Massa Jefferson, his own self, once took him by the arm to the barbecue pit to meet the new state senator, whom Ole Jeff had just bought and who might come in handy.

Josh resented his cousin—so much so that he continued to hope that he would someday own even more slaves himself and maybe even reach the pinnacle of success. Some day he might even be able to make Cousin Jeff a low-interest loan to cover his famous gambling debts, not to mention those debts for somewhat unclear expenditures in New Orleans. But, how far could he carry his resentment toward Cousin Jeff? Everyone, including Josh, knew that his cousin might be a little stuffy, might put on airs, but that he always had a helping hand for anyone in the neighborhood, black or white. Josh raised some extra corn and a few hogs. What was he supposed to do? Hand-carry them to Cincinnati? Wait to sell them to unreliable drovers, who specialized in hard bargains? Cousin Jeff always stood ready to pay a fair price even though he could just as easily have increased the orders through his factors and not have bothered with such local trifles.

Josh also knew any number of local farmers who raised two or three bales of cotton. If they had to spend $125 each for a cotton gin and then pay the costs of individual marketing, they could not have covered costs. Yet, there was good ole Jefferson Venable, and two or three other such worthies, ready to gin the cotton for a fair service charge of 9 or 10 percent and market it with their own large crops to insure a fair price for their poorer neighbors. No one ever accused Ole Jeff of trying to make a dollar off his neighbors. To the contrary, he was quick to send food supplies to help someone down and out. And everyone saw how he sent a few of his hands to help a sick neighbor get in his small crop when everything hung in the balance. If it were not for Ole Jeff and a few others like him, how could many of the poorer farmers make it?

The planters occasionally hired the sons of poor neighbors to do odd jobs or even to help with the cotton picking. They hired a relative here or there to oversee their plantations. If a small farmer got lucky and was able to buy a slave before he could profitably use him, there was Jeff ready to rent him for a year. Alternatively, if a farmer got lucky and needed the temporary services of a slave he could not yet afford to buy, there was Jeff ready to send one over at the going rate. And everyone remembered how the local planters sent their slaves to throw up houses for new settlers and did everything possible to help them get started.

Certainly, that kind of neighborliness was normal in rural areas throughout the United States. But in the South, population was much more scattered, and it would have been hard to help people get on without the work of those slaves. What then could lead Jefferson Venable's neighbors to see him as an enemy? He in no way exploited them, except perhaps for the poor white trash he occasionally hired to do odd jobs, and treated with contempt. And they were no-account anyway.

Consider the financial relation of the planters to the yeomen on the one side and the country storekeepers on the other. Most yeomen sold their cotton not to planters at all but to storekeepers or even itinerant merchants and speculators. These storekeepers and merchants represented merchant capital in its independent or pure form; that is, they had no direct part in the production process and made their profits as a rake-off on the surplus product of others. Buying cheap and selling dear was their stock in trade, and they provided the yeomen with a wide variety of commodities, which the planters, for their part, normally obtained through their factors. In this way, the storekeepers functioned as customers as well as virtual agents of the big factors, who were themselves largely hostage to the northern and the British financial centers. The storekeepers may have wished to be as neighborly as the planters; certainly, they extended all too easy credit to the yeomen. They also applied two sets of prices, one for cash business, the other for business on credit.

Two things kept the yeomen from sinking into the usual enslavement to merchant capital and virtual usury. First and more important, they resisted cotton mania and produced for themselves before they produced for market. At least the sensible ones did, and most seem to have been sensible. But second, the planters unostentatiously offered an alternative to the merchants and thereby set limits to any gouging. Wherever planters were willing to step in and market the yeomen's crops along with their own, the merchants found themselves confronting an elastic demand for their services, and they could not impose monopolistic policies. Some planters even bought up their neighbors' cotton outright and, in consequence, found themselves denounced as "fools" who knew nothing about proper cotton pricing. In other words, they found themselves denounced by merchants for paying their neighbors too much.

Plantation-belt yeomen either aspired to become slaveholders or to live as marginal farmers under the limited protection of their stronger neighbors. They displayed nothing irrational or perverse with this attitude. White labor was scarce and unreliable, at least if a farmer needed steady help. Any farmer who wanted to expand his operations and make a better living had to buy slaves as soon as possible. It was therefore natural, as a matter of inclination and social conscience, to be ready to ride patrol, to help discipline the slaves, and to take part in the political and police aspects of the slave regime—in short, to think and act like slaveholders even before becoming one. No doubt many were motivated by money, racism, sadism, or a penchant for putting-on-dog, but even without those pleasantries, the path of social duty emerged as the path of self-interest.

Under the best of circumstances, a class of independent proprietors, with limited spatial range and cultural horizons, could hardly be expected to ask hard questions about these socioeconomic relations. No matter how poor or marginal, small farmers were in no position to make sophisticated analyses of the indirect workings of the slave system as a whole and to conclude that they were oppressed by the very planters who played Lord Bountiful or in any case did not bother them. But this particular class of farmers had had its own positive political history in relation to the planters.

As shorthand for a complicated historical development, consider one or two features of the democratic upsurge of the Jacksonian era. If one reads the political speeches and dwells on the rhetoric, the South after 1819 was torn by the bitterest kind of class warfare. The farmers rose against the aristocracy, the debtors against the creditors, the people against the privileged. The ensuing political reforms, as Fletcher Green and Charles Sydnor in particular have so well shown, were in fact formidable. Politically, the South underwent substantial democratization. The haughty aristocrats were beaten, although more thoroughly in Mississippi and Alabama than in Louisiana, not to mention South Carolina.

And yet, this period of democratization coincided precisely with the great period of territorial, demographic, and ideological expansion of the slave regime. In its wake came the suppression of southern liberalism. Those who brought democracy to the Southwest also brought plantation slavery and the hegemony of the master class. At this point, the Herrenvolk thesis is usually trotted out to resolve all contradictions. Unfortunately, it cannot explain how the racism of the yeomanry, no matter how virulent, led the farmers to surrender leadership to the slaveholders instead of seizing it for themselves. And they did surrender it.

It is not merely or essentially that lawyers attached to the plantation interest often dominated politics; after all, in a democratic society lawyers usually do. The social interests they serve, not their own class origins, remain at issue. Quantitative studies of social origin and class have solemnly revealed what we might have expected: politicians are not themselves usually bankers, industrialists, planters, or in general very rich men, at least not until they take office. The democratic movement in the South nonetheless effectively removed the slavery question from politics and thereby guaranteed the property base of the slaveholding class—which is all a hegemonic politics is supposed to do.

This process of democratic expansion under slaveholder hegemony emerges from a critical view of antiaristocratic rhetoric. Consider some of the major recurring issues: a more equitable legislative apportionment; transfer of the state capital to the interior and away from the centers of entrenched wealth; credit and banking policies to aid debtors rather than creditors; internal improvements designed to open up those areas suitable to staple-crop production; redistribution of the tax burden; and a final solution to the Indian question. In each case, we find the rhetoric of class war—the poor against the rich, the people (defined as white) against the aristocrats. But, "the people" turn out to be planters on the make as well as yeomen farmers who were trying to move up the social and economic scale.

In Mississippi, for example, the goal was to break the power of the arrogant nabobs of Natchez and to permit the rapid settlement and development of the interior. But that development always concerned the extension and development of the slave-plantation system itself. The struggle, above all, pitted old and conservative slaveholders against bold new men whose commitment to the social order did not deviate one whit from that of the nabobs. Room had to be made for free competition, which, despite pretenses, required public power in Mississippi as elsewhere. The new men required new money, and the old banking monopoly, tailored to the limited interests of the Natchez aristocracy, had to give way before a policy that would create the credit necessary to buy land and slaves for the interior.

The demands, by their very nature, brought a significant portion of the planter class of the interior into coalition with the democratic yeomanry, whose interests appeared largely the same. Thus, wealthier and more successful men in the interior easily assumed leadership of the movement. Among those of common interest, the men of wealth, education, and influence, or at least men who looked like a good bet to become so, were obviously better equipped to formulate policy. And when the crash came, the interior planters themselves retreated into the conservative policies they had helped to overthrow: by that time they were established and needed sound money rather than loose policies designed to advance the interests of some new competitors. By that time, also, the farmers of the upcountry as well as of the plantation belt had felt the ravages of speculative banking and were ready to accept the lure of hard money or at least of fiscal responsibility.

In short, so long as the yeomen accepted the existing master-slave relation as either something to aspire to or something peripheral to their own lives, they were led step by step into willing acceptance of a subordinate position in society. They accepted the position not because they did not understand their interests, or because they were panicked by racial fears, and certainly not because they were stupid, but because they saw themselves as aspiring slaveholders or as nonslaveholding beneficiaries of a slaveholding world that constituted the only world they knew. To have considered their position in any other terms would have required a herculean effort and a degree of sophistication capable of penetrating the indirect and subtle workings of the system as a whole.

Ordinary farmers might in fact have accomplished that herculean effort and attained that sophistication. The secession crisis and especially the defection from the Confederacy demonstrated the fragility of the upcountry's loyalty to the regime. And even in the plantation belt, the slaveholders wondered aloud whether such arguments as those of Hinton Helper would not take hold among a basically literate, politically experienced, and fiercely proud white population, if economic conditions deteriorated or free discussion were to blossom. The slaveholders contained the threat by preventing the message from reaching the people—by placing the slavery question beyond discussion. It did not, however, require a genius to recognize that a hostile free-soil regime in Washington, the constant agitation of the slavery question within the national Union, or some internal crisis that upset the delicate ideological balance within the South might lead to the emergence of an antislavery movement at home. Secession and independence had much to recommend them to the dominant property holders of so dangerous a world.

How loyal, then, were the nonslaveholders? Loyal enough to guarantee order at home through several tumultuous decades, loyal enough to allow the South to wage an improbable war in a hopeless cause for four heroic years, but by no means loyal enough to guarantee the future of the slaveholders' power without additional measures. The full assessment of this problem lies ahead of us, for the yeomen, of both the upcountry and the plantation belt, have yet to receive the careful attention they deserve. Without it, much of the southern experience must remain in the shadows.

Until recently, we knew little about the actual lives of the slaves, and many said we could never know since the data were not available. Yet, during the last decade many scholars—too many to name—have demonstrated the value of the old adage "Seek and ye shall find." In retrospect, the work of Frank Owsley, Blanche Clark, Herbert Weaver, and others of their school appears all the more impressive despite sins against statistical method and a tendency toward romantic reconstruction. Much as a new generation of scholars has been able to uncover the story of the slaves by taking a sympathetic view of their lives, their aspirations, and their struggles for survival, so did the Owsley school point a similar direction with regard to the yeomen. We may expect a new wave of researchers to pay close attention to the fundamental cultural as well as economic cleavages that separated the farmers of the upcountry from those of the plantation belt.

One thing is certain: we shall never understand fully the triumph and eventual demise of the slave system of the South, or the secret of the slaveholders' success in establishing their hegemony in society, or the nature and extent of the persistent pressure from below that threatened that hegemony until we study the daily lives, the religion, the family and courting patterns, and the dreams of the ordinary farmers of the slave South. And we shall have to study them with the same kind of sympathetic understanding and fundamental respect that so many fine scholars have been bringing to the study of the slaves.

Independent and Rebellious Yeomen

PAUL D. ESCOTT

North Carolina, along with a few other states, had successfully blunted the tide of democratic constitutional reform that swept across the South in the 1830s. Its Constitution of 1776 had established "a representative democracy in form but an oligarchy in spirit and practice," and the convention of 1835 made only modest changes. Election of a governor became the choice of the voters, not the legislature, but few other democratizing measures prevailed.

From Paul D. Escott, *Many Excellent People*, pp. 15–17, 23–27, 69, 81–83. © 1985 The University of North Carolina Press. Reprinted by permission.

White men who owned fewer than fifty acres of land—a large minority—still could not vote for state senator, whereas free blacks lost all rights of suffrage. Though all white adult male taxpayers could vote for members of the house of commons, a property requirement of one hundred acres disqualified more than half of them from running for the legislature. Property qualifications for senators were higher and for governor higher still. In 1860 more than 85 percent of the members of the general assembly were slaveholders (the highest percentage in the South), and more than 36 percent owned at least twenty slaves (one of the highest percentages in the South). Formulas for apportioning the legislature conceded something to the west's grievances against the east but nothing to democratic principle. The senate was to be chosen from districts paying equal amounts of taxes, thus overrepresenting wealthy areas; membership in the house of commons was based on the "federal ratio," which counted each slave as three-fifths of a person and thus overrepresented slaveholding areas. State funds for schools also were distributed in accord with the federal ratio.

Moreover, the "oligarchic, undemocratic" system of local government lived on. In an era when local government was very powerful, North Carolinians could not elect their local officials, except sheriff and clerk of court. Justices of the peace laid down county policies, elected various county officers, and made important decisions on tax rates, the location of roads, provisions for education and the poor, and many other social and economic matters. In their judicial capacity they judged most ordinary crimes and settled law suits and other civil matters vital to the affected parties such as the division of estates and disputes over boundaries. These justices of the peace, or "squires," were not elected but recommended by the county's representatives and appointed by the governor. Their term was for life. In many parts of the state a leading family, such as the Hawkinses of Warren County, the Riddicks of Gates and Perquimans counties, and the Speights of Greene County, dominated the county court and state offices for decades or generations. Samuel Finley Patterson chaired the Caldwell County Court for much of his adult life and continuously after 1845, except for brief intervals when he served as state senator, representative, or delegate to a constitutional convention. This "squirarchy" was so powerful that justices "generally were able to control the vote of the county in the choice of representatives in the General Assembly and in state and national elections."

What kept democratic attitudes alive in the face of a hierarchical, undemocratic government and social structure? Jacksonian democracy had thrived in the South, and the pervasive democratic values of America were part of the answer, as Weldon Edwards had ruefully observed. For the American Revolution had set loose upon hierarchical societies the idea of natural, inherent human rights, and the words "all men are created equal" swiftly made the Declaration of Independence an imperishable document. As America grew, it filled up with men and women eager to grasp new opportunities of equality. The surging democracy that Alexis de Tocqueville described had, just a few years previously, carried thousands of simple citizens into the White House, where they raucously celebrated the inauguration of Andrew Jackson. The election of this hero of the common man, writes one scholar, "marked the coming of age in the United States of a new political idea—the idea that people had a right to a voice in choosing their rulers and lawmakers, not because they possessed special qualifications of education or of wealth, but simply because they were people." Elites might contain the democratic impulse, but they could not remove it.

The influence of frontier traditions also was extremely important in a sparsely settled state that retained a strong, rural ambiance (there were only 20.4 persons per square mile, on the average, in 1860). On the frontier individuals had taken care of their own needs and provided for themselves; most North Carolinians continued in fact to live in economic independence on their family farms. On the frontier men also had settled their own scores without reliance on others, for a man was not worthy of respect if he failed to rise to a challenge; this frontier attitude about violence also remained influential. Whereas the wealthy fought duels, commoners settled disputes in fistfights or worse. Judge William Battle was shocked in 1851 to see how thoroughly the informal code of honor supplanted the law. A Burke County lawyer named William Waightstill Avery shot and killed another man in the courtroom in front of the judge and dozens of spectators; ten days later a jury of citizens speedily acquitted Avery of murder because the victim previously had cowhided Avery on a public street, thus calling into question his honor.

Encounters with others had an extra bite amid the isolation of rural life, and conflict in such communities, whose members all were known to each other, became very personal. People managed their own affairs, and their own district became their world. They knew well their problems, their friends, and their enemies. As they contested issues with other individuals, they were prone to take the law into their own hands. To many the rules of law were distant and abstract compared to the small realm that was home, a realm in which they sought to establish their will. One visitor found such attitudes in a man who spoke openly of avenging himself on "six or seven creeturs up in my district." "I don't speak fur nothin' but my deestric,' " the man specified, "an' what I tell ye is what me an' my neighbors 'll stand to." Thus community standards, hammered out through the clash of wills, could take the place of formal statutes, and the direct action of assault could inject a rough form of equality among individuals into the social order.

But there was another important agent of democratic values in the culture of many yeomen. Evangelical religion exercised a powerful influence over many North Carolinians, impelling them to concentrate upon religious priorities whose sacred character superseded all worldly strivings. This religious world created its own, autonomous standards beside which the pretensions of secular powers were, by definition, dross. A sizable portion of the state's ordinary citizens followed evangelical faiths and thus participated in an emotionally compelling way of life that stood apart from society's rules of hierarchy.

Methodists and Baptists dominated evangelical circles in much of North Carolina. In 1860 Alamance County had seven Methodist churches and two Baptist congregations; Caldwell County had sixteen Methodist and fifteen Baptist churches; for Edgecombe the figures were eight and nine; and for New Hanover and Randolph they were eighteen and fourteen and fifty-one and seven, respectively. Various other dissenting sects, such as the Christians, Presbyterians, or Lutherans as well as Primitive and Missionary Baptists claimed adherents throughout the state, but the higher-status Episcopalian churches were rare outside plantation areas. Randolph County had an unusually varied mixture of religions that included a strong community of Friends.

An important quality of evangelical congregations was the seriousness of their devotion to pious living and the rigor of their discipline. Both Methodists and Baptists, for example, believed that the church had a responsibility to monitor the conduct of its members. Methodists periodically examined the character of delegates to their conferences and of exhorters, licensed preachers, and other officers; those found wanting lost their place or failed to have their licenses renewed. New members generally were admitted "on trial" before gaining acceptance into "full communion." The Baptists likewise supervised the behavior of their communicants in virtually any area of personal or business life. Baptist churches, each acting independently as an autonomous body, appointed committees of their members to investigate rumors or charges of sinful behavior. Called into the presence of the congregation, a wrongdoer had to hear the committee's report and answer to the membership, on pain of expulsion.

The evangelical sought through conversion and faith to enter into a new and holier life, and therefore any signs of falling away from God's path were relevant. The Mount Zion Baptist Church in Alamance County scrutinized a dispute between two members "about some unmarked hogs" as readily as it appointed "a Committee of females . . . to inquire into a Report in circulation against Kisia Wheeler for the sin of fornication." The nearby Mount Olive Baptist Church heard "A report laid in by the Commity [Committee] Against Brother Levi Crutchfield for Drinking too Mutch and Swaring"; it also investigated "A Charg" that "Brother J. F. Cheek . . . was the Father of A [il]legitimate child" and delegated "Brother Alston Smith . . . to see Brother John Edwards for reported absence." Orange County's Mount Herman Baptist Church expelled a number of members in the 1850s for "neglect in attending Church Meetings" as well as for more notorious sins. Similarly, the nine churches in the conference of Lenoir Crescent Methodist Church regularly reported the number of expulsions as well as conversions and heard appeals in which the member under question had to appear in person.

Given the individualism of the ordinary farmer, it was not remarkable that Brother Oliver Foster after being absent "for some time" from Mount Zion Baptist Church defiantly told the investigating committee "that he had as good right to stay away as others." But most church members had committed themselves fervidly to a new way of living and therefore regarded their summons before the congregation as a serious crisis. Kisia Wheeler admitted her fornication and "Requested the church to forgive her." Her repentence resulted in a successful "motion [that] the church forgive her." Similarly an Orange County Baptist "made his confession" of drunkenness and was "forgiven" with a "Serious Charge" from the "Moderator . . . to abstain from even the appearance of that evil." Although Edward Edwards, a Caldwell County Methodist, had been expelled from the church at Lenoir for profanity, his "particular temperament . . . the very vexing cause . . . his great desire to remain . . . and the probability of his doing better in the future" won him a pardon. The first time Alamance County Baptists investigated Sister Anne Kimery for "sinful conduct," she "confessed she had done wrong," sought forgiveness, and remained in fellowship. A year later, however, the congregation excommunicated her "for not Complying with the Requirements of the Church and for sinful Conduct and fornication."

In the eyes of the church faith, zeal, devotion to righteous living, and other spiritual qualities counted, not secular social status. Committees had a duty to investigate according to God's law, and though they might find a rumor to be false, they took stands against wrongdoing no matter what the position of its perpetrator. Some politically influential men belonged to the Lenoir Crescent Methodist Conference, and they found that the rituals of politics could conflict with the requirements of the church. In 1850 the Quarterly Conference resolved that "no member . . . will hereafter support or vote for any candidate for office who shall treat to ardent Spirits"; it judged the distilling of liquor a violation of the "Rule of Discipline." Because treating was virtually obligatory in politics yet forbidden in religion, the politically ambitious Methodist faced a difficult choice. By 1853 the conference had demonstrated the strength of its resolve on three occasions: it found a steward of the church guilty of "treating and allowing treating to be done" and dismissed him from his office; and twice, by increasing majorities, it reaffirmed the church's policy.

Evangelical religion symbolized an alternative, more democratic set of values in a rigid hierarchical social order. Beginning with the Second Great Awakening after 1800, evangelicalism brought "a new sense of worthiness and hope to people at every level of society. . . . Faith and worship instilled a sense of competence and dignity into ordinary people in the South." The thrust of evangelicalism was to democratize religion and make salvation available to all, not just a few elect. One of its tendencies was to breach racial barriers and involve black and white together in worship (a phenomenon which occurred in some of the churches described above). In fact, evangelicalism had a "soaring ambition to unite and relate all individual experiences in ways which blur and obscure the larger society with its resistant substrata of habit and injustice." Another tendency of evangelicalism was to lead people to renounce the "temptations . . . vain amusements . . . and the allurements of the world"; indeed it sometimes denounced wealth, power, and prestige as worldly vanities unimportant before God. More explicitly than any other source, evangelical Christianity proclaimed to antebellum Southerners "that wisdom and authority and fame belonged to people equally and could be appropriated and celebrated by anyone with the gumption and virtue to do so."

This faith was a powerful element in North Carolina (and southern) culture. It worked against and moderated the aristocratic tendencies in the social order. To the extent that it reached people at all levels of society, it tended to blur the line between aristocracy and democracy, hierarchy and equality. In this way it rendered society a more ambiguous and complex whole. But evangelicalism had not united all levels of society or created a uniform consciousness. The social order remained highly divergent and stratified, and therefore the functional significance of evangelicalism lay in its strengthening of democratic values.

At some times and in some circumstances white North Carolinians felt almost no class tension or separation, but the potential for such awareness was strong. . . .

As 1864 advanced, desertion and violence spread all over North Carolina. Governor Vance received pleas for help from Richmond and Chatham counties in August; in the latter instance he learned that deserters had "threatened to burn Pittsbraugh [Pittsboro]." Another man claimed that "Robbing houses and stealing and shooting down Cattle in the woods has become to be the order *of the day*." Although many felt problems in Randolph County had been solved in the fall of 1864, by January 1865 Jonathan Worth reported that "theft, robbery, and almost every other crime are common in almost all the rural districts" and were increasing. "We bolt & bar our doors every night, not knowing what hour they [Bushwackers] may make their appearance," declared a member of Caldwell County's gentry. By February and March 1865 reports were common of bands of three to four hundred deserters "committing the most tyrannical outrages," of "bold & defiant" deserters who "had a fight . . . with our *Cavalry*," and of "Union men . . . defying the Confederate authorities."

In addition to the areas mentioned above, frequent complaints of robbery and violence came from counties such as Avery, Wilkes, and Jackson in the mountains; Forsyth, Moore, and Montgomery in the piedmont; and Cumberland, Robeson, Bladen, Columbus, Johnston, and Edgecombe in the east. The problem had expanded all over the state and become a general phenomenon. Order was dissolving and disorder spreading like an epidemic in the last months of the war. Not only had violence become a daily affair, but also the forces of illegal opposition to authority had become so formidable that in many places the power to enforce obedience was in doubt. Bemoaning the fact that a judge had not dared to hold court in Pittsboro and Asheboro, Jonathan Worth admitted, "it is an acknowledgment to the deserters that they have overawed the courts." If the courts, which could command the presence of armed forces of the state, were so threatened, it was far more clear to the ordinary citizen that the state was struggling with a massive tide of violence within.

In fact, as the breadth of the evidence indicates, North Carolina experienced internal war as well as the anguish of war with the forces of the

United States. Citizens within the state had resorted to violence to achieve change. By turning their backs on the established political process, they revealed a breakdown in the legitimacy of the social order. Their actions pointed also toward the existence of a startling amount of collective frustration and aggression in the population at large. Deeply divisive conflict was at work within. . . .

. . . The crisis of internal war destroyed interclass unity and revealed a fissure that had run beneath the surface of the antebellum social system. The proud and independent yeomen had managed their own affairs and held to a Jacksonian, indeed an American, faith that they were as good as anybody. Their evangelical religion and their slow but steady economic progress had nourished a strong devotion to democratic values. At the same time they had lived in quite an undemocratic state and coexisted with aristocratic leaders who exercised major control over social processes. The yeomen could not help but know these facts, yet in the antebellum era they often had been able to ignore them.

The prewar social system, despite growing signs of conflict, had been able to maintain an appearance of calm because the yeomen customarily had enjoyed a large degree of functional independence. Their daily routines of subsistence farming and livestock raising took place in a sparsely settled, rural world that left them fairly isolated from the larger society. Most yeomen did not frequently confront the facts of class privilege, and they were free to seek salvation in company with a self-governing, evangelical congregation or to devote their attention to family ties, hunting and recreation, or other activities of their choice. In normal times many of these people tolerated power realities that were difficult to change, and thus a combination of yeoman independence and aristocratic privilege was usually possible. The rich largely dominated what the poor largely ignored, and both groups concentrated primarily on their own affairs. This meant that there had been an unrecognized condition to yeoman cooperation with authority. In effect the price of North Carolina's autocratic government was substantial independence for the lower classes and acceptable living conditions among them.

During the war all the essential conditions of coexistence were violated. After a long prewar period of economic improvement for nonslaveholders and slaveholders alike, ordinary North Carolinians experienced a sudden and drastic deterioration in their standard of living. For tens of thousands penury and hunger became constant companions. Government, which traditionally had borne lightly upon the people, now reached deeply into society, imposed unprecedented burdens, and demanded painful sacrifices. Moreover, government took these actions in ways that were inequitable and discriminatory and without successful results; thus it seemed both oppressive and ineffectual. Nor could efforts to aid the yeomen offset these deficiencies. Poor relief, even in adequate quantities, would have been unsatisfactory because it meant the end of people's precious independence and a demeaning reliance on those who arrogantly claimed superiority. The conditions of wartime added up to an attack on the core of yeomen culture.

Given the assertive individualism that characterized them, it was predictable that they would rebel and struggle against the decline in their status.

The independent thinking and outspoken resentment of many ordinary North Carolinians are evident in a rare letter of protest from a Randolph County man named Emsley Beckerdite to the editor and politician Marmaduke Robins. Although he wrote "in a homely back woods stile," Beckerdite lost no pointedness thereby. Blasting the irresponsibility of the newspapers, he recalled that, "according to [them], cecession was to be peacable. Cotton was to be King, and if by any possibility war should ensue, it was to be a *mighty* little thing. The Yankees would not fight &c., &., &c." Then he asked, addressing himself to a basic question, "Was ours a republican government? You answer in the affirmative. Then I ask again if the people, the bone and sinew of this once great country were ever legitimately consulted upon the question of cecession. You would not like to risk your well earned title to intelligence by answering affirmatively." The war, Beckerdite charged, was the responsibility of a minority and its "ignorance, madness or selfish policy."

Then he proceeded to describe frankly the feelings of the common people who were bearing the resulting burdens. "I have not known a man in the last two years [1863 and 1864] who would not willingly have given all he had and would have pledged all that his friends had to keep out of the army. . . . I tell you plainly that the people of the Confederate states would welcome with ovations any power upon earth that was able to deliver them from Conscription impressments taxation and the other ills imposed upon them by those who have deceived them." Beckerdite even declared that racial justifications for continuing the war could not stand: "We cannot afford to give up the white race for the negro." Then he drew the implication of his arguments very plainly. "The common people, the bone and sinew of the southern states are looking to other sources than the Confederate authorities for deliverance."

These independent, individualistic people looked to themselves for deliverance. They refused to be pushed too far, and once the essential conditions of cooperation had been violated, they adamantly resisted all attempts to force their compliance. After the common people's personal independence had been taken away and their sense of justice violated, they paid no attention to diversionary mechanisms. The elite's cause suffered from the large-scale defection of stubbornly independent individuals who continued to act in an individualistic way. Relatively few engaged in highly organized subversion or laid plans to overthrow the government, but many thousands drew the line at further cooperation and acted instead upon their own concepts of fairness and social justice. They demonstrated that there were limits to society's power over them, and after those limits had been reached they replaced acquiescence with disobedience.

In a very real sense society had embraced not just a white community and a black one but several separate communities of whites. The yeomen constituted a class that was dedicated to the preservation of its way of life. The painful experience of war had deepened the yeomen's sense of their identity as opposed to other groups and shown that they were quite capable of violence in defense of their class position. But the yeomen's social attitudes tended to emphasize disengagement rather than engagement with society. Normally they preferred not to impose their desires on other groups but to continue an independent style of life free from extensive involvement with, or dependence on, others. When necessity required they acted strongly to protect their independence.

Both yeomen and gentry had oriented themselves toward their own group and had dealt with others from a distance. Feisty and sure of themselves, Tar Heels were both reserved and assertive; they sprang to the defense of whatever they valued but otherwise asked to be left alone and generally were willing to accord others the same treatment. In terms used by sociologist John Shelton Reed to describe contemporary social relations, southern whites lived in "different communities" and "pretty well succeed[ed]" both in "ignoring one another" and in "disguis[ing] indifference as cordial respect." The Civil War exposed lines of division that had been invisible in normal times.

人 *F U R T H E R   R E A D I N G*

Fred Arthur Bailey, *Class and Tennessee's Confederate Generation* (1987)

Frederick A. Bode and Donald E. Ginter, eds., *Farm Tenancy and the Census in Antebellum Georgia* (1986)

Randolph B. Campbell, "Intermittent Slave Ownership: Texas as a Test Case," *Journal of Southern History* 51 (February 1985), 15–30.

Bruce Collins, *White Society in the Antebellum South* (1985)

Paul D. Escott, *Many Excellent People: Power and Privilege in North Carolina, 1850–1900* (1985)

Lacy K. Ford, Jr., *Origins of Southern Radicalism: The South Carolina Upcountry, 1800–1860* (1988)

Eugene D. Genovese, "Yeoman Farmers in a Slaveholders' Democracy," in Elizabeth Fox-Genovese and Eugene D. Genovese, *Fruits of Merchant Capital* (1983)

Steven Hahn, *The Roots of Southern Populism* (1983)

J. William Harris, *Plain Folk and Gentry in a Slave Society: White Liberty and Black Slavery in Augusta's Hinterlands* (1985)

James Oakes, *The Ruling Race* (1982)

Frank L. Owsley, *Plain Folk of the Old South* (1949)

Gavin Wright, *The Political Economy of the Cotton South* (1978)

Women's Culture in the Old South

One of the fastest-growing fields of scholarship in southern history is the study of women, both black and white. Initially oriented toward comparisons with the North, research on southern women is now generating its own models and theories and producing information valuable for a better understanding of half of the South's population and of the dynamics of southern society itself.

The South's women lived in a variety of social environments and were divided not only by class lines but also by race. Compared to the North, the South had greater portions of women who were rural, enslaved, and cut off from most associations beyond family and church. How should those realities affect scholars' conceptualization of the social world of southern women? How were women in the South joined by common experiences based on gender and divided by social barriers of race or class? What were the key experiences of socialization for women at different ages and in different groups? What does the evidence reveal of distinct female perspectives on experience or of gender-based patterns of behavior? The agenda for research in this new field is long, but scholars have rapidly made strides toward a fuller understanding of southern women.

⅄ D O C U M E N T S

Free women were constrained in numerous ways, legally and socially, by marriage, family, and community expectations of proper behavior. Evangelical churches, however, were one setting in which southern women could sometimes play an influential role. These churches usually elevated the status of women by allowing them to vote on church matters and giving them a role in church governance. The minutes of a North Carolina congregation, reprinted in the first document, show how women participated in church affairs and helped the church enforce community norms of sexual and matrimonial conduct. Southern women recorded some of the most telling comments on their lives in their diaries. Lucy Breckinridge, who belonged to Virginia's slaveholding elite, kept an unusually frank diary that recorded her unromantic perspective on the decisions a woman made about her life when she married; excerpts from it are reprinted in the second document. Mary Boykin Chesnut, a member of South Carolina's planter class, made biting comments in her diary about slavery and women's subordination. The selections in the third document also contain Mrs. Chesnut's description of the insecurity and even fear felt by white women surrounded by slaves. (Chesnut's references to "Mr. C." and "JC" apply to her husband, James Chesnut.) Fanny Kemble, a famous British actress who married an American, kept a journal when she went to live on his Georgia rice plantation. Her foreigner's perspective, evident in the excerpts contained in the fourth selection, prompted her to make many strong comments on the status of women, particularly slave women. Harriet Jacobs, a woman who escaped from slavery, describes in the fifth document some of the trials that enslaved black women had to endure. One experience that virtually all women in the nineteenth-century South shared was illness, including constant threats to health associated with childbearing. The letters in the last document describe the rapid course of puerperal, or "childbed," fever in Maria Lamar. Many other women in the South (and the North also) shared her fate before the development of antibiotics.

Kisia Wheeler and Anne Kimery Face the Church, 1859, 1864–1865

The [Baptist] Church of Mt. Zion [in Alamance County, North Carolina] met in Conference on Saturday before the 2nd Sunday in September [1859]. . . . On motion a Committee of females was appointed, to wit Rebecca Euliss & Margaret Fogleman, to inquire into a Report in circulation against Kisia Wheeler for the sin of fornication & Report at next meeting.

The Church of Mt. Zion met in Conference on Saturday before the 2nd Sunday in October. . . . The female Committee called on to Report & they Brought a writen Report & [said] that she (Kisia Wheeler) acknowledged she had Done wrong & Requested the Church to forgive her. On motion the church forgive her.

The Church of Mt. Zion met in Conference on Saturday before the 2nd Sunday in May [1864]. . . . Sister Nelly Foster reported that she had seen sinful conduct by sister Anne Kimery. The Church appointed Sisters Peggy Fogleman [and] Rebecca Euliss to go with the same Nelly Foster to see and labour with said Anne Kimery & invite her to next meeting.

The Church of Mt. Zion met in Conference on Saturday before the 2nd Sunday in June. . . . The case of sister Anne Kimery taken up the Committee not Ready to Report.

Kisia Wheeler and Anne Kimery Face the Church, 1859, 1864–1865, reprinted courtesy of North Carolina Division of Archives and History.

The Church of Mt. Zion met in Conference on Saturday before the 2nd Sunday in July. . . . The case of Sister Kimery taken up the Committee Reported that she did not deny the charge. She confessed she had done wrong & asked the church to forgive her, that she believed God had forgiven her. On motion she was forgiven.

The Church of Mt. Zion met in Conference on Saturday before the 2nd Sunday in September [1865]. . . . It is reported that sister Anne Kimery is living with a man unmarried. On motion Sister Fogleman and sister Euliss was appointed to see her and invite her to church meeting.

The Church of Mt. Zion met in Conference on Saturday before the 2nd Sunday in February [1866]. . . . The case of Anne Kimery taken up and she was Excommunicated for not Complying with the Requirements of the Church and for sinful Conduct and fornication.

Lucy Breckinridge Comments on Marriage, 1862–1864

Tuesday, August 12, 1862 . . .

Brother Gilmer indulged his taste for saying original things by advising us not to marry for love. He says that no one knows the person they marry until *it is too late;* that gentlemen are actors and hide their real feelings and characters. The reasons he urged for not marrying for love are that if we do it we are sure to be bitterly disappointed. We find after marriage that the gentleman is not at all what we expected, and if we love him we cannot but feel that very bitterly, whereas, if we only liked him and were disappointed, it would not touch our hearts at all. Very few people can expect happiness after they are married; but then they ought to love each other enough to be willing to make many sacrifices and excuse many faults. From observation, my theory is that wives generally love their husbands more than their lovers. The wife's love grows, becomes deeper, more patient and fonder than ever the girl's could be, while the husband's almost invariably cools down into a sort of patronizing friendship. If they care for their wives at all it is only as a sort of servant, a being made to attend to their comforts and to keep the children out of the way. It is very inconsistent of Brother Gilmer to give us such advice. If ever a couple did marry for love, it was Brother Gilmer and Sister Julia. And he is one of the few husbands I ever saw who I think does and always will love his wife as much as she does him. Seeing their happiness in each other is almost enough to reconcile anyone to matrimony.

Eliza and Miss Fannie have been arguing one question for three weeks. Eliza generally gets the better of it. Miss Fannie maintains that men are

From *Lucy Breckinridge of Grove Hill: The Journal of a Virginia Girl, 1862–1864.* Edited by Mary D. Robertson. Kent State University Press, 1979, used by permission.

in every way superior to women, while Eliza argues warmly in defense of woman. I am neutral and listen to their discussions with great interest. Eliza brings forward so many instances where the woman is the superior or equal that she nearly always vanquishes her opponent. Sometimes they forget the argument and commence talking of their acquaintances, and Miss Fannie will say, "What a pity Miss Blank married Mr. Blank. She has to support the family." Then Eliza exclaims, "Another instance, Miss Fannie, of woman's superiority!" And where Miss Fannie can mention only one instance of the husband's superiority, Eliza can bring forward ten where the wife is the laborer, the head of the family, the gentle and good angel of the household. I rather incline to the opinion that women are purer and better than men, but, then, they are so guarded from evil and temptation, while men are exposed to every temptation to wickedness, and have so many disadvantages to struggle with; and (I think) they have not the moral courage that women have. When a man is good he is certainly the noblest work of God.

One part of the question they argue, I can entertain no doubt upon, viz., which has the most trouble and suffering. A woman's life after she is married, unless there is an immense amount of love, is nothing but suffering and hard work. I never saw a wife and mother who could spend a day of unalloyed happiness and ease. The children are constantly getting hurt, and crying and tearing their dresses, thereby keeping "Mamma" miserable and busy. And then "husband" is cross, and all of her patience and gentleness is necessary to prevent a quarrel. Bless the little babies, though, the trouble they give is almost pleasure. "Mamma" can be quite happy and contented, even with an ill-natured husband, if the "baby" will only sleep well and not have the colic. I wish I was a man! I would make my wife so happy. She would never repent having married me.

Friday, Oct. 3rd, 1862

Cousin Kate put the children into a state of great joy by giving them each a beautiful present and as much candy as they could eat. I found the sock I knit for Robbie was too small so I walked over to Amanda's and got her to knit one the right size for a model for Cousin Kate. Eliza got a letter from Rosa Burwell enclosing a letter from Brother James. Ma got a letter from Aunt Lizzie, telling us of poor Aunt Marianna's death. It is a happy release for her, for her married life has been a long term of suffering. She has been married about seven years and had five children. I never heard of anyone who suffered as much. Her death was very unexpected. They all thought she was doing well after the birth of a dead child, and Uncle Wilmer went to the bed and felt her hand and brow and finding they were very cold, he called the Doctor; they found she had died without anyone's knowing it. I cannot help thinking that Uncle Wilmer is a Bluebeard. I was saying the other day that some relative or connection of ours had died every month since June. John died in June, Aunt Watts and Cousin Edward in July, Fan in August and now Aunt Marianna in September, on Saturday, 27th.

Monday, December 22, 1862 . . .

Capt. Clarke said I must not be an old maid, that I would be too good a wife and mother to sacrifice myself on the altar of Diana, but I do not agree with him. I don't want any grumblesome husband to be sewing and cooking for all the time, nor any disagreeable, colicky little babies, always getting their little noses and mouths soiled and keeping me awake all night. I beg to be excused. Help me, chaste Diana, to keep resolutely this wise determination!! And may all the young maidens who are disposed to laugh at old ladies of my class be brought to believe that there can be such a thing as a happy, contented "old maid" when they look upon the happy face of old "Miss Lucy Breckinridge!"

Sunday, July 5th, 1863

Little Emma and I spent the day together reading the bible and learning hymns. She wrote a note to her Mamma, but the poor child shows very little literary taste and cares for nothing but Ella. She has depreciated very much of late. I missed Ma, Eliza and Emma very much. I read all of Capt. H.'s letters. I ought to destroy them, but cannot make up my mind to do so. I wonder if I shall ever love anyone as much as I did him. I am afraid to think of him much, the old love comes back; but I am so thankful that our engagement is broken off, for all of my family objected so strongly to the match, and I should not have been happy if I had married him. Ma came late this evening having had a pleasant visit. Poor Johnny Clarke was drowned in the river on Thursday; two of his brothers met with a similar fate. Mr. Anthony sent me the only ripe apricot, dear, old gentleman! Oh, dear! how dismally the frogs are singing. There is something in the idea that ever since I or anyone else can remember those or some other frogs have been singing that very same song, which always reminds me of eternity. I love to hear them, but it has the same effect on me that drowning is said to have—recalling all the incidents of the past, more particularly those of my childhood, to my mind, and it is impossible to think of the past without being melancholy—even when we remember happy things. We are generally alone and in some private place when we indulge in the pleasures of memory, and the very contrast between what we are recalling and our present position produces melancholy. It is very sweet to look upon "the blue mountains of our dim childhood" as Richter calls the past, and a very good little simile it is. The farther we get from the mountain the more softened is the outline, the less distinct the rocks and rugged places. The mountain is not *blue* enough yet for me to be thinking so sadly. What will my reflections be 10 years hence if I begin so early to moralize, then I'll have cause, I expect, for mournfulness, being quite a desolate old maid or still worse a married woman with ever so many crying babies and a cross, horrid husband as all husbands are. Oh, dear! Oh, dear!! How gloomy the prospect.

Saturday, January 16, 1864 . . .

Let people talk as much as they choose about engagements being happy; my late experience does not increase my faith in the idea. Engagements lead too certainly to matrimony. It is happy to be "in maiden expectation fancy free." I envy girls who are free—they cannot realize the blessedness of it. I hate the idea of marrying. I saw a quotation tonight that expressed my ideas exactly, "The hour of marriage ends the female reign! And we give all we have to buy a chain; Hire men to be our lords, who were our slaves; And bribe our lovers to be perjured knaves. O, how they swear to heaven and the bride, They will be kind to her and none beside; And to themselves, the while in secret swear, They will be kind to everyone but her." Perhaps I am unjust in my opinion of man and too partial to woman. Sometimes I am wild and school-girlish enough to dream of connubial bliss. I am going to try very hard "a gude wife to be," at any rate, and I expect I shall be enabled to endure all the hardships. I feel certain, as if I had a peep into the book of fate, that I shall never marry Lieut. Bassett, not that I shall prove false, but something will prevent it. Maybe *he'll jilt me*! That would be funny. Mamma and Eliza love him so much they would make me remain faithful if I needed any compulsion. I got a letter from him a day or two ago. He had sprained his wrist. I wish he was here so I could make him well.

Saturday, May 21, 1864

On Tuesday, the 17th, I worked very hard all day, and was right much discomfited at being interrupted by Eliza's exclaiming, "There's a white-faced horse"—and sure enough there was dear Selim and Lieut. B. He staid until Friday the 20th. I did not tell him goodbye. I enjoyed his visit somewhat—enjoyed teasing him about being bald, etc. We are D. V. [*Deo volente*] to be married next September. I do not look forward to that time with much pleasure though I do love him a great deal more than he loves me—more than any selfish, wicked man *can* love—not meaning to insinuate that he is more afflicted with those qualities than all the rest of mankind. He has some qualities that I admire very much. I always wanted to love someone upon whom I could lean, someone to protect me, to be firm for me and help me to do what is right. I am so weak and yielding with those whom I love. It is woman's nature to love in a submissive, trusting way, but it is better and safer to rely altogether upon themselves—poor creatures! God help them! I got a letter from Tommy the day he left, a very smart letter as all of his are.

[Lucy Breckinridge married "Tommy" Bassett on January 28, 1865. On June 16, 1865, she died of typhoid fever.]

Mary Boykin Chesnut on Women and Slavery, 1861

March 4, 1861 . . .

Yesterday I dined with Brewster, Mallory, Hill, Mr. C & the Judge. What a merry dinner it. I introduced Mallory & Hill at last. After dinner slept until evening—the same dish at evening. Until half past ten, Mallory, Hill, Frank Campbell, Brewster, Gov. Moore, the Judge, Mr. C, I the only lady. I must say the stories 'tho' rich & rare were rather strongly spiced for my presence. Mr. Mallory's were the best. 'Tho' they say his mother was a washer woman, he is the most refined in the group who surround me here except my husband. Mallory told the tale here of Judge Butler in the Senate—giving way to "flounce tail." I understand now some of Mrs. Clay's jokes.

Frank Campbell told me Dallas had refused to allow Buchanan to visit his house in Philadelphia—& Buchanan was afraid to recall Dallas for fear of ripping up the old story. Sat at home this morning eating my own heart—but knew that would never do. So rushed, first got my watch, left a card for Mrs. Davis, called a Mrs. Farley who lives in a beautiful house—& then left a card at the top of a high hill for Mrs. Fitzpatrick. Came home in a more sane state of mind with a bunch of flowers. Had a letter from Kate Withers—she improves evidently. Says she can sing.

I saw to day a sale of Negroes—Mulatto women in *silk dresses*—one girl was on the stand. Nice looking—like my Nancy—she looked as coy & pleased at the bidder. South Carolina slave holder as I am my very soul sickened—it is too dreadful. I tried to reason—this is not worse than the willing sale most women make of themselves in marriage—nor can the consequences be worse. The Bible authorizes marriage & slavery—poor women! poor slaves!—"Still—slavery tho art a bitter draught disguise it as we will & ten thousands have drunk," &c.

March 18, 1861 . . .

I wonder if it be a sin to think slavery a curse to any land. Sumner said not one word of this hated institution which is not true. Men & women are punished when their masters & mistresses are brutes & not when they do wrong—& then we live surrounded by prostitutes. An abandoned woman is sent out of any decent house elsewhere. Who thinks any worse of a Negro or Mulatto woman for being a thing we can't name. God forgive *us*, but ours is a *monstrous* system & wrong & iniquity. Perhaps the rest of the world is as bad. This *only* I see: like the patriarchs of old our men live all in one house with their wives & their concubines, & the Mulattoes one sees in every family exactly resemble the white children—& every lady tells you who is the father of all the Mulatto children in every body's

From *The Private Mary Chesnut* edited by C. Vann Woodward and Elisabeth Muhlenfeld. Permission granted by Harold Ober Associates Incorporated.

household, but those in her own, she seems to think drop from the clouds or pretends so to think—Good women we have, *but* they talk of all *nastiness*—tho they never do wrong, they talk day & night of [six unrecoverable words, apparently a quote]. My disgust sometimes is boiling over—but they are, I believe, in conduct the purest women God ever made. Thank God for my country women—alas for the men! No worse than men every where, but the lower their mistresses, the more degraded they must be.

My mother in law told me when I was first married not to send my female servants in the street on errands. They were there tempted, led astray—& then she said placidly, "So they told *me* when I came here—& I was very particular, *but you see with what* result." Mr. Harris said it was so patriarchal. So it is—flocks & herds & slaves—& wife Leah does not suffice. Rachel must be *added,* if not *married.* & all the time they seem to think themselves patterns—models of husbands & fathers.

Mrs. Davis told me "every body described my husband's father as an odd character—a Millionaire who did nothing for his son whatever, left him to struggle with poverty," &c. I replied, "Mr. Chesnut Senior thinks himself the best of fathers—& his son thinks likewise. I have nothing to say—but it is true, he has no money but what he makes as a lawyer," &c. Again I say, my countrywomen are as pure as angels—tho surrounded by another race who are—the social evil!

September 21, 1861
Last night Mary Witherspoon wrote to JC that her mother [in] law, dear old cousin Betsey, had been murdered by her negroes. Mr. C concluded to go at once. She was smothered—arms & legs bruised & face scratched. William, a man of hers, & several others suspected of her own negroes, people she has pampered & spoiled & done every thing for. Next day I came here, that is, to day. Told David & JC good bye at Bonney's. Came to Aunt B's; had a pleasant visit but drank port wine. Judge very kind. Then I went to the Perkinses' but did not see Cally. As I expected, her Mother is tormenting her to death.

Came here, found Mr. Borman and the children as I left them—& was *ill.* Aunt Sally H & Mary came. I had to rush in & was really ill.

September 22, 1861
Sunday did not leave my bed—in the evening Aunt B came—in the most wretched state about this most foul murder.

September 23, 1861
Sat in the piazza—& kind Mary Boykin—Mary Edward—sent me some lemons. Nothing pleasant in the northern or rather Richmond papers. Pickens wrote to JC to offer him a rifle regiment but in Confederate Service.

Retire now to the Caxtons'. Mrs. Cureton sends scuppernongs. Col. & Mrs. Deas at Sandy Hill.

September 24, 1861
Tuesday. Mrs. Cureton sat the morning—& I knit a sock. At night David
& JC returned—nothing definite. William & Rhody & several others in
jail.

George Williams has not been [to see] his sister since the murder.
Society Hill in a ferment. John Wallace & Kirby there & Sam Evans,
wanting all the Negroes burnt.

September 25, 1861
Wednesday. Spent at Kate's & came down in the evening & came by. *Saw*
the Rangers but did not drive near enough to say good bye. Came home
& Col. C & Miss Sally came to hear the news.

September 26, 1861
Thursday. Rainy day—knit—& arranged my things.

September 27, 1861
Friday, Sandy Hill. Mr. Chesnut wrote 4 pages of foolscap for his mother
with the details of that fiendish murder at Society Hill. The papers are
dreary—if our army retires into winter quarters woe be unto us.

Read a frantic article in the *Mercury*—arranging a party for Barnwell
Rhett. I do not see what Mr. C means—he writes to no one—knows nothing
that is going on. If he has *one* active friend in the state I do not know it
unless it be Wilmot DeSaussure & Bob McCaw. In the mean time at these
fiery times he is as peaceful here & as *secure!* Making arrangements to
spend the winter in Richmond. John C writes capital letters—pitches into
Capt. B. Bonham, Douglas, DeSaussure, &c, &c, as boldly.

Davis has given Tom Drayton a *generalcy*. If JC made Jeff Davis
President has he not been *rewarded* as usual. Wm. T. Martin [is] Gen. of
Cavalry—the post JC could have gotten by lifting a finger.

I went to see the Perkinses—but only saw Miss Ossear while I was in
Kirkwood. She says it is the same as if Cally was twice widowed—poor
thing. Such comforters. Mr. Chesnut treated Mrs. Lee shamefully. I do
not know how she will feel towards us.

Poor old cousin Betsey—Murdered! I always felt that I had never
injured any one black especially & therefore feared nothing from them—
but *now*. She was so good—so kind—the ground is knocked up from under
me. I sleep & wake with the horrid vision before my eyes of those vile
black hands—smothering her.

October 9, 1861 . . .
John Witherspoon writes that Rhody & Romeo have confessed that they
& William & Silvy murdered Mrs. W——William holding the counterpane
over her face & the others her arms & feet—& then they changed her
clothes. Hicks the detective says it was one of the best managed plots he
has ever had any thing to do with.

The Philadelphia Smiths have come. Mrs. Edward Stockton another
baby. Mrs. John Williams did not come but sent a piece of worsted work

& a letter. None of them have taken any concern about Mrs. Witherspoon's death—in any way, shape or form. JC had a letter from F. J. Moses offering a company for *his* regiment!

October 10, 1861

Went up to Cool Spring. Stopped at Aunt B's, had a very pleasant morning. *No Joe.* Got to Kate's to dinner. Found as I feared that Negroes & over seer & all had tried to make it unpleasant for her & she wishes to go to Buncombe. Thompson is the worst.

Circumstantial details of Mrs. Witherspoon's death. Wm. came home & Rhody told him John had threatened them with punishment next day. Wm. said, "Do as I bid you & there will be no whipping here tomorrow." John had found out about them having a party & using Mrs. W's silver & house linen. They went to sleep & William woke them up in time. They went in one by one. Wm. stood at her head with the counterpane & Rhody at her feet & Romeo & Silvy at each arm. She struggled very hard & a long time. After they thought her dead she revived—& they commenced their hellish work again. Next day while Molly was so scared, Rhody saw her cap was bloodied & changed it—& she saw that the counterpane on the crib was bloodied & showed it herself that she might not be suspected.

Mr. Chesnut found a superb crop on John's place—but sulky & dissatisfied negroes.

December 7, 1861

I have been busy all day reading old letters. What a meek, humble little thing I was—how badly JC has played his cards to let me develop into the self sufficient thing I am now. For I think this last bitter drop was for *me.* He will care very little—but I had grown insufferable with my arrogance. Some times I feel it a righteous retribution for the rage I got into a year ago about JC's writing those letters for his nephew.

Team thinks the war may leave us a great & independent nation but *slavery* is over. I have thought so six months (& *hoped* it). He told several overseer's anecdotes, *which* made [illegible word] not *sigh* to believe it, of one of Powell McRae's Negroes, driven to despair by the driver, tying her baby on her back & walking into the river. Found drowned—baby still strapped to her back—& said Team, "The man who caused it was not hung!" Ho for honest poverty!

Fanny Kemble on Slave Women, 1839

[January 1839]

Dear E[lizabeth],

. . . [Slaves'] tasks, of course, profess to be graduated according to the sex, age, and strength of the laborer; but in many instances this is not the

Reprinted by permission of the University of Georgia Press from *Journal of a Residence on a Georgian Plantation in 1838–1839*, edited, with an introduction, by John A. Scott, pp. 66–72, 94–96. Copyright 1984 by John A. Scott.

case, as I think you will agree when I tell you that on Mr. [Butler]'s first visit to his estates he found that the men and the women who labored in the fields had the same task to perform. This was a noble admission of female equality, was it not?—and thus it had been on the estate for many years past. Mr. [Butler], of course, altered the distribution of the work, diminishing the quantity done by the women.

I had a most ludicrous visit this morning from the midwife of the estate—rather an important personage both to master and slave, as to her unassisted skill and science the ushering of all the young Negroes into their existence of bondage is entrusted. I heard a great deal of conversation in the dressing room adjoining mine while performing my own toilet, and presently Mr. [Butler] opened my room door, ushering in a dirty, fat, good-humored looking old Negress, saying: "The midwife, Rose, wants to make your acquaintance."

"Oh massa!" shrieked out the old creature, in a paroxysm of admiration, "where you get this lilly alabaster baby!"

For a moment I looked round to see if she was speaking of my baby; but no, my dear, this superlative apostrophe was elicited by the fairness of *my skin:* so much for degrees of comparison. Now I suppose that if I chose to walk arm in arm with the dingiest mulatto through the streets of Philadelphia, nobody could possibly tell by my complexion that I was not his sister, so that the mere quality of mistress must have had a most miraculous effect upon my skin in the eyes of poor Rose. But this species of outrageous flattery is as usual with these people as with the low Irish, and arises from the ignorant desire, common to both the races, of propitiating at all costs the fellow creature who is to them as a Providence—or rather, I should say, a fate—for 'tis a heathen and no Christian relationship.

Soon after this visit, I was summoned into the wooden porch or piazza of the house, to see a poor woman who desired to speak to me. This was none other than the tall, emaciated-looking Negress who, on the day of our arrival, had embraced me and my nurse with such irresistible zeal. She appeared very ill today, and presently unfolded to me a most distressing history of bodily afflictions. She was the mother of a very large family, and complained to me that, what with childbearing and hard field labor, her back was almost broken in two. With an almost savage vehemence of gesticulation, she suddenly tore up her scanty clothing, and exhibited a spectacle with which I was inconceivably shocked and sickened. The facts, without any of her corroborating statements, bore tolerable witness to the hardships of her existence. I promised to attend to her ailments and give her proper remedies; but these are natural results, inevitable and irremediable ones, of improper treatment of the female frame; and, though there may be alleviation, there cannot be any cure when once the beautiful and wonderful structure has been thus made the victim of ignorance, folly, and wickedness.

After the departure of this poor woman, I walked down the settlement toward the infirmary or hospital, calling in at one or two of the houses along the row. These cabins consist of one room, about twelve feet by fifteen, with a couple of closets smaller and closer than the staterooms of a ship, divided off from the main room and each other by rough wooden partitions, in which the inhabitants sleep. They have almost all of them a rude bedstead, with the gray moss of the forests for mattress, and filthy, pestilential-looking blankets for covering. Two families (sometimes eight and ten in number) reside in one of these huts, which are mere wooden frames pinned, as it were, to the earth by a brick chimney outside, whose enormous aperture within pours down a flood of air, but little counteracted by the miserable spark of fire, which hardly sends an attenuated thread of lingering smoke up its huge throat. A wide ditch runs immediately at the back of these dwellings, which is filled and emptied daily by the tide. Attached to each hovel is a small scrap of ground for a garden, which, however, is for the most part untended and uncultivated.

Such of these dwellings as I visited today were filthy and wretched in the extreme, and exhibited that most deplorable consequence of ignorance and an abject condition, the inability of the inhabitants to secure and improve even such pitiful comfort as might yet be achieved by them. Instead of the order, neatness, and ingenuity which might convert even these miserable hovels into tolerable residences, there was the careless, reckless, filthy indolence which even the brutes do not exhibit in their lairs and nests, and which seemed incapable of applying to the uses of existence the few miserable means of comfort yet within their reach. Firewood and shavings lay littered about the doors, while the half-naked children were cowering round two or three smouldering cinders. The moss with which the chinks and crannies of their ill-protecting dwellings might have been stuffed was trailing in dirt and dust about the ground, while the back door of the huts, opening upon a most unsightly ditch, was left wide open for the fowls and ducks, which they are allowed to raise, to travel in and out, increasing the filth of the cabin by what they brought and left in every direction.

In the midst of the floor, or squatting round the cold hearth, would be four or five little children from four to ten years old, the latter all with babies in their arms, the care of the infants being taken from the mothers (who are driven afield as soon as they recover from child labor), and devolved upon these poor little nurses, as they are called, whose business it is to watch the infant, and carry it to its mother whenever it may require nourishment. To these hardly human little beings I addressed my remonstrances about the filth, cold, and unnecessary wretchedness of their room, bidding the older boys and girls kindle up the fire, sweep the floor, and expel the poultry. For a long time my very words seemed unintelligible to them, till, when I began to sweep and make up the fire, etc., they first fell to laughing, and then imitating me. The incrustations of dirt on their hands, feet, and faces were my next object of attack, and the stupid Negro practice (by-the-by, but a short time since nearly universal in enlightened Europe) of keeping the babies with their feet bare, and their heads, already well capped by nature with their woolly hair, wrapped in half a dozen hot, filthy coverings.

Thus I traveled down the "street," in every dwelling endeavoring to awaken a new perception, that of cleanliness, sighing, as I went, over the futility of my own exertions, for how can slaves be improved? Nathless, thought I, let what can be done; for it may be that, the two being incompatible, improvement may yet expel slavery; and so it might, and surely would, if, instead of beginning at the end, I could but begin at the beginning of my task. If the mind and soul were awakened, instead of mere physical good attempted, the physical good would result, and the great curse vanish away; but my hands are tied fast, and this corner of the work is all that I may do. Yet it cannot be but, from my words and actions, some revelations should reach these poor people; and going in and out among them perpetually, I shall teach, and they learn involuntarily a thousand things of deepest import. They must learn, and who can tell the fruit of that knowledge alone, that there are beings in the world, even with skins of a different color from their own, who have sympathy for their misfortunes, love for their virtues, and respect for their common nature—but oh! my heart is full almost to bursting as I walk among these most poor creatures.

The infirmary is a large two-story building, terminating the broad orange-planted space between the two rows of houses which form the first settlement; it is built of whitewashed wood, and contains four large-sized rooms. But how shall I describe to you the spectacle which was presented to me on entering the first of these? But half the casements, of which there were six, were glazed, and these were obscured with dirt, almost as much as the other windowless ones were darkened by the dingy shutters, which the shivering inmates had fastened to in order to protect themselves from the cold. In the enormous chimney glimmered the powerless embers of a few sticks of wood, round which, however, as many of the sick women as could approach were cowering, some on wooden settles, most of them on the ground, excluding those who were too ill to rise; and these last poor wretches lay prostrate on the floor, without bed, mattress, or pillow, buried in tattered and filthy blankets, which, huddled round them as they lay strewed about, left hardly space to move upon the floor. And here, in their hour of sickness and suffering, lay those whose health and strength are spent in unrequited labor for us—those who, perhaps even yesterday, were being urged on to their unpaid task—those whose husbands, fathers, brothers, and sons were even at that hour sweating over the earth, whose produce was to buy for us all the luxuries which health can revel in, all the comforts which can alleviate sickness. I stood in the midst of them, perfectly unable to speak, the tears pouring from my eyes at this sad spectacle of their misery, myself and my emotion alike strange and incomprehensible to them. Here lay women expecting every hour the terrors and agonies of childbirth, others who had just brought their doomed offspring into the world, others who were groaning over the anguish and bitter disappointment of miscarriages—here lay some burning with fever, others chilled with cold and aching with rheumatism, upon the hard cold ground, the draughts and dampness of the atmosphere increasing their sufferings, and dirt, noise, and stench, and every aggravation of which sickness is capable, combined in their condition—here they lay like brute beasts, absorbed in physical suffering; unvisited by any of those Divine influences which may ennoble the dispensations of pain and illness, forsaken, as it seemed to me, of all good; and yet, O God, Thou surely hadst not forsaken them! Now pray take notice that this is the hospital of an estate where the owners are supposed to be humane, the overseer efficient and kind, and the Negroes remarkably well cared for and comfortable.

As soon as I recovered from my dismay, I addressed old Rose the midwife, who had charge of this room, bidding her open the shutters of such windows as were glazed, and let in the light. I next proceeded to make up the fire; but, upon my lifting a log for that purpose, there was one universal outcry of horror, and old Rose, attempting to snatch it from me, exclaimed: "Let alone, missis—let be; what for you lift wood? you have nigger enough, missis, to do it!" I hereupon had to explain to them my view of the purposes for which hands and arms were appended to our bodies, and forthwith began making Rose tidy up the miserable apartment, removing all the filth and rubbish from the floor that could be removed, folding up in piles the blankets of the patients who were not using them, and placing, in rather more sheltered and comfortable positions, those who were unable to rise. It was all that I could do, and having enforced upon them all my earnest desire that they should keep their room swept, and as tidy as possible, I passed on to the other room on the ground floor, and to the two above, one of which is appropriated to the use of the men who are ill. They were all in the same deplorable condition, the upper rooms being rather the more miserable, inasmuch as none of the windows were glazed at all, and they had, therefore, only the alternative of utter darkness, or killing draughts of air from the unsheltered casements. In all, filth, disorder, and misery abounded; the floor was the only bed, and scanty begrimed rags of blankets the only covering. I left this refuge for Mr. [Butler]'s sick dependents with my clothes covered with dust, and full of vermin, and with a heart heavy enough, as you will well believe. My morning's work had fatigued me not a little, and I was glad to return to the house, where I gave vent to my indignation and regret at the scene I had just witnessed to Mr. [Butler] and his overseer, who, here, is a member of our family. The latter told me that the condition of the hospital had appeared to him, from his first entering upon his situation (only within the last year), to require a reform, and that he had proposed it to the former manager, Mr. K[ing], and Mr. [Butler]'s brother, who is part proprietor of the estate, but, receiving no encouragement from them, had supposed that it was a matter of indifference to the owners, and had left it in the condition in which he had found it, in which condition it has been for the last nineteen years and upward.

This new overseer of ours has lived fourteen years with an old Scotch gentleman, who owns an estate adjoining Mr. [Butler]'s, on the island of St. Simons, upon which estate, from everything I can gather, and from what I know of the proprietor's character, the slaves are probably treated with as much humanity as is consistent with slavery at all, and where the management and comfort of the hospital in particular had been most carefully and judiciously attended to. With regard to the indifference of our former manager upon the subject of the accommodation for the sick, he was an excellent overseer, *videlicet* the estate returned a full income under his management, and such men have nothing to do with sick slaves: they are tools, to be mended only if they can be made available again; if not, to be flung by as useless, without further expense of money, time, or trouble.

[January 1839]

Dear E[lizabeth],

This morning I paid my second visit to the infirmary, and found there had been some faint attempt at sweeping and cleaning, in compliance with my entreaties. The poor woman Harriet, however, whose statement with regard to the impossibility of their attending properly to their children had been so vehemently denied by the overseer, was crying bitterly. I asked her what ailed her, when, more by signs and dumb show than words, she and old Rose informed me that Mr. O———had flogged her that morning for having told me that the women had not time to keep their children clean. It is part of the regular duty of every overseer to visit the infirmary at least once a day, which he generally does in the morning, and Mr. O———'s visit had preceded mine but a short time only, or I might have been edified by seeing a man horsewhip a woman. I again and again made her repeat her story, and she again and again affirmed that she had been flogged for what she told me, none of the whole company in the room denying it or contradicting her. I left the room because I was so disgusted and indignant that I could hardly restrain my feelings, and to express them could have produced no single good result. . . .

Among our visitors from St. Simons today was Hannah's mother (it seems to me that there is not a girl of sixteen on the plantations but has children, nor a woman of thirty but has grandchildren). Old House Molly, as she is called, from the circumstance of her having been one of the slaves employed in domestic offices during Major [Butler]'s residence on the island, is one of the oldest and most respected slaves on the estate, and was introduced to me by Mr. [Butler] with especial marks of attention and regard; she absolutely embraced him, and seemed unable sufficiently to express her ecstasy at seeing him again. Her dress, like that of her daughter, and all the servants who have at any time been employed about the family, bore witness to a far more improved taste than the half-savage adornment of the other poor blacks, and upon my observing to her how agreeable her neat and cleanly appearance was to me, she replied that her old master (Major [Butler]) was extremely particular in this respect, and that in his time all the house servants were obliged to be very nice and careful about their persons.

She named to me all her children, an immense tribe; and, by-the-by, E[lizabeth], it has occurred to me that whereas the increase of this ill-fated race is frequently adduced as a proof of their good treatment and well-being, it really and truly is no such thing, and springs from quite other causes than the peace and plenty which a rapidly increasing population are supposed to indicate. If you will reflect for a moment upon the overgrown families of the half-starved Irish peasantry and English manufacturers, you will agree with me that these prolific shoots by no means necessarily spring from a rich or healthy soil. Peace and plenty are certainly causes of human increase, and so is recklessness; and this, I take it, is the impulse in the instance of the English manufacturer, the Irish peasant, and the Negro slave. Indeed here it is more than recklessness, for there are certain indirect premiums held out to obey the early commandment of replenishing the earth which do not fail to have their full effect. In the first place, none of the cares, those noble cares, that holy thoughtfulness which lifts the human above the brute parent, are ever incurred here by either father or mother. The relation indeed resembles, as far as circumstances can possibly make it do so, the short-lived connection between the animal and its young. The father, having neither authority, power, responsibility, or charge in his children, is of course, as among brutes, the least attached to his offspring; the mother, by the natural law which renders the infant dependent on her for its first year's nourishment, is more so; but as neither of them is bound to educate or to support their children, all the unspeakable tenderness and solemnity, all the rational, and all the spiritual grace and glory of the connection, is lost, and it becomes mere breeding, bearing, suckling, and there an end. But it is not only the absence of the conditions which God has affixed to the relation which tends to encourage the reckless increase of the race; they enjoy, by means of numerous children, certain positive advantages. In the first place, every woman who is pregnant, as soon as she chooses to make the fact known to the overseer, is relieved of a certain portion of her work in the field, which lightening of labor continues, of course, as long as she is so burdened. On the birth of a child certain additions of clothing and an additional weekly ration are bestowed on the family; and these matters, small as they may seem, act as powerful inducements to creatures who have none of the restraining influences actuating them which belong to the parental relation among all other people, whether civilized or savage. Moreover, they have all of them a most distinct and perfect knowledge of their value to their owners as property; and a woman thinks, and not much amiss, that the more frequently she adds to the number of her master's livestock by bringing new slaves into the world, the more claims she will have upon his consideration and good will. This was perfectly evident to me from the meritorious air with which the women always made haste to inform me of the number of children they had borne, and the frequent occasions on which the older slaves would direct my attention to their children, exclaiming: "Look, missis! little niggers for you and massa; plenty little niggers for you and little missis!" A very agreeable apostrophe to me indeed, as you will believe.

Harriet Jacobs's Trials as a Slave Girl (1828), 1861

During the first years of my service in Dr. Flint's family, I was accustomed to share some indulgences with the children of my mistress. Though this seemed to me no more than right, I was grateful for it, and tried to merit the kindness by the faithful discharge of my duties. But I now entered on my fifteenth year—a sad epoch in the life of a slave girl. My master began to whisper foul words in my ear. Young as I was, I could not remain ignorant of their import. I tried to treat them with indifference or contempt. The master's age, my extreme youth, and the fear that his conduct would be reported to my grandmother, made him bear this treatment for many months. He was a crafty man, and resorted to many means to accomplish his purposes. Sometimes he had stormy, terrific ways, that made his victims tremble; sometimes he assumed a gentleness that he thought must surely subdue. Of the two, I preferred his stormy moods, although they left me trembling. He tried his utmost to corrupt the pure principles my grandmother had instilled. He peopled my young mind with unclean images, such as only a vile monster could think of. I turned from him with disgust and hatred. But he was my master. I was compelled to live under the same roof with him—where I saw a man forty years my senior daily violating the most sacred commandments of nature. He told me I was his property; that I must be subject to his will in all things. My soul revolted against the mean tyranny. But where could I turn for protection? No matter whether the slave girl be as black as ebony or as fair as her mistress. In either case, there is no shadow of law to protect her from insult, from violence, or even from death; all these are inflicted by fiends who bear the shape of men. The mistress, who ought to protect the helpless victim, has no other feelings towards her but those of jealousy and rage. The degradation, the wrongs, the vices, that grow out of slavery, are more than I can describe. They are greater than you would willingly believe. Surely, if you credited one half the truths that are told you concerning the helpless millions suffering in this cruel bondage, you at the north would not help to tighten the yoke. You surely would refuse to do for the master, on your own soil, the mean and cruel work which trained bloodhounds and the lowest class of whites do for him at the south.

Every where the years bring to all enough of sin and sorrow; but in slavery the very dawn of life is darkened by these shadows. Even the little child, who is accustomed to wait on her mistress and her children, will learn, before she is twelve years old, why it is that her mistress hates such and such a one among the slaves. Perhaps the child's own mother is among those hated ones. She listens to violent outbreaks of jealous passion, and cannot help understanding what is the cause. She will become prematurely knowing in evil things. Soon she will learn to tremble when she hears her master's footfall. She will be compelled to realize that she is no longer a child. If God has bestowed beauty upon her, it will prove her greatest curse. That which commands admiration in the white woman only hastens the degradation of the female slave. I know that some are too much brutalized by slavery to feel the humiliation of their position; but many slaves feel it most acutely, and shrink from the memory of it. I cannot tell how much I suffered in the presence of these wrongs, nor how I am still pained by the retrospect. My master met me at every turn, reminding me that I belonged to him, and swearing by heaven and earth that he would compel me to submit to him. If I went out for a breath of fresh air, after a day of unwearied toil, his footsteps dogged me. If I knelt by my mother's grave, his dark shadow fell on me even there. The light heart which nature had given me became heavy with sad forebodings. The other slaves in my master's house noticed the change. May of them pitied me; but none dared to ask the cause. They had no need to inquire. They knew too well the guilty practices under that roof; and they were aware that to speak of them was an offence that never went unpunished.

I longed for some one to confide in. I would have given the world to have laid my head on my grandmother's faithful bosom, and told her all my troubles. But Dr. Flint swore he would kill me, if I was not as silent as the grave. Then, although my grandmother was all in all to me, I feared her as well as loved her. I had been accustomed to look up to her with a respect bordering upon awe. I was very young, and felt shamefaced about telling her such impure things, especially as I knew her to be very strict on such subjects. Moreover, she was a woman of a high spirit. She was usually very quiet in her demeanor; but if her indignation was once roused, it was not very easily quelled. I had been told that she once chased a white gentleman with a loaded pistol, because he insulted one of her daughters. I dreaded the consequences of a violent outbreak; and both pride and fear kept me silent. But though I did not confide in my grandmother, and even evaded her vigilant watchfulness and inquiry, her presence in the neighborhood was some protection to me. Though she had been a slave, Dr. Flint was afraid of her. He dreaded her scorching rebukes. Moreover, she was known and patronized by many people; and he did not wish to have his villainy made public. It was lucky for me that I did not live on a distant plantation, but in a town not so large that the inhabitants were ignorant of each other's affairs. Bad as are the laws and customs in a slaveholding community, the doctor, as a professional man, deemed it prudent to keep up some outward show of decency.

O, what days and nights of fear and sorrow that man caused me! Reader, it is not to awaken sympathy for myself that I am telling you truthfully what I suffered in slavery. I do it to kindle a flame of compassion in your hearts for my sisters who are still in bondage, suffering as I once suffered.

I once saw two beautiful children playing together. One was a fair white child; the other was her slave, and also her sister. When I saw them embracing each other, and heard their joyous laughter, I turned sadly away from the lovely sight. I foresaw the inevitable blight that would fall on the little slave's heart. I knew how soon her laughter would be changed to sighs. The fair child grew up to be a still fairer woman. From childhood to womanhood her pathway was blooming with flowers, and overarched by a sunny sky. Scarcely one day of her life had been clouded when the sun rose on her happy bridal morning.

How had those years dealt with her slave sister, the little playmate of her childhood? She, also, was very beautiful; but the flowers and sunshine of love were not for her. She drank the cup of sin, and shame, and misery, whereof her persecuted race are compelled to drink.

Letters Concerning Maria Cumming Lamar's Impending Death, 1873

Maria Cumming Lamar to Emily C. Hammond

Sunday night, July 13, 1873

Dear Sister Emily:

Mother insists that I should write you a few lines to tell you of my condition tonight, thinking you may have heard through Mrs. Hammond of our sending for Dr. Campbell yesterday evening. Dr. C has just left here and after talking with him I don't think any one could tell what he thought or what to think themselves. As well as I can tell you the state of the case is this.

Julia being sick with measles last week (she has entirely recovered) and having no nurse at all part of the time, I was obliged to lift her about a little and yesterday while stooping over a clothes basket taking out clothes I "ruptured the membrane" as the Dr. says, and tho' having no pain had every other symptom of immediate labor. The Dr. assured me that there was no danger about it, and *pretended* to believe that it had come to the full time and everything would be over safely in the course of the night. He even wished to wait up here but I would not hear of that. I know it is not the time and I have not the *feeling* that it will come on yet, tho' this symptom continued all through last night and today until a late hour this evening. It has however passed off now and the Dr. says the membrane may have reformed, in which case I may go on till September (a thing he told me would be impossible last night). So what is one to believe? In the meantime I am sitting up and walking about my room but not going down-stairs and Derry is ready to send for Dr. C at a moment's notice, and the worse thing to me about the matter is the uncertainty as I am about as comfortable as usual, and Margaret is here with the children. We will send you word when I am *really* sick, but as I don't think it will be for a month or two yet, can't you come up and see us if only for a day? It would be so pleasant to us all. I have written much more than I intended, on this not very agreeable subject, and now I must close as it is getting very late. Will you please hurry up my work. I literally have not one garment ready and last night was in despair. I am going to beg you to lend me a double gown or so. Any thing in fact that you can spare for a while. I am so afraid to go back to the machine again. All are pretty well, Mother about as usual. Do come up and hear all about us. Mother says she would send for you if she had any horses of her own.

Goodnight dear sister Emily. I would give anything if you were here.

From *The Hammonds of Redcliffe*, edited by Carol Bleser, Oxford University Press, 1981.

I am not frightened, but I wish it was all natural. Love to Mr. H and Julia. Derry and Mother send love,

Affectionately,
M.C.L.

Julia A. Cumming to Emily C. Hammond

July 16, 1873

My Dear Emmie:

As I promised I write a line or two now quarter past 12 to let you know of Maria's condition, as according to my own judgment, and Dr. C.'s opinion. After you left she continued sleeping heavily with but little fever, but complaining of great soreness and pain when she would make the slightest movement. About 5 P.M. she became extremely nervous and agitated declaring she felt worse than ever, but this state was very soon overcome by the use of Bromide and red Lavender. The fever had abated very much, and in that respect she seemed better. Dr. C. came as usual after dark, and hearing from Mrs. Meté [midwife] how she has passed the day he immediately knelt by her and passed his hands about to ascertain if there was any tendency to Peritonitis, and when he left her he told me he apprehended the pain of which she complained was of that character. Mrs. Meté thought differently [that it] arose from the contraction which was slowly taking place in the womb. Dr. C., I thought, looked very anxious and enquired of her how Morphine affected her, when she herself asked him to try a portion, which he did, and since then, or as soon as it began to affect her, she fell off into a pleasant sleep. A full, warm perspiration soon broke out all over her, and the skin soft and natural, and when she was roused (from some apprehension she was sleeping too heavily, Mrs. Meté felt) she sent down for Dr. C. to know if she could use coffee to counteract the effect of the Morphine. She was made anxious, I think, merely because she snored a little, which habit Derry charges her with doing habitually. At any rate, the Dr. declared the treatment was having the happiest effect, "it had developed the fact that it was not inflammation," and that he was immensely [relieved] and thought better of the case than he had at any previous time. She herself says "she feels a great deal better, she is free from pain, and her sleep is delightful." I may be too hopeful, but I bless God for what I consider the favourable change.

You must not fatigue yourself and run the risk of hurting your baby by coming over tomorrow. I will try very hard to send you another Bulletin tomorrow. I am certainly much relieved, but I find myself startled at every sound, especially when Derry or any of the nurses come stealing down to my door and softly calling "Mrs. Cumming." I like Mrs. Meté more and more.

Much love to all your household and to Mrs. Hammond.

Ever So dear Emmie,

P.S. It seems like a week since you were here. . . .   J.A. Cumming

[Maria Bryan Cumming Lamar died four days later on July 20, 1873, at the age of twenty-nine.]

⚹ *E S S A Y S*

Historian Suzanne Lebsock of Rutgers University made a careful study of legal and other records revealing the status of women in Petersburg, Virginia from 1784 to 1860. Although Petersburg was only one town in a rural South, her thorough examination produced interesting evidence, described in the first essay, of increasing female autonomy and attitudes of personalism that marked women's culture. Elizabeth Fox-Genovese of Emory University has recently offered a rigorous conceptualization of women's status in the South, as determined by class, race, and gender. The second essay outlines some of her basic concepts and delves more deeply into the gender conventions that affected southern ladies. Deborah Gray White of Rutgers University has written about the world of those southern women who were slaves. The last essay contains her conclusions that the work routines of slavery often divided according to gender and that female slaves had common experiences and faced common dilemmas that encouraged them to cooperate as women.

Female Autonomy and Personalism

SUZANNE LEBSOCK

When this project was first begun [in the 1970s], the prevailing interpretation in the history of nineteenth-century American women was the thesis of decline. The most influential work was Elisabeth Anthony Dexter's *Colonial Women of Affairs*, first published in 1924. Dexter found colonial women engaged in every imaginable trade and enterprise, and she concluded by proposing that women's economic opportunities contracted in the decades following the American Revolution. Although Dexter herself reversed that decision in a later study, her initial thesis of decline was quickly established as conventional wisdom when the rebirth of feminism in the 1960s gave rise to a new wave of historical writing on women. This made sense, given what we were learning about the nineteenth century's ideas about woman's proper place; with the cult of true womanhood, as Barbara Welter named it, women were told, more stridently and more frequently than ever before, to stay home. Putting Dexter and Welter together, it was easy to imagine a female variation on the Rip Van Winkle theme: In 1750, a busy, brassy woman pauses from setting type for her newspaper to catch a few winks and wakes up blinking in 1850, becorseted and a prisoner in her own house.

    Subsequent research has made it plain that no such easy scheme will do, and the evidence from Petersburg affirms that the experience of women in the nineteenth century cannot be readily classified as either decline or progress. In one respect, however, there was development in a nearly straight line: Women in Petersburg experienced increasing autonomy, autonomy in the sense of freedom from utter dependence on particular men. Relatively speaking, fewer women were married, more women found work for wages, and more married women acquired separate estates, that is, property that their husbands could not touch.

This is about as straight as any line we will be looking at. When we explore how this new autonomy was acquired and what changes it inspired in turn, the line curves in intriguing ways. To cite the clearest example, women acquired separate estates, not because anyone thought women deserved more independence, but because of the nineteenth century's sudden panics and severe economic depressions. A separate estate was a means of keeping property in the family when times were hard and families stood to lose everything because of the husband's indebtedness. It did not take organized feminism to bring about positive change in the status of women. Petersburg provides a case study of how the condition of women could change for the better in a nonfeminist, even antifeminist culture.

This is also a study in the limits of such change. Petersburg's women were not able to translate what they gained at home into bolder action in the public sphere. The 1850s, in fact, saw a sharp turn in the direction of less autonomy for women in the public sphere, as men co-opted causes formerly championed only by women, while the new organizations open to women, organizations devoted to temperance, agricultural progress, and the local library, were all auxiliaries to organizations run by men. It was as though the women were required to pay for their private gains with some visible, public currency. . . .

. . . The transmission of property can provide a surprisingly clear window on human values. When we compare what women and men did with what they had, we find the outlines of a distinctive women's value system or culture.

At the center of this culture was personalism, a tendency to respond to the particular needs and merits of individuals. When women wrote wills, for example, they tended to pick and choose among their potential heirs, rewarding personal loyalty and taking note of special economic need. Women were also more likely than men to reward the exceptional slave with emancipation. They were more likely than men to grant separate estates to their daughters, thus placing a particular woman's need for economic security above the general principle of male dominance in the family. Altogether, women as a group were more personalistic, more attuned to the needs and interests of other women, more concerned with economic security, more supportive of organized charity, and more serious about the spiritual life than were men. This is not to say that no woman ever committed a greedy or evil deed or that the sexes shared no values. It is to say that women at times behaved according to standards of their own. With local records we can find out what some of these standards were.

This is of critical significance to the continuing development of women's history as a distinct field of inquiry. Much of what has been written on the history of women is, to use Gerda Lerner's term, "contribution history." That is, the scholar marks off some endeavor that has traditionally been regarded as important and proceeds to outline women's previously unacknowledged contributions to it. One result is a relatively large literature on organized feminism and social reform, areas in which women were extremely active and in which traditional scholarly neglect is proportionally inexcusable. This is the kind of women's history that is now appearing in textbooks, as well it should.

The problem with the contribution approach is that it does not challenge traditional assumptions about what matters in history. It takes men as the measure; it allows women into history only when they thought as men thought, achieved what men achieved, or fought for what men had already won. With contribution history, we are forever testing how women measured up on a masculine scale of achievement.

But if we believe that women all along created cultures of their own, our approach to the past is different. With enough imaginative research, it should be possible to reconstruct women's cultures. We could then busy ourselves with testing how men measured up—not a very high-minded approach, but one with enormous therapeutic potential. Better yet, we can learn more about what women and men shared and where they diverged, about how women and men experienced change, and about the ways in which gender influenced their choices as active agents in history. The reward lies not only in giving women their due, but also in recognizing that in all societies the range of human values and aspirations was greater than we had allowed. . . .

Marriage contracts were always relatively rare; from 1784 to 1860, only ninety-five of them were recorded in Petersburg. Their frequency rose a little in the antebellum period, however, and this was an important indicator of increased leverage for some middle- and upper-class women. Marriage contracts were drawn up and signed before the wedding, and they did not ordinarily give the husband a chance to try his managerial hand. Rather, the convention of male command was shoved aside for the sake of the security of the wife's property. (And it *was* the wife's property: In only four of the ninety-five cases did the groom contribute any of the property covered by the contract.) Moreover, marriage contracts showed that the protection of the wife's property need not sentence her to passivity. Marriage contracts were empowering documents on the whole, and their terms grew more liberal with time. Finally, as time went on, marriage contracts were democratized somewhat, as the parties to them became a more ordinary group.

From 1784 to 1810, marriage contracts were distinguished by their scarcity, for only one marriage in sixty-two (7/433) was regulated by a publicly recorded agreement. The parties to these novel arrangements belonged to two groups. Four were women of affairs—women who were not about to let marriage interfere with the economic independence to which they had become accustomed. The others were members of Petersburg's first families, young women with a great deal of property to protect. . . .

Through 1825, a third of the women who signed marriage agreements (6/18) were documentably in business before or at the time of marriage. The proportion fell to less than a tenth (6/78) in the years from 1826 to 1860. The female parties to marriage contracts in the antebellum period, in short, were less exceptional than their predecessors. They were also more likely to be marrying for the first time, or so it appears from the information available. The change came in the 1840s. From 1784 to 1840, the majority of the women who signed marriage contracts (20/32, with 9 additional cases unknown) were widows. This is no surprise, for a widow was more likely than a single woman to own property. More to the point, the widow was more likely to have children, and a marriage contract could do much to protect the child's interests from waste at the hands of an ill-disposed or unlucky stepfather. From 1841 to 1860, however, the majority of marriage contracts (23/41, with 13 additional cases unknown) were signed by women who had never married. As time went on, then, the female parties to marriage agreements less often had a fortune, a business, or a child to protect. For women of the privileged classes, commencing marriage with a contract was becoming less exceptional.

Marriage contracts did, in any case, become more frequent. From 1821 to 1860, one marriage in twenty-six (84/2,224) was covered by a contract, a substantial increase over the earlier ratio of one in sixty-two. There was also measurable improvement in the terms. Before the 1840s, only 14.3 percent (6/42) of the contracts empowered the woman to sell her property; from 1841 to 1860, that figure jumped to 62.3 percent (33/53). Authority to write a will had always been more readily reserved; even before the 1840s, two-thirds of the agreements included this power. From 1841 to 1860, the proportion grew to over 80 percent (43/53).

We can only guess whether the women themselves insisted on those liberal terms. There is no question, however, that women were increasingly assertive in matters of property and that the overall growth in the number of separate estates owed much to female initiative. A few women found in their dower rights a new means of establishing separate estates for themselves. And by will and deed of gift, women were increasingly active in establishing separate estates for one another.

Under the common law, the married woman's one power was the power to refuse to relinquish her dower rights in property her husband wished to convey. From the 1830s on, some Petersburg women began to use it—to trade their contingent rights of dower for active control over a separate estate. Mary Boswell showed how it was done. Mary's husband William was a merchant, and for more than twenty years, he was one of Petersburg's biggest real estate owners. The crash came in 1842. William mortgaged one lot after another in a desperate effort to keep faith with his creditors, and time after time, Mary signed away her dower rights. "How submissively and cheerfully she bore this reverse of fortune," her obituary later chirped. But Mary Boswell was no martyr. There were two lots on High Street that Mary wanted for herself. In these, she refused to give up her dower, and in exchange for the promise that she would relinquish her rights in all of

William's remaining lands, the two lots, along with five slaves, were conveyed to a trustee for Mary's separate use. The following year, William's mortgaged property went under the hammer. Mary's separate property was preserved, and when she died a few years later, she left all of it to her married daughter, likewise, as a separate estate.

From the mid 1830s until 1860, there were only twenty-five recorded cases in which women parlayed dower rights into separate estates. But that was twenty-five cases more than in the previous fifty years, a significant if small indicator of women's growing assertiveness. The more arresting measure was the frequency with which women established separate estates for other women. Of the separate estates established by deed of gift from 1784 to 1840, one-fifth were granted by women (11/52). In the twenty years that followed, two-fifths (42/118) were granted by women. Wills were less often used to establish separate estates, but here the agency of women was even more pronounced. Among the eighteen testators who left separate estates from 1784 to 1840, five were women. After 1840, women moved into the lead; fifteen of the twenty-six testators leaving separate estates were women. Altogether a large third of the separate estates established by will and deed of gift were established by women (88/234 = 37.6 percent).

This third was large indeed given women's place in the structure of property holding. Although women as a group were making gains, never did they add up to a third of Petersburg's property owners. And they controlled nowhere near a third of the wealth. Relative to the amount of property they possessed, women were far more active than men in establishing separate estates.

Their gifts expose the fraudulence of the adage that women were their own worst enemies. From the letters and diaries of nineteenth-century women, historians have begun to recover evidence of an emotional universe in which intimate relationships between women were central. Based on common work and shared experience, this universe was characterized by strong bonds between mothers and daughters and by friendships between women that were long-lived and emotionally, sometimes sensually, rich. The Petersburg women who granted separate estates to other women add an economic dimension to this portrait. Most often the grants were from mothers to their daughters. Women understood what it was to be legally and financially vulnerable; more often than men, they tried to see to it that their daughters were spared.

Yet this was not feminism. Or if it can be called feminism, it was feminism of the most inchoate and defensive kind. The woman who granted her daughter a separate estate was not rejecting male dominance for the sake of equality or female autonomy. Equality and autonomy were not ordinarily among the choices. Rather, the choice was between the maintenance of the husband's dominance on the one hand, and on the other, the guarantee of some economic security to a woman and her family, ends that were both desired but often incompatible in the capricious economy of the nineteenth century. The provisions of estates established by women did not differ a great deal from those of estates set up by men. Women granted power to make a will somewhat more often than men did; provisions for writing a will were included by 20.7 percent of the women grantors (12/58) and 13.4 percent of the men (15/112). Power to sell the property was also granted a little more often by the women (18/58 = 31 percent) than by the men (25/112 = 22.3 percent). The great majority of grantors of both sexes, meanwhile, granted no powers at all. The principal and common target was security; the essential point was not to free the wife but to restrain the husband's creditors. The most that can be said for the women grantors is that they were somewhat less likely than were the men to equate security with utter passivity.

The rise of separate estates owed a great deal to female assertiveness and to sisterhood. The central, usually implicit demand was not, however, for equality, nor was it for autonomy. What was asked for was protection from gross exploitation. . . .

. . . Among free black women, refraining from legal marriage was commonplace all along. Among white women, the proportion of widows and spinsters appears to have grown substantially over time. By 1860, more than a third of the white women living in Petersburg were either widowed or had never married at all. Not all of these women were property owners, of course, but women as a group did by 1860 have more to work with than ever before. In 1790, only 7.3 percent of Petersburg's property taxpayers were women. By 1860, a full quarter of the town's taxpayers were women. A large minority of Petersburg's women were facing life as legally autonomous persons. . . .

. . . While Petersburg's women tended toward the conservative in their financial dealings, they appear to have become increasingly active in the acquisition and disposition of property. [Legal records show] the growth of women's participation in real estate and credit transactions. The significance of this growth would be clearer if we knew, for each period, what proportion of Petersburg's women had the legal capacity to make property transactions. We do know that after 1830 there was a marked increase in the numbers of women who were able to buy more than one parcel of real estate. Most of these women bought two properties, but a few bought as many as eight or ten or . . . fourteen. By 1860, 28.7 percent of Petersburg's real estate owners were women. In 1820, the proportion had been 14 percent; in 1790, only 8.4 percent.

The most dramatic upsurge in women's economic activity, meanwhile, was in the writing of wills. Here the numbers are startling. In the early going, women hardly ever left wills. From 1784 to 1800, only 7.1 percent (5/70) of the wills recorded in Petersburg had been written by women. In the first decade of the new century, women's wills appeared more frequently, and there was another spurt in the 1830s. By the 1840s, the activism of the women was nothing less than phenomenal. From 1841 to 1860, 44.4 percent of the wills recorded in Petersburg (99/223) were the work of women.

Once again, caution was not the same thing as passivity. With the writing of wills, women were, relatively speaking, more active than were men. The same was true of deeds of gift; all along, about 40 percent of Petersburg's deeds of gift (77/192) were executed by women. Exploring why women were so active in the writing of wills and deeds of gift is in part a study of the peculiar legal constraints that bore on women. It is also, and more significantly, a study in values.

To understand why women wrote so many of the recorded deeds of gift, it helps to understand that a deed of gift could serve a variety of purposes. Some deeds of gift represented genuine acts of generosity, others were social security arrangements for the givers, and still others were substitutes for wills. And there were always the swindlers. In 1798, Moses Jeffreys made a deed of gift to his daughter-in-law Elizabeth, conveying to her his household furnishings and all his other movable property. Several years later, Jeffreys revealed his motive: ". . . a certain execution [was] issued against me for a debt, which I was not able to pay without entire ruin, and to avoid which I conveyed said property to my daughter-in-law; and without any consideration only as above." Jeffreys assumed that as soon as he got straight with his creditors, Elizabeth would reconvey the property to him. Bamboozled. Elizabeth not only refused, but by 1805 was remarried and to a man who, not surprisingly, supported her in her determination to maintain possession of the gift. Jeffreys vowed to fight their claim in court, but as he did not have a prayer at law, he probably derived his only satisfaction from taking out a newspaper ad to denounce the woman who "proved unworthy of my confidence. . . ." It did not seem to trouble him that he might damage his own reputation in the process. . . .

Families are full of inequalities, inequalities of love and loyalty, inequalities of need. Women recognized this in the terms of their wills, and they were occasionally explicit about it. "I have not given any thing to my son Seth and daughter Susan purposely for reasons which they are apprized of"; "I do not wish for Henry Johnson'[s] child to have any posion of my estate being he is well enough off without my little estate"; "I hope my brother Robert and Sister Mary will not think that there is any want of affection on my part for them, I am only anxious to secure my little property to those of my family who need it most"; "I love all my children alike but my daughters I feel most attached to and think they ought to have what I own at my death, and therefore this disposition."

While men for the most part distributed their property according to formula, women tended to pick and choose. There may have been an element of the power play in this; a propertied woman could keep her heirs on their good behavior for years, as long as she kept them guessing as to the terms of her last will. The women's wills were, in any case, highly personalized. They rewarded special qualities of loyalty and affection. They also funneled property into the hands of the heirs who needed it most, and here again the women's penchant for economic security was revealed. . . . Women were more likely than were men to protect the legacies they gave their female heirs by making the legacies separate estates. (The desire to exempt bequests to married women from the control of husbands and husbands' creditors was in itself a major incentive for writing a will.) What is more, the women took the lead in a more novel procedure of establishing extra measures of economic security for sons. After 1820, there were ten wills that set up trusts for the benefit of adult sons. Eight of them were written by women.

Thus women had good reason to avoid intestacy: They wanted their property divided on the basis of personal merit and particular need, and they often wanted it conveyed on more protective terms than the ordinary course of probate law would permit. They also wanted, more often than did the men, special treatment for their slaves. "It is my first desire to make some comfortable provision for my servants as a just reward for their affection and fidelity." So began the will that Dorothy Mitchell wrote in 1837, and as more women began to write wills, they left more evidence of a special relationship between southern white women and chattel slavery. It has been proposed by some observers that the white women of the South were covert abolitionists, or, at the least, that they lacked a full-scale commitment to the slave system. The wills of Petersburg's white slaveholders, though their numbers are relatively small, give us a first opportunity to put this proposition to the test.

The results appear to be positive. First of all, more women than men used their wills to set slaves free. After 1840, twelve white women emancipated slaves by will; only eight white men did the same. (A much larger number of emancipations were performed by deed, and here, too, white women appear to have outdone the men in liberating slaves.) Second, more women than men (again after 1840, eight women and five men) inserted clauses either to prevent their slaves from being moved or sold or to restrict the terms of sale. Lucy Frances Branch, a single woman of fifty, made herself very clear: "It is my express wish and desire to make such a disposition of my woman *Martha Graves* as to prevent her being removed farther from her mother and husband than she now lives." To that end, Branch stipulated that Graves was not to be moved or mortgaged, and that if a sale ever became unavoidable, Graves be permitted to choose her purchaser.

Finally, women more often than men (twelve women, seven men) gave their slaves legacies, single cash payments in some cases, maintenance for life in others. For Mary Lithgow, the central clauses of her will, written more lovingly and in more detail than any of the provisions concerning her son and her grandchildren, were those written for the benefit of William Alexander, a seven-year-old boy whom she had recently freed. Lithgow directed that William be given fifty dollars a year until he turned twenty-one, that he receive five hundred dollars on his majority along with some furniture and traveling trunks, that he be put to a good trade, that he be educated in morals and religion, that he be allowed to stay in Virginia, and that, if this last request were impossible, he be placed with a gentleman of good standing in the North. Lithgow subsequently revised her will twice, and each revision brought a bonus for William Alexander. The first allotted the three hundred dollars Lithgow had stashed in her savings account to William's "plain education, so as to fit him for business." The second authorized him to buy members of his family, and at a fair price.

So far as the wills let us judge, white women were kinder to their slaves than were men, and the women were more likely to set their slaves free. But was this a quiet form of abolitionism? Was it an implicit critique of the slave system?

The best answer seems to be that white women were in fact a subversive influence on chattel slavery, not so much because they opposed slavery as a system (the abstract merits of systems did not concern them much), but because they operated out of an essentially personal frame of reference. The women who wrote special provisions for their slaves into their wills worked from the same mentality that caused women as a group to divide property unevenly among their heirs: Women indulged particular attachments—they were alert to the special case, to the personal exception.

Constraints of the Plantation Household

ELIZABETH FOX-GENOVESE

Southern women belonged to a slave society that differed decisively from the northern bourgeois society to which it was politically bound. Slavery as a social system shaped the experience of all its women, for slavery influenced the nature of the whole society, not least its persisting rural character. Southern slave society consisted largely of a network of households that contained within themselves the decisive relations of production and reproduction. In the South, in contrast to the North, the household retained a vigor that permitted southerners to ascribe many matters—notably labor relations, but also important aspects of gender relations—to the private sphere, whereas northerners would increasingly ascribe them to the public spheres of market and state. The household structure and social relations of southern society had multiple and far-reaching consequences for all spheres of southern life, including law, political economy, politics, and slaveholders' relations with yeomen and other nonslaveholding whites. And it had special consequences for gender relations in general and women's experience in particular.

The persistence in the South of the household as the dominant unit of production and reproduction guaranteed the power of men in society, even as measured by nineteenth-century bourgeois standards. During the period in which northern society was undergoing a reconversion of household into home and ideologically ascribing it to the female sphere, southern society was reinforcing the centrality of plantation and farm households that provided continuities and discontinuities in the experience of women of different classes and races. Variations in the wealth of households significantly

From *Within the Plantation Household: Black and White Women of the Old South* by Elizabeth Fox-Genovese, pp. 38–39, 43–44, 192–195, 203–206. © 1988 The University of North Carolina Press. Reprinted by permission.

differentiated women's experience, but the common structure as a unit of production and reproduction under men's dominance provided some basic similarity. Effectively, the practical and ideological importance of the household in southern society reinforced gender constraints by ascribing all women to the domination of the male heads of households and to the company of the women of their own households. In 1853 Mary Kendall, a transplanted New Englander, wrote to her sister of her special pleasure in receiving a letter from her, for "I seldom see any person aside from our own family, and those employed upon the plantation. For about three weeks I did not have the pleasure of seeing *one white female face,* there being no white family except our own upon the plantation." The experience of black slave women differed radically from that of all white women, for they belonged to households that were not governed by their own husbands, brothers, and fathers. But even black slave women shared with white women of different social classes some of the constraints of prevalent gender conventions.

As members of a slave society, southern women differed in essential respects from other American women, although their experience has not figured prominently in the development of American women's history, much less influenced the theory that informs generalizations about the experience of American women. Southern women's history should force us to think seriously about the relation between the experiences that unite women as members of a gender and those that divide them as members of specific communities, classes, and races. It should, in other words, challenge us to recognize class and race as central, rather than incidental to, women's identities and behavior—to their sense of themselves as women. . . .

Class and race deeply divided southern women, notwithstanding their shared experience of life in rural households under the domination of men. There is almost no evidence to suggest that slaveholding women envisioned themselves as the "sisters" of yeoman women, although there may have been some blurring at the margins when kin relations crossed class lines. In contrast, there is reason to believe that some slaveholding women felt minimal kinship with their female slaves, with whom they might have intimate, if tension-fraught, relations in everyday life. In general, but for women in particular, class relations in southern society remained essentially hierarchical. If anything, relations among women of different classes strengthened and reaffirmed class distance among free white families and served as an antidote to the elements of egalitarianism—or at least formal political democracy—that characterized relations among free white men. The relations among women also reaffirmed the special race relations of slave society, for the more established slaveholding women viewed their female slaves as somehow part of their affective universe in a way that they did not view yeoman women or even arrivistes. But they unavoidably viewed those slaves as social and racial inferiors whose station in life was that of perpetual servants. Thus, the arrivistes could in time "arrive," whereas the slaves had no prospects and the nonslaveholders could be perceived as having none.

Gender, race, and class relations constituted the grid that defined southern women's objective positions in their society, constituted the elements from which they fashioned their views of themselves and their world, constituted the relations of different groups of southern women to one another. The class relations that divided and interlocked southern women played a central role in their respective identities. Slaveholding, slave, yeoman, poor white, and middle-class town women, as members of a gender, shared the imposition of male dominance, but their experience of that dominance differed significantly according to class and race.

The forms of male prejudice and dominance differ among societies that assign specific purposes and forms to prejudice and domination. The distinctive forms of male dominance in the South developed in conjunction with the development of slavery as a social system and reflected the rural character that slavery reinforced in southern society. In the South, as in many other societies, church and state substantially reinforced the prevalent forms of male dominance, some of which were national and some regionally specific. Within the South, the forms varied considerably according to community. Like religion and the law, the rural character of southern slave society impinged upon women of all classes and races in innumerable, albeit different, ways. Above all, it circumscribed their mobility and the size of the communities to which they belonged or within which they developed their sense of themselves. For most women, male dominance appeared specifically as a direct manifestation of the social and gender relations of particular communities, however much accepted as a general law of life. . . .

Within the household, the everyday lives of slaveholding women, and in some measure those of slaves, conformed closely to prevailing notions of the appropriate division of labor by gender, following earlier British, European, and, to some extent, African conceptions of male and female spheres. Although some Euro-American and Afro-American views coincided, slaveholders and slaves did not contribute equally to the gradual crystallization of distinct southern patterns. With their power over slaves, slaveholders could set the terms of everyday life and could, if they chose, violate their slaves' notions of gender relations. Convention declared that the household responsibilities of slaveholding women were natural extensions of their personal relations as wives, mothers, and daughters, all of whom answered to a master who was husband or father. Slave women, in contrast, answered to a master who was not of their natural family, class, or race and who at any moment could exercise his power according to imperatives that had nothing to do with family feeling. They knew that he frequently exercised his power severely and might even make sexual demands that mocked the prevalent norms of gender relations to which he claimed to subscribe.

For slaveholding women, gender relations merged seamlessly with the sense of their own social roles and personal identities. Modern sensibilities may view them as the oppressed victims of male dominance, but few of them would have agreed, notwithstanding some bad moments. Their men's abuse of prerogatives, notably sexual philandering but also excessive drinking and the squandering of family resources, caused them untold distress. But their resentment of these abuses rarely passed into rejection of the system that established their sense of personal identity within a solid community.

For slave women, the power of masters over their lives and the lives of their men distorted their sense of the links between their relations with men and their roles and identities as women. For black women, social relations with black men did not necessarily mesh with work relations. They did not primarily devote themselves to the care of their own children and houses, and their gender roles did not necessarily emanate directly from their relations with black men or from African traditions. Within the big house, they performed the labor deemed appropriate to the gender roles of white women, but they worked as servants—the opposite of mistress. Even the exceptions—cook, mammy, and a few especially well-trained maids—did work that bore no necessary relation to their roles as mother or wife. Their field labor departed even further from Euro-American notions of women's gender roles, although it may have fit more comfortably with Afro-American traditions. From the perspective of the dominant culture, slave women were regularly assigned to men's work. White farm women, North and South, might work in the fields, but they were not expected to do the kind of heavy work routinely assigned to black women. The only concession to a notion of orderly gender roles for slave women lay in their being primarily assigned to work with other women rather than with men, and even that norm was frequently breached. Within the slave community women's activities were tied more directly to their personal relations with men, as, for example, when they cooked and sewed for their own families. But their roles as daughters, wives, and mothers depended upon the sufferance of a master who could always break up families. Under these conditions the slave's sense of herself as a woman—her gender identity—remained separable from the gender relations and roles that depended heavily on the vicissitudes of power in a slave society.

Both slave and slaveholding women lived in a world in which gender afforded a principle of the practical, political, and symbolic organization of society. Norms of appropriate gender conventions could be violated. Black women could be set to work considered unfit for white women. Slave women could be separated from their children and husbands and could be subject to a sexual violation that would have offended the honor and evoked the murderous retaliation of the husbands and fathers of white women. Violations of the norm painfully reminded slaves that they did not enjoy the full status of their gender, that they could not count on the "protection"—however constraining and sometimes hypocritical—that surrounded white women. Yet the norms also governed the opportunities available to slave women, for ruling men, like enslaved men, were unlikely to violate the norms in ways that would promote the independence of slave women. Slave women may not have had access to the privileges of slaveholding women, but they, too, remained excluded from a host of male prerogatives. In this respect, the gender conventions of slave society weighed equally on all women, regardless of race or class. Gender relations, in both their observance and their breach, constituted an essential aspect of the relations of power between classes and races.

The household worlds of slave and slaveholding women embodied and contributed to the dominant gender relations of southern society, forming a system of conventions that guided women's behavior and identities. Southern gender conventions simultaneously derived from and influenced social relations and operated like a language or discourse that helped individuals to make sense of their place in their world. The constant flux of relations between individual women and men, as with those among women of different classes and races, unfolded as discrete stories—the result of personality and circumstance—but gender conventions offered a way of interpreting those stories and linking them to society. The widespread acceptance of gender conventions limited a woman's freedom to write her life exactly as she might have chosen.

Gender conventions direct fundamental human impulses into socially acceptable and useful channels and thereby serve the needs of individuals as well as of society. They derive as much from custom and practice as from ideology. Influenced both by tradition and circumstances, they constitute compelling ideals disseminated through literate, visual, and oral cultures. They figure among society's most influential and binding elements, for, in telling people how to be men and women, they tell them how to relate to society. Modern cynicism about the observance of social rules has celebrated the breach rather than the observance of conventions in past societies. A healthy appreciation of people's determination to create their own lives and to resist the imprint of official values has led to doubts that official prescriptions had anything to do with life as it was actually lived.

Yet although the dominant gender conventions of the antebellum South reflected the values, aspirations, and anxieties of the dominant class, they also encoded a slave society's essential conditions of life for yeomen and slaves as well as for masters. The yeomen, not to mention the slaves, did not always share most of the slaveowners' concerns. They resisted many of their pretensions, not least because the slaveholders' conventions linked gender relations closely to attitudes toward class relations. But they could not readily forge alternate gender conventions, at least not in the great heartland dominated by the system of plantation households, whatever success they may have had in the yeoman-dominated upcountry. Slaveholders, slaves, and nonslaveholding whites—whatever their differences over specifics—shared an ideal of the universal division between women and men. They agreed that defined male and female spheres constituted the bedrock of society and community, even if they did not subscribe to emerging bourgeois notions about the nature of the spheres.

For southerners, gender spheres interlocked with networks of families and households; men represented those families and households in the larger worlds of politics and warfare, or, to reverse matters, women belonged within families and households under the governance and protection of their men. As Henry Wise wrote to his first wife, Anne: "My wife is not competent to advise the statesman or the politician—her knowledge, her advice, her ministry is in a kindlier sphere." Yet southerners, unlike northerners, did not view either families or households as primarily female preserves, but as terrain that contained woman's sphere. According to this view, women did not belong abroad alone; a woman alone on the public thoroughfares was a woman at risk. Women had no business to bear arms and no place in politics. They were not fit to meet men on equal terms in the combat of public life and, should they attempt to, they would open themselves to being bested by superior physical strength.

Rural women lived within the constraints of these fundamental attitudes toward gender relations and spheres—within a set of firmly entrenched expectations about appropriate behavior for women and for men. Although rooted in the specific conditions of their everyday lives in rural households in a slave society, these expectations derived from longstanding Euro-American and Afro-American notions about the natural relations between women and men. At all levels, southern culture reflected and reinforced a view of the world in which women were subordinate to men. The view proved the more powerful because it conformed so closely to intuitive notions about "natural" differences between women and men. . . .

The ideal of the lady constituted the highest condition to which women could aspire, but the lady, like other women, remained bound by a broad vision of appropriate gender relations. The activities of even the most prestigious lady remained carefully circumscribed by the conventions ordained for women in general, but southern culture placed a premium on her meeting her responsibilities in accordance with her station. The lady, like less privileged women, accepted the dominance of men but cultivated her own sense of honor, which depended heavily on her embodiment of the privileges of her class. In her case, the male dominance that weighed so heavily on black slave and many nonslaveholding white women was, in many respects, experienced as protection. Even as male prerogative hedged her in, it shielded her from direct contact with the disorderly folks who populated the world beyond her household.

A concern with locking women firmly into coverture and domesticity prevailed throughout the United States during the first half of the nineteenth century. No region encouraged divorce or the ownership, much less the effective control, of property by married women, but southerners and their courts proved especially intransigent, the precocious married woman's property act of Mississippi (1839) notwithstanding. As Wyatt-Brown has insisted, southern women's legal standing affected "not only their livelihood but also their sense of themselves." In his judgment, "the effect of the law upon gender relations" has been so little considered that "the hard economic and legal reasons for women's passivity have been hidden from historical view. Too often advances in church life, opening new vistas for usefulness, have obscured the implications of restraints in law."

In a world dominated by male strength, women could not aspire to be the head of a household. They might answer for the household as delegates of their families, but even then they required extensive support from male kin or friends. Slaveholding women might inherit households from their fathers or husbands, but they almost invariably turned the management over to men in practice, even if a will or marriage settlement had left them legally in the woman's control. In general, a widow's ability to assume command depended upon the age of her sons. Should they still be minors, she would have to make do, normally with the help of an overseer; should one son be an adult, he would probably try to assume control himself. Natalie de DeLage Sumter of South Carolina ranked as one of the few women who, as a widow, genuinely managed a plantation, and even she had ample assistance from overseers. Keziah Brevard, who was a widow, did the same, relying upon male advice and the everyday assistance of her difficult driver, Jim.

Whenever possible the male kin of heiresses assumed legal or de facto control. James Henry Hammond braved the wrath of the family of his bride, Catherine Fitzsimmons, to secure complete control of her large inheritance and made his "duties as plantation master . . . the focus of his existence." Anna Matilda King participated more actively than Catherine Fitzsimmons in the management of her extensive inheritance, for her husband, Thomas Butler King, was more often absent than present on the estate. Yet she always treated him as master of the household, consulting him on everything from the marketing of crops to the education of their children, and in everyday matters she relied heavily on the advice of male neighbors, factors, and kin. Eventually, to her delight and relief, her oldest son, Butler, took over completely. Margaret Campbell, who inherited Argyle Plantation in the Mississippi Delta from her husband, ran the place with the assistance of an overseer and neighbors and on the basis of constant consultation with her cousin, Robert Campbell.

David Outlaw spent long periods fulfilling his obligations in the U.S. House of Representatives, leaving his wife, Emily, to preside over the household in Bertie County, North Carolina. He regularly wrote to her about the details of management but expected to provide her with male assistance for their execution. Emily Outlaw consulted him on everything, including the hiring of a governess and the appropriateness of letting their daughter give a party. "Really," he responded on the question of the governess, "I shall quarrel with you if you do not quit asking my advice and permission about matters of this kind." She was implying, whatever her intentions, "that I exact from you to do nothing without my permission." He did not deserve the reproach and had always considered theirs at least "a partnership of equals." He had the "most unlimited confidence in your prudence and discretion." Yet on the matter of the party, to which he had "no objection" and in which he could see no "impropriety," he admonished her "not to give your guest [*sic*] liquor enough to get drunk and get Joe Cherry or some other gentleman to assist you."

John Quitman did not take so tolerant a view. His wife, Eliza, reported that things were going badly on their Springfield Plantation, where the overseer "was in a constant state of intoxication," the "negroes were idle doing nothing whatever," the cotton had not been weighed, and the overseer had "shot some of the cattle for mere sport." She had requested Mr. Kent, who brought the news, to go up and discharge Rees, the delinquent overseer, at once. "I hope my dear John," she concluded, "that what I have done may meet your approbation. It appeared to me to be the only course to pursue in your absence." She hoped in vain. Quitman replied, "I fear you have done wrong in discharging Rees—These reports are generally exaggerated and at any rate no more harm could have been done before my return." He did not add that had he been present the harm might never have occurred at all.

Like Sarah Gayle, many women cared deeply about having a plantation household—a farm—as a basis for family security, and some, like Floride Calhoun, preferred to remain at home while their husbands were off attending to politics or business. Yet few had the training or taste to oversee the management of farming or business activities themselves. Mrs. James Polk insisted on keeping the family plantation when her husband became president, but she had a competent overseer to run it. She apparently possessed uncommon business sense. The overseer consulted her on the timing of the marketing of the crop, but she consulted him on the specifics of managing the slaves. When John Grimball was away, he meticulously instructed his wife, Meta, on innumerable details, from the feeding of mulch cows to care of the horses to distributing molasses to sick slaves. As a widow, Hugh Legaré's mother retained the family plantation, but she always begged her son to assume responsibility for its management. Legaré, although devoted to his mother, did not respond to her pleas. Rachel O'Connor, a widow who presided over a cotton plantation in Feliciana Parish, Louisiana, had terrible trouble with her overseers and regularly wrote to her brother, David, for advice.

A lack of business knowledge constituted only part of the problem for these southern women—romance aside—they could not exercise mastery of their own slaves, much less contribute to the control of the slaves in their communities. Women who managed plantations were, like all other planters, responsible for contributing to the patrols and to other community responsibilities such as building and repairing the levees on the delta, but women could not meet those obligations in person. Some women, in fact, relied heavily on slave drivers to manage the other slaves and even the basic farm operations of the household. During the Civil War, with many overseers as well as slaveholders away, the use of drivers to run plantations became even more common. When the driver was accomplished and loyal the results could be excellent; when he chafed under the direction of a mistress they could leave a good deal to be desired. Keziah Brevard was at her wits' end with Jim, her driver. Jim enjoyed the requisite authority over the other slaves: "Every servant knuckles to him. If they do not his family will put them down." But he was also "an impudent negro," whom Keziah Brevard mistrusted yet dared not punish. She believed him to be "a self willed negro" who "wants every servant on the place to look to him as a superior & he certainly has great influence over my negroes." She could only hope that he "begins to cave a little" and that "his power is on the wane." As Keziah Brevard, like Sarah Gayle and many others, knew, slaveholding women could not, in their own persons, embody the physical attributes of a master, who could, if circumstances demanded, whip his strongest male field hand himself.

Thus, although some women owned plantations and more had to assume responsibility when their husbands were away, they "managed" them through men in all except the rarest of cases. Overseers exercised much wider authority when working for women than they would have dared to claim when working for men. Overseer or no, a woman planter almost always had a male relative or close friend in the neighborhood to look in on her plantation affairs. Not surprisingly, southern men assumed women's incapacity and discussed its consequences for the maintenance of community order. It will not do to dismiss their judgment as so much male prejudice, for the diaries and correspondence of these women with their husbands and others sustains it, and, more to the point, the evidence from the war years, when many women were put to the test, is overwhelming.

Bonds Among Slave Women

DEBORAH GRAY WHITE

Slave women have often been characterized as self-reliant and self-sufficient because, lacking black male protection, they had to develop their own means of resistance and survival. Yet, not every black woman was a Sojourner Truth or a Harriet Tubman. Strength had to be cultivated. It came no more naturally to them than to anyone, slave or free, male or female, black or white. If they seemed exceptionally strong it was partly because they often functioned in groups and derived strength from numbers.

Much of the work slaves did and the regimen they followed served to stratify slave society along sex lines. Consequently, slave women had ample opportunity to develop a consciousness grounded in their identity as females. While close contact sometimes gave rise to strife, adult female cooperation and interdependence was a fact of female slave life. The self-reliance and self-sufficiency of slave women, therefore, must not only be viewed in the context of what the individual slave woman did for herself, but what slave women as a group were able to do for one another.

It is easy to overlook the separate world of female slaves because from colonial times through the Civil War black women often worked with black men at tasks considered by most white Americans to be either too difficult or inappropriate for females. All women worked hard but when white women consistently did field labor it was considered temporary, irregular, or extraordinary, putting them on a par with slaves. Swedish actress Frederika Bremer, visiting the antebellum South, noted that usually only men

Reprinted from *Ar'n't I A Woman? Female Slaves in the Plantation South*, by Deborah Gray White, by permission of W. W. Norton & Company, Inc. Copyright © 1985 by Deborah Gray White.

and black women do field work. Commenting on what another foreign woman sarcastically claimed to be a noble admission of female equality, Bremer observed pointedly that "black [women] are not considered to belong to the weaker sex."

Bremer's comment reflects what former slaves and fugitive male slaves regarded as the defeminization of black women. Bonded women cut down trees to clear lands for cultivation. They hauled logs by leather straps attached to their shoulders. They plowed using mule and ox teams and hoed, sometimes with the heaviest implements available. They dug ditches, spread manure fertilizer, and piled coarse fodder with their bare hands. They built and cleaned Southern roads, helped construct Southern railroads, and of course, they picked cotton. In short, what fugitive slave Williamson Pease said regretfully of slave women was borne out in fact: "Women who do outdoor work are used as bad as men." Almost a century later Green Wilbanks was less remorseful than Pease but in his remembrances of his Grandma Rose, he implied that the work had a kind of neutering effect. Grandma Rose was a woman who could do any kind of job a man could do, a woman who "was some worker, a regular man-woman."

However, it is hardly likely that slave women, especially those on large plantations with sizable female populations, lost their female identity. Harvesting season on staple crop plantations may have found men and women gathering the crop in sex-integrated gangs, but at other times women often worked in exclusively or predominantly female gangs. Thus women were put in one another's company for most of the day. This meant that those with whom they ate meals, sang work songs, and commiserated during the work day were people with the same kind of responsibilities and problems. If anything, slave women developed their own female culture, that is, a way of doing things and a way of assigning value that flowed from the perspective that they had on Southern plantation life. Rather than being diminished, their sense of womanhood was probably enhanced, and their bonds to one another made stronger.

Since slave owners and managers seemingly made little of the slave woman's lesser strength, one wonders why they separated men and women at all. Gender must have provided a natural and easy way to divide the labor force. Despite their limited sensitivity regarding female slave labor, and the double standard they used when evaluating the uses of white and black female labor, slave owners did reluctantly acquiesce to female physiology. For instance, depending on their stage of pregnancy, pregnant women were considered half or quarter hands. Healthy, nonpregnant women were considered three-quarter hands. Three-quarter hands were not necessarily exempt from some of the herculean tasks performed by men who were full hands, but usually, when work assignments were being parceled out men were given the more physically demanding work unless there was a shortage of male hands to do the very heavy work or a rush to get that work completed. A case in point was the most common differentiation: men plowed and women hoed.

Like a lot of field labor, nonfield labor was structured so that women could identify with one another. In the Sea Islands slave women sorted cotton lint according to color and fineness and removed the cotton seeds the gin had crushed into the cotton and lint. Fence building often found men splitting rails in one area and women doing the actual construction in another. Men usually shelled corn, threshed peas, and cut potatoes for planting and platted shucks. Grinding corn into meal or hominy was woman's work; as were spinning, weaving, sewing, and washing.

Female slave domestic work sealed the bonds of womanhood that were forged in the fields and other work places. Usually women spun thread, wove cloth, sewed, and quilted apart from men. Sylvia King grew up on a Texas plantation where women sewed together in the "spinnin' and weavin' cabins." On Captain Kinsler's South Carolina plantation, as on countless others, "old women and women bearin' chillun not yet born did cardin' wid hand-cards." Some would spin, others would weave, but all would eventually learn from some skilled woman "how to make clothes for the family . . . knit coarse socks and stockins." Saturday afternoon was usually reserved for doing laundry, although sometimes women did it at night after coming from the fields.

It is not at all clear what role slave women had in shaping their domestic work, or how they felt about it; what is clear is that they sometimes worked long after their return from the fields, and long after the men had retired. Frances Willingham of Georgia remembered that when slaves came in at night "woman's cleant up deir houses atter dey et, and den washed and got up early next mornin' to put de clothes out to dry." In contrast, men would "set 'round talkin' to other mens and den go to bed." Women also sometimes sat up sewing. "When the work in the fields was finished women were required to come home and spin one cut a night," reported another Georgian. "Those who were not successful in completing this work were punished the next morning." Women had to spin, weave, and sew in the evenings partly because slave owners bought few ready-made clothes, and when they did, the white family and single slave men were the most likely recipients. On one South Carolina plantation each male slave received a fall allotment of one cotton shirt, one pair of woolen pants, and one woolen jacket. In the spring each man got one shirt and two pairs of cotton pants. Slave women, on the other hand, received six yards of woolen cloth and three yards of cotton shirting in the fall. In the spring they got six yards of cotton drillings and three yards of shirting. In both the spring and the fall women got one needle and a half dozen buttons.

Perhaps a saving grace to this "double duty" was that women got a chance to interact with each other. On a Sedalia County, Missouri, plantation women looked forward to doing laundry on Saturday afternoons because, as Mary Frances Webb explained, they "would get to talk and spend the day together." Quiltings, referred to by former slaves as female "frolics" and "parties," were especially convivial. South Carolinian Sallie Paul explained that "when dey would get together den, dey would be glad to get together."

Women also spent a lot of their nonworking hours with each other.

Anna Peek recalled that when slaves were allowed to relax they gathered around a pinewood fire in Aunt Anna's cabin to tell stories. At that time "the old women with pipes in their mouths would sit and gossip for hours." Missourian Alice Sewell told of women occasionally slipping away to hold their own prayer meetings. They cemented their mutual bonds at the end of every meeting when they walked around shaking hands singing "fare you well my sisters, I am going home." Impromptu female religious services were a part of Minksie Walker's mother's life, too. Her mother, Walker testified, would stop and talk with other women after Sunday services on a Missouri plantation. "First thing I would know dey would be jumpin' up and dancin' around and pattin' their hands until all de grass was wore slick."

Residential arrangements further reinforced the bonds forged during work, social, and religious activities. The women of the slave quarters lived within a stone's throw of one another. Living at such close quarters could sometimes be unsettling since rumors, with or without foundation, spread faster in the confined environment. Yet, close living allowed for informal palavers during which females could share their joys, concerns, gossip, and heartbreak.

The organization of female slave work and social activities not only tended to separate women and men, but it also generated female cooperation and interdependence. . . . The pregnant female slave could usually depend on the company of her peers during delivery and convalescence. The midwife or "doctor woman" who delivered the baby was often a member of that peer group. One Virginia physician estimated that nine tenths of all deliveries among the black population in his state were conducted by midwives, most of whom were also black. Another Virginia physician set the number at five sixths.

Slave women and their children could depend on midwives and "doctor women" to treat a variety of ailments. Menstrual cramps, for example, were sometimes treated with a tea made from the bark of the gum tree, and at least one woman treated colic by giving the fretting infant a syrup made from a boiled rat's vein. Midwives and "doctor women" administered various other herb teas to ease the pains of many ailing slaves. Any number of broths, made from the leaves and barks of trees, from the branches and twigs of bushes, from turpentine, catnip, or tobacco were used to treat whooping cough, diarrhea, toothaches, colds, fevers, headaches, and backaches.

Male slave herb "doctors" and professionally trained white doctors did play a limited role in female slave medical care but more often than not it was elderly and middle-aged black women who tended to the slave population. William Howard Russell noted this phenomenon during his stay on a plantation outside of New Orleans where the cabin that served as a hospital for slaves was supervised by an old woman. While visiting an estate in Mississippi Frederick Olmsted overheard an elderly slave woman request medicines for a sick woman in her charge. According to a Georgia ex-slave, "one had to be mighty sick to have the services of a doctor." On his master's plantation "old women were . . . responsible for the care of the sick." This was also the case on Rebecca Hooks' former Florida residence. "The doctor," she noted, "was not nearly as popular as the 'granny' or midwife, who brewed medicines for every ailment."

Female cooperation in the realm of medical care helped foster bonding that led to collaboration in the area of resistance. Frances Kemble could attest to the concerted efforts of the black women on her husband's Sea Island plantations. More than once she was visited by groups of women imploring her to get her husband to extend the lying-in period for child-bearing women. On one occasion the women had apparently prepared beforehand the approach they would take with the foreign-born and sympathetic Kemble, for their chosen spokeswoman took care to play on Kemble's own maternal sentiments, and pointedly argued that slave women deserved at least some of the care and tenderness that Kemble's own pregnancy had elicited.

Usually, however, slave women could not be so outspoken about their needs, and covert cooperative resistance prevailed. Slaveowners suspected that midwives conspired with their female patients to induce abortions, and on Charles Colcock Jones' Georgia plantation such seems to have been the case. A woman named Lucy gave birth in secret and then denied that she had ever been pregnant. Although the midwife attended her, she too claimed not to have delivered a child, as did Lucy's mother. Jones had a physician examine Lucy, and the doctor confirmed what Jones had suspected, that Lucy had indeed given birth. Twelve days later, the decomposing body of a full-term infant was found, and Lucy, her mother, and the midwife were all hauled off to court. Another woman, a nurse, managed to avoid prosecution but not suspicion. Whether Lucy was guilty of murder and whether the others were accessories will never be known because the court could not shatter their collective defense that the child had been stillborn.

The inability of slave owners to penetrate the private world of female slaves is probably what kept them from learning of many abortions. The secrets kept by a midwife named Mollie became too much for her to bear. When she embraced Christianity it was the first thing for which she asked forgiveness. As she recalled: "I was carried to the gates of hell and the devil pulled out a book showing me the things which I had committed and that they were all true. My life as a midwife was shown to me and I have certainly felt sorry for all the things I did, after I was converted."

Health care is not the only example of how the organization of slave work and slave responsibilities led to female cooperation and bonding; slave women were also dependent on each other for child care. During his investigation of the domestic slave trade E. A. Andrews queried a slave trader as to how slave women could be expected to do a full day's work and raise their children, too. The trader dismissed the question as if it challenged the natural order of things: "Oh yes, they'll do a smart chance of work and raise the children besides." Such expectations reveal that slave traders and slave owners either were not conscious of the time and energy child raising consumed or knew what efforts had to be expended and just did not care. In hindsight their demands, whether based on ignorance or callousness, seem unreasonable. Slave women had an intensive work day before child care was added. Few could satisfy the demands made by the master on the one hand and their children on the other. Fatigue was a hard enemy to conquer. Some women, like Booker T. Washington's mother, set aside time to spend with their children every evening, but others, like the parents of Laugan Shiphard, found their offspring asleep when they returned from the fields.

Slave women had to have help if they were to survive the dual responsibilities of laborer and mother. Sometimes, especially on small farms or new plantations where there was no extra hand to superintend children, bondwomen took their offspring to the field with them and attended to them during scheduled breaks. Usually, however, infants and older children were left in the charge of an elderly female or females whose sole job was to baby-sit during working hours. These women did not assume the full maternal burden but they did spend as much or more time with a slave child than did the biological mother.

And they took their charge seriously. Said Robert Shepherd of the Georgia slave woman who looked after him: "Aunt Viney . . . had a big old horn what she blowed when it was time for us to eat, and us knowed better dan to git so fur off us couldn't hear dat horn, for Aunt Viney would sho' tear us up." Josephine Bristow spent more time with Mary Novlin, the nursery keeper on Ferdinand Gibson's South Carolina plantation, than she spent with her mother and father who came in from the fields after she was asleep: "De old lady, she looked after every blessed thing for us all day long en cooked for us right along wid de mindin'." In their complementary role as nurse, nursery superintendents ministered to the hurts and illnesses of infants and children. It was not at all uncommon for the children's weekly rations to be given to the "grannies" rather than to the children's parents. Neither the slaveowner nor slave society expected the biological mother of a child to fulfill all of that child's needs. Given the circumstances, the responsibilities of motherhood had to be shared, and this required close female cooperation.

FURTHER READING

Carol Bleser, *The Hammonds of Redcliffe* (1981)

Jane Turner Censer, *North Carolina Planters and Their Children, 1800–1860* (1984)

Catherine Clinton, *The Plantation Mistress* (1982)

Beth G. Crabtree and James W. Patton, eds., *"Journal of a Secesh Lady": The Diary of Catherine Ann Devereux Edmondston, 1860–1866* (1979)

Carl N. Degler, *At Odds: Women and the Family in America from the Revolution to the Present* (1980)

Elizabeth Fox-Genovese, *Within the Plantation Household* (1988)

Walter J. Fraser, Jr., R. Frank Saunders, Jr., and Jon L. Wakelyn, eds., *The Web of Southern Social Relations: Women, Family, and Education* (1985)

Jean E. Friedman, *The Enclosed Garden: Women and Community in the Evangelical South, 1830–1900* (1985)

Joanne V. Hawks and Sheila L. Skemp, eds., *Sex, Race, and the Role of Women in the South* (1983)

Harriet A. Jacobs, *Incidents in the Life of a Slave Girl: Written by Herself*, ed. Jean Fagan Yellin (1987)

Jacqueline Jones, *Labor of Love, Labor of Sorrow* (1985)

Suzanne Lebsock, *The Free Women of Petersburg* (1984)

Elisabeth Muhlenfeld, *Mary Boykin Chesnut* (1981)

Mary D. Robertson, ed., *Lucy Breckinridge of Grove Hill* (1979)

Ann Firor Scott, *The Southern Lady* (1970)

Deborah Gray White, *Ar'n't I a Woman?* (1985)

Sectionalism and Slavery

人

*As the nineteenth century advanced, sectionalism became a major theme in na-
tional politics, and southern challenges to federal authority became increasingly
emotion charged and serious. The defense of slavery was an explicit theme of
southern protests—as central and dominant as were discussions of state rights
and constitutional theory.*

*The South shared in some important political developments that were na-
tionwide in scope. During the Jacksonian era, vigorous two-party competition
between Whigs and Democrats characterized the southern states as much as their
northern counterparts. During the 1820s and 1830s, however, an unapologetic
proslavery argument emerged in the South. Thereafter it became steadily more
influential. Southern leaders began to erect barriers to and defenses for the "peculiar institution," and efforts to secure the loyalty of the yeoman farmer multiplied. Long before the 1850s, sectionalism and the defense of slavery had become
major themes of southern politics.*

*How and why did the slavery issue come to the fore in southern politics?
Were slaveowners or nonslaveholders more responsible for pressing this issue?
How different was the South from the North in politics, and how dominant was
the influence of slavery? How did nonslaveholding small farmers view their particular interests within a society whose politics were tightly bound up with slavery? These questions are at the heart of any analysis of the southern political
system.*

人 *D O C U M E N T S*

It is universally accepted that the long, deepening confrontation between the federal government and the South began no later than the nullification controversy
in 1832 in which South Carolina declared null and void a congressional tariff act.
The text of the Ordinance of Nullification, reprinted in the first document, states
South Carolina's grievances. The next two documents provide insight into the
reasons behind South Carolinians' actions. George McDuffie was a South Carolina congressman who became the nullifiers' leading orator. John C. Calhoun,
who developed the theoretical justifications for nullification, served as vice-presi-

dent until his resignation in 1833, at which time the South Carolina legislature sent him to the U.S. Senate. It was in the Senate in 1837 that Calhoun asserted that slavery was "a good"; his resolutions of 1838 indicate both his determination to defend slavery and the reasoning he used to develop its constitutional defense. Calhoun also pioneered in an activity that became common among southern leaders: arguing the benefits of slavery to nonslaveholders. The fourth document, an account of a speech by Jefferson Davis of Mississippi opposing the Compromise of 1850, is an able statement of these arguments in defense of slavery to nonslaveholders. Many southern intellectuals developed religious and sociological defenses of slavery, especially from the 1830s to the Civil War. Reverend Thornton Stringfellow, a Baptist minister from Virginia, penned one of the most popular and widely read scriptural defenses of the South's "peculiar institution"; it appears as the last selection.

South Carolina Nullifies the Tariff, 1832

An Ordinance to Nullify certain acts of the Congress of the United States, purporting to be laws laying duties and imposts on the importation of foreign commodities.

Whereas the Congress of the United States, by various acts, purporting to be acts laying duties and imposts on foreign imports, but in reality intended for the protection of domestic manufactures, and the giving of bounties to classes and individuals engaged in particular employments, at the expense and to the injury and oppression of other classes and individuals, and by wholly exempting from taxation certain foreign commodities, such as are not produced or manufactured in the United States, to afford a pretext for imposing higher and excessive duties on articles similar to those intended to be protected, hath exceeded its just powers under the Constitution, which confers on it no authority to afford such protection, and hath violated the true meaning and intent of the Constitution, which provides for equality in imposing the burthens of taxation upon the several States and portions of the Confederacy: *And whereas* the said Congress, exceeding its just power to impose taxes and collect revenue for the purpose of effecting and accomplishing the specific objects and purposes which the Constitution of the United States authorizes it to effect and accomplish, hath raised and collected unnecessary revenue for objects unauthorized by the Constitution:—

We, therefore, the people of the State of South Carolina in Convention assembled, do declare and ordain, . . . That the several acts and parts of acts of the Congress of the United States, purporting to be laws for the imposing of duties and imposts on the importation of foreign commodities, . . . and, more especially, . . . [the tariff acts of 1828 and 1832] . . . , are unauthorized by the Constitution of the United States, and violate the true meaning and intent thereof, and are null, void, and no law, nor binding upon this State, its officers or citizens; and all promises, contracts, and obligations, made or entered into, or to be made or entered into, with purpose to secure the duties imposed by the said acts, and all judicial proceedings which shall be hereafter had in affirmance thereof, are and shall be held utterly null and void.

And it is further Ordained, That it shall not be lawful for any of the constituted authorities, whether of this State or of the United States, to enforce the payment of duties imposed by the said acts within the limits of this State; but it shall be the duty of the Legislature to adopt such measures and pass such acts as may be necessary to give full effect to this Ordinance, and to prevent the enforcement and arrest the operation of the said acts and parts of acts of the Congress of the United States within the limits of this State, from and after the 1st day of February next, . . .

And it is further Ordained, That in no case of law or equity, decided in the courts of this State, wherein shall be drawn in question the authority of this ordinance, or the validity of such act or acts of the Legislature as may be passed for the purpose of giving effect thereto, or the validity of the aforesaid acts of Congress, imposing duties, shall any appeal be taken or allowed to the Supreme Court of the United States, nor shall any copy of the record be printed or allowed for that purpose; and if any such appeal shall be attempted to be taken, the courts of this State shall proceed to execute and enforce their judgments, according to the laws and usages of the State, without reference to such attempted appeal, and the person or persons attempting to take such appeal may be dealt with as for a contempt of the court.

And it is further Ordained, That all persons now holding any office of honor, profit, or trust, civil or military, under this State, (members of the Legislature excepted), shall, within such time, and in such manner as the Legislature shall prescribe, take an oath well and truly to obey, execute, and enforce, this Ordinance, and such act or acts of the Legislature as may be passed in pursuance thereof, according to the true intent and meaning of the same; and on the neglect or omission of any such person or persons so to do, his or their office or offices shall be forthwith vacated, . . . and no person hereafter elected to any office of honor, profit, or trust, civil or military, (members of the Legislature excepted), shall, until the Legislature shall otherwise provide and direct, enter on the execution of his office, . . . until he shall, in like manner, have taken a similar oath; and no juror shall be empannelled in any of the courts of this State, in any cause in which shall be in question this Ordinance, or any act of the Legislature passed in pursuance thereof, unless he shall first, in addition to the usual oath, have taken an oath that he will well and truly obey, execute, and enforce this Ordinance, and such act or acts of the Legislature as may be passed to carry the same into operation and effect, according to the true intent and meaning thereof.

And we, the People of South Carolina, to the end that it may be fully understood by the Government of the United States, and the people of the co-States, that we are determined to maintain this, our Ordinance and Declaration, at every hazard, *Do further Declare* that we will not submit to the application of force, on the part of the Federal Government, to reduce this State to obedience; but that we will consider the passage, by

Congress, of any act . . . to coerce the State, shut up her ports, destroy or harass her commerce, or to enforce the acts hereby declared to be null and void, otherwise than through the civil tribunals of the country, as inconsistent with the longer continuance of South Carolina in the Union: and that the people of this State will thenceforth hold themselves absolved from all further obligation to maintain or preserve their political connexion with the people of the other States, and will forthwith proceed to organize a separate Government, and do all other acts and things which sovereign and independent States may of right to do.

The Motives of South Carolina's Leaders, 1830, 1832

George McDuffie, from Speech of May 28, 1832

Any course of measures which shall hasten the abolition of slavery by destroying the value of slave labor, will bring upon the southern States the greatest political calamity with which they can be afflicted. . . . It is the clear and distinct perception of the irresistible tendency of this protecting system to precipitate us upon this great moral and political catastrophe, that has animated me to raise my warning voice, that my fellow-citizens may foresee, and, foreseeing, avoid the destiny that would otherwise befal them.

John C. Calhoun, from Letter to Virgil Maxcy, September 11, 1830

I consider the Tariff, but as the occasion, rather than the real cause of the present unhappy state of things. The truth can no longer be disguised, that the peculiar domestick institutions of the Southern States, and the consequent direction which that and her soil and climate have given to her industry, has placed them in regard to taxation and appropriation in opposite relation to the majority of the Union; against the danger of which, if there be no protective power in the reserved rights of the states, they must in the end be forced to rebel, or submit to have . . . their domestick institutions exhausted by Colonization and other schemes, and themselves & children reduced to wretchedness. Thus situated, the denial of the right of the state to interfere constitutionally in the last resort, more alarms the thinking than all other causes.

John C. Calhoun Defends Slavery, 1837–1838

Speech on the Reception of Abolition Petitions

However sound the great body of the non-slaveholding States are at present, in the course of a few years they will be succeeded by those who will have been taught to hate the people and institutions of nearly one-half of this Union, with a hatred more deadly than one hostile nation ever entertained towards another. It is easy to see the end. By the necessary course of events, if left to themselves, we must become, finally, two people. It is impossible under the deadly hatred which must spring up between the two great sections, if the present causes are permitted to operate unchecked, that we should continue under the same political system. The conflicting elements would burst the Union asunder, powerful as are the links which hold it together. Abolition and the Union cannot co-exist. As the friend of the Union I openly proclaim it,—and the sooner it is known the better. The former may now be controlled, but in a short time it will be beyond the power of man to arrest the course of events. We of the South will not, cannot surrender our institutions. To maintain the existing relations between the two races, inhabiting that section of the Union, is indispensable to the peace and happiness of both. It cannot be subverted without drenching the country in blood, and extirpating one or the other of the races. Be it good or bad, it has grown up with our society and institutions, and is so inter-woven with them, that to destroy it would be to destroy us as a people. But let me not be understood as admitting, even by implication, that the existing relations between the two races in the slaveholding States is an evil:—far otherwise; I hold it to be a good, as it has thus far proved itself to be to both, and will continue to prove so if not disturbed by the fell spirit of abolition. I appeal to facts. Never before has the black race of Central Africa, from the dawn of history to the present day, attained a condition so civilized and so improved, not only physically, but morally and intellectually. It came among us in a low, degraded, and savage con-dition, and in the course of a few generations it has grown up under the fostering care of our institutions, reviled as they have been, to its present comparatively civilized condition. This, with the rapid increase of numbers, is conclusive proof of the general happiness of the race, in spite of all the exaggerated tales to the contrary.

In the mean time, the white or European race has not degenerated. It has kept pace with its brethren in other sections of the Union where slavery does not exist. It is odious to make comparison; but I appeal to all sides whether the South is not equal in virtue, intelligence, patriotism, courage, disinterestedness, and all the high qualities which adorn our nature. I ask whether we have not contributed our full share of talents and political wisdom in forming and sustaining this political fabric; and whether we have not constantly inclined most strongly to the side of liberty, and been the first to see and first to resist the encroachments of power. In one thing only are we inferior—the arts of gain; we acknowledge that we are less wealthy than the Northern section of this Union, but I trace this mainly to the fiscal action of this Government, which has extracted much from, and spent little among us. Had it been the reverse,—if the exaction had been from the other section, and the expenditure with us, this point of superiority would not be against us now, as it was not at the formation of this Government.

But I take higher ground. I hold that in the present state of civilization, where two races of different origin, and distinguished by color, and other physical differences, as well as intellectual, are brought together, the re-lation now existing in the slaveholding States between the two, is, instead of an evil, a good—a positive good. I feel myself called upon to speak freely upon the subject where the honor and interests of those I represent are involved. I hold then, that there never has yet existed a wealthy and civilized society in which one portion of the community did not, in point of fact, live on the labor of the other. Broad and general as is this assertion, it is fully borne out by history. This is not the proper occasion, but if it were, it would not be difficult to trace the various devices by which the wealth of all civilized communities has been so unequally divided, and to show by what means so small a share has been allotted to those by whose labor it was produced, and so large a share given to the non-producing classes. The devices are almost innumerable, from the brute force and gross superstition of ancient times, to the subtle and artful fiscal contrivances of modern. I might well challenge a comparison between them and the more direct, simple, and patriarchal mode by which the labor of the African race is, among us, commanded by the European. I may say with truth, that in few countries so much is left to the share of the laborer, and so little exacted from him, or where there is more kind attention paid to him in sickness or infirmities of age. Compare his condition with the tenants of the poor houses in the more civilized portions of Europe—look at the sick, and the old and infirm slave, on one hand, in the midst of his family and friends, under the kind superintending care of his master and mistress, and compare it with the forlorn and wretched condition of the pauper in the poor house. But I will not dwell on this aspect of the question; I turn to the political; and here I fearlessly assert that the existing relation between the two races in the South, against which these blind fanatics are waging war, forms the most solid and durable foundation on which to rear free and stable political institutions. It is useless to disguise the fact. There is and always has been in an advanced stage of wealth and civilization, a conflict between labor and capital. The condition of society in the South exempts us from the disorders and dangers resulting from this conflict; and which explains why it is that the political condition of the slaveholding States has been so much more stable and quiet than that of the North. The advantages of the former, in this respect, will become more and more manifest if left undisturbed by interference from without, as the country advances in wealth and numbers. We have, in fact, but just entered that condition of society where the strength and durability of our political institutions are to be tested; and I venture nothing in predicting that the experience of the next generation will fully test how vastly more favorable our condition of society is to that of other sections for free and stable institutions, provided we are not disturbed by the interference of others, or shall have sufficient intelligence and spirit to resist promptly and successfully such interference. It rests with ourselves to meet and repel them. I look not for aid to this Government, or to the other States; not but there are kind feelings towards us on the part of the great body of the non-slaveholding States; but as kind as their feelings may be, we may rest assured that no political party in these States will risk their ascendency for our safety. If we do not defend ourselves none will defend us; if we yield we will be more and more pressed as we recede; and if we submit we will be trampled under foot. Be assured that emancipation itself would not satisfy these fanatics:—that gained, the next step would be to raise the negroes to a social and political equality with the whites; and that being effected, we would soon find the present condition of the two races reversed. They and their northern allies would be the masters, and we the slaves; the condition of the white race in the British West India Islands, bad as it is, would be happiness to ours. There the mother country is interested in sustaining the supremacy of the European race. It is true that the authority of the former master is destroyed, but the African will there still be a slave, not to individuals but to the community,—forced to labor, not by the authority of the overseer, but by the bayonet of the soldiery and the rod of the civil magistrate.

Surrounded as the slaveholding States are with such imminent perils, I rejoice to think that our means of defence are ample, if we shall prove to have the intelligence and spirit to see and apply them before it is too late. All we want is concert, to lay aside all party differences, and unite with zeal and energy in repelling approaching dangers. Let there be concert of action, and we shall find ample means of security without resorting to secession or disunion. I speak with full knowledge and a thorough examination of the subject, and for one, see my way clearly. One thing alarms me—the eager pursuit of gain which overspreads the land, and which absorbs every faculty of the mind and every feeling of the heart. Of all passions avarice is the most blind and compromising—the last to see and the first to yield to danger. I dare not hope that any thing I can say will arouse the South to a due sense of danger; I fear it is beyond the power of mortal voice to awaken it in time from the fatal security into which it has fallen.

Speech on the Importance of Domestic Slavery

Resolved, That in the adoption of the Federal Constitution, the States adopting the same acted severally, as free, independent, and sovereign States; and that each, for itself, by its own voluntary assent, entered the Union with the view to its increased security against all dangers, *domestic* as well as foreign, and the more perfect and secure enjoyment of its advantages, natural, political, and social.

Resolved, That in delegating a portion of their powers to be exercised by the Federal Government, the States retained, severally, the exclusive and sole right over their own domestic institutions and police, and are alone responsible for them, and that any intermeddling of any one or more States, or a combination of their citizens, with the domestic institutions and police of the others, on any ground, or under any pretext whatever, political, moral, or religious, with the view to their alteration, or subversion, is an assumption of superiority not warranted by the Constitution, insulting to the States interfered with, tending to endanger their domestic peace and tranquility, subversive of the objects for which the Constitution was formed, and, by necessary consequence, tending to weaken and destroy the Union itself.

Resolved, That this Government was instituted and adopted by the several States of this Union as a common agent, in order to carry into effect the powers which they had delegated by the Constitution for their mutual security and prosperity; and that, in fulfilment of this high and sacred trust, this Government is bound so to exercise its powers as to give, as far as may be practicable, increased stability and security to the domestic institutions of the States that compose the Union; and that it is the solemn duty of the Government to resist all attempts by one portion of the Union to use it as an instrument to attack the domestic institutions of another, or to weaken or destroy such institutions, instead of strengthening and upholding them, as it is in duty bound to do.

Resolved, That domestic slavery, as it exists in the Southern and Western States of this Union, composes an important part of their domestic institutions, inherited from their ancestors, and existing at the adoption of the Constitution, by which it is recognised as constituting an essential element in the distribution of its powers among the States; and that no change of opinion, or feeling, on the part of the other States of the Union in relation to it, can justify them or their citizens in open and systematic attacks thereon, with the view to its overthrow; and that all such attacks are in manifest violation of the mutual and solemn pledge to protect and defend each other, given by the States, respectively, on entering into the Constitutional compact, which formed the Union, and as such is a manifest breach of faith, and a violation of the most solemn obligations, moral and religious.

Resolved, That the intermeddling of any State or States, or their citizens, to abolish slavery in this District, or any of the Territories, on the ground, or under the pretext, that it is immoral or sinful; or the passage of any act or measure of Congress, with that view, would be a direct and dangerous attack on the institutions of all the slaveholding States.

Jefferson Davis on Slavery and White Equality, 1851

[Reviewing the debates in Congress on the Compromise of 1850, Jefferson Davis expressed regret that the border states,] after we of the planting states had labored to give them the law by which they might perchance recover their slaves, had refused to co-operate with us, to enable our people to obtain an outlet for the black population of the country; joining in the cry of the "glorious Union," sustaining the odious so-called adjustment measures, and thus aiding in the attempt of the free-soilers to encircle us about with a cordon of free States, the direct tendency of which is to crowd upon our soil an overgrown black population, until there will not be room

Text from Dunbar Rowland, ed., *Jefferson Davis: Constitutionalist*, Vol. II, 1929, pp. 70–75. Quoted courtesy of Jackson, MS: Mississippi Department of Archives and History.

in the country for the whites and the blacks to subsist in; and in this way destroy the institution and reduce the whites to the degraded position of the African race. He, therefore, was in favor of excluding the slaves of the *border states* from the *planting states,* and he hoped that this policy would be adopted.

Col. Davis said that he had heard it said that the poor men, who own no negroes themselves, would all be against the institution, and would, consequently, array themselves on the side of the so called Union men— that the submissionists claimed them. But that he could not believe, that the poor men of the country, were so blind to their own interests, as to be thus cheated out of their privileges, which they now enjoy. That *now they stand upon the broad level of equality with the rich man.* Equal to him in every thing, save that they did not own so much property; and that, even in this particular, the road to wealth was open to them, and the poor man might attain it; and, even if he did not succeed, the failure did not degrade him. That no white man, in a slaveholding community, was the menial servant of any one. That whenever the poor white man labored for the rich, he did so upon terms of distinction between him and the negro. It was to the interest of the master to keep up a distinction between the white man in his employment, and his negroes. And that this very distinction elevated, and kept the white laborer on a level with the employer; because the distinction between the classes throughout the slaveholding states, is a distinction of color. Between the classes there is no such thing, here, as a distinction of property; and he who thinks there is, and prides himself upon it, is grossly mistaken. Free the negroes, however, and it would soon be here, as it is in the countries of Europe, and in the North, and everywhere else, where negro slavery does not exist. The poor white man would become a menial for the rich, and be, by him, reduced to an equality with the free blacks, into a degraded position; and the distinction, at once, would be made that of—*Property*—of *Wealth*—between the classes, between the *Rich* and the *Poor.* The *rich man,* with his lands, and his other property, and his money, would be a rich man still. The *poor* would be *poor* still, and with much less chance than he now has of acquiring property, because of the numbers of mean and worthless free negroes, in competition with whose labor his own would have to come. And yet the tendency of the doctrines of the submissionists, is directly to invite further aggression from the North, and by this invitation, to bring about this very state of things. The non-slaveholder can see this, as well as the slaveholder. And seeing, and knowing his rights, he will defend and maintain them, as soon, if not sooner, than the rich man will. Then, he did not believe that the submission party had the exclusive right, which they claimed, or expect that the middle and poorer classes would co-operate with them upon this important question, affecting, as it does, their interests—their standing in the community— more than all others.

Col. Davis said that he had always thought, and sincerely believed, that the institution of negro slavery, as it now exists among us, is necessary to the *equality* of the *white* race. Distinctions between classes have always existed, everywhere, and in every country, where civilization has been established among men. Destroy them to-day, and they will spring up to-morrow; and we have no right to expect, or even to hope, that this Southern climate of ours, would be exempt from the operation of this Universal law.

Menial services have to be performed, by some one; and every where the world over, within the range of civilization, those persons, by whom the menial services have been performed, as a class, have been looked upon, as occupying, and are reduced to a state of inferiority. Wherever a distinction in color has not existed to draw the line, and mark the boundary, the line has been drawn, by *property,* between the rich and poor. *Wealth* and *poverty* have marked the boundary. The poor man stands in need of all his rights, and all his privileges, and therefore, this question is of the greatest, and the gravest importance to him; much more so than it is to the rich. The rich by siding with the party in power—the authorities that be, may always be safe. Not so with the poor. Their all is suspended upon their *superiority* to the *blacks*—their all of equality, in a political and social point of view—the social equality of their wives, daughters, and sons, are all suspended upon, and involved in this question. It will not do to say that this is a fancy sketch, or that these things are too far in the distance, to be seriously contemplated. The tendencies are all in that direction, and if they are not met, and met promptly, and rolled back, or stayed forever in their progress, the wheel of revolution will roll on until the institution is crushed, the great object of the freesoilers accomplished, and the negroes freed.

But they have, if possible, still higher grounds than these. The constitution, the palladium of the liberties of the people, in more respects than one, has been violated, and that violation is to be continued, under the *implied* invitation of the submissionists, if they succeed in the present contest. And when once it becomes an established principle, that repeated violations of that instrument will be tolerated by the people—that they will submit—the poor man's liberties are all gone, and gone forever.

Reverend Thornton Stringfellow's Defense of Slavery, 1856

Jesus Christ recognized this institution [slavery] as one that was lawful among men, and regulated its relative duties.

. . . I affirm then, first, (and no man denies,) that Jesus Christ has not abolished slavery by a prohibitory command: and second, I affirm, he has introduced no new moral principle which can work its destruction, under the gospel dispensation; and that the principle relied on for this purpose, is a fundamental principle of the Mosaic law, under which slavery was instituted by Jehovah himself: and third, with this absence of positive prohibition, and this absence of principle, to work its ruin, I affirm, that

Thornton Stringfellow, *Scriptural and Statistical Views in Favor of Slavery, 1856* from the book, *Slavery Defended: The Views of the Old South*, edited by Eric L. McKitrick, © 1963. Used by permission of the publisher, Prentice-Hall, Inc., Englewood Cliffs, NJ.

in all the Roman provinces, where churches were planted by the apostles, hereditary slavery existed, as it did among the Jews, and as it does now among us, (which admits of proof from history that no man will dispute who knows any thing of the matter,) and that in instructing such churches, the Holy Ghost by the apostles, has recognized the institution, as one *legally existing* among them, to be perpetuated in the church, and that its duties are prescribed.

Now for the proof: To the church planted at Ephesus, the capital of the lesser Asia, Paul ordains by letter, subordination in the fear of God,— first between wife and husband; second, child and parent; third, servant and master; *all, as states, or conditions, existing among the members.*

The relative duties of each state are pointed out; those between the servant and master in these words: "Servants be obedient to them who are your masters, according to the flesh, with fear and trembling, in singleness of your heart as unto Christ; not with eye service as men pleasers, but as the servants of Christ, doing the will of God from the heart, with good-will, doing service, as to the Lord, and not to men, knowing that whatsoever good thing any man doeth, the same shall he receive of the Lord, whether he be bond or free. And ye masters do the same things to them, forbearing threatening, knowing that your master is also in heaven, neither is there respect of persons with him." Here, by the Roman law, the servant was property, and the control of the master unlimited, as we shall presently prove.

To the church at Colosse, a city of Phrygia, in the lesser Asia,—Paul in his letter to them, recognizes the three relations of wives and husbands, parents and children, servants and masters, as relations existing among the members; (here the Roman law was the same;) and to the servants and masters he thus writes: "Servants obey in all things your masters, according to the flesh: not with eye service, as men pleasers, but in singleness of heart, fearing God: and whatsoever you do, do it heartily, as to the Lord and not unto men; knowing that of the Lord ye shall receive the reward of the inheritance, for ye serve the Lord Christ. But he that doeth wrong shall receive for the wrong he has done; and there is no respect of persons with God. Masters give unto your servants that which is just and equal, knowing that you also have a master in heaven."

The same Apostle writes a letter to the church at Corinth;—a very important city, formerly called the eye of Greece, either from its location, or intelligence, or both, and consequently, an important point, for radiating light in all directions, in reference to subjects connected with the cause of Jesus Christ; and particularly, in the bearing of its practical precepts on civil society, and the political structure of nations. Under the direction of the Holy Ghost, he instructs the church, that, on this particular subject, *one general principle* was ordained of God, applicable alike in all countries and at all stages of the church's future history, and that it was this: *"as the Lord has called every one, so let him walk."* "Let every man abide in the same calling wherein he is called." "Let every man wherein he is called, therein abide with God."—1 Cor. vii: 17, 20, 24. *"And so ordain I in all churches;"* vii: 17. The Apostle thus explains his meaning:

"Is any man called being circumcised? Let him not become uncircumcised."

"Is any man called in uncircumcision? Let him not be circumcised."

"Art thou called, being a servant? Care not for it, but if thou mayest be made free, use it rather;" vii: 18, 21. Here, by the Roman law, slaves were property,—yet Paul ordains, in this, and all other churches, that Christianity gave them no title to freedom, but on the contrary, required them not to care for being slaves, or in other words, to be contented with their *state*, or *relation*, unless they could be *made free*, in a lawful way.

Again, we have a letter by Peter, who is the Apostle of the circumcision—addressed especially to the Jews, who were scattered through various provinces of the Roman empire; comprising those provinces especially, which were the theater of their dispersion, under the Assyrians and Babylonians. . . . He thus instructs them: "Submit yourselves to every ordinance of man for the Lord's sake." "For so is the will of God." "Servants, be subject to your masters with all fear, not only to the good and gentle, but also to the froward."—1 Peter ii: 11, 13, 15, 18. What an important document is this! enjoining political subjection to *governments of every form*, and Christian subjection on the part of servants to their masters, whether good or bad; for the purpose of showing forth to advantage, the *glory of the gospel*, and putting to silence the ignorance of foolish men, who might think it seditious.

By "every ordinance of man," as the context will show, is meant governmental regulations or laws, as was that of the Romans for enslaving their prisoners taken in war, instead of destroying their lives.

When such enslaved persons came into the church of Christ let them (says Peter) "be subject to their masters with all fear," whether such masters be good or bad. It is worthy of remark, that he says much to secure civil subordination to the State, and hearty and cheerful obedience to the masters, on the part of servants; yet he says nothing to masters in the whole letter. It would seem from this, that danger to the cause of Christ was on the side of *insubordination among the servants*, and a *want of humility with inferiors*, rather than *haughtiness among superiors* in the church. . . .

. . . It is taken for granted, on all hands pretty generally, that Jesus Christ has at least been silent, or that he has not personally spoken on the subject of slavery. Once for all, I deny it. Paul, after stating that a slave was to honor an unbelieving master, in the 1st verse of the 6th chapter, says, in the 2d verse, that to a believing master, he is the rather to do service, because he who partakes of the benefit is his brother. He then says, if any man teach otherwise, (as all abolitionists then did, and now do,) and consent not to wholesome words, "even the words of our Lord Jesus Christ." Now, if our Lord Jesus Christ uttered such words, how dare we say he has been silent? If he has been silent, how dare the Apostle say these are the words of our Lord Jesus Christ, if the Lord Jesus Christ never spoke them? . . .

We will remark, in closing under this head, that we have shown from the text of the sacred volume, that when God entered into covenant with Abraham, it was with him as a slaveholder; that when he took his posterity by the hand in Egypt, five hundred years afterward to confirm the promise made to Abraham, it was done with them as slaveholders; that when he gave them a constitution of government, he gave them the right to perpetuate hereditary slavery; and that he did not for the fifteen hundred years of their national existence, express disapprobation toward the institution.

We have also shown from authentic history that the institution of slavery existed in every family, and in every province of the Roman Empire, at the time the gospel was published to them.

We have also shown from the New Testament, that all the churches are recognized as composed of masters and servants; and that they are instructed by Christ how to discharge their relative duties; and finally that in reference to the question which was then started, whether Christianity did not abolish the institution, or the right of one Christian to hold another Christian in bondage, we have shown, that "the words of our Lord Jesus Christ" are, that so far from this being the case, it adds to the obligation of the servant to render service with good-will to his master, and that gospel fellowship is not to be entertained with persons who will not consent to it!

⅄ *E S S A Y S*

In the first selection, historian Robert F. Durden of Duke University appraises the contributions of various groups to slavery consciousness and the degree of integration of the South in national political patterns. His analysis relates the advance of political democracy among whites to proslavery ideology and notes that, despite regional concerns about slavery, southerners threw themselves into the national political competition between Whigs and Democrats. But William J. Cooper, Jr., professor of history at Louisiana State University, places greater emphasis on the dominating power of the slavery question. He argues in the second essay that the issue was of paramount importance within the South as early as the 1830s. Historian Steven Hahn of the University of California, San Diego, focuses on the yeomen farmers of upcountry Georgia and their place in a politics of slavery. Arguing in the final selection that localism and attitudes toward the market economy shaped their politics, he describes the importance to them of independence and shows how the yeomen were sometimes the opponents and sometimes the allies of the planters.

Regional and National Patterns in Southern Politics

ROBERT F. DURDEN

Some influential historians . . . argue . . . that the large slaveholders formed a ruling class, an aristocratic or elite group that enjoyed a hegemonic control over the whole of southern life. If white southerners in all classes became fanatic in defense of slavery, these historians maintain, it was because such

From Robert F. Durden, *The Self-Inflicted Wound*, 1985, pp. 40–48. Copyright © 1985 by The University Press of Kentucky. Reprinted by permission of the publishers.

a policy was in the class interests of the great slaveholders and was successfully carried out by and for them.

An alternative explanation of the South's gradual freezing up in defense of slavery from the 1820s on focuses not on class but on race. The racial dimension of slavery in North America—that is, the fact that black Africans were the slaves of whites of European ancestry—loomed large from the beginning and had always differentiated American slavery from that which had been known in the civilizations of the Greeks, Romans, and others in antiquity.

While the racial aspect of American slavery was always important, not until the nineteenth century did educated Europeans and Americans begin self-consciously to think and write a great deal about the distinct races of mankind. In the eighteenth century, universalist ideas about mankind—such as natural rights allegedly belonging to all men—had prevailed. In the nineteenth century, however, attention shifted markedly to the distinct races of human beings, and inevitably to the allegedly scientifically proven superiority or inferiority of certain races. In the United States the assumption of the superiority of the white race, or, as it was often called, the "Anglo-Saxon" race, over both the Negro and Indian races became a most important fact before and after the Civil War, a fact that massively influenced national politics and policies. And while the Mason-Dixon line came after 1800 to separate the slaveholding states from those states that had eliminated slavery, there was certainly never a Mason-Dixon line for white racism.

Just as whites, South and North, began to think self-consciously about race in the early nineteenth century, so political democracy, as that century defined the term, arrived on the scene at about the same time. There were some exceptions, especially in South Carolina and the other South Atlantic states, but as a result of popular agitation and constitutional reform in the 1820s and 1830s, the advance of political democracy in most of the South matched that of the rest of the nation. By the mid-1830s in Alabama, Mississippi, and Tennessee, government was quite democratic by the standards of that era: the voters, not the legislature, elected the governor; there was universal manhood suffrage (that is, white adult males could vote); the legislatures were based on the white population and were reapportioned regularly; and the voters elected county officials. When Arkansas (1836) and Texas (1845) entered the Union and thus joined the ranks of the slaveholding states, they too had the same democratic features. Three other states in the Deep South—Georgia, Florida (1845), and Louisiana—were not far behind in the advance of political democracy. Neither was Kentucky, except that its county governments continued to be undemocratic.

In the older seaboard states of Maryland, Virginia, North Carolina, and South Carolina the popular push for democratic reforms had more mixed results. In both Maryland and North Carolina constitutional reforms gave the voters power to elect the governor and moved the basis of apportionment in the legislature in a more democratic direction. In Virginia, while suffrage was broadened, it was still tied to property-holding or taxpaying.

And though the traditionally dominant eastern counties in Virginia made concessions to the western ones in the matter of representation in the legislature, the east kept power that was out of proportion to its white population. Both Virginia and South Carolina resisted political reform more than the other southern states: property qualifications for voting and officeholding were kept, county government remained undemocratic, and the legislatures still chose the governors. But despite necessary qualifications, the fact remains that political democracy for white adult males became a reality in most of the South long before the Civil War.

One of the first tangible results of that democratic advance may well have been a more positive and vigorous defense of slavery, for as countless antebellum white southerners as well as later historians have pointed out, slavery was an arrangement of the races as well as a system of labor. By the arrangement, all white persons, no matter how rich or poor they may have been or what social class they may have belonged to, were drastically separated from—and, they believed, kept raised above—the vast majority of the blacks who were slaves. "Break down slavery," one prominent Virginia declared, "and you would with the same blow destroy the great democratic principle of equality among men." He meant, of course, that all whites could allegedly enjoy equality precisely because the blacks were slaves. A Georgian explained that since the black slaves were not citizens, every white who was a citizen felt that he belonged to an elevated class. "It matters not that he is no slaveholder," the Georgian continued, "he is not of the inferior race; he is a freeborn citizen; he engages in no menial occupation. The poorest meets the richest as an equal; sits at his table with him; salutes him as a neighbor; meets him in every public assembly, and stands on the same social platform. Hence there is no war of classes."

There were, despite such assertions as the Georgian's, quite real class tensions among whites, but the argument that there were not was often used by upper-class slaveholders to try to stifle opposition and protect their own interests. Yet nonslaveholding whites also used the argument that all whites were equal, and when they did so they were asserting their hotly claimed superiority to the black slaves.

The classic statement about the racial aspect not only of slavery but of southern history in general was made by historian Ulrich B. Phillips in 1928. In a now-famous essay entitled "The Central Theme of Southern History," Phillips argued that the absolute essence or core of southernism was "a common resolve indomitably maintained" that the South be and always remain "a white man's country." Whether expressed "with the frenzy of a demagogue or maintained with a patrician's quietude," a belief in and adherence to white supremacy was "the cardinal test of a Southerner and the central theme of Southern history." Before the Civil War, the most basic fact about slavery, according to Phillips' interpretation, was that it maintained white supremacy.

Regardless of why the white South gradually closed ranks in defense of slavery—because of the alleged domination of the great slaveholders or, as the evidence increasingly suggests, because of the pride and fears of the race-conscious and politically active nonslaveholding majority—the fact remains that the old necessary-evil concept gave way to the newer and more dynamic idea of slavery as a positive good, and whites of all classes became militant defenders of slavery. An outpouring of speeches and pamphlets in South Carolina beginning in the 1820s marked the beginning of the shift. In the late eighteenth century the Methodist and Baptist leaders in the South had disapproved of slavery, but in 1823 the Reverend Richard Furman, president of the Baptist State Convention in South Carolina, published a biblical defense of slavery. In 1826 the learned Dr. Thomas Cooper, president of South Carolina College (later the University of South Carolina), spoke out in defense of slavery, and in 1829 Governor Stephen Miller of South Carolina asserted: "Slavery is not a national evil; on the contrary, it is a national benefit . . . [and] upon this subject it does not become us to speak in a whisper, betray fear, or feign philanthropy."

That the proslavery argument gained powerful champions in Virginia too became clear in 1832. Having closely followed the slavery debates in the Virginia legislature, Thomas R. Dew, a professor at the College of William and Mary and soon to become its president, published a powerful defense of slavery. Numerous other defenses of slavery continued to appear, right on down to the collapse of the institution in 1865, for the construction and elaboration of the proslavery argument was perhaps the most sustained intellectual activity of the antebellum South. A milestone in the advance of the argument was reached in 1837 when Senator John C. Calhoun, the widely acknowledged possessor of perhaps the keenest political mind in the South, declared on the floor of the United States Senate: "When two races of different origin and distinguished by color, and other physical differences, as well as intellectual [differences] are brought together, the relation now existing in the slave-holding states between the two, is instead of an evil, a good—a positive good." Calhoun and other defenders of slavery usually spoke first and foremost to their fellow white southerners, for lingering doubts about slavery had to be removed and uneasy consciences constantly assuaged.

The attack on the institution from the outside, however, reached new heights in the 1830s. Growing partially out of a religious revival in the North led by Charles G. Finney and partially out of the humanitarian and reforming zeal of certain wealthy New York merchant-philanthropists, the American Anti-Slavery Society was established late in 1833. Although angry northern mobs assailed the abolitionists, who remained unpopular in much of the North until the Civil War, their number did grow. In the mid-1830s they attempted to flood the South with antislavery pamphlets and newspapers, only to inspire mobs in some southern cities to seize the material from the post offices and burn it. In addition, many southern states enacted laws making the distribution of abolitionist literature a felony. Next the Anti-Slavery Society began to flood the United States Congress with petitions demanding the abolition of slavery and the slave trade in the District of Columbia, over which the Constitution gave Congress sole power. Opponents of President Jackson and his Democratic party were happy to see

Congress paralyzed as southern congressmen angrily responded to the petitions, and a bitter fight ensued over how the petitions should be handled.

By the late 1830s, however, the American Anti-Slavery Society had fallen into disarray. Not only did the leadership divide over various questions of policy, but the severe economic depression that began in 1837 dried up most of the Society's sources of funds. By the time William Lloyd Garrison and his fellow abolitionists from New England captured control of the organization in 1840, many of the original leaders were turning to the type of political action that the Garrisonians scorned.

For all of the controversy, North and South, that the abolitionists stirred up in the 1830s, they and their cause did not significantly affect the mainstream of the nation's political life. The reason for this was that a vigorous two-party system emerged in the same decade. Since both parties were national in scope and abolitionism was unpopular in the North and anathema in the South, the leaders of both parties did their utmost to avoid touching the slavery question.

The Democrats, galvanized by the bold and therefore controversial leadership of Andrew Jackson, saw their National Republican opponents metamorphose around 1834 into the Whig party. With a name that recalled British as well as American resistance to the powers of the Stuart kings and George III, the Whigs were an amorphous coalition which formed initially to oppose "King Andrew" and his minions. Despite the fragility of the Whig coalition, for almost two decades the nation witnessed a vigorous two-party system in operation, and southern voters as much as those in any other section of the country divided passionately into Democrats and Whigs.

The southern Whigs were an incredibly mixed lot. The hemp growers of Kentucky and the great sugar planters of Louisiana were traditional friends of the protective tariff in the South, and they gravitated naturally to the support of Clay's American System, which was at the heart of northern Whiggery. Businessmen in Baltimore, Richmond, and Norfolk tended to be Whigs just as many had earlier been Federalists and then National Republicans.

The black-belt counties of the South, so-called because of the fertile dark soil, were, outside of the tidewater, the areas of greatest slaveholding in the South, and these counties were generally Whig. The claim was sometimes made, in fact, that three-fourths of the slaves in the South were owned by Whigs. Many of these planters were Whigs not so much because they liked the whole American System—though there were parts of it, such as a central bank, which they did support—but because the Whigs presented themselves as champions of order and property and as the conservative, gentlemanly opponents of the Democratic "rabble." Some southerners, such as John Tyler of Virginia, became Whigs mainly because they feared and disliked Andrew Jackson's unprecedented display of executive power and the disdain for states' rights that he revealed in the nullification crisis. Southern Whigs were by no means recruited only from the ranks of the larger slaveholders, however. In the North Carolina up-country and in eastern Tennessee, yeoman farmers, who hoped for internal improvements in the form of railways, joined the Whig party. In their eyes, the Whigs were the champions of progress and economic development.

Wildly heterogeneous though the southern Whigs were, they offered the Democrats a vigorous, frequently successful opposition. With both parties claiming nationally to be the true champion of liberty and the people—and each painting the other as a menace to freedom and the Republic—the two southern wings of the parties faced the additional task of assuring the voters that they were solidly behind slavery and the equality of all whites that the peculiar institution allegedly made possible.

Sharing the goal of protecting and promoting liberty and equality for whites, Whigs and Democrats differed as to the best way of achieving those goals. There were numerous variations and issues from state to state, but generally the Whigs favored a positive role for government in encouraging economic development and therefore economic opportunities for all. The Democrats, on the other hand, opposed federal or state financing of internal improvements such as railroads or canals on the grounds that such policies aided the rich and powerful few at the ultimate expense of the impoverished masses and that public debt, the inevitable by-product of an activist role for the government, would lead to corruption. With Democrats stressing the government's obligation merely to protect the equal rights of all white men, Whigs looked less fearfully upon government and the help it might give to the capitalistic market economy.

In an Upper South state such as North Carolina, where historian Marc Kruman has carefully studied the workings of the second party system, the Whigs took the lead in having the state government aid in financing major railroads and in launching banks for which the state provided a minority share of the capital. Tar Heel Democrats bitterly oppposed such measures on the grounds that they favored special interests and threatened liberty and equality.

Studying Alabama in the Deep South, historian J. Mills Thornton III likewise argues that Whigs there maintained that positive state action would benefit society as a whole while the Democrats feared any increase of power in government or in such private institutions as state-chartered corporations. Fierce political battles raged in Alabama about a host of issues ranging from banking to the removal of the Creek Indians, but Thornton suggests that there was actually only one issue in the state's politics: how to protect liberty and white equality, or, to put the matter another way, how to avoid slavery. While this same republican ideology, the legacy of the American Revolution, animated northerners as well as southerners, the presence of large numbers of black slaves in the South served as a constant reminder to southern whites of the grim reality that lay behind the politicians' rhetoric.

Whether in the Upper or the Deep South, both parties claimed to be staunch defenders of slavery. Each party, in fact, claimed superiority in that respect and attempted to arouse suspicion among the voters as to the soundness or trustworthiness of the opposition in championing "southern rights." Paradoxically, by constantly stressing the centrality of southern rights and the alleged threats to the institution of slavery from various northern groups, the state political parties actually increased southern sectional sensitivity at the same time that the national parties worked to lessen the dangers of sectionalism.

As a two-party region, moreover, the South and its interests were important to both parties. The paradox was that the South's political sectionalism actually diminished in the very same period in which its feelings about and defense of the peculiar institution moved farther and farther from the older national consensus about slavery. That is, although political sectionalism waned, the South's cultural sectionalism increased. But as long as the national leaders of both parties scrupulously avoided offending the South on the slavery question, the region seemed well integrated into the nation's vigorous and often clamorous political life.

The Dominance of Slavery

WILLIAM J. COOPER, JR.

[In the 1830s] even Whigs who were primarily interested in economic matters had to turn to states' rights and sectional issues to arouse southern voters against the Democratic party.

Although Whigs espoused states' rights, a political cry that tended to rally southerners, that chorus alone did not make the Whigs such a powerful threat to the Democrats. While the old shibboleth of states' rights could arouse a certain, but unknown, number of southern voters, it could never generate the mass excitement and exuberance necessary to harness the energy of tens of thousands of southern voters behind the Whig cause. In 1833 and 1834 the Whig party stood on the threshold. It seemed to have three alternatives: the fledgling party could disintegrate amidst the ideological squabbles of National Republicans and nullifiers; it could prove incapable of growth . . . ; [or] it could build on its early momentum and become a major party. That last possibility required a galvanizing issue, for no great popular figure in the Jackson image donned a Whig cloak. In fact none existed. The Whigs ended up taking the third course because they found their issue. The rise of an organized abolition movement in the North matched the growth of anti-Jackson sentiment in the South. The southern anti-Jackson men, the Whigs, went after the abolition issue with unabashed vigor and glee.

The rise of an organized, militant abolition movement in the United States is normally dated from 1831 when William Lloyd Garrison began the publication of his *Liberator* in Boston. By 1835 the South confronted this uncompromising opposition to slavery, which took the form of petitions to Congress praying chiefly for emancipation in the District of Columbia

William J. Cooper, Jr., *The South and the Politics of Slavery, 1828–1856*, pp. 58–69 (Baton Rouge: Louisiana State University Press, 1978). Reprinted by permission of the publisher.

and in abolitionist pamphlets sent by mail to southern communities. The South, always keenly sensitive to any outside intervention regarding slavery, was horrified. That this abolition crusade followed so rapidly the great slave revolt led by Nat Turner sent visions of cataclysm through the slave states.

Immediately and in unison the South struck back. Meetings to protest abolition in general and the incendiary publications (the name given by southerners to the abolitionist pamphlets) in particular were held in southern cities. In Charleston a group of irate citizens broke into the post office and burned the hated pamphlets. The South Carolina legislature declared that it was simply "impossible" for the South to permit the reception of abolitionist literature. Other state legislatures passed resolutions like those adopted in Virginia that affirmed that the South, or states in the South, retained sole control of slavery and that right must "be maintained at all hazards." "Upon this point," asserted the Georgia legislature, "there can be no discussion—no compromise—no doubt." In Louisiana governor and legislature agreed and moved for a southern convention to consider the crisis. United States Senator Hugh Lawson White of Tennessee told the Senate that slavery was "sacred" to the South. Never, proclaimed White, would southerners stand for any outside meddling with slavery. This turmoil stemming from the collision between abolition and an aroused South exposed the raw nerve of slavery.

And the institution of slavery formed the bedrock of southern society. Perceptive as usual, Alexis de Tocqueville in the early 1830s recognized this centrality of slavery in southern society. From Tocqueville's time to break up of the Union nothing shoved slavery out of that central place. Practically every white southerner agreed with Mississippi Governor John A. Quitman's assertion in his 1850 inaugural address: "This institution [slavery] is entwined with our political system and cannot be separated from it." Theresa Pulszky, accompanying Louis Kossuth on his southern tour in 1852, found slavery "so thoroughly interwoven with life and habits of Southerners that it 'form[ed] a part of their existence.' " To the Savannah physician and politician Richard Arnold slavery was no abstract question; for southerners it "involve[d] life and property, safety and security." Slavery meant "life and death to the South," wrote Colonel Arthur Hayne of South Carolina in 1835 to his friend Andrew Jackson. In January 1849 the General Assembly of Florida resolved unanimously that no division existed in the South on questions involving "the institution of slavery." To a Little Rock audience in the summer of 1850 United States Senator Solon Borland described slavery as "underlying as a sort of substratum, and inseparably connected with, the structure of all our institutions." "It affects," Borland emphasized, "the personal interest of every white man."

For many southerners slavery also provided the foundation for their civilization; it became "the very foundation of Liberty." A broad-based intellectual defense became the cardinal goal of southern ministers, scientists, academicians, writers, and politicians. Together they agreed with William Gilmore Simms: "We believe also that negro slavery is one of the greatest and most admirable agents of Civilization." By the hundreds and even the thousands, books, speeches, pamphlets, editorials, and sermons affirming the joy and value of slavery inundated southern readers and listeners. Many historians have cataloged and explicated the many facets of the proslavery argument. Even with their work, it is impossible to say how many southerners accepted or believed in the orthodox doctrine. But the number of true believers is of little import.

Although an indefinite number of white southerners refused to join the proslavery offensive, they remained steadfast behind slavery and reinforced the powerful hold it exerted on southern society. Concentrated in the upper South, especially in Virginia, these southerners followed the lead of men like Thomas Jefferson and John Randolph of Roanoke who, in an earlier day, had decried slavery as an evil but who had envisioned no remedy. More important, slavery was for them a southern problem not to be touched by outside hands. "In the name of wonder," Thomas Ritchie asked Martin Van Buren, "what business have our Brethren of the North with our Slaves?" While governor of Virginia in 1837, David Campbell spoke directly: "I am not decidedly opposed to any interference on the part of the non-slaveholding States or people about this question—*I do not even want their advice.*" For emphasis Campbell added, "I would not consent that any power upon earth should interfere with us about it." In 1835 the Richmond *Whig* admitted that it had supported a gradual emancipation program during the great Virginia debate of 1831, but the *Whig* declared that it lagged behind no man in opposing the abolitionists. They were outsiders and the South had no intention of ever allowing outsiders to make any decisions regarding slavery. A toast at a public dinner for Congressman Henry Wise summed up this view: "Slavery—Whatever differences of opinion may exist among us Virginians upon this vexed subject, we are unanimous on one point, a positive determination that no one shall think or act for us."

This possessiveness spanned the South. Slavery was a misfortune said North Carolina's Kenneth Rayner to Congress in 1841, "But if it were ten times greater an evil than it is, we will never suffer those who are uninterested [northerners] in the matter to interfere with us." Calling emancipation "this delicate question," the Milledgeville *Federal Union* asserted, "the people of the South will be the keepers of their consciences, the protectors of their own interests, and the guardian of their own interests." During the abolitionist outburst of the mid-1830s the legislature of North Carolina resolved "with almost entire unanimity" that "North Carolina alone has the right to legislate over the slaves in her territory, and any attempt to change the condition, whether made by the congress, the legislatures, or the people of other states will be regarded as an invasion of our just rights." Declaring that the South could never liberate her slaves, Sam Houston of Texas, in his direct way, told the North to keep hands off.

This unanimity of southern opinion certainly affected travelers in Dixie. E. A. Andrews of Boston visited northern Virginia in 1835 and quoted Virginians, even those who had supported emancipation Virginia style, as saying, "Our people have become exasperated, the friends of the slaves alarmed, and nothing remains, but that we should all unite in repelling the officious intermeddling of persons who do not understand the subject [read northerners] with which they are interfering." The Scotsman William Thomson reported conversing with planters who opposed slavery, but raised no hands against it because they saw no conceivable way of ending it. Joel Poinsett of South Carolina told Fredrika Bremer that though he felt slavery a "moral obliquity," he foresaw only one solution—the future. To Poinsett insurmountable difficulties barred any possible changes for the present. The peripatetic Frederick Law Olmsted found several southerners, particularly of the lower social classes, opposed to slavery in theory but he found all accepting it and none working against it. A "poor white" in northeastern Mississippi told the traveler that he knew many who wanted slavery ended, but, the Mississippian continued, "it wouldn't never do to free 'em [the slaves] and leave 'em here [because] Nobody couldn't live here then." An Alabamian heading for Texas expressed identical sentiments: "I'd like it if we could get rid of 'em to yonst. I wouldn't like to hev' 'em freed, if they gwine to hang 'round."

This kind of opposition really amounted to no opposition. Strong and positive assaults on slavery simply did not occur in the South. Impressed by this unity the world-traveled Englishman James Buckingham thought that it would be easier to attack popery in Rome, Mohammedanism in Constantinople, and despotism in St. Petersburg than to move against slavery in the South.

Thus in practical terms it mattered little whether or not a southerner accepted or rejected the argument that slavery was a positive good. Standing "one and indivisible" on slavery, white southerners of all political persuasions and all social classes built a massive fortress around it. None could touch it but them, and they never did because even those who disliked slavery believed it untouchable and unchangeable. Any serious move against slavery was, as James H. Hammond, the South Carolina planter-politician, boldly put it, "a naked impossibility." This absence of even minimal dissent struck the historian of southern dissent Carl Degler, who described "an overall unity that embraces the diversity." This conviction that slavery had to remain solely a southern concern made southerners acutely sensitive to any outside discussions or attacks on slavery and on any attempts to connect them with such views or movements.

From the Jackson period onward, southerners were quick to find even the worth of the Union wanting when it seemed to foster or harbor antislave sentiments. In the 1830s nullifiers and their extremist brethren continually spoke about the danger of the Union for southern interests. Repeatedly they, like James H. Hammond, declared that any government interference with slavery would "disolve the Union." But the extremists did not cry out alone. Although Virginia Democrats worked hard to defuse the nullification crisis, their rhetoric often paralleled that of the nullifiers. William C. Rives, Virginia's loyal Jacksonian senator, asserted "that for the people of the non-slaveholding States to discuss the question of slavery, at all, is to attack the foundations of the union itself." From the pulpit of his Richmond

Enquirer, Thomas Ritchie in 1833 preached that any tampering with slavery meant that the "Union [would] inevitably fall in pieces." Writing to Martin van Buren four years later Ritchie declared that the South "would freely and voluntarily, coolly and deliberately withdraw from the Confederation" before allowing the federal government to strike against slavery. With outcries such as "The North must put down the fanatics, or the Union is gone like a wreath of sand before the flood tide," Whigs kept pace with Democrats. During the petition controversy in the House, Whig orators in clarion-call style emphasized that the Union did not come before southern determination to maintain slavery as a southern question.

Later, when the issue of slavery in the territories erupted during the Mexican War, southerners equated their right to carry slavery into the territories with the existence of slavery itself. To southerners the exclusion of slavery from the territories by the federal government was just as unacceptable as emancipation. Freesoil and freesoilers became ogres in the exact image of abolition and abolitionists. The adamant southern stand against restricting slavery in the territories rested on constitutional theory, on considerations of political power, and on southern honor. Although southerners developed a constitutional defense of their position, political and psychological motives were paramount. Each reinforced the other. Southerners viewed the exclusion of slavery with hostility and horror, for they saw it as the preface to ultimate abolition. Moreover, they feared adoption of a restrictive policy as a first step toward permanent political inferiority, an inferiority that would eventually mean that the South could no longer protect its peculiar institution. Furthermore restriction branded southern society as un-American and dishonorable. Committed to slavery as the southerners were, they could not think otherwise. Restriction equaled insult and the southern code forbade accepting insults.

Because southerners never distinguished between free soil and abolition, the cry of restriction engendered all the charged emotion associated with the cry of emancipation. Talk and threats of restriction, just as talk and threats of abolition, stirred the innermost soul of southern society. Thus the emergence of the extension issue in the late 1840s only intensified the volatility of southern politics, a politics easily and often convulsed by any hint of outside moves against slavery.

Because slavery occupied such a crucial position in southern society, slavery dwarfed all other political issues. John Quincy Adams, who knew firsthand whereof he spoke, recognized in 1835 that the slave question was "paramount to all others" in the South. Southern politicians, Adams noted, "never failed to touch upon this key . . . and it has never yet failed of success." In that same year, Governor William Schley told his fellow Georgians that they could and did differ over the tariff and nullification, but not over slavery, the most important issue. To the South Carolina nullifier Thomas Cooper "the question of *Domestic Servitude* ultimately like Aaron's rod swallow[ed] up all the rest." Traveling in the South just before the 1840 presidential contest James Buckingham reported that when slavery took to the political field, all other issues fled. The slavery issue assumed "paramount importance" to southern parties and politicians, observed the Richmond *Whig* in 1846. Toward the close of the 1840s William P. Duval, a grand old man among Florida Democrats, described the tariff and banks as "mere subjects of policy" about which southerners "may honestly differ." But, Duval continued, "The slave question is the rock."

Party partisans certainly tried to benefit from the political potency of slavery. Whigs constantly accused Democrats of trying "to make a party issue of the slavery question." Denouncing such tactics William B. Campbell, a Whig congressman from Tennessee, defined the congressional hassles over abolition in the late 1830s as an effort "by the Van Buren party & the Nullifiers to disturb the question of abolition." In 1850 the Raleigh *Register* proclaimed that southern Democrats had always engaged in "the aggravated *agitation* of the Slavery issue, as an end to be sought after." According to the Arkansas Whig, Charles F. M. Noland, southern Democrats "use[d] it for the purpose of injuring Whigs in advancing Democracy." Announcing that the Democrats "have ever used, and attempted to use, every question connected with the rights of the South, to a mere selfish political and party purpose," the leading Whig newspaper in Florida echoed Noland's charge. Democratic practices aroused the ire of the Vicksburg *Whig* while the Richmond *Whig* seemed resigned: "Agitation on the subject of Slavery has been a favorite game with the Locofoco party for many years." The general Whig assessment, in Alexander Stephens' pithy summary, had Democrats using "the slave question for nothing but political capital."

Although the Whigs continuously berated the Democrats for politicizing slavery, the Democrats, in turn, castigated the Whigs for attempting to make the slave issue their own. A rising North Carolina Democrat was disturbed because the Whigs adopted "rash measures in the hope of aiding the cause of *party*." The Whig goal in 1835, according to William H. Haywood, Jr., was to "alarm the Southern feelings" by agitating the slavery question. The Raleigh *Standard* claimed that the slavery issue had become "an electioneering hobby" with Whigs. John H. Cocke, Sr., of Virginia decried Whig strivings "to lash up, & appeal to the morbid sensibility of the South." Florida Democrats protested vehemently against Whig attempts to use the slave issue for partisan advantage. In 1850 United States Senator James M. Mason, a Virginia Democrat, wrote that the slavery question had become "the touchstone of party" for Whigs in the South.

Party politicians bedeviled each other in a personal way over the unending topic of slavery. Virginia Whigs tried to embarrass the prominent Democrat William C. Rives by publicizing certain comments on gradual emancipation that Rives had made in private correspondence. The North Carolina gubernatorial contest of 1840 found both sides plagued with efforts to connect each with abolition. Democrats tried to blemish the strongest Whig candidate "by representing that he had introduced Abolition memorials in the Legislature last winter." The Whigs responded in kind, for the Democratic nominee felt compelled to proclaim publicly that he opposed abolition "in any and every shape, form or fashion, except as the owners of slaves themselves desire"; Romulus Saunders' letter covered four newspaper columns. During the bitter gubernatorial race of 1851 in Mississippi, Henry Stuart Foote gave firsthand testimony on the use of slavery as an issue when he railed against his accusers: "I never voted with the Abolitionists—never—never—so help me God!"

Candidates for national office also found themselves hounded by the omnipresent slavery issue. Opponents of Whig John M. Berrien's reelection to the United States Senate from Georgia worked zealously to cast doubt on Berrien's slavery stance. Evidently these efforts paid some dividends, if only briefly, for one of Berrien's supporters wrote the senator, "I was astonished to have it insinuated . . . that perhaps I was tainted with abolitionism" and just because he favored Berrien. In Arkansas both parties tried to elect congressmen by painting opponents with the abolition brush. In 1848 the Democrats charged the Whig candidate with supporting the Wilmot Proviso, but the Whigs, at least to their own satisfaction, proved the Democrats wrong. Then in 1851 while attacking the Democratic candidate for supporting restriction, the Whigs urged Arkansans to vote for their candidate with "his sturdy support of the true rights of the South."

Aware that the slavery issue stirred up more excitement and enthusiasm than any other, southern politicians quite consciously invoked it as often and as forcefully in the 1830s as they did twenty years later. Many of them, in James H. Hammond's graphic language, "[thought] that you have to say but nigger to the South to set it on fire, as one whistles to a Turkey to make him gobble." Southern politicians of all persuasions recognized that discussion of the slave question "excite[d] feelings allied to madness."

Slavery and the Politics of the Yeomen

STEVEN HAHN

"Slavery," Georgia Governor Joseph E. Brown proclaimed [in 1863], "is the poor man's best Government." Trumpeting familiar refrains from the score of proslavery doctrine, Brown argued that, despite the inequalities of wealth in Southern society, black bondage served as the foundation of white social and political democracy: "Among us the poor white laborer is respected as an equal. His family is treated with kindness, consideration, and respect. He does not belong to the menial class. The negro is in no sense his equal. . . . He belongs to the only true aristocracy, the race of white men." With special reference to Upcountry yeomen, Brown acknowledged that "some contemptible demagogues have attempted to deceive [them] by appealing to their prejudices and asking them what interest they have in maintaining the rights of wealthy slaveholders." But he felt that such efforts were to little effect. "They [the yeomen] know that the Government of our State protects their lives, their families, and their property," he announced, "that every dollar the wealthy slaveholder has may be taken by the Government of the State, if need be, to protect the rights and liberties of all." . . .

To the extent that it limited the development of market relations, slavery also served the interests of poorer whites, or so the institution's outspoken supporters vehemently claimed as they paraded evidence touching the concerns of all strata of nonslaveholders. Because the significant element of the region's work force was black and enslaved, propertyless whites received higher wages for their labor than did Northern counterparts; because the elite invested in slaves as well as real estate, landownership was widely distributed; and because Upcountry farmers grew nonstaple crops, they did not have to compete with the slave-based plantations. Warning of the consequences of Emancipation, Joseph Brown wove these threads into an ominous tapestry. There are always rich and poor men, he stated, and "if we had no negroes the rich would still be in a better position to take care of themselves than the poor. They would still seek the most profitable and secure investment for their capital." "What would this be?" Brown asked rhetorically. "It would be land. The wealthy would soon buy all the lands of the South worth cultivating [and] . . . the poor would all become tenants . . . as in all old countries where slavery does not exist." "It is sickening to contemplate the miseries of our poor people under these circumstances," Georgia's governor concluded. "They now get higher wages for their labor than the poor of any other country on the globe. Most of them are now landowners, and they are now respected. . . . Abolish slavery . . . and you very soon make them all tenants and reduce their wages to the smallest pittances that will sustain life." By shielding the lower classes from what one contributor to the Cassville *Standard* termed the "fluctuations of commerce," slavery proved to be the guardian of their personal and local independence. As the Atlanta *Daily Intelligencer* chimed in 1856, "It is a fact well known in the South, but which is surprisingly hard to beat into the heads of the Yankees, that it is to preserve their own independence that the nonslaveholding voters of the South have ever been staunch supporters of slavery. They well know that wealth always commands service and that there can be no such thing as equality between a boot-black and his master."

Yeoman farmers, especially in nonplantation areas, did not need to accept—and generally did not accept—the paternalist underpinnings of the proslavery argument to feel a certain affinity with its social and cultural premises. Fundamentally committed to producing for household consumption and local exchange, wary of "economic development," and often hostile to outside authority, they shared important ideological ground with wealthy planters. As small property holders born into a society sanctioning racial bondage, they saw blacks as symbols of a condition they most feared— abject and perpetual dependency—and as a group whose strict subordination provided essential safeguards for their way of life. Whatever the differing milieu of slavery on farms and whatever the force of racism in its own right, the attitudes of the yeomanry toward Afro-Americans must be understood, historically, as attitudes of petty property owners toward the propertyless poor—attitudes which at certain junctures led smallholders to join with the upper class in defining the dispossessed out of the political community.

But while the planters and their spokesmen prated about the common stake all Southern whites had in slavery, their continuing pronouncements seemed to reveal nagging doubts. The yeomanry, and nonslaveholders in general, they occasionally admitted, would likely be the very people most receptive to free-labor ideology. Wealthy slaveholders certainly could not fail to recognize that yeomen and poorer whites rarely had patience for their haughty pretensions. Indeed, the planters might pose as much of a threat to the independence of small farmers as did the slaves, for it required no keen analytical mind to see that the dependency of the blacks and the domineering, aristocratic stance of the masters went hand in glove. Racism and antiplanter sentiment, in short, could represent two sides of the same coin, with potentially explosive repercussions by the 1850s.

The sources of class cohesion and conflict in the antebellum South, which the proslavery argument sought to enunciate and resolve, found special expression in the structure and dynamic of local and state politics. In a region embracing diverse physical and economic settings, the political process provided the means through which social and cultural tensions as well as social and cultural power found public articulation, display, and reinforcement. It was in the workings of the county courthouse that the social relations of the Black Belt and Upcountry took political form, while it was in the statehouse and party system that conflicting claims within the elite, between the elite and other social groups, and between different geographical locales were mediated. And, as the core of the proslavery argument suggested, the issues of independence and the role of the marketplace served as the bridges of political consensus and as the elements of political discord.

Politics in the Georgia Upcountry had a distinctive flavor—local in orientation, at once democratic and deferential in substance—that complemented the relations of social and economic life. In an era of limited transportation and communication, the courthouse, not the state legislature, the Congress, or the presidency, stood as the symbol of political authority; local, rather than state or national, concerns elicited the greatest popular attention. And that attention was considerable. By the 1840s, a series of reforms stretching back into the eighteenth century had broadened the suffrage to include all adult white males and expanded the number of elective offices on every level of government. This process of democratization grew out of extended agitation, much of which originated in the Upcountry, but in many ways it bolstered instead of challenged the influence of the well-to-do. For although reflecting and contributing to the yeoman commitment to local autonomy and political independence, the contours of local politics also mitigated class conflict by encouraging the formation of patron-client relations. . . .

In rural societies containing weak commercial and industrial bourgeoisies, such as the South, smallholders often surrender political leadership to their richer neighbors. A common concern for the protection of property, the need to discipline a labor force, and the visibly higher cultural attainments of the economic elite help explain this phenomenon. Yet, as the experience of the Black Belt indicates, this pattern of deference is ultimately founded upon the prestige of wealthy landowners in the spheres of production and exchange and upon the relations they enter into with other social groups. That Black Belt yeomen frequently depended on the planters for various services enormously strengthened the planters' claims to authority beyond the bounds of their plantations, and nurtured networks of patronage which account, in large sum, for local political alignments and the personal factionalism that undergirded much of the political discord in the antebellum era. In a social order that conferred status upon the ability to command the allegiances of lesser men, intracounty rivalries often reflected competition among members of the elite and their followers for influence. Thus, the electoral process offered poorer whites the advantages and favors that good connections might bring, while it reinforced the political and cultural hegemony of the master class.

Consider the nature of officeholding itself. For planters, election to a county post could be an affirmation of their personal power, a means of enlarging their patronage, and perhaps a stepping-stone to bigger things. Aspiring planters doubtless saw political preferment as a possible avenue for social mobility. But for yeoman farmers, local office held a special lure—a steady source of income. Given the uncertainties of agriculture, this was no small attraction, especially since the salary could easily equal the annual earnings derivable from the farm, if not surpass them. Men, in fact, commonly announced their candidacy by emphasizing circumstances of hardship, and political contests normally drew large numbers of office seekers. Yet, whatever their local popularity, these individuals could rarely hope to win unless they had a wealthy sponsor who wielded some leverage in other districts. The legal requirements for officeholding made such relations particularly compelling. According to Georgia law, all county officials had to post bond as part of their oath, and the bonds were rather substantial. Sheriffs had to put up $20,000, tax receivers and collectors had to put up double the taxes due the state from their county, and even the clerk of the Inferior Court had to put up $3,000. Clearly, few smallholders had the resources to stand for these sums, so they turned to neighboring planters who would sign as security. This loosely organized, but nonetheless widespread, patron-client structure strengthened the slaveholders' political influence in the Black Belt and in the South as a whole. . . . But in a region where the turnout for elections could exceed 80 percent of the eligible voters, where literacy was widespread, and where partisan leanings expressed an ideological stance, [slaveholders] had to pay keen attention to the sentiments of the yeomanry, if they did not share those sentiments themselves. . . .

. . . Sensitivity to external power and authority had deep roots and emerged with special force in state politics. As early as the first decades of the nineteenth century, representatives from the Upcountry joined with rising slaveholders in Georgia's central Cotton Belt in a concerted attempt to loosen the hold of Low Country planters on the legislature. Apportionment on the basis of the federal ratio and the creation of new coastal counties had given the seaboard gentry sway in both the state house and the senate even as the hinterlands rapidly boasted a substantially larger white population. Reform forces succeeded in enlarging the franchise, abolishing property qualifications for most offices, and facilitating the popular election of the governor, who previously had been selected by the seaboard-dominated senate; they fared worse in attacks on the federal ratio, which the old elite managed to keep firmly entrenched. Under threat of ad hoc action, however, the legislature consented to a formal constitutional convention in 1833. . . .

. . . The class and regional divisions that surfaced during the battle for political reform became very much a part of Southern politics in the 1840s and 1850s. There is no need to accept the simplified equation of Whiggery with planters and the Black Belt and Democracy with yeomen and the Upcountry in order to recognize that each party appealed to certain constituencies. In Georgia and other states of the Lower South, a distinct correlation could be found between high per capita wealth, commercial agriculture, large slaveholdings, and strong support for the Whig party. Indeed, from the personal factionalism of the 1820s to the formation of the Union and State Rights parties during the Nullification controversy, to the linkages with emerging national parties in the late 1830s and 1840s, to the realignments of the 1850s, and eventually to the movement for secession, political rifts in Georgia often tapped antagonisms between plantation and nonplantation areas. . . .

At bottom, partisan divisions reflected deeper cleavages between those social groups and locales participating extensively in the market economy and those on the periphery or virtually isolated from it. On issues such as banking, credit, and internal improvements, party stances diverged. The Whigs hoped to facilitate and expand commercial interchange, while the Democrats, certainly by the 1840s, sought to limit or regulate it. Both parties spoke to the ideal of independence and defined it in economic terms, but as the Whigs believed that independence required the accumulation of wealth, the Democrats contended that it could survive only by circumscribing involvement in the market. The Democrats' suspicion of and hostility toward corporate power and the cash nexus in general appealed to many planters who resented outside authority, feared industrial development, and groaned about Northern and Southern middlemen and the fluctuations of cotton prices. As election returns strikingly illustrated, however, the party also captured the spirit of Upcountry yeomen.

The bank question offers a cogent example of the nature of social and political discord. During the first decades of the nineteenth century, alignments remained hazy, partly because of the constitutional issues surrounding the Bank of the United States. But by the 1830s, and especially after the Panic of 1837, battle lines in Georgia crystallized between supporters of independent commercial banking—generally Whigs in the Black Belt and market towns—and a broad spectrum of reformers—congregating primarily in the Democratic party—who pressed for strict regulation, state control, or the outright abolition of banks. As early as 1823, Governor John Clark, a hard-money man whose following would eventually side with the Democrats, favored restricting banks to major marketing cities, where convertibility of paper into specie would be required, and the establishment of a state-owned institution. Although the ensuing years saw the multiplication of commercial banks, as the plantation economy spread through middle Georgia, Clark's recommendation for a public corporation designed to extend long-term loans came to fruition in 1828 with the founding of the Central Bank.

A more firmly entrenched banking system in Georgia mitigated both the effects of economic depression and the rise of vehement antibank sentiment that took hold in the southwest during the late 1830s. Nevertheless, some legislative representatives from small farming areas argued that commercial banking should be confined to the wholesale trade, and hard-money Democrats played a leading role in agitating for debtor relief and bank regulation. They inspired a series of laws demanding the issuance of semi-annual reports detailing bank transactions, preventing the circulation of small notes, and penalizing banks for failing to make specie redemptions. One measure passed by the assembly in 1840 sought to enforce strict convertibility with the threat of immediate suit for foreclosure and liquidation. Amid a widespread conservative response to the commercial panic, the 1840s witnessed a halt to bank charters in Georgia and, under Democratic auspices, the virtual prohibition of banking in two other Southern states.

During the prosperous 1850s, commercial banking in Georgia expanded once again, with twenty-seven new institutions chartered between 1850 and 1856. But a new crisis accompanied the Panic of 1857, for while state banks operated on a relatively stable basis, they defied the law and suspended specie payments. Although the out-going governor, Herschel V. Johnson, took no action, his successor, Joseph E. Brown, who spoke for the hard-money wing of the Democratic party, issued a scathing attack and warned that when he received evidence of a bank's transgression, he would "order proceedings for the forfeiture of its charter." Moving to forestall such retribution, the banking interest obtained enabling legislation from the General Assembly; Brown then summarily vetoed it. "The people [will] sustain him," the Upcountry Clarksville *Georgian* proclaimed, and meetings in several north Georgia counties which passed resolutions in support of the governor's stand seemed to bear testimony to the paper's prediction. An intensive lobbying campaign waged by the banks ultimately won enough legislators to the side of moderation to override Brown's veto, but the controversy continued to bristle in the press.

For the Whiggish Athens *Southern Watchman*, "Brown was strictly carrying out Democratic principles in opposing banks, railroads, factories, and internal improvements." And as another paper of similar disposition sneered: "By his Bank Veto Message [Brown] . . . got his name up with the 'wool hat boys' and that class of our *Democratic* friends, who have little or no correct knowledge of the practical science of Banking. . . ." Yet, neither a flat rejection of commercial intercourse nor a muddled understanding "of the practical science of Banking" led Brown's supporters, the staunchest of whom resided in the Upcountry, to join his "war" on the banks. Rather, notions about the proper relations of production and exchange and the threat that banks posed to those relations fueled the agitation. Through the "unguarded grant of corporate powers and privileges" denied to "the laboring masses," the hard-money forces thundered in the language of Jacksonianism, the banks had become "monied monopolies" exercising inordinate power in the marketplace. By "extend[ing] their paper circulation . . . in a wild spirit of speculation," they were also responsible for the frequent cycles of economic dislocation. "The great fundamental defect of our present banking system," an Upcountry representative told the state legislature, "is that the office or province of furnishing a circulating medium and of supplying our commercial exchange is vested in the same institution."

Perhaps more importantly, commercial banking challenged the deepest popular sensibilities by divorcing wealth from productive labor. "What is the use of money?" a contributor to the Cassville *Standard* asked. "Money is not bread to eat nor clothes to wear. Money is not wealth—it is only the representation of wealth. . . . Bread is wealth, clothes is wealth; a bed to lie on; a horse to ride, to plow—whatever meets man's necessities is wealth. . . ." Unfortunately, he lamented, "the idea . . . has extensively obtained, that . . . money is wealth . . . that just as money is multiplied, so is wealth increased, and shrewd and far-seeing men have taken advantage of this popular delusion, upon which to engraft the banking system—a system which *makes the money* and *avoids the labor*. . . ."

Corporate domination of the marketplace, the antibank forces insisted, lay only a short step from corporate domination of the political process. "It is already claimed by some," Governor Brown charged, "that [the banks] now have the power by combinations and free use of large sums of money to control the political conventions and elections of our State and in this way to crush those who may have the independence to stand by the rights of the people in opposition to their aggressive power. . . ." Acknowledging the "sudden shock" that "harsh [and] . . . radical . . . measures" might precipitate, Brown nonetheless counseled that "we should do all in our power to bring about [the] complete reformation . . . of our banking system . . . and if this not be possible, we should abandon it entirely. . . ." He and his supporters in the General Assembly suggested the rigid regulation of charters or the establishment of a state subtreasury. "Let it not be forgotten . . . by those who have watched with anxiety the growing power of corporate influence," the governor reminded his constituents, "that the price of Republican liberty is perpetual vigilance."

The strong backing that Brown received from the Upcountry in the gubernatorial election of 1859, when the opposition attempted to make political capital out of the bank issue, further evidenced the yeomanry's identification with the governor's point of view. In county after county, Brown mustered well over 60 percent of the votes, and in several counties he won over 80 percent. Only in those areas blending into the Black Belt or containing large commercial centers did Brown's margin of victory prove less than overwhelming. For most Upcountry yeomen, to be sure, the "monied monopolists" could have appeared, at worst, a distant threat. No county north of the Black Belt had a chartered bank, circulating currency always remained scarce, and few cultivators had more than limited involvement with the export market and its attendant financial structure. But at a time when commercial agriculture was expanding, railroad development being promoted, and court dockets being cluttered with actions for debt, the bank question had a special symbolic importance.

⅄ F U R T H E R   R E A D I N G

James Broussard, *Southern Federalists, 1800–1816* (1978)
Margaret L. Coit, *John C. Calhoun: American Portrait* (1950)
Arthur C. Cole, *The Whig Party in the South* (1913)
William J. Cooper, Jr., *Liberty and Slavery* (1983)
———, *The South and the Politics of Slavery* (1978)
George Dangerfield, *The Awakening of American Nationality, 1815–1828* (1965)
Clement Eaton, *The Growth of Southern Civilization, 1790–1860* (1961)
Drew G. Faust, *James Henry Hammond and the Old South* (1982)
William W. Freehling, *Prelude to Civil War: The Nullification Controversy in South Carolina, 1816–1836* (1965)
Fletcher M. Green, *Constitutional Development in the South Atlantic States, 1776–1860: A Study in the Evolution of Democracy* (1930)
Steven Hahn, *The Roots of Southern Populism* (1983)
Holman Hamilton, *Prologue to Conflict: The Crisis and Compromise of 1850* (1966)
Richard P. McCormick, *The Second American Party System: Party Formation in the Jacksonian Era* (1966)
Glover Moore, *The Missouri Controversy, 1819–1821* (1953)
Chaplain W. Morrison, *Democratic Politics and Sectionalism: The Wilmot Proviso Controversy* (1967)
John Niven, *John C. Calhoun and the Price of Union* (1988)
Robert Remini, *Andrew Jackson and the Bank War* (1967)
Norman K. Risjord, *The Old Republicans: Southern Conservatism in the Age of Jefferson* (1965)
Marshall Smelser, *The Democratic Republic, 1801–1815* (1968)
Charles S. Sydnor, *The Development of Southern Sectionalism, 1819–1848* (1948)
J. Mills Thornton III, *Politics and Power in a Slave Society: Alabama, 1800–1860* (1978)

CHAPTER

11

The Sectional Crisis and Secession

⋏

In the 1850s the country entered its period of greatest crisis. As sectional conflict deepened, the white South increasingly debated the wisdom and desirability of leaving the Union. Ultimatums and threats of secession that were made in 1850 became reality ten years later.

The issue of slavery in the territories was troublesome throughout the decade. From the Compromise of 1850 through the controversial Dred Scott *decision, and in the last-minute attempts to save the Union, this issue remained at the core of North-South disagreements. What position did defiant southern leaders take on slavery in the territories in 1850? Did their view and that of the rest of the South change during the decade? What impact did the* Dred Scott *decision have on southern attitudes about this question?*

Among the significant changes that took place during the 1850s were the rise of the Republican party and the splitting of the Democratic party into a northern and a southern wing. How did southern whites view the Republican party, and on what points did southern Democrats differ from their northern counterparts?

The road to secession was not the same in all parts of the South, nor was it an easy one for all southern whites to travel. What kind of opposition to secession developed within the South? What were its sources? And in what kind of atmosphere did the South ultimately decide to leave the Union?

⋏ *D O C U M E N T S*

The status of slavery in the territories convulsed the U.S. Congress for almost nine months in 1850. During that period representatives from nine slave states met in Nashville to formulate southern demands. Although "moderates" controlled the Nashville convention, note how the convention's closing resolutions, set out in the first document, describe southerners' rights in the territories and the obligations of Congress. In 1857 the Supreme Court addressed the issues of slavery in the territories and Congress's powers. Dred Scott, a Missouri slave, had sued for his freedom on the grounds that previously he had been taken to live in free territory. The Court's decision in *Dred Scott* v. *Sandford*, the second document, immediately attracted national attention. What effect would this

453

decision have on white southerners' opinions? The next selection contains a famous statement of southern self-confidence, voiced in 1858 by Senator James H. Hammond of South Carolina. Note how Hammond's declarations about King Cotton led into an analysis of slavery and the strengths of southern society. Southern Democrats broke with their party in 1860. Nominating John C. Breckenridge of Kentucky for president over Stephen A. Douglas of Illinois, the southern Democrats explained themselves—and the controversies at the heart of the party's split—by issuing their own platform, reprinted as the fourth document. Kentucky's Senator John J. Crittenden devised a final compromise proposal. Although Lincoln and the Republicans rejected it, this proposal, which appears as the fifth selection, seemed acceptable to southern leaders in the Senate, and thus it sheds light on what was essential to them on the eve of secession. The final excerpts, taken from newspapers in the South, give further insight into how southern spokesmen viewed secession.

Resolutions of the Nashville Convention, 1850

1. *Resolved*, That the territories of the United States belong to the people of the several States of this Union as their common property. That the citizens of the several States have equal rights to migrate with their property to these territories, and are equally entitled to the protection of the federal government in the enjoyment of that property so long as the territories remain under the charge of that government.

2. *Resolved*, That Congress has no power to exclude from the territory of the United States any property lawfully held in the States of the Union, and any act which may be passed by Congress to effect this result is a plain violation of the Constitution of the United States. . . .

4. *Resolved*, That to protect property existing in the several States of the Union the people of these States invested the federal government with the powers of war and negotiation and of sustaining armies and navies, and prohibited to State authorities the exercise of the same powers. They made no discrimination in the protection to be afforded or the description of the property to be defended, nor was it allowed to the federal government to determine what should be held as property. Whatever the States deal with as property the federal government is bound to recognize and defend as such. Therefore it is the sense of this Convention that all acts of the federal government which tend to denationalize property of any description recognized in the Constitution and laws of the States, or that discriminate in the degree and efficiency of the protection to be afforded to it, or which weaken or destroy the title of any citizen upon American territories, are plain and palpable violations of the fundamental law under which it exists.

5. *Resolved*, That the slaveholding States cannot and will not submit to the enactment by Congress of any law imposing onerous conditions or restraints upon the rights of masters to remove with their property into the territories of the United States, or to any law making discrimination in favor of the proprietors of other property against them. . . .

8. *Resolved*, That the performance of its duties, upon the principle we declare, would enable Congress to remove the embarrassments in which

the country is now involved. The vacant territories of the United States, no longer regarded as prizes for sectional rapacity and ambition, would be gradually occupied by inhabitants drawn to them by their interests and feelings. The institutions fitted to them would be naturally applied by governments formed on American ideas, and approved by the deliberate choice of their constituents. The community would be educated and disciplined under a republican administration in habits of self government, and fitted for an association as a State, and to the enjoyment of a place in the confederacy. A community so formed and organized might well claim admission to the Union and none would dispute the validity of the claim. . . .

9. *Resolved,* That a recognition of this principle would deprive the questions between Texas and the United States of their sectional character, and would leave them for adjustment, without disturbance from sectional prejudices and passions, upon considerations of magnanimity and justice. . . .

11. *Resolved,* That in the event a dominant majority shall refuse to recognize the great constitutional rights we assert, and shall continue to deny the obligations of the Federal Government to maintain them, it is the sense of this convention that the territories should be treated as property, and divided between the sections of the Union, so that the rights of both sections be adequately secured in their respective shares. That we are aware this course is open to grave objections, but we are ready to acquiesce in the adoption of the line of 36 deg. 30 min. north latitude, extending to the Pacific ocean, as an extreme concession, upon consideration of what is due to the stability of our institution.

12. *Resolved,* That it is the opinion of this Convention that this controversy should be ended, either by a recognition of the constitutional rights of the Southern people, or by an equitable partition of the territories. That the spectacle of a confederacy of States, involved in quarrels over the fruits of a war in which the American arms were crowned with glory, is humiliating. That the incorporation of the Wilmot Proviso in the offer of settlement, a proposition which fourteen States regard as disparaging and dishonorable, is degrading to the country. A termination to this controversy by the disruption of the confederacy or by the abandonment of the territories to prevent such a result, would be a climax to the shame which attaches to the controversy which it is the paramount duty of Congress to avoid.

Dred Scott v. Sandford, 1857

Taney, C. J. . . . The question is simply this: Can a negro, whose ancestors were imported into this country, and sold as slaves, become a member of the political community formed and brought into existence by the Constitution of the United States, and as such become entitled to all the rights, and privileges, and immunities, guaranteed by that instrument to the citizen? One of which rights is the privilege of suing in a court of the United States in the cases specified in the Constitution. . . .

The words "people of the United States" and "citizens" are synonymous terms, and mean the same thing. They both describe the political body who, according to our republican institutions, form the sovereignty, and who hold the power and conduct the government through their representatives. They are what we familiarly call the "sovereign people," and every citizen is one of this people, and a constituent member of this sovereignty. The question before us is, whether the class of persons described in the plea in abatement compose a portion of this people, and are constituent members of this sovereignty? We think they are not, and that they are not included, and were not intended to be included, under the word "citizens" in the Constitution, and can, therefore, claim none of the rights and privileges which that instrument provides for and secures to citizens of the United States. On the contrary, they were at that time considered as a subordinate and inferior class of beings, who had been subjugated by the dominant race, and whether emancipated or not, yet remained subject to their authority, and had no rights or privileges but such as those who held the power and the government might choose to grant them. . . .

In the opinion of the court, the legislation and histories of the times, and the language used in the Declaration of Independence, show, that neither the class of persons who had been imported as slaves, nor their descendants, whether they had become free or not, were then acknowledged as a part of the people, nor intended to be included in the general words used in that memorable instrument.

It is difficult at this day to realize the state of public opinion in relation to that unfortunate race, which prevailed in the civilized and enlightened portions of the world at the time of the Declaration of Independence, and when the Constitution of the United States was framed and adopted. . . .

They had for more than a century before been regarded as beings of an inferior order; and altogether unfit to associate with the white race, either in social or political relations; and so far inferior that they had no rights which the white man was bound to respect; and that the negro might justly and lawfully be reduced to slavery for his benefit. . . . This opinion was at that time fixed and universal in the civilized portion of the white race. It was regarded as an axiom in morals as well as in politics, which no one thought of disputing, or supposed to be open to dispute; and men in every grade and position in society daily and habitually acted upon it in their private pursuits, as well as in matters of public concern, without doubting for a moment the correctness of this opinion. . . .

The legislation of the different Colonies furnishes positive and undisputable proof of this fact. . . .

The language of the Declaration of Independence is equally conclusive. . . .

And upon a full and careful consideration of the subject, the court is of opinion that, upon the facts stated in the plea in abatement, Dred Scott was not a citizen of Missouri within the meaning of the Constitution of the United States, and not entitled as such to sue in its courts; and, consequently, that the Circuit Court had no jurisdiction of the case, and that the judgment on the plea in abatement is erroneous. . . .

We proceed, therefore, to inquire whether the facts relied on by the plaintiff entitled him to his freedom. . . .

In considering this part of the controversy, two questions arise: 1st. Was he, together with his family, free in Missouri by reason of the stay in the territory of the United States hereinbefore mentioned? And 2d, If they were not, is Scott himself free by reason of his removal to Rock Island, in the State of Illinois, as stated in the above admissions?

We proceed to examine the first question.

The Act of Congress, upon which the plaintiff relies, declares that slavery and involuntary servitude, except as a punishment for crime, shall be forever prohibited in all that part of the territory ceded by France, under the name of Louisiana, which lies north of thirty-six degrees thirty minutes north latitude, and not included within the limits of Missouri. And the difficulty which meets us at the threshold of this part of the inquiry is, whether Congress was authorized to pass this law under any of the powers granted to it by the Constitution; for if the authority is not given by that instrument, it is the duty of this court to declare it void and inoperative, and incapable of conferring freedom upon any one who is held as a slave under the laws of any one of the States.

The counsel for the plaintiff has laid much stress upon that article in the Constitution which confers on Congress the power "to dispose of and make all needful rules and regulations respecting the territory or other property belonging to the United States;" but, in the judgment of the court, that provision has no bearing on the present controversy, and the power there given, whatever it may be, is confined, and was intended to be confined, to the territory which at that time belonged to, or was claimed by, the United States, and was within their boundaries as settled by the treaty with Great Britain, and can have no influence upon a territory afterwards acquired from a foreign Government. It was a special provision for a known and particular territory, and to meet a present emergency, and nothing more. . . .

. . . If the Constitution recognizes the right of property of the master in a slave, and makes no distinction between that description of property and other property owned by a citizen, no tribunal, acting under the authority of the United States, whether it be legislative, executive, or judicial, has a right to draw such a distinction, or deny to it the benefit of the provisions and guarantees which have been provided for the protection of private property against the encroachments of the Government.

Now . . . the right of property in a slave is distinctly and expressly affirmed in the Constitution. The right to traffic in it, like an ordinary article of merchandise and property, was guaranteed to the citizens of the United States, in every State that might desire it, for twenty years. And the Government in express terms is pledged to protect it in all future time, if the slave escapes from his owner. . . . And no word can be found in the Constitution which gives Congress a greater power over slave property, or which entitles property of that kind to less protection than property of any other description. The only power conferred is the power coupled with the duty of guarding and protecting the owner in his rights.

Upon these considerations, it is the opinion of the court that the Act of Congress which prohibited a citizen from holding and owning property of this kind in the territory of the United States north of the line therein mentioned, is not warranted by the Constitution, and is therefore void; and that neither Dred Scott himself, nor any of his family, were made free by being carried into this territory; even if they had been carried there by the owner, with the intention of becoming a permanent resident. . . .

Upon the whole, therefore, it is the judgment of this court, that it appears by the record before us that the plaintiff in error is not a citizen of Missouri, in the sense in which that word is used in the Constitution; and that the Circuit Court of the United States, for that reason, had no jurisdiction in the case, and could give no judgment in it.

Its judgment for the defendant must, consequently, be reversed, and a mandate issued directing the suit to be dismissed for want of jurisdiction. WAYNE, J., NELSON, J., GRIER, J., DANIEL, J., CAMPBELL, J., AND CATRON, J., filed separate concurring opinions. McLEAN, J., and CURTIS, J. dissented.

James Henry Hammond Praises King Cotton, 1858

[W]ould any sane nation make war on cotton? Without firing a gun, without drawing a sword, should they make war on us we could bring the whole world to our feet. The South is perfectly competent to go on, one, two, or three years without planting a seed of cotton. I believe that if she was to plant but half her cotton, for three years to come, it would be an immense advantage to her. I am not so sure but that after three years' entire abstinence she would come out stronger than ever she was before, and better prepared to enter afresh upon her great career of enterprise. What would happen if no cotton was furnished for three years? I will not stop to depict what every one can imagine, but this is certain: England would topple headlong and carry the whole civilized world with her, save the South. No, you dare not make war on cotton. No power on earth dares to make war upon it. Cotton *is* king. Until lately the Bank of England was king; but she tried to put her screws as usual, the fall before the last, upon the cotton crop, and was utterly vanquished. The last power has been conquered. Who can doubt, that has looked at recent events, that cotton is supreme? When the abuse of credit had destroyed credit and annihilated confidence; when thousands of the strongest commercial houses in the world were coming down, and hundreds of millions of dollars of supposed property evaporating in thin air; when you [Northerners] came to a dead lock, and revolutions were threatened, what brought you up? Fortunately for you it was the commencement of the cotton season, and we have poured in upon you one million six hundred thousand bales of cotton just at the crisis to save you from destruction. That cotton, but for the bursting of your speculative bubbles in the North, which produced the whole of this convulsion, would have brought us $100,000,000. We have sold it for $65,000,000, and saved you. Thirty-five million dollars we, the slaveholders of the South, have put into the charity box for your magnificent financiers, your "cotton lords," your "merchant princes."

But, sir, the greatest strength of the South arises from the harmony of her political and social institutions. This harmony gives her a frame of society, the best in the world, and an extent of political freedom, combined with entire security, such as no other people ever enjoyed upon the face of the earth. Society precedes government; creates it, and ought to control it; but as far as we can look back in historic times we find the case different; for government is no sooner created than it becomes too strong for society, and shapes and moulds, as well as controls it. In later centuries the progress of civilization and of intelligence has made the divergence so great as to produce civil wars and revolutions; and it is nothing now but the want of harmony between governments and societies which occasions all the uneasiness and trouble and terror that we see abroad. It was this that brought on the American Revolution. We threw off a Government not adapted to our social system, and made one for ourselves. The question is, how far have we succeeded? The South, so far as that is concerned, is satisfied, harmonious, and prosperous, but demands to be let alone.

In all social systems there must be a class to do the menial duties, to perform the drudgery of life. That is, a class requiring but a low order of intellect and but little skill. Its requisites are vigor, docility, fidelity. Such a class you must have, or you would not have that other class which leads progress, civilization, and refinement. It constitutes the very mud-sill of society and of political government; and you might as well attempt to build a house in the air, as to build either the one or the other, except on this mud-sill. Fortunately for the South, she found a race adapted to that purpose to her hand. A race inferior to her own, but eminently qualified in temper, in vigor, in docility, in capacity to stand the climate, to answer all her purposes. We use them for our purpose, and call them slaves. We found them slaves by the common "consent of mankind," which, according to Cicero, "*lex naturæ est.*" The highest proof of what is Nature's law. We are old-fashioned at the South yet; slave is a word discarded now by "ears polite;" I will not characterize that class at the North by that term; but you have it; it is there; it is everywhere; it is eternal.

The Senator from New York [William H. Seward] said yesterday that the whole world had abolished slavery. Aye, the *name,* but not the *thing;* all the powers of the earth cannot abolish that. God only can do it when he repeals the *fiat,* "the poor ye always have with you;" for the man who lives by daily labor, and scarcely lives at that, and who has to put out his labor in the market, and take the best he can get for it; in short, your whole hireling class of manual laborers and "operatives," as you call them, are essentially slaves. The difference between us is, that our slaves are hired for life and well compensated; there is no starvation, no begging, no want of employment among our people, and not too much employment either. Yours are hired by the day, not cared for, and scantily compensated, which may be proved in the most painful manner, at any hour in any street in any of your large towns. Why, you meet more beggars in one day, in any single street of the city of New York, than you would meet in a lifetime in the whole South. We do not think that whites should be slaves either by law or necessity. Our slaves are black, of another and inferior race.

The Platform of the Breckinridge Democrats, 1860

Resolved, That the platform adopted by the Democratic party at Cincinnati be affirmed, with the following explanatory resolutions:

1. That the Government of a Territory organized by an act of Congress is provisional and temporary, and during its existence all citizens of the United States have an equal right to settle with their property in the Territory, without their rights, either of person or property being destroyed or impaired by Congressional or Territorial legislation.

2. That it is the duty of the Federal Government, in all its departments, to protect, when necessary, the rights of persons and property in the Territories, and wherever else its constitutional authority extends.

3. That when the settlers in a Territory, having an adequate population, form a State Constitution, the right of sovereignty commences, and being consummated by admission into the Union, they stand on an equal footing with the people of other States, and the State thus organized ought to be admitted into the Federal Union, whether its Constitution prohibits or recognizes the institution of slavery.

Resolved, That the Democratic party are in favor of the acquisition of the Island of Cuba, on such terms as shall be honorable to ourselves and just to Spain, at the earliest practicable moment.

Resolved, That the enactments of State Legislatures to defeat the faithful execution of the Fugitive Slave Law are hostile in character, subversive of the Constitution, and revolutionary in their effect.

Resolved, That the Democracy of the United States recognize it as the imperative duty of this Government to protect the naturalized citizen in all his rights, whether at home or in foreign lands, to the same extent as its native-born citizens.

WHEREAS, One of the greatest necessities of the age, in a political, commercial, postal and military point of view, is a speedy communication between the Pacific and Atlantic coasts, Therefore be it

Resolved, That the National Democratic party do hereby pledge themselves to use every means in their power to secure the passage of some bills, to the extent of the constitutional authority of Congress for the construction of a Pacific Railroad from the Mississippi River to the Pacific Ocean, at the earliest practicable moment.

The Proposed Crittenden Compromise, 1860

Whereas, serious and alarming dissensions have arisen between the Northern and Southern States, concerning the rights and security of the rights of the slave-holding States, and especially their rights in the common territory of the United States; and whereas it is eminently desirable and proper that these dissensions which now threaten the very existence of this Union, should be permanently quieted and settled, by constitutional provision, which shall do equal justice to all sections, and thereby restore to the people that peace and good will which ought to prevail between all the citizens of the United States: Therefore,

Resolved by the Senate and House of Representatives of the United States of America in Congress Assembled, That the following articles be, and are hereby, proposed and submitted as amendments to the Constitution of the United States, . . .

Article 1. In all the territory of the United States now held, or hereafter acquired, situate North of Latitude 36° 30', slavery or involuntary servitude, except as a punishment for crime, is prohibited while such territory shall remain under territorial government. In all the territory south of said line of latitude, slavery of the African race is hereby recognized as existing, and shall not be interfered with by Congress, but shall be protected as property by all the departments of the territorial government during its continuance. And when any Territory, north or south of said line, within such boundaries as Congress may prescribe, shall contain the population requisite for a member of Congress according to the then Federal ratio, of representation of the people of the United States, it shall, if its form of government be republican, be admitted into the Union, on an equal footing with the original States, with or without slavery, as the constitution of such new State may provide.

Art. 2. Congress shall have no power to abolish slavery in places under its exclusive jurisdiction, and situate within the limits of States that permit the holding of slaves.

Art. 3. Congress shall have no power to abolish slavery within the district of Columbia so long as it exists in the adjoining States of Virginia and Maryland, or either, not without the consent of the inhabitants, nor without just compensation first made to such owners of slaves as do not consent to such abolishment. Nor shall Congress at any time prohibit officers of the Federal Government, or members of Congress, whose duties require them to be in said District, from bringing with them their slaves, and holding them as such during the time their duties may require them to remain there, and afterwards taking them from the District.

Art. 4. Congress shall have no power to prohibit or hinder the transportation of slaves from one State to another, or to a Territory in which slaves are by law permitted to be held, whether that transportation be by land, navigable rivers, or by the sea. . . .

Art. 6. No future amendment of the Constitution shall affect the five preceding articles . . . and no amendment shall be made to the Constitution which shall authorize or give to Congress any power to abolish or interfere with slavery in any of the States by whose laws it is, or may be, allowed or permitted.

And whereas, also, besides these causes of dissension embraced in the foregoing amendments proposed to the Constitution of the United States, there are others which come within the jurisdiction of Congress, and may be remedied by its legislative power; Therefore

1. Resolved. . . . That the laws now in force for the recovery of fugitive slaves are in strict pursuance of the plain and mandatory provisions of the Constitution, and have been sanctioned as valid and constitutional by the judgment of the Supreme Court of the United States; that the slave-holding States are entitled to the faithful observance and execution of those laws, and that they ought not to be repealed, or so modified or changed as to impair their efficiency; and that laws ought to be made for the punishment of those who attempt by rescue of the slave, or other illegal means, to hinder or defeat the due execution of said laws.

2. That all State laws which conflict with the fugitive slave acts of Congress, or any other Constitutional acts of Congress, or which, in their operation, impede, hinder, or delay, the free course and due execution of any of said acts, are null and void by the present provisions of the Con-stitution of the United States; yet those State laws, void as they are, have given color to practices, and led to consequences which have obstructed the due administration and execution of acts of Congress, and especially the acts for the delivery of fugitive slaves, and have thereby contributed much to the discord and commotion now prevailing. Congress, therefore, in the present perilous juncture, does not deem it improper, respectfully and earnestly to recommend the repeal of those laws to the several States which have enacted them, or such legislative corrections or explanations of them as may prevent their being used or perverted to such mischievous purposes.

3. That the Act of the 18th of September, 1850, commonly called the fugitive slave law, . . . the last clause of the fifth section of said act, which authorizes a person holding a warrant for the arrest or detention of a fugitive slave, to summon to his aid the *posse comitatus*, and which declares it to be the duty of all good citizens to assist him in its execution, ought to be so amended as to expressly limit the authority and duty to cases in which there shall be resistance or danger of resistance or rescue.

4. That the laws for the suppression of the African slave trade, and especially those prohibiting the importation of slaves in the United States, ought to be made effectual, and ought to be thoroughly executed: and all further enactments necessary to those ends ought to be promptly made.

Southern Editors Speculate on Secession, 1860, 1861

Charleston Mercury, *November 3, 1860*

The issue before the country is the extinction of slavery. No man of common sense, who has observed the progress of events, and who is not prepared to surrender the institution, with the safety and independence of the South, can doubt that the time for action has come—now or never. The Southern States are now in the crisis of their fate; and, if we read aright the signs of the times, nothing is needed for our deliverance, but that the ball of revolution be set in motion. There is sufficient readiness among the people to make it entirely successful. Co-operation will follow the action of any State. The example of a forward movement only is requisite to unite Southern States in a common cause. Under these circumstances the Legislature of South Carolina is about to meet. It happens to assemble in advance of the Legislature of any other State. Being in session at this momentous juncture—the Legislature of that State which is most united in the policy of freeing the South from Black Republican domination—the eyes of the whole country, and most especially of the resistance party of the Southern States, is intently turned upon the conduct of this body. We have innumerable assurances that the men of action in each and all of the Southern States, earnestly desire South Carolina to exhibit promptitude and decision in this conjuncture. Other states are torn and divided, to a greater or less extent, by old party issues. South Carolina alone is not. Any practical move would enable the people of other States to rise above their past divisions, and lock shields on the broad ground of Southern security. The course of our Legislature will either greatly stimulate and strengthen, or unnerve the resistance elements of the whole South. A Convention is the point to which their attention will be chiefly directed.

The question of calling a Convention by our Legislature does not necessarily involve the question of separate or co-operative action. That is a question for the Convention when it assembles, under the circumstances which shall exist when it assembles. All desire the action of as many Southern States as possible, for the formation of a Southern Confederacy. But each should not delay and wait on the other. As these States are separate sovereignties, each must act separately. . . .

. . . What is really essential is this—that by the action of one or more States, there shall be the *reasonable probability* that a Southern Confederacy will be formed.

Richmond Semi-weekly Examiner, *November 9, 1860*

It would seem that the sectional game has been fairly played out in the North. New York has gone for Lincoln by a majority larger than she cast for Fremont in 1856. Of the free States we see no reason to hope that the Black Republicans have lost more than two, and they amongst the smallest and weakest in political power—those on the Pacific. The solid, compact mass of free States has solemnly given its sanction and its political power to the anti-slavery policy of the Black Republicans.—The idle canvass prattle about Northern conservatism may now be dismissed. A party founded on the single sentiment, the exclusive feeling of hatred to African slavery, is now the controlling power in this Confederacy. Constitutional limitations on its powers are only such, in its creed, as its agents or itself shall recognize. It claims power for the Government which it will control, to construe the measure of its own authority, and to use the entire governmental power of this Confederacy to enforce its construction upon the people and States of this Union. No man can fail to see and know this who reads and understands what he reads. The fact is a great and a perilous truth. No clap trap about the Union, no details of private conversations of Northern men can alter it or weaken its force. It is here a present, living, mischievous fact. The Government of the Union is in the hands of the avowed enemies of one entire section. It is to be directed in hostility to the property of that section.

What is to be done, is the question that presses on every man.

New Orleans Daily Crescent, *November 13, 1860*

We have abated not one jot or tittle of our attachment to the "Constitution, the Union and the Enforcement of the Laws"—the proud and unexceptional motto of the party for which we battled during the long and exciting contest so recently closed. . . .

But, we cannot say, and we have never said, that we were in favor of a Union to be maintained at the sacrifice of a violated Constitution, by a persistent refusal to obey the mandates of the Supreme Court, and by a general nullification of the laws of Congress, by the majority section, to oppress and outrage the minority portion of the confederacy. We have never been in favor of *such* a Union, and never shall be. The fathers of the Republic would have spurned such a confederation with as much loathing as they did the treason of Benedict Arnold. The Declaration of Independence itself says: "Whenever any form of government becomes destructive of these ends, (life, liberty and the pursuit of happiness) it is the right of the people to alter or to abolish it, and to institute a new government, laying its foundation on such principles, and organizing its powers in such form, as to them shall seem most likely to effect their safety and happiness." Higher authority than the above is not to be found in the history of the United States. The principle it enunciates constitutes the very corner stone of the temple of American liberty—of liberty everywhere. Wherever the principle is unrecognized, sheer and unadulterated despotism prevails. There is no such thing as civil and religious freedom where it is ignored. The right to change a government, or to utterly abolish it, and to establish a new government, is the inherent right of a free people; and when they are deprived of that right they are no longer free—not a whit more so than the serfs of Russia or the down-trodden millions of Austria.

The history of the Abolition or Black Republican party of the North is a history of repeated injuries and usurpations, all having in direct object the establishment of absolute tyranny over the slaveholding States. And all without the smallest warrant, excuse or justification. We have appealed to their generosity, justice and patriotism, but all without avail. From the beginning, we have only asked to be let alone in the enjoyment of our plain, inalienable rights, as explicitly guaranteed in our common organic law. We have never aggressed upon the North, nor sought to aggress upon the North. Yet every appeal and expostulation has only brought upon us renewed insults and augmented injuries. They have robbed us of our property, they have murdered our citizens while endeavoring to reclaim that property by lawful means, they have set at naught the decrees of the

Supreme Court, they have invaded our States and killed our citizens, they have declared their unalterable determination to exclude us altogether from the Territories, they have nullified the laws of Congress, and finally they have capped the mighty pyramid of unfraternal enormities by electing Abraham Lincoln to the Chief Magistracy, on a platform and by a system which indicates nothing but the subjugation of the South and the complete ruin of her social, political and industrial institutions.

New Orleans Bee, *December 14, 1860*

The political charlatans of the North and the patriotic but mistaken public men of the border slave States appear to outvie each other in efforts to discover a remedy for existing evils. They do not perceive that the wound inflicted by the North upon the South is essentially incurable. They think, on the contrary, it may be plastered, and bandaged, and dressed in some sort of fashion and will do very well. The Union is broken in two, but the political doctors fancy that the ruptured extremities can be readily brought together, and that by the aid of the world-renowned "compromise" machine, the integrity of the fractured parts may be completely restored. Without further figure of speech, let us say that we hardly know whether to smile or sigh over the innumerable devices resorted to by members of Congress to save the Union. With just about as much hope of success might they expect to breathe life into a corpse, or look for green leaves, bright flowers, and savory fruit from the blackened and withered trunk of a blasted tree, as imagine that the Union may yet be preserved. This *might* have been done a few months ago. The Union might have received a new lease of life, had the Abolition party been overwhelmingly defeated in the recent contest; but after its signal triumph to seek to bolster up the Union is as fruitless a task as would be the attempt to teach [William Lloyd] Garrison moderation, [Charles] Sumner national patriotism, and [Henry] Wilson the feelings and instincts of a gentleman. . . .

But the grand, overwhelming objection to these feeble and fruitless projects is the absolute impossibility of revolutionizing Northern opinion in relation to slavery. Without a change of heart, radical and thorough, all guarantees which might be offered are not worth the paper on which they would be inscribed. As long as slavery is looked upon by the North with abhorrence; as long as the South is regarded as a mere slave-breeding and slave-driving community; as long as false and pernicious theories are cherished respecting the inherent equality and rights of every human being, there can be no satisfactory political union between the two sections. If one-half the people believe the other half to be deeply dyed in iniquity; to be daily and hourly in the perpetration of the most atrocious moral offense, and at the same time knowing them to be their countrymen and fellow-citizens, conceive themselves authorized and in some sort constrained to lecture them, to abuse them, to employ all possible means to break up their institutions, and to take from them what the Northern half consider property unrighteously held, or no property at all, how can two such antagonistic nationalities dwell together in fraternal concord under the same government? Is not the thing clearly impossible? Has not the experiment been tried for more than seventy years, and have not the final results demonstrated its failure? The feelings, customs, mode of thought and education of the two sections, are discrepant and often antagonistic. The North and South are heterogeneous and are better apart. Were we foreign to the North, that section would treat us as our Government now treats Mexico or England—abstaining from interference in the internal policy of a country with which we have nothing to do, and with which we are at peace. As it is, we are persuaded that while the South continues a part of the American confederacy, there is no power which can prevent her progressive degradation, humiliation and spoliation by the victorious North. We are doomed if we proclaim not our political independence.

Republican Banner, *Nashville, January 25, 1861*

The Resolutions adopted by the General Assembly, published in our paper a few days since, define the position of Tennessee satisfactorily, as we believe, to the great mass of the people. They substantially adopt the Crittenden Compromise as a basis of adjustment of the pending issues between the North and South, and Tennessee will say to the people of the North, not in a spirit of blustering defiance and braggadocio, but firmly and calmly, and with a sincere and honest desire that this adjustment may be accepted—we demand nothing more—*we will accept of nothing less.* This settlement can be agreed upon by the people of both sections without the sacrifice of a principle or of any material interest. It would be acceptable, we believe, to a majority of the people in the seceding States, and the State of Tennessee could take no course better calculated to befriend and conserve the interests of those States than by maintaining such a position as will enable her, in conjunction with other Southern States, to negotiate the adoption of this compromise with the North. That the sympathies of Tennessee are emphatically Southern, no one will deny. She will take no course, in any event, calculated to militate against the interests of her Southern sisters. But the question for her to decide—and it is a question upon which hangs her own and the destiny of the South and the Union—is what course is most judicious, most patriotic, and best calculated to conserve the interests of her Southern sisters, and if possible preserve the Union? Upon this question there is a difference of opinion. Some are for precipitate secession. Others for maintaining our present attitude, prepared, when the time comes, to act as mediators upon the basis of the Crittenden adjustment. If the policy of the former party is pursued, we lose the advantage of our position as pacificators, and gain nothing that we could not gain at any future time, when it shall be demonstrated, as it unfortunately may be, that a settlement is impracticable. We are therefore opposed to hasty action. We do not think the friends of a fair and honorable settlement, in the seceding States, desire Tennessee to follow their example until all honorable endeavors to secure such a settlement are exhausted. Doubtless there are many in those States who do not desire a settlement—who prefer disunion and a Southern Confederacy to any reconstruction of the Government. There are a few, even in Tennessee, who sympathize with these disunionists *per se*, but they are very few, and thus far have been very modest in the avowal of such sentiments. Tennessee is emphatically a Union State, if the Union can be preserved upon terms of equality and justice, and is for making an attempt to preserve it before abandoning the hope. The difference of opinion among her people is merely as to the best policy to be pursued to accomplish a given end, at which all seem to be driving. We should rejoice to see this difference of opinion reconciled or compromised, so that we might all move in solid phalanx, and as a unit. It would add immensely to our influence in the crisis, and might, indeed, be the means of securing what, under existing circumstances, may not be attained—a perpetuation of the Government.

⅄ *E S S A Y S*

Professor of history J. Mills Thornton III of the University of Michigan has closely studied the politics of Alabama in the decades before secession. In the first essay, he analyzes the social and political assumptions that made the argument for secession convincing to many southerners. Historians have always noted that secession seemed less desirable to many voters in the Upper South than to those in the Lower South. Historian Daniel W. Crofts of Trenton State College describes in the second essay the enormous political shifts that occurred in Virginia, North Carolina, and Tennessee as many Unionists and nonslaveholders mobilized to oppose secession. For many voters in these states, secession became inevitable only after war had begun. In many parts of the Lower South, however, the political and racial atmosphere was highly charged for months before the 1860 presidential election. The last essay, by historian Steven Channing, who formerly taught at the University of Kentucky, depicts the climate of feeling in South Carolina on the eve of disunion and describes South Carolinians' fear that their way of life was doomed under a Republican administration.

The Argument for Secession

J. MILLS THORNTON III

A not inconsiderable portion of historians' misunderstanding of secession perhaps derives from a general failure to reflect seriously upon the social and political assumptions in the arguments offered in favor of that step. Numerous arguments of many different types were presented, by politicians, editors, theorists, and ordinary citizens. But the student who ponders them will come to see that almost all of them are, unconsciously, buttressing one or another aspect of a single, general case. The case is so logical and so internally consistent that it may almost be presented syllogistically. Its logic and consistency, however, were not dictated by one thinker, or even

J. Mills Thornton III, *Politics and Power in a Slave Society*, excerpts from pp. 204–222 (Baton Rouge: Louisiana State University Press, 1978). Reprinted by permission of the publisher.

by a group of them, but by the society in which Alabamians lived. The skeleton of the case was formed of unquestioned social axioms, and the marrow of that skeleton was political reality.

At the beginning of the 1850s the arguments seemed to most people unconvincing; ten years later this situation had been altered. But the arguments themselves did not really change. The unfolding of events merely lent them more empirical weight. Thus, an analysis of the appeals made during the Crisis of 1850 will prepare us to understand the questions at issue in the coming decade's bitter contests. . . .

The case begins with portraits of what the South would be like without slavery. These portraits emphasize two complementary appeals—one to the race fears of the readers, the other to their sense of race superiority. The appeal to fears is typified by the following quotation.

Hemmed in on the North, West and Southwest by a chain of nonslave-holding States; fanaticism and power, hand in hand, preaching a crusade against her institutions; her post offices flooded with incendiary documents; her by-ways crowded with emissaries sowing the seeds of a servile war, in order to create a more plausible excuse for Congressional interference; the value of her property depreciated and her agricultural industry paralyzed, what would become of the people of the Southern States, when they would be forced at last to let loose among them, freed from the wholesome restraints of patriarchal authority, a population whose only principle of action has ever been animal appetite? With an idle, worthless, profligate set of free negroes prowling about our streets at night and haunting the woods during the day armed with whatever weapons they could lay their hands on, and way-laying every road through every swamp in the South, what would be our situation? The farmer, when his stock were all killed up, his corn house plundered, and perhaps his stable set on fire, would be forced to make a block house of his dwelling and sleep every night with his musket by his side. There would remain but one remedy for the evils thus inflicted upon our social system—a war of extermination against the whole negro race.

Another vision of the future was set in 1871.

The slave population will then be doubled in the few remaining slave States that are likely to hold on to that institution. Missouri, Kentucky, Maryland and Delaware, harrassed [*sic*] by the constant thefts of their slaves by citizens of the free States, will have sent them nearly all South, and will stand ready (some of them will have already done so) to abolish the institution in their limits. Many of the whites in the remaining slave States, being inconvenienced by this dense population of the negroes will sell out, being prevented by the free States from taking their slaves with them, and go themselves to free States. So will many others through fear and interest; and even the patriot Southerner, who is now branded as an "ultra and traitor" by the tories of the present day, tired of being abused and vilified, and disgusted with the pusalanimity [*sic*] and cowardice of his fellow-citizens of the South will, in many instances, take up his departure from a people that have shown so little willingness to defend their rights and honor. The negroes will become insupportable when they shall have doubled and trebled the white population South, with the sympathies of three-fourths of the whites in the United States against the institution. The sequel may be easily discerned. We have an illustration in point in St. Domingo. This is but an imperfect picture of the prospect before us. Gloomy, indeed—but is it not true?

The two examples suffice to show the tone of these arguments. The sustaining vision of Jacksonian America was the prospect for future advancement. But the southern future held only horror. The prophecies would have their most profoundly depressing effect upon those citizens who had not yet arrived in the society, who counted upon America's continued march towards the sunlit uplands of tomorrow for the fulfillment of their personal dreams. And it is to be noted that the simple farmer, defending his corn house and his stable from the sneak attacks of alien guerrillas, is the hero of the descriptions. This point is even clearer in the arguments based upon appeals to race superiority.

The farmers were told that slavery "promotes equality among the free by dispensing with grades and castes among them, and thereby preserves republican institutions." They were told:

> The total abolition of slavery would affect more injuriously the condition of the poor white man in the slaveholding States than that of the rich slaveholder; for the slaveholder, having the means which attends upon the possession of slaves, would be able to maintain his *position*, whilst the poor man would have to doff that native, free-born and independent spirit which he now possesses, and which he prizes above all wealth, and would have to become virtually the slave (barring color) of the rich man. This would be one of the consequences of the abolition of negro slavery, and the poorest white man who walks, barefoot, our hills is wise enough to see it; and though he may only leave to his children the heritage of *freedom* and *poverty*, yet he is determined that neither they nor his children's children, to the latest generation, shall ever occupy, through their remissness of duty, the position of *servants*.

Future governor John Gill Shorter warned that "should the time ever arrive when four millions of slaves congregated in the South Atlantic and Gulf States were turned loose upon the country, there would then be a contest between the two races for supremacy; that while the rich would be able to leave a land thus cursed, the poor white man would be left in a most lamentable condition. He would, then, perhaps, instead of occupying the position of master, find his case reversed, and he reduced to the most abject and degrading servitude." . . .

. . . Every one of these portraits of the future had the nonslaveholder principally in mind. It was always he who was driven from his home, plunged into the midst of an ocean of hostile, animal-like blacks, forced to fight to the death to retain his little plot of earth, threatened with becoming the menial of the wealthy. Secession was a political act and two-thirds of the electorate owned no slaves.

Not only would the abolition of slavery harm primarily the nonslaveholder, but it appeared that he was a major beneficiary of its existence. It kept the wages of working whites high, for it insured that they would never have to occupy the lowest rungs of the economic ladder. It gave the small farmer a ready market for his produce, because of the massive, local demand of the great plantations. But most importantly, it gave him a world in which he could govern his own life without the interference of society, or of social tumult. "In his social progress he encounters no mobs, no riots, no violent political excitements, no communism, no agrarianism, no mormonism, no antimasonism, no lawless leagues of rabble. In his labor he has to contend with no foreign pauperism, no home pauperism, no daily laborers going about begging but unable to obtain employment."

The next step in the southern rights case was to link the exclusion of slavery from the territories with the forecast catastrophes. This relation was established by two arguments. In the first place, given the rapid rate of increase which the slave population showed, if slaves were limited to the South, the whites would soon find themselves a minority in a black sea. As in the case of emancipation, rich whites might flee, leaving the poor to deal with the increasingly restless blacks. Alternatively, the increasing number of Negroes could force the occupation of a greater and greater percentage of the arable land by plantations, forcing the nonslaveholders off their farms and driving them homeless into the world. On the other hand, the export of slaves to new areas and their employment in new pursuits would diminish overproduction of cotton, raise the price of the staple, and thus increase the small farmer's income.

The second argument through which the territorial issue was connected to the interests of the electorate was even more revealing. The southern farmer—indeed, the American farmer—in the nineteenth century suffered from a sort of claustrophobia. He could not tolerate the prospect of being irrevocably condemned to his existing farm, of being shut out of the possibility of migration to a new life if events should ever require it. But his vision was not of migration to a new world and a new life-style; rather, he wanted the assurance that there was an accessible alternate community in which he could engage in fundamentally the same pursuits, but in circumstances which might produce greater success. Southern rights advocates constantly reminded him that the Yankee culture was very different from his own, and that if he allowed the territories to become re-creations of the northern states, he could thereafter migrate to them only at the cost of giving up his own egalitarian, democratic world for a socially stratified society swept by the gales of class conflict and unbridled meliorist ferment. It is that condition which the writer quoted earlier was seeking to define with his long list of social ills and reformist movements. In the South, the farmer "lives quietly, and if he be industrious, comfortably"; his taxes were low, particularly because the government had few paupers to support; nor did he really compete with Negro labor, for he did not usually raise the staple crops.

> Under this system of things all thrived and all were happy. From father to son, through a long succession of years, they progressed, and have gone

on accumulating at a steady rate until, without apparently being aware of the fact, we, their posterity, have become a prosperous and wealthy people—not in the sense in which these terms are applied to England and the North—not by the concentration of capital in the hands of a few enterprising individuals, to whom the many are the mere "hewers of wood and drawers of water"—but by a general diffusion of wealth and happiness over the whole community.

The fear of the antebellum reform movements—of the "communism, agrarianism, mormonism, anti-masonism and lawless leagues of rabble" which the earlier quotation deplored—reflects a deep-seated uneasiness which constitutes the next link in the southern rights case. Its advocates were frightened by the prospect that the sort of commotion observable elsewhere in the world would invade their own peaceful realm, and their apprehensions led them to see nascent danger in small circumstances. When Senator Clemens introduced into Congress a constitutional amendment for popular election of senators, the Mobile *Register* was concerned, despite its approval of the measure's object. "Let the instrument [the Constitution] pass under the hands of the political tinkers who are ever and anon thinking themselves wiser than its framers, and our habitual reverence for it as something sacred will be extinguished." When a writer ventured kind words about Aaron Burr, one editor lamented feelingly that it had now become the fashion to defend people formerly execrated. The heated debates in Congress dismayed observers; the absence of polite discourse in the halls of legislation seemed to many an omen of imminent social disintegration. . . .

Looking at the example of the North, then, these men felt uneasy at the ability of the South to maintain its unique social stability, and they sought actively to communicate their apprehensions. In the past, they liked to believe, the world had left the ordinary citizen alone; he had been his own master, an autonomous unit; neither society nor other men had sought to dictate his course. But that day might be drawing to a close. Society, it appeared, was about to materialize on an Alabama farm, and its avatar would assuredly be mounted upon a storm. Could freedom survive the manifestation? With that question, we reach the core and motive force of the southern rights case.

So often that it became a sort of litany, southern rights advocates reiterated that freedom and equality were in imminent danger. Southerners had intimate experience with slavery, and it was their greatest dread. Now those with acute vision professed to see the very shackles being forged. There were two interlocking appeals, one to freedom and the ideal of individual autonomy, and one to equality and the alleged threat to manhood and self-respect. In either guise the argument touched the very meaning of the American experiment as the Jacksonian generations understood it. . . .

Congressman David Hubbard informed the voters:

It is clear that the power to dictate what sort of property the State may allow a citizen to own and work—whether oxen, horses or negroes; or what religion he may preach, teach or practice, on account of its morality, is alike despotic and tyrannical, whether such power is obtained by conquest in battle or by a majority vote and is equally galling and oppressive upon those whose consciences are made to conform to the standard of morality which the majority sets up; and was never surpassed by the British crown during the reign of her most absolute and despotic kings.

When a constituent expressed a willingness to accept emancipation with colonization if it would restore harmony to the Union, the congressman wrote him that

the white people in the Southern States had better exterminate both the negroes and their owners, who would turn them loose upon them, than allow any such scheme to be carried out, as you appear to be willing to adopt, rather than meet it as you ought. Because, the assumed power to put an end to slavery, or take the first steps towards that object, being a higher power than the Constitution has given Congress, is a violation of its provisions, and a destruction of liberty itself. It was constitutional liberty which our fathers fought to establish and *not* union! they *had* union with the mother country when they rebelled; they had *more* of it than they wanted, and the revolution was fought to get clear of such union as they then had, and to obtain liberty in its stead.

After they had gained liberty in battle, they established peaceable union, for strength to *protect* liberty. Now if the strength which union gives, is used for the purpose of *destroying* and not protecting liberty, we must get clear of such strength and keep liberty. This seems to me to be our plain duty. . . .

The southern rights advocates pictured southerners as a persecuted minority—indeed, "the most oppressed, insulted and plundered of all"—fighting valiantly for "the maintenance and perpetuation of those great principles of civil liberty transmitted to us by a glorious and venerated ancestry." They referred constantly, therefore, to two examples—the revolutionaries of 1776 and the contemporary European struggles against monarchy. The issue which southerners faced was "whether they are to be free or slaves—whether they are to be subjugated as Ireland and Hungary—whether they are to be partitioned as Poland, or erect themselves into an independent State"; and there could be but a single choice "as long as one drop of revolutionary blood courses our veins." . . .

A Jefferson County meeting asserted that the South faced a "return to a colonial vassalage more galling than the one our fathers resisted." A Jackson County paper believed, "The same spirit of freedom and independence that impelled our Fathers to the separation from the British Government, will induce the liberty loving people of the Southern States to a separation" in the face of continued northern aggressions. The Huntsville *Democrat* said that the South's cause was "the cause of freedom, of constitutional liberty," and reminded all of "the Jeffersonian doctrine that 'Resistance to tyranny is obedience to God.' " A Fourth of July editorial from the Black Belt hailed the day "of our release from thraldom—from the insult, injury, tyranny and oppression of *power*" and proclaimed that in

1776 "the bloody ghost of anarchy, civil commotion" was held up to our ancestors as reason for compromise, but it "had no such terrors as to drive them from the assertion and maintenance of their rights. Why should we, the descendants of those people, suffer ourselves to be frightened by the same stories, from similar sources of the present day? . . .

At least as important as the threat to liberty was the threat to equality. Southerners were being stripped of all self-respect by their treatment as second-class citizens. A Talladega County meeting resolved "that whenever an abolition majority in Congress, by aid of the interference of any officer of the Federal Government or by any other mode, shall deprive us of the inestimable right of *political equality,* and appropriate to themselves the vast territories of the United States (the common property of all the States)—it is then *their* Government, not ours. Then we shall be compelled to regard it as our enemy." Thaddeus Sanford concluded, "To resist such arrogant assumptions is but the ordinary impulse of manhood—to submit to them is voluntary degradation. An American freeman acknowledges no master but his God." . . .

The emphasis upon equality led to frequent appeals to the memory of Andrew Jackson. "Gen. Jackson knew that this Government was formed on the great principle of equality, that it was a partnership of sovereign States, each equal to the other, and all entitled alike to a full share of its benefits, as all had alike to bear its burdens"; therefore, he could never have accepted "that under the Constitution Congress had the power to declare that a free citizen of Massachusetts was a better man and entitled to more privileges than a free citizen of Alabama." Of course, Jackson had opposed nullification, but southern rights men dismissed that point. "Gen. Jackson is the last man in the world that should be quoted by the submissionists to aggression and oppression; his whole life vindicates his character from such contamination—it is well known he bore to his grave the mark of a sword cut from a British officer because he would not clean his boots." Since southern rights advocates equated Unionism with self-abasement and slavish conduct, it naturally followed that Jackson's refusal to clean a British officer's boots placed the Old Hero in the southern rights camp.

For the student who fails to realize the importance of the argument from equality, it must often seem that southern rights reasoning has, as in this instance, a peculiarly metaphorical character. But these are not metaphors. The society was structured so as to demand, and to appear to allow, the achievement of individual autonomy. Therefore, each man's self-respect was absolutely essential to his existence as a part of the social organism. Doubtless it is ironic that the antebellum world encouraged—indeed, was founded upon—a concept which in its very nature is socially disorganizing. The necessity for reconciling an antisocial ideal with the obvious imperative for communal cooperation induced the fascination with symbols which we have encountered so often in political propaganda. Observers focused their comments so intensely upon the symbolic issue or verbal formulation that the issue or formulation could pass beyond a mere hint at truth to the substance of truth in the minds of antebellum Americans. A metaphrastic rendering of the oratory of the period must miss the point, but just as the monster bank became the sum of evils, so the free-soil territory became the embodiment of humiliation. . . .

The northern threat to southern self-respect could come in many guises. Its chief form was the free-soil movement. But cited with almost equal frequency by the press were personal insults to individual southerners who traveled to the north, and northern statements which indicated supercilious contempt for the South. Indeed, one beat [district] meeting resolved that even if free-soil aggressions should cease, "the unwillingness of Northern men to sit around the same altars with Southern men—the denunciations of us by the press and people of the North—the false slanders circulated in their periodicals and reviews—the rending of churches for a theoretical sentiment, and then appropriating to their use what they sanctimoniously call the price of blood—have alienated the two sections of a common country, and would alone, at some future day, terminate in a dissolution of the union." . . .

The southern rights case was complete. We may recapitulate it in deductive form. The essence of Jacksonian society was the worship of the idols Liberty and Equality. Southerners, because of their daily contact with genuine slavery, were even more fanatically devoted to the Jacksonian cult than were most Americans; they did not exclude human sacrifice in order to sustain it. Since absolute individual autonomy is antisocial, the society tended to use symbols with which to reaffirm to itself its professed ideals. But the ideals were consciously held, and any action which appeared to the citizenry to threaten individual autonomy was regarded as a challenge to democracy and a portent of thralldom.

Upon these assumptions, which Alabamians held without question or examination, was founded the portion of the southern rights case more susceptible of explicit expression. Insults to individual southerners, the division of the churches, and similar circumstances proved that northerners held their fellow citizens of the South in contempt. The goal of Yankee South-haters was domination of the general government. The adoption of a free-soil policy would follow immediately upon their gaining that control. Once free-soil was enacted, the South would be condemned to inferiority in the Union. Southerners would be imprisoned within existing southern boundaries, for to settle in the territories would be to abandon a truly democratic, truly free, truly American community for a community riven by social conflict, in which the many were directly dependent upon the few for their livelihood and in which genuine egalitarianism was therefore impossible. Given the rate of Negro population increase, confining southerners to the South meant trapping them to be drowned by a rising black tide. When the population imbalance became excessive, by perhaps 1870, the weak and rich would flee, leaving the yeomen to fight a race war or, alternatively, to accept equality with slaves. Equality with slaves destroyed the meaning of equality—the pride of manhood which flows from the knowledge of freedom. Now if the northern masses, under the guidance of their fanatical manipulators, were indeed committed to free-soil, then their numbers would inevitably give them eventual mastery within the federal government. At that time only secession—escape from the tyrannical exercise of power which would follow—could preserve the substance of equality and freedom. But since free-soilism would ultimately become governmental policy, it was dangerous to tarry while the South was stealthily ensnared in the net of despotism. If southerners were to remain Americans, they must secede as soon as possible, while they were still able to do so.

The Unionist Groundswell in the Upper South

DANIEL W. CROFTS

One must take into account both slaveholding and previous patterns of party allegiance to understand why the upper and lower South took such different stances during the months after Lincoln's election. High-slave-owning areas across the South generally displayed more support for secession, and slaveowning was more concentrated in the lower than the upper South. Deep South secessionists also benefited from virtually unchallenged statewide Democratic majorities. The party's radical Southern Rights wing planted seeds of poisonous suspicion that suddenly sprouted in late 1860. . . . Closer two-party competition in the upper South, however, gave Whiggish opponents of secession a substantial nucleus from which to build. Antisecessionists there, using a new "Union party" label, could thus overwhelm the initial secessionist challenge.

Three waves of change, each successively larger than the other, washed over and fundamentally reshaped political contours in Virginia, North Carolina, and Tennessee during the brief six-month interval between November 1860 and April 1861. Promoters of secession tried to spur the upper South to follow the example of the lower South. At first it appeared they might succeed. Those favoring secession were active, ardent, and outspoken after Lincoln's election. They had a program to confront northern menace and insult. And, not least among their assets, they had leverage in the Democratic party, which maintained a modest majority in all three states. Many Democrats, especially the officeholding elite, either supported secession overtly or allowed disunionists to lead. For perhaps two months, secession strength grew, creating a wave that surged formidably as it crested in late December and early January. In parts of "lower Virginia" and the Democratic plantation counties of North Carolina, the initial secessionist wave looked irresistible.

But in the upper South—unlike the lower South—the first wave did not dislodge any state from the Union. Instead, the push for secession created an explicitly antisecession countermobilization. Upper South Unionists organized, campaigned, and deeply stirred popular feeling, especially in

From *Reluctant Confederates* by Daniel W. Crofts, pp. 130–133, 154–156, 193–194. © The University of North Carolina Press. Reprinted by permission.

nonplantation areas. They generated a second wave, greater than the first, that appeared to sweep away the popular underpinnings of secession in February 1861. Voters in all three states decisively rejected southern independence. To be sure, Unionists usually attached conditions to their allegiance, pledging to resist federal "coercion" of the seceding states. They nevertheless expected that secessionists would reconsider their rash action, thereby allowing peaceful restoration of the Union.

The Unionist coalition in the upper South was composed primarily of Whigs, often simply called "Opposition" by the late 1850s, after the collapse of their national party. The survival of competitive Opposition parties in the upper South, in contrast to the experience of the lower South during the 1850s, provided institutional barriers against secession. In nonplantation areas of the upper South, substantial increments of Union Democrats and previous nonvoters also voted against secession. Many other Democrats, uneasy about secession and about alliance with Whiggish Unionists, did not vote at all, thereby further depressing prosecession vote totals.

The action of the upper South stunned secessionists, as one famous example will illustrate. Edmund Ruffin, the elderly prophet of southern nationalism, fled from his native Virginia to South Carolina in early March 1861. He arrived just before Lincoln's inauguration, to avoid living "even for an hour" in a country with a Republican president. Ruffin had reason to feel frustrated as he traveled south. Lincoln's election had not united the South, as Ruffin had hoped. On February 4, 1861, the very day that representatives from the seven seceding states met in Montgomery, Alabama, to organize the Confederate States of America, Ruffin's home state delivered a crippling blow against upper South secession. Strongly affirming their hopes for peaceful restoration of the Union, Virginia voters rejected most prosecession candidates for the state convention. More than two out of three of those voting also specified that any convention action be made subject to popular referendum, a provision secessionists bitterly opposed. Just before leaving Virginia, Ruffin visited the convention, by then in session in Richmond. "The majority of this Convention is more basely submissive than I had supposed possible," he fumed.

The ability of Unionists to prevent the upper South from seceding gave legitimacy to the efforts of conciliatory Republicans, headed by the incoming secretary of state, William H. Seward. He tried to persuade President Lincoln that a noncoercive "hands-off" policy toward the seceded states would maintain the dominance of Unionists in the upper South and lead eventually to peaceful restoration of the Union. During March and early April, upper South Unionists believed Lincoln had agreed to the conciliatory plan.

Lincoln's proclamation calling for seventy-five thousand troops on April 15, in effect asking the upper South to fight the lower South, stirred the third and greatest wave. It immediately engulfed upper South Unionism. The three states studied here seceded in a frenzy of patriotic enthusiasm. Only in northwestern Virginia and East Tennessee did an unconditionally Unionist leadership and electorate resist the majority current. Elsewhere, original secessionists rolled out the red carpet for new converts. Believing they had been betrayed by the Lincoln administration, countless thousands who had earlier rejected secession embraced the cause of southern independence. Original and converted secessionists joined hands to defend southern honor and constitutional principles against what they perceived as corrupt, tyrannical oppression. They believed themselves fighting for the same cause as the patriots of 1776. So it was that Edmund Ruffin could return in triumph to Richmond on April 23. By then, a common resolve to resist "northern domination" had undermined Virginia's earlier Unionism, and the "submissive" convention had voted for secession. "There has been a complete and wonderful change here since I left," Ruffin exulted. . . .

Upper South Unionism coalesced during the first two months of 1861. Though confronted by grave obstacles, Unionists possessed one key advantage: popular support for secession had grown since November but had not yet gained a majority in any upper South state. Unionists faced the task of arresting and reversing the growth of secession sentiment in their home states, while also urging Congress to enact Union-saving measures. . . .

The great Unionist achievement, during a winter otherwise marked by frustration and failure, was the mobilizing of popular majorities across the upper South to thwart secession. Why did the upper South refuse to follow the lead of the lower South? That crucial question requires a two-pronged answer, involving both slavery and party. Relatively smaller concentrations of slaves and slaveowners, plus statewide political arenas in which the two major parties competed on close terms, made the upper South less receptive to secessionist appeals. The combination of fewer slaveowners and more formidable political opposition to the secession-leaning Democratic party kept Virginia, North Carolina, and Tennessee in the Union during early 1861.

Plantation regions dominated the seven seceding states in the deep South. It was no coincidence that the first states to leave the Union had the greatest commitment to slavery. Support for secession, both in the upper and lower South, tended to be strongest in high-slaveowning areas and weakest in the low-slaveowning regions of the upcountry. However formidable the slaveowning interest in Virginia, North Carolina, and Tennessee, a larger share of each state's electorate resided in the upcountry than anywhere in the lower South.

Somewhat less well known, but of comparable importance in understanding the relative weakness of secession in the upper South, was a set of partisan arrangements that differed markedly from those in the lower South. Competitive two-party politics in the upper South gave antisecessionists an indispensable base. The Whig party organization and electorate provided the foundation for what would soon be called the Union party in Virginia, North Carolina, and Tennessee.

Whig and Opposition parties throughout the lower South were much weaker and generally weakest in the upcountry. The tendency for lower South Whigs to reside in the "black belts" enervated whatever latent

Unionism they possessed. But in the Upper South, Whigs had greater residual strength, which was by no means confined to plantation regions. In North Carolina, notably, a cluster of low-slaveowning counties in the piedmont regularly provided the largest Whig margins in the state. Voters in this Whiggish "Quaker Belt" spearheaded statewide opposition to secession. They gained reinforcements from party loyalists in the mountains and the northeast. Each Tennessee party received comparable support from high- and low-slaveowning regions. But a bloc of strong Whig counties around Knoxville provided a militantly antisecession nucleus for the broader East Tennessee region, and Whiggish counties in the fertile Cumberland Valley of Middle Tennessee proved especially hospitable to a qualified wait-and-see conditional Unionism. Western Virginia was slightly more Democratic than eastern Virginia, but the unique geographical position of the trans-Allegheny, coupled with its long history of estrangement from the east, made the west almost unanimously pro-Union. Whig strongholds in the Virginia valley and western piedmont also rejected secession, including, for example, Jefferson County, the site of John Brown's assault in October 1859. Even in Southampton County, the Virginia tidewater locale where the slave rebel Nat Turner had rampaged thirty years before, Whigs voted overwhelmingly pro-Union. The inability of secessionists to carry even a bare majority in Southampton well illustrated the linkage between Unionism and Whig party loyalties.

Upper South Unionism thus had both a regional and a party base. A popular outpouring of antisecession sentiment among upcountry nonslaveowners provided the most conspicuous element of Union strength. But Unionism had the potential to become a dominant political force because it extended beyond the upcountry to draw support from the Whig rank and file. The latter included a broad spectrum of southerners, among them more than a few slaveowners from the fertile lowlands. Thomas P. Devereux, one of the wealthiest plantation owners in North Carolina, berated South Carolina for her "folly" and confidently awaited a Union-saving compromise. A conservative orientation was especially pronounced among Union Whigs in eastern Virginia, many of whom deplored the democratic revisions in the 1851 Virginia constitution. They blamed secession on the new breed of "worthless, disgusting politicians" who pandered to popular fears.

Although some embraced Unionism to preserve or rebuild existing social hierarchies, the antisecession insurgency in the upper South had unmistakable egalitarian overtones. Far more than in the lower South, class resentments surfaced in late 1860 and early 1861. One of Edmund Ruffin's correspondents told him in late November that secession sentiment in the Southside Virginia counties of Lunenburg and Nottoway had increased greatly since the election but that "disaffection" among "the poorer class of non slaveholders" had also appeared. Some antisecessionists stated flatly that "in the event of civil war or even servile insurrection, they would not lift a finger in defense of the rights of slaveholders." An observer in Hertford County, North Carolina, a tidewater area just below the Virginia border, was similarly "mortified" to find many nonslaveowning "plain country people" unwilling to fight "to protect rich men's negroes." Nor were nonslave-owning Virginians in the Shenandoah Valley willing "to break up the government for the mere loss of an election." Similar reports emanated from West Tennessee, where "the nonslave holders (or a large majority of them) when approached on the subject declare that they will not fight if war fol[l]ows a dissolution of the union." And in towns and cities across the upper South, "workingmen" organized and demonstrated against secession.

Sensitive to the egalitarian stirrings, some secession sympathizers cautioned against trying to rush the states of the upper South out of the Union prematurely. "You cannot unite the *masses* of any southern State much less those of North Carolina against the Union and in favor [of] slavery *alone*," surmised an astute secessionist. Nonslaveowners would resist any movement that appeared controlled by "the *avarice* and the *selfishness* of *Negro Slavocracy*." But by prudently waiting until the federal government attacked the seceding states, secessionists could "change the issue" to "a question of popular liberty." Once the second consideration was introduced, nothing could hold North Carolina in the Union. A Southern Rights supporter from Virginia reasoned along the same lines. "You can't make the great mass of the people, especially the non slaveholders understand . . . the nice principles on which the secessionists are now attempting to act," he observed. Indeed, he feared that secessionist clamor ran the potential danger "of creating a party with sympathies for the incoming administration, here in our midst." He therefore thought it best "to *prepare* for resistance" without seeming to follow the lead of "disunionists *per se*." He foresaw, too, that "the non slaveholder will fight for his section as soon as the slaveholder if you can convince him that *his* political rights are really threatened."

Such caution was appropriate. Large regions of Virginia, North Carolina, and Tennessee opposed secession with at least as much fervor and with even greater unanimity than it was supported in other areas of those states. Spontaneous Union meetings gathered in upcountry locations at the same time secessionists seized the organizational initiative in many plantation districts. For example, a well-attended public meeting on November 29 in Hawkins County, East Tennessee, resolved that "the doctrine of secession" was "subversive of all just principles of government." The meeting reaffirmed Andrew Jackson's view that secession was "treason." An estimated eight hundred to a thousand people likewise gathered on December 28 in intensely Unionist Randolph County, in the North Carolina piedmont, to condemn secession as "unwise and suicidal" and to deplore the "folly and madness" of extremists North and South.

For the Breckinridge wing of the Democratic party, which provided the political backbone for the secession movement, the antisecession groundswell in parts of Virginia, North Carolina, and Tennessee posed a deadly threat. Breckinridge had readily carried most Democratic areas of the upcountry. Any significant slippage of Democratic loyalties there, when coupled with the already manifest disaffection from the party of those who voted for Douglas in 1860, seriously endangered the prospects for statewide secession. It likewise threatened the narrow statewide Democratic majorities in all three states. . . .

. . . The majority of Unionist politicians and newspapers supported calling state conventions in North Carolina and Tennessee, for fear of alienating conditional Unionists who were willing to support antisecession delegates but who still wanted a convention held. The election results suggested, however, that "the people determined for once to think and act for themselves" and that in so doing they discovered "*their power* over politicians, and party organizations." The high turnouts in Union strongholds in Tennessee and North Carolina revealed an unusual intensity of popular feeling. Randolph County, North Carolina, in the heart of the Quaker Belt, normally cast fewer than 2,000 votes but voted against a convention by a majority of 2,466 to 45. The county sheriff, J. W. Steed, reported: "The people of Randolph believed that all the warm advocates of a Convention wanted to withdraw this State from the Union, and voted accordingly. Not quite all of the 45 who voted 'Convention' are disunionists. Every one of the 2,466 are Union men. We regarded the question as of infinitely greater moment than any on which we had ever before been called upon to vote, and large numbers went to the polls who often neglect the privilege of voting."

Many slaveowners in the upper South reacted nervously to the triumph of "the people." The recent furor about Hinton Helper's book *The Impending Crisis* had revealed a large reservoir of anxiety about the loyalty of nonslaveowning southern whites. The secession crisis rekindled such doubts. Observers noted with dismay "a disposition on the part of the *non* slave holders to back out." Pessimistic secessionists predicted that the convention elections would give "bright visions of coming glory" to Unionist leaders, whose political ambitions would inevitably lead them to sacrifice "the rights of the slaveholder" by creating "a party with supporters for the incoming administration here in our midst." Former Secretary of War John B. Floyd bitterly condemned the willingness of Virginia voters to submit "to the long continued aggressions of the North" and to value "peace and quiet" over an assertion of southern rights. "Far seeing and sagacious men begin already to see symptoms of a coming contest in Virginia for the emancipation of the slaves," he noted. Virginia had dealt "the Southern cause" a "fearful defeat." Historian Roy Franklin Nichols shrewdly assessed the motives of powerful southern Democrats: their "very real and often overlooked fear was loss of power at home" and a "shift of power to poorer farmers and artisans," who would reject the extreme proslavery politics of the 1850s.

A specific case nicely illustrates why upper South slaveowners could become alarmed about the nonslaveowning majority during the secession crisis. William S. Pettigrew, of Washington County, North Carolina, on Albemarle Sound—an eminent large slaveowner, conservative Whig, and heir to one of the great family names in his state—decided to run for the convention as a conditional Unionist, expecting that "he would unite the vote of all parties and not have the shadow of an opposition." Instead, local Unionists challenged Pettigrew by nominating incumbent state legislator Charles Latham. The latter "avowed himself as the poor man's candidate" and circulated rumors that Pettigrew, "the property-holders candidate," would not permit the poor to enter his house, "but would send a servant to meet them at the gate to ask their business." Latham and his friends also spread word that Pettigrew was a secret secessionist who had been urged to run for office by his brother in the South Carolina army. The whispering campaign, conducted behind Pettigrew's back on election day and the day before, gave him no chance to respond. Having aroused what Pettigrew considered "a furious agrarian spirit" in the upper part of the county, Latham handily carried the election, 396 to 276. The convention lost even more decisively, 418 to 238.

Hysterical Southern Rights fulminations about the rise of a Black Republican–abolitionist-submissionist and pro-Lincoln party in the upper South were based upon a kernel of truth. In Tennessee, for example, secessionists tried to woo nonslaveowners by insisting that a Republican president threatened their interests too. Secessionists contended that slavery prevented class antagonisms among whites, thereby making the social and economic status of nonslaveowning southerners enviably better than that of northern workers. Southern white artisans were better paid, secessionists asserted; they were treated with dignity and respect. Secessionists furthermore predicted that Tennessee's material prosperity would be enhanced by joining the Confederacy. The already well-established pattern of selling grain and livestock to the cotton states would expand, and Tennessee would become "the chief manufacturer for the South."

The voting results baffled and frustrated Southern Rights supporters. As they saw it, Unionist nonslaveowners had been misled and had failed to perceive their own best interests. Memphis secessionists, especially, complained bitterly that their city faced a miserable future if isolated economically from the planters of Alabama and Mississippi. The two secessionist newspapers in Memphis warned that economic calamity would "fall most heavily" on the "laboring men" and "artisans," who had "voted in a solid phalanx for the Union ticket." Memphis secessionists attempted to reassure Alabama and Mississippi customers that "the great mass of our property-holders" and "the solid, substantial and reliable business men" had voted secessionist and therefore deserved continued patronage. But the initial response from the deep South was not encouraging. One Alabama newspaper proposed an economic boycott of Tennessee products. Mississippi secessionists sneered that people in Tennessee were "too cowardly" to stand up for their rights and were "willing to be treated as inferiors—as serfs." The "dastard Tennesseeans," having submitted their necks "to a yoke worse than death to an honorable people," were "trotting like a cur to the beck and call of Lincoln." The *Memphis Avalanche* despondently agreed that Tennessee had been "plunged" into "disgrace" and "shame."

Warning that Unionists had resurrected the heresy of Hinton Helper, the *Avalanche* predicted editorially that "the germ of Abolitionism is budding in our midst and will soon blossom."

Secessionists may well have exaggerated the dangers of internal disunity, but the upper South in 1861 was no monolith and never had been. The survival of a competitive two-party system there institutionalized the means to challenge existing power relationships. Of course, no serious challenge occurred before 1861. But during the preceding decade, popular discontents had spilled decisively into the arena of party politics in the North. There, Know-Nothings and subsequently Republicans had incorporated most of the old Whig party and given the new grouping a politically appealing antiaristocratic ethos; Unionists in the upper South in early 1861 were moving in a parallel direction. The Union party thus threatened to disrupt the ground rules for political competition. For the first time nonslaveholders in the upper South would have found a political framework within which to develop a consciousness of separate interests. . . .

The pro-Union mobilization of nonslaveowners in the upper South certainly did not, by itself, signal an overt challenge to planter hegemony, let alone opposition to slavery. Most upper South Unionists were not trying to subvert the social order in the style of Hinton Helper. They were, however, rejecting the program of Southern Rights Democrats who claimed to champion the slave interest. They were also broadly hinting that they intended to extinguish the political power of the secession-tainted Democratic party at the first possible opportunity. And by refusing even to countenance a state convention, nonslaveowners in North Carolina and Tennessee defied the upper-class slaveowning leadership in the Union coalition itself, thereby alerting aspiring new political entrepreneurs to potential opportunity.

Most fundamentally, the February 1861 elections in Virginia, North Carolina, and Tennessee created a situation within each state very much like what had happened nationally in November 1860. A gnawing sense of political irrelevance was one of the principal sources of southern distress following Lincoln's election. By sweeping the North, Lincoln had accomplished the unprecedented feat of winning the presidency without needing southern support. That stunning demonstration of apparent southern political powerlessness in the Union probably fueled the secession movement as much as any other single factor. For the proud, assertive leaders of the Southern Rights wing of the Democratic party, Lincoln's election was too great a humiliation to bear. Even those who had private doubts about secession soon found that their core constituencies—the substantial slaveowning areas that voted for Breckinridge—demanded radical action.

But then, to the surprise and horror of the Southern Rights leaders in the upper South, the Unionist groundswell in January and February 1861 jeopardized their power at home just as Lincoln had jeopardized their power in the nation. The secession stigma suddenly crippled the Democratic parties of the upper South, the instruments through which Southern Rights leaders had long wielded power. To make matters worse, the challenge to the

Democrats came from new political entities, the emerging Union parties, whose most distinguishing characteristic was a base of support in which slaveowners were incidental and irrelevant. Union victories could easily have been achieved in all three states without the vote of a single slaveowner. Stung by Lincoln's victory, the self-designated custodians of southern interests found themselves facing a situation in the upper South which, to say the least, added insult to injury. And because nobody had demonstrated very conclusively how Lincoln might injure the South—his victory was more of an insult than an injury—the rise of Union party power and the eclipse of Democratic party power was perhaps the true injury.

All things considered, the Union party of 1861 contained in embryo something as close to the outer limits of change in the social basis of political power as could ever be expected from electoral politics. That was its strength and also its weakness. It threatened not only to thwart secession but also to overthrow the structure of power Southern Rights Democrats had amassed in the upper South, while isolating most slaveowners in a minority party. Though led for the most part by a comfortable elite of Whig politicians whose property-holding and social position better fit the secessionist profile, the Union party constituency came closer to being nonplanter, if not yet antiplanter, than any political coalition ever to hold power in a slaveowning state. To flourish, the Union party desperately needed to bring about a peaceful resolution to the crisis that had spawned it. Failing that, it was peculiarly vulnerable to disruption. Leading Unionists well knew that war could destroy their new party even more quickly than it had been formed.

Fear and Secession in South Carolina

STEVEN CHANNING

Secession was the product of logical reasoning within a framework of irrational perception. The party of Abraham Lincoln was inextricably identified with the spirit represented by John Brown, William Lloyd Garrison, and the furtive incendiary conceived to be lurking even then in the midst of the slaves. The election of Lincoln was at once the expression of the will of the Northern people to destroy slavery, and the key to that destruction. The constitutional election of a president seemed to many, North and South, an unjustifiable basis for secession. But it was believed that that election had signalled an acceptance of the antislavery dogmas by a clear majority of Northerners, and their intention to create the means to abolish slavery in America. Lincoln was elected, according to South Carolinians, on the platform of an "irrepressible conflict." This, as James Hammond believed, was "no mere political or ethical conflict, but a social conflict in which there is to be a war of races, to be waged at midnight with the torch, the knife & poison." Submission to the rule of the Republicans would be more than a dishonor. It would be an invitation to self-destruction. Implementing the power of the Presidency, and in time the rest of the Federal machinery, slavery would be legally abolished in time. What would that bring? Baptist minister James Furman thought he knew.

> Then every negro in South Carolina and every other Southern State will be his own master; nay, more than that, will be the equal of every one of you. If you are tame enough to submit, Abolition preachers will be at hand to consummate the marriage of your daughters to black husbands.

South Carolinians were repeatedly called on to explain the reasons for secession to their uncomprehending Northern friends and relatives. The description these Northerners received of the dominant new party—and of themselves—must have shocked them. "Who are these Black Republicans?" Sue Keitt, wife of the congressman, wrote to a woman in Philadelphia. "A motley throng of Sans culottes and Dames des Halles, Infidels and freelovers, interspersed by Bloomer women, fugitive slaves, and," worst of all, "amalgamationists." The Republican party was the incarnation of all the strange and frightening social and philosophical doctrines which were flourishing in free Northern society, doctrines which were not only alien but potentially disruptive to the allegedly more harmonious and conservative culture of the slave South. It has been suggested that slavery was merely a handle seized upon by extremists in both sections to wage a battle founded in far deeper antagonism. The election of 1860 proclaimed to the South that it must accept a new order of consolidation, industrialization, and democratization. According to this interpretation, secession spelled the rejection of these terms for the preservation of the Union by the old ruling classes.

There is no doubt that those who dominated political life in South Carolina feared the nature of the new social order rising in the North, and feared the party that stood for this order. "The concentration of absolute power in the hands of the North," Lawrence Keitt predicted, "will develop the wildest democracy ever seen on this earth—unless it shall have been matched in Paris in 1789—What of conservatism?—What of order?—What of social security or financial prosperity?" Many Carolinians believed that two separate and distinct civilizations existed in America in 1860, one marked by "the calculating coolness and narrow minded prejudices of the Puritans of New England in conflict with the high and generous impulses of the cavalier of Virginia and the Carolinas." By pecuniary choice and racial compulsion the South had "opted" for slavery and out of that decision had arisen a superstructure of social attitudes and institutions which marked the uniqueness of the slaveholding South.

Moreover, just as Northerners failed to comprehend the Southern view of the world, many Carolinians refused to admit that there was, or could be, any moral or idealistic quality in the antislavery pillar of the Republican party. Hammond affirmed that if the Republicans could have been defeated at the polls in 1860 and 1864, abolitionism would have been abandoned, for "no great party question can retain its vitality in this country that cannot make a President." A number of his fellow citizens declared that they too rejected the "mock humanity" of the Republicans. The issue was one of political power, they said, of controlling the national government, of party spoils. There was an almost pathetic element in this refusal to admit, and inability to see, the sincerity of the moral quality of abolitionism. Nevertheless, particularly in the private correspondence of unassuming soldiers and farmers, one can see frequent references to resistance to the threat of Northern despotism, to the need to protect certain vaguely understood "rights and privileges," often guaranteed by the Constitution. "I care nothing for the 'Peculiar institution' " claimed one former Unionist, "but I cant stand the idea of being domineered over by a set of Hypocritical scoundrels such as Sumner, Seward, Wilson, Hale, etc. etc."

Still, the conclusion is inescapable that the multiplicity of fears revolving around the maintenance of race controls for the Negro was not simply the prime concern of the people of South Carolina in their revolution, but was so very vast and frightening that it literally consumed the mass of lesser "causes" of secession which have inspired historians. James Hammond recognized the question of economic exploitation, and the fact that Southerners believed in Northern financial and commercial domination is clear. Nonetheless, the issue went virtually unnoticed in private exchanges throughout the year. Some leaders denounced what they thought was the injustice of the colonial status of the economic South, but this did not touch the hearts of the people, great and low. Attempts to organize such devices as direct steamship trade with Europe, use of homespun cloth, and conventions to promote Southern economic self-sufficiency were, like the more transparent plans for commercial non-intercourse, aimed at wielding the economic power of the region to gain political ends, specifically an end to agitation of the slavery question.

The glorious potential of an independent Southern nation held great emotional appeal for many, but no one was prepared to enter into the perilous business of nation building without some more basic incentive. South Carolina's spokesmen revelled in the contemplation of the political, economic, and social power of the South. They were eager to prove to the North and to the entire world that the South could establish a great nation in her own right. Yet who could fail to see that this was in part a rationalization for the strong desire to escape the moral obloquy heaped upon slaveholders by the North for so many years past; in part an element in the pro-slavery argument, which held a civilization based upon the peculiar institution to be the highest possible culture; and in part a function of the secession persuasion designed to attract and calm adherents to the cause.

As for the "dry prattle" about the constitution, the rights of minorities, and the like, there never was any confusion in the minds of most contemporaries that such arguments were masks for more fundamental emotional issues. Trescot welcomed the speeches of William Seward because they eschewed textual interpretations of the Constitution, and frankly posed the only true and relevant question: "Do the wants of this great Anglo Saxon race, the need of our glorious and progressing free white civilization require the abolition of negro slavery?" Charles Hutson, son of William F. Hutson, a Beaufort rice planter and a signer of the secession ordinance, phrased the matter more directly. Writing from an army camp near Mt. Vernon, Virginia, in September 1861, Hutson commented on a sermon which described the cause of secession as the defense of the noble right of self-government. "It is insulting to the English common sense of the race which governs here," the young soldier retorted, "to tell them they are battling for an abstract right common to all humanity. Every reflecting child will glance at the darkey who waits on him & laugh at the idea of such an abstract right." And when the family of planter John Berkeley Grimball was torn apart by the secession crisis, his son Louis bitterly denounced his sister for charging that South Carolina had willfully destroyed the Union. "What are you writing?" he gasped. "You speak as if we are the aggressors, and would dissolve the union in Blood shed upon a *mere abstract principle,* when the fact is we are oppressed and are contending for all that we hold most dear—our Property—our institutions—our Honor—Aye and our very lives!" To understand what the revolution was all about, he advised his sister to return home from the North, and become a slaveholder herself. So, writing on a broader canvass, Arthur Perroneau Hayne assured President Buchanan that his acquiescence in secession was a noble act of humanity to the white people of the South.

> Slavery with us is no abstraction—but a *great* and *vital fact.* Without it our every comfort would be taken from us. Our wives, our children, made unhappy—education, the light of knowledge—all *all* lost and our *people ruined for ever. Nothing short of separation from the Union can save us.*

The people of 1860 were usually frank in their language and clear in their thinking about the reasons for disunion. After the war, for many reasons men came forward to clothe the traumatic failure of the movement in the misty garments of high constitutional rights and sacred honor. Nevertheless, there were two "abstract rights" which were integral to secession, state sovereignty and property rights. No historian could surpass the discussion of these questions by wartime governor Andrew Gordon Magrath. From the fastness of his imprisonment in Fort Pulaski in 1865 Magrath looked back upon the cause of secession with a detachment which had not yet been colored by the sterilization and obfuscation of the post-war remembrance. There were tangential reasons for the revolution, Magrath allowed, but the central "motive power" was the belief that the ascendancy of the Republican party threatened to disturb their "right of property in slaves." To his credit, Magrath did see the rich variety of implications enmeshed in this property right. For those who did not own a slave, Lincoln's election implied that they might never be able to purchase that essential key to social and economic elevation. In addition, the former jurist understood that the people of the antebellum South conceived slavery to be the basis of stability for their social order, the foundation of their economy, and the source of their moral and cultural superiority. State sovereignty was an issue only because the retreat to the inviolability of state's rights had always been a refuge for those fearful of a challenge to their property. Certainly, the "right of property in slaves" is closer to the heart of the problem than "fear of the antislavery movement," or similar propositions which raise more questions than they answer.

Mid-nineteenth century Americans lived in an age of romanticism. Men had fought for lesser glories than independence and Southern nationalism; and once the terrible momentum was begun, who could say for certain what myths, compulsions, and desires drove men on into revolution and civil war. But somewhere in the intellectual hiatus of the war the clear and concrete understanding of the cause of it all, an understanding shared by those who joined to tear away from the Union, was lost. For the people of South Carolina perpetuation of the Union beyond 1860 meant the steady and irresistible destruction of slavery, which was the first and last principle of life in that society, the only conceivable pattern of essential race control. Perpetuation of the Union, according to Senator Hammond, meant servile insurrection, and ultimately abolition. "We dissolve the Union to prevent it," he told a Northerner in 1861, "and [we] believe, I believe it will do it." Secession was a revolution of passion, and the passion was fear.

> Here we have in charge the solution of the greatest problem of the ages. We are here two races—white and black—now both equally American, holding each other in the closest embrace and utterly unable to extricate ourselves from it. A problem so difficult, so complicated, and so momentous never was placed in charge of any portion of Mankind. And on its solution rests our all.

The nation was led into war in 1861 by the secession of the lower South, not by the desire of the Northern people either to end slavery or bring equality to the Negro. Subsequent generations of Americans came to condemn the racist fears and logic which had motivated that secession, yet the experience of our own time painfully suggests that it was easy to censure racism, but more difficult to obliterate it. If the history of race relations in the United States is an accurate measure, we can assume that there will not and perhaps cannot be a genuine reconciliation between the races, that white and black will never achieve equality because of the fears of the one, and their oppression of the other. But human experience also indicates the possibility of transcending history, for history is neither a lawgiver nor an impenetrable obstacle. As Hammond could not foresee, the solution must and will go on.

⋏ *F U R T H E R   R E A D I N G*

Thomas B. Alexander, *Sectional Stress and Party Strength* (1967)
William F. Barney, *The Secessionist Impulse* (1974)
Randolph B. Campbell, *An Empire for Slavery: The Peculiar Institution in Texas, 1821–1865* (1989)
Steven A. Channing, *A Crisis of Fear: Secession in South Carolina* (1970)

William J. Cooper, Jr., *The South and the Politics of Slavery, 1828–1856* (1978)
Avery O. Craven, *The Growth of Southern Nationalism, 1848–1861* (1953)
Daniel W. Crofts, *Reluctant Confederates: Upper South Unionists in the Secession Crisis* (1989)
Drew G. Faust, *A Sacred Circle: The Dilemma of the Intellectual in the Old South* (1978)
Lacy K. Ford, Jr., *Origins of Southern Radicalism: The South Carolina Upcountry, 1800–1860* (1988)
Eugene D. Genovese, *The Political Economy of Slavery* (1967)
Michael F. Holt, *The Political Crisis of the 1850s* (1978)
Michael P. Johnson, *Toward a Patriarchal Republic: The Secession of Georgia* (1977)
Marc W. Kruman, *Parties and Politics in North Carolina, 1836–1865* (1983)
Ernest M. Lander, Jr., *Reluctant Imperialists: Calhoun, the South Carolinians, and the Mexican War* (1980)
Robert E. May, *John A. Quitman* (1985)
——, *The Southern Dream of a Caribbean Empire, 1854–1861* (1973)
John Niven, *John C. Calhoun and the Price of Union* (1988)
David M. Potter, *The Impending Crisis, 1848–1861* (1976)
——, *The South and the Sectional Conflict* (1968)
James L. Roark, *Masters Without Slaves* (1977)
Thomas E. Schott, *Alexander H. Stephens of Georgia* (1988)
Charles S. Sydnor, *The Development of Southern Sectionalism, 1819–1848* (1948)
J. Mills Thornton III, *Politics and Power in a Slave Society* (1978)
Ralph Wooster, *The Secession Conventions of the South* (1962)
Gavin Wright, *The Political Economy of the Cotton South* (1978)

CHAPTER
12

The Confederate Experience

✝

The Civil War was a massive event, deeply affecting the entire nation. In the South it brought about profound changes. The fact that most of the war's battles took place on southern soil was only a contributing factor to change. More fundamental was the need to organize and mobilize the South's resources to fight a contest of unprecedented scale. The South had seceded in order to avoid change; the realities of war compelled it to make and accept sweeping transformations in almost all areas of life.

Such changes occasioned intense conflict. Controversies raged over such issues as the importance of state rights versus the need for an effective central government, and the sanctity of slavery versus the necessity of making better use of southern blacks in the war effort. Conflicts between nonslaveholders and slaveholders, and between rich and poor, reached unaccustomed proportions, and hunger and suffering spread extensively among the civilian population.

These striking changes and struggles have also produced controversies among the historians striving to understand them. How deeply did change affect the South, and how much was it accepted or resisted? How strong was a spirit of Confederate nationalism that could inspirit southerners to fight on to independence? What were the sources of unity or division in the society and the political system? What did the Confederate debate on emancipation signify? Why did the Confederacy fail?

✝ *D O C U M E N T S*

Governor Joseph E. Brown of Georgia was one of the most outspoken among many state leaders who criticized the Confederate administration in Richmond, Virginia, for taking too much power into its hands and threatening state rights. Brown's letter to President Jefferson Davis, contained in the first document, is an example of his frequent protests and indicates the seriousness of these confrontations. The two letters in the second selection, one to a Georgia newspaper and the other from a North Carolina private to his state's governor, exemplify another kind of discontent—that of nonslaveholders. Injustices perceived by ordinary soldiers and concerns about the welfare of their families threatened the ability of the Confederacy to keep troops in the field. Letters to the Confederate secretary of war, and the endorsements, or comments, added to them by Assistant Secretary of War John A. Campbell, which appear in the third selection, testify to the seriousness of the problems of desertion and resistance to Confederate authority. The excerpts in the fourth selection from the diaries and letters of southern women suggest the privations and hardship that gripped the homefront. Suffering and need drove them to take actions that affected Confederate strength. Among the public issues that caused division, none was more prominent than the debate, evident in the last selection, over the Davis administration's proposal to enlist slaves as soldiers and subsequently reward them for their service with emancipation. Robert E. Lee's letters to a Confederate congressman make the case for the administration's proposal. Editorials from the *Richmond Examiner* and the *Charleston Mercury* suggest the nature of the opposition, which prominent politician Howell Cobb of Georgia expressed strongly.

Joseph E. Brown Attacks Conscription, 1862

Canton, Ga., Oct. 18, 1862.

His Excellency Jefferson Davis:

Dear Sir: The act of Congress passed at its late session extending the Conscription Act, unlike its predecessor, of which it is amendatory, gives you power, in certain contingencies, of the happening of which you must be the judge, to suspend its operation, and accept troops from the States under any of the former acts upon that subject. By former acts you were authorized to accept troops from the States organized into companies, battalions and regiments. The Conscription Act of 16th April last, repealed these acts, but the late act revives them when you suspend it.

For the reasons then given, I entered my protest against the first conscription act on account of its unconstitutionality, and refused to permit the enrollment of any State officer, civil or military, who was necessary to the integrity of the State government. But on account of the emergencies of the country, growing out of the neglect of the Confederate authorities to call upon the States for a sufficient amount of additional force to supply the places of the twelve months' troops, and on account of the repeal of the formal laws upon that subject having, for the time, placed it out of your power to accept troops organized by the States in the constitutional mode, I interposed no active resistance to the enrollment of persons in this State between 18 and 35, who were not officers necessary to the maintenance of the government of the State.

The first Conscription Act took from the State only part of her military force. She retained her officers and all her militia between 35 and 45. Her military organization was neither disbanded nor destroyed. She had permitted a heavy draft to be made upon it, without Constitutional authority, rather than her fidelity to our cause should be questioned, or the enemy should gain any advantage growing out of what her authorities might consider unwise councils. But she still retained an organization subject to the command of her constituted authorities, which she could use for the protection of her public property, the execution of her laws, the repulsion of invasion, or the suppression of servile insurrection which our insidious foe now proclaims to the world that it is his intention to incite, which if done may result in an indiscriminate massacre of helpless women and children.

At this critical period in our public affairs, when it is absolutely necessary that each State keep an *organization* for home protection, Congress, with your sanction, has extended the Conscription Act to embrace all between 35 and 45 subject to military duty, giving you the power to suspend the Act as above stated. If you refuse to exercise this power, and are permitted to take all between 35 and 45 as conscripts, you *disband and destroy* all military organization in this State, and leave her people utterly powerless to protect their own families even against their own slaves. Not only so, but you deny to those between 35 and 45 a privilege of electing the officers to command them, to which, under the Constitution of the Confederacy and the laws of this State, they are clearly entitled, which has been allowed to other troops from the State, and was to a limited extent allowed even to those between 18 and 35 under the Act of 16th of April, as that Act did allow them thirty days within which to volunteer under such officers as they might select, who chanced at the time to have commissions from the War Department to raise regiments.

If you deny this rightful privilege to those between 35 and 45, and refuse to accept them as *volunteers* with officers selected by them in accordance with the laws of their State, and attempt to compel them to enter the service as *conscripts,* my opinion is, your orders will only be obeyed by many of them when backed by an armed force which they have no power to resist. . . .

The late act of Congress, if executed in this State, not only does gross injustice to a large class of her citizens, utterly destroys all State military organizations, and encroaches upon the reserved rights of the State, but strikes down her sovereignty at a single blow, and tears from her the right arm of strength, by which she alone can maintain her existence, and protect those most dear to her and most dependent upon her. The representatives of the people will meet in General Assembly on the 6th day of next month, and I feel that I should be recreant to the high trust reposed in me, were I to permit the virtual destruction of the government of the State, before they shall have had time to convene, deliberate and act.

Referring, in connection with the considerations above mentioned, to our former correspondence, for the reasons which satisfy my mind beyond doubt of the unconstitutionality of the conscription acts; and to the fact that a Judge of this State, of great ability, in a case regularly brought before him in his judicial capacity, has pronounced the law unconstitutional; and to the further fact that Congress has lately passed an additional act authorizing you to suspend the privilege of the writ of habeas corpus, doubtless with a view of denying to the judiciary in this very case the exercise of its constitutional functions, for the protection of personal liberty, I can no longer avoid the responsibility of discharging a duty which I owe to the people of this State, by informing you that I cannot permit the enrollment of conscripts, under the late act of Congress entitled "An act to amend the act further to provide for the common defence," until the General Assembly of this State shall have convened and taken action in the premises.

The plea of necessity set up for conscription last spring, when I withheld active resistance to a heavy drain upon the military organization of the State under the first conscription act, cannot be pleaded, after the brilliant successes of our gallant armies during the summer and fall campaign, which have been achieved by troops who entered the service, not as conscripts but as volunteers. If more troops are needed to meet coming emergencies, call upon the State, and you shall have them as *volunteers* much more rapidly than your enrolling officers can drag *conscripts,* like slaves, "in chains," to camps of instruction. And who that is not blinded by prejudice or ambition, can doubt that they will be much more effective as volunteers than as conscripts? The volunteer enters the service of his own free will. He regards the war as much his own as the government's war, and is ready, if need be, to offer his life a willing sacrifice upon his country's altar. Hence it is that our *volunteer armies* have been invincible when contending against vastly superior numbers with every advantage which the best equipments and supplies can afford. Not so with the conscript. He may be as ready as any citizen of the State to volunteer, if permitted to enjoy the constitutional rights which have been allowed to others, in the choice of his officers and associates. But if these are denied him, and he is seized like a serf and hurried into an association repulsive to his feelings, and placed under officers in whom he has no confidence, he then feels that this is the Government's war, not his; that he is the mere instrument of arbitrary power, and that he is no longer laboring to establish constitutional liberty, but to build up a military despotism for its ultimate but certain overthrow. Georgians will never refuse to volunteer as long as there is an enemy upon our soil, and a call for their services. But if I mistake not the signs of the times, they will require the government to respect their constitutional rights.

Surely no just reason exists why you should refuse to accept volunteers when tendered, and insist on replenishing your armies by conscription and coercion of free-men.

The question then is, not whether you shall have Georgia's quota of troops, for they are freely offered—*tendered in advance*—but it is whether you shall accept them when tendered as volunteers, organized as the Constitution and laws direct, or shall, when the decision is left with you, insist on rejecting volunteers and dragging the free citizen of this State into your armies as conscripts. No act of the government of the United States prior to the secession of Georgia struck a blow at constitutional liberty, so fell, as has been stricken by the conscription acts. The people of this State had ample cause, however, to justify their separation from the old government. They acted cooly and deliberately in view of all the responsibilities, and they stand ready to day to sustain their action, at all hazards; and to resist submission to the Lincoln government, and the reconstruction of the old Union, to the expenditure of their last dollar and the sacrifice of their last life. Having entered into the revolution freemen, they intend to emerge from it freemen. And if I mistake not the character of the sons, judged by the action of their fathers against Federal encroachments under Jackson, Troup, and Gilmer, respectively, as executive officers, they will refuse to yield their sovereignty to usurpation, and will require the government, which is the common agent of all the States, to move within the sphere assigned it by the constitution.

Very respectfully, your obedient servant,

JOSEPH E. BROWN.

Nonslaveholders Protest Wartime Inequities, 1861, 1863

Letter to the Candidates of Floyd County

Rome (Georgia) Weekly Courier, *September 27, 1861*

Please give your views concerning our present condition—about the war, and the cause of said war, the Stay Law, and our present condition of taxation for the support of the war. Is it right that the poor man should be taxed for the support of the war, when the war was brought about on the slave question, and the slave at home accumulating for the benefit of his master, and the poor man's farm left uncultivated, and a chance for his wife to be a widow, and his children orphans? Now, in justice, would it not be right to levy a direct tax on that species of property that brought about the war, to support it?

Now, we have many candidates out, will they give their views on these questions?

MANY ANXIOUS TO HEAR.

Letter from Confederate Soldier to Governor Zebulon Vance of North Carolina

Fayetteville NC 27th Feb/63

Gov Vance

Dr Sir

Please pardon the liberty which a poor soldier takes in thus addressing you as when he *volunteered* he left a wife with four children to go to fight for his country. He cheerfully made the sacrifices thinking that the Govt. would protect his family, and keep them from starvation. In this he has been disappointed for the Govt. has made a distinction between the rich man (who had something to fight for) and the poor man who fights for that he never will have. The exemption of the owners of 20 negroes & the allowing of substitutes clearly proves it. Healthy and active men who have furnished substitutes are grinding the poor by speculation while their substitutes have been discharged after a month's service as being too old or as invalids. By taking too many men from their farms they have not left enough to cultivate the land thus making a scarcity of provisions and this with unrestrained speculation has put provs. up in this market as follows Meal $4 to 5 per Bus, flour $50 to 60 per Brl, Lard 70¢ per lb by the brl, Bacon 75¢ per lb by the load and every thing else in proportion.

Now Govr. do tell me how we poor soldiers who are fighting for the "rich mans negro" can support our families at $11 per month? How can the poor live? I dread to see summer as I am fearful there will be much suffering and probably many deaths from starvation. They are suffering now. A poor little factory girl begged for a piece of bread the other day & said she had not had anything to eat since the day before when she eat a small piece of Bread for her Breakfast.

I am fearful we will have a revolution unless something is done as the majority of our soldiers are poor men with families who say they are tired of the rich mans war & poor mans fight, they wish to get to their families & fully believe some settlement could be made were it not that our authorities have made up their minds to prosecute the war regardless of all suffering since they receive large pay & they and their families are kept from suffering & exposure and can have their own ends served. There is great dissatisfaction in the army and as a mans first duty is to provide for his own household the soldiers wont be imposed upon much longer. If we hear our families are suffering & apply for a furlough to go to them we are denied & if we go without authority we are arrested & punished as deserters. Besides not being able to get provs. the factories wont let us have cloth for love or money & are charging much over 75 per ct profit. Now Govr you are looked upon as the soldiers friend and you know something of his trials & exposures by experience. But you do not know how it is to be a poor man serving your country faithfully while your family are crying for bread because those who are enjoying their property for which you are fighting are charging such high prices for provs & the necessaries of life and still holding on for higher prices.

I would also request in behalf of the soldiers generally (for I know it is popular with the army) for you to instruct our representatives in Congress to introduce a resolution as follows. That all single young men now occupying salaried positions as Clerks Conductors or Messengers in the Depts of Govt & State & Rail Road & Express Cos. be discharged immediately & sent into the services and their places filled by married men & men of families who are competent to fill the positions.

Such a move as this would enable many a poor man to support his wife & family & prevent them from becoming public charges & at the same time it would fill our ranks with a very large no. of young active men who have no one dependent upon them for a support and who are shirking service. This would be very acceptable to the army generally. Our soldiers cant understand why so many young magistrates are permitted to remain at home and especially so many militia officers there being no militia and two sets of officers.

> Respy your obt svt
> O. GODDIN
> Private Co D. 51st Regt. N.C.T.
> on detached service

The Confederacy Struggles with Desertion and Disaffection, 1863

STATE OF NORTH CAROLINA, EXECUTIVE DEPT.,
Raleigh, July 25, 1863

Hon. J. A. SEDDON,
Secretary of War:
DEAR SIR: A large number of deserters, say 1,200, are in the mountains and inaccessible wilds of the west. I have found it impossible to get them out, and they are plundering and robbing the people. Through their friends they have made me propositions to come out and enlist for defense of this State alone. Shall I accept it? The effect on the Army might be injurious, but they can never otherwise be made of service or kept from devastating the country. If you advise favorably, I think I can get at least 1,000 effective men. Please answer soon.
Very respectfully, your obedient servant,

Z. B. VANCE.

[Indorsement.]

SECRETARY OF WAR:
There is a great necessity for some practical dealing with the crime of desertion, if so general a habit is to be considered a crime.
There are from 50,000 to 100,000 men who are in some form or other evading duty. Probably there are 40,000 or 50,000 of absentees without leave. The accommodation of the Department to the necessity of the case is, in my judgment, the best policy. To allow those who belong to other organizations than those in which they enlisted to remain, to allow all persons not in the Army to connect themselves with new organizations, to pronounce a general amnesty, and to make a new departure seems to me a measure of prudence under the existing circumstances. I notice that desertion during the French Revolution was a great source of complaint. There were at one time 12,000 on furlough, and there had been ten times that number of desertions.

[J. A. CAMPBELL.]

OFFICE OF INSPECTOR OF CONSCRIPTION,
Salisbury, N. C., September 2, 1863.

Col. J. S. PRESTON,
Superintendent of Conscription:
SIR: When the conscript service was organized the direction that among its duties should be embraced that of collecting and forwarding deserters and skulkers by the use of force was doubtless based on the supposition that such characters would be found lurking about singly, unarmed, acting in no concert, and supported by no local public opinion or party. Even for such work our means at command have been inadequate in many parts of the country, and whatever auxiliary force time may prove to be available under the special efforts indicated in my letter of July———, approved and adopted by the War Department, cannot be expected to accomplish more than to meet the condition of things above described.
The utter inadequacy now of any force that we can command without potential aid from armies in the field will become apparent when it is realized that desertion has assumed (in some regions, especially the central and

western portions of this State) a very different and more formidable shape and development than could have been anticipated. It is difficult to arrive at any exact statistics on the subject. The unquestionable facts are these: Deserters now leave the Army with arms and ammunition in hand. They act in concert to force by superior numbers a passage against bridge or ferry guards, if such are encountered. Arriving at their selected localities of refuge, they organize in bands variously estimated at from fifty up to hundreds at various points. These estimates are perhaps exaggerated in some cases. The patrols sent out from the conscript guard and bringing back a few prisoners each report that they have only captured these by surprise, and have been compelled to make good their retreat in returning by circuitous routes to avoid arrangements made to intercept them by superior force. His Excellency Governor Vance credits official information received by him, that in Cherokee County a large body of deserters (with whom I class also those in resistance to conscription) have assumed a sort of military occupation, taking a town, and that in Wilkes County they are organized, drilling regularly, and intrenched in a camp to the number of 500. Indeed, the whole number of deserters in the latter county is said to be much larger. The reports of our patrols indicate 300 or 400 organized in Randolph County, and they are said to be in large numbers in Catawba and Yadkin, and not a few in the patriotic county of Iredell. These men are not only determined to kill in avoiding apprehension (having just put to death yet another of our enrolling officers), but their esprit de corps extends to killing in revenge as well as in prevention of the capture of each other. So far they seem to have had no trouble for subsistence. While the disaffected feed them from sympathy, the loyal do so from fear. The latter class (and the militia) are afraid to aid the conscript service lest they draw revenge upon themselves and their property.

The present quiet of such lawless characters of course cannot be expected to continue, and the people look for a reign of marauding and terror, protection against which is loudly called for. Letters are being sent to the Army stimulating desertion and inviting the men home, promising them aid and comforts. County meetings are declaring in the same spirit and to hold back conscripts. As desertion spreads and enjoys impunity, in the same proportion do the enrolled conscripts hang back from reporting where there is not force enough to compel them, and the more dangerous and difficult becomes the position of our enrolling officers. All this trouble is of very rapid, recent growth, and is intimately connected with—indeed, mainly originates in and has been fostered by—the newly developed but active intrigues of political malcontents, having the Raleigh Standard for their leader, and, it is said, a majority in the capital itself. The resolutions of the several county meetings, central and western, have evidently issued from the same mint, the common stamp being that North Carolina has not received due justice or credit, that she has done more than her share, and that her people ought to contribute no further. I allude to the political aspect only to show that there is danger of marked political division and something like civil war if the military evils reported be not at once met by strong measures of military repression. Such appears the calm opinion, without panic, of loyal and substantial men, and such are my own impressions from observation. They all think the evil is spreading, and such are likely to find themselves in a bad position in some regions—for the balance of physical force is on the wrong side, the loyal having contributed most freely to the Army, even their sons still in early boyhood and not liable to serve. So far it does not appear that men of political weight have come forward publicly to any great extent to meet the intriguing demagogues on their own arena and prevent the ignorant masses from following their lead in ovine style. A reference to the faithful reports of Colonel Mallett, the vigilant State commander of conscripts, will show that he has been anticipating such evils, though their rapid increase has surpassed expectation.

In considering the remedies to be applied but two appear feasible of sufficient promptness to be effective—the one consisting of detachments of troops by the nearest local commanders, the other in like detachments from the larger armies depleted by desertion and demanding re-enforcement.

The nearest local commanders on whom I have the authority of the Secretary of War to call for aid are General Whiting (whose troops are mainly about Weldon and Wilmington, at a great distance for detachment to the districts where most needed) and Major-General Buckner, if he be still posted near the western frontier of this State. To the former general I have written that, learning how largely he has detached to Charleston, I did not suppose it feasible now to procure any force from him, but urgently requested him to aid the conscript service by designating a military commandant to take post at Raleigh, and recommended that our present State commandant of conscripts be clothed with the additional authority. To General Buckner I will write a representation of the state of things as soon as I can procure official and authentic information after arriving at Morganton or Asheville. I have conversed with Governor Vance as commander of the militia and home guards organized by State legislation. Of the first class of force he remarked that it had been practically well-nigh absorbed by the new levy, and at all events he did not consider it well adapted for the sort of work now demanded. In regard to the second, he stated that its organization had proceeded slowly, and that what had been accomplished was in counties other than those where the service in question is required. Hence, I have received from him the impression that although he is earnest in the purpose of aid, he does not expect to be able to furnish it to any great extent yet awhile. I hope to meet His Excellency again at Asheville. The State Legislature has passed a law against harboring deserters, which may help us somewhat, though doubt is expressed if its terms are broad enough for practical effect. I will communicate it hereafter. Your attention is invited to the inclosed proclamation addressed to the public at large by Colonel Mallett at my instance. He had already instructed his subordinates in a like sense. All other details of our efforts to invigorate the conscript service here I reserve for a future report. Assuming that it is of vital import to crush out without the least delay the evils I have described as threatening to develop indefinitely, I am led by the foregoing exhaustive discussion to tender boldly, though reluctantly, an unpalatable conclusion. It is that the sort of success demanded by the crisis can only be attained by a prompt detachment of effective force (say two or three selected regiments of fidelity) from the main army which suffers most from desertion and evasion of service, and which it is to be hoped can best spare the remedial agencies. Such a force should proceed to occupy the infected districts, surround the traitors, bring the disloyal to punishment, fortify the loyal, and decide the wavering. The adoption of this plan, if practicable, may be rendered more palatable by the reflection that its rejection will probably involve a loss of numbers at least equal to those proposed to be detached under a system which would secure not only their own return, but that of large re-enforcements in, say, probably five or six weeks.

I am, sir, very respectfully, your obedient servant,

GEO. W. LAY,
Lieutenant-Colonel and Inspector.

P.S.—I have advised Colonel Mallett not to send away for the present any conscripts whose fidelity may be trusted for the home service.

BUREAU OF CONSCRIPTION,
Richmond, Va., September 7, 1863.

Respectfully referred to the War Department for information.   Please order the paper returned.

JNO. S. PRESTON,
Colonel and Superintendent.

[Second indorsement.]

SECRETARY OF WAR:

The condition of things in the mountain districts of North Carolina, South Carolina, Georgia, and Alabama menaces the existence of the Confederacy as fatally as either of the armies of the United States.   This report does not state the danger as so imminent as it has been stated in a number of letters that have been received at this Department.

Respectfully submitted.

J. A. CAMPBELL,
Assistant Secretary of War.

[Third indorsement.]

SEPTEMBER 8, 1863.

Respectfully submitted for the information of the President.

J. A. SEDDON,
Secretary of War.

[Fourth indorsement.]

SECRETARY OF WAR:

The orders to Brigadier-General Hoke anticipate the proposed remedy. It might be advantageous to correspond with Governor Vance and inform him of the traitorous efforts made to induce desertion and the agents at work to effect it.

J. D.

Women React to Suffering at Home, 1862–1864

Excerpts from the Diary of Margaret Junkin Preston

April 3d, 1862: . . .

Darkness seems gathering over the Southern land; disaster follows disaster; where is it all to end? My very soul is sick of carnage. I loathe the word—*War*. It is destroying and paralyzing all before it. Our schools are closed—all the able-bodied men gone—stores shut up, or only here and there one open; goods not to be bought, or so exorbitant that we are obliged to do without. I actually dressed my baby all winter in calico dresses made out of the lining of an old dressing-gown; and G. in clothes concocted out of old castaways. As to myself, I rigidly abstained from getting a single article of dress in the entire past year, except shoes and stockings. Calico is not to be had; a few pieces had been offered at 40 cents per yard. Coarse, unbleached cottons are very occasionally to be met with, and are caught up eagerly at 40 cents per yard. Such material as we used to give ninepence for (common blue twill) is a bargain now at 40 cents, and then of a very inferior quality. Soda, if to be had at all, is 75 cents per lb. Coffee is not to be bought. We have some on hand, and for eight months have drunk a poor mixture, half wheat, half coffee. Many persons have nothing but wheat or rye.

These are some of the *very trifling* effects of this horrid and senseless war. Just now I am bound down under the apprehension of having my husband again enter the service; and if he goes, he says he will not return until the war closes, if indeed he come back alive. May God's providence interpose to prevent his going! His presence is surely needed at home; his hands are taken away by the militia draught, and he has almost despaired of having his farms cultivated this year. His overseer is draughted, and will have to go, unless the plea of sickness will avail to release him, as he has been seriously unwell. The [Virginia Military] Institute is full, two hundred and fifty cadets being in it; but they may disperse at any time, so uncertain is the tenure of everything now. The College [Washington College] has five students; boys too young to enter the army.

April 10th: Ground white with snow; no mails still: Mr. P. consents to postpone his going to the army, till there is a more decided change in George (an ill child). How this unnatural war affects everything! Mr. P. asks me for some old pants of Willy's or Randolph's, for a boy at the farm. I tell him that on them I am relying wholly to clothe John and George this summer.

August 2d: . . . What straits war reduces us to! I carried a lb. or so of sugar and coffee to Sister Agnes lest she should not have any, and she gave me a great treasure—a *pound of soda!* When it can be had, it is $1.25 per lb.

August 23d: . . . Willy Preston has been in a battle (Cedar Run), and we hear behaved with remarkable gallantry—rallied a disorganized regiment, or rather parts of many companies, and with a lieutenant led them to the charge.

Sept. 3d: . . . Yesterday asked the price of a calico dress; "Fifteen dollars and sixty cents!" Tea is $20. per lb. A merchant told me he gave $50. for a pound of sewing silk! The other day our sister, Mrs. Cocke, purchased 5 gallons of whiskey, for which, by way of favor, she only paid $50.! It is selling for $15. per gallon. Very coarse unbleached cotton (ten cent cotton) I was asked 75 cts. for yesterday. Eight dollars a pair for servants' coarse shoes. Mr. P. paid $11. for a pair for Willy. These prices will do to wonder over after a while.

10 *o'clock P. M.* Little did I think, when I wrote the above, that such sorrow would overtake this family so soon! News came this afternoon of the late fearful fight on Manassas Plains, and of Willy Preston *being mortally wounded*—in the opinion of the surgeons! His Father was not at home, and did not hear the news for some time. Oh! the anguish of the father-heart! This evening he has gone to Staunton; will travel all night in order to take the cars tomorrow morning. I am afraid to go to bed, lest I be roused by some messenger of evil tidings, or (terrible to dread) the possible arrival of the dear boy—dead! Father in Heaven! Be merciful to us, and spare us this bitterness!

Sept. 4th: The worst has happened—our fearful suspense is over: Willy, the gentle, tender-hearted, brave boy, lies in a soldier's grave on the Plains of Manassas! This has been a day of weeping and of woe to this household. I did not know how I loved the dear boy. My heart is wrung with grief to think that his sweet face, his genial smile, his sympathetic heart are gone. My eyes ache with weeping. But what is the loss to me, compared to the loss to his Father, his sisters, his brothers! Oh! his precious stricken Father! God support him to bear the blow! The carriage has returned, bringing me a note from Mr. P. saying he had heard there was faint hope. Alas! the beloved son has been five days in his grave. My poor husband! Oh! if he were only here, to groan out his anguish on my bosom. I can't write more.

Letter of Martha Revis to Her Husband

Marshall, Madison County, North
Carolina
July 20 [?], 1863

H. W. Revis:

Dear Husband: I seat myself to drop you a few lines to let you know that me and Sally is well as common, and I hope these few lines will come to hand and find you well and doing well. I have no news to write to you at this, only I am done laying by my corn. I worked it all four times. My wheat is good; my oats is good. I haven't got my wheat stacked yet. My oats I have got a part of them cut, and Tom Hunter and John Roberts is cutting to-day. They will git them cut to-day.

I got the first letter yesterday that I have received from you since you left. I got five from you yesterday; they all come together. This is the first one I have wrote, for I didn't know where to write to you. You said you hadn't anything to eat. I wish you was here to get some beans for dinner. I have plenty to eat as yet. I haven't saw any of your pap's folks since you left home. The people is generally well hereat. The people is all turning to Union here since the Yankees has got Vicksburg. I want you to come home as soon as you can after you git this letter. Jane Elkins is living with me yet. That is all I can think of, only I want you to come home the worst that I ever did. The conscripts is all at home yet, and I don't know what they will do with them. The folks is leaving here, and going North as fast as they can, so I will close.

Your wife, till death,

MARTHA REVIS

Petition from Women of Miller County, Georgia, to Secretary of War James Seddon and President Jefferson Davis, September 8, 1863

Our crops is limited and so short . . . cannot reach the first day of march next . . . our fencing is unanamosly allmost decayed . . . But little [illegible] of any sort to Rescue us and our children from a unanamus starveation. . . . We can seldom find [bacon] for non has got But those that are exzempt from service by office holding and old age and they have no humane feel-inging nor patraotic prinsables. . . . An allwise god ho is slow to anger and full of grace and murcy and without Respect of persons and full of love and charity that he will send down his fury and judgement in a very grate manar [on] all those our leading men and those that are in power ef thare is no more favors shone to those the mothers and wives and of those hwo in poverty has with patrootism stood the fence Battles . . . I tell you that with out som grate and speadly alterating in the conduckting of afares in this our little nation god will frown on it and that speadly.

Plea by Mrs. R. H. Hinolin of Clarksville, Virginia, to Secretary of War James Seddon, October 27, 1864

I have felt so dieply the wrongs and sufferings of our people . . . the wail of the widows and orphans, the poor and oppressed . . . that I can stand it no longer, and am induced to say to you that if you will grant my Husband a 60 day furlough, I will go on to Washington and see if I can penetrate those hard hearts. Do you believe a *Lady* could do anything with them? . . .

My own deplorable condition will cause me to exhaust every effort in paving the way to peace.

Letter from Nancy Mangum to Governor Zebulon Vance of North Carolina

Mcleanesville N c
Aprile 9th 1863

Gov Vance

I have threatend for some time to write you a letter—a crowd of we Poor wemen went to Greenesborough yesterday for something to eat as we had not a mouthful meet nor bread in my house what did they do but put us in gail Jim Slone, Linsey Hilleshemer and several others I will not mention—thes are the one that put us to gail in plase of gieving us aney thing to eat and I had to com hom without aneything—I have 6 little children and my husband in the armey and what am I to do Slone wont let we Poor wemen have thread when he has it we know he has evry thing plenty he say he has not got it to spair when we go but just let thes big men go they can git it withou aney trouble. when we go for aney thing they will not hardley notis us Harper Linsey has money for the Poor weman it was put in his handes for the Poor weman I have not got one sent of it yet since my husband has bin gon he has bin gon most 2 years I have went to Linsey for money he told me to go to a nother man and he said . . . he could not do nothing for me—Lindsey would grumble at him for him takeing such a big bil if you dont take thes yankys a way from greenesborough we wemen will write for our husbans to come . . . home and help us we cant stand it the way they are treating us they charge $11.00 Per bunch for their thread and $2.50 for their calico—They threatend to shoot us and drawed their pistols over us that is hard.

Jim Slone sid he would feed we poor weman on dog meet and Roten egges. I tel you if you dont put Slone and Linsey out of offis the Poor weman will perish for the want of something to eat my brother sent home for some shirtes I went to Slone for bunch coten he would not let me have one thread and he had plenty their is bound to be a fammon if I dont git help soon.

if their ant beter better times in greenesborough the waar will end in in that plase The young men has runaway from newburn and come to this plase about to take the country they are speclating evry day their is old Ed. Holt where has a factory on alamance he has maid his Creiges [?] if this war holds on 2 years longer he would own all of alamance county he has cloth and thread and wont let no body have it without wheat or Corn or meet what am I to do I cant git it to eat—three and four men gatherd hold of one woman and took thir armes away from them and led them all up to gail—you have no ide how the men in Greenesborough has treated we poor weman we have to pay $3.50 per bushel for goverment corn and half measure and have the exact change or dont git the corn for the meel we dont git nun they seling sugar sugar at $1.50 per pound and black peper $9.00 per pound and say it not half as much as a soldier wife ought to pay and asking $50.00 for a barel of flour so no more

Yours very
Respectfuly
NANCY MANGUM

The Confederacy Debates Emancipation, 1865

Robert E. Lee to Congressman Ethelbert Barksdale, February 18, 1865

I have the honor to acknowledge the receipt of your letter of the 12th instant [February], with reference to the employment of negroes as soldiers. I think the measure not only expedient but necessary. The enemy will

---

Lee's letter to Ethelbert Barksdale from James D. McCabe, Jr., *Life and Campaigns of General Robert E. Lee* (Atlanta, 1866), pp. 574–575.

certainly use them against us if he can get possession of them; and, as his present numerical superiority will enable him to penetrate many parts of the country, I cannot see the wisdom of the policy of holding them to await his arrival, when we may, by timely action and judicious management, use them to arrest his progress. I do not think that our white population can supply the necessities of a long war without overtaxing its capacity, and imposing great suffering upon our people; and I believe we should provide resources for a protracted struggle,—not merely for a battle or a campaign.

In answer to your second question, I can only say that, in my opinion, the negroes, under proper circumstances, will make efficient soldiers. I think we could at least do as well with them as the enemy, and he attaches great importance to their assistance. Under good officers and good instructions, I do not see why they should not become soldiers. They possess all the physical qualifications, and their habits of obedience constitute a good foundation for discipline. They furnish a more promising material than many armies of which we read in history, which owed their efficiency to discipline alone. I think those who are employed should be freed. It would be neither just nor wise, in my opinion, to require them to serve as slaves. The best course to pursue, it seems to me, would be to call for such as are willing to come with the consent of their owners. An impressment or draft would not be likely to bring out the best class, and the use of coercion would make the measure distasteful to them and to their owners.

I have no doubt that if Congress would authorize their reception into service, and empower the President to call upon individuals or States for such as they are willing to contribute, with the condition of emancipation to all enrolled, a sufficient number would be forthcoming to enable us to try the experiment. If it proved successful, most of the objections to the measure would disappear, and if individuals still remained unwilling to send their negroes to the army, the force of public opinion in the States would soon bring about such legislation as would remove all obstacles. I think the matter should be left, as far as possible, to the people and to the States, which alone can legislate as the necessities of this particular service may require. As to the mode of organizing them, it should be left as free from restraint as possible. Experience will suggest the best course, and it would be inexpedient to trammel the subject with provisions that might, in the end, prevent the adoption of reforms suggested by actual trial.

Richmond Examiner, *February 25, 1865*

The question of employing negroes in the army is by no means set at rest by the Senate majority of one. The debates having been secret, the publick can have no knowledge of the reasons and arguments urged on either side. Undoubtedly the arming of negroes, whether as slaves or not, is a very serious step; justifies earnest deliberation, and accounts for honest differences of opinion. It is a great thing which General Lee asks us to do, and directly opposite to all the sentiments and principles which have heretofore governed the Southern people. Nothing, in fact, but the loud and repeated demand of the leader to whom we already owe so much, on whose shoulders we rest so great a responsibility for the future, could induce, or rather coerce, this people and this army to consent to so essential an innovation. But still the question recurs—can we hope to fight successfully through a long war without using the black population? Evidently General Lee thinks not; because at the same moment that he makes new efforts to recall the absentees and deserters to their posts, he also urgently demands that Congress and the several States pass at once such legislation as will enable him to fill his ranks with negro troops. On this point of military necessity, there are few in the Confederacy who would not defer to the judgment of the General.

There is another very material consideration. If we arm negroes can they be made serviceable soldiers? This journal has heretofore opposed the whole project upon the last named ground; and has not changed its opinion. Yet General Lee has, on this question also, very decidedly expressed a different judgment in his letter to a member of Congress. And this is another question purely military; upon which, therefore, the whole country will be disposed to acquiesce silently in the opinion of the commander who undertakes to use that species of force efficiently for our defence. There are many other considerations, which are not military, but moral, political and social, relating to the future of the black race as well as of the white,— all of which oppose themselves strongly to the revolutionary measure now recommended. On these General Lee cannot be admitted as an authority without appeal: indeed, his earnestness in providing that "those who are employed should be freed," and "that it would be neither just nor wise to require them to serve as slaves," suggests a doubt whether he is what used to be called a "good Southerner"; that is, whether he is thoroughly satisfied of the justice and beneficence of negro slavery as a sound, permanent basis of our national polity. Yet all these considerations must also give way, if it be true that, to save our country from Yankee conquest and domination it is "not only expedient but necessary" to employ negroes as soldiers. *He* is the good Southerner who will guaranty us against that shameful and dreadful doom. To save ourselves from that, we should of course be willing not only to give up property and sacrifice comfort, but to put in abeyance political and social theories, which in principle we cannot alter.

The whole matter depends practically on the question—Is this necessary, or not necessary, to the defeat of the Yankee invaders and the establishment of Confederate independence? The Senators who voted against the measure are entitled to credit for purity of purpose. It would be very invidious, and is unnecessary, to assume that any of them refuse the aid of negroes in this war from any silly and sneaking sort of a lingering secret hope that if the country is subdued they will not perhaps be deprived of their slaves by the Yankee conquerers. If any Senator, or any constituent of any Senator, is at this day so hopelessly idiotick as to imagine that in case of subjugation the enemy will not take from him both his negroes and his plantation to boot, that Senator, or constituent, is not to be argued with. Leaving that out of the question, then, it may be assumed that the majority of the Senate objected to the employment of negro soldiers, either because they think the "Necessity" spoken of by General Lee does not exist—or because they are of opinion that negroes would make bad soldiers; and that if the whites confess themselves unable to continue the contest, negroes would not save them; or because they are inflexibly opposed in principle to altering the relative *status* of white and black from these moral, political and social considerations alluded to before. As to the two first objections, the only answer that can be made is that General Lee is of a different opinion; he thinks he can make efficient soldiers of negroes, and he thinks the time has come when it is necessary to take and use them. It is one thing to be quite converted to his opinion, and another to acquiesce in his decision. As to those other and larger considerations, which do not depend upon military necessity, nor on the present exigency, but go down to the foundations of society and the natural relation of races, those Senators who hold that it would be a cruel injury, both to white and black, to sever their present relation of master and slave; that to make "freedom" a reward for service, is at war with the first principles of this relation, and is the beginning of abolition, and that abolition means the abandonment of the black race to inevitable destruction upon this continent, those Senators are undoubtedly right. This is the true Southern principle, and the only righteous principle. But what then? What good will our principle do if the Yankees come in over us? Will there be any comfort in going down to perdition carrying our principles with us intact? The principle of slavery is a sound one; but is it so dear to us that rather than give it up we would be slaves ourselves? Slavery, like the Sabbath, was made for man; not man for slavery. On this point also, as well as all the others, the only practical question now ought to be: Is it necessary, in order to defend our country successfully, to use negroes as soldiers—not abandoning any principle, but reserving for quieter times the definitive arrangements which may thus become needful? If it is necessary, as General Lee has said—that is, if the alternative is submission to the enemy—then no good Southern man will hesitate. It may be under protest that we yield to this imperious necessity; but still we yield.

Charleston [S.C.] Mercury, *January 13, 1865*

In 1860 South Carolina seceded alone from the old union of States. Her people, in Convention assembled, invited the *slaveholding* States (none others) of the old Union to join her in erecting a separate Government of *Slave States,* for the protection of their common interests. All of the slave states, with the exception of Maryland and Kentucky, responded to her invitation. The Southern Confederacy of slave States was formed.

It was on account of encroachments upon the institution of *slavery* by the sectional majority of the old Union, that South Carolina seceded from that Union. It is not at this late day, after the loss of thirty thousand of her best and bravest men in battle, that she will suffer it to be bartered away; or ground between the upper and nether mill stones, by the madness of Congress, or the counsels of shallow men elsewhere.

By the compact we made with Virginia and the other States of this Confederacy, South Carolina will stand to the bitter end of destruction. By that compact she intends to stand or to fall. Neither Congress, nor certain make-shift men in Virginia, can force upon her their mad schemes of weakness and surrender. She stands upon her institutions—and there she will fall in their defence. *We want no Confederate Government without our institutions.* And we will have none. Sink or swim, live or die, we stand by them, and are fighting for them this day. That is the ground of our fight—it is well that all should understand it at once. Thousands and tens of thousands of the bravest men, and the best blood of this State, fighting in the ranks, have left their bones whitening on the bleak hills of Virginia in this cause. We are fighting for our system of civilization—not for buncomb, or for Jeff Davis. We intend to fight for *that,* or nothing. We expect Virginia to stand beside us in that fight, as of old, as we have stood beside her in this war up to this time. But such talk coming from such a source is destructive to the cause. Let it cease at once, in God's name, and in behalf of our common cause! It is paralizing [*sic*] to every man here to hear it. It throws a pall over the hearts of the soldiers from this State to hear it. The soldiers of South Carolina will not fight beside a nigger—to talk of emancipation is to disband our army. We are free men, and we chose to fight for ourselves—we want no slaves to fight for us. Skulkers, money lenders, money makers, and blood-suckers, alone will tolerate the idea. It is the man who won[']t fight himself, who wants his nigger to fight for him, and to take his place in the ranks. Put that man in the ranks. And do it at once. Control your armies—put men of capacity in command, re-establish confidence—enforce thorough discipline—and there will be found men enough, and brave men enough, to defeat a dozen Sherman's. Falter and hack at the root of the Confederacy—our institutions—our civilization—and you kill the cause as dead as a boiled crab.

The straight and narrow path of our deliverance is in the reform of our government, and the discipline of our armies. Will Virginia stand by us as of old in this rugged pathway? We will not fail her in the shadow of a hair. But South Carolina will fight upon no other platform, than that she laid down in 1860.

Howell Cobb to [Secretary of War] James Seddon, January 8, 1865

Your letter of the 30th of December received by yesterday's mail. I beg to assure you that I have spared no efforts or pains to prosecute vigorously the recruiting of our Army through the conscript camp. It is true, as you say, there are many liable to conscription who have not been reached, and for reasons I have heretofore given I fear never will be reached. Rest assured, however, that I will not cease my efforts in that regard. In response to your inquiries, how our Army is to be recruited, I refer with strength and confidence to the policy of opening the door for volunteers. I have so long and so urgently pressed this matter that I feel reluctant even to allude to it, and yet I should not be true to my strong convictions of duty if I permitted any opportunity to pass without urging and pressing it upon the proper authorities. It is in my opinion not only the best but the only mode of saving the Army, and every day it is postponed weakens its strength and diminishes the number that could be had by it. The freest, broadest, and most unrestricted system of volunteering is the true policy, and cannot be too soon resorted to. I think that the proposition to make soldiers of our slaves is the most pernicious idea that has been suggested since the war began. It is to me a source of deep mortification and regret to see the name of that good and great man and soldier, General R. E. Lee, given as authority for such a policy. My first hour of despondency will be the one in which that policy shall be adopted. You cannot make soldiers of slaves, nor slaves of soldiers. The moment you resort to negro soldiers your white soldiers will be lost to you; and one secret of the favor with which the proposition is received in portions of the Army is the hope that when negroes go into the Army they will be permitted to retire. It is simply a proposition to fight the balance of the war with negro troops. You can't keep white and black troops together, and you can't trust negroes by themselves. It is difficult to get negroes enough for the purpose indicated in the President's message, much less enough for an Army. Use all the negroes you can get, for all the purposes for which you need them, but don't arm them. The day you make soldiers of them is the beginning of the end of the revolution. If slaves will make good soldiers our whole theory of slavery is wrong—but they won't make soldiers. As a class they are wanting in every qualification of a soldier. Better by far to yield to the demands of England and France and abolish slavery, and thereby purchase their aid, than to resort to this policy, which leads as certainly to ruin and subjugation as it is adopted; you want more soldiers, and hence the proposition to take negroes into the Army. Before resorting to it, at least try every reasonable mode of getting white soldiers. I do not entertain a doubt that you can by the volunteering policy get more men into the service than you can arm. I have more fears about arms than about men. For heaven's sake try it before you fill with gloom and despondency the hearts of many of our truest and most devoted men by resorting to the suicidal policy of arming our slaves.

⋏ *E S S A Y S*

Historian Emory M. Thomas of the University of Georgia has done more than any other scholar to show the extent of the changes that swept over Confederate society. In the first essay, he describes the dimensions of these wartime changes. Professor of history Paul D. Escott of Wake Forest University argues in the second essay that the South's class system generated major opposition to the changes that occurred and that this opposition damaged Confederate nationalism. In the final selection, Richard E. Beringer, Herman Hattaway, Archer Jones, and William N. Still, Jr., authors of *Why the South Lost the Civil War*, argue that Sherman's march to the sea did not have to spell the end of the Confederate war effort. They pinpoint the reason for the South's defeat in a failure of will and explain that failure in terms of southern religious attitudes and guilt over slavery.

The Revolution Brings Revolutionary Change

EMORY M. THOMAS

Southerners since 1865 have been peculiarly squeamish about the terms "rebel" and "revolution." Long ago they convinced the nation at large to drop "War of Rebellion" as the name of their Confederate experience. Even now many Southerners recoil at the use of "Civil War." They prefer "War between the States," which implies, it would seem, some kind of sterile conflict over antique political principles. Perhaps Reconstruction was never so successful as in the realm of semantics. For even otherwise "unreconstructed" Southerners have in the years since Appomattox outdone themselves to become 100 percent Americans. The recent South has been a bastion of American orthodoxy in which revolution is a nasty word. Corporately Americans remember the Confederacy as the vehicle through which brave men fought a gallant though tragic war. Somehow the dust and smoke of battles, real and reenacted, has obscured the revolutionary nature of the struggle.

The time has come to recognize anew that Southern Confederates made a revolution in 1861. They made a "conservative revolution" to preserve the antebellum status quo, but they made a revolution just the same. The "fire-eaters" employed classic revolutionary tactics in their agitation for secession. And the Confederates were no less rebels than their grandfathers had been in 1776.

The supreme irony was that the Confederate revolution was scarcely consummated when the radicals lost control. Moderate elements of the Southern political leadership took charge and attempted to carry out the radicals' program. In the process, however, the Confederacy underwent an internal revolution—one revolution became two. In the name of independence the Southerners reversed or severely undermined virtually every tenet of the way of life they were supposedly defending. The substantive revolution came only after the Confederacy was engaged in a fight for its life. That fight itself was in part characterized by revolutionary strategy and guerrilla tactics.

The Confederates sacrificed a state rights polity and embraced centralized nationalism. The Davis administration outdid its Northern counterpart in organizing for total war. Economically, the nation founded by planters to preserve commercial, plantation agrarianism became, within the limits of its ability, urbanized and industrialized. A nation of farmers knew the frustration of going hungry, but Southern industry made great strides. And Southern cities swelled in size and importance. Cotton, once king, became a pawn in the Confederate South. The emphasis on manufacturing and urbanization came too little, too late. But compared to the antebellum South, the Confederate South underwent nothing short of an economic revolution.

Pre-Confederate Southerners had thought themselves stable people. The Confederacy and its war changed their minds. Wartime brought varieties of experience hitherto unknown below the Potomac. Riot and disaffection rocked the nation. An incipient proletariat exhibited a marked degree of class awareness. Southern women climbed down from their pedestals and became refugees, went to work in factories, or assumed responsibility for managing farms. The upheaval of war severely tested the aristocracy and brought "new people" to financial and social prominence. The military and governmental hierarchies created new avenues to social status and to a large extent democratized Southern social mores. Southerners, some of them for the first time, became aware of their corporate as well as their individual identities. Organized religion underwent structural and doctrinal change. And the war rudely shocked the Confederates out of many of their romantic self-delusions.

Ultimately even racial slavery changed. Although the Confederates "used" free and bonded black people in ways unknown in the Old South, the institution of slavery underwent a fundamental change in the wartime South. White mastery declined and in turn black dependence faded. In the cities and in the countryside slavery was a "dying institution." Finally the Confederates were willing to sacrifice their "peculiar institution" for the sake of independence. The Congress provided for black troops, and the administration was willing to exchange emancipation for foreign recognition.

By 1865, under the pressure of total war, the Confederate South had surrendered most of its cherished way of life. Independence became an end, not a means. The South had revolutionized herself. This is not to say that the origins of the Confederate revolution were not present in the antebellum South, or that all the tendencies in Confederate national life came to full flower. Rather, the movement of the Confederate South in so many new directions in so short a time constituted a genuine revolution in Southern life.

Ironically the internal revolution went to completion at the very time that the external revolution collapsed. Both died at Appomattox. In 1865 the Confederacy did more than surrender—it disintegrated. The Union not only destroyed and devastated; it eradicated the rebel nation. All that was positive in the Confederate experience went down with all that was negative. The Davis administration and Southern nationalism were no more. Southern industry and cities were largely rubble. Social structure disappeared in individual struggles for survival. Slaves were freedmen by fiat of the Yankee. Few "nations" have suffered defeat more thorough than that of the rebel South.

The Confederate revolutionary experience did not survive the total defeat and destruction of the Confederate state. And Reconstruction finished the job. The program of the radical Republicans may have failed to restructure Southern society. It may, in the end, have "sold out" the freedmen in the South. Yet Reconstruction did succeed in frustrating the positive elements of the revolutionary Southern experience. In 1865 Southerners, while accepting military defeat, were blind to its implications. They hoped to rejoin the Union and continue "business as usual," and they found the presidential plans for Reconstruction encouraging. But then Congress took a hand in Reconstruction. Northern legislators were understandably displeased by the ease with which the rebel states reentered the Union. The "black codes" enacted by Southern state legislatures alarmed Northern solons, and the race riots in Southern cities appalled them. Senators and congressmen from these unrepentant states were ex-Confederate leaders, grinning and primed to pick up the old sectional quarrels where they had left off in 1860. The Republican majority would have none of it. The South had fulfilled the president's conditions for rejoining the Union without fulfilling the war aims of that Union. The radical Republicans imposed new conditions, sent troops to occupy the Southern states, and hoped for genuine repentance. The South yielded only bitterness. The bitterness of Reconstruction outlasted the bitterness of the war. It survives still in the persistent myth of "black Reconstruction."

From Reconstruction and its aftermath arose the New South. Yet nothing is so striking about the New South as its resemblance to the Old South. The New South rhetoric preached reunion and economic progress. But beginning with the "Redeemers," those men who credited themselves with restoring white, conservative rule, the New Southerners reasserted state rights, racial bondage, agrarianism, and all the rest of those conditions rejected by Confederate Southerners. The New South was the thermidor of the Confederate revolutions—the conservative reaction. "Freed" black men belonged to company stores and landlords. The issue of race submerged class awareness on the part of poor and middle-class white men. The South remained predominantly rural and agricultural. Money and land raised up a New South aristocracy who longed for nothing so much as the brave old world, that mythical South that existed before the "late unpleasantness." In short, most of the positive, substantive changes wrought during the Confederate experience drowned in a sea of "Bourbonism."

There are some far-reaching implications here. If indeed the Confederacy was a revolutionary experience, however much it failed, it should stand at the center of Southern historical consciousness. The Confederacy was not simply the end of the Old South, nor simply the beginning of the New South. It was a unique experience in and of itself. For four brief years Southerners took charge of their own destiny. In so doing they tested their institutions and sacred cows, found them wanting, and redefined them. In a sense the Confederacy was the crucible of Southernism. And as such it provides a far better source of Southern identity than the never-never world of agrarian paradise in the Old South or the never-quite-new world of the New South. In the context of the Confederate revolutionary experience, when "unreconstructed" Southerners venerate the Confederacy, they are right for the wrong reasons. And when liberated Southerners vilify the Confederacy, they are wrong for the right reasons.

There are broader implications still. It is a truism that history, the process of human development, enslaves its products. No people should be more aware of this than Southerners. No other Americans seem to have so thoroughly bound themselves to the past. The study of history, however, can liberate. An honest awareness of the past can sever the bonds of that past. An honest awareness of the past can reveal to us who we are, and enable us to live with the past in the present.

The challenge here is to be honest to the Confederate past. Honesty requires that myths and historical apology be put to rest, along with many of the negative clichés about the Confederate South. To be honest to the Confederate experience requires that we accept its revolutionary aspects and rethink many outworn judgments of its positive and negative accomplishments.

The task is not simple. But the rewards are rich. Present Americans have much in common with the Confederate past. Both people have experienced revolution. Both have known corporate guilt and shame amid triumph. The Confederate experience is "usable past."

The Failure of Confederate Nationalism

PAUL D. ESCOTT

For Southerners the Confederacy was an unwelcome experience, a change that the majority of Southerners came to oppose. A spirit of Confederate nationalism failed to develop, and voluntary support for the war effort progressively disintegrated. The roots of this failure lay in the Southern class system as it responded to the stresses of war. The nation did not cohere; and the Old South was not fundamentally changed. It retained a class system based on contradiction and a regional identity that was inescapable, even though it was insufficient to constitute a nation-state.

On the eve of the Civil War the South had attained a regional identity, a sense of itself as a place and as a distinct social system. The creation of the Confederacy, however, was an assertion of something more, a declaration of a sense of nationalism that was not yet present. In 1860 most southerners felt they belonged to the American nation. Some new bond, some sense of Confederate purpose was required to efface those loyalties and establish a Confederate identity. Moreover, in terms of the harsh realities of war, a sense of Confederate nationalism *had* to grow and inspire southerners if they were to emerge from their ordeal as an independent nation.

From Paul D. Escott, "The Failure of Confederate Nationalism" in Harry P. Owens and James J. Cooke, eds., *The Old South in the Crucible of War*, 1983. Published by permission of University Press of Mississippi.

The responsibility for fostering commitment to the nation fell to Jefferson Davis, who, as a determined but distant personality, was both well and poorly qualified for the task. Davis devoted himself irrevocably to Confederate independence, and initially he nurtured the frail spirit of nationalism with skill. He organized a government and articulated an ideology that avoided potential disagreements. By emphasizing that the Confederacy was the embodiment and continuation of American political principles, his ideology invited the many southerners who still had affection for the United States to transfer their loyalty to the new government. Collisions with Northern armies stimulated an outpouring of regional loyalty for the sake of self-defense. In the late summer of 1861 Southern unity was at its zenith, and the prospects for growth of a national spirit seemed bright.

By early 1862, however, "the spirit of volunteering had died out," and serious problems multiplied thereafter—long before the military situation became hopeless. The next year, 1863, brought further deterioration and calamities that put the growth of disaffection beyond the government's control; by 1864 the Davis administration was struggling against disintegration. What had happened? The sources of these ills provide a clue to their cause.

The Confederacy's internal problems appeared at the top and bottom levels of white society—at the extremes of the class system. The centralizing efforts of the Davis administration offended prominent state rightists, who began a continuing attack on the policies, and even legitimacy, of their own government. Opposition from planters grew as the Richmond government impressed slaves and interfered with plantation routines. Meanwhile poverty invaded the homes of ordinary Southerners who had reason to wonder whether they had as much at stake as the wealthy planters. Worse, Congress' unpopular conscription law discriminated against the poor by giving exemptions to those who managed twenty or more slaves, and the stringent tax-in-kind added to the burdens of an "unequal and odious" impressment law.

In the face of such troubles, Davis' ideology degenerated into little more than racial scare tactics, a desperate effort (often repeated in Southern history) to force white Southerners to pull together out of fear. During 1864 a lack of consensus over war aims and widespread reluctance to continue the war were painfully evident. Despite the absence of a two-party system, which tarnished those who proposed alternate policies with the taint of treason, a variety of peace movements appeared. Long before the end of the war (in 1863 or certainly in 1864) most Confederates knew the feeling voiced by one bitter farmer: "The sooner this damned Government [falls] to pieces the better it [will] be for us." . . .

. . . As hundreds of thousands of yeomen sank rapidly into poverty, class tensions flared. The proud individualism and democratic outlook of the yeomen stirred them to demand justice (in no uncertain terms). Why was it, asked even a supporter of the government, that "nine tenths of the youngsters of the land whose relatives are conspicuous in society, wealthy, or influential obtain some safe perch where they can doze with their heads under their wings?" A Georgian denounced the "notorious fact [that] if a man has influential friends—or a little money to spare he will never be enrolled." The yeomen believed, as a hill-country newspaper put it, that, "*All classes of the community* MUST *do their share of the fighting,* the high, the low, the rich and poor, and those who have *the means* MUST *pay the expense. . . .*" Hundreds of letters to the War Department echoed this warning: "the people will not *always* submit to this *unequal, unjust* and partial distribution of favor. . . ."

In response to these angry protests the aristocrats of the South too often answered with assertive individualism of their own. Consider these phenomena: Robert Toomb's defiant refusal to grow less cotton, the wealthy men who "spent a fortune in substitutes," Congress' refusal to end substitution until the start of 1864, and the arrogant opinion of the *Richmond Examiner* that "this ability to pay [for a substitute] is, in most cases, the best proof of the citizen's social and industrial value." Planters continued to expect privileged treatment, as shown by men like North Carolina's Patrick Edmondston who declined to serve unless given a high command and by the fact that in September, 1864, when the army was desperately short of mules and horses, the War Department was lending them to prominent citizens.

Such self-serving, callous acts by the elite were a slap in the face to the yeomen, and they responded with quiet rebellion. Men who saw themselves as "we poor soldiers who are fighting for the 'rich mans [N]egro' " stopped fighting. Wives urged husbands to "desert again. . . . come back to your wife and children." With calm determination and self-assurance in their course, "many deserters . . . just pat[ted] their guns and . . . sa[id], 'This is my furlough.' " Thousands of others refused to cooperate with tax collectors, enrollment officers and other officials or went into open opposition.

As for the slaveowners, they too had a frustrating and bitter experience, but one they had brought on themselves. For as political leaders they had made a profound mistake. They had launched a revolution to secure conservative ends, and they found that their means and ends were incompatible. To keep their lives and plantations unchanged, they had plunged into a vortex of change. The gamble that secession might be peaceful or war brief was lost, and with it went any hope of attaining their goal amid total war.

To this fact they could not, as a class, adjust. Reality required strong measures, changes of many kinds. Jefferson Davis understood the situation and inaugurated change, but the planter class was frozen in the past and inflexible. As Davis responded to reality, his unpopularity with slaveowners grew. They had used the shibboleth of state rights so often, and resisted central power so long, that they fought against their own government and opposed measures necessary for survival. Their capacity for creative statesmanship had withered, and they ended the war hostile and uncooperative prisoners of their own initiative.

Moreover, the planter class failed to offer a vision for the society it wished to lead and the nation it attempted to create. The planters had no unifying goal in mind and little inclination to seek one; they merely wanted to be left undisturbed in their way of life, their privileges, and their possession of slaves. When the debate over Confederate emancipation occurred, the response of slaveowners was overwhelmingly negative. Thus, they revealed that they valued slavery above independence and had led their society into a cataclysm for nothing beyond a selfish reason: to safeguard their class interests. . . .

The failure of Confederate nationalism is apparent in this sequence of events and has been documented in various ways. Thomas Alexander and Richard Beringer have shown that Congress' spirit was marked by a declining willingness to sacrifice, rather than by revolutionary zeal. They confirmed, as well, Buck Yearns' finding that as opposition grew the Davis administration relied more and more heavily on the votes of congressmen whose districts lay in enemy hands. Popular governors like North Carolina's Zeb Vance and Georgia's Joe Brown won people's loyalty by expressing the dissatisfactions of poor and rich alike and by shielding all their citizens, as far as they were able, from the Confederacy's relentless demands for sacrifice. Successful politics became the art of playing on dissatisfactions without offering a solution. Politicians who sought solutions by making the hard choices necessary for survival became unpopular, while those who denounced stern but necessary policies of the Confederacy won gratitude and devotion.

The Confederacy did not fall apart. Some ardent secessionists—like Robert B. Rhett of the Charleston *Mercury*—swallowed their hatred of Davis to support his insistence on independence. Many Southerners endured their dislike of the Confederacy because their dislike of Yankees was growing even more rapidly. Because the army rounded up deserters and the bureaucracy enforced war measures, because Jefferson Davis was unbending and many soldiers were gritty and courageous, the South doggedly stayed in the fight until Appomattox. But no sense of unity or purpose had emerged to turn southern society into a nation.

Religion, Guilt, and Southern Defeat

RICHARD E. BERINGER, HERMAN HATTAWAY, ARCHER JONES, AND

WILLIAM N. STILL, JR.

[General William] Sherman was not irrevocably committed to capturing Atlanta before beginning his march to the sea. And Sherman's movement toward the coast caused [General John] Hood to counter with his Nashville campaign, raising the question of the contribution to Confederate defeat made by the innovative Union strategy and whether Grant's plan rather

Reprinted by permission of the University of Georgia Press from *Why the South Lost the Civil War* by Richard E. Beringer, et al., pp. 337–339, 342–351, 354–361. Copyright 1986 by the University of Georgia Press.

than Hood's loss of the Army of Tennessee may have provided a military reason that precluded a Confederate campaign in 1865.

Grant's way of war, though differing in objective from any envisioned by Clausewitz or Jomini [European experts], fit well with the evolution of Union strategy along lines anticipated by Clausewitz. For total defeat of an enemy he had prescribed "*the destruction of his armed forces and the conquest of his territory,*" pointing out that "the destruction of his armed forces is the most appropriate action and the occupation of his territory only a consequence." But Clausewitz would have known as well as the Union commanders that they lacked adequate superiority to destroy the South's armed forces. Instead, Union leaders adopted as their objective the "necessary evil," to "occupy land" before defeating the hostile armies.

Clausewitz had seen value in ways "to influence the enemy's expenditure of effort; in other words, how to make the war more costly to him." Casualties inflicted in battle and conquest of territory provided two obvious means, but he noted three others all relevant to this discussion: "*the seizure of enemy territory; not with the object of retaining it* but in order to exact financial contributions, or even to lay it waste"; giving "priority to operations that will increase the enemy's suffering" with the essentially political object of increasing his desire for peace; and finally, outlasting him, "using *the duration of the war to bring about a gradual exhaustion of his physical and moral resistance.*" Clearly, in such a war it was unlikely that one army could annihilate the adversary's physical existence; it was necessary to lay siege to his spiritual-moral resources.

The Union had followed all of these prescriptions. Yet through its successful resistance, the Confederacy relied more than the Union did upon the strategy of wearing out the opponent's will to win. In a sense Grant's strategy made irrelevant the continuance of Hood's army in its old form. It had recovered from defeat, heavy casualties, and retreat after Shiloh, Murfreesboro, and the battles at Lookout Mountain and Missionary Ridge. That it did not display the same resilience after the Battle of Nashville and could not, as in the past, replace its casualties illustrates how much its morale and faith in victory had changed. But the army owed its loss of effectiveness as much to the collapse of Confederate morale as to Hood's generalship.

Although the Confederate supply organization still provided the essentials for the South's forces in April 1865, it could not have continued much longer with the mainline railroads broken and Wilmington, Charleston, Savannah, and Mobile completely closed by capture. At this late date a raid north was hardly feasible for Lee, with his animals debilitated and his men's physical and spiritual condition weakened by inadequate rations, distressing news from home, and doubtful notions about the Confederacy's ultimate prospects. No western concentration of troops could be created to conduct a major raid, for Davis had transferred the remains of the Army of Tennessee east to resist Sherman. Moreover, Wilson's cavalry raid to Selma and the readiness to raid northward of the powerful landing force at Mobile would have imposed on a reinvigorated Army of Tennessee, had one existed in the West, the same logistic constraints that hampered Lee in the East. And without functioning trunk-line railways, the Confederacy probably could not have kept its men together and could not have made a frontal resistance against any advance by the major Union troop concentrations.

To campaign in 1865 the main Confederate forces would have had to withdraw into the interior, closer to their sources of supply, and disperse into smaller groups. This strategy would increase the availability of food and fodder but would not have worked as well to connect with sources of ammunition, weapons, and shoes. Because of the simplicity involved in equipping and sustaining mid-nineteenth-century armies, however, the Confederates still would have remained formidable. John Shy notes that "when the Confederacy gave up, its main armies had been destroyed, its people were tired, and its resources depleted." But "continued military resistance . . . was possible and was seriously considered at the time." The Confederacy still possessed important advantages, considering that "the vast spaces, rural economy, and poor transportation system of the South were ideal factors for an effective large-scale resistance movement along guerrilla lines." Under such conditions, Shy contends, "the South could have been made virtually indigestible for a Federal army." He believes that the Confederacy had the weaponry and manpower to continue effective resistance; he also believes Confederates had retained the will to resist, but that is unlikely. Still, given sufficient weapons and a handful of men with the will to use them, a Confederate remnant could have created no end of difficulty for the Federal government after Appomattox and Durham Station.

No longer opposed by major concentrations of force, the Union army would then have had the task of occupying the entire Confederacy. The area then rendered defenseless by Grant's strategy of exhaustion would have been enormous, for until then the Union actually had conquered only a small part of the South. And in moving to occupy a vast land defended only by small, dispersed forces Grant might have opened himself to serious difficulties. Clausewitz and Jomini surely would have anticipated that Union armies would feel most acutely that they were engaged in a national war in which "a people enthusiastic in its political opinions" rushed "to meet the enemy in defense of all it holds dear." When, in a national war, the defeated withdrew into the interior, defenders employed as a "last resort" the guerrilla warfare of a "general insurrection." In this way they could mobilize new strength, "not otherwise available" until that time. Jomini, who had fought against such a resistance in Spain, knew how formidable it could be: "The whole country is the scene of hostilities. . . .

The Union commanders need not have feared an expansion of guerrilla warfare. Little did they realize that, after a long war against such a determined opposition, the spiritual underpinnings of Confederate resistance had almost melted away. The Confederates lacked enough nationalism to continue a conventional defense, much less have the motivation to engage in an ongoing guerrilla war. This is not to deny, however, that there might be issues so deeply felt that southerners would resort to partisan warfare to assert their interests; it is just that Confederate nationhood was not one of them.

Like many leaders on both sides, Johnston and Sherman did not look favorably upon guerrilla warfare; most professional soldiers in the nineteenth century felt the same way. The Civil War had generated enough such hostilities already. The internal war in Missouri saw a few hundred pro-Confederate guerrillas holding down several thousand Union troops, and similar activities had taken place in Kentucky and Tennessee; Sherman himself had had to contend with the problem when he commanded in Memphis in 1862.

The Confederates' refusal to consider the guerrilla alternative may be a major reason why the South lost the Civil War. At the very least, it is certain that if they had adopted such a strategy in 1865 the Union would have had a much larger job on its hands than the one it had just concluded. . . .

. . . Whatever the future, whatever the duration of the war, southerners came to acknowledge that they could not envision a favorable end. There was no reservoir of national determination to fall back upon when the military no longer possessed the power to sustain itself by military means alone. The time had come when the struggle would depend almost totally on the will of the people in arms. But by the winter of 1865, the people were too demoralized to provide the supplementary strength that they had provided in the past.

In the closing months of the war the military and psychological bases of Confederate defeat became closely intertwined. The fall of Atlanta, Sheridan's victories, and the impact of the strategy of raids starkly brought home to Confederates that God did not support their side, at least in the ways they previously had believed; clearly, if He had preferred them, the fortunes of war would have favored the South. Facing defeat, southerners felt compelled to reconcile the ways of God and man. They could do this by changing the perception of God, which led to the conclusion that perhaps He was not on the Confederate side after all. They could also manipulate God by appeasement, supplication, and prayer. If these efforts did not work, however, the only way to reconcile man to his God was for man to change his perceptions of himself. This led to self-examination that obliged Confederates to confess that God punished them for not being in step with His ways. "Can we believe in the justice of Providence, or must we conclude that we are after all wrong?" asked Josiah Gorgas. "Such visitations give me to great bitterness of heart, and repinings at His decrees. It is apparent that we are not yet sufficiently tried," he confessed, for he saw the hand of God directly punishing the people for not being in step with His ways. His people had the duty to confess their sins, accept His punishment, and invoke His blessing. "If repentance, humiliation and faith were unfeigned," then He would prosper southern arms and the war would go well.

If they were sincerely to repent, Confederates had to determine wherein their sins lay. As they searched for examples of their apostasy, many of them came to conclude, even if grudgingly, that the difficulty lay in the institution of slavery. Northern Protestants had long since reached this conclusion, for ever since the Emancipation Proclamation and the subsequent movement toward enacting the Thirteenth Amendment they had made the war one to end slavery and had seen northern arms prosper thereafter. Thus, as Moorhead has observed, "to an unprecedented extent, the war had broken down distinctions between the sacred and the secular, endowing the arms and policies of the Union with religious significance."

Thus the strategy of raids not only vindicated and intensified by reinforcement the Protestant religious convictions espoused by each side but also forced the South to reconsider its own domestic institutions. The Confederates' religious views predisposed them toward this conclusion. They saw God's hand in history and believed events would reflect His will. By late 1864, therefore, God's will was becoming apparent; His people had the task of accounting for and adjusting to it. "What have we done," asked Gorgas, "that the Almighty should scourge us with such a war—so relentless and so repugnant. . . . Is the cause really hopeless? Is it to be abandoned and lost in this way?"

Since the discomfort created by the dissonant knowledge of alternative decisions surely caused great pain, it took much thinking to reduce it and accept new ideas of the Confederate future. Some southerners could not envision and accept even the possibility of defeat, so understandably painful the prospect loomed. At the end of March 1865, one Confederate expressed his "unshaken faith in the ultimate triumph of that cause" and confessed himself "provoked and annoyed that any human being, who had *faith in God,* should doubt." Others felt equally certain of the outcome, even on the brink of defeat. The editor of the *Lynchburg Virginian* thought that the side devoted to "right and justice, against wrong and oppression," inevitably would win, and concluded that, since the Confederacy had right on its side, "if we . . . do not falter, we must succeed." A Georgia congressman agreed. God would never "desert a cause so pure and just as ours." "I do not see, but I feel," said Senator R. M. T. Hunter, "that there is a righteous God in Heaven, who holds our destinies in his hand, and I do not believe He will allow us to be cast down and the wicked to prosper."

Many southerners had expressed similar sentiments at an earlier period of the war, but by 1865 patience with God's slow process was wearing thin. "It is time for thee, Lord, to work," reminded the Lynchburg editor. God was clearly putting His people to the test. Jefferson Davis believed this, and so did others. Josiah Gorgas thought that God sent afflictions "to assure us of our strength," but he also observed that "even those whose faiths remain unshaken find it difficult to give a reason for their faith."

For most Confederates, however, after the fall of Atlanta and the reelection of Lincoln, and certainly after Sherman's march to the sea, the time had come to face the inevitable. Their religious views made this process easier. Their brand of Christianity and the religious fatalism they espoused allowed them to overcome more easily than otherwise the dissonance created by the knowledge of the attractive features of rejected alternatives.

God's will became a psychological bridge to the acceptance of defeat. Confederates reminded their countrymen that they "must walk by faith, as well as sight," for it was "not vouchsafed to mortals to control events that own a higher Power. There is a divinity that shapes our ends." For whatever reason, God might be punishing southerners. In any event, He was making His displeasure known. We cannot deny, said a refugee editor from Tennessee, "that we are mere instrumentalities in the hand of Omnipotence." In such situations, one must necessarily rely on a merciful God.

Reliance on God meant repentance of sin. Southerners fully realized that they had shortcomings. God had punished them and would continue to do so "until the whole people shall have repented of their sins in sackcloth and ashes," for they "have sinned grievously." Here the clergy had a vital role to play. A Richmond editor called upon the preachers to "preach until every man thinks the Devil has gotten into his pew, and is chasing him up to the corner of it." The clergy, rigidly scrupulous and ambitious, proved only too ready to respond and thundered attacks on such vices as alcohol, sexual pleasure, merrymaking, and gambling, among others. Obviously, some ministers were using the war for complex ends, to promote the church, or their version of it, rather than the Confederacy; nevertheless, most clergymen preached that a "return to Christ" would bring victory. Others pointed to the apparent manifestation of God's wrath and complained that people had not learned the obvious lesson. Rather, they had been "driven away from God's commandments" at a time when they ought to be learning to submit to His will. The Episcopal bishop of Virginia, John Johns, asserted that God's displeasure resulted from the collective guilt of all southerners, and he expressed amazement that God had not punished His people sooner and more drastically.

Psychologists emphasize the role of guilt in shaping behavior. This emotion would have equal importance in any age, for Christians believed, and still do, in the omnipresence of sin. Bishop Johns gave voice to this belief, but what sin or sins so oppressed Confederates as to cause God to spread His wrath over the people? Some thought God might be punishing southerners for extortion (charging high prices) or violation of His commandments. Others looked to other sins. In his study *Confederate Morale and Church Propaganda*, James W. Silver points to the role of slavery and touches upon the two aspects of the institution that caused Confederates to ponder. Many thought the institution inherently wrong; but even if it were right, the people did not administer it according to God's will. The institution itself, plus failure to respect slave marriages, to encourage sabbath worship among slaves, to provide religious instruction to slaves, or to protect them from unkind masters, clearly involved sins that led to God's condemnation. Thus the Roman Catholic bishop of Savannah called upon the South to make slavery "conform to the law of God" because He would not bless "a state of things which would be a flagrant violation of His holy commandments." Such perceptions sometimes resulted in an effort to reform slavery, as discussed, for example, by Bell I. Wiley, who noted the efforts of some Confederates "to humanize the institution, and to bring it up to 'Bible standards.' " Some reformers contended that the war was a punishment, not for slavery but for the South's "refusal to cleanse slavery of its abuses." More important, as a consequence of this guilt, some southerners even questioned the entire institution. This questioning had a close relation to the problem of morale and to Confederate nationalism, for slavery constituted the major difference between North and South. If Confederates lost confidence in its legitimacy, sooner or later they would lose confidence in their country as well. . . .

We argue that many southerners did feel guilt over slavery and thus unconsciously looked to a Union victory and emancipation as desirable outcomes of a disastrous war, as Stampp suggests. Clearly this sentiment served as a self-fulfilling prophecy, causing southerners to accept past and current defeats in such a way as to encourage future defeats as well. We would add further, however, that these Confederates, and many other southerners as well, came to believe that God willed that slavery should end, and from that point they logically progressed to a sense of guilt over the war itself, a guilt that could only increase as both the war and the casualty lists grew longer. Still others had their crisis of conscience when it became apparent that the South would lose the war, and these souls were joined by others who had become greatly disillusioned when Jefferson Davis and other members of the Confederate leadership abandoned the earlier war goal of preserving slavery by proposing to arm and emancipate slaves. All of these negative attitudes together amounted to enough to provide the margin of Union victory, especially when reinforced by the religious fatalism that permeated the South's brand of Christianity.

This is not to say that a significant number of southerners consciously desired defeat. But many of them had unconscious inclinations in that direction, and defeat would have its rewards. For some, the loss of slavery would be a favorable outcome, if the collective behavior of the postwar South is any indication. Few southerners ever admitted a desire to restore slavery, but thousands confessed relief that war had destroyed the peculiar institution. The loss of slaves would make defeat less fearsome and hence easier to accept. By the same token, defeat would mean the end of a war that most of them had not wanted. In defeat, Confederates could recapture the clear advantages of the rejected alternatives, Union and peace, thereby reducing the postdecision dissonance between their knowledge of the horror of the war in which they were engaged and their knowledge that the South had had other, more attractive alternatives in 1861.

A nationalism based on an institution about which many southerners felt guilt could not sustain the Confederacy past the losses and disappointments of late 1864. And with military reverses inducing many to believe that God did not favor their cause, religion, which had originally buoyed up Confederate confidence, not only no longer supported morale but even inspired in some southerners a fatalism about defeat. When Confederates read in their Bibles the verses that assured them that "there is none righteous, no, not one. . . . For all have sinned, and come short of the Glory of God," they saw the inextricable connection of religion and guilt. So strong was the relationship of the two concepts that both of them must constitute key words in the lexicon of those who would isolate the causes of the Confederate defeat.

⅄ *F U R T H E R   R E A D I N G*

Thomas B. Alexander and Richard E. Beringer, *The Anatomy of the Confederate Congress* (1972)

Fred Arthur Bailey, *Class and Tennessee's Confederate Generation* (1987)

Richard E. Beringer, Herman Hattaway, Archer Jones, and William N. Still, Jr., *Why the South Lost the Civil War* (1986)

James H. Brewer, *The Confederate Negro* (1969)

Thomas L. Connelly and Archer Jones, *The Politics of Command* (1973)

David P. Crook, *The North, the South, and the Powers, 1861–1865* (1974)

Charles P. Cullop, *Confederate Propaganda in Europe* (1969)

Robert F. Durden, *The Gray and the Black: The Confederate Debate on Emancipation* (1972)

Paul D. Escott, *After Secession: Jefferson Davis and the Failure of Confederate Nationalism* (1978)

——, *Many Excellent People: Power and Privilege in North Carolina, 1850–1900* (1985)

Drew G. Faust, *The Creation of Confederate Nationalism* (1988)

Shelby Foote, *The Civil War, a Narrative*, 3 vols. (1958–1974)

Joseph T. Glatthaar, *The March to the Sea and Beyond* (1985)

Archer Jones, *Confederate Strategy from Shiloh to Vicksburg* (1961)

Ella Lonn, *Desertion During the Civil War* (1928)

Malcolm C. McMillan, *The Disintegration of a Confederate State* (1986)

James M. McPherson, *Battle Cry of Freedom* (1988)

Grady McWhiney and Perry D. Jamieson, *Attack and Die* (1982)

Mary Elizabeth Massey, *Bonnet Brigades* (1966)

——, *Refugee Life in the Confederacy* (1964)

Clarence L. Mohr, *On the Threshold of Freedom* (1986)

Harry P. Owens and James J. Cooke, eds., *The Old South in the Crucible of War* (1983)

Frank L. Owsley and Harriet Owsley, *King Cotton Diplomacy* (1959)

Charles W. Ramsdell, *Behind the Lines in the Southern Confederacy*, ed. Wendell H. Stephenson (1944)

Georgia Lee Tatum, *Disloyalty in the Confederacy* (1934)

Emory M. Thomas, *The Confederacy as a Revolutionary Experience* (1971)

——, *The Confederate Nation* (1979)

——, *The Confederate State of Richmond* (1971)

C. Vann Woodward and Elisabeth Muhlenfeld, eds., *Mary Chesnut's Civil War* (1981)

Bell Irvin Wiley, *The Life of Johnny Reb* (1943)

——, *The Plain People of the Confederacy* (1943)

——, *Southern Negroes, 1861–1865* (1938)

W. Buck Yearns, *The Confederate Congress* (1960)

——, ed., *The Confederate Governors* (1985)

Emancipation

The emancipation of 4 million slaves catalyzed momentous change in American politics, society, and the economy. Full of intense meaning for the men, women, and children who had endured bondage and prayed for freedom, emancipation carried especially profound implications for southern society. It immediately challenged long-established patterns in race relations and economics, as it would in politics by 1868.

The traditional dominance and subservience between masters and slaves had to give way to relations between free citizens, or, more precisely, between resentful whites and hopeful blacks. Landowners and agricultural laborers had to devise new arrangements under which crops could be cultivated and workers paid. The position of blacks in southern society had to be redefined. As black aspirations and white resistance collided in the South, the victorious North watched intently and began to establish ground rules through policies made in Washington.

Emancipation was a process begun during the Civil War. On every plantation in the South, but especially in areas that fell under federal control, slaves began to free themselves. Black southerners had their own ideas about the economic, social, and political future they desired, and they pressed carefully but vigorously to secure as much progress as possible. White southerners, by and large, resisted any significant change with adamant determination. During the war and after, the federal government influenced the outcome of this struggle.

What did emancipation mean to black southerners? What did they want and seek from freedom? How did southern whites respond to the epochal changes sweeping over their region? What was the federal government's stance, and what attitudes guided northerners?

DOCUMENTS

In the 1930s the Federal Writers' Project conducted interviews with elderly ex-slaves who recalled their experiences in slavery and freedom. The first document records the reaction of three slaves to the news of their freedom. Affidavits from federal archives, reprinted in the second document, describe some of the efforts slaves made to gain freedom, assist the Union armies, and provide for themselves during the war. In the next document a newspaper reports the views of Garrison Frazier, a black minister in Savannah, Georgia, who was invited to a wartime meeting with Major General William T. Sherman and Secretary of War Edwin M. Stanton. Reverend Frazier spoke for other black leaders about the hopes and expectations of his people. Blacks' desire for better treatment and for land, and the "prejudice" about which Frazier spoke, are prominent subjects discussed in the fourth selection, the journal and a family letter of Mrs. Mary Jones of Georgia. In freedom, blacks quickly showed a concern for their rights, as the petition of a delegation of Kentucky blacks to the president, the fifth document, shows. The sixth selection contains a letter to President Lincoln from Don Carlos Butler, a freedman in the South Carolina Sea Islands, describing the fondest hope of most black southerners: to gain land, on which they could raise crops and lay the foundations for social independence. Unfortunately, as the last excerpt, from General O. O. Howard's autobiography, reveals, this central hope was crushed when President Andrew Johnson ordered abandoned southern lands returned to their former owners.

Ex-Slaves Recall Their First Taste of Freedom, 1937

Betty Jones, b. 1863, Charlottesville, Virginia

Gramma used to tell dis story to ev'ybody dat would lissen, an' I spec' I heered it a hundred times. Gramma say she was hired out to de Randolphs during de war. One day whilst she was weedin' corn another slave, Mamie Tolliver, come up to her an' whisper, "Sarah, dey tell me dat Marse Lincum done set all us slaves free." Gramma say, "Is dat so?" an' she dropped her hoe an' run all de way to de Thacker's place—seben miles it was— an run to ole Missus an' looked at her real hard. Den she yelled, "I'se free! Yes, I'se free! Ain't got to work fo' you no mo'. You can't put me in yo' pocket now!" Gramma say Missus Thacker started boo-hooin' an' threw her apron over her face an' run in de house. Gramma knew it was true den.

Charlotte Brown, b. c. 1855, Woods Crossing, Virginia

De news come on a Thursday, an' all de slaves been shoutin' an' carryin' on tell ev'ybody was all tired out. 'Member de fust Sunday of freedom. We was all sittin' roun' restin' an' tryin' to think what freedom meant an' ev'ybody was quiet an' peaceful. All at once ole Sister Carrie who was near 'bout a hundred started in to talkin':

> Tain't no mo' sellin' today,
> Tain't no mo' hirin' today,
> Tain't no pullin' off shirts today,
> Its stomp down freedom today.
> Stomp it down!

An' when she says, "Stomp it down," all de slaves commence to shoutin' wid her:

> Stomp down Freedom today—
> Stomp it down!
> Stomp down Freedom today.

Wasn't no mo' peace dat Sunday. Ev'ybody started in to sing an' shout once mo'. Fust thing you know dey done made up music to Sister Carrie's stomp song an' sang an' shouted dat song all de res' de day. Chile, dat was one glorious time!

Georgianna Preston, b. c. 1855, Residence Unspecified

Us young folks carried on somep'n awful [that first night of freedom]. Ole Marse let us stay up all night, an' didn't seem to mind it at all. Saw de sun sot an' befo' we know it, it was a-risin' again. Ole folks was shoutin' an' singin' songs. Dar's one dey sung purty nigh all night. Don't know who started it, but soon's dey stopped, 'nother one took it up an' made up some mo' verses. Lawdy, chile, I kin hear dat song a-ringin' in my haid now:

> Ain't no mo' blowin' dat fo' day horn,
> Will sing, chillun, will sing,
> Ain't no mo' crackin' dat whip over John,
> Will sing, chillun, will sing.

Slaves Remember Their Wartime Experience, 1864, 1865

Affidavit of a Mississippi Fugitive Slave, 1864

Jack, *Cold* Being sworn, deposes & says—I was the slave of Wylie Boddy who lives 6 miles north of Jackson on the road to Canton. Miss—he owns a plantation & lives upon it, I left my home (at Boddys) Thursday sept 8th—five days ago—intending to make my escape & come to this city [Vicksburg]. I took my way thrgh the woods & cane brakes. swam Big Black River on Sunday evening (11th Inst) & came to this City yesterday. Before I left home I heard my master (he is a hard rebel) tell my mistress, that Forest was on the other side of Pearl river near or below Jackson with six (6) thousand cavly & right smart of artillery—& that Forest had a lot of boats on wagons (15 I think) & that Forest intended to cross Pearl river way down at some place & attack Natchez & then come up the river and attack Vicksburg on the south side of the city & take it if possible. I heard the son of my masters brother say that there was a right smart lot of cavalry at Livingston (above Yazoo City) He said it was all Cav'ly—no artillery, or Infantry—this son said he was up there & saw them come into Livingston, I did not hear him say who commanded them. I did not see any troops as I came through the woods—only a few rebel scouts I dodged them through the woods—I have not been in Jackson for 4 weeks when there I saw seven peices of artillery which I saw & examined, the (witness stated that the diameter of the muzzle was about six inches).

Affidavit of a Mississippi Freedman, 1865

My name is Nat. Green, I am 23 years old. I was raised as a slave in the state of Mississippi I was owned by Miss Betty Jones of De Soto County in that state, but I always worked for her brother Col. Thos. Jones of the same place, I was working for Col. Jones in the year 1864, in October of that year all his men servants left him, having been told by Union men that the were freed by Mr. Lincoln, I was sick the night the others left or I would have left with them. the next day Col. Jones told me if I would remain with him he would pay me and on this understanding I remained with him eight months, namely from October 1864 till the latter part of May 1865, for which I have never received any pay whatever,

When I left Col. Jones' place I left there a pig which I raised myself two or three months old which was of considerable value, I could not take any thing with when I left, Col. Jones having threatened my life I was obliged to leave in the night,

Affidavit of a Tennessee Freedman, 1865

My name is Makey Woods. I am 43 years old. I have lived with Mr. William Woods, of Hardaman County, Tennessee for about twenty years. I was his slave. about three years ago when the Union Army was in possession of Bolivar Tenn. and when nearly all the Black people were leaving their Masters and going to the Union Army Mr. Woods told me and such others as would stay with him that he would give us *one fourth* of the crop that we would raise while we stayed with him that he would clothe us and feed us and pay our doctor's bills. Since which time Mr. Wood has given *me* nothing but my clothing: about that time and soon after he made this statement to us he ran off down South into the Rebel lines *fourteen of his slaves* among whom were three of my children, Mr. Woods is now living in Memphis and refus to perform his contract or fulfil his promises to me in any respect, and when I spoke to him a few days ago about carrying out his contract he told me that he was sorry he made such a bargain with us:

There has been raised on Mr. Woods' place this year 48 bales of Cotton most of which Mr. Wood has taken to Memphis last year there were 26 bales raised which Mr. Wood sold I do not know exactly how many black people on Mr. Woods' place at present. Mr. Woods told us that any little patches we might cultivate at odd hours he would not take into the count but would let us have it besides the 1/4 of the regular crop

Reverend Garrison Frazier on the Aspirations of His Fellow Blacks, 1865

Minutes of an interview between the colored ministers and church officers at Savannah with the Secretary of War and Major-General Sherman.

On the evening of Thursday, the 12th day of January, 1865, [twenty] persons of African descent met, by appointment, to hold an interview with Edwin M. Stanton, Secretary of War, and Major-General Sherman, to have a conference upon matters relating to the Freedmen of the State of Georgia. . . .

Garrison Frazier, being chosen by the persons present to express their common sentiments upon the matters of inquiry, makes answers to inquiries as follows:—

First. State what your understanding is in regard to the Acts of Congress, and President's Lincoln's Proclamation, touching the condition of the colored people in the rebel States.

Answer. So far as I understand President Lincoln's Proclamation to the rebellious States, it is, th[at] if they would lay down their arms and submit to the laws of the United States before the 1st of January, 1863, all should be well, but if they did not, then all the slaves in the rebel States should be free, henceforth and forever; that is what I understood.

Second. State what you understand by slavery, and the freedom that was to be given by the President's Proclamation.

Answer. Slavery is receiving by irresistible power the work of another man, and not by his consent. The freedom, as I understand it, promised by the Proclamation, is taking us from under the yoke of bondage, and placing us where we could reap the fruit of our own labor, and take care of ourselves, and assist the Government in maintaining our freedom.

Third. State in what manner you think you can take care of yourselves, and how you can best assist the Government in maintaining your freedom.

Answer. The way we can best take care of ourselves is to have land, and turn in and till it by our labor—that is, by the labor of the women, and children, and old men—and we can soon maintain ourselves, and have something to spare; and to assist the Government, the young men should enlist in the service of the Government, and serve in such manner as they may be wanted—(the rebels told us that they piled them up, and made batteries of them, and sold them to Cuba; but we don't believe that.) We want to be placed on land until we are able to buy it, and make it our own.

Fourth. State in what manner you would rather live, whether scattered among the whites, or in colonies by yourselves.

Answer. I would prefer to live by ourselves, for there is a prejudice against us in the South that will take years to get over; but I do not know that I can answer for my brethren.

[*Mr. Lynch* says he thinks they should not be separated, but live together. All the other persons present being questioned, one by one, answer that they agree with "brother *Frazier*."]

Fifth. Do you think that there is intelligence enough among the slaves of the South to maintain themselves under the Government of the United States, and the equal protection of its laws, and maintain good and peaceable relations among yourselves and with your neighbors?

Answer. I think there is sufficient intelligence among us to do so.

Sixth. State what is the feeling of the black population of the South towards the Government of the United States; what is the understanding in respect to the present war, its causes and object, and their disposition to aid either side; state fully your views.

Answer. I think you will find there is thousands that are willing to make any sacrifice to assist the Government of the United States, while there is also many that are not willing to take up arms. I do not suppose there is a dozen men that is opposed to the Government. I understand, as to the war, that the South is the aggressor. President Lincoln was elected President by a majority of the United States, which guaranteed him the right of holding the office, and exercising that right over the whole United States. The South, without knowing what he would do, rebelled. The war was commenced by the rebels before he came into office. The object of the war was not, at first, to give the slaves their freedom, but the sole object of the war was, at first, to bring the rebellious States back into the Union, and their loyalty to the laws of the United States. Afterwards, knowing the value that was set on the slaves by the rebels, the President thought that his Proclamation would stimulate them to lay down their arms, reduce them to obedience, and help to bring back the rebel States; and their not doing so has now made the freedom of the slaves a part of the war. It is my opinion that there is not a man in this city that could be started to help the rebels one inch, for that would be suicide. There was two black men left with the rebels, because they had taken an active part for the rebels, and thought something might befall them if they staid behind, but there is not another man. If the prayers that have gone up for the Union army could be read out, you would not get through them these two weeks.

Seventh. State whether the sentiments you now express are those only of the colored people in the city, or do they extend to the colored population through the country, and what are your means of knowing the sentiments of those living in the country.

Answer. I think the sentiments are the same among the colored people of the State. My opinion is formed by personal communication in the course of my ministry, and also from the thousands that followed the Union army, leaving their homes and undergoing suffering. I did not think there would be so many; the number surpassed my expectation.

Eighth. If the rebel leaders were to arm the slaves, what would be its effect?

Answer. I think they would fight as long as they were before the bayonet, and just as soon as they could get away they would desert, in my opinion.

Ninth. What, in your opinion, is the feeling of the colored people about enlisting and serving as soldiers of the United States, and what kind of military service do they prefer?

Answer. A large number have gone as soldiers to Port Royal to be drilled and put in the service, and I think there is thousands of the young men that will enlist; there is something about them that, perhaps, is wrong; they have suffered so long from the rebels, that they want to meet and have a chance with them in the field. Some of them want to shoulder the musket, others want to go into the Quartermaster or the Commissary's service.

Tenth. Do you understand the mode of enlistment of colored persons in the rebel States, by State agents, under the act of Congress? If yea, state what your understanding is.

Answer. My understanding is that colored persons enlisted by State agents are enlisted as substitutes, and give credit to the States, and do not swell the army, because every black man enlisted by a State agent leaves a white man at home; and, also, that larger bounties are given or promised by the State agents than are given by the States. The great object should be to push through this rebellion the shortest way, and there seems to be something wanting in the enlistment by State agents, for it don't strengthen the army, but takes one away for every colored man enlisted.

Eleventh. State what, in your opinion, is the best way to enlist colored men for soldiers.

Answer. I think, sir, that all compulsory operations should be put a stop to. The ministers would talk to them, and the young men would enlist. It is my opinion that it would be far better for the State agents to stay at home, and the enlistments to be made for the United States under the direction of General Sherman.

In the absence of General Sherman, the following question was asked:

Twelfth. State what is the feeling of the colored people in regard to General Sherman, and how far do they regard his sentiments and actions as friendly to their rights and interests, or otherwise.

Answer. We looked upon General Sherman, prior to his arrival, as a man, in the providence of God, specially set apart to accomplish this work, and we unanimously felt inexpressible gratitude to him, looking upon him as a man that should be honored for the faithful performance of his duty. Some of us called upon him immediately upon his arrival, and it is probable he did not meet the Secretary with more courtesy than he met us. His conduct and deportment towards us characterized him as a friend and a gentleman. We have confidence in General Sherman, and think that what concerns us could not be under better hands. This is our opinion now from the short acquaintance and intercourse we have had.

Mary Jones on the Concerns of Ex-Slaves, 1865

Mary Jones in Her Journal, 1865

Friday, January 6th. No enemy appeared here today, but we have heard firing around on different places.

The people are all idle on the plantations, most of them seeking their own pleasure. Many servants have proven faithful, others false and rebellious against all authority or restraint. Susan, a Virginia Negro and nurse to my little Mary Ruth, went off with Mac, her husband, to Arcadia the night after the first day the Yankees appeared, with whom she took every opportunity of conversing, informing them that the baby's father was Colonel Jones. She has acted a faithless part as soon as she could. Porter left three weeks since, and has never returned to give any report of Patience

---

Letters of the C. C. Jones family as found in Robert Manson Myers, editor, *The Children of Pride,* 1972, Yale University Press. Charles Colock Jones Papers, Howard-Tilton Memorial Library, Tulane University, reprinted with permission.

or himself or anyone at Arcadia. Little Andrew went to Flemington and returned. I sent him back to wait on our dear sister and family and to be with his own. I hope he will prove faithful. Gilbert, Flora, Tenah, Sue, Rosetta, Fanny, Little Gilbert, Charles, Milton and Elsie and Kate have been faithful to us. . . .

Tuesday, January 10th. We have been free from the presence of the enemy thus far today, although in great apprehension for several hours, as Sue came in at dinner time and advised us to hasten the meal, as she heard firing in the woods between this and White Oak, which is not much over a mile distant. It was reported they would return today with a large forage train of several hundred wagons going on to the Altamaha.

One thing is evident: they are now enlisting the Negroes here in their service. As one of the officers said to me, "We do not want your women, but we mean to take the able-bodied men to dredge out the river and harbor at Savannah, to hew timber, make roads, build bridges, and throw up batteries." They offer twelve dollars per month. Many are going off with them. Some few sensible ones calculate the value of twelve dollars per month in furnishing food, clothing, fuel, lodging, etc., etc. Up to this time none from this place has joined them. I have told some of those indisposed to help in any way and to wander off at pleasure that as they were perfectly useless here it would be best for me and for the good of their fellow servants if they would leave and go at once with the Yankees. They had seen what their conduct was to the black people—stealing from them, searching their houses, cursing and abusing and insulting their wives and daughters; and if they chose such for their masters to obey and follow, then the sooner they went with them the better; and I had quite a mind to send in a request that they be carried off. . . .

Thursday and Friday, January 12th and 13th. . . . Everything confirms the raid south. The enemy are in full possession of Savannah; Negroes in large numbers are flocking to them. . . .

Saturday Night, January 21st. On Thursday Mr. L. J. Mallard visited us. He is now with his family. Gave us various accounts of the enemy. They encamped near his house; at one time on his premises over a thousand. They entered his dwelling day and night. They were forced to obtain a guard from the commander of the post, who was stationed at Midway, to protect his family. The house was repeatedly fired into under pretense of shooting rebels, although they knew that none but defenseless women and children were within. And Mrs. Mallard, who is almost blind, was then in her confinement. They rifled the house of every article of food or clothing which they wished. Mr. Mallard had nothing left but the suit of clothes he wore. . . .

Kate, Daughter's servant who has been cooking for us, took herself off today—influenced, as we believe, by her father. Sent for Cook Kate to Arcadia; she refuses to come.

Their condition is one of perfect anarchy and rebellion. They have placed themselves in perfect antagonism to their owners and to all government and control. We dare not predict the end of all this, if the Lord in mercy does not restrain the hearts and wills of this deluded people. They are certainly prepared for any measures. What we are to do becomes daily more and more perplexing. It is evident if my dwelling is left unoccupied, everything within it will be sacrificed. Wherever owners have gone away, the Negroes have taken away all the furniture, bedding, and household articles.

Mary Jones to Her Daughter, Mary S. Mallard, November 17, 1865

As I wrote you, Sue had left. She is still at the Boro, and I am told has hired Elizabeth to work at Dr. Samuel Jones's. Flora is in a most unhappy and uncomfortable condition, doing very little, and that poorly. . . . I think Flora will certainly leave when she is ready. I overheard an amusing conversation between Cook Kate and herself: they are looking forward to gold watches and chains, bracelets, and *blue veils* and silk dresses! Jack has entered a boardinghouse in Savannah, where I presume he will practice attitudes and act the Congo gentleman to perfection. Porter and Patience will provide for themselves. I shall cease my anxieties for the race. My life long (I mean since I had a home) I have been laboring and caring for them, and since the war have labored with all my might to supply their wants, and expended everything I had upon their support, directly or indirectly; and this is their return.

You can have no conception of the condition of things. I understand Dr. Harris and Mr. Varnedoe will rent their lands to the Negroes! The conduct of some of the citizens has been very injurious to the best interest of the community. At times my heart is so heavy I feel as if it would give way, and that I cannot remain. But I have no other home, and if I desert it, everything will go to ruin. Mr. Fennell has done all he could to protect my interest; but he is feeble physically, and I do not know that he has any special gift at management. I believe him to be an honest and excellent man. We planted only a half-crop of provisions here, and they did not work one-fourth of their time. Judge the results: not a pod of cotton planted, and all I had stolen, and the whole of that at Arcadia gone. You know I wished Little Andrew to return to Montevideo after Mr. Buttolph decided not to go to Baker, as he was our best plowman. He did not do so. Wanting help at this time in grinding cane, I wished him to come down. He did so, stayed part of a day, and walked off. I have not heard of him since. This is a specimen of their conduct. It is thought there will be a great many returning to the county; I do not believe so.

I have mentioned all the news I could collect in Aunty's letter, and refer you to that.

I hope Robert received your brother's letter in reference to the circulars. All we want at present is to obtain subscribers. The work probably cannot be published under a year. I have requested Joseph to confer with Mr. Rogers about the paper he so generously and kindly offered to give for printing the first edition. Do let him know where Mr. Rogers is.

I have just called Charles and asked if he had any messages. "He sends love to Lucy and Tenah, and begs to be remembered to you, and says he will make an opportunity to come and see them before long." This is the sum and substance of his message. It is impossible to get at any of their intentions, and it is useless to ask them. I see only a dark future for the whole race. . . . Do write me all about yourself and the dear children and Robert and the church. . . . Kiss my precious grandchildren. If they were here they should eat sugar cane all day and boil candy at night. . . . The Lord bless you, my dear child!

Ever your affectionate mother,
Mary Jones.

Freedmen Assert Their Rights, 1865

Mr President Haveing been delegated by the Colored People of Kentuckey to wait upon you and State their greiveances and the terrible uncertainty of their future, we beg to do so in as respectfull and concise a manner as Posible—

First then, we would call your attention to the fact that Kentuckey is the only Spot within all the bounds of these United States, where the People of colour Have No rights *whatever* Either in Law or in fact—and were the Strong arm of Millitary Power no longer to curb her—Her jails and workhouses would Groan with the Numbers of our people immured within their walls—

Her Stattutes are disgraced by laws in regard to us, too barbarous Even for a community of Savages to Have Perpetrated. Not one of those laws have Even yet become obsolete, all Have been Executed Promptly and Rigoursly up to the time the government intervened—and will be again Executed in the Most remorseless Manner and with four fold the Venom and Malignanty they were Every Heretofore Enforced—the Very Moment the Government ceases to Shield us with the broad aegeis of her Power—

Not only that—but the brutal instincts of the Mob So Long restrained will Set no bounds to its ferocity but like an uncaged wild beast will rage fiercely among us—Evidence of which is the fact that a member of the present common council of the city of Louisville who when formerly Provost Marshall of that city caused his guards to carry bull whips and upon meeting colored men, women or children in the Public High ways any time after dark to surround them and flay them alive in the public Streets) is allready a petitioner to Genl Palmer to remove the Millitary Restrictions that he and others May again renew the brutaleties that Shocked Humanity during that Sad Period—therefore to Prevent all the Horrible calamities that would befall us and to shut out all the terrors that So fiercely Menace us in the immediate future—we Most Humbly Petition and Pray you that you will Not Remove Marshall Law from the State of Kentuckey Nor her Noble Millitary commander under whose Protection we have allmost learned to Realise the Blessings of a Home under the Safeguard and

Sanction of law for in him and him alone do we find our Safety—we would Most Respectfully call your attention to a few of the laws that bear Most cruelly upon us—

1st we have No Oath

2nd we have no right of domicil

3rd we have no right of Locomotion

4th we have no right of Self defence

5th a Stattute law of Kentuckey makes it a penal crime with imprisonment in the Penitentiary for one year for any free man of colour under any Sircumstances whatever to pass into a free State Even although but for a Moment any free man Not a Native found within her Borders is Subject to the Same penalty and for the Second offence Shall be sold a slave for life—

the State of Kentuckey Has contributed of her colored Sons over thirty thousand Soldiers who have illustrated their courage and devotion on Many battle fields and Have Poured out their blood Lavishly in defence of their Country and their Country's flag and we confidently hope this Blood will be carried to our credit in any Political Settlement of our Native State— yet if the government Should give up the State to the control of her civil authorities there is not one of these Soldiers who will Not Suffer all the grinding oppression of her most inhuman laws if not in their own persons yet in the persons of their wives their children and their mothers—

Therefore your Excellency We Most Earnestly Petition and pray you that you will give us Some security for the future or if that be impracticable at least give us timely warning that we may fly to other States where law and Christian Sentiment will Protect us and our little ones from Violence and wrong.

Chas A. Roxborough	Jerre Meninettee
R M Johnson	Henry H. White
Thomas James	Wm F. Butler

Don Carlos Butler on Freedmen's Yearning for Land, 1864

I hope my letter will find you and your family in perfect health. Will you please to be so kind, Sir as to tell me whether the land will be sold from under us or no, or whether it will be sold to us at all. I should like to buy the very spot where I live. It ain't but six acres, and I have got cotton planted on it, and very fine cotton too; and potatoes and corn coming on very pretty. If we colored people have land I know we shall do very well— there is no fear of that. Some of us have as much as three acres of corn, besides ground-nuts, potatoes, peas, and I don't know what else myself. If the land can only be sold we can buy it all, for every house has its cotton planted, and doing well, and planted only for ourselves. We should like to know how much we shall have to pay for it—if it is sold.

I am pretty well struck in age Sir, for I waited upon Mrs. Alston that was Theodosia Burr, daughter of Aaron Burr, and I remember well when she was taken by pirates.—but I can maintain myself and my family well on this land. My son got sick on the Wabash (Flagship at Hilton Head) and he will never get well, for he has a cough that will kill him at last. He cannot do much work, but I can maintain him. I had rather work for myself and raise my own cotton than work for a gentleman for wages for if I could sell my cotton for [illegible] cents a pound it would pay me.

Whatever you say I am willing to do and I will attend to whatever you tell me.

O. O. Howard Recalls Andrew Johnson's 1865 Policy on Abandoned Lands, 1907

With reference to the land in General Saxton's States, South Carolina, Georgia, and Florida, I will endeavor to explain the effect of the President's pardons upon my own actions, and the special tasks he assigned to me in connection with the abandoned and other real property. In fact, my own special efforts covered the land question for the southern coast.

In order to establish a definite and uniform policy relative to confiscated and abandoned lands, as commissioner, I issued a circular (July 28th) [1865] quoting the law and limiting and regulating the return of the lands to former owners; I authorized assistant commissioners to restore any real property in their possession not *abandoned;* the cultivators were protected in the ownership of growing crops on land to be restored, and careful descriptions were required of such land, and monthly records of amounts which remained in the possession of the Government. I further directed the assistant commissioners to select and set apart in orders, with as little delay as possible, as some had been already doing, such confiscated and abandoned property as they deemed necessary for the immediate use for the life and comfort of refugees and freedmen; and we also provided for rental or sale when that was possible. Surely the pardon of the President would not be interpreted to extend to the surrender of abandoned or confiscated property which in strict accordance with the law had been "set apart for refugees and freedmen" or was then in use for the employment and general welfare of all such persons within the lines of national military occupation in insurrectionary States. Did not the law apply to all formerly held as slaves, who had become or would become free? This was the legal status and the humane conclusion. Then naturally I took such action as would protect the *bona fide* occupants, and expected the United States to indemnify by money or otherwise those Confederates who were pardoned; assuredly we would not succor them by displacing the new settlers who lawfully were holding the land.

My circular of instructions did not please President Johnson. Therefore, in order to avoid misunderstandings now constantly arising among the people in regard to abandoned property, particularly after the President had set on foot a systematic method of granting to the former holders a formal pardon, he made me draw up another circular worded better to suit his policy and submit it to him before its issue. But he, still dissatisfied, and with a totally different object in view than mine, had the document redrawn at the White House and instructed me September 12, 1865, to send it out as approved by him, and so with reluctance I did. This document in great part rescinded former land circulars. Besides allowing assistant commissioners to return all land not abandoned, it instructed them to return all abandoned lands to owners who were pardoned by the President, and provided no indemnity whatever for the occupants, refugees, or freedmen, except a right to the growing crops.

In the definition of confiscated estates the words were: "Land will not be regarded as confiscated until it has been condemned and sold by decree of the United States court for the district in which the property may be found, and the title thereto thus vested in the United States."

On the face of it this approved circular appeared fair and right enough; but with masterly adroitness the President's draft had effectually defeated the *intention* of all that legislation which used the abandoned estates and the so-called confiscated property; that intention was to give to loyal refugees and freedmen allotments of and titles to land. In Virginia, a considerable amount had been libeled and was about to be sold, when Mr. Stanton considerately suspended the sales, that these lands might be turned over more directly to the Bureau for the benefit of the freedmen. I insisted that these lands, condemned for sale, though not actually sold, were already the property of the Government; therefore, I made objection to the President against the insertion of the world "sold" into the definition of confiscated property; but after reference to the attorney general, the President decided adversely to me and so the word "sold" was inserted in the definition that was published in the order. This was what caused the return to former owners of *all property* where slaves had been suspended and never consummated. It was further strongly recommended by me to the President that all men of property to whom he was offering pardon should be conditioned to provide a small homestead or something equivalent to each head of family of his former slaves; but President Johnson was amused and gave no heed to this recommendation. My heart ached for our beneficiaries, but I became comparatively helpless to offer them any permanent possession.

When the former owner had not as yet been pardoned the burden was after this time put upon my officers to prove that property had ever been voluntarily abandoned by a disloyal owner. I soon saw that very little, if any, had been confiscated by formal court decision; so that wholesale pardons in a brief time completed the restoration of the remainder of our lands; all done for the advantage of the late Confederates and for the disadvantage and displacement of the freedmen. Very many had in good faith occupied and cultivated the farms guaranteed to them by the provision and promise of the United States.

My heart was sad enough when by constraint I sent out that circular letter; it was chagrined when not a month later I received the following orders issued by President Johnson:

"Whereas certain tracts of land, situated on the coast of South Carolina, Georgia, and Florida, at the time for the most part vacant, were set apart by Major General W. T. Sherman's special field order No. 15 for the benefit of refugees and freedmen that had been congregated by the operations of the war, or had been left to take care of themselves by their former owners; and whereas an expectation was thereby created that they would be able to retain possession of said lands; and whereas a large number of the former owners are earnestly soliciting the restoration of the same, and promising to absorb the labor and care for the freedmen:

"It is ordered: That Major General Howard, Commissioner of the Bureau of Refugees, Freedmen and Abandoned Lands, *proceed* to the several above-named States and endeavor to effect an agreement mutually satisfactory to the freedmen and the land owners, and make report. And in case a mutual satisfactory arrangement can be effected, he is duly empowered and directed to issue such orders as may become necessary, after a full and careful investigation of the interests of the parties concerned." Why did I not resign? Because I even yet strongly hoped in some way to befriend the freed people.

Obeying my instructions I reached Charleston, S. C., October 17, 1865. General Saxton's headquarters were then in that city. I had a conference with him and with many of the land owners concerned. The truth was soon evident to me that nothing effective could be done without consulting the freedmen themselves who were equally interested. Therefore, accompanied by several officers and by Mr. William Whaley, who represented the planters, I went to Edisto Island, and met the freedmen of that vicinity who came together in a large meeting house. The auditorium and the galleries were filled. The rumor preceding my coming had reached the people that I was obliged by the President's orders to restore the lands to the old planters, so that strong evidence of dissatisfaction and sorrow were manifested from every part of the assembly. In the noise and confusion no progress was had till a sweet-voiced negro woman began the hymn "Nobody knows the trouble I feel—Nobody knows but Jesus," which, joined in by all, had a quieting effect on the audience. Then I endeavored as clearly and gently as I could to explain to them the wishes of the President, as they were made known to me in an interview had with him just before leaving Washington. Those wishes were also substantially embodied in my instructions. My address, however kind in manner I rendered it, met with no apparent favor. They did not hiss, but their eyes flashed unpleasantly, and with one voice they cried, "*No, no!*" Speeches full of feeling and rough eloquence came back in response. One very black man, thick set and strong, cried out from the gallery: "Why, General Howard, why do you take away our lands? You take them from us who are true, always true to the Government! You give them to our all-time enemies! That is not right!"

At my request, the assembly chose three of their number, and to them I submitted with explanations the propositions to which the land owners were willing to subscribe. Then I faithfully reiterated to the whole body the conditions of the existing tenure under our President's action, they having no absolute title but simply occupying the homesteads. I urged them to make the best terms they could with the holders of the titles. These simple souls with singular unanimity agreed to leave everything to my decision with reference to restorations to be made, and also the conditions attending them. But their committee after considering all the matters submitted to them said that on no condition would the freedmen work for their late owners as formerly they did under overseers; but if they could rent lands from them, they would consent to all the other arrangements proposed. Some without overseers would work for wages; but the general desire was to rent lands and work them.

At last, to be as fair to all parties as possible, I constituted a board of supervisors in which the Government, the planters, and the freedmen were equally represented. This board was to secure and adjust contracts and settle cases of dispute and controversy. The freedmen and the planter could form contracts for rental or for labor with wages as elsewhere; but before the latter could do so his land must be formally restored. To effect this restoration, there was drawn up for his signature an obligation in which he promised substantially: To leave to the freedmen the existing crop; to let them stay at their present homes so long as the responsible freedmen among them would contract or lease; to take proper steps to make new contracts or leases, with the proviso that freedmen who refused would surrender any right to remain on the estate after two months; the owners also engaged to interpose no objections to the schools; all the obligations to hold for only one year unless renewed.

At the time, I placed in charge of the whole adjustment Captain A. P. Ketchum, One hundred and Twenty-eighth United States Colored Infantry, acting assistant adjutant general, an officer of acknowledged acumen and conscientiousness. He was in this business my representative with power to extend the arrangement above given to all estates embraced in General Sherman's original provision in South Carolina, Georgia, and Florida.

Upon our return to Charleston, I sent Mr. Stanton this dispatch:

> I met several hundred of the colored people of Edisto Island to-day, and did my utmost to reconcile them to the surrender of their lands to the former owners. They will submit, but with evident sorrow, to the breaking of the promise of General Sherman's order. The greatest aversion is exhibited to making contracts, and they beg and plead for the privilege of renting or buying land on the island. My task is a hard one and I am convinced that something must be done to give these people and others the prospect of homesteads.

> Six days later, on October 25th, Mr. Stanton replied, his message reaching met at Mobile, Ala. He telegraphed: "I do not understand that your orders require you to disturb the freedmen in possession at present, but only ascertain whether a just mutual agreement can be made between the pardoned owners and the freedmen; and if we can, then carry it into effect."

The very rumor of my coming disturbed them. I answered Mr. Stanton that I had set Captain Ketchum to restore lands to the pardoned, provided they signed the obligatory instrument which I have described; that this was as nearly satisfactory to all parties as anything that I could devise. I had given the freedmen a supervising board to guard their interests during the transition.

After the work under the President's instructions extending as far as Mobile had been finished, I returned to Washington November 18th, and submitted an account of the journey to Mr. Stanton. These were my closing words:

> It is exceedingly difficult to reconcile the conflicting interests now arising with regard to lands that have been so long in possession of the Government as those along the coast of South Carolina, Georgia, and Florida. I would recommend that the attention of Congress be called to the subject of this report at as early a day as possible, and that these lands or a part of them be purchased by the United States with a view to the rental and subsequent sale to the freedmen.

Congress soon had the situation clearly stated, but pursued its own plan of reconstruction, as did the President his own, regardless of such minor justice as making good to thousands of freedmen that promise of land which was at that time so essential to their maintenance and their independence.

ᛋ E S S A Y S

Professor of history Willie Lee Rose of Johns Hopkins University studied an unusual experiment in freedom that took place under federal supervision at Port Royal, South Carolina, and on the adjacent Sea Islands during the war. The selections from her work, presented in the first essay, focus on northern missionaries' initial impressions of the newly freed blacks and on the economic and social progress the islanders had made by the end of 1865. Historian Leon Litwack of the University of California, Berkeley, conducted massive research on the responses of black southerners to the coming of freedom. The second essay portrays the deepest feelings of ex-slaves as they faced their former owners and an uncertain future. The last selection is by Eric Foner, professor of history at Columbia University, who has written widely on the economic issues that lay at the heart of all post-emancipation changes. He illuminates the divergent economic assumptions of northern whites and southerners of both races and suggests how white attitudes foreclosed the possibility of land for the freedmen and promoted the sharecropping of staple crops.

A Federal Experiment in Freedom

WILLIE LEE ROSE

In the few days between the [federal] bombardment and the occupation of Beaufort [in 1861], life took a turning on the islands that would never be retraced. Those who streamed off to the interior could not know that they would be away for four years, that some would never return. They could not know what changes would take place in their absence. They could not know that their particular part of South Carolina would undergo Reconstruction before the Civil War was over, or that their own social revolution would be accomplished before the process had fairly begun in other parts of the South.

The revolution began with considerable destruction of property. The Negroes on many plantations, thinking to release themselves from the next task in the cotton, broke the cotton gins. In other cases they began looting their masters' houses and furniture, an activity which the Federal soldiers took up enthusiastically until their officers restrained them. The inward significance of these destructive acts on the part of the colored people could scarcely be grasped aside from an understanding of their previous pattern of life, which only a few Northerners then on the islands had attained.

The masters themselves were responsible for a large amount of destruction. Of the three sorts of property they were leaving behind—land, slaves, and cotton—real estate seems to have given them least concern. Many came back under cover of darkness in the first few weeks of the Federal occupation in order to set fire to their cotton houses and to attempt, usually without success, to make their slaves come inland with them. Numbers of cotton barns were burned, but cotton in the field was difficult to destroy. One fugitive planter, an advocate of the scorched-earth policy who intended to "make hot work" of his own cotton, explained that the stakes were much higher than the crop itself. The Negroes could be put to work harvesting the crop for the Yankees if it were not burned. *With* the cotton the Negroes were an asset to the invaders; *without* it they were a liability. The slaves would, he thought, in the latter case go hungry, and return to their masters in preference to starvation.

Despite the cluster of doubtful assumptions in the planter's reasoning, he had touched the salient point. For the first time in their long mutual history, the black man would find his relationship to King Cotton a fortunate thing. Although it would not immediately be apparent why this was true, in the long run the circumstance that the slaves and the cotton were taken together as "abandoned property" had more than a little to do with justifying the belief of many slaves that they could date their freedom from the day of the "gun-shoot at Bay Point." The collection of abandoned property was the responsibility of the Treasury Department, and Secretary Salmon P. Chase had emerged as "the mainspring of anti-slavery influence within the councils of the President." As a result of his official position, Chase had the opportunity to foster the first important experiment testing newly released slaves in the responsibilities of free laborers; because of his anti-slavery convictions, he seized it. . . .

The Negroes of the islands, wrote Edward Pierce, "had become an abject race, more docile and submissive than those of any other locality." Nowhere else had "the deterioration from their native manhood been carried so far. . . ." Pierce was by no means alone in this conclusion, for all the missionaries were struck with certain childish qualities manifested by many of the Negroes. Elizabeth Botume described a class of young adults:

They rolled up their eyes and scratched their heads when puzzled, and every line in their faces was in motion. If any one missed a word, or gave a wrong answer, he looked very grave. But whenever a correct answer was given, especially if it seemed difficult, they laughed aloud, and reeled about, hitting each other with their elbows. Such "guffaws" could not be tolerated in regular school hours. They joked each other like children; but, unlike them, they took all goodnaturedly.

A superintendent concluded that the Negroes were entirely dependent, lacking in initiative, and that they needed "the positive ordering that a child of five or ten years of age requires." The sum of these observations added up to a picture of the personality known in American literature as "Sambo," the plantation slave, "docile but irresponsible, loyal but lazy, humble but chronically given to lying and stealing."

But it is well to remember that although "Sambo" finds many illustrations in the observations of the teachers on the islands, he remains a *statistical* concept, and the record contains as many stories of protest, disloyalty to the late masters, and manly independence as of servile acquiescence. The extent to which the personality of the common field hand had been fundamentally altered by the experience of slavery finds a good test in his response to the opportunities offered by the new order inaugurated in the wake of the Northern occupation. The first reaction can be found in the large numbers of slaves willing to risk severe punishment and even death by running away from their masters. The wild sacking of Beaufort and the plantation houses and the complete destruction of the cotton gins show a bitter and long dammed-up hostility that, if perhaps childish in its discharge, is yet remarkably similar to the venting of spleen demonstrable among more "civilized" peoples. Other and more positive tests as to the fundamental damage to the slaves' personality would be provided as time went on in the success, or lack thereof, of the missionaries' labors to make the people self-reliant.

A more probable and immediate explanation of the obsequious and infantile behavior of the majority of slaves who demonstrated childish traits is that playing "Sambo" had its rewards and that failing to play him incurred many risks. That the role could be one of conscious hypocrisy is illustrated by the case of Elijah Green. This ancient veteran of slavery remembered with rancor, many long years after his freedom came, having been obliged to give an affectionate endorsement of the new brides and grooms who joined his master's family, whether he liked them or not.

The main effect of slavery was a thick residue of accumulated habits and responses that a slave child learned early in life. It was a culture, in short, that invested its members with a number of character traits useful in slavery but unbecoming in free men. The extent to which these traits developed in an individual slave depended in part upon the class to which he belonged. It has been a general assumption that more enlightenment and self-respect were to be found among house servants and the Negroes of the towns than among field slaves. The common corollary, however, that these "Swonga" people, as they were denominated by the field hands, also possessed a greater spirit of *independence* is, at the very least, a debatable point. They had merely absorbed more of the white man's culture, and they paid for it in daily contacts with the "superior" beings whose very presence was a reminder of their own inferior status. Sometimes the loyalty of a well-treated house servant could make war on the very notion of independence. There is considerable evidence to support the idea that, while the Swonga people had perhaps more self-esteem and were better dressed, the field hands had more self-reliance. It would be hard to conceive of a more independent spirit than that shown by the six strapping sons of "Mom Peg." They had all been field slaves, and they defied an overseer to whip them. When one brother was threatened, all took to the woods in a body and had to be guaranteed immunity before returning. Described as "tall and handsome," the brothers held "high rank in church and council" and were to enjoy a bright future in freedom. . . .

The story of Lydia Smalls is most instructive. When she was a girl, her mistress had taken her away from field work on the Ashdale plantation on Ladies Island and had brought her to Beaufort, where she became a trusted house servant. When Lydia's own son was growing up as a pampered pet in the Prince Street house of their master, Henry McKee, Lydia was afraid he did not realize the meaning of slavery or the full indignity of his position. Ever a rebel in her heart, Lydia forced her son to watch a slave being whipped in the yard of the Beaufort jail. Then young Robert went himself to stay for a time at the Ashdale plantation. He had seen the seemingly dull and cringing plantation people every week when he had come with his master to bring their rations. He never understood much about them, however, until the day he stayed and his master rode away. The apathetic people suddenly found the spirit to grumble and complain heartily about their diet. It was on the plantation that Robert Smalls first heard about Frederick Douglass and decided that he too would become a free man. . . .

The missionaries complained now [late in 1865] frequently of the freedman's agricultural and social failings, with a significant emphasis on his ingratitude and faithlessness. The Negro continued to rate cotton culture distinctly second-place in his farming interests; he was reluctant to haul the "salt marsh" so necessary to its success, and after enough freedmen owned their own land to make detection difficult, he was also apt to steal it. John Hunn, the Quaker evangel of underground railroad fame, frankly told a reporter for the *Nation* that "as a friend of the colored people, he would . . . not wish a final judgment of them to be deduced from their present condition in the Sea Islands." "Father Hunn," as he was called, was operating at a loss, and his condemnation of a labor system that allowed the people living on the properties so much liberty was "unqualified." He complained to the reporter that "for every acre that his people planted for him for wages they planted precisely two acres for themselves, and it was hard to induce them to take up more cotton ground than would supply them with spending money." . . .

Arthur Sumner came to the heart of the matter when he explained that

"The negro has always been oppressed by the white man, and knows that even now . . . [the white man] has it in his power to cheat him. Even the best of the young men sent down here by the benevolent societies at the North, have failed to gain their confidence. [The Negroes] . . . are stupid and ignorant, and therefore incapable of comprehending that a man who has it in his power to cheat them, should fail to do so." Even Sumner understood that there was some ground for mistrust. When Edward Philbrick introduced a new superintendent at Coffin Point, the Negroes thronged about, demanding promptly, "A dollar a task, A dollar a task!" Their spokesman, the ubiquitous John Major, told Philbrick he was sure he could afford it, for he had seen him "jamming the bills into that big iron cage (meaning . . . the safe at R[uggle]s) for six months, and there must be enough in it now to bust it." Major may have been right.

The real problem was that many Gideonites could not recognize the signs of the growth of freedom. Harriet Ware reduced a host of peevish observations to a single sentence when she said that she was glad to see the Negroes losing some of their old *servility,* but sorry that they were no longer very *obedient.* The freedmen's mounting protests were to many evangels simply signs of ingratitude. The wisest observers were looking for independent thought and action.

Laura Towne knew how to recognize the small gains. When she drove out with a Negro family to meet an aged grandmother who had arrived with a band of refugees brought from the mainland by Higginson's regiment, she noticed a significant reaction. The old woman was amazed to see how freely the little grandchildren expressed their joy at the reunion in the presence of the "buckra" lady! One Northern observer of several years' experience on the islands saw that the freedmen were busy building homes in the spring after the war, as well as "cornhouses, fences, [and] carts." He thought the colored people were working harder than in any year since slavery, and that they were cultivating their crops better, concentrating on provision crops, especially vegetables. They were also learning to read and to conduct their own business affairs. The same observer commented that the freedmen were "rising in the scale of civilization, however much they may be traduced by those who only look at single specimens of their race, or who from mismanagement or fraud have failed to gain the respect, or good-will of the people."

In the same summer that many Gideonites were experiencing so much difficulty with the freedmen as laborers, a Northern reporter for the *Nation* observed that in the Sea Island communities where Negroes were cultivating crops for themselves, the result was "highly encouraging." He saw large fields of corn under good cultivation and described a "crazy little steam flat, . . . crowded with colored people who were carrying their produce to market—tomatoes, okra, huckleberries, water melons, chickens, eggs, and bundles of kindling." The same reporter judged that the freedmen were perhaps not working "according to the Northern standard," but they were able to care for themselves, which was "all we have a right to require of any set of people. . . ." Dr. Richard Fuller, who toured the islands in the distinguished company of Salmon P. Chase in the summer following the war, was favorably impressed with the progress of the freedmen who had once been his slaves. He told Whitelaw Reid, who was reporting the tour, that St. Helena was thriving under the new order. "I never saw as much land there under cultivation—never saw the same general evidences of prosperity, and never saw the negroes themselves appearing so well or so contented."

Elizabeth Botume wrote that "some of the finest cotton brought to market on the islands" in the year after the war was raised by a group of freedmen who "hired and bought land, and worked independent of any white superintendent." That was the main point. Joseph Parrish, who visited the islands in the spring of 1866, noticed a great difference between St. Helena Island, which was denominated "A Negro's Heaven" because the freedmen had by that time come into possession of most of the land there, and Port Royal Island, where much land was worked on a contract basis for superintendents or larger white owners. "Wherever the lands are held in fee by the people they work better."

The Promised Land of Freedom

LEON LITWACK

From the very outset of the war, black Southerners were placed in an anomolous and dangerous position—in an impossible position. On the one hand, they were the cause of the war; on the other, they were necessary for the war's success—that is, their labor and loyalty were essential to the Confederacy. But could they be trusted? The answer came slowly in some cases, quickly in others: the more desperate the Confederate cause became, the more the white South depended on the labor and loyalty of its blacks. And the more they were needed, the less they could be trusted.

Neither whites nor blacks were untouched by the physical and emotional demands of the war. Both races suffered, and each evinced some sympathy for the plight of the other. But there was a critical difference, and that difference grew in importance with each passing month. If slaves evinced a compassion for beleaguered masters and mistresses, if they deplored the ravagement of the land and crops by Union soldiers who brutalized and looted whites and blacks alike, many of these same slaves and still others came to appreciate at some moment in the war that in the very suffering and defeat of their "white folks" lay their only hope for freedom. That revelation was no less far-reaching in its implications than the acknowledgment by white Southerners that they were facing danger on both sides—from the Yankees and from their own blacks. "We have already been twice betrayed by negroes," Joseph LeConte lamented, as he made his way to the safety of Confederate lines; "we avoid them as carefully as

From Leon F. Litwack, "Many Thousands Gone" in Harry P. Owens and James J. Cooke, eds., *The Old South in the Crucible of War*, 1983. Published by permission of University Press of Mississippi.

we do Yankees." No less distraught, the mistress of a plantation in the Abbeville district of South Carolina wondered how the remaining whites could possibly survive if the home guard was called up to combat the Yankees. "If the men are going, then awful things are coming, and I don't want to stay. My God, the women and children, it will be murder and ruin. There are many among the black people and they only want a chance."

The tensions and tragedies introduced into the lives of white families during the Civil War made them seem, in the eyes of their slaves, less than omnipotent. Rarely, after all, had slaves perceived their owners so beleaguered, so helpless, so utterly at the mercy of circumstances over which they had no control. It was the kind of vulnerability a slave could readily understand. If privation, betrayed expectations, fear of the unknown, and the forced separation from loved ones were new experiences for many whites, they were not for many slaves. To witness the anguish of white men and women experiencing some of the same personal tragedies and disruptions they had visited upon others no doubt generated considerable ambivalence in the slave quarters, if not some private or shared gratification. Levi Ashley, a former Mississippi slave, sorted out his thoughts some years later about the plight of his "white folks" during and after the war. He had worked for "de hardes' man ever lived" and for a mistress who had been equally "mean an' hard." The war left its mark on the plantation in ways he could easily appreciate.

> When Marse John was in de war he had his arm shot off an' afte' he come back, he didn' live long. Miss Elviry an' her mother, Miss Fanny, was lef' alone. Dey sho' got to be po' folks. Dey had to sell dey beddin' an' furniture in de house fer suppo't. All de old slaves sho' was glad to hear it. Dey was so mean to 'em. You know, lady, 'whut goes over de Devil's backbone is boun' to pass under his stomach'—an' dey got whut was comin' to 'em.

Contrary to the legends of "docility" and "rebelliousness," the variety of slave personalities does not permit any easy division of the nearly four million enslaved blacks into Uncle Toms and Nat Turners. Rebelliousness, resistance, accommodation, and submission might manifest themselves at different times in the same slave, depending on his or her own perception of reality. Few slaves, no matter how effusively they professed their fidelity to "marse" and "missus," did not contain within them a capacity for outrage. Whether or not that outrage ever surfaced was the terrible reality every white man and woman had to live with and could never really escape. The experiences of war and emancipation made this abundantly clear, playing upon and exacerbating white fears and fantasies that were as old as slavery itself. The tension could prove to be unbearable. Midway through the war, a Southern white woman noted in her diary that a room in the house had accidentally caught fire. "But we at once thought Jane [the cook] was wreaking vengeance on us all by trying to burn us out. We would not have been surprised to have her slip up & stick any of us in the back."

The importance of the nearly four million slaves could not be measured in economic terms alone. What black novelist Ralph Ellison said of the black presence in the South one century later was no less true of the war years: "Southern whites cannot walk, talk, sing, conceive of laws or justice, think of sex, love, the family, or freedom without responding to the presence of Negroes." Whether by their conversations or daily conduct, slaveholding families revealed a relationship with their blacks that was riddled with ambiguity, doubt, and suspicion. No matter how much they flaunted their pretensions to security and professed to believe in the fidelity of their own blacks, the doubts and the apprehension surfaced with every rumor of an uprising, with every case of insubordination and desertion, with every perceived change in the demeanor of their slaves.

The almost studied indifference of some slaves was perhaps most troubling of all. For white families to determine how their slaves felt about the war could be a downright frustrating and exasperating experience. To listen to their slaves' professions of fidelity was seldom as reassuring as it should have been. If white families complained with increasing frequency of the deceitfulness of their slaves, that suggested how well the blacks played their roles, invoking the "darky act" at the appropriate moment. If some slaves internalized the ritual of deference, few whites knew for certain. The slave's "mask of meekness," Ralph Ellison has suggested, "conceals the wisdom of one who has learned the secret of saying the 'yes' which accomplishes the expressive 'no.' " Generations of blacks made the same point when they taught their children, "Be sho' you knows 'bout all you tells, but don't tell all you knows," or when they sang,

> Got one mind for white folks to see,
> 'Nother for what I know is me;
> He don't know, he don't know my mind.

Louis Manigault, the Georgia planter, conceded as much when he reflected on his wartime experience, "So deceitful is the Negro that as far as my own experience extends I could never in a single instance decipher his character."

To endure enslavement, black men and women had learned how to placate the fears of the white owners, how to stroke their egos, how to anticipate their moves and moods. During the Civil War, when the white family's temperament fluctuated even more violently, it became imperative for the slave to remain circumspect in his views, to feign stupidity or indifference at the right moment, to mask his feelings, to adopt the appropriate facial expressions and gestures in his responses to whites, to exploit the various ploys that made up the "darky act"—the hat in hand, the downcast eyes, the shuffling feet, the fumbling words. When questioned about the war, slaves shaped their responses to the tone of the question and the requirements of the occasion, and some sought refuge in a pretense of incomprehension. "Why, you see, master," one elderly slave responded, " 'taint for an old nigger like me to know anything 'bout politics." But when he was pressed further to indicate his preference for the Union or the Confederacy, he smiled and carefully phrased his reply, "I'm on de

Lord's side." If the "darky act" was performed for Yankees and Confederates alike, that reflected a slave's sense of reality. The Civil War would not last forever, a Texas slave advised his son, but "our forever was going to be spent living among the Southerners, after they got licked."

No matter how cautiously a master screened news of the war and emancipation, slaves employed time-tested devices to obtain and communicate information. "Shucks," a former Louisiana slave recalled, "we knew ev'rything de master talked er bout. The house girl would tell us an we would pass it er round. Dats how we knew dat master was er fraid of de yankees." Even if the "grapevine telegraph" broke down, slaves possessed an extraordinary insight into the minds and moods of their "white folks." To gaze at their faces, to feel the growing tension was to know how the war was progressing, that the expected early victory had become instead a prolonged, costly, and apparently fated slaughter. Even if the precise causes of the war remained unclear, what was at stake became increasingly clear. Slaves remained reticent about openly revealing their feelings. But they found it increasingly difficult to mask them, particularly as the outcome of the war became more predictable. The more perceptive masters and mistresses sensed the changes. On some plantations, the prayer meetings in the quarters and fields were noticeably louder and more effusive; songs about the war and freedom suddenly surfaced as well, some of them composed for the occasion, many of them variations on older songs whose contents had seemed innocuous to whites.

Even if the words of many slave spirituals and songs did not change during the Civil War, their immediacy did, and that was often reflected in the emphasis with which certain phrases were intoned. Near the end of the war, with Lee's surrender imminent, a white woman in the Alabama black belt overheard a service conducted by slaves. With particular fervor, they were singing:

> Where oh where is the good old Daniel,
> Where oh where is the good old Daniel,
> Who was cast in the lion's den?
> Safe now in the promised land;
> By and by we'll go home to meet him,
> By and by we'll go home to meet him,
> Way over in the promised land.

Listening to the voices, she "could almost imagine they were on wing for 'the promised land' as they seemed to throw all the passion of their souls into the refrain." Whatever meaning she chose to attach to the words in the song, the entire scene only reinforced her feelings of despondency and impending disaster. "I . . . seemed to see the mantle of our lost cause descending." It was as though these slaves, in their own devious way, understood even better than she did or could admit to herself that "the promised land" lay in the ruins of the Confederacy. And in "Many Thousands Gone," a spiritual composed during the war, slaves would begin to define that "promised land" as a release from the most oppressive aspects of bondage: "No more peck o'corn for me," "No more driver's lash for me," "No more pint o'salt for me," "No more hundred lash for me," and "No more mistress' call for me."

To reach that "promised land," flight to the North had become unnecessary. The proximity of Union soldiers, not the Emancipation Proclamation, made the critical difference in most instances. Every plantation, every farm, every community had its version of how the slaves responded. For some masters and mistresses, the behavior of individual slaves was inexplicable, for others a confirmation of what they had long suspected. What made the "faithful few" so exemplary, in the eyes of the white South, were the slaves who fled to the Union lines without the slightest warning, the servants who turned over the house and barn keys to the Yankees, the slaves who piloted the troops to where the family valuables had been secreted (often the same slaves who had helped to hide them), the slaves who told the Yankees everything, and the slaves who vented their bitterness on the most glaring and accessible symbols of their enslavement—the Big House and the cotton gin. John F. Andrews, an Alabama planter, stood by helplessly while his slaves assisted the Union soldiers in burning his residence and gin house. "The 'faithful slave' is about played out," he observed afterwards. "They are the most treacherous, brutal, and ungrateful race on the globe."

More than any government proclamation, the slaves themselves undermined the authority of the planter class. How they chose to do so—and when—varied with each slave. How slaveholding whites chose to make sense out of what was happening around them assumed a more familiar and uniform pattern. The terms used by masters and mistresses to describe the disaffection of enslaved black workers—"insolence," "impertinence," "impudence," "ingratitude," "betrayal," "desertion," "demoralization"—suggest how many of them perceived the "moment of truth." In the past, such terms had been employed to denote slave transgressions or departures from expected behavior. During the war, however, they took on added dimensions, as they recorded the very destruction of the slave order. To talk about "ingratitude" was to describe slaves who "defected" without a word to their masters. To talk about "insolence," "impudence," and "impertinence" was to describe slaves who refused to obey orders and to submit to punishment. (To a Virginia white woman, the blacks were acting "very independent and impudent," and like most whites she equated the two traits.) To talk about "demoralized" slaves was to describe slaves who were unwilling to work "as usual." To talk about a "rebellion" or a "state of mutiny" was to describe slaves who staged plantation strikes or slowdowns and who in some instances seized control of the plantations, ousting the overseers left in charge. To talk about "betrayal" was invariably to report the behavior of slaves in whom masters and mistresses had reposed the greatest trust and confidence. The plaintive cries of "betrayal" and "desertion" were heard most often, perhaps because they were the least comprehensible: "Those we loved best and who loved us best—as we thought—were the first to leave us." Neither "rebellious" nor "faithful" in the fullest sense of those terms, most slaves seemed to have balanced the habit of obedience against the intense desire for freedom. But as the war progressed, few owners found themselves able to predict with any confidence when the habit of obedience would become less compelling than the desire for freedom.

What the Civil War did was to sweep away the pretenses, dissolve the illusions, lay bare the tensions and instability inherent in the master-slave relationship, and reveal the many-sided personalities of enslaved black men and women. It taught the masters who claimed to "know" the Negro best that they knew him least of all, that they had mistaken the slave's outward demeanor for his inner feelings, his docility for contentment, his deference and accommodation for submission. Few sensed this more clearly than Louis Manigault, when he came to assess the wartime conduct of his slaves. The slave he had esteemed most highly, who had been his "constant companion" for thirty years, had been the first to create trouble. Subsequent "instances of ingratitude" persuaded Manigault that he could place no confidence in any of his slaves. "In too numerous instances those we esteemed the most have been the first to desert us." And when Manigault returned to the plantation after the war, he found his newly freed slaves even less recognizable. "I almost imagined myself with Chinese, Malays or even the Indians in the interior of the Philippine Islands."

For whites and blacks alike, the Civil War was an experience as traumatic and far-reaching as any in their lives. The Confederate States of America would assume legendary proportions in the annals and minds of white Southerners. But for black men and women, the ultimate significance of the Confederacy lay in its destruction. What for generations of whites remained a heroic struggle for independence took on a very different meaning for black southerners. To have prolonged the life of the Confederacy was to have prolonged their own enslavement and debasement. Understandably, few of them could embrace such a cause with any degree of enthusiasm, even if it was rooted in a southland they called their home. When he first heard of the act to recruit blacks for the Confederate Army, a Virginia slave could no longer restrain his emotions. "I never felt at liberty to speak my mind until they passed an act to put colored men into the army. That wrought upon my feelings so I couldn't but cry. . . . They asked me if I would fight for my country. I said, 'I have no country.' "

Freedom, Land, and Labor

ERIC FONER

Among white southerners, the all-absorbing question of 1865 and 1866 was, "Will the free Negro work?" For it was an article of faith among white southerners that the freedmen were inherently indolent and would work only under supervision and coercion by whites. The papers of planters, as well as newspapers and magazines, were filled with complaints of black labor having become "disorganized and repugnant to work or direction." As one group of Mississippi blacks observed, "Our faults are daily published by the editors, not a statement will you ever see in our favor. There is surely some among us that is honest, truthful and industrious." But to whites, the problem was clear-cut: as a member of South Carolina's Middleton family put it, "there is no power to make the negroes work and we know that without that they will not work."

In the years following the Civil War, a complex triangular debate was played out among freedmen, northern whites, and southern planters, over the nature of the South's new free labor system. For northerners, the meaning of "free labor" derived from the anti-slavery crusade, at the heart of which stood a critique of slavery dating back at least as far as Adam Smith. Slavery, Smith had insisted (more as an ideological article of faith than on the basis of empirical investigation) was the least efficient, most expensive method of making people work. The reason lay in unalterable facts of human nature. Labor was distasteful, and the only reason men worked productively was to acquire property and satisfy their material wants. Since the slave had no vested interest in the results of his labor, he worked as little as possible. Smith's message had been hammered home by the anti-slavery movement in the years before the Civil War: slavery was costly, inefficient, and unproductive; freedom meant prosperity, efficiency, and material progress.

An elaborate ideology defending the northern system of "free labor" had developed in the two decades before the Civil War. To men like Abraham Lincoln the salient quality of northern society was the ability of the laborer to escape the status of wage earner and rise to petty entrepreneurship and economic independence. Speaking within a republican tradition which defined freedom as resting on ownership of productive property, Lincoln used the term "free labor" to embrace small farmers and petty producers as well as wage laborers. But within this definition a question persisted: why should the independent artisan or farmer work at all, except to satisfy his immediate wants? The answer, once again, derived from the classical paradigm of Adam Smith, as elaborated by his American descendants Henry Carey, E. Pershine Smith, and others. The ever-increasing variety of human wants, desires, and ambitions was, for these writers, the greatest spur to economic progress. It was these "wants" which led northern farmers to produce for the market; indeed, from the northern point of view, participation in the marketplace honed those very qualities that distinguished northern labor from that of the slave—efficiency, productivity, industriousness.

Thus, there was no contradiction, in northern eyes, between the freedom of the laborer and unrelenting personal effort in the marketplace. As General O. O. Howard, head of the Freedmen's Bureau, told a group of blacks in 1865, "he would promise them nothing but their freedom, and freedom means work." Such statements, as well as the coercive labor policies adopted by the Bureau in many localities, have convinced recent scholars that an identity of interests existed between the Bureau and southern planters. Certainly, many Bureau practices seemed designed to serve the needs of the planters, especially the stringent orders of 1865 restricting blacks' freedom of movement and requiring them to sign labor contracts, while withholding relief rations from those who refused. On the other hand, it is difficult to reconcile this recent view of the Bureau with the unrelenting hostility of southern whites to its presence in the South.

The Freedmen's Bureau was not, in reality, the agent of the planters, nor was it precisely the agent of the former slaves. It can best be understood as the agent of the northern free labor ideology itself; its main concern was to put into operation a viable free labor system in the South. To the extent that this meant putting freedmen back to work on plantations, the Bureau's interests coincided with those of the planters. To the extent that the Bureau demanded for the freedmen the rights to which northern laborers were accustomed, it meant an alliance with the blacks. The issue was how the freedmen should be induced to work. Northerners looked to the market itself to provide the incentive, for it was participation in the marketplace which would make self-disciplined free laborers of the blacks, as well as generating a harmony of interests between capital and labor and allowing for social mobility, as, ostensibly, existed in the North. The northern preference for a system in which skilled and educated men worked voluntarily to satisfy ever-expanding wants, generating an endless spiral of prosperity for both capital and labor, was strikingly articulated by the Maine-born Georgia Bureau agent, John E. Bryant:

> Formerly, you were obliged to work or submit to punishment, now you must be induced to work, not compelled to do it. . . . You will be better laborers if educated. Men do not naturally love work, they are induced to work from necessity or interest. That man who has the most wants will usually labor with the greatest industry unless those wants are supplied without labor. The more intelligent men are the more wants they have, hence it is for the interest of all that the laborers shall be educated.

Although Bryant, like so many other Army and Bureau agents in 1865, issued stringent regulations against black "idleness and vagrancy," he essentially viewed the problem of southern economic readjustment through the lens of labor, rather than race. The same psychology that governed white labor, applied to blacks: "*No* man loves work naturally. . . . Why does the *white man* labor? That he may acquire property and the means of purchasing the comforts and luxuries of life. The *colored man* will labor for the same reason."

Spokesmen for the free labor ideology like Bryant viewed the contract system inaugurated by the Freedmen's Bureau in 1865 not as a permanent framework for the southern economy, but as a transitional arrangement, a way of reestablishing agricultural production until cash became readily available and a bona fide free labor system could emerge. General Robert K. Scott, head of the Bureau in South Carolina, explained rather cavalierly to Governor James L. Orr that the state could not hope to escape "the fixed principles which govern [free labor] all over the world." "To the establishment of these principles," he added, "the Bureau is committed." Even Wager Swayne, considered one of the most pro-planter state Bureau chiefs, believed the contract system was "only excusable as a transient." Eventually, as in the North, the natural internal mechanisms of the labor market would regulate employment: "This is more and better than all laws."

Men like Swayne and Scott, however, quickly became convinced that the planters did not comprehend the first principles of free labor. Scott found in 1866 that their idea of a contract was one "that would give the land owner an absolute control over the freedman as though he was his slave." Northern visitors to the South reached the same conclusion. Whitelaw Reid found planters "have no sort of conception of free labor. They do not comprehend any law for controlling laborers, save the law of force." Carl Schurz, one of the most articulate spokesmen for the free labor ideology before the war, concluded that white southerners were unable to accept the cardinal principles that "the only incentive to faithful labor is self-interest," and that a labor contract must be "a free transaction in which neither coercion nor protection is necessary."

Northern and southern perceptions of "free labor" did indeed differ. Planters did not believe that freedmen could ever achieve the internal self-discipline necessary for self-directed labor. The free labor ideology, they insisted, ignored "the characteristic indolence of the negro, which will ever be manifested and indulged in a condition of freedom." It was pointless, therefore, to speak of white and black labor in the same breath: the black was "*sui generis,* and you must argue for him upon his own characteristics." Only legal and physical compulsion could maintain the discipline and availability of plantation labor, in the face of the collapse of the planters' authority and the "indolence" of the laborers. "Our little sovereignties and Feudal arrangements are all levelled to the ground," bemoaned one South Carolina planter. As a result, planters turned to the state to provide the labor discipline which they could no longer command as individuals. "A new labor system," declared a New Orleans newspaper in 1865, must be "prescribed and enforced by the state." Hence, the southern legislatures of 1865–66 enacted a series of vagrancy laws, apprenticeship systems, criminal penalties for breach of contract, and all the other coercive measures of the Black Codes, in an effort to control the black labor force. As one Georgian explained, despite the general conviction that "the negro will not work. . . . we can control by wise laws."

The differences in outlook which divided northern and southern whites were strikingly expressed by a southern planter who told a northern visitor, "all we want, is that our Yankee rulers should give us the same privileges with regard to the control of labor which they themselves have." When informed that northern workers were not legally obligated to sign yearly contracts, and that there were no criminal penalties for leaving one's employment, he was incredulous: "How can you get work out of a man unless you *compel* him in some way?" This very question as Joyce Appleby has observed, haunted seventeenth- and eighteenth-century English economic theorists: how could individual freedom and the need for labor be reconciled, especially if it were assumed that men naturally desired to avoid labor? The answer was to posit a labor force imbued with economic rationality, that is, the willingness to subordinate itself to the incentives of the marketplace. "The acceptance of the idea of universal economic rationality," according to Appleby, "was the key step in the triumph of modern liberalism."

"Modern liberalism," however, had implications the leaders of southern society could not accept. The ideological underpinning of economic liberalism is freedom of choice among equals, however much free contract and equality may in fact diverge. By the time of the Civil War, the symbiotic relationship between political and economic liberty had become an article of faith in the North. "Everything which secures freedom and equality of rights at the South," a Republican newspaper stated in 1865, "tends directly to the benefit of trade." And, it might have added, vice versa. As Smith had argued, the market was egalitarian. It freed men from dependent relationships and paternalist obligations, and threatened traditional ruling classes with its guarantee of perpetual social and economic change. By breaking down traditional economic privileges, it fostered the idea of equality.

Yet planter spokesmen did not want a laboring force, black or white, with such ideas. The central premise of the free labor ideology—the opportunity for social mobility for the laborer—was anathema to planters, who could not conceive of either a plantation economy or their own social privileges surviving if freedmen were able to move up the social scale. "You must begin at the bottom of the ladder and climb up," General Howard informed a black New Orleans audience in 1865, but at least he offered the opportunity to climb. A Natchez newspaper at the same time was informing its readers, "the true station of the negro is that of a servant. The wants and state of our country demand that he should remain a servant." A delegate to the Texas Constitutional Convention of 1866 agreed: the freedmen must remain "hewers of wood and drawers of water." As for white labor, there was a concerted, though unsuccessful effort to attract immigrants to the South during Reconstruction. Pamphlets appeared singing the praises of "the thrifty German, the versatile Italian, the sober Englishman, the sturdy sons of Erin," in contrast to blacks who did not understand "the moral obligations of a contract." Yet others noted that such immigrants might bring with them unwanted ideas. "Servants of this description may please some tastes," said a southern newspaper in 1867, "but the majority of our people would probably prefer the sort we have, who neither feel nor profess equality with their employer."

Nor could white southerners accept the other half of the free labor equation—market-oriented rationality on the part of their laborers. In the recent work of "cliometricians" investigating post-bellum southern history, the freedmen emerge from slavery as, to use their terminology, rational, market-oriented profit-maximizers. It is difficult, however, to accept the idea that slavery produced workers socialized to the discipline of capitalist wage labor. The slave's standard of consumption, and his experience with the marketplace, was, of necessity, very limited. The logic of ever-greater effort to meet ever-expanding needs (what capitalist society calls "ambition") had no meaning for him. As one planter complained, freedmen did not respond to the marketplace incentives to steady labor: "released from the discipline of slavery, unappreciative of the value of money, and but little desirous of comfort, his efforts are capricious."

Here, indeed, lies the ultimate meaning of the innumerable complaints about the freedman's work habits—so reminiscent, it might be noted, of labor "problems" in the Third World today. Why did so many whites constantly claim that blacks were lazy and idle? The tendency of historians has been to deny the accuracy of such complaints, attributing them to simple racism. Doubtless, there is justification for this response, but it does not go to the heart of the matter. Consider two examples of such complaints. The first is from a Maryland newspaper in 1864, just after emancipation in that state: "The ambition of the negro, as a race, when left to his own volition, does not rise above the meagre necessities of life. . . . One fruitful source of idleness has been the ability to possess themselves of a hut and a few acres of land, thereby enabling them to preserve the semblance of a means of living." The second is a remark by the North Carolina planter and political leader Kemp P. Battle in 1866: "Want of ambition will be the devil of the race, I think. Some of my most sensible men say they have no other desire than to cultivate their own land in grain and raise bacon."

On the face of it, a desire to cultivate one's own land in food crops does not appear to warrant the charge of "want of ambition." The term "indolence," it appears, encompassed not simply blacks unwilling to work at all, but those who preferred to work for themselves. The same plantation blacks arraigned for idleness spent considerable time and effort on their own garden plots and, as is well known, it was the universal desire of the freedmen to own their own plots of land. What one Mississippi white called the freedman's "wild notions of right and freedom" were actually very traditional in republican America. Blacks believed, according to another Mississippi planter, "that if they are hirelings they will still be slaves." Whether in withdrawing from churches dominated by whites, refusing to work under drivers and overseers, or in their ubiquitous desire for forty acres and a mule, blacks made clear that, for them, freedom meant independence from white control. "Their great desire," wrote a Georgia planter, "seems to be to get away from all overseers, to hire or purchase land, and work for themselves." From the freedmen's point of view, an Alabama Bureau agent reported, this would "complete their emancipation."

The vast majority of freedmen, of course, were compelled by necessity to labor on the plantations, but they too appeared to respond only imperfectly to the incentives and demands of the marketplace. Many freedmen did seek the highest wages available, whether this meant moving to states like Texas and Arkansas where labor was scarce and wages high, or seeking employment in railroad construction crews, turpentine mills, and lumber companies. Others, however, seemed to value things like freedom of movement off the plantations and personal autonomy more than pecuniary rewards. "Let any man offer them some little thing of no real benefit to them, but which looks like a little more freedom," Georgia's Howell Cobb observed, "and they catch at it with alacrity." And a Mississippi Bureau agent reported, "many have said to me they cared not for the pay if they were only treated with kindness and not over worked."

Instead of working harder than they had as slaves, as Adam Smith would have predicted, the freedmen desired to work less, and black women sought to withdraw from field labor altogether. "The women say that they never mean to do any more outdoor work," said a report from Alabama. "White men support their wives and they mean that their husbands shall support them." Those women who did remain in the fields were sometimes even more "undisciplined" than the men. One rice plantation worker told her employer in 1866 on being ordered to complete a task, "she did not know if she would . . . and could 'not work herself to death before her time came.' "

Most distressing of all, many freedmen evinced a strong resistance to growing the "slave crop" cotton. As one Georgia freedman said, "If ole massa want to grow cotton, let him plant it himself." On the Sea Islands, they refused to repair broken cotton gins and displayed more interest in subsisting on garden plots, fishing, and hunting than producing a crop for the marketplace. Freedom, for Sea Island blacks, seemed to mean "no more driver, no more cotton." The South Carolina planter Edward B. Heyward noted the irony of the situation:

> It seems the belief among planters, that negroes *will not plant cotton* but are interested only in *food*. Wouldn't it be curious if by the voluntary act of the emancipated blacks, the New England manufacturers should fail. . . . They are going to worry somebody, and I think it will be their friends the Yankees. They say we can't *eat cotton* and there they stop.

As Heyward suggested, on the question of cotton a community of interest did indeed exist between northern and southern whites interested in the revitalization of the plantation economy. Their great fear was that the freedmen might retreat into self-sufficiency. "The products of these islands are absolutely necessary to supply the wants of the commercial world," wrote a northern investor from St. Helena, South Carolina, in 1865. Two years later another northerner with an eye to southern investments commented on the absolute necessity of reviving an export cotton crop to "pay our debts and get the balance of trade in our favor." To such men, and many others who looked to the post-war South for the investment of war-generated surplus capital, the idea of granting subsistence plots to the freedmen was disastrous. As Willie Lee Rose has shown, the arguments between land reform and cotton production were articulated during the war itself, in the conflict on the Sea Islands between the freedmen and moral reformers like Laura Towne on the one hand, and representatives of northeastern business like Edward Atkinson and Edward Philbrick, who envisioned a post-war economy in which blacks worked cotton plantations for reasonable wages.

To Atkinson and Philbrick, the Port Royal experiment provided a golden opportunity to prove "that the abandonment of slavery did not mean the abandonment of cotton," that free blacks could raise the crop more efficiently and profitably than as slaves. Cotton was the measure of freedom, for as Philbrick put it, "as a general thing, the amount of cotton planted will always be a pretty sure index to the state of industry of the people." In order to "multiply their simple wants" as a means of stimulating interest in cotton among blacks, Philbrick established plantation stores, placing a variety of new products within the freedmen's reach. His great fear was that they might retreat into self-sufficiency, removing themselves from the disciplines of the marketplace, eliminating them as consumers of northern goods, and enabling them to resist the exploitation of their labor (except by themselves).

Of course, complete self-sufficiency was rarely possible in nineteenth-century America. But the Sea Island experience—where many blacks did acquire small plots of land—as well as scattered evidence from other states, suggests that black landowners and renters preferred to farm much in the manner of ante-bellum upcountry white yeomen, concentrating on food crops as a first priority, and only to a lesser extent on cotton, for ready cash. The pattern persisted into the 1870s, except where rental contracts specifically required, in the words of one, that "all of said land is to be cultivated in cotton." The ambition of the freedmen to own or rent land, therefore, cannot be understood as simply a quest for material accumulation and social mobility; it reflected above all a desire for autonomy from both individual whites, and the impersonal marketplace. And it was this ambition which frightened both southern planters and the Atkinsons and Philbricks.

The experience of labor in other post-emancipation situations was hardly reassuring to such men. Southerners were well aware of the aftermath of emancipation in the West Indies, which appeared to demonstrate that the end of slavery spelled the end of plantation agriculture. Plantations could not be maintained with free labor, wrote a prominent Charlestonian; "the experiments made in Hayti and Jamaica settled that question long ago." On those islands the freedmen had been able to drift off the plantations and take up small farming, and the result had been a catastrophic decline in sugar production. "See what ruin emancipation brought on that paradise of the tropics," observed one southern writer. Comparative studies of emancipation in the West Indies and South America reveal that nearly every plantation society enacted vagrancy, contract, and debt peonage laws in an attempt to keep freedmen on the plantations. But only where land was not available—or another source of unfree labor was—did the plantation survive. Trinidad, with little free land, was a success: "land . . . is owned by the white man and the negro is unable to get possession of a foot of it." So was Guyana, where imported East Indian coolies replaced the blacks on sugar plantations. But not Jamaica, where uninhabited land was available for the freedmen.

The lesson of the West Indies seemed clear: without "some well regulated system of labor . . . devised by the white man . . . the South would soon become a second Haiti." Basically, the problem seemed to be that free people do not like to work on plantations. This was why slavery had been "necessary" in the first place, and why the chimera of white immigration was bound to fail. As a Georgia newspaper observed in 1866, "everybody must know that no white man is going to work as a negro on a large estate, to rise at the sound of a horn and return when the dews are heavy." But the myth that they would persisted for years, as did the reluctance of white immigrants to move South. The Selma *Southern Argus*, one of the most perceptive spokesmen for the planter class, explained the problem: "Our people . . . have vainly expected an impossibility—white immigrants to take the place of the negro as hewers of wood and drawers of water. . . . They want . . . labor to occupy the social position of negroes and to be treated like negroes." Others looked to the Chinese immigrant, who, it was believed, was more manageable than the black. "He is not likely to covet ownership of the soil, and . . . he is not likely to become a politician," commented a Mississippi planter.

In the end, if the plantations were to continue, it would have to be with black labor. This was why white southerners absolutely insisted that blacks not be allowed access to land. Unlike the West Indies, the "availability" of land in the South was a political issue, not a matter determined by geography, for there was an abundance of uncultivated land. Less than a tenth of Louisiana's thirty million acres, for example, were being tilled at the end of Reconstruction. The fear that access to land for blacks would lead to the disintegration of staple production was graphically expressed by an Alabama newspaper, commenting on the Southern Homestead Act of 1866, which offered public land to black farmers:

> The negroes will become possessed of a small freehold, will raise their corn, squashes, pigs and chickens, and will work no more in the cotton, rice and sugar fields. In other words, their labor will become unavailable for those products which the world especially needs. . . . The title of this law ought to have been, "A bill to get rid of the laboring class of the South and make Cuffee a self-supporting nuisance."

Even if relatively few independent black farmers succeeded economically, the result would be disastrous. As a Mississippi planter put it, in that case, "all the others will be dissatisfied with their wages no matter how good they may be and thus our whole labor system is bound to be upset."

Thus, the problem of adjustment from slave to free labor was compounded by racial and class assumptions, ideas about the nature of labor itself, which dictated to white southerners that blacks not be allowed to escape the plantations, and led many northerners to agree that the road to black landownership should lie through patient wage labor—while market values and responses were learned—rather than a sudden "gift" of land.

⅄ *F U R T H E R   R E A D I N G*

Martin Abbott, *The Freedmen's Bureau in South Carolina, 1865–1872* (1967)
Roberta Sue Alexander, *North Carolina Faces the Freedmen* (1985)
Ira Berlin et al., eds., *Freedom: A Documentary History of Emancipation* (1985)
James A. Brewer, *The Confederate Negro* (1969)
John Cimprich, *Slavery's End in Tennessee* (1986)
Dudley Cornish, *The Sable Arm* (1956)
Paul D. Escott, *Slavery Remembered* (1979)
Barbara Jeanne Fields, *Slavery and Freedom on the Middle Ground* (1985)
Eric Foner, *Nothing but Freedom* (1983)
——, *Politics and Ideology in the Age of the Civil War* (1983)
Louis S. Gerteis, *From Contraband to Freedman* (1973)
Herbert G. Gutman, *The Black Family in Slavery and Freedom, 1750–1925* (1976)
Peter Kolchin, *First Freedom* (1972)
Leon Litwack, *Been in the Storm So Long* (1979)
William S. McFeely, *Yankee Stepfather* (1968)
James M. McPherson, *The Negro's Civil War* (1965)
Edward Magdol, *A Right to the Land* (1977)
Clarence L. Mohr, *On the Threshold of Freedom* (1986)
Claude F. Oubre, *Forty Acres and a Mule* (1978)
Benjamin Quarles, *The Negro in the Civil War* (1953)
Peter C. Ripley, *Slaves and Freedmen in Civil War Louisiana* (1976)
Armstead Robinson, *Bitter Fruits of Bondage* (forthcoming)
Willie Lee Rose, *Rehearsal for Reconstruction* (1964)
Clarence G. Walker, *A Rock in a Weary Land* (1982)
Bell I. Wiley, *Southern Negroes, 1861–1865* (1938)

Reconstruction

⊥
人

At one time, historians echoed the assessment of Reconstruction prevailing among white southerners: that Reconstruction had been a disastrous episode in which unscrupulous northern carpetbaggers, aided by traitorous scalawags and unqualified blacks, wrested power in southern governments and inaugurated an orgy of corruption, robbery, and misrule. But the civil-rights movement and new historical research since 1960 has led to a complete revision of this once-standard interpretation. While noting the importance of many white southerners' opposition to racial and other changes, revisionist studies have presented a much more factual assessment of the personnel and policies of Reconstruction. The twists and turns of policymaking in Washington, from Andrew Johnson's first and apparently harsh plan to the adoption of so-called Radical Reconstruction, are now better understood, and more objective attention has been given to the actions and character of Republicans—white and black—in the South.

What exactly did Reconstruction policies require? What consideration was given to land reform or land redistribution? What kind of competition prevailed between Democrats (or Conservatives) and Republicans in the South? What policies did Republican governments follow? And what impact did the Ku Klux Klan and other terrorist organizations have on Reconstruction? This chapter explores these probing questions.

人 *D O C U M E N T S*

Andrew Johnson's proclamations, reprinted as the first document, described the first plan of Reconstruction, which he implemented and then partially abandoned during 1865. His Amnesty Proclamation applied to the entire South; separate proclamations for reestablishing governments in each state followed the model of the North Carolina Proclamation. Although portions of the Amnesty Proclamation suggest that Johnson intended to remove prominent slaveholders from power, the President issued wholesale pardons to leading Confederates, even those who had violated his proclamations and sought office without a pardon. Alarmed by the return of Confederate leaders to power and upset by state laws that restricted southern blacks' liberty—the Black Codes—the northern Congress stepped in. Congress's involvement in Reconstruction is summarized in the proposed Fourteenth Amendment, which Johnson's white governments in the southern states rejected, and then in the Military Reconstruction Act of 1867— the second and third documents, respectively. Certain "Radical" Republicans urged stronger measures that were not taken. Thaddeus Stevens, a leading Radical in the House, was the principal, but one of the few, advocates of land confiscation and redistribution. Note the features in his proposal, outlined in the fourth document, that are designed to make it appealing to the many who disapproved of it. The fifth document contains excerpts from the *Raleigh* (North Carolina) *Sentinel* that reveal how quickly southern opponents of Congress's measures began to construct the legend of Reconstruction misrule. As these excerpts show, Southern Conservatives or Democrats also typically blamed all violence on the Republicans; their views are revealed in the sixth and seventh documents. To many southern whites, the granting of the right to vote to black people was simply intolerable, as shown in document eight. The ninth document reprints instructions to South Carolina's Red Shirts, armed supporters of Democratic gubernatorial candidate Wade Hampton. These instructions make clear that white Democrats were determined to regain control of the government at any price. The final selection comprises cartoons by Thomas Nast for *Harper's Weekly* that comment graphically on the issues of Reconstruction.

Andrew Johnson Begins Reconstruction, 1865

Amnesty Proclamation

. . . To the end that the authority of the Government of the United States may be restored and that peace, order, and freedom may be established, I, Andrew Johnson, President of the United States, do proclaim and declare that I hereby grant to all persons who have, directly or indirectly, participated in the existing rebellion, except as hereinafter excepted, amnesty and pardon, with restoration of all rights of property, except as to slaves, . . . but upon the condition, nevertheless, that every such person shall take and subscribe the following oath (or affirmation) and thenceforward keep and maintain said oath inviolate, . . . to wit:

I, ———, do solemnly swear (or affirm), in presence of Almighty God, that I will henceforth faithfully support, protect, and defend the Constitution of the United States and the Union of the States thereunder, and that I will in like manner abide by and faithfully support all laws and proclamations which have been made during the existing rebellion with reference to the emancipation of slaves. So help me God.

The following classes of persons are excepted from the benefits of this proclamation:

First. All who are or shall have been pretended civil or diplomatic officers or otherwise domestic or foreign agents of the pretended Confederate government.

Second. All who left judicial stations under the United States to aid the rebellion.

Third. All who shall have been military or naval officers of said pretended Confederate government above the rank of colonel in the army or lieutenant in the navy.

Fourth. All who left seats in the Congress of the United States to aid the rebellion.

Fifth. All who resigned or tendered resignations of their commissions in the Army or Navy of the United States to evade duty in resisting the rebellion.

Sixth. All who have engaged in any way in treating otherwise than lawfully as prisoners of war persons found in the United States service as officers, soldiers, seamen, or in other capacities. . . .

Eighth. All military and naval officers in the rebel service who were educated by the Government in the Military Academy at West Point or the United States Naval Academy.

Ninth. All persons who held the pretended offices of governors of States in insurrection against the United States. . . .

Thirteenth. All persons who have voluntarily participated in said rebellion and the estimated value of whose taxable property is over $20,000. . . .

Provided, That special application may be made to the President for pardon by any person belonging to the excepted classes, and such clemency will be liberally extended as may be consistent with the facts of the case and the peace and dignity of the United States.

North Carolina Proclamation

. . . Whereas the rebellion which has been waged by a portion of the people of the United States against the properly constituted authorities of the Government thereof in the most violent and revolting form, but whose organized and armed forces have now been almost entirely overcome, has in its revolutionary progress deprived the people of the State of North Carolina of all civil government; and

Whereas it becomes necessary and proper to carry out and enforce the obligations of the United States to the people of North Carolina in securing them in the enjoyment of a republican form of government:

Now, therefore, in obedience to the high and solemn duties imposed upon me by the Constitution of the United States and for the purpose of enabling the loyal people of said State to organize a State government whereby justice may be established, domestic tranquillity insured, and loyal citizens protected in all their rights of life, liberty, and property, I, Andrew Johnson, President of the United States and Commander in Chief of the Army and Navy of the United States, do hereby appoint William W. Holden provisional governor of the State of North Carolina, whose duty it shall be, at the earliest practicable period, to prescribe such rules and regulations as may be necessary and proper for convening a convention composed of delegates to be chosen by that portion of the people of said State who are loyal to the United States, and no others, for the purpose of altering or amending the constitution thereof, and with authority to exercise within the limits of said State all the powers necessary and proper to enable such loyal people of the State of North Carolina to restore said State to its constitutional relations to the Federal Government and to present such a republican form of State government as will entitle the State to the guaranty of the United States therefor and its people to protection by the United States against invasion, insurrection, and domestic violence: *Provided,* That in any election that may be hereafter held for choosing delegates to any State convention as aforesaid no person shall be qualified as an elector or shall be eligible as a member of such convention unless he shall have previously taken and subscribed the oath of amnesty as set forth in the President's proclamation of May 29, A.D. 1865, and is a voter qualified as prescribed by the constitution and laws of the State of North Carolina in force immediately before the 20th day of May, A.D. 1861, the date of the so-called ordinance of secession; and the said convention, when convened, or the legislature that may be thereafter assembled, will prescribe the qualification of electors and the eligibility of persons to hold office under the constitution and laws of the State—a power the people of the several States composing the Federal Union have rightfully exercised from the origin of the Government to the present time.

And I do hereby direct—

First. That the military commander of the department and all officers and persons in the military and naval service aid and assist the said provisional governor in carrying into effect this proclamation. . . .

Second. That the Secretary of State proceed to put in force all laws of the United States the administration whereof belongs to the State Department applicable to the geographical limits aforesaid.

Third. That the Secretary of the Treasury proceed to nominate for appointment assessors of taxes and collectors of customs and internal revenue and such other officers of the Treasury Department as are authorized by law and put in execution the revenue laws of the United States within the geographical limits aforesaid. . . .

Fourth. That the Postmaster-General proceed to establish post-offices and post routes and put into execution the postal laws of the United States within the said State. . . .

Fifth. That the district judge for the judicial district in which North Carolina is included proceed to hold courts within said State in accordance with the provisions of the act of Congress. . . .

Sixth. That the Secretary of the Navy take possession of all public property belonging to the Navy Department within said geographical limits and put in operation all acts of Congress in relation to naval affairs having application to the said State.

Seventh. That the Secretary of the Interior put in force the laws relating to the Interior Department applicable to the geographical limits aforesaid.

Congress Proposes the Fourteenth Amendment, 1866

Sec. 1. All persons born or naturalized in the United States, and subject to the jurisdiction thereof, are citizens of the United States and of the State wherein they reside. No State shall make or enforce any law which shall abridge the privileges or immunities of citizens of the United States; nor shall any State deprive any person of life, liberty or property, without due process of law, nor deny to any person within its jurisdiction the equal protection of the laws.

Sec. 2. Representatives shall be apportioned among the several States according to their respective numbers, counting the whole number of persons in each State, excluding Indians not taxed. But when the right to vote at any election for the choice of electors for President and Vice President of the United States, representatives in Congress, the executive and judicial officers of a State, or the members of the Legislature thereof, is denied to any of the male inhabitants of such State, being twenty-one years of age, and citizens of the United States, or in any way abridged, except for participation in rebellion or other crime, the basis of representation therein shall be reduced in the proportion which the number of such male citizens shall bear to the whole number of male citizens twenty-one years of age in said State.

Sec. 3. No Person shall be Senator or Representative in Congress, or elector of President or Vice President, or hold any office, civil or military, under the United States, or under any State, who, having previously taken an oath as a member of Congress, or as an officer of the United States, or as a member of any State Legislature, or as an executive or judicial officer of any State, to support the Constitution of the United States, shall have engaged in insurrection or rebellion against the same, or given aid or comfort to the enemies thereof. But Congress may, by a vote of two-thirds of each House, remove such disability.

Sec. 4. The validity of the public debt of the United States, authorized by law, including debts incurred for payment of pensions and bounties for services in suppressing insurrection or rebellion, shall not be questioned. But neither the United States nor any State shall assume or pay any debt or obligation incurred in aid of insurrection or rebellion against the United States or any claim for the loss or emancipation of any slave; but all such debts, obligations, and claims shall be held illegal and void.

Sec. 5. The Congress shall have power to enforce, by appropriate legislation, the provisions of this article.

The Military Reconstruction Act, 1867

Whereas no legal State governments or adequate protection for life or property now exists in the rebel States of Virginia, North Carolina, South Carolina, Georgia, Mississippi, Alabama, Louisiana, Florida, Texas, and Arkansas; and whereas it is necessary that peace and good order should be enforced in said States until loyalty and republican State governments can be legally established: Therefore

Be it enacted, . . . That said rebel States shall be divided into military districts and made subject to the military authority of the United States . . .

Sec. 2. . . . It shall be the duty of the President to assign to the command of each of said districts an officer of the army, not below the rank of brigadier general, and to detail a sufficient military force to enable such officer to perform his duties and enforce his authority within the district to which he is assigned.

Sec. 3. . . . It shall be the duty of each officer assigned as aforesaid to protect all persons in their rights of person and property, to suppress insurrection, disorder, and violence, and to punish, or cause to be punished, all disturbers of the public peace and criminals, and to this end he may allow local civil tribunals to take jurisdiction of and to try offenders, or, when in his judgment it may be necessary for the trial of offenders, he shall have power to organize military commissions or tribunals for that purpose; and all interference under color of State authority with the exercise of military authority under this act shall be null and void. . . .

Sec. 5. . . . When the people of any one of said rebel States shall have formed a constitution of government in conformity with the Constitution of the United States in all respects, framed by a convention of delegates elected by the male citizens of said State twenty-one years old and upward, of whatever race, color, or previous condition, . . . and when such constitution shall provide that the elective franchise shall be enjoyed by all such persons as have the qualifications herein stated for electors of delegates, and when such constitution shall be ratified by a majority of the persons voting on the question of ratification who are qualified as electors of delegates, and when such constitution shall have been submitted to Congress for examination and approval, and Congress shall have approved the same, and when said State, by a vote of its legislature elected under said constitution, shall have adopted the amendment to the Constitution of the United States, proposed by the thirty-ninth Congress, and known as article fourteen, and when said article shall have become a part of the Constitution of the United States, said State shall be declared entitled to representation in Congress, and senators and representatives shall be admitted therefrom on their taking oaths prescribed by law, and then and thereafter the preceding sections of this act shall be inoperative in said State: *Provided,* That no person excluded from the privilege of holding office by said proposed amendment to the Constitution of the United States shall be eligible to election as a member of the convention to frame a constitution for any of said rebel States, nor shall any such person vote for members of such convention.

Sec. 6. . . . Until the people of said rebel States shall be by law admitted to representation in the Congress of the United States, any civil governments which may exist therein shall be deemed provisional only, and in all respects subject to the paramount authority of the United States at any time to abolish, modify or control, or supersede the same; and in all elections to any office under such provisional governments all persons shall be entitled to vote, and none others, who are entitled to vote under the provisions of the fifth section of this act; and no person shall be eligible to any office under any such provisional governments who would be disqualified from holding office under the provisions of the third article of said constitutional amendment.

Thaddeus Stevens Advocates the Redistribution of Land, 1865

Reformation *must* be effected; the foundation of their institutions, both political, municipal and social *must* be broken up and *relaid*, or all our blood and treasure have been spent in vain. This can only be done by treating and holding them as a conquered people. Then all things which we can desire to do, follow with logical and legitimate authority. As conquered territory Congress would have full power to legislate for them; for the territories are not under the Constitution except so far as the express power to govern them is given to Congress. They would be held in a territorial condition until they are fit to form State Constitutions, republican in fact not in form only, and ask admission into the Union as new States. If Congress approve of their Constitutions, and think they have done works meet for repentance they would be admitted as new States. If their Constitutions are not approved of, they would be sent back, until they have become wise enough so to purge their old laws as to eradicate every despotic and revolutionary principle—until they shall have learned to venerate the Declaration of Independence. . . .

We propose to confiscate all the estate of every rebel belligerent whose estate was worth $10,000, or whose land exceeded two hundred acres in quantity. Policy if not justice would require that the poor, the ignorant, and the coerced should be forgiven. They followed the example and teachings of their wealthy and intelligent neighbors. The rebellion would never have originated with them. Fortunately those who would thus escape form a large majority of the people, though possessing but a small portion of the wealth. The proportion of those exempt compared with the punished would be I believe about nine tenths.

There are about six millions of freemen in the South. The number of acres of land is 465,000,000. Of this those who own above two hundred acres each, number about 70,000 persons, holding in the aggregate (together with the States) about 394,000,000 acres, leaving for all the others below 200 each about 71,000,000 of acres. By thus forfeiting the estates of the leading rebels, the Government would have 394,000,000 of acres beside their town property, and yet nine tenths of the people would remain untouched. Divide this land into convenient farms. Give if you please forty acres to each adult male freed man. Suppose there are one million of them. That would require 40,000,000 of acres, which deducted from 394,000,000 leaves three hundred and fifty-four millions of acres for sale. Divide it into suitable farms and sell it to the highest bidders. I think it, including town property, would average at least ten dollars per acre. That would produce $3,540,000,000,—Three billions, five hundred and forty millions of dollars.

Let that be applied as follows to wit:

1. Invest $300,000,000 in six per cent. government bonds, and add the interest semi-annually to the pensions of those who have become entitled by this villainous war.

2. Appropriate $200,000,000 to pay the damages done to loyal men North and South by the rebellion.
3. Pay the residue being $3,040,000,000 towards the payment of the National debt.

What loyal man can object to this? Look around you, and everywhere behold your neighbors, some with an arm, some with a leg, some with an eye carried away by rebel bullets. Others horribly mutilated in every form. And yet numerous others wearing the weeds which mark the death of those on whom they leaned for support. Contemplate these monuments of rebel perfidy, and of patriotic suffering, and then say if too much is asked for our valient soldiers.

Look again, and see loyal men reduced to poverty by the confiscations by the Confederate States, and by the rebel States—see Union men robbed of their property, and their dwellings laid in ashes by rebel raiders, and say if too much is asked for them. But above all, let us inquire whether imperative duty to the present generation and to posterity does not command us to compel the wicked enemy to pay the expenses of this unjust war. In ordinary transactions he who raises a false clamor and prosecutes an unfounded suit, is adjudged to pay the costs on his defeat. We have seen that, by the law of nations, the vanquished in an unjust war must pay the expenses.

Our war debt is estimated at from three to four billions of dollars. In my judgment, when all is funded and the pensions capitalized, it will reach more than four billions.

The interest at 6 per cent only, (now much more)	$240,000,000
. . . .	120,000,000
For some years the extraordinary expenses of our army and navy will be	110,000,000
	$470,000,000

Four hundred and seventy millions to be raised by taxation—our present heavy taxes will not in ordinary years, produce but little more than half that sum. Can our people bear double their present taxation? He who unnecessarily causes it will be accursed from generation to generation. It is fashionable to belittle our public debt, lest the people should become alarmed, and political parties should suffer. I have never found it wise to deceive the people. They can always be trusted with the truth. Capitalists will not be effected for they can not be deceived. Confide in the people, and you will avoid repudiation. Deceive them, and lead them into false measures, and you may produce it.

We pity the poor Englishmen whose national debt and burdensome taxation we have heard deplored from our childhood. The debt of Great Britain is just about as much as ours, ($4,000,000,000) four billions. But in effect it is but half as large,—it bears but three per cent interest. The current year the Chancellor of the Exchequer tells us, the interest was $131,806,990, ours, when all shall be funded, will be nearly double.

The plan we have proposed would pay at least three fourths of our debt. The balance could be managed with our present taxation. And yet to think that even that is to be perpetual is sickening. If it is to be doubled, as it must be, if "restoration" instead of "reconstruction" is to prevail, would to God the authors of it could see themselves as an execrating public and posterity will see them. . . .

But, it is said, by those who have more sympathy with rebel wives and children than for the widows and orphans of loyal men, that this stripping the rebels of their estates and driving them to exile or to honest labor would be harsh and severe upon innocent women and children. It may be so; but that is the result of the necessary laws of war. But it is revolutionary, say they. This plan would, no doubt, work a radical reorganization in southern institutions, habits and manners. It is intended to revolutionize their principles and feelings. This may startle feeble minds and shake weak nerves. So do all great improvements in the political and moral world. It requires a heavy impetus to drive forward a sluggish people. When it was first proposed to free the slaves, and arm the blacks, did not half the nation tremble? The prim conservatives, the snobs, and the male waiting maids in Congress, were in hysterics.

The whole fabric of southern society *must* be changed, and never can it be done if this opportunity is lost. Without this, this Government can never be, as it never has been, a true republic. Heretofore, it had more the features of aristocracy than of democracy.—The Southern States have been despotisms, not governments of the people. It is impossible that any practical equality of rights can exist where a few thousand men monopolize the whole landed property. The larger the number of small proprietors the more safe and stable the government. As the landed interest must govern, the more it is subdivided and held by independent owners, the better. What would be the condition of the State of New York if it were not for her independent yeomanry? She would be overwhelmed and demoralized by the Jews, Milesians and vagabonds of licentious cities. How can republican institutions, free schools, free churches, free social intercourse exist in a mingled community of nabobs and serfs; of the owners of twenty thousand acre manors with lordly palaces, and the occupants of narrow huts inhabited by "low white trash?"—If the south is ever to be made a safe republic let her lands be cultivated by the toil of the owners or the free labor of intelligent citizens. This must be done even though it drive her nobility into exile. If they go, all the better.

It will be hard to persuade the owner of ten thousand acres of land, who drives a coach and four, that he is not degraded by sitting at the same table, or in the same pew, with the embrowned and hard-handed farmer who has himself cultivated his own thriving homestead of 150 acres. This subdivision of the lands will yield ten bales of cotton to one that is made now, and he who produced it will own it and *feel himself a man*.

It is far easier and more beneficial to exile 70,000 proud, bloated and defiant rebels, than to expatriate four millions of laborers, native to the soil and loyal to the Government. This latter scheme was a favorite plan of the Blairs with which they had for awhile inoculated our late sainted President. But, a single experiment, made him discard it and its advisers. Since I have mentioned the Blairs, I may say a word more of those persistent apologists of the South. For, when the virus of Slavery has once entered the veins of the slaveholder, no subsequent effort seems capable of wholly eradicating it. They are a family of considerable power, some merit, of admirable audacity, and execrable selfishness; with impetuous alacrity they seize the White House, and hold possession of it, as in the late Administration, until shaken off by the overpowering force of public indignation. Their pernicious course had well nigh defeated the reelection of Abraham Lincoln; and if it should prevail with the present Administration, pure and patriotic as President Johnson is admitted to be, it will render him the most unpopular Executive—save one—that ever occupied the Presidential chair. But there is no fear of that. He will soon say, as Mr. Lincoln did: "YOUR TIME HAS COME!"

This remodeling the institutions, and reforming the rooted habits of a proud aristocracy, is undoubtedly a formidable task; requiring the broad mind of enlarged statesmanship, and the firm nerve of the hero. But will not this mighty occasion produce—will not the God of Liberty and order give us such men? Will not a Romulus, a Lycurgus, a Charlemagne, a Washington arise, whose expansive views will found a free empire, to endure till time shall be no more?

This doctrine of restoration shocks me.—We have a duty to perform which our fathers were incapable of, which will be required at our hands by God and our Country. When our ancestors found a "more perfect Union" necessary, they found it impossible to agree upon a Constitution without tolerating, nay guaranteeing Slavery. They were obliged to acquiesce, trusting to time to work a speedy cure, in which they were disappointed. *They* had some excuse, some justification. But we can have none if we do not thoroughly eradicate Slavery and render it forever impossible in this republic. The Slave power made war upon the nation. They declared the "more perfect Union" dissolved. Solemnly declared themselves a foreign nation, alien to this republic; for four years were in fact what they claimed to be, We accepted the war which they tendered and treated them as a government capable of making war. We have conquered them, and as a conquered enemy we can give them laws; can abolish all their municipal institutions and form new ones. If we do not make those institutions fit to last through generations of free men, a heavy curse will be on us. Our glorious, but tainted republic has been born to new life through bloody, agonizing pains. But this frightful "Restoration" has thrown it into "cold obstruction, and to death." If the rebel states have never been out of the Union, any attempt to reform their State institutions either by Congress or the President, is rank usurpation.

A Southern Newspaper Denounces Reconstruction, 1869

That the State has been cursed and almost ruined by a class of "carpet bag" vultures from the North, aided by degenerate and too often corrupt natives, is patent to anybody who opens his eyes. We have not been slow to tell the people of the villianies that have been perpetrated and are yet being perpetrated, day and night, by the present State government, at the expense and injury of the people, black and white. We intend to continue to do so regardless of cost or consequences.

Our firm conviction is that the people will not tolerate these villainies a great while longer; the day of reckoning cometh, and it will be terrible. The "carpet bagger" race will then hurry off to some other field of spoils and laugh at the calamity of their dupes and co-workers in iniquity; but the *native* culprit must answer at the bar of public opinion, and in many cases at the bar of the Court for high crimes. We tell the native scalawags that the day is not far distant, when the thin vail that now hides their crimes from public gaze will be withdrawn, and they will be exposed to the scorn and indignation of an outraged people. Yes, and that small class of our people who claim to be good and true men, who, for the sake of a little gain, have *secretly* colluded with the bad wretches who have plundered and impoverished the people without mercy, they, too, will be exposed. Yes, we repeat, the day will be mercilessly exposed. And such perpetration or crime will thenceforth be a *stench* in the nostrils of all decent men, white and black. Everybody will bate them, mock and hiss at them as they pass by. The Penitentiary fraud will be exposed, the Railroad frauds will be exposed; it will yet be known how much money was used to corrupt the members of the Legislature, who used it, who paid it, and where it came from; it will yet be known how many warrants have been made on the Treasury not authorized by law. We have the best of reasons for saying that the passage of the Railroad acts cost the State tens and hundreds of thousands of dollars. The people will yet ferret out those who so recklessly and criminally spent the treasure of the people. Yes, gentlemen, the day of reckoning will come. Mark what we say! Let every man watch how he connects himself even innocently with those who have so outraged the State and the people.

Southern Conservatives' View of Violence, 1869

Gov. Holden seems much exercised about the recent murders in Jones county, and it is proper he should be.

When a negro who offered brute violence to a respectable lady of Alamance was chastised, and the men who chastised him appeared with sheets over their heads at the house of Mr. Badham and Colonel Albright to scare them out of the Leagues, the Governor sent up his militia for their protection.

When the Governor's "beloved" son Joseph William, Speaker of the House, accompanied by the Governor's friends who hold office in the Capitol, made an attack upon the Editor of the SENTINEL, armed with pistols, clubs, and bowie knives, the Governor applauded their murderous attempt in a public speech to five hundred negroes who crowded in and about the City Hall. When the Governor and his son left the Hall the negroes left huzzahing for Joe.

When three barns were recently burnt in Orange, in which were consumed grain, forage and horses, the Governor sent out no militia or even detectives. This burning was no doubt done by men who belonged to the Governor's secret oath bound association of which he is the head centre.

The Foscue family of Jones county were murdered by League men; a whole family was put to death, Colonel Nethercutt, of Jones, was murdered in his own house in the night time and no doubt by members of their diabolical Leagues, organized throughout the State by the Governor himself.

Old Mr. Briley, of Pitt, was most inhumanly murdered by a carpet-bag Leaguer and three negroes belonging to the League.

In Wilson county a negro was beaten with 300 stripes by Leaguers for voting the Democratic ticket. Judge Thomas, signer of the ordinance of secession and League Judge, refused to allow the negro's counsel to prove that this outrage was committed by order of the League. Notwithstanding, the Leaguers were convicted and sentenced to jail, and the Governor, being President of the League, pardoned the perpetrators of this outrage. No wonder that murder, assassination, and all manner of lawlessness are on the increase.

The Constitution, the law and the Courts are disregarded by the Executive himself. He rescued a prisoner from the hands of the Marshal in defiance of law, and in contempt of the Supreme Court.

The Governor, as head of a secret political club, has trampled on all subordination and broken or borne down the unarmed laws of the State. He has uselessly called in a lawless militia to execute the civil law; nor did he desist from such lawless calls until his own militia murdered and cut each other's throats.

This state of things, though most extraordinary, for this country and this State, is not to be wondered at. It is all the workings, doings and proceedings of secret oathbound political clubs and societies. Where there is two there will be murder, arson, burglary and all manner of attrocious crimes.

We tell the Governor that his Leagues are the secret cause of all the troubles, tumults, barn burnings and assassinations which have occurred in this once quiet land of law and order. Things cannot remain much longer in their present confusion and disorder. The murders and burnings will go on between the two secret political clubs until the whole people will be hurried into the rage of civil discord, revenge and violence.

It is time,—high time that the Executive should dissolve his Leagues and quit his rings.

Congressional Testimony on the Ku Klux Klan, 1871

General John B. Gordon on the Loyal Leagues and the Origin of the Ku Klux Klan

The instinct of self-protection prompted that organization; the sense of insecurity and danger, particularly in those neighborhoods were the negro population largely predominated. The reasons which led to this organization were three or four. The first and main reason was the organization of the Union League, as they called it, about which we knew nothing more than this: that the negroes would desert the plantations, and go off at night in large numbers; and on being asked where they had been, would reply, sometimes, "We have been to the muster;" sometimes, "We have been to the lodge;" sometimes, "We have been to the meeting." These things were observed for a great length of time. We knew that the "carpet-baggers," as the people of Georgia called these men who came from a distance and had no interest at all with us; who were unknown to us entirely; who from all we could learn about them did not have any very exalted position at their homes—these men were organizing the colored people. We knew that beyond all question. We knew of certain instances where great crime had been committed; where overseers had been driven from plantations, and the negroes had asserted their right to hold the property for their own benefit. Apprehension took possession of the entire public mind of the State. Men were in many instances afraid to go away from their homes and leave their wives and children for fear of outrage. Rapes were already being committed in the country. There was this general organization of the black race on the one hand, and an entire disorganization of the white race on the other hand. . . . It was therefore necessary, in order to protect our families from outrage and preserve our own lives, to have something that we could regard as a brotherhood—a combination of the best men of the country, to act purely in self-defense. . . .

Ben Hill on the Klan

Question. You have not studied this organization?

Answer. I have only investigated a few cases for the purpose of ascertaining who were the guilty offenders. One reason for investigating the few cases was upon the attempt to reconstruct Georgia some time ago, and these Ku-Klux outrages were made to bear very, very heavily against even Union parties [who opposed returning Georgia to military rule]. I wanted to know if that was the case, and if so, I wanted the people to put down the Ku-Klux. In the second place, I arrived at the conclusion that a great many of these outrages were committed by gentlemen who wanted a reconstruction of the State, and committed those outrages to give an excuse for it. I have always thought that two or three of the most outrageous murders committed in the State were really committed by persons of the same political faith of the parties slain.

Question. And committed for the political effect they would have?

Answer. I think so. And a great many of us who have really wanted to be reconstructed have been between fires.

Question. Will you have the kindness to state to what cases you last referred, where persons were killed by their friends?

Answer. I think Ashburn [a Republican] was killed by his own political friends.

Question. So as to have the benefit of the political capital that could be made out of it?

Answer: I do not think the motive for killing Ashburn was altogether that; I think there was a personal grudge, or jealousy on the part of some of his political friends. And though my mind is not positive, I am inclined to believe that this fellow Adkins was killed expressly for political capital by his own friends. I was positive about that at one time, but I am not so positive about it now.

Question. Killed by his own friends?

Answer. Yes, sir; though I think it likely some of the others were in it also. I may be wrong, but that was the conclusion to which I arrived. . . .

Question. So far as I have observed your papers, (and I have examined them both before I came into the State and since, I mean the democratic papers,) two lines of thought on this subject seem to run along through them; one is to deny the existence of this organization, and the other is to discountenance with unmeasured abuse every effort to punish such offenses, and even to inquire and ascertain whether in fact they exist. . . . Why is that?

Answer. I am unable to give you a very satisfactory reason. I think myself that the great body of our people are really anxious to put down anything of this sort, the great body of our people of the best class, almost without exception. There are a very few, however, who, as you have stated, have denied unconditionally the existence of such things at all, even in the local and sporadic form I have mentioned, for I do not myself believe that they have existed in any other form. I think they have discountenanced the effort of some people to investigate them, first, because they professed to believe that they did not exist; second, because I think a great many of them have honestly been actuated by a simple desire to pander to what was considered sectional prejudice on this subject. I think we have a class of people in our State, and democrats, too, who are willing to use this occasion, as a great many politicians use all occasions to make themselves popular, by simply pandering to what they consider the sectional prejudices of the hour. I think some have been extreme and ultra in denouncing all pretense of lawlessness, merely for the purpose of making political capital for themselves individually.

Question. Take the case of an honest man, desirous to do justice and to know the truth, who reads nothing but the democratic papers in Georgia, would he believe that there had been any of these outrages and enormities committed from anything he would see in those papers, published as matters of information or for the purpose of denouncing them and rebuking them?

Answer. Heretofore, I believe, that if a man was shut up to the information derived from the democratic press of Georgia, he would have believed that there was no such thing; but I believe now the thing would be different. A great many of our papers are awakening to the fact that there is such a thing as I say, local and temporary in its character. I have believed, myself, for a long time, that there have been these local organizations, and I believe they have been . . . not political in their character. Some few have been political, no doubt; I think that in some cases democrats have availed themselves of the public sentiment for the purpose of exterminating a radical; and I believe some colored people have organized for plunder and robbery. But I believe there have been some cases where men have been made victims by their own political friends for party purposes and ends. I think democrats have been guilty; that plunderers and robbers have been guilty; and I believe that radicals have been guilty for the purpose of making [political] capital.

Question. Can you state any particulars you may have heard in reference to the attack on Ware?

Answer. Yes, sir; I can state what I heard. A body of about twenty-five or thirty disguised men went one night and met him upon the road. (I think this was the case of Jourdan Ware.) I am not certain that they went to his house. I believe they met him on the road, somewhere or other, and demanded of him his arms and his watch. I believe he gave up his arms, and they shot him upon his refusal to surrender the watch, and he died a day or two afterward.

Question. Did you ever hear that there was any accusation of his having done anything wrong?

Answer. No, sir; I think not, except I believe I did hear that there was some complaint of his impudence, or something of that sort.

Question. We hear from a great many witnesses about the "impudence" of negroes. What is considered in your section of the country "impudence" on the part of a negro?

Answer. Well, it is considered impudence for a negro not to be polite to a white man—not to pull off his hat and bow and scrape to a white man, as was always done formerly.

Question. Do the white people generally expect or require now that kind of submissive deportment on the part of the negroes that they did while the negroes were slaves?

Answer. I do not think they do as a general thing; a great many do.

Question. Are there many white people who do require it?

Answer. Yes, sir; I think there are a great many who do require it, and are not satisfied unless the negroes do it.

Question. Suppose that a negro man has been working for a white man, and they have some difference or dispute in relation to wages, will your people generally allow a negro man to stand up and assert his rights in the same way and in the same language which they would allow to a white man without objection?

Answer. O, no sir, that is not expected at all.

Question. If the colored man does stand up and assert his rights in language which would be considered pardonable and allowable in a white man, that is considered "impudence" in a negro?

Answer. Yes, sir; gross impudence.

Question. Is that species of "impudence" on the part of the negro considered a sufficient excuse by many of your people for chastising a negro, or "dealing with him?"

Answer. Well, some think so. . . .

Question. In your judgment, from what you have seen and heard, is there something of a political character about this organization?

Answer. I think it is entirely political.

Question. What makes you think so?

Answer. Because the parties who are maltreated by these men are generally republicans. I have never known a democrat to be assaulted. . . .

Question. Give the committee your judgment in relation to the object with which this organization has been gotten up. What do its members intend to attain by it?

Answer. Well, sir, my opinion is that the first object of the institution of the Ku-Klux, or these disguised bands, was to cripple any effect that might be produced by Loyal Leagues. That is my opinion—that this organization was an offset to the Loyal Leagues.

Question. But the Ku-Klux organization kept on increasing after the Loyal Leagues were disbanded?

Answer. Yes, sir.

Question. What, in your opinion, is the object of keeping up the Ku-Klux organization and operating it as they do? What do they intend to produce or effect by it?

Answer. My opinion is, that the purpose was to break down the reconstruction acts; that they were dissatisfied with negro suffrage and the reconstruction measures and everybody that was in favor of them.

Question. Do you think this organization was intended to neutralize the votes of the negroes after suffrage had been extended to them?

Answer. Yes, sir, I think so.

Question. How? By intimidating them?

Answer. Any way. Yes, sir, by intimidation.

Question. Making them afraid to exercise the right of suffrage?

Answer. Yes, sir.

Question. Do you believe that the organization and its operations have, in fact, produced that effect?

Answer. I think they have to some extent.

Question. What is the state of feeling which has been produced among the colored people by this armed, disguised organization, and the acts they have committed?

Answer. Well, in my section of the country, the colored people, generally, are afraid now, and have been for some time, to turn out at an election. They are afraid to say much, or to have anything to do with public affairs. I own a plantation on Coosa River, upon which I have, perhaps, about 40 negroes, and some of them have been pretty badly alarmed, afraid to say much. Some have lain out in the woods, afraid to stay at home.

White Conservatives Petition Congress, 1868

It is well known by all who have knowledge on the subject, that while the negroes of the South may be more intelligent and of better morals than those of the same race in any other part of the world where they exist in equal density, yet they are in the main, ignorant generally, wholly unacquainted with the principles of free Governments, improvident, disinclined to work, credulous yet suspicious, dishonest, untruthful, incapable of self-restraint, and easily impelled by want or incited by false and specious counsels, into folly and crime. Exceptions, of course, there are; chiefly among those who have been reared as servants in our domestic circles, and in our cities. But the general character of our colored population is such as we have described. . . .

Are these the people in whom should be vested the high governmental functions of establishing institutions and enacting and enforcing laws to prevent crime, protect property, preserve peace and order in society, and promote industry, enterprise and civilization in Alabama, and the power and honor of the United States? Without property, without industry, without any regard for reputation, without control over their own caprices and strong passions, and without fear of punishment under laws, by courts and through juries which are created by and composed of themselves, or of those whom they elect, how can it be otherwise than that they will bring, to the great injury of themselves as well as of us and our children, blight, crime, ruin and barbarism on this fair land? . . .

Continue over us, if you will do so, your own rule by the sword. Send down among us, honorable and upright men of your own people, of the race to which you and we belong: and ungracious, contrary to wise policy and the institutions of the country, and tyrannous as it will be, no hand will be raised among us to resist by force their authority. But do not, we implore you, abdicate your own rule over us, by transferring us to the blighting, brutalizing and unnatural dominion of an alien and inferior race: a race which has never shown sufficient administrative capacity for the good government of even the tribes into which it has always been broken up in its native seats; and which in all ages, has itself furnished slaves for all the other races of the earth.

Instructions to Red Shirts in South Carolina, 1876

1. That every Democrat in the Townships must be put upon the Roll of the Democratic Clubs. . . .
2. That a Roster must be made of every white and of every Negro in the Townships and returned immediately to the County Executive Committee.

3. That the Democratic Military Clubs are to be armed with rifles and pistols and such other arms as they may command. They are to be divided into two companies, one of the old men, the other of the young men; an experienced captain or commander to be placed over each of them. . . .

12. Every Democrat must feel honor bound to control the vote of at least one Negro, by intimidation, purchase, keeping him away or as each individual may determine, how he may best accomplish it.

13. We must attend every Radical meeting that we hear of whether they meet at night or in the day time. Democrats must go in as large numbers as they can get together, and well armed, behave at first with great courtesy and assure the ignorant Negroes that you mean them no harm and so soon as their leaders or speakers begin to speak and make false statements of facts, tell them then and there to their faces, that they are liars, thieves and rascals, and are only trying to mislead the ignorant Negroes and if you get a chance get upon the platform and address the Negroes.

14. In speeches to Negroes you must remember that argument has no effect upon them: they can only be influenced by their fears, superstitions and cupidity. Do not attempt to flatter and persuade them. . . . Treat them so as to show them, you are the superior race, and that their natural position is that of subordination to the white man. . . .

16. Never threaten a man individually. If he deserves to be threatened, the necessities of the times require that he should die. . . .

29. Every club must be uniformed in a red shirt and they must be sure and wear it upon all public meetings and particularly on the day of election.

30. Secrecy should shroud all of our transactions. Let not your left hand know what your right hand does.

Thomas Nast Views Reconstruction, 1865, 1874

"Worse Than Slavery"

And Not This Man?"

Columbia.—"Shall I Trust These Men,

⅄ E S S A Y S

Historian William C. Harris of North Carolina State University has reexamined both the actions and the motives of the much-maligned carpetbaggers. Although some northerners in the Reconstruction South were corrupt or scoundrels, Harris shows in the first essay that most of those called carpetbaggers had quite different, and often laudable, motives. Their chief crime was to challenge traditional racial, political, and social arrangements in the region. In the second selection, Eric Foner, professor of history at Columbia University, has delineated with care the role that blacks played in Reconstruction and the importance of the Ku Klux Klan. Historian J. Mills Thornton of the University of Michigan focuses in the third essay on fiscal and tax policies of the Republican administrations in the South. His findings show that the cost of Republican programs damaged the party's political prospects, particularly its ability to appeal to small white farmers.

Carpetbaggers in Reality

WILLIAM C. HARRIS

The tainted reputation of the carpetbagger during the post–Civil War period is undergoing a remarkable revision. Viewed for decades as the chief of villains in the melodrama known as Radical Reconstruction, the carpetbagger, or northerner who went south after the war and engaged in politics, has attracted during the last few years a number of defenders among historians of the postwar era. The image that now emerges, though far from exculpating them for their failures and abuses of power, represents carpetbaggers as basically decent individuals who in most cases entered the South seeking the main chance through commercial and planting endeavors rather than through political activity. Many became insolvent as a result of the disastrous agricultural failure of 1866, and some of the less enterprising abandoned the region at this time, returning to the North to inveigh against the inhospitable South. Only after the passage of the military Reconstruction Acts of 1867, enfranchising blacks and temporarily disfranchising the former leadership class in the South, did many of the remaining northerners become involved in the politics of their adopted states. Regarded as liberators by the freedmen, the influence of these newcomers among the new citizens virtually ensured their rapid rise to positions of state and local leadership in the young Republican organizations of the region.

   In office, the performance of the carpetbaggers was mixed in the opinion of present-day historians. While some were extravagant and corrupt, others, like Governors Adelbert Ames of Mississippi and Daniel Henry Chamberlain of South Carolina, "were economy-minded and strictly honest." Even those who pursued material gain through political power often did so in

---

From "The Creed of the Carpetbaggers" by William C. Harris, *Journal of Southern History* XL (May 1974), pp. 199–224. Copyright © 1974 by the Southern Historical Association. Reprinted by permission of the Managing Editor.

collaboration with acquisitive southern Democrats. Of course, the carpet-baggers disturbed race relations in the South: to have done otherwise would have been an abject abandonment of the freedmen to the devices of un-sympathetic southern whites. But carpetbaggers, revisionist historians find, did not incite blacks to violence against their former masters; in fact, they frequently took the position of their conservative neighbors on inflammatory racial issues, notably the question of social integration.

These revisionist perspectives are both provocative and suggestive. However, they are views derived from limited research. The revisionist generalization, for example, that carpetbaggers were a variegated lot is based upon vignettes of a handful of the more prominent northerners, not upon grass-roots studies of the motives, policies, and activities of a rela-tively large number. Additional research, testing, and refining of hypotheses concerning this class of politicians is needed. Data should be sought to reveal in full measure the experience and character of carpetbagger lead-ership in southern Reconstruction.

This essay suggests the utility of such basic research. The focus is upon a single aspect of the story of the carpetbaggers—their objectives and ideals in participating in the politics of postwar Mississippi. . . .

The politically active carpetbag class in Mississippi was never very numerous, probably at no time exceeding two hundred men and never including the majority of the postwar northern settlers in the state. Most of the newcomers from above the Ohio were of the farmer class and, either because of their fear of ostracism by local whites or their hostility to the advanced doctrines of Negro rights, shunned affiliation with the Republican party. On the other hand, carpetbaggers, or those northerners who joined and labored for the Republican party, generally were the most affluent and best educated of the northern immigrants in the state. And these men frequently accumulated considerable property in Mississippi before entering politics. Such elite qualities were especially true of carpetbaggers whose influence was statewide, but evidence exists that a number of relatively obscure members of this political class, those who organized and led local Republican clubs and Union Leagues, often serving in county and town offices, were also men of means and some erudition.

Carpetbagger ideology in Mississippi was a product of the intense re-publican idealism that swept the North during the Civil War era, finding its most profound expression in the minds of young, educated officers in the Union army. Generally men of some mobility even before the war, the northerners who came to the state after the conflict had never felt the constraints of provincial ties usually characteristic of life in a single com-munity. To an impressive extent their allegiance was to the stirring national ideals produced by the sectional conflict and the subsequent northern com-mitment to freedom; their vision was broad and optimistic, with a belief in progress through the revitalized republican institutions of the Founding Fathers.

The principal goal of the carpetbaggers was the eradication of the ves-tiges of slavery and rebellion which they believed still existed in the South.

They sought to replace these baneful anachronisms with the progressive spirit of Union and freedom. These were broad and ambiguous concepts, but northerners in Mississippi thought they knew their precise meaning and the requirements for fulfilling them. In their view, slavery and secession were coexistent if not synonymous; similarly, Union and freedom were paired. The slavery-secession syndrome, according to these agents of a new order for the state, had not only caused the internecine war but had also been the reason for the destitution, economic inefficiency, ignorance, intolerance, and violence they found to a deplorable extent in the postwar South. "The effects of the [slave] institution upon the character of its devotees," a leading carpetbagger observed after living in the state for two years, "are a thousandfold more appalling than the most vivid imagination ever dreamed. What slavery failed to touch has been wrecked by secession and treason. The social, business, religious, and political history of the south will show more bad faith, deception, and treachery in a single State [there] than in all the States of the north together." Not until the "hydra-headed monster" of secession had been completely expelled could the South and Mississippi hope to be regenerated and become like the progressive states of the North.

Secession and rebellion had become institutionalized in the Democratic party, carpetbaggers believed, and it followed that the national agency for the redemption of the South should be the Republican party. Triumphant in the war against Democratic copperheads and secessionists, the Republican party must ensure in Reconstruction that Union sacrifices had not been made in vain. Specifically, the South should be reconstructed along lines that would guarantee loyalty to the Union, bona fide freedom for blacks, and tolerance of the opinions of all. Despite the intensity of their views, most carpetbaggers in Mississippi would probably not have agreed with [Governor] Adelbert Ames that Reconstruction was merely an extension of the Civil War and that their purpose in the state was "Mission with a large M," but most of them accepted the necessity of certain changes in the South designed to preserve the fruits of the national victory. . . .

Once in power, carpetbaggers, who proved to be the predominant element in the Republican administrations from 1870 to 1876, set about to implement the progressive features of the new constitution. Shunning a conception of themselves as revolutionary agents or as ultra-Radicals, these northerners were nonetheless convinced that certain reforms were essential before Mississippi could advance into the mainstream of American life. After five years of peace the state still suffered from lawlessness, violence, ignorance, and intolerance of the rights of those who disagreed with the white majority. These vestiges of the blighted past, they believed, must be stamped out before the spirit of progress and equality could take permanent root in the state.

In the minds of the reformers the most important prescription for the retrogressive ills of Mississippi society was a comprehensive system of public schools for both races. Even the shadowy Ku Klux Klan owed its existence to the ignorance of the masses, according to carpetbagger Amos Lovering, a former Indiana judge. Such lawless activities as those practiced by the Klan, he declared, could only be permanently suppressed through the power of "universal education in morals and mind." Charles W. Clarke, the thirty-year-old native of Vermont who drafted the public-school article in the constitution, asserted that education was "the energizing agent of modern civilization" and a necessity for the continuance of republican government and institutions. Furthermore, Clarke and others of his class believed that education was the answer to the race problem in southern society. Enlighten the white masses and their prejudices against Negroes would fade away, they argued; at the same time schooling for the blacks would elevate them to a position in society nearly equal to whites, and their irresponsible behavior in freedom would inevitably cease. In the Republican press, on the campaign stump, and in the legislature, carpetbaggers trumpeted the virtues of public education. Much of their rhetoric was simply promotional, but the emphasis and zeal with which they pursued educational reform suggest strongly the faith of these northerners in its remedial and progressive qualities.

On the question of mixed schools most carpetbaggers preferred to remain silent or ambiguous, hoping to avoid a commitment to equality for blacks that would arouse the prejudices of the bulk of white Republicans, incite conservatives to violent opposition, and inevitably destroy the infant school system. Some, like their southern white neighbors, were simply antagonistic to any social mixing of the races, although they generally were able to keep their racism subdued for political, if for no other, reasons. A few northerners such as Clarke, Henry R. Pease, the state superintendent of education, and Albert T. Morgan probably favored the principle of integration, but they shied away from public statements suggesting that they questioned the dual arrangement established by the legislature of 1870. The only white Republican in Mississippi during Reconstruction to advocate publicly the integration of the public schools was a scalawag and a former slaveholder, Robert W. Flournoy.

After only one year's experience with the free school system, Superintendent Pease reported outstanding progress, including a remarkable improvement in white attitudes toward public education, despite the burning of several Negro schools by the Klan. But difficulties developed as the financial costs of the system proved greater than anticipated, and the goodwill of whites toward it declined. As a result Pease and his associates turned to the federal government for aid. Writing in the state educational journal, Hiram T. Fisher asserted: "It is the utmost folly to talk about establishing free schools permanently in the South without national aid. . . . The little that has been done [already] . . . far surpasses anything that the friends of education can or will do in the South for the next twenty years if they are compelled to rely solely upon their own resources." Congress, he declared, must act before it was too late to save free schools in the financially depressed region. Although viewed as radical and unconstitutional in most quarters, the demand for federal aid received the strong support both of Mississippi carpetbaggers of Radical tendencies and those of the moderate persuasion as well.

To effectuate these demands for national aid, carpetbag congressman Legrand Winfield Perce of Natchez on January 15, 1872, introduced in the House of Representatives a bill to apply the annual proceeds from the sale of federal lands to education in the states. Even though the measure did not single out the South for special treatment, the amended version of the bill had this effect, since it provided that the distribution of the funds during the first ten years would be based on the proportion of illiterates in the population of each state, a category in which the southern states clearly led the nation. The first federal-assistance bill for public school to be given serious consideration by Congress, the far-reaching Perce proposal passed the House but failed in the Senate. . . .

Though never achieving the society of virtue and enlightenment that the educational program was supposed to produce, the carpetbag principle of free schools did not die in Mississippi when the Republican political edifice collapsed. The conservative Redeemers of the late 1870s and the 1880s, despite their public resolves to purge the state of carpetbag innovations and to economize in state expenditures, found it desirable to maintain the semblance of the comprehensive system of public education that their bitter enemies had established during Reconstruction.

Even though public education was the cornerstone of the carpetbaggers' reform program, they realized somewhat vaguely that other measures were also required to transform Mississippi into a progressive commonwealth. Perhaps most carpetbaggers, especially those of moderate leanings, believed that the adoption of the Fifteenth Amendment and the establishment of Republican civil rule in the state made further legislation guranteeing fundamental rights unnecessary. The ferociousness of Ku Klux Klan attacks in 1870 and 1871 and the continuation of general lawlessness, however, convinced many that additional laws, either state or federal, along with a vigorous enforcement, were essential to the security of the new order. In the United States Senate during the zenith of Klan activity in the South, Adelbert Ames, who was always suspicious of the intentions and behavior of southern whites, led the effort to reawaken Republicans in Mississippi, and especially blacks, to the dangers posed by the resurgence of the "Ku Klux Democracy." At the same time, encouraged by his Radical colleagues in Mississippi, the young, idealistic native of New England urged Congress to apply the full power of the army to end the spreading political violence in the South.

Moderate carpetbaggers, on the other hand, sought frantically to prevent this, believing, as so many of their brethren in the North did, that "The ready resort to the military is one of the most dangerous precedents which we can establish as a party." In an effort to prevent federal intervention, Governor Alcorn and his associates, including carpetbaggers, secured the passage of a state Ku Klux Klan law, legislated against the carrying of concealed weapons, and organized the militia. When these measures failed, many moderate carpetbaggers abandoned their reservations and supported the federal Klan law of 1871, designed to put down terror societies in the South.

Northerners in Mississippi were even more reluctant to accept the necessity for further legislation protecting the rights of blacks. During the early, exuberant days of the new order they seemed genuinely to believe that the ballot for blacks and universal education for whites would lead to an end of racial hostility and prejudice in the state. Many carpetbaggers obviously held racial attitudes similar to those of native whites, but it is also clear that an impressive number of them viewed black inferiority as only temporary, and they believed that Negroes would soon come up to or approach closely the standards set by whites. At any rate, most northerners in the state interpreted black capacity in a far more sympathetic light than did their white neighbors.

In the beginning carpetbaggers especially objected to proposals advanced by a handful of Negro leaders in the legislature to guarantee the rights of freedmen in public places. Believing that the Constitution already required the equal treatment of blacks on railroads and steamboats, even the Radical state senator Albert T. Morgan, who married a mulatto schoolteacher, at this time denounced as premature and politically disastrous any measure that would go beyond this right in the direction of social equality. Reflecting the position of those northerners with strong racial prejudices, the carpetbag editor of the Vicksburg *Times and Republican* minced no words in castigating lawmakers who proposed such schemes, especially the state civil rights bill of 1872, which resembled Charles Sumner's national measure. Holding views amazingly similar to those of southern conservatives during the age of segregation, this editor announced that Radical legislators in Jackson should "recognize the fact that the pathway of the colored man through life shall not be higher and shall not be lower than the pathway of the white race, but that it shall be seperate [*sic*] and distinct, and yet be equal. The two races can not be hurled together into an indiscriminate mass without the consent of both. . . . We know that it [the civil rights bill] is repugnant to the feelings of both races; we know that both races look upon such attempts with horror, as foreboding the destruction of both." Nonetheless, after some reflection many moderate carpetbaggers, as well as Radicals, came to support the bill, and in 1873 it became law.

Probably more representative of carpetbag opinion on the treatment of blacks in public was the position of Governor Ridgely C. Powers, generally a moderate in politics, who signed the civil rights bill in 1873. Addressing the state Senate in 1870, he explained that he could "see some reason for refusing to ride in the same car or steamboat, or for declining to sit in the same assembly with drunkards, gamblers, robbers and murderers, but to refuse to come into such proximity with men because they happened to bear a different complexion from my own, would be to acknowledge a mean prejudice, unworthy of an age of intelligence. . . . The time, I apprehend, has past for estimating a man by the color of his skin rather than by the qualities of his heart, or the strength of his intellect." . . .

. . . As might be expected, carpetbaggers were caught up in the mania for railroad construction, although most of them probably did not view such internal improvements as the *sine qua non* for economic rehabilitation and progress that conservatives did. On one occasion the editor of the Jackson *Mississippi Pilot* had to reassure his readers that, regardless of its concern with other issues, the Republican leadership in the state had no intention of slighting Mississippi railroads. As "the great civilizer of nations," railroads, carpetbaggers asserted, should receive the financial support of all levels of government—federal, state, county, and community. Such aid would be repaid in many ways: lands would appreciate in value, economic activity would be stimulated, new enterprises would arise, tax revenues would increase, and a large number of immigrants would be attracted to Mississippi. The Vicksburg *Times and Republican* confidently claimed that the railroads "will certainly bring prosperity and population" to the state.

Although equally as interested as the old citizens in promoting internal improvements, leading carpetbaggers warned against haphazardly conceived railroad projects. Unlike overanxious conservative leaders during the Johnsonian period, they urged legislative planning for the construction of roads that would serve the general interests of the state. As Stafford of the Jackson *Mississippi Pilot* put it, railroads should be constructed for the benefit of Mississippi and her people "without regard to section, locality, race, color, or previous condition." The provision in the constitution against extending the state's credit to aid private corporations, Stafford and others of his class believed, should be no barrier; they fully expected the legislature to evade the clause by providing direct assistance to the railroads. When the chips were down, transplanted northerners, as much as their conservative associates in railroad development, abandoned their good intentions and succumbed to local influences and interests in supporting the construction of roads that would benefit only their own communities or districts.

Black Activism and the Ku Klux Klan

ERIC FONER

In 1867, politics emerged as the principal focus of black aspirations. In that *annus mirabilis*, the impending demise of the structure of civil authority opened the door for political mobilization to sweep across the black belt. Itinerant lecturers, black and white, brought the Republican message into the heart of the rural South. A black Baptist minister calling himself Professor J. W. Toer journeyed through parts of Georgia and Florida with a "magic lantern" exhibiting "the progress of reconstruction. . . . He has a scene, which he calls 'before the proclamation,' another 'after the proclamation' and then '22nd Regt. U. S. C[olored] T[roops] Duncan's Brigade'."

Voting registrars instructed freedmen in American history and government and "the individual benefits of citizenship." In Monroe County, Alabama, where no black political meeting had occurred before 1867, freedmen crowded around the speaker shouting, "God bless you," "Bless God for this." Throughout the South, planters complained of blacks neglecting their labor. Once a week during the summer of 1867, "the negroes from the entire county" quit work and flocked to Waco, Texas, for political rallies. In Alabama, "they stop at any time and go off to Greensboro" for the same purpose. On August 1, Richmond's tobacco factories were forced to close because so many black laborers attended the Republican state convention.

So great was the enthusiasm that, as one ex-slave minister later wrote, "Politics got in our midst and our revival or religious work for a while began to wane." The offices of the black-controlled St. Landry (Louisiana) *Progress*, where several hundred freedmen gathered each Sunday to hear the weekly issue read aloud, temporarily displaced the church as a community meeting place. More typically, the church, and indeed every other black institution, became politicized. Every AME [African Methodist Episcopal] preacher in Georgia was said to be actively engaged in Republican organizing, and political materials were read aloud at "churches, societies, leagues, clubs, balls, picnics, and all other gatherings." One plantation manager summed up the situation: "You never saw a people more excited on the subject of politics than are the negroes of the south. They are perfectly wild."

The meteoric rise of the Union League reflected and channeled this political mobilization. Having originated as a middle-class patriotic club in the Civil War North, the league now emerged as the political voice of impoverished freedmen. Even before 1867, local Union Leagues had sprung up among blacks in some parts of the South, and the order had spread rapidly during and after the war among Unionist whites in the Southern hill country. Now, as freedmen poured into the league, "the negro question" disrupted some upcountry branches, leading many white members to withdraw altogether or retreat into segregated branches. Many local leagues, however, achieved a remarkable degree of interracial harmony. In North Carolina, one racially mixed league composed of freedmen, white Unionists, and Confederate Army deserters, met "in old fields, or in some out of the way house, and elect candidates to be received into their body."

By the end of 1867, it seemed, virtually every black voter in the South had enrolled in the Union League or some equivalent local political organization. Although the league's national leadership urged that meetings be held in "a commodious and pleasant room," this often proved impossible; branches convened in black churches, schools, and homes, and also, when necessary, in woods or fields. Usually, a Bible, a copy of the Declaration of Independence, and an anvil or some other emblem of labor lay on a table, a minister opened the meeting with a prayer, new members took an initiation oath, and pledges followed to uphold the Republican party and the principle of equal rights, and "to stick to one another." Armed black sentinels—"a thing unheard of in South Carolina history," according to one alarmed white—guarded many meetings. Indeed, informal self-defense organizations sprang up around the leagues, and reports of blacks drilling with weapons, sometimes under men with self-appointed "military titles," aroused considerable white apprehension.

The leagues' main function, however, was political education. "We just went there," explained an illiterate North Carolina black member, "and we talked a little; made speeches on one question and another." Republican newspapers were read aloud, issues of the day debated, candidates nominated for office, and banners with slogans like "Colored Troops Fought Nobly" prepared for rallies, parades, and barbecues. One racially mixed North Carolina league on various occasions discussed the organization of a July 4 celebration, cooperation with the Heroes of America (itself experiencing a revival among wartime Unionists in 1867), and questions like disenfranchisement, debtor relief, and public education likely to arise at the state's constitutional convention. A York County, South Carolina, league "frequently read and discussed" the Black Code, a reminder of injustices in the days of Presidential Reconstruction.

The detailed minute book of the Union League of Maryville, Tennessee, a mountain community with a long-standing antislavery tradition, offers a rare glimpse of the league's inner workings. It records frequent discussions of such issues as the national debt and the impeachment of President Johnson, as well as broader questions: "Is the education of the Female as important as that of the male?" "Should students pay corporation tax?" "Should East Tennessee be a separate state?" Although composed largely of white loyalists—mainly small farmers, agricultural laborers, and town businessmen, many of them Union Army veterans—and located in a county only one-tenth black, the Maryville league chose a number of black officers, called upon Tennessee to send at least one black to Congress, and in 1868 nominated a black justice of the peace and four black city commissioners, all of whom won election.

The local leagues' multifaceted activities, however, far transcended electoral politics. Often growing out of the institutions blacks had created in 1865 and 1866, they promoted the building of schools and churches and collected funds "to see to the sick." League members drafted petitions protesting the exclusion of blacks from local juries and demanding the arrest of white criminals. In one instance, in Bullock County, Alabama, they organized their own "negro government" with a code of laws, sheriff, and courts. (The army imprisoned its leader, former slave George Shorter.)

This hothouse atmosphere of political mobilization made possible a vast expansion of the black political leadership (mostly, it will be recalled, freeborn urban mulattoes) that had emerged between 1864 and 1867. Some, like the Charleston free blacks who fanned out into the black belt spreading Republican doctrine and organizing Union Leagues, did have years of political activism behind them. Others were among the more than eighty "colored itinerant lecturers" financed by the Republican Congressional Committee—men like William U. Saunders, a Baltimore barber and Union

Army veteran, James Lynch, who left the editorship of the *Christian Recorder* to organize Republican meetings in Mississippi, and even James H. Jones, former "body servant" of Jefferson Davis. Of the black speakers who crisscrossed the South in 1867 and 1868, Lynch was widely regarded as the greatest orator. "Fluent and graceful, he stirred the audience as no other man did or could do," and his eloquence held gatherings of 3,000 freedmen or more spellbound for hours at a time.

Not a few of the blacks who plunged into politics in 1867 had been born or raised in the North. Even in South Carolina, with its well-established native leadership, Northern blacks assumed a conspicuous role. One white participant in the state's first Republican convention, "astonished" by "the amount of intelligence and ability shown by the colored men," singled out Ohio-born William N. Viney, a young veteran (he was twenty-five in 1867) who had purchased land in the low country and, after the passage of the Reconstruction Act, organized political meetings throughout the region at his own expense. Many Northern blacks, like Viney, had come south with the army; others had served with the Freedmen's Bureau, or as teachers and ministers employed by black churches and Northern missionary societies. Still others were black veterans of the Northern antislavery crusade, fugitive slaves returning home, or the children of well-to-do Southern free blacks who had been sent north for the education (often at Oberlin College) and economic opportunities denied them at home. Reconstruction was one of the few times in American history that the South offered black men of talent and ambition not only the prospect of serving their race, but greater possibilities for personal advancement than existed in the North. And as long as it survived, the southward migration continued. As late as 1875, twenty-two year old D. B. Colton came to South Carolina from Ohio and promptly won a position as election manager. As a consequence, Northern black communities were drained of men of political ambition and of lawyers and other professionals. Having known discrimination in the North—Jonathan C. Gibbs had been "refused admittance to eighteen colleges" before finding a place at Dartmouth—black migrants carried with them a determination that Reconstruction must sweep away racial distinctions in every aspect of American life.

Even more remarkable than the prominence of Northern blacks was the rapid emergence of indigenous leadership in the black belt. Here, where few free blacks had lived before the war, and political mobilization had proceeded extremely unevenly before 1867, local leaders tended to be ex-slaves of modest circumstances who had never before "had the privilege" of expressing political opinions "in public." Many were teachers, preachers, or individuals who possessed other skills of use to the community. Former slave Thomas Allen, a Union League organizer who would soon win election to the Georgia legislature, was a propertyless Baptist preacher, shoemaker, and farmer. But what established him as a leader was literacy: "In my county the colored people came to me for instructions, and I gave them the best instructions I could. I took the New York Tribune and other papers, and in that way I found out a great deal, and I told them whatever

I thought was right." In occupation, the largest number of local activists appear to have been artisans. Comprising 5 percent or less of the rural black population, artisans were men whose skill and independence set them apart from ordinary laborers, but who remained deeply embedded in the life of the freedmen's community. Many had already established their prominence as slaves, like Emanuel Fortune, whose son, editor T. Thomas Fortune, later recalled: "It was natural for [him] to take the leadership in any independent movement of the Negroes. During and before the Civil War he had commanded his time as a tanner and expert shoe and bootmaker. In such life as the slaves were allowed and in church work, he took the leader's part." The Union League catapulted others into positions of importance. James T. Alston, an Alabama shoemaker and musician and the former slave of Confederate Gen. Cullen A. Battle, had "a stronger influence over the minds of the colored men in Macon county" than any other individual, a standing he attributed to the commission he received in 1867 to organize a local Union League.

And there were other men, respected for personal qualities—good sense, oratorical ability, having served in the army, or, like South Carolina Republican organizer Alfred Wright, being "an active person in my principles." Calvin Rogers, a Florida black constable, was described by another freedman as "a thorough-going man; he was a stump speaker, and tried to excite the colored people to do the right thing. . . . He would work for a man and make him pay him." Such attributes seemed more important in 1867 than education or political experience. "You can teach me the law," wrote one black Texan, "but you cannot [teach] me what justice is." Nor, in a region that erected nearly insuperable barriers against black achievement, did high social status appear necessary for political distinction. "All colored people of this country understand," a black writer later noted, "that what a man does, is no indication of what he is."

In Union Leagues, Republican gatherings, and impromptu local meetings, ordinary blacks in 1867 and 1868 staked their claim to equal citizenship in the American republic. Like Northern blacks schooled in the Great Tradition of protest, and the urban freemen who had dominated the state conventions of 1865 and 1866, former slaves identified themselves with the heritage of the Declaration of Independence, and insisted America live up to its professed ideals. In insistent language far removed from the conciliatory tones of 1865, an Alabama convention affirmed its understanding of equal citizenship:

> We claim exactly *the same rights, privileges and immunities as are enjoyed by white men*—we ask nothing more and will be content with nothing less. . . . The law no longer knows white nor black, but simply men, and consequently we are entitled to ride in public conveyances, hold office, sit on juries and do everything else which we have in the past been prevented from doing solely on the ground of color. . . .

Violence . . . had been endemic in large parts of the South since 1865. But the advent of Radical Reconstruction stimulated its further expansion.

By 1870, the Ku Klux Klan and kindred organizations like the Knights of the White Camelia and the White Brotherhood had become deeply entrenched in nearly every Southern state. One should not think of the Klan, even in its heyday, as possessing a well-organized structure or clearly defined regional leadership. Acts of violence were generally committed by local groups on their own initiative. But the unity of purpose and common tactics of these local organizations makes it possible to generalize about their goals and impact, and the challenge they posed to the survival of Reconstruction. In effect, the Klan was a military force serving the interests of the Democratic party, the planter class, and all those who desired the restoration of white supremacy. Its purposes were political, but political in the broadest sense, for it sought to affect power relations, both public and private, throughout Southern society. It aimed to reverse the interlocking changes sweeping over the South during Reconstruction: to destroy the Republican party's infrastructure, undermine the Reconstruction state, reestablish control of the black labor force, and restore racial subordination in every aspect of Southern life. . . .

By and large, Klan activity was concentrated in Piedmont counties where blacks comprised a minority or small majority of the population and the two parties were evenly divided. But no simple formula can explain the pattern of terror that engulfed parts of the South while leaving others relatively unscathed. Georgia's Klan was most active in a cluster of black belt and Piedmont cotton counties east and southeast of Atlanta, and in a group of white-majority counties in the northwestern part of the state. Unknown in the overwhelmingly black South Carolina and Georgia lowcountry, the organization flourished in the western Alabama plantation belt. Scattered across the South lay counties particularly notorious for rampant brutality. Carpetbagger Judge Albion W. Tourgée counted twelve murders, nine rapes, fourteen cases of arson, and over 700 beatings (including the whipping of a woman 103 years of age) in his judicial district in North Carolina's central Piedmont. An even more extensive "reign of terror" engulfed Jackson, a plantation county in Florida's panhandle. "That is where Satan has his seat," remarked a black clergyman; all told over 150 persons were killed, among them black leaders and Jewish merchant Samuel Fleischman, resented for his Republican views and reputation for dealing fairly with black customers.

Nowhere did the Klan become more deeply entrenched than in a group of Piedmont South Carolina counties where medium-sized farms predominated and the races were about equal in number. An outbreak of terror followed the October 1870 elections, in which Republicans retained a tenuous hold on power in the region. Possibly the most massive Klan action anywhere in the South was the January 1871 assault on the Union county jail by 500 masked men, which resulted in the lynching of eight black prisoners. Hundreds of Republicans were whipped and saw their farm property destroyed in Spartanburg, a largely white county with a Democratic majority. Here, the victims included a considerable number of scalawags and wartime Unionists, among them Dr. John Winsmith, a member of "the old land aristocracy of the place" wounded by Klansmen in March 1871. In York County, nearly the entire white male population joined the Klan, and committed at least eleven murders and hundreds of whippings; by February 1871 thousands of blacks had taken to the woods each night to avoid assault. The victims included a black militia leader, found hanging from a tree in March with a note pinned to his breast, "Jim Williams on his big muster," and Elias Hill, a self-educated black teacher, minister, and "leader amongst his people." Even by the standards of the postwar South, the whipping of Hill was barbaric: A dwarflike cripple with limbs "drawn up and withered away with pain," he had mistakenly believed "my pitiful condition would save me." Hill had already been organizing local blacks to leave the region in search of the "peaceful living, free schools, and rich land" denied them in York County. Not long after his beating, together with some sixty black families, he set sail for Liberia.

Contemporary Democrats, echoed by subsequent scholars, often attributed the Klan's sadistic campaign of terror to the fears and prejudices of poorer whites. (More elevated Southerners, one historian contends, could never have committed these "horrible crimes.") The evidence, however, will not sustain such an interpretation. It is true that in some upcountry counties, the Klan drove blacks from land desired by impoverished white farmers and occasionally attacked planters who employed freedmen instead of white tenants. Sometimes, violence exacerbated local labor shortages by causing freedmen to flee the area, leading planters to seek an end to Klan activities. Usually, however, the Klan crossed class lines. If ordinary farmers and laborers constituted the bulk of the membership, and energetic "young bloods" were more likely to conduct midnight raids than middle-aged planters and lawyers, "respectable citizens" chose the targets and often participated in the brutality.

Klansmen generally wore disguises—a typical costume consisted of a long, flowing white robe and hood, capped by horns—and sometimes claimed to be ghosts of Confederate soldiers so, as they claimed, to frighten superstitious blacks. Few freedmen took such nonsense seriously. "Old man, we are just from hell and on our way back," a group of Klansmen told one ex-slave. "If I had been there," he replied, "I would not want to go back." Victims, moreover, frequently recognized their assailants. "Dick Hinds had on a disguise," remarked an Alabama freedmen who saw his son brutally "cut to pieces with a knife." "I knew him. Me and him was raised together." And often, unmasked men committed the violence. The group that attacked the home of Mississippi scalawag Robert Flournoy, whose newspaper had denounced the Klan as "a body of midnight prowlers, robbers, and assassins," included both poor men and property holders, "as respectable as anybody we had there." Among his sixty-five Klan assailants, Abram Colby identified men "not worth the bread they eat," but also some of the "first-class men in our town," including a lawyer and a physician.

Personal experience led blacks to blame the South's "aristocratic classes" for violence and with good reason, for the Klan's leadership included planters, merchants, lawyers, and even ministers. "The most respectable citizens are engaged in it," reported a Georgia Freedmen's Bureau agent, "if there can be any respectability about such people." Editors Josiah Turner of the Raleigh *Sentinel*, Ryland Randolph of the Tuscaloosa *Monitor* (who years later recalled administering whippings "in the regular *ante bellum style*"), and Isaac W. Avery of the Atlanta *Constitution* were prominent Klansmen, along with John B. Gordon, Georgia's Democratic candidate for governor in 1868. When the Knights of the White Camelia initiated Samuel Chester in Arkansas, the pastor of his church administered the oath and the participants included Presbyterian deacons and elders "and every important member of the community." In Jackson County, Florida, the "general ring-leader of badness . . . the generalissimo of Ku-Klux" was a wealthy merchant; elsewhere in the black belt, planters seem to have controlled the organization. Even in the upcountry, "the very best citizens" directed the violence. "Young men of the respectable farming class" composed the Klan's rank and file in western North Carolina, but its leaders were more substantial—former legislator Plato Durham, attorney Leroy McAfee (whose nephew, Thomas Dixon, later garbed the violence in romantic mythology in his novel *The Clansman*), and editor Randolph A. Shotwell. As the Rutherford *Star* remarked, the Klan was "not a gang of *poor trash*, as the leading Democrats would have us believe, but men of property . . . respectable citizens." . . .

. . . Violence had a profound effect on Reconstruction politics. For the Klan devastated the Republican organization in many local communities. By 1871, the party in numerous locales was "scattered and beaten and run out." "They have no leaders up there—no leaders," a freedman lamented of Union County, South Carolina. No party, North or South, commented Adelbert Ames, could see hundreds of its "best and most reliable workers" murdered and still "retain its vigor." Indeed, the black community was more vulnerable to the destruction of its political infrastructure by violence than the white. Local leaders played such a variety of roles in schools, churches, and fraternal organizations that the killing or exiling of one man affected many institutions at once. And for a largely illiterate constituency, in which political information circulated orally rather than through newspapers or pamphlets, local leaders were bridges to the larger world of politics, indispensable sources of political intelligence and guidance. Republican officials, black and white, epitomized the revolution that seemed to have put the bottom rail on top. Their murder or exile inevitably had a demoralizing impact upon their communities.

The violence of 1869–71 etched the Klan permanently in the folk memory of the black community. "What cullud person dat can't 'membahs dem, if he lived dat day?" an elderly Texas freedman asked six decades later. The issue of protection transcended all divisions within the black community, uniting rich and poor, free and freed, in calls for drastic governmental action to restore order. To blacks, indeed, the violence seemed an irrefutable denial of the white South's much-trumpeted claims to superior morality and higher civilization. "Pray tell me," asked Robert B. Elliott, "who is the barbarian here?"

More immediately, violence underscored yet again the "abnormal" quality of Reconstruction politics. Before the war, Democrats and Whigs had combated fiercely throughout the South, but neither party, as Virginia Radical James Hunnicutt pointed out, advised its supporters "to drive out, to starve and to perish" its political opponents. Corrupt election procedures, political chicanery, and even extralegal attempts to oust the opposition party from office were hardly unknown in the North, but not pervasive political violence. "I never knew such things in Maine," commented an Alabama carpetbagger. "Republicans and Democrats were tolerated there." Democracy, it has been said, functions best when politics does not directly mirror deep social division, and each side can accept the victory of the other because both share many values and defeat does not imply "a fatal surrender of . . . vital interests." This was the situation in the North, where, an Alabama Republican observed, "it matters not who is elected." But too much was at stake in Reconstruction for "normal politics" to prevail. As one scalawag pointed out, while Northern political contests focused on "finances, individual capacity, and the like, our contest here is for life, for the right to earn our bread . . . for a decent and respectful consideration as human beings and members of society."

Most of all, violence raised in its starkest form the question of legitimacy that haunted the Reconstruction state. Reconstruction, concluded Klan victim Dr. John Winsmith, ought to begin over again: "I consider a government which does not protect its citizens an utter failure." Indeed, as a former Confederate officer shrewdly observed, it was precisely the Klan's objective "to defy the reconstructed State Governments, to treat them with contempt, and show that they have no real existence." The effective exercise of power, of course, can command respect if not spontaneous loyalty. But only in a few instances had Republican governments found the will to exert this kind of force. Only through "decided action," wrote an Alabama scalawag, could "the state . . . protect its citizens and vindicate its own authority and *right to be*." Yet while their opponents acted as if conducting a revolution, Republicans typically sought stability through conciliation.

Tax Policy and the Failure of Radical Reconstruction

J. MILLS THORNTON III

One of the most pernicious difficulties afflicting the historiography of Reconstruction is that few historians of Reconstruction have done much research on the antebellum period that preceded it. White Southern voters who judged Reconstruction policies at the polls viewed those policies from the perspective of a lifetime's experience with their state government; history did not begin for them in 1867. But too many historians approach Reconstruction as the carpetbaggers at the time did: devoid of any thorough

---

"Fiscal Policy and the Failure of Reconstruction in the Lower South" by J. Mills Thornton III from Kousser and McPherson, eds., *Region, Race, and Reconstruction*. Copyright © 1982 by Oxford University Press. Used by permission.

knowledge of what the earlier policies of Southern governments had been, relying instead on a few facts and hostile legends. This absence of an accurate conception of the antebellum context is arguably a principal reason that the carpetbaggers were so markedly unsuccessful in their efforts to hold the allegiance of native white voters. And it is the principal reason, I believe, that recent historians have so misunderstood the factors underlying white small farmers' desertion of the Republican cause.

In his first book [*Tom Watson: Agrarian Rebel*], published more than forty years ago, Professor C. Vann Woodward laid much stress upon the necessity of appreciating the connections between antebellum political assumptions and postbellum discontent among white small farmers. He sought to show that the lines of descent in Southern history join antebellum policies and the attitudes of the Populists. But that lesson has still not been learned. Recent historians of Reconstruction, displaying little sensitivity to the world view of nineteenth-century Southern small farmers, have therefore been unable to offer any compelling explanation for small farmers' behavior during the decade. Small farmers' increasing distrust of the Republicans, and their eventual cooperation with the Redeemer Democrats in overthrowing Reconstruction, have been attributed simply to racism.

I would certainly not wish to question the power of racial antipathies in shaping the course of Southern history. Racism cannot serve, however, as an all-purpose explanation for small farmers' electoral behavior. Another essential concern of the work of Professor Woodward has been his effort to demonstrate that lower-middle- and lower-class whites have often been willing to rise above their racial attitudes when presented, as in Populism, with a political or economic movement that offered real hope of ameliorating their hard lot. As depicted in much of the recent historiography, Republicanism ought to have been just such a movement. Republicans, we are told, established or greatly increased support of public schools. They aided the building of railroads into the hill counties. They looked with favor on a wide variety of eleemosynary institutions. If white small farmers were not wholly averse to cooperating with blacks in the Populist effort to make the government the defender of the masses, one must wonder why their racism had so inhibited such cooperation only fifteen years earlier.

The answer, of course, is that Republicanism was not at all like Populism. One important difference between them, I should admit, reinforces the notion that racism was at the root of small-farmer behavior: the Populists did not take nearly so strong a stand in favor of legal guarantees of equal rights for blacks. But the Populist experience seems to me to indicate that small farmers might even have tolerated on practical political grounds the passage of state and federal civil-rights acts, if the Republican party had otherwise been vigorously espousing policies that promised small farmers important benefits. Far from promising them benefits, however, Republican policies may actually have seemed to be inimical to their interests. Many poorer whites did indeed support the Republicans early in Reconstruction, even though doing so meant working with blacks and Yankees. But the fiscal policies that the Republicans implemented, once in power, drove, I think, white small farmers into the arms of the Redeemers. And the final irony of this process is that many Republicans, particularly those who were carpetbaggers, never really comprehended why the small farmers were so hostile to these policies.

The explanation I would offer for the white small farmers' perception of Republican fiscal policies turns upon an understanding of the fiscal policies that they replaced. The principal source of tax revenue in all of the Lower South states during most of the antebellum period was the tax on slaves. The slave tax constituted some 60 percent of the total receipts in South Carolina and 30 to 40 percent in the others. The substantial revenues from this source allowed the states to hold their land taxes at quite low levels. Even toward the end of the antebellum period, when the land tax rose somewhat to meet greatly increased expenditures, it generally remained under two mills on the dollar. In addition, the states levied a variety of specific taxes on luxuries and capital. Only the modest land tax and a small poll tax—a levy of from 25 cents to one dollar on white males between twenty-one and forty-five—were broad-based taxes. The result of this tax structure was in large measure to exempt poorer whites from direct taxation. It would appear that the wealthiest third of the citizenry in the Lower South paid at least two-thirds of its taxes.

The abolition of slavery brought dramatic changes to the Southern tax structure, as to all areas of Southern life. Reconstruction legislators turned to the land tax to make up for the loss of the slave tax; the land tax produced some two-thirds, and in a few cases an even larger proportion, of the state revenues during the decade. At the same time, disbursements rose far above those of antebellum levels. The greater reliance on the land tax and the increase in disbursements together forced extraordinary increases in the millage rates. In Mississippi, for instance, the tax rose from 1.6 mills near the end of the antebellum years, to 9 mills in 1871 and $12\frac{1}{2}$ mills in 1873. Alabama taxed at a rate of 2 mills in 1860 and $7\frac{1}{2}$ mills in 1870. In Louisiana the millage rate was 2.9 in 1860, but $20\frac{1}{2}$ in 1872, and $14\frac{1}{2}$ in 1874. In Florida the millage rate went from $1\frac{2}{3}$ mills in 1860 to 7 mills in 1870 and 13 mills in 1874. These rates reflect only state taxes, of course. In Florida in 1874 the counties assessed an additional $11\frac{1}{2}$ mills, for a total rate of $24\frac{1}{2}$ mills. These large new taxes fell on every property owner. For the first time in Southern history the burden of taxation came home to the small farmer. Largely exempted from taxation throughout the antebellum years, he was suddenly called upon to support a very active government.

It might be said, of course, that in return for this new contribution the small farmer received much in disbursements for social-service programs. But such a contention would, I believe, misrepresent the small farmer's own perspective. Because the citizenry to be served had been virtually doubled by the emancipation of the slaves, and because the inflation of prices caused by the war required, until the panic of 1873, the expenditure of more money in order to purchase the same amount of goods and services, so that disbursements for many programs were apparently but not really larger, white small farmers had in many cases in the antebellum period actually received benefits equal to or greater than those they received during Reconstruction, and for a great deal less in taxes. Recent historiography, for instance, has emphasized Republican generosity to the public-school systems in the South. However, public-school expenditures per eligible child, measured in constant dollars, remained about the same in one state, rose in two, but still only to quite modest levels, and actually declined in two others. I need hardly add that the freedmen, because they owned very little property, paid directly only a small proportion of the taxes: 2.3 percent of the property-tax receipts and 7.4 percent of the total tax receipts in Georgia in 1874, when they composed some 46 percent of the population. As the white small farmer could well have seen his situation, therefore, he was paying far more in taxes, but his contribution was in considerable measure state-enforced altruism; he was getting back little more in services than he had received earlier. . . .

It does not seem to me that the recent historiography of Reconstruction has shown a sufficient awareness of just how large the receipts and disbursements of the Southern state governments during the decade were, in comparison with the figures from preceding and following years. They dwarfed the totals from the 1850s, though the 1850s had been a period of massive expansion in governmental activity in most of the Lower South states. . . . I do not, of course, mean to endorse the assumption . . . that the size of the figures is prima facie evidence of wastefulness. On the contrary, I believe that the heart of the Republicans' political dilemma . . . is that the vast social needs of a devastated region peopled with millions of destitute citizens, black and white, clearly justified the states in undertaking expenditures on a scale equal to the problem. Indeed, one can make a persuasive argument that the expenditures, far from being excessive, were insufficient. But such an argument looks at the matter from the perspective of an administrator seeking to deal with the demands of a difficult situation. The reality of democracy demands that the politician look at matters from the perspective of the voter as well, and the two perspectives are by no means always congruent. In the case of Reconstruction, however great the social needs apparent from the capital may have been, it would not have been irrational for the white small farmer to have felt himself overtaxed and underserved by Republican policies. In the present section, I shall attempt to suggest what may have been his viewpoint on what was happening to him, as opposed to the viewpoint of his governors, which dominates the current secondary literature.

In the first place, it is necessary to underscore . . . that taxes increased rapidly in this decade. . . . I need not belabor this point further; it in any case is generally acknowledged. Far less often recognized is the apparent shift in tax incidence which accompanied the abolition of slavery. Slaves had, of course, been a very large part of the total wealth in the antebellum South. One index to their value is that in nine of the fifteen slave states in 1860, according to the federal census of that year, the assessed value of personal property exceeded that of real estate, whereas this situation obtained in only three of the nineteen free states. Slaves were a form of property whose ownership was concentrated almost exclusively in the hands of wealthier citizens. And slaves were an obvious and readily assessable asset. The slave tax had therefore been chiefly responsible for the progressive features of the antebellum tax structure.

After the abolition of slavery, only intangible personal property—stocks, bonds, notes, money at interest—remained as a form of property whose ownership was essentially limited to the wealthy. A property tax on intangibles is, however, notoriously easy to evade, and intangibles did not constitute a substantial part of Southern wealth in any case. Nor is the property tax a very effective method of taxing a business corporation. The Reconstruction statutes insisted that capital and the property of corporations had to be taxed, of course. But receipts from these sources were never very large, perhaps 15 percent of the totals. An additional 15 percent came from other personalty, including wagons, farming implements, furniture, and livestock. The poll tax usually contributed another 5 to 10 percent. It was not the taxes from these sources, however, that really sustained the rapidly expanding Reconstruction governments. Sixty percent or more of this burden fell on a single object of taxation—land.

In the antebellum period, the land tax had seldom exceeded a third of the tax receipts. The presence of the slave tax had allowed legislators to keep land-tax rates low. Just as governmental activity and the consequent need for revenue soared to levels unexampled in peacetime, however, the states faced a newly, and markedly, constricted tax base. It was the decision of Republican legislators to let the land tax alone bear the burden formerly divided between the land and slave taxes.

Of course the value of real estate in the South during this unsettled period had declined markedly from the late 1850s, returning to the levels of the early 1850s. Therefore, the fact that tax rates increased by four to eight times does not imply that actual taxes rose so much. Still, the increase in taxes was steep enough. The following [data] illustrate the taxes due on a 160-acre farm in Alabama and Mississippi in various years, assuming that the farm was worth the average assessed value per acre in the year. In Alabama, though the value per acre had declined by a third between 1860 and 1870, the tax on the farm had multiplied by almost two and a half times, and the average tax in the Reconstruction years was double the level of 1860. In Mississippi, the tax in 1871 was three and a half times what it had been in 1857, and in 1873 it was almost five times the figure for 1857, though in 1873 the value of the farm was almost 40 percent less than in 1857.

It might be argued, on the other hand, that the actual tax, in dollar terms, was still a modest one. But such a contention misunderstands the situation of a small farmer operating on the edge of the cash economy. For him these taxes were indeed significant, because his cash income was so small. We may form a rough estimate of what the cash income of the owner of a 160-acre farm was in these two states. The federal censuses of 1860 and 1870 inform us that approximately two-thirds of the farm was unimproved acreage; let us assume that our farmer has 60 of his 160 acres in cultivation. Perhaps two-thirds of the improved acreage was given over to the growth of food crops for use by the farmer's family. On the remaining 20 acres, he might plant cotton to be marketed for cash. During Reconstruction, and we may assume also during the 1850s, the average yield of cotton was a bit less than four-tenths of a bale per acre. Thus our farmer marketed some eight bales. In the marketing years 1855–56 to 1860–61, the weighted average of ordinary-grade cotton sold at New Orleans was 8.445 cents a pound. In the marketing years 1870–71 to 1875–76, the comparable figure was 12.9 cents a pound. These figures, after we deduct 5 percent for factorage fees and transportation costs, produce a cash income for the farmer of about $257 a year in the late 1850s and about $392 a year in the early 1870s. The latter amount is, incidentally, less than 18 percent greater than the former one in constant dollar terms, because of the postwar inflation of prices. If these estimates are reasonable, then the state land tax alone represented 1 percent or more of the farmer's total cash income in Alabama during the Reconstruction years, except for the brief period in 1871–72 when the Democrats regained power. And it was some $1\frac{1}{2}$ to 2 percent of his income in Mississippi during the period. The Alabama percentage is nearly double that for 1855 and 50 percent above that for 1860. The Mississippi percentage in 1873 is more than treble that for 1857.

To the state land tax must be added the county and school-district land taxes, the personalty tax on livestock, farm implements, and similar possessions, and the poll tax, which in Alabama was $1.50, and in Mississippi was $2.00 in 1870 but $1.00 in 1873. It is not at all unreasonable, therefore, to estimate that our owner of a 160-acre farm paid some 2 to 4 percent of his total cash income to the tax collector during Reconstruction. And when we reflect that a considerable part of the farmer's cash income necessarily went to pay the immediate expenses of his farming operation—to pay for seed, supplies, and, very probably, interest on his debts—then it becomes apparent that the taxes would have been an even larger percentage of his discretionary income. If a fourth of his cash income remained after the payment of unavoidable farming expenses, he would have paid some 8 to 10 percent or more of that remainder in taxes. Taxation at this level would most certainly not have been inconsequential for the small farmer. Nor are we reduced to mere speculation about its effect, in Mississippi at least. We need only note that by the spring of 1871, that state was reporting nearly 3,330,000 acres—14 percent of its entire taxable acreage—as having been forfeited to the government for nonpayment of taxes.

The abolition of slavery, then, because it moved so much of the burden of taxation to land, apparently brought about in the Lower South a marked shift in tax incidence downward in the social scale. At the same time, rapidly rising tax rates brought taxes to a level at which they became genuinely onerous to the small farmer. But, it might be said, if the small farmer was paying large taxes for the first time, he was also receiving substantial governmental services for the first time. Though at first glance this position looks very plausible, it does not, I think, accurately depict the small farmer's situation as he may well have perceived it. . . .

. . . Whites paid almost all of the direct taxes both before and after the Civil War. In the antebellum period the only blacks who were taxpayers were, of course, the handful of free Negroes. But even after the war, the freedmen owned virtually no property, and therefore for all practical purposes they were subject directly only to the poll tax. Beginning in 1874 Georgia reported tax receipts segregated by race. The returns for 1874 indicate that blacks, who made up some 46 percent of the population in that year, paid only 2.3 percent of the property taxes. The addition of the poll taxes brings the black percentage of the total tax receipts to 7.4. Indeed, it was precisely the ability of the poll tax to extract a contribution from the propertyless that made it seem to Southern legislators—during Reconstruction, as before and afterward—the ideal tax for the support of the public schools. It was the one tax paid by a significant minority—and just after emancipation probably the majority—of the parents whose children used the schools. This attitude among the legislators is connected with the view general among white voters that they were being taxed to provide services to nontaxpayers. Now, this attitude was in part a misconception. Blacks who were renters or sharecroppers contributed to tax receipts indirectly by providing a part of the income out of which the white property owner paid the tax on the farm. But however unfair the attitude was, it was certainly real. After redemption, indeed, it produced a vigorous campaign throughout the South to expend on black schools only those school taxes actually paid by black citizens. . . .

. . . While the number of taxpayers remained essentially constant after emancipation, the number of citizens needing state services was doubled at a stroke. Disbursements expressed in aggregate terms seem quite small in the antebellum era and much larger during Reconstruction. But the reality is almost the reverse. Because the citizenry was half as large before the Civil War, disbursements per citizen actually declined during Reconstruction. Republicans were well aware of this distinction; it was their standard reply to Democratic charges of profligate waste. But we must note that it was the Democratic charge rather than the Republican reply which appears to have struck home with the white small farmer. As I have said, the Republican argument looked at the problem from the point of view of the administrators, of those in charge of the government. It was necessary for expenditures to expand rapidly even to maintain services at their former levels, they said, because prices were higher and because twice as many people had to be served. But such an explanation, however cogent it was in fact, would probably have seemed to the white farmer only an elaborate rationalization for a gross injustice. . . . The reality for the white farmer was a sharp increase in taxes and a decline in services. From this perspective, it was quite natural that the notion that the large new taxes were going into the pockets of corrupt officials—bolstered as the notion was by a number of cases of genuine corruption among the Republicans—was convincing. And even if it had not been, the simple fact of high taxes and small returns, produced by dividing the tax receipts between hard-pressed whites and "nontaxpaying" blacks, would probably have been damning enough.

FURTHER READING

Michael Les Benedict, *A Compromise of Principle* (1974)
Carol R. Bleser, *The Promised Land* (1969)
Orville Vernon Burton, *In My Father's House Are Many Mansions* (1985)
Dan T. Carter, *When the War Was Over* (1985)
Richard N. Current, *Those Terrible Carpetbaggers* (1988)
Edmund L. Drago, *Black Politicians and Reconstruction in Georgia* (1982)
W. E. B. Du Bois, *Black Reconstruction* (1935)
Paul D. Escott, *Many Excellent People* (1985)
W. McKee Evans, *Ballots and Fence Rails* (1966)
Roger A. Fischer, *The Segregation Struggle in Louisiana, 1862–1877* (1974)
Eric Foner, *Reconstruction* (1988)
William Gillette, *Retreat from Reconstruction, 1869–1879* (1979)
William C. Harris, *Day of the Carpetbagger* (1979)
James Haskins, *Pinckney Benton Stewart Pinchback* (1973)
Thomas Holt, *Black over White* (1977)
Elizabeth Jacoway, *Yankee Missionaries in the South* (1979)
Jacqueline Jones, *Soldiers of Light and Love* (1985)
J. Morgan Kousser and James M. McPherson, eds., *Region, Race, and Reconstruction* (1982)
Peggy Lamson, *The Glorious Failure* (1973)
Edward Magdol, *A Right to the Land* (1977)
Robert C. Morris, *Reading, 'Riting, and Reconstruction* (1981)
Elizabeth Studley Nathans, *Losing the Peace* (1968)
Otto H. Olsen, *Carpetbagger's Crusade* (1965)
———, ed., *Reconstruction and Redemption in the South* (1980)
Claude F. Oubre, *Forty Acres and a Mule* (1978)
Joseph H. Parks, *Joseph E. Brown of Georgia* (1976)
Lillian A. Pereyra, *James Lusk Alcorn* (1966)
Michael Perman, *Reunion Without Compromise* (1973)
———, *The Road to Redemption* (1984)
Lawrence N. Powell, *New Masters* (1980)
Howard N. Rabinowitz, ed., *Southern Black Leaders in Reconstruction* (1964)
George C. Rable, *But There Was No Peace* (1984)
James Roark, *Masters Without Slaves* (1977)
Kenneth M. Stampp, *The Era of Reconstruction, 1865–1877* (1965)
Mark W. Summers, *Railroads, Reconstruction, and the Gospel of Prosperity* (1984)
Emma Lou Thornbrough, ed., *Black Reconstructionists* (1972)
Albion W. Tourgee, *A Fool's Errand* (1879)
Allen W. Trelease, *White Terror* (1971)
Okon E. Uya, *From Slavery to Public Service* (1971)
Charles Vincent, *Black Legislators in Louisiana During Reconstruction* (1976)
Vernon L. Wharton, *The Negro in Mississippi, 1865–1890* (1947)
Sarah Woolfolk Wiggins, *The Scalawag in Alabama Politics, 1865–1881* (1977)
Joel Williamson, *After Slavery* (1966)